MOVING ON

The American People Since 1945

Second Edition

George Donelson Moss

The City College of San Francisco

Prentice
Hall

Upper Saddle River New Jersey 07458

Library of Congress Cataloging-in-Publication Data

Moss, George,
    Moving on : the American people since 1945 / George Donelson Moss.—2nd ed.
       p. cm.
    Includes bibliographical references and index.
    ISBN 0-13-017191-3
    1. United States—History—1945–   I. Title.

    E741 .M673   2000
    973.92—dc21   00-020144

Editor-in-Chief: Charlyce Jones Owen
Editorial Assistant: Chris Glynn
Production Editor: Jean Lapidus
Prepress and Manufacturing Buyer: Lynn Pearlman
Copy Editor: Michele Lansing
Artist: Mirella Signoretto
Photo Researcher: Teri Stratford
Photo Permissions Coordinator: Michelina Viscusi
Cover Design: Bruce Kenselaar

**For the "baby boomers"
and their descendants:
this is the story of their America.**

This book was set in 10/12 Times Roman by The Composing Room
of Michigan, Inc. and was printed and bound by RR Donnelley & Sons Company.
The cover was printed by Phoenix Color Corp.

© 2001, and 1994 by Prentice-Hall, Inc.
A Division of Pearson Education
Upper Saddle River, New Jersey 07458

Printed in the United States of America
10   9   8   7   6   5   4   3   2

ISBN 0-13-017191-3

PRENTICE-HALL INTERNATIONAL (UK) LIMITED, *London*
PRENTICE-HALL OF AUSTRALIA PTY. LIMITED, *Sydney*
PRENTICE-HALL CANADA INC., *Toronto*
PRENTICE-HALL HISPANOAMERICANA, S.A., *Mexico*
PRENTICE-HALL OF INDIA PRIVATE LIMITED, *New Delhi*
PRENTICE-HALL OF JAPAN, INC., *Tokyo*
PEARSON EDUCATION ASIA PTE. LTD., *Singapore*
EDITORA PRENTICE-HALL DO BRASIL, LTDA., *Rio de Janeiro*

Contents

Preface

Moving On: The American People Since 1945 covers the half-century of American history from the end of World War II to the present; it endeavors to explain how the American nation has become what it is today and how the American people have become what they are today. It represents my best efforts to probe the deeper meanings of the recent historical experiences that have shaped our country and forged the social character of our people. It has been an exciting book to write and revise for a second edition, because our recent past has been, and no doubt will continue to be, supercharged with energy, conflict, and drama. Recent American history is a compelling saga of human struggle, achievement, and failure, full of irony, tragedy, and comedy. I confess that it has been a formidable challenge to try to impose coherent patterns of description, analysis, and interpretation on the mighty spectacle of recent American history—to discern order and purpose amid so much chaos and diversity.

The era that began amidst the storm of the planet's largest war and continues to the present forms a coherent unit of study. It is no wonder that students have made recent U.S. history courses among the most popular currently being offered on the nation's college and university campuses. Paradoxically, most students, even the best and the brightest who have had good high school survey courses in U.S. history, are unlikely to know well the recent history of their country—even though it is that recent history that most usefully illuminates the present and suggests the shape of the future rapidly exploding upon us.

Most U.S. history survey courses scurry through the 1940s and 1950s, only to peter out sometime during the 1960s. Consequently, students do not have a historical understanding of recent events; for most young people, Watergate and the Iran-Contra scandal are merely rhetorical labels, names for events that scarcely one student in ten can discuss meaningfully. Young people often know more about the Spanish-American War than they do about the Persian Gulf War. Having scant historical understanding of recent events, they have little sense of causation or consequences. They lack the experience of constructing meaningful patterns of explanation and interpretation that creates out of these recent events an intelligible, usable past. Did the upheavals of the 1960s have an enduring impact on the status of minorities, women, and young people? How has the legacy of the Vietnam War influenced subsequent American diplomatic and strategic policies? To what extent has the presidency of Bill Clinton been influenced by recent political history? Only a close study of the past fifty years can provide answers to these and the myriad of other questions that thoughtful students bring to the recent U.S. past.

The year 1945 is an appropriate one to begin our story of recent America. World War II signified one of the most profound turning points in the history of the Republic. Out of that horrific conflict came America's involvement in the postwar world, giving rise to the long Cold War struggle with the Soviet Union that dominated U.S. foreign policy for nearly a half-century. Out of World War II came a revitalized, transformed American economy that undergirded the remarkable prosperity that most American families enjoyed for nearly thirty years. Forged within the terrible crucible of war, a new, more egalitarian society emerged that influenced the historical experience of Americans for decades.

During the late 1960s, Americans found themselves embroiled in twin convulsions, full-blown political and cultural crises. These crises occurred because of American involvement in a controversial war in Indochina and because of the rise of domestic insurgencies, of which the militant civil rights movement was the most powerful. War and domestic rebellions combined to polarize Americans in 1968. Political activists clashed with defenders of traditional values and institutions. During the presidential election of 1968, Richard Nixon rallied traditional forces, who then defeated the forces of reform and social activism, ushering in a conservative era that stretched from the 1970s through the 1990s.

Moving On draws upon the work of many scholars who have studied all facets of recent American history. In some instances, most notably in those sections concerned with U.S. interventions in Southeast Asia, culminating in the Vietnam War, I have been able to utilize my own research. Mostly, however, this book is a work of synthesis, a comprehensive narrative that conveys a sizable portion of what professional historians know about recent American history.

I have written a book that retains what is most valuable from traditional public policy approaches to U.S. history: it incorporates political history, economic history, military history, and foreign policy history. These histories are usually told from the top down, from the perspectives of elite groups that have dominated governmental and economic institutions. While retaining some elements of these traditional approaches, I have also integrated much demographic, ecological, and cultural history. During the past fifty years, Americans have developed a vital popular culture. Its most important forms reach most Americans through the mass media of radio, movies, and, most important, television. Sections of many chapters chart the rise of a multimedia-saturated popular culture that is flourishing as the 21st century dawns. Further, I have devoted a good deal of space to the new social history that has enriched our historical literature and greatly expanded our understanding of what constitutes mainstream American history. Much of this new social history, with its focus on issues of class, gender, race, and ethnicity, is told from the perspective of those groups that in the past were either ignored or were perceived as passive objects of more powerful historical agents. Social history is often told from the ground up. Thus you will find that I have given much attention to immigration history, labor history, women's history, gay-lesbian history, African-American history, Hispanic-American history, Asian-American history, and Native American history. The story of recent America includes the stories of all individuals and groups who have played active roles in the unfolding drama.

My inclusive approach amounts to a work of restoration. I aim to restore to the recent past as much of its diversity and complexity as my knowledge and talent permit. Within the traditional framework of public policy history, I have crafted innovative multicultural structures as diverse and dynamic as American society itself. *Moving On* is a book for everyone, for traditionalists and multiculturalists alike. If I have created the book that I intended, it will be the first study of the recent American past that one reads, not the last. If historical study represents a kind of journey, consider *Moving On* a point of departure, not a destination.

As a teacher and a textbook writer, I have two important goals: the first is to help the student learn how to think about recent American history, not what to think. The second is to provide the student with a vocabulary to enable him or her to engage in an informed conversation about the recent past, especially about topics that are personally meaningful and relevant.

Acknowledgments

Most *Homo historienses* belong to that privileged category of human beings that has found useful work that is also enjoyable. One of the many features of the historian's profession that makes it so rewarding, so much fun to be a part of, is the incredible generosity of others who so willingly give their time, energies, talents, and knowledge in countless ways. In the creation and revision of *Moving On,* I am grateful to many people: my students and colleagues at City College of San Francisco and the University of California, San Diego, and friends and other scholars, some of whom embrace disciplines other than history, who also contributed in ways that improved the content, organization, and writing of this book.

To mention a few of the many others who helped: among my colleagues at City College, Edward W. Moreno, Mary Adams, Richard Oxsen, Stephen Moorhouse, and most of all, "Old Faithful," Austin White, who shares my passion for teaching recent U.S. history; among my colleagues at the University of California, San Diego, Daniel Hallin, Michael Schudsen, and Michael Bernstein.

A few of the other scholars who provided invaluable help, either while writing or revising the book, include: Thomas Wolf, Laney College; Bruce Dierenfield, Canisius College; Jeffrey Kimball, Miami University, Oxford, Ohio; Garen Burbank, the University of Winnipeg; Kevin O'Keefe, Stetson University; Paul Conway, Oneonta College; David Hollinger, the University of California, Berkeley; and Ronald G. Walters, the Johns Hopkins University.

Special thanks go to Todd Armstrong, executive editor at Prentice Hall, for giving me an opportunity to create a second edition of *Moving On.* I only hope that it meets his expectations. I also am grateful to Jean Lapidus, who once again expertly took charge of the production process.

And final thanks to two special people: Mary Chatelier, who used her detective's skills to tease original and wonderfully expressive photographs out of the not-entirely-friendly confines of the Photo Collections of the National Archives, and the lovely Linda, who, forsaking all others, has hitched her team to my wagon. Together it is a grand ride! (But we are a little worried about the horses!)

The author also thanks the following reviewers for their helpful suggestions and comments: Professor Gene A. Sessions, Weber State University; and Professor William Issel, San Francisco State University.

George Donelson Moss

1

Prologue: The American People in 1945

On August 14, 1945, the Japanese government announced Japan's unconditional surrender, bringing history's largest war to a triumphant conclusion for the United States and its allies. Across America, its people erupted in frenzied victory celebrations. Tumultuous parades occurred in New York, Chicago, San Francisco, and in other great cities. In the American heartland, in small towns and villages everywhere, citizens joined in spontaneous, joyous victory parades. All Americans rejoiced at the final destruction of the Axis menace and the advent of peace throughout a battered world.

In Blythe, California, an agricultural community of perhaps 2,500 people, amidst the honking cars, pickup trucks, and tractors, a ten-year-old boy, astride his chestnut pony, shouted, "We won! We won!" The high school marching band played "The Star-Spangled Banner," "America the Beautiful," and John Philip Sousa's rousing "Stars and Stripes Forever." Immediately behind the band came a black car draped with a large gold star. Inside of the car, their grief and loss temporarily masked as they waved and smiled at bystanders gathered along Main Street, rode three women whose sons had died in battle. The parade constituted a motley column of vehicles, horse-drawn wagons, cowboys on horseback, pedestrians, Native Americans from a nearby reservation, and soldiers from an air base at the edge of town. At the tail end of the parade, riding in their wagon pulled by a team of mules, came an African-American couple whose son had been fighting in the great war to preserve democracy.

The mood of the paraders was exultant. Americans had just won history's greatest war! At last the killing and dying would stop. Husbands, fathers, brothers, and sweethearts could come home. Wartime shortages and rationing would soon end. Thirty miles north of Blythe, Japanese Americans interned at Camp Poston quietly observed the end of the war. They too could go home.

After the paraders had traversed Main Street, they turned onto a side road that led to the fairgrounds, which also served as a rodeo arena and a football stadium. As they reached the fairgrounds, the paraders dispersed. George Donelson Moss, tired but immensely proud to be an American on that long-ago, glorious summer day, his little boy's imagination fired by the sense that he had played a small part in a great historical drama, rode his pony home. It was dinner time.

WAR AS SOCIAL REVOLUTION

At war's end, the United States was vastly changed from the nation that had been thrust suddenly into the cauldron of war by the Japanese surprise attack on Pearl Harbor on December 7, 1941. During the intervening three years and nine months of fighting and winning World War II, America had undergone profound transformations that forever changed the social landscape and created new possibilities for its people.

During the war years, huge military forces were raised and sent to fight on the land, on the sea, and in the air around the globe. The most productive economy the world had ever seen sustained America's large civilian population and simultaneously supplied its and its allies' military forces fighting the Axis powers. The war revitalized the American economy, extricated the American people from the lingering clutches of the Great Depression, and inaugurated a cycle of affluence that stretched into the 1970s. War enhanced the power and reach of the federal government. War thrust America irrevocably into the center of world affairs and destroyed forever isolationist tendencies that had lingered tenaciously until the morning that Japanese aircraft bombed Pearl Harbor.

War transformed the nation's social structure. Well-paying jobs in war industries located in coastal cities triggered a vast folk migration that rapidly depopulated the countryside. War opened up unprecedented economic opportunities for women, African Americans, and Hispanic Americans. War, hysteria, and race prejudice combined to harm gravely the Japanese-American population that lived along the West Coast when America entered the war. Army troops uprooted 120,000 people from their homes and interned them in desolate camps in isolated desert regions for the duration of the war.

DEMOGRAPHIC CHANGE

In 1945, approximately 140,000,000 Americans inhabited the nation and its territories and served overseas in the armed forces. World War II had had a dramatic impact on the lives of nearly all Americans—on where they lived and what kind of work they did. It also affected family life and patterns of leisure and recreation. The war experience established demographic patterns that would persist for the rest of the twentieth century.

Between 1941 and 1945, approximately 16 million men, about 95 percent of whom were drafted, and 250,000 women served in the armed forces. About half of those who went into the military during the war never left the Continental United States. But many of those servicemen who never left the states were assigned to bases in different parts of the coun-

Figure 1.1   Americans celebrating V-J day in Times Square. All across the country, people erupted into spontaneous celebrations of victory.   *Source:* Bettmann Archive.

try that they had never before seen. After the war ended and they had been discharged, they often returned with their families to become permanent residents of the locales where they had performed military service. In addition to service personnel, millions of civilian war workers moved from rural areas to the cities, where jobs in war industries could be found. In many cases, those transplanted civilian war workers, refugees from rural poverty and isolation, did not go home after the war. They and their families joined the burgeoning postwar urban and suburban populations.

Several important population shifts occurred in wartime that would shape the demographic contours of postwar America for decades. Population flowed from the rural interior of the country outward toward the cities along the Pacific, Atlantic, and Gulf coasts. People also left inland farms and villages for the cities of the Upper Midwest, because it was in the coastal and Midwestern cities that the major military installations, shipyards, aircraft assembly plants, and other war industries were located. Population also made a major shift westward, particularly to California. California's population increased by 40 percent from 1940 to 1945, and millions of the military personnel and war workers who came to California in wartime remained or returned after the war to become permanent residents of the Golden State.

The Sunbelt, that southern rim of states stretching from South Carolina to Southern California, also began to grow rapidly during the war years. The Sunbelt states, especially Florida, Texas, and Southern California, would become the nation's most dynamic centers of population growth and economic expansion in the postwar decades. Another important demographic trend, induced by World War II, was the good-paying jobs in war industries

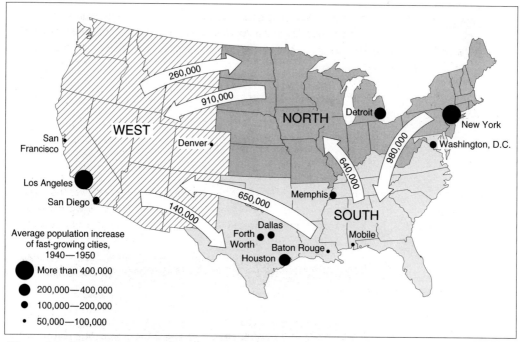

Figure 1.2   Internal migration in the United States during World War II.   *Source: Statistical Abstract of the United States, 1974 ed.*

that lured over 1 million African Americans out of the Old South and on to New York, Chicago, Philadelphia, Detroit, and the rapidly growing cities along the West Coast. Most African Americans and their families also remained in these new locales after the war, becoming permanent residents of New York, Ohio, Pennsylvania, Illinois, Michigan, and California. The geographic mobility induced by the war resulted in permanent relocations for millions of American families. Rural America declined, regional differences among Americans diminished; and the demographic foundations for the postwar surge of urban and suburban communities were laid.

Despite the mobilization of the nation's vast human and economic resources for the war effort, there occurred more social reform affecting the quality of American lives during the war than had occurred during the previous years of New Deal reforms. Medical and dental care improved dramatically. Prepaid health insurance for working people became available for the first time. Some progressive employers such as Kaiser Shipyards offered medical care as a fringe benefit. Millions of young men from disadvantaged backgrounds drafted into the armed forces enjoyed a nutritious diet and adequate medical and dental care for the first time in their lives. Even with the nation at war and with the dangers inherent in war work, the overall health of the nation's population improved dramatically. The birthrate rose rapidly; the death rate sharply diminished. Median life expectancy increased by five years!

A huge increase in the size of the American middle class was the most significant demographic transformation of the war years. The United States became, for the first time in its history, a middle-class nation in the sense that a statistical majority, more than half of its families, enjoyed middle-class incomes and lifestyles. Real personal income more than doubled during the war years, and national income was more equitably distributed than ever before. Perhaps one-third of the nation's families remained poor, but even poor families often enjoyed relative improvements in their living standards. It was during the early 1940s that prosperity levels that had been reached in this country during the late 1920s before the Great Crash were finally eclipsed.

ECONOMIC TRANSFORMATIONS

It was American industrial output that largely determined the Allied victory over the Axis. According to historian Glen Jeansonne, "The war was won as much on the assembly lines as on the front lines." Hitler fatally underestimated U.S. economic power when he sneered that Americans "only know how to make refrigerators and razor blades." During forty-five months of war, American factories built 86,000 tanks, 5,500 merchant ships, 6,000 naval vessels, 300,000 planes, and 15 million rifles. U.S. military production more than doubled the output of its enemies, eventually winning a war of attrition.

In addition to raising a vast military force, the United States had to gear its economy for global war. America's factories had to produce arms for itself and its major allies, the British, the Soviets, and the Chinese. During the first half of 1942, the federal government placed orders for over $100 billion in war contracts, more goods than the economy had ever produced in a year. Federal spending surged in wartime—$35 billion in 1942, $75 billion in 1943, and $98 billion in 1945. These gigantic wartime federal expenditures dwarfed New Deal spending, which had never exceeded $10 billion for any year. Unprecedented federal spending, 90 percent of which was for war or war-related enterprises, fueled the economic and social transformations that had created a new American society by the summer of 1945.

Converting the economy to a war footing challenged American industrialists and government bureaucrats. To manage the gigantic wartime effort, Roosevelt created a central planning agency, the Office of Economic Stabilization, headed by James F. Byrnes. To spur industrial production, the Justice Department suspended antitrust laws, and the Pentagon awarded lucrative cost-plus contracts to manufacturers, whereby the government paid all research and development costs and then purchased the products at a price that guaranteed companies a substantial profit. Because of such incentives, America's corporate industrialists not only accomplished the "miracle of production" that defeated the Axis, they also earned historic high profits for their shareholders.

Fueled by vast federal expenditures, total productivity increased at the remarkable rate of 25 percent per annum, a growth rate never approached before or since World War II. The gross domestic product more than doubled during the war years, from $95 billion in 1940 to more than $211 billion by 1946. During those years, economic expansion added 10 million new jobs. The federal government during World War II spent more than twice as much money than all previous governments combined had spent since the creation of the Republic.

To help pay for these prodigious wartime expenditures, Congress broadened and deepened the tax structure. The Revenue Acts of 1942 and 1943 created the modern federal income tax system. Most Americans had never filed an income tax return before World War II, because the income tax, on the books since 1913, had been a small tax on upper-income families and corporations. Starting in 1942, anyone earning $600 or more annually had to file an income tax return. A withholding tax went into effect in 1943, which made employers the nation's principal tax collectors. Income tax revenues rose from $5 billion in 1940 to $49 billion in 1945, a tenfold increase. These wartime tax increases were by far the largest in the nation's history.

Although the government presented the new income tax system to the American people as a temporary wartime necessity, it remained a permanent feature of national life in the postwar era. Even though taxes were increased significantly, tax revenues paid only 41 percent of the cost of the war. Government paid the rest of the war bills by borrowing. War bonds, peddled by movie stars, war heroes, and professional athletes, added $135 billion. But ordinary citizens bought only about one-third of these bonds; large institutional investors purchased the bulk of them. By war's end, the national debt had climbed to $280 billion, up from $40 billion when it began. And by war's end, the national debt was larger than the economy, that is, the debt exceeded the gross domestic product.

Vast federal spending for war ended the lingering depression that had afflicted Americans for a decade. The New Deal had failed to find a cure for economic depression. On the eve of war, over 7 million Americans were out of work, or 14 percent of the labor force. Real wages in 1941 were below 1929 levels. By New Year's Day in 1943, unemployment in America had vanished. Wartime economic expansion, fueled by unprecedented levels of government spending, combined with mass conscription to create severe labor shortages. By war's end, the nation's workers still enjoyed full employment at the highest wages in history.

The discovery that government spending could banish the specter of depression confirmed the claims of the world's foremost economist, England's John Maynard Keynes. Keynes contended that government spending could cure economic depression. If private sector investment proved inadequate, government could cut taxes and begin large-scale spending programs to stimulate demand and restore the business cycle. During the New Deal of the mid-1930s, government spending was not large enough and taxes were generally regressive, so Keynes' theories could not be confirmed until the war years. Their wartime success in eliminating the depression also gave American political leaders a confidence that they could regulate the business cycle, a confidence that lasted for the next thirty years. They believed that they now possessed the fiscal tools to monitor spending levels, maintain prosperity, keep unemployment low, and prevent the recurrence of recession, all the while controlling inflation. Americans also looked to government after the war to maintain a prosperous, growing, and full-employment economy.

Farmers and industrial workers, two classes devastated by the depression, prospered during the war years. Farm output rose 20 percent, even though the farm population declined more than 50 percent and farmers struggled with chronic labor shortages. Big labor prospered along with big business in wartime. Congress created the War Labor Board in 1942, which set guidelines for wages, hours, and collective bargaining. Employers, unions, and government officials generally cooperated during the war. Union membership grew from 10.5 million in 1941 to over 15 million in 1945, one-third of the non-farm workforce. Proportionally, this wartime growth represented the high watermark of union membership in American history. During the war, trade union leaders consolidated their new status as members of the nation's political and economic elites.

There were some labor problems that the War Labor Board could not resolve. The American Federation of Labor and the Congress of Industrial Organizations engaged in bitter, sometimes violent, jurisdictional disputes. Although organized labor had given a no-strike pledge for the duration of the war, it could not be enforced. The United Mine Workers, led by the crusty John L. Lewis, went on strike in 1943. The coal strike disrupted the nation's economic life, but most work stoppages during the war years lasted only a few days. These strikes never caused serious production delays in the industries that cranked out the huge amounts of war materials required by the armed forces.

Vastly increased federal spending, full employment, and shortages of consumer items sent powerful inflationary forces surging through the wartime economy. The shift from peacetime to wartime production sharply reduced the amount of consumer goods available to buy just at the time when people had significantly more money to spend. By 1943, the production of new cars and other durable goods had ceased. A giant inflationary gap generated by too much money chasing too few goods threatened to drive prices way up and to rob Americans of their wartime economic gains. To clamp a lid on inflation, the government imposed price controls, joining them to a rationing system that used coupon allotments to consumers for scarce items such as sugar, butter, coffee, beef, tires, and gasoline.

Roosevelt created the Office of Price Administration (OPA) to administer the control apparatus nationally. The OPA had a daunting task. Economic interests accepted controls on the other fellow's prices but regarded controls on their prices as subversive. Business lobbyists, farm bloc politicians, and union leaders waged unceasing "guerrilla warfare" against the OPA for the duration of the war. Consumers chafed under rationing restrictions, particularly those on beef and gasoline. A ban on all "pleasure driving" and a 35 mph speed limit accompanied gasoline rationing. The average motorist received three gallons of gas a week. Most people walked to work or took public transportation. Auto touring practically vanished. Black markets in gasoline flourished; racketeers had not had it so good since Prohibition. At times, motorists could not obtain any gas, legal or illegal. Service stations often closed, stranding motorists and truckers. When a station could get gas, customers lined up their cars for miles waiting to buy it.

Beef rationing caused the worst problems. Butcher display cases were frequently empty. Butchers sometimes favored old customers, infuriating new ones. Frustrated shoppers often abused butchers and occasionally rioted. Horse meat and muskrat meat appeared in several places as beef substitutes. Despite grievances and injustices, the universally unpopular OPA maintained price stability and distributed scarce goods equitably. Most people complied with the system of controls, considering it both a wartime necessity and to their economic advantage. The cost of living rose only 3 percent in 1944 and 1945. Government controls and rationing effectively contained inflation in wartime.

Even as ordinary citizens chafed under the restrictions of rationing and price controls, purchased war bonds, and saved grease, scrap metals, and used tires, a quite remarkable redistribution of income occurred. During the war years, real wages for workers employed in manufacturing rose over 50 percent, from twenty-four dollars to thirty-seven dollars a week. The share of national wealth owned by the richest 5 percent of American families dropped from 23.7 percent to 16.8 percent. The number of families earning less than $2,000 annually declined by 50 percent from 1941 to 1945, and the number of families earning $5,000 or more quadrupled during the same time span. World War II was the most successful war on poverty in American history; it also created the social foundations for the affluent society that flowered during the postwar era.

Despite shortages and rationing, people with money to spend in wartime found ways to spend it and to enjoy it. Wartime prosperity strengthened materialistic values and revived consumerism, which largely had been suspended during the depression decade. Americans spent money on entertainment, on going to the movies, and on going out to dinner. People resorted to black markets when rationed goods could not be found. Many people saved their money for new cars, new homes, new appliances, and new radios that they would purchase after the war. Advertisers promised consumers new and better goods when civilian production patterns were restored following victory over the Axis powers. Consumerism, reborn amidst war, would become a powerful engine driving the postwar affluent economy.

WOMEN IN WARTIME

Between 1941 and 1945, over 6 million women entered the labor force, about half of whom worked in the manufacturing sector. Women also joined the branches of military service open to them. They served in the WACS (Women's Auxiliary Army Corps) and in the WAVES (Women Accepted for Voluntary Emergency Service). They also served in women's units in the Coast Guard and Marine Corps, and thousands of women became noncombat military pilots.

Married women, many with children, made up three-quarters of working women in wartime. Before the war, the typical working woman had been young and single; only about 15 percent of married women worked outside of the home. By 1945, more than half of working women had married, and their median age was thirty-seven. Most women in the prewar-war labor force had been confined to low-paying, low-status jobs in the service, clerical, and light manufacturing fields. Employers considered women unsuitable for heavy labor amidst the masculine atmosphere prevailing in factories. Acute wartime labor shortages quickly changed those attitudes. Women learned skilled trades, joined unions, and earned high wages. They performed certain jobs better than men, such as those requiring close attention to detail and manual dexterity. Women worked in munitions factories and foundries. They became riveters, welders, crane operators, tool and die makers, and iron workers. They operated heavy equipment, drove trucks, and became train engineers. Women increased their geographic and occupational mobility tremendously in wartime. Thousands of black women quit work as domestics to join the factory labor force. Millions of women moved from the rural South and Midwest to coastal cities where the war-generated jobs were located. In Southern California, hundreds of thousands of women went to work in aircraft assembly plants.

Opinion polls showed that the general public favored wartime work by women. Cor-

Figure 1.3   Over 6 million women entered the labor force during World War II. Many of them worked in industries such as these two "Rosie the Riveter," helping to build military aircraft.   *Source:* National Archives.

porate public relations campaigns encouraged women to obtain jobs in war industries. A government propaganda agency, the Office of War Information (OWI), mounted publicity campaigns to persuade women to join the war labor force. These media campaigns portrayed women's work in shops and factories as both noble and absolutely necessary to the war effort. A fictional "Rosie the Riveter" became a popular wartime symbol of women working in war industries. She was celebrated in an eponymous hit tune of the era, and her picture appeared on posters and magazine covers. "Do the Job HE Left Behind" exhorted the billboards.

Patterns of gender discrimination persisted in wartime. Surveys showed that women in manufacturing earned about 60 percent of what men received for comparable work. Factories offered limited promotional opportunities and supervisorial positions for women. Even though the war emergency opened up hitherto closed occupations to women, most jobs in the sex-segregated labor market remained classified as "male" or "female" work. Where women worked in factories, they often worked on all-female shop floors, under male supervisors. Women resented the unequal pay and working conditions, and the sexual harassment from chauvinistic males. But they loved the opportunity to do important work that contributed to winning the war, and they also enjoyed the camaraderie and support of their female co-workers.

The most serious problem faced by working mothers in wartime was the almost complete absence of child care centers. During the war, juvenile delinquency, venereal disease, and teenage pregnancies rose sharply. "Latchkey children," children left alone while their mothers worked their shifts at a factory, became a national scandal. Children roamed the streets, were put in all-day movie houses, or were locked in cars outside of defense plants. Police arrested many teenage girls for prostitution and apprehended boys for theft and vandalism.

Because so many men went to war, millions of women found themselves the de facto heads of single-parent households. They had a much greater range of responsibilities than just working full-time shifts in factories and shipyards. They became the centers of family life. Many also found time for neighborhood volunteer work. They served on civil defense committees, attended club meetings and went to PTA meetings, and gave blood and worked as hostesses at USO (United Service Organizations) centers. Often women simply never found enough hours in the day to do their jobs, fulfill all of their family obligations, attend union meetings, and meet the myriad of other demands on their time and energy.

Increasing numbers of women got married at the same time they went to work in war industries. Marriage rates rose sharply in 1942. Many young couples got married to spend time together before the man got shipped overseas. The birthrate also climbed sharply. Many births enabled men to qualify for military deferments. Others conceived "good-bye babies" to perpetuate the family, even if the fathers were killed in the war. Returning prosperity provided the main reason for the increase in marriages and in the rising birthrate. A parent, often two parents with good jobs in a war industry, headed the new families. The population, which had grown by only 3 million during the decade of the 1930s, added 6.5 million people during the war years. The baby boom that would be one of the most significant demographic trends of the postwar decades had begun.

Women's wartime factory work was considered only a temporary response to a national emergency. Once victory was achieved and the soldiers returned, women were expected to surrender their jobs to returning GIs. The president of the National Association of Manufacturers intoned, "Too many women should not stay in the labor force. The home is the basic American institution." But surveys showed that most women wanted to continue working after the war. Indeed, 75 percent of Detroit's female factory workers wanted to keep working. After the war, with their war contracts canceled, employers fired their female employees. Others were pressured by their husbands to quit and return to the kitchen. Single working women continued to work. But often they could find only low-paying jobs in domestic service, restaurants, and department stores. Many of these women expressed disappointment and felt a keen sense of personal defeat over having to resume work in low-status, low-paying fields from which they had temporarily escaped for a few years during the war.

But the roots of the modern feminist movement can be found in the work experience, financial independence, and attitudinal changes achieved by millions of women during World War II. They had found new opportunities and met new challenges that traditionally had been denied women. They developed talents that they did not realize they could until the war came along. They discovered that they could work at skilled trades, join unions, support a family, and head a household. Many derived a larger sense or their own worth and felt a strong sense of empowerment. Many reared their daughters to have greater self-esteem and to demand much more from life than their own mothers had taught them to expect. When their children were grown in the 1960s and 1970s, many of these middle-aged Rosie the Riveters rejoined the workforce.

AFRICAN AMERICANS AT WAR

World War II proved a mixed blessing for African Americans: it provided both unprecedented economic opportunities and continuing encounters with the hardships of segregation and racism. About 1 million black men and women, nearly all of the men draftees, served in the armed forces during the war, entering all branches of military service. Even though the American military was still segregated during World War II, African Americans attained far more opportunities than had been available during World War I. The Army Air Corps trained black pilots who flew in all-black squadrons. African American Marines, fighting in all-black units, fought heroically in savage island battles in the Pacific war.

Black-white race relations within the military reflected the racist society it served. Many race riots occurred on military bases. White civilians often attacked African American soldiers stationed in the South. The morale and motivation of black soldiers frequently suffered from encounters with racist whites. African American soldiers often found themselves serving in menial positions in wartime. Black troops were sometimes commanded by white Southern officers who subjected them to harsh and humiliating treatment. African American soldiers sometimes found enemy prisoners of war treated better than they were. But most black soldiers found reasons to fight the Axis powers, even if at times they could see little difference between German racism and the homegrown kind. They also kept up steady pressures for better assignments, fairer treatment, and improved statuses. African Americans planned to trade their wartime military service for improved educational and job opportunities after the war. A NAACP (National Association for the Advancement of Colored People) spokesman asserted that the war gave African Americans the chance "to . . . compel and shame our nation . . . into a more enlightened attitude toward a tenth of its people." African Americans fought for a double victory: over the Axis powers abroad and Jim Crow at home. Many returning black veterans could not celebrate the victorious end of the war as enthusiastically as white Americans could, because they knew that they were coming home to face a segregated society and the racist attitudes that sustained it.

The war also opened up many new employment opportunities for African Americans. In January 1941, A. Philip Randolph, angered because employers with war contracts refused to hire African American workers, threatened to stage a march on Washington to protest both employer discrimination and segregation in the armed forces. President Roosevelt, wanting to avoid the embarrassment of a protest march and possible violence, persuaded Randolph to call off the proposed march in return for an executive order establishing a President's Fair Employment Practices Committee (FEPC), which ordered employers in defense industries to make jobs available "without discrimination because of race, creed, color, or national origin." The FEPC was understaffed and underfunded, and it had limited enforcement powers. It was a symbolic gesture that proved to be of little use during the war. Acute labor shortages far more than government policy opened up war employment opportunities for African Americans.

Over 2 million African American men and women left the South to find work in the industrial cities of the North and West. Many joined CIO unions. Black voters in Northern cities became an important constituency in local and state elections. Most African American families who left the South during the war remained a permanent part of the growing

Figure 1.4   African Americans made a major contribution to American victories during World War II. Here the Army Air Force's all-black 99th Fighter Group assembles at the beachhead of Anzio, Italy, in 1944.   *Source:* National Archives.

Northern urban population in the postwar era. Southern black migrants often encountered racist hostility as they struggled to adapt to their new lives in Northern cities. They discovered that there was little difference between Northern and Southern white racial attitudes. Many Northern whites hated blacks for competing with them for housing, jobs, and schools for their children. They resented coming into contact with African Americans at parks, beaches, and other public facilities.

These racial antagonisms flared violently during the summer of 1943. About 250 race riots occurred in nearly fifty Northern cities; the largest riots were in Detroit and Harlem, but the worst violence was in Detroit, where it had been building for years. The immediate provocation had been an angry struggle for access to a public housing project demanded by both African American workers and white workers during a time of acute housing shortages for everyone. One hot night in June, things got out of control. A full-scale race riot exploded, which lasted several days. Before order could be restored, twenty-five African Americans and nine whites had died.

Despite these outbreaks of homefront racial violence, World War II proved to be a watershed for African Americans; the war experience aided the black struggle for civil rights and full citizenship. Military service gave most African American veterans greater self-esteem and a sense of empowerment. It also raised expectations. Many black veterans did not return to the rural South after the war but chose to settle in one of the Northern or Western states, perhaps one in which they had spent time while in the military. Others took advantage of the GI Bill to go to college, learn a skilled trade, or start a business after the war. These black professionals, technicians, and businessmen formed a new and much larger African American middle class. A combination of vastly improved economic opportunities and continuing encounters with racism generated a new militancy among black people. They were determined not to accept second-class citizenship after the war. These African American veterans and their children took the lead in challenging Jim Crow and racism in the postwar era. The roots of the modern civil rights movement can be found in black experiences during World War II.

HISPANIC AMERICANS IN WARTIME

According to the 1940 census, about 2.7 million Hispanic people lived among the American population. Most were of Mexican descent living in California, Texas, and the Southwest. Much of this predominantly rural population endured poverty, discrimination, and segregation. These people lacked decent jobs, housing, and educational opportunities and had no political influence. However, World War II created opportunities for Hispanics; thousands of Mexican Americans moved to urban areas to find work in war industries.

About 350,000 went into the armed forces, nearly all of them draftees. Although the military never segregated Hispanics in the thorough way in which they did African Americans, many served in predominantly Hispanic units. Mexican-American warriors joined elite units such as the airborne rangers, and they often volunteered for dangerous missions. Eleven Mexican Americans won the nation's highest military award, the Congressional Medal of Honor. At the same time, the war created acute shortages of agricultural workers. American growers persuaded the government to make arrangements with Mexico to import farm workers from Mexico. Under a program established in 1942, nearly 2 million Mexican *braceros* (laborers) entered the United States. Because of lax government supervision, employers often ruthlessly exploited these imported contract laborers. The *braceros* often worked for fifty cents a day, had no fringe benefits, and were housed in shacks and converted chicken coops.

Hispanics in the war labor force often suffered discriminations similar to those encountered by African Americans and women. They sometimes got paid less than "Anglo" employees for doing the same work. They found their problems most acute in the crowded cities. Many young Mexican Americans belonged to neighborhood gangs. They called themselves *pachucos* and favored a distinctive style of dress called a "zoot suit." The "zoot suit" consisted of baggy trousers that flared at the knees and were fitted tightly around the ankles, complemented by a wide-brimmed felt hat. These costumes were an assertion of a distinct cultural identity and a defiance of Anglo values.

In June 1943, at a time when black-white racial tensions were erupting in cities, ethnic relations in Los Angeles also were strained. Hundreds of sailors and Marines on leave from bases in Southern California assaulted Mexican Americans on the streets of Los An-

geles and tore off their "zoot suits." Police either looked the other way or arrested only Mexican-American youths during these encounters. The local media supported the attacks on
the *pachucos*. Only after the president of Mexico threatened to cancel the *bracero* program
did President Roosevelt intervene to stop the violence.

Despite the zoot-suit incidents, Hispanic-American wartime experiences brought
some advances. As was the case for African Americans, military service gave thousands of
Mexican Americans an enhanced sense of self-worth. They returned from the war with
greater expectations and enlarged views of life's possibilities. Many Hispanic veterans took
advantage of the GI Bill. In the postwar years, Mexican-American veterans and their sons
assumed leadership roles in organizations that challenged discrimination against Hispanic
people in Southwestern states.

NATIVE AMERICANS IN WARTIME

In addition to the 25,000 Native Americans who served in the armed forces during World
War II, thousands more left their reservations to work in war industries around the country.
Most of these mobile people did not return to their reservations and tribal life after the war;
they remained in the cities and became part of the rapidly growing postwar urban and suburban population. Some of those who returned to the reservations brought with them new
ideas, technologies, and plans for the future.

In 1944, in California, lawyers representing a group of Native Americans filed suit in
federal court for $100 million as compensation for lands taken illegally from Native Amer-
icans' ancestors during the 1850s. Congress enacted legislation to pay them for their lands,
but President Roosevelt vetoed the bill. Litigation on this matter continued on and off for
the next thirty-five years, until finally, both parties reached a compromise. The Native
Americans accepted a settlement that brought them about forty-seven cents per acre.

ASIAN AMERICANS IN WARTIME

The war to save democracy featured many home front violations of democracy. In some areas, civil liberties violations during World War II were not as severe as during World War
I. German Americans were not harassed or persecuted as in World War I. Congress never
enacted repressive measures like the Espionage Act or the Sedition Act. But during the
spring and summer of 1942, about 120,000 Japanese Americans, two-thirds of them native-
born American citizens, were uprooted from their homes along the Pacific Coast and taken
to internment centers in remote, desolate interior regions of the country. There they lived in
tar paper barracks behind barbed wire for three years. The internment of Japanese Americans for the duration of World War II represented the worst violation of civil liberties in
wartime in American history.

The initiative was taken by the military commander in charge of security along the
West Coast, General John Dewitt. Dewitt and other officials claimed that the relocation of
Japanese Americans was necessary to guarantee military security along the West Coast.

Figure 1.5   Three Native American Marine Corps Woman Reservists at Camp Lejuene, North Carolina, October 1943. They are (from left to right): Minnie Spotted Wolf (Blackfoot), Celia Mix (Potawatomi), and Viola Eastman (Chippewa).   *Source:* National Archives.

They argued that if the Japanese Americans were not relocated, some of them would aid the enemy in case of attack. Since the "disloyals" could not be separated from the "loyals," all would have to go. Their accusations were demonstrably false. FBI agents admitted that they never discovered a single proven act of disloyalty committed by any Japanese American. The real reasons for their removal included anti-Japanese race prejudice, wartime hysteria, and greed. The claim of military necessity was based on unfounded suspicion, not evidence. The relocation of Japanese Americans in wartime also was the culminating act of a half-century of anti-Japanese agitation and assaults in California, Oregon, and Washington.

Japanese-American spokesmen asserted their loyalty, to no avail. No political leaders or newspaper editors defended the Japanese Americans, nor did any question the need for relocation. Earl Warren, California's attorney general in 1942, strongly advocated removal. The removal order, Executive Order No. 9066, came from President Roosevelt and could not be challenged. In 1944, the U.S. Supreme Court placed the constitutional seal of approval upon the relocation of Japanese Americans. In the case of *Fred Korematsu v. the United States,* the Court accepted the claim of army lawyers that relocation was a wartime military necessity. A 5 to 3 majority ruled that in time of war, individual rights could be sacrificed to military necessity. Associate Justice Frank Murphy filed a powerful dissenting opinion, stating that the relocation of Japanese Americans fell "into the ugly abyss of racism."

Following the advice of their leaders, virtually the entire Japanese-American population complied with the relocation order without resistance or protest. They submitted in accordance with the spirit of *Shikata Ga Nai* (realistic resignation). Because they were given little time to gather at assembly centers and were allowed to take only what they could carry to the camps, families lost homes, businesses, farms, and personal property worth an estimated $400 million. They arrived at the camps to find hastily built tar paper barracks amidst

Figure 1.6   U.S. soldiers uprooted about 120,000 Japanese Americans, most of them U.S. citizens, from their homes in early 1942 and imprisoned them in various internment centers. The move, spawned by panic and prejudice, was both unnecessary and wrong. Here a family awaits a bus to haul them away. *Source:* National Archives.

bleak desert landscapes that would be their homes for three years. The internment centers were de facto prisons. People were not free to come and go. The camps were under continuous surveillance by armed guards and enclosed by barbed wire fencing. During the war, some internees were allowed to leave the camps, provided that they agreed to settle in Eastern states. By the summer of 1945, all were allowed to leave. A few fortunate families had friends who had saved their homes or businesses for them while they were incarcerated, but many internees had no homes or businesses to return to. They found that interlopers now resided in their former residences and owned their former businesses.

Even though their families were imprisoned in camps, thousands of young Japanese-American men volunteered for military service. They were determined to prove their loyalty to a government that had betrayed them. Japanese-American soldiers contributed much to the war effort. They fought in the European theater, and many served in the Pacific war as translators, interpreters, and intelligence officers. They proved themselves brave warriors, winning medals and suffering severe casualties. One Japanese-American unit, the 442nd Regimental Combat Engineers, was the most decorated unit in American military history.

Ironically, the government refused to relocate Japanese Americans living in Hawaii. Thousands of them continued to work for the American military at Pearl Harbor and other installations following the Japanese attacks. They were not removed because of military necessity; they made up one-fifth of the Hawaiian population, and their labor was essential; and there was no place to put them, nor ships to transport them.

In truth, loyal Americans were the victims of an egregious injustice, a vicious example of the tyranny of the white majority in wartime. Congress authorized token restitution for Japanese Americans in 1948, and a total of about $38 million was paid to claimants during the 1950s. These payments totaled about ten cents for each dollar of loss claimed. Years later, after much litigation and quiet political pressure, Japanese Americans belatedly received vindication and additional restitution. In 1983, U.S. District Court Judge Marilyn Hall Patel vacated Fred Korematsu's conviction. Judge Patel's action came after Korematsu's attorneys discovered secret government documents proving that government officials knew that Japanese Americans posed no dangers to national security in wartime, and they withheld this evidence from the Supreme Court.

In 1988, President Ronald Reagan, speaking for all Americans, acknowledged that wartime relocation had been unnecessary and wrong, and he apologized to the Japanese-American community. In 1989, Congress agreed to pay each of the estimated 60,000 survivors of the wartime relocation experience $20,000. Although some embittered victims dismissed the money as "too little, too late," others were grateful and appreciated the symbolic significance of the gesture. Ten years later, in the summer of 1998, after paying out over $1.6 billion to survivors, their heirs, and to some people whose property had been confiscated by the government, the government closed the books on the matter of compensating the internees.

After the war, Japanese Americans did not protest the gross injustices that they were forced to endure in wartime. They internalized the anger, shame, and humiliation associated with the relocation experience and rarely talked about those experiences, even among close friends and family. Instead, Japanese Americans vowed to put their wartime experiences behind them and to go forward—to prove to the government and to the white majority that had abused them that they were good citizens and productive members of society. Their postwar record of achievement was astonishing. Japanese Americans, by any measure, are among the most successful and prosperous groups in the country. They have integrated themselves into mainstream society and have achieved distinction in the sciences, the arts, medicine, law, engineering, academic life, business, finance, athletics, and politics. They are among the leaders in the amount of education attained and in annual per capita income. In the half-century following their harrowing wartime experiences, Japanese Americans and their descendants have emphatically demonstrated that they are good Americans.

In contrast to the brutal mistreatment of Japanese Americans in wartime, Chinese Americans fared comparatively well. Chinese Americans enjoyed the sympathy and goodwill of most Americans, because China was a wartime ally of the United States. Americans also felt much sympathy for the Chinese, who were suffering terribly at the hands of Japanese soldiers during the war. Because of their status as allies and because of acute labor shortages in war industries, unprecedented opportunities for Chinese workers suddenly opened up. By the thousands, Chinese families streamed out of the Chinatown ghettos into the mainstream of American life. Most of these mobile families never returned to the Chinatown ghettos, and in the years following World War II, they headed for the suburbs.

In 1943, Congress at long last repealed the Chinese Exclusion Act, that egregious artifact of anti-Asian racism that had been in place since 1882. For the first time in over sixty years, it was now possible for people to emigrate from China to the United States. In addition, the government finally extended citizenship to thousands of Chinese, many of them quite elderly, long-time residents of the United States who had hitherto been ineligible for citizenship.

THE POLITICS OF WAR

War moved the country toward the Right. Resurgent Republicans gained seventy-seven seats in the House and ten seats in the Senate in the 1942 midterm elections. A conservative coalition of Northern Republicans and Southern Democrats, which had emerged following the 1938 elections, consolidated its control of Congress. Roosevelt, sensing the political drift and preoccupied with the immense task of running history's largest war, put social reform on the back burner. Conservatives snuffed out many New Deal agencies in 1942 and 1943, on the grounds that wartime economic revival had rendered them obsolete. Among their most prominent victims were the WPA (Work Progress Administration) and the CCC (Civilian Conservation Corps). Federal spending for social programs declined sharply in wartime.

Antitrust activity ceased. Businessmen poured into Washington to run new wartime bureaucracies. They regained much of the popularity and prestige that they had lost during the 1930s. Depression-bred popular resentment of business greed and social irresponsibility gave way to a new image of businessmen as patriotic partners providing the tools needed to win the war. Roosevelt, needing business cooperation for the war effort, cultivated a cordial relationship among his former adversaries. Populistic, antibusiness rhetoric vanished from public discourse. Secretary of War Henry Stimson observed: "If you are going to go to war . . . in a capitalist country, you have got to let business make money out of the process or business won't work." Many corporate leaders abandoned their bitter criticisms of Roosevelt and New Deal policies, having discovered that they could profit from the policies of the welfare state turned warfare state. Businessmen switched their political strategy from one of trying to dismantle big government to trying to use it to their advantage. Corporate executives would continue these new political strategies in the postwar era.

The war effort further centralized the corporate economy, because 90 percent of the billions of dollars the government spent on war contracts went to 100 large corporations. Big business got bigger in wartime, and most companies enjoyed historic high profits, surpassing anything earned during the best years of the 1920s. Wartime politics showed that the positive state, erected by liberals to fight the Great Depression and to promote social reform, could be manned by conservatives who would use its power to promote business interests, curtail reform, and attack trade unions—while winning a war. Conservatives continued to apply what they had learned in wartime during the postwar era.

The huge increase in the size and scope of the federal government, particularly in the executive branch, represented the most important wartime political development. As government spent more and more money, it became far more centralized than ever before. Federal bureaucracies assumed many economic functions previously performed by the private sector. The number of federal employees rose from 1 million in 1940 to 3.8 million in 1945, the most ever in the nation's history. Wartime agencies proliferated, generating an alphabetical avalanche that dwarfed the New Deal. President Roosevelt issued more executive orders during World War II than all previous presidents had during the entire history of the nation. The most powerful politicians in the country, after Roosevelt, were the men he appointed to run the war agencies. The president recruited most of these "war lords" of Washington from the ranks of business.

As the executive branch made a quantum leap in size and power, Congress suffered a relative decline in power and prestige. Through his active participation in foreign conferences and various domestic agencies coordinating the gigantic war effort, Roosevelt significantly enhanced the powers of the presidency and set an example followed by all postwar presidents. Both the power of the national government and the power of the presidency grew tremendously in wartime. The "imperial" presidency had its origins in World War II.

The Supreme Court, dominated by Roosevelt's eight liberal appointees, refused to review any cases involving wartime extensions of federal power into economic affairs, an arena in which it had been especially active during the New Deal years. The Court also refused to intervene in cases involving wartime violations of civil liberties, except to affirm the relocation of Japanese Americans from the Pacific Coast. The FBI, in wartime, acquired enhanced authority to spy on Americans and to tap telephones in national security cases.

The war multiplied the points of contact between the federal government and its citizens. Millions of names were added to the Social Security rolls, and everyone who worked had to pay federal income taxes. War experiences strengthened the tendency of people to look to Washington for solutions to their problems. This trend weakened social bonds and undermined state and local governments. People traded some of their personal freedom for greater government control and an enhanced sense of social security. This trade-off, of liberty for security, carried into the postwar era.

Washington became the biggest of all war boomtowns. In 1942, the Pentagon, the world's largest office building, opened. It housed over 35,000 bureaucrats, and its offices consumed thirty tons of paper annually. Lobbyists stalked the corridors of political power seeking ever-larger shares of the vast wartime expenditures flowing outward from Washington into corporate coffers. The broker-state, a creation of New Dealers, was much refined and significantly expanded in wartime. The government also subsidized the creation of new industries required by the necessities of war. With supplies of natural rubber from Southeast Asia cut, Washington spent nearly $1 billion to create a synthetic rubber industry to provide substitute products.

Much basic research for new weaponry and war industries had come from universities and colleges, which became committed to meeting the needs of military research. Most colleges and universities suffered no loss of enrollment during the war, despite massive conscription, because the government utilized their campuses for training enlisted men and officers. After the war, the GI Bill, which paid for millions of veterans' college educations, ensured the continuing growth and expansion of higher education.

World War II created a wartime partnership among businesses, universities, Congress, and the Pentagon, engaged in the procurement of war contracts. This "military-industrial complex," as President Eisenhower would later call it during his famed farewell address, nurtured during the war, came of age during the Cold War. It became a powerful lobby for creating a kind of permanent war economy in the postwar decades. The military-industrial complex guaranteed that the vastly enhanced authority of government in American economic and scientific affairs would continue after the war.

THE ELECTION OF 1944

During the 1944 election, President Roosevelt faced the challenge of Republican New York Governor Thomas E. Dewey. Roosevelt, to keep his party unified in wartime, dumped his vice president, Henry Wallace. Wallace, a fervent New Dealer, had alienated powerful big-city bosses and conservative Southerners within the Democratic Party. Roosevelt replaced Wallace with a candidate acceptable to all factions within the party, Missouri Senator Harry Truman. Truman had rendered valuable service to the country in wartime, heading a watchdog committee that had investigated government war contracts. Senator Truman's energetic, scrupulous efforts saved taxpayers billions of dollars and expedited the delivery of crucial war materials. Despite his wartime service, Truman was still a relative unknown in 1944, an undistinguished political journeyman acceptable to all powerful factions within the Democratic Party.

The contest between Roosevelt and Dewey was a rather dull, one-sided affair. In the eyes of many observers, Dewey did not appear presidential. He was a short, neat little man who came across as rather aloof, cold, and stiff. He also did not cultivate good relations with the media: Alice Roosevelt Longworth asked, "How can we be expected to vote for a man who looks like the bridegroom on a wedding cake?"

Newly empowered, organized labor played a major role in the 1944 campaign. The CIO, through its Political Action Committee, circumvented laws restricting union activities and funneled millions of dollars into the campaign for the Roosevelt ticket and many liberal congressional candidates. It also registered voters, circulated campaign literature, and got out the vote on Election Day.

Dewey's campaign strategy differed from previous Republican efforts. He accepted the New Deal welfare state but accused New Dealers of waste and inefficiency. He endorsed U.S. membership in a postwar United Nations. He also refused to make Roosevelt's foreign policy a campaign issue, not wishing to revive isolationist issues amidst the war. By embracing the welfare state and internationalism, Dewey placed both the New Deal and the war beyond partisan debate. His campaign proved ineffective.

Roosevelt, who did not campaign much, exploited his prestige as wartime commander in chief of a vast military effort that was winning everywhere. He attacked Republicans for their isolationism and reminded the electorate that they had been responsible for the Great Depression of the 1930s. He called attention to legislation benefiting veterans, including the G.I. Bill of Rights. Ominously, Roosevelt had aged dramatically by 1944. Friends and close political associates noticed that he had grown frail and thin. His hands trembled, and there were dark circles under his eyes. His doctors knew that he was suffering from heart disease and hypertension, however, the American public was not informed and apparently took no notice of Roosevelt's failing health. Journalists, if they noted anything, kept it to themselves.

In November, Roosevelt easily won his fourth presidential election victory, carrying thirty-six states to Dewey's twelve. His electoral vote count was 432 to 99, but his popular vote tally was only 25.6 million to 22 million for Dewey. Roosevelt's 53.4 percent of the popular vote was his smallest margin ever. The conservative coalition retained its control of Congress. The 1944 vote revealed an important demographic change that was occurring in the country. The Democratic Party was becoming more urban as a result of the wartime migration that had lured millions of workers from rural regions into the cities.

WAR AND CULTURE

During the war, television had not yet come of age. Print journalism (newspapers and magazines), radio, and "movies" flourished in vigorous variety. The three major mass media enjoyed a rough equality. People spent hours each week listening to radio programs in their homes or while driving their cars, but they also read one or two daily newspapers, subscribed to several magazines, and went to the movies on the average of twice a week.

Sales of books, both fiction and nonfiction, increased sharply in wartime. People had more money to spend on books and more time available for reading. Writers were generally less alienated than they had been during the 1920s and 1930s. In 1943, Ayn Rand wrote *The Fountainhead,* a best-seller that praised individualism over collectivism. Friedrich Hayek, an expatriate Austrian economist living in the United States, wrote *The Road to Serfdom,* a conservative tract that argued that modern liberalism was the path to tyranny. Although a difficult book to read, *The Road to Serfdom* enjoyed wide sales. It should be noted that by no means did most Americans read serious fiction or non-fiction books in wartime. By far, the most popular literary genre was comic books. One-third of young adults read comic books regularly; some adults read only comic books. Special editions of the most popular comic books were made available to soldiers.

An emerging generation of young writers found in World War II the defining experience of their lives, among them Saul Bellow, Irving Shaw, and John Hersey. Many war novels and journalistic accounts of the war made the best-seller charts. The best and most popular war correspondent was Ernie Pyle, a quiet Midwesterner who wrote with great insight and accuracy about ordinary soldiers in combat. His *Brave Men,* published in 1945, after he had been killed covering the Okinawa campaign, remains the finest account of GI life ever written.

Ballroom dancing also flourished during the war. The popularity of jitterbugging, a carryover from the late 1930s, continued unabated, especially among young people for whom it offered a distinctive world with its own clothes, language, and ritualistic behaviors. Energetic, athletic youngsters spun, whirled, and tossed their partners to the pulsing rhythms of hot jazz. Older couples enjoyed the more sedate pleasures of fox trots and waltzes. Night life, particularly New York night life, sparkled. Patrons of the Copacabana or the Latin Quarter could spend $100 on an evening of drinking, dancing, and enjoying the singing of young crooners such as Frank Sinatra and Perry Como or the sounds of big bands such as Tommy Dorsey's or Frankie Carle's.

Professional spectator sports drew large crowds, and racetracks enjoyed historic high attendance in wartime. Since most of its outstanding players were in military service, major league baseball continued its pennant races and annual World Series using mostly teenagers, castoffs, and overage players. One of these wartime athletes was in his way remarkable. Pete Gray, an outfielder for the Saint Louis Browns, played in seventy-seven games during the 1945 season, even though he had only one arm. Gray symbolized both the wartime circumstances of sports and the courageous overcoming of a handicap at a time when many disabled veterans were returning from war. A women's professional baseball league started up and, after a rugged start, flourished in wartime. Many of the women were fine athletes who played a spirited and highly skilled brand of baseball. The women's league continued its run into the 1950s before disbanding, mainly because of a lack of fan interest.

HOLLYWOOD GOES TO WAR

Hollywood prospered in wartime, even though the major studios produced far fewer movies a year than they had during the late 1930s. Before-tax profits increased from $42 million in 1939 to $239 million in 1945. Attendance at the nation's 18,000 movie houses trebled between 1941 and 1945. Surveys showed that about 75 percent of all Americans went to the movies. The typical moviegoer patronized a neighborhood theater at least twice a week during the war years. Millions of moviegoers also avidly read Hollywood fan magazines and newspaper stories about prominent movie stars. Two Hollywood gossip columnists, Hedda Hopper and Louella Parsons, were syndicated and had millions of devoted readers nationwide. The film industry was dominated by five major studios—Metro-Goldwyn-Mayer (MGM), Paramount, Warner Brothers, RKO, and Twentieth Century Fox. Each of the Big Five employed a small army of actors, directors, writers, technicians, and production personnel who turned out hundreds of pictures each year to slake the great American thirst for celluloid entertainment in wartime. In 1945, the five major studios enjoyed vertical control over both the creation and distribution of their films. They made the pictures and then distributed them through theater chains that they owned. In 1945, studio-owned theater chains earned over 70 percent of total box office receipts.

Hollywood had to adapt to wartime conditions. Most top male stars either got drafted or they enlisted, and thousands of technicians and production personnel went off to war. Jimmy Stewart flew bombing missions over Germany. Henry Fonda joined the Navy and served in the South Pacific. Clark Gable, "The King," joined the Army Air Corps. A lesser star from Warner Brothers, Ronald Reagan, was assigned to an Army Air Corps motion picture unit in Hollywood that made documentary and propaganda films. Many actors not in the armed forces and top women stars like Dorothy Lamour, Rita Hayworth, and Betty Grable entertained the troops both in the States and around the world.

Even though the major studios continued to turn out the standard genres—Westerns, detective thrillers, adventure films, romances, gangster pictures, and musicals, wartime Hollywood mostly made war movies. The studios churned out a flood of war and spy stories. Many Chinese actors got work in Hollywood films for the first time, playing Japanese villains in war movies. John Wayne starred in a series of war epics glorifying various branches of the military service—*Flying Tigers, Fighting Seabees,* and *The Sands of Iwo Jima,* the last about the U.S. Marine Corps. The best war film was *The Story of GI Joe,* adapted from Ernie Pyle's reporting. It contained no preaching, no propaganda, no hateful enemy stereotypes, and no heroes. It depicted American soldiers as skilled professionals doing a dirty job, trying mainly to survive and return home after the war. Hollywood also made several excellent war documentaries, the best one a series produced by Frank Capra and John Huston. Another wartime film genre was the "canteen film." It was a celluloid USO show, hosted by a big-name star featuring celebrity guests who sang, danced, and told jokes—all promoting the war effort.

Hollywood films in wartime continued to project cultural stereotypes onto the silver screen. African American soldiers occasionally appeared in war films, usually as "happy Negroes," jiving, dancing, grinning and laughing. Jewish soldiers were portrayed as guys named "Brooklyn" who looked forward to returning to Ebbets Field after the war and jeering at the Giants. Women were usually portrayed as the "weaker sex," dependent upon men and totally involved with their homes, children, and marriage. Native Americans continued to be depicted as primitive and duplicitous savages. The Japanese were portrayed as depraved, cruel, and vicious, with many references to "slant-eyed rats," "little yellow monkeys," and "beasts."

Responding to governmental pressure applied through the Office of War Information, war films portrayed American allies such as the Chinese, the British, and the French as heroic. Wartime movie Russians were hearty, simple people and gallant fighters. In *Mission to Moscow,* an American diplomat goes off to Moscow to meet the Russians. He is tailed by two jolly KGB agents who cheerfully inform the American star that the infa-

**Figure 1.7   Hollywood does its bit for the war effort . . .
Pin-up photos of Betty Grable, famed for her "million
dollar legs," adorned thousands of soldiers' footlockers
around the world.**   *Source:* National Archives.

mous purge trials of the 1930s were necessary to save the Soviet Union from a Fascist
coup.

Wartime Hollywood had to continue to conform to strict moral codes and observe political limits as well. Churches, especially the Catholic Church's Legion of Decency, functioned as moral watchdogs for the movie industry. The major studios were scrupulous in
placating these powerful censors, especially the Legion of Decency, which purportedly
spoke for the nation's Catholics, representing 20 percent of the national movie audience.
The studios tried to anticipate Legion objections and to pre-censor their movies. The major
film factories also resorted to considerable self-regulation to placate the self-appointed
guardians of movie morality. Criminals could never escape unpunished in a Hollywood
film. Sexual contact was carefully limited to gentle kissing between fully-clothed adults.
Homosexuality was never mentioned, much less displayed. Profanity was forbidden. Characters were statically portrayed either as total villains with no redeeming features or as
heroic figures with no faults or weaknesses. Ideas were censored, as was moral conduct.
Films had to stay within mainstream ideological boundaries. Radical ideas or serious social
criticism were excised from Hollywood pictures. Serious political discourse rarely found
its way into Hollywood films, and when it did, it usually parroted the bland patriotic liberalism emanating from Franklin Roosevelt's wartime White House.

Most wartime films were mediocre, but a few qualified as serious art. In 1945, Billy
Wilder directed *Lost Weekend,* a story about an alcoholic, starring Ray Milland and Jane
Wyman. It was a serious, sensitive treatment of alcoholism and its ruinous effects upon the
lives of people. *Lost Weekend* won an Academy Award for best picture, and both Milland
and Wilder also received Oscars. One World War II film became a classic. In 1942, Warner
Brothers brought out a low-budget melodrama set in Morocco. It told a tale of an American nightclub owner, Rick Blaine, who hides patriotic idealism beneath a hard-boiled sur-

face. In the end, Blaine sacrifices both his business and the woman he loves to rescue an anti-Nazi resistance fighter. Humphrey Bogart played Blaine in *Casablanca,* becoming a cult hero to millions of moviegoers in the postwar era.

WARTIME RADIO

In the pre-television years, another electronic medium, radio, became more popular than ever in wartime. Just as the film industry was dominated by five major studios, the radio industry was controlled by four major national networks. The National Broadcasting Company (NBC) was the oldest and largest. Columbia Broadcasting System (CBS) was second, followed by the American Broadcasting Company (ABC), which began as a spin-off from NBC in 1941, and the Mutual Broadcasting System. More than half of the country's 75,000 radio stations were affiliated with one of the major networks, and the networks all had affiliates in the large metropolitan centers of the nation.

Radio programming fell into different categories or genres. The most popular in 1945 were musical shows. One of the top musical shows was the *Lucky Strike Hit Parade.* Other popular musicals featured well-known singers such as Kate Smith and Bing Crosby. For aficionados of serious music, there was the NBC symphony orchestra, sponsored by Standard Oil, and the New York Metropolitan Opera, sponsored by Texaco. After musicals, the second most popular programs were drama, including the daytime dramas or "soap operas," whose large audiences consisted mostly of women. Prime-time programming featured a variety of action-adventure dramas with a cast of heroic detectives, cowboys, and space warriors who overcame villains and upheld law and order. Other genres included quiz programs and situation comedies. The longest-running and one of the most popular of these weekly comedies in 1945 was *Amos 'n Andy.* The show highlighted the hilarious adventures of two African Americans from the South, now living in Harlem, but the characters of Amos and Andy were played by two white actors.

Radio was a prime source of news about the war. World War II was the first war that was ever given live media coverage. War correspondent Edward R. Murrow described the Battle of Britain for American radio audiences in the summer of 1940. People listened to his deep, solemn voice, hearing shrill air raid sirens and the roar of exploding bombs in the background, as Murrow vividly described the "blitz" of London. He brought the European war into American living rooms. Throughout the war, foreign correspondents in Europe and Asia often risked their lives to go everywhere the soldiers went and to transmit firsthand accounts of battles to the folks back home. Radio correspondents hit the beaches at Normandy with the invading forces. Many of these correspondents were killed or wounded in action. Never had war journalism been so direct or authentic.

But censors often edited the news. Broadcasters frequently sacrificed factual accuracy for dramatic effect. War news had entertainment as well as informational value. Wartime radio remained essentially an entertainment medium, always accompanied by incessant commercial messages urging listeners to buy cigarettes, soap, and chewing gum. Radio often appeared to be little more than a conduit through which advertisers poured their commercials for the myriad of products they manufactured. Advertisers also had great influence on the contents of the shows that they sponsored, including news and news commentaries. Sponsors favored the largest possible audiences and frowned upon any programming that was artistically or politically controversial, because they feared it might alienate viewers. The biggest single purchaser of airtime, Proctor and Gamble, the giant cleaning products company, had a policy of never offending a single listener. In 1945, good radio often was subordinated to good salesmanship.

WORLD WAR AND ITS LEGACIES

World War II was an intense, transforming experience for most Americans. The war fundamentally changed American society in many ways. These war-induced changes were more profound and permanent than any occurring in this country since the Industrial Revolution. On the eve of war, Americans suffered from the lingering effects of the Great Depression—high unemployment, low productivity, and massive poverty—accompanied by lurking doubts about the vitality of American institutions and the purpose of national life. Americans looked out at a threatening world engulfed in war, a world in which their nation played only a peripheral role. Within the nation, Americans quarreled bitterly among themselves over President Roosevelt's conduct of foreign policy, until the bombing of Pearl Harbor abruptly ended the debate.

Four years later, a unified, proud, and powerful nation emerged victoriously from war. Its armed forces and industrial might had played decisive roles in destroying Fascism, militarism, and imperialism around the globe. America had won the largest war in human history. War revitalized the American economy; it emerged far more productive and prosperous than ever. More Americans lived better than they ever had before, and the proportion of poor Americans had been reduced to historic lows. American faith in capitalism and democratic institutions also had been restored. Compared to other nations at war, American casualties had been light. American civilians had been spared the devastations and terrors of a war fought outside of its continental boundaries. Fewer than 12 percent of the nation's population had served in the armed forces; over half of those who did never left the States, and the majority of those who got sent overseas never experienced a moment's combat.

The day the war against Japan ended, the United States reached its apogee as a world power. It strode the world as an international colossus; its armed forces, linked to its nuclear monopoly, made it the most powerful nation-state in the history of the planet. Its statesmen took the lead in creating a new international agency to preserve peace in the postwar era. Fittingly, the United Nation's permanent home would be New York, the financial and cultural capital of the new imperium.

The war was a watershed from which emerged the dominant patterns of postwar life. It forced Americans to accept involvement with the world beyond national boundaries; there could be no reversion to isolationism after 1945. Their war experiences gave Americans new confidence that they could solve all serious problems, both internal and external. They had proved that they had both the will and the means to lick depression at home and aggression abroad.

The major contours of post–1945 American history originated in the war experience.

The long Cold War with the Soviet Union that dominated international affairs for decades after the war stemmed from the tensions and conflicts that strained the Grand Alliance in wartime. Soviet leader Joseph Stalin distrusted the Western leaders, whom he suspected of deliberately delaying the opening of a second front against the Germans. Postwar economic policies were derived from the awareness that federal spending in wartime had finally ended economic depression. Political leaders during the postwar era assumed that similar fiscal practices could stabilize the business cycle and promote economic growth. A new understanding of the role of consumerism in sustaining economic growth meant that government would promote spending instead of saving after the war. The struggles and achievements of women and minorities in wartime planted the seeds of their postwar drives for equal access to the American Dream.

The war shifted American politics to the Right. Americans generally became more conservative, fundamentally because the restoration of prosperity gave most Americans more to conserve. The Republican Party made a significant comeback during the war years, and the informal conservative coalition of Southern Democrats and Northern Republicans consolidated its control of the legislative process. Leviathan was the most important political legacy of World War II. Big government became the foundation of the modern social welfare/warfare state that would dominate national politics in the decades following the war. Washington regulated the economy and was the conservator of the natural environment. In the postwar era, huge federal bureaucracies became a fourth branch of the national government; most of the actions taken by the federal government directly affecting the lives of its citizens were taken by the legions of bureaucrats staffing these large federal agencies. The organizational society, a society increasingly dominated by large public and private sector bureaucracies that characterized the postwar era, came of age during World War II.

The war left a mixed environmental legacy. On the one hand, it heightened awareness that the American economy was becoming less self-sufficient and increasingly dependent on foreign sources for strategic minerals and oil. On the other hand, the crash production programs of wartime to outproduce the enemy accelerated the depletion of natural resources. During the war, energy sources, technology, and industrial capacity were all maximally utilized. Trees were cut down. Air and water were polluted. Farmers made far greater use of chemical fertilizers and pesticides to enhance output. Ecological awareness and conservation issues were neglected in wartime; these were seen as luxuries that a nation engaged in total war for its survival could not afford. Trends established in wartime continued into the postwar era. Deteriorating environmental conditions finally brought about a surge of interest in the environment, which surfaced during the 1960s.

The war restored America's philosophic birthright, an optimistic sense of individual and national potential that would shape the national experience for the next three decades. The Axis powers were destroyed, the Soviet Union was exhausted, and Western Europe was depleted. But America was strong, prosperous, and free. Its people felt ready for the "American Century" they knew lay ahead. America's economy was powerful, its resources were abundant, and it had the scientific and technological talent to use them. Success in wartime gave Americans confidence and great expectations for a future that appeared to stretch limitlessly before them.

Americans also soberly confronted a future that they feared could bring a recurrence of the Great Depression. Could prosperity, growth, and full employment be sustained in the postwar era without the stimulus of a war economy? Could jobs be found for the millions of returning veterans and displaced war workers? Americans also worried about threats to their peace and security posed by the Soviet Union, an expanding Communist power. Perhaps the war had not made the world safe for democracy. Perhaps there was not going to be an American Century. Most of all, Americans were alarmed by the nuclear shadow that they had cast over the postwar era.

Americans, in the summer of 1945, faced the future with mixed feelings: feelings of pride, confidence, and hope, but also feelings of fear—of the return of depression, of expanding Soviet power, and of a nuclear catastrophe.

BIBLIOGRAPHY

Many fine studies of America during World War II are available. The following is a select list of those books that are especially well written and easily accessible. They will make informative, enjoyable reading for students who want to learn more about the prominent individuals and major events that dominated the war years and influenced the course of recent American history. Most of these books are available in paperback editions and can be found in any good college, university, or public library.

The best studies of the home front are Richard Polenberg's *War and Society: The United States, 1941–1945* and John Morton Blum's *"V" Was for Victory: Politics and American Culture during World War II.* The best social history of the United States at war is Geoffrey Perrett's *Days of Sadness, Years of Triumph.* Roland Young's *Congressional Politics in the Second World War* is a good political history. Susan M. Hartmann's *The Homefront and Beyond: American Women in the 1940s* is an account of women and the war. Another fine account of women's experiences during the war is Karen Anderson's *Wartime Women.* See also Sherna B. Gluck's *Rosie the Riveter Revisited: Women, the War, and Social Change.* Neil A. Wynn's *The Afro-American and the Second World War* has recorded the crucial experiences of black people in wartime. The best account of the wartime relocation of Japanese Americans is Edward Spencer's *Impounded People: Japanese Americans and World War II.* See also Peter Irons' *Justice at War: The Story of the Japanese-American Internment Cases.* Jeanne Wakatsuki Houston's and James D. Houston's *Farewell to Manzanar* is a compelling story of a Japanese family interned for the duration of the war. Richard R. Lingeman's *Don't You Know There's a War On?* is a general account of popular culture in wartime. Joel Greenberg's *Hollywood in the Forties* is an account of wartime movies and their effects on the populace. James L. Baughman's *The Republic of Mass Culture* has an informative chapter about the major mass media—print journalism, radio, and movies—during the war years. John Brooks' *The Great Leap: The Past Twenty-Five Years in America* is an important book highlighting the immense changes brought about in this country by World War II that shaped the postwar era. Two fine regional studies of the impact of world war include Gerald D. Nash's *World War II and the West: Reshaping the Economy* and Avram Mezerick's *The Revolt of the South and West.* The best novel about the war experience in this country is Harriet Arnow's *The Dollmaker,* which movingly describes its disruptions and dislocations.

2

The Rise of the Cold War

When World War II ended, much of the world faced the daunting task of digging itself out from rubble. The world's first global war had left a large part of Europe and many nations of Asia and elsewhere in ruins and had shattered the old balance of power. Even most of the victors had fared badly. The Soviets had lost 30 million people, and much of their economy had been ruined by war. It would be years before the Soviet Union would regain the industrial and agricultural productivity it had enjoyed when Germany invaded that country in 1941. The British, depleted economically and militarily, faced the imminent loss of much of their vast empire and the painful necessity of adjusting to the new status of being a second-rate power in the postwar world. After 1945, Britain's ability to play a major role in world affairs would depend mainly on American friendship and support. France had been humiliated by defeat and occupation during the war. The French economy was weak, its government was unstable, and the French Communist Party was a rising force.

The war had so weakened the British, French, and Dutch nations that they could no longer control many of their rebellious colonies in Asia, Africa, and the Middle East. Throughout the postwar era, the decolonization process that had begun during World War II accelerated, presenting challenges to the United States in what became known as the Third World. In the Far East, China was sinking into the chaos of civil war, dashing any hopes that Americans still entertained that it would be a major factor in postwar Asian diplomacy. Only America emerged from the war with its wealth and power enhanced and with most of its citizens better off than they had ever been before. The United States, for the first time in its history, had become a global power, the mightiest nation in the history of the world.

Postwar American celebrations of victory and expectations of a peaceful and prosperous world order dominated by the United States quickly gave way to conflicts between

America and its erstwhile ally, the Soviet Union. A multitude of challenging postwar political problems generated over forty years of tension, ideological warfare, and a thermonuclear arms race that historians called the Cold War. Beginning in 1945 and 1946, the Cold War would remain the dominant international reality influencing the conduct of U.S. foreign policy for over four decades.

THE UNITED NATIONS

It was a grim world into which the United Nations (UN) was born. President Roosevelt had made the creation of a postwar international organization to prevent aggression in the world his major diplomatic objective. Most influential Americans shared his goal, determined not to repeat the mistake the United States had made after World War I, when they refused to join the League of Nations. Many Americans believed that the United States' failure to join the League had undermined it, contributing to the breakdown of international order during the 1930s that had led to World War II.

The UN experienced significant birthing pains. Soviet and American delegates quarreled frequently over many features of the new organization. A young journalist on special assignment from the Hearst press syndicate covering the founding conference (himself a combat veteran) wrote angrily about the lack of a conciliatory spirit among the delegates: John F. Kennedy could not see that the statesmen had learned anything from the destruction of war. He saw delegates from the gathered nations all playing politics as usual. Eventually they wrote and signed a charter. Despite some concessions to the Soviets to ensure their participation, the UN was largely an American creation. It was Woodrow Wilson's League of Nations Covenant reborn and slightly revised.

The UN Charter created an "upper house," the Security Council, and a "lower house," the General Assembly. It also fashioned a permanent administrative apparatus, called the Secretariat, and many allied agencies, including the International Court of Justice, the International Monetary Fund, the Export-Import Bank, and the United Nations Relief and Rehabilitation Agency (UNRRA). The Security Council consisted of the five major world powers—the United States, the Soviet Union, Great Britain, France, and China—and six associate members elected from the General Assembly to serve for two years on a rotating basis. Action on all important matters required unanimous approval from the five permanent Security Council members, giving each an absolute veto of any UN action it found contrary to its interests. In the General Assembly, every nation was represented, but only for debate, not decision. The UN was a federation of sovereign states. It had only the powers that the major nations permitted it to have. It had no tax powers, depending on member contributions for funds. It had no military forces of its own. It quickly proved to be powerless to prevent aggression by the major powers. With the advent of the Cold War, the UN often was ignored or bypassed by the United States and the Soviet Union. Sometimes delegates representing the two superpowers would use the UN Security Council meetings as a propaganda forum to defend their actions and to recruit supporters.

U.S. officials were mainly responsible for creating an international agency with contingent powers. President Roosevelt had insisted upon devising an organization that would not impair national sovereignty but would allow the major powers to police their regional spheres of influence. There was a core of realpolitik underlying Roosevelt's commitment to Wilsonian internationalism. Neither the United States nor the Soviet Union would have joined any postwar international agency that did not permit them to retain an absolute veto over its actions.

Immediately after the war, the UN provided relief to the war-ravaged populations of Europe and Asia. The United States funneled billions of dollars through the UNRRA for food, clothing, and medicine for needy people in Germany, Japan, China, and Eastern Europe. The British borrowed $3.75 billion from the United States in 1946, much of which was used to pay for food imports. Postwar Germany faced economic disaster. Germans had no money. German industrial and agricultural production had shrunk to pitiful fractions of prewar levels. Germany's population had swelled from the addition of 10 million "displaced persons," German refugees who had either been expelled or had fled from Eastern Europe. Churchill called postwar Europe "a rubble heap, a charnel house."

The United States shared occupation responsibilities in Germany with the Soviets, the British, and the French, but it had sole authority in Japan. In the American occupation zone in Germany, U.S. officials worked hard to root out all traces of Naziism. Special courts punished over 1,500 major Nazi offenders and over 600,000 minor Nazi officials. The most famous trial occurred at Nuremberg, the former site of huge Nazi Party rallies during the 1930s. An international tribunal put twenty-two former high Nazi officials on trial, nineteen of whom were convicted and twelve hanged for "war crimes and atrocities." In Japan, U.S. officials, under the command of the American proconsul General Douglas MacArthur, staged a Tokyo equivalent of Nuremberg. Twenty-eight former high Japanese officials were tried, and all were convicted of war crimes. Seven were hanged, including former Premier Hideki Tojo.

Americans also completely refashioned Japanese society. They broke up industrial monopolies, abolished feudal estates, and implemented land reform. They introduced political democracy and established independent trade unions. They forced the Japanese to destroy all military weapons and to renounce war as an instrument of national policy. The Japanese have depended on America's nuclear shield to protect their national security ever since. Most important for the future of Japan, American engineers modernized Japanese industry, introducing new management and quality control techniques and modern industrial technology. From the ashes of war, with help from their conquerors, the Japanese fashioned a working system of political economy. By the early 1970s, Japan had become both a major trading partner and a potent commercial rival of the United States.

TRUMAN TAKES CHARGE

On April 12, 1945, President Franklin Roosevelt died suddenly of a cerebral hemorrhage at his vacation retreat in Warm Springs, Georgia. The titan's death immediately thrust Harry Truman into the White House, leader by chance of history's mightiest wartime coalition of nations. At the time of his accession to the presidency, Truman was ill-prepared and virtually unknown. Chairman of the Joint Chiefs of Staff Admiral William Leahy spoke for millions of his fellow Americans when he asked, "Who the hell is Harry Truman?"

During Truman's three-months' tenure as vice president, Roosevelt, who did not know him well nor have a very high opinion of his talents, met with him infrequently. The president had not kept his vice president informed of his major military, political, and diplomatic decisions. Truman learned most of what he knew about the Roosevelt administration's actions from reading the newspapers and listening to the radio news. But now it was Truman who would have to bring history's largest war to a successful conclusion and shape the peace that would follow. It was Truman who would have to manage the German surrender, maintain good relations with America's thorny Communist ally, the Soviet Union, and make the awesome decision whether to use atomic bombs on Japanese cities. No president ever began office under less promising circumstances or had to face greater pressures than did Harry Truman.

ORIGINS OF COLD WAR

During 1945 and 1946, American and Soviet leaders clashed over many postwar political issues. Their wartime alliance deteriorated. Even before war's end, the Allies had quarreled over the opening of a second front in Western Europe and the future political status of Eastern European countries. The proximate origins of the Cold War conflict lay in these wartime strains within the Grand Alliance. Historians, concerned with putting the origins of the Cold War into a larger framework, have traced the roots of the Cold War to the American response to the 1917 Bolshevik Revolution and Lenin's profound hatred of Western liberal capitalist culture. From 1917 until 1933, a succession of American presidents refused to recognize the Soviet state. Even after the normalization of U.S.-USSR relations in 1933, friendly relations between the two nations did not evolve. When Stalin concluded the non-aggression pact with Hitler in August 1939, most Americans equated the Soviet Union with Nazi Germany. It was the wartime alliance between the Americans and the Soviets, born of strategic necessity, that represented a departure from the historic norm of mutual distrust and ideological hostility.

During the war, the leaders of the major allies, the Big Three—Roosevelt, Stalin, and Churchill—met on occasion to discuss political problems and to plot grand strategy. The most famous meeting of the Big Three took place at Yalta, a resort on the Black Sea coast, on February 4, 1945, to February 11, 1945. At Yalta, Roosevelt, Churchill, and Stalin charted the final drives of the European war, discussed the Pacific war, talked about the postwar political status of Eastern European countries, planned for occupying Germany, and arranged for the creation of a proposed United Nations.

It was at Yalta that the Big Three agreed to divide Germany into four occupation zones, with France assigned the fourth zone. They also agreed to a joint occupation of Berlin, which lay deep within the Soviet zone in Eastern Germany, an arrangement that both sides deeply regretted after the rise of the Cold War. Berlin became one of the recurring flash points of the Cold War in Europe for thirty years. All parties accepted the principle of German reparations for the Soviet Union and referred the matter to an appointed commission to determine specific amounts.

Roosevelt initiated discussions at Yalta on the pending formation of the United Nations. Vigorous American participation in an international organization armed with power to maintain peace by using economic sanctions or military force was Roosevelt's chief concern at Yalta. He wanted Stalin, without whose cooperation it could not succeed, to commit himself to full support for the new agency to be created at San Francisco in April 1945. To ensure Soviet cooperation, he accepted Stalin's demand for three votes in the General Assembly.

The postwar political status of Poland caused the most controversy at the Yalta conference, particularly the composition of its new government. There were, at the time, two governments claiming to represent all Poles, one headquartered in London, championed by the British, and one in Lublin, backed by the Soviets. Stalin, making it clear that Poland was a vital Soviet interest, proposed that the Communist-controlled government at Lublin become the government of a new Poland. Roosevelt proposed a government comprised of representatives of Poland's five major political parties. The Soviets rejected it, but Stalin agreed to add "democratic elements" to the Lublin regime. To avoid letting differences over Poland undermine conference harmony, the Allies worked out an agreement that papered over significant differences with vague, elastic language. Stalin agreed to "free and unfettered elections" at an unspecified time in the future. Roosevelt settled for a reorganized Lublin regime that included "other" political leaders, language susceptible to differing interpretations.

At Yalta, Roosevelt also wanted to commit the Soviets to entering the Asian war against Japan as soon as possible. On February 10, Stalin and Roosevelt signed a secret treaty in which the Soviet Union agreed to enter the war within three months following Germany's surrender. In return, the Soviets were given several concessions: a Soviet-controlled satellite in Outer Mongolia; the guaranteed return of the southern portion of Sakhalin Island; the internationalization of the port of Darien; a lease for the use of Port Arthur as a naval base; the establishment of a joint Chinese-Soviet consortium to operate the Manchurian railways; and the Japanese transference of the Kurile Islands to them.

Figure 2.1   The Big Three. Prime Minister Winston Churchill of Great Britain, President Franklin Roosevelt of the United States, and Premier Joseph Stalin of the Soviet Union held several wartime conferences. At Yalta, a Black Sea resort in the Crimea, they met for the last time in February 1945. *Source:* U.S. Army Photo.

President Roosevelt and his advisers considered the price of Soviet entry into the Asian war reasonable at the time. The expectation that an atomic bomb would be ready in August did not alter Roosevelt's goal of getting the Soviets into the war. His military advisers told Roosevelt that Soviet participation at the earliest possible moment would ensure the defeat of Japanese forces in Manchuria, and that Soviet air raids on Japan flown from Siberia would ensure the disruption of Japanese shipping from the Asian mainland. Most important, Soviet intervention would shorten the war and save thousands of American lives.

The atmosphere at Yalta was cordial, as befitted members of a wartime coalition who still needed one another to achieve victory over their enemies. Both sides made compromises and concessions. Controversies and disagreements were covered over or deferred; they were not allowed to disrupt proceedings. But the Soviets achieved more important diplomatic victories at Yalta than the United States. Stalin used the military situation favoring the Soviet Union at the time to achieve his objectives. The role of the Allied military in the ultimate defeat of the Germans was relatively minor compared to the Soviet effort. Hundreds of Soviet divisions fighting the best Wehrmacht armies in the Soviet Union and Eastern Europe eventually broke the spine of German power. As Red forces overran Eastern and Southern Europe, Stalin used military occupation to gain political control of countries within these strategic regions. Stalin also used the American desire for Soviet entry into the war against Japan to exact major diplomatic concessions in the Far East. Roosevelt did not "sell out" China to the Soviets at Yalta as Republican critics later charged, but the Yalta agreements amounted to a significant diplomatic victory for the Soviet Union.

Cordiality among the Allies began to dissipate soon after the Yalta conference. In March 1945, President Roosevelt perceived Soviet efforts to impose a Communist regime on Poland as a violation of the Yalta agreements and protested to Stalin. Truman, who succeeded Roosevelt in April, was inexperienced in the craft of diplomacy and lacked FDR's poise and style. Truman also believed that Roosevelt had been too easy on Stalin and that he would stand up to the Soviets. Truman personally rebuked Soviet Foreign Minister V. M. Molotov over Yalta violations. Truman's outburst shocked and angered the Soviet foreign minister, but Truman's tough words to the Soviet diplomat had no effect on Soviet foreign policy. Stalin made it bluntly clear that maintaining a security zone in Eastern Europe was much more vital to Soviet interests than maintaining cordial relations with wartime allies. Besides, military force gave the Soviet Union control of Eastern Europe's political destinies. In 1945 and 1946, Soviet military forces installed puppet Communist regimes in Poland, Bulgaria, and Rumania. In 1947 and 1948, the Soviets used local Communist forces to install Communist regimes in Hungary and Czechoslovakia. Stalin, determined to protect his empire and its Communist system from future security threats, and perhaps also from Western cultural influences and U.S. investment, erected a ring of submissive client states along the Soviet Union's western periphery.

American political leaders and prominent journalists strongly condemned Soviet domination of Poland and other Eastern European countries. American statesmen would not concede, at least for the record, that the new Soviet empire in Eastern Europe constituted a legitimate "sphere of influence," for several reasons: besides the sense of betrayal felt over Yalta, there were domestic political considerations. Millions of Americans of East European background were enraged at the Soviet Union's brutal domination of their ancestral homelands. Americans also anticipated having trade and investment opportunities in Eastern European countries in the postwar era until Communist control sealed them off. American leaders also felt a sense of righteous, missionary power, that they could move Eastern Europe toward democratic capitalism. Soviet intrusions frustrated American intentions and imposed an abhorrent system of political economy on the region that many Americans equated with Fascism.

At a time when American-Soviet relations were strained because of Stalin's intrusions into Eastern Europe, the Soviets applied for a $6 billion loan from the United States to rebuild their wrecked economy. American officials tried to apply pressure on the Soviets to make them more receptive to American goals for Eastern Europe. The State Department refused to consider the loan unless, as U.S. Ambassador to the Soviet Union Averill Harriman put it, the Soviets "work cooperatively with us on international problems in accordance with our standards." The Soviets refused, and Americans rejected the loan request. A later Soviet request for $1 billion was made, contingent upon the Soviets permitting American trade and investment in Eastern Europe. Stalin refused to accept those terms, and the loan was denied. The Soviets rebuilt their economy using their own resources, plus whatever they could extract from Germany and Eastern Europe. Although U.S. efforts to extract Soviet concessions in exchange for credits had failed to change Soviet behavior in Eastern Europe, they angered Stalin, reinforcing his distrust of Western capitalist powers. Stalin also resented America's refusal to accept Soviet domination of Eastern Europe while excluding the Soviets from Italian and Japanese occupations.

But there were clear limits to what actions the Truman administration would take to prevent Soviet domination of Eastern Europe. It could denounce Soviet actions and apply economic and diplomatic pressures, but the United States never threatened the Soviets with military action. In the judgment of American leaders, the freedom of Eastern Europe from Soviet domination was not worth a war with the Soviet Union. When Stalin forcibly incorporated the eastern half of Europe into the Soviet empire between 1945 and 1948, the United States grudgingly accepted the creation of a de facto Soviet sphere of influence.

The Potsdam conference, held in late July 1945, the final wartime meeting of leaders of the United States, Great Britain, and the Soviet Union, revealed the strains within the Grand Alliance. The leaders often quarreled—over German boundaries and reparations, over the composition of the new Polish government, and over when the Soviet Union would enter the Pacific war against Japan. At Potsdam, a suburb north of Berlin, the Soviets pressed their demand, made at Yalta, for $20 billion of reparations to be taken from the German occupation zones. The Americans and British again refused to fix a dollar amount for reparations, but they permitted the Soviets to remove some industry from their zones. But in May 1946, the American military governor suddenly halted all reparations shipments from the U.S. zone. The angry Soviets denounced this U.S. unilateral action that canceled an agreement important to Soviet postwar reconstruction. Continual conflicts between the Soviets and the Western powers over occupation policy in occupied Germany were major causes of the Cold War. In fact, conflicts among former allies over Germany were the core causes of the Cold War, which originated in the heart of Europe.

It was at Potsdam that President Truman learned of the first successful testing of an atomic device. The U.S. atomic bomb project was history's most expensive scientific undertaking. Between 1941 and 1945, American and British scientists, engineers, and technicians, many of them émigré European Jews who had fled Nazi tyranny, labored intensively to build atomic bombs. U.S. Army Corps of Engineers General Leslie Groves headed the secret, top-priority program, code-named the "Manhattan District Project." A brilliant scientific team, gathered under the leadership of Dr. J. Robert Oppenheimer and working at Los Alamos, New Mexico, eventually solved the complex theoretical and technical problems involved in creating the immensely powerful new weapons.

The Manhattan Project was so secret that Congressmen who appropriated the vast sums of money for the bomb had no idea what the money was for. Harry Truman came to the presidency ignorant about the project. He was astonished to learn from Secretary of War Stimson, a few days after becoming president in April 1945, that the United States would soon have "the most terrible weapon ever known in human history, one bomb of which could destroy a whole city." In July, the world's first atomic device was exploded in the desert near Los Alamos at a site called Trinity. An awed Dr. Oppenheimer, witnessing the enormous fireball created by the explosion, was reminded of a passage from Hindu scriptures: "I am become Death, destroyer of worlds."

Before the weapon was completed, Stimson convened an Interim Committee that recommended unanimously to the president that the atomic bomb, when ready, be used without warning against Japan. Truman had concurred. Some scientists who had worked on the project opposed this recommendation at Committee hearings and proposed instead that the United States invite Japanese observers to witness a harmless demonstration of the bomb's power, perhaps inducing their surrender. Committee members unanimously rejected their recommendation, and Truman never learned of their proposal. Other high-ranking officials also urged holding back and trying to get Japan to surrender without having to use atomic weapons, perhaps by offering them better surrender terms. Truman consistently rejected such advice.

Meanwhile, a new government took power in Japan. Its civilian faction sought a way to end the hopeless war. Unaware of the secret Yalta agreements that would soon bring the Soviet Union into the war against Japan, a member of the peace faction sought Soviet mediation to get a modification of the unconditional surrender terms that would permit the Japanese to keep their emperor. The Soviets rebuffed the Japanese approach and informed Washington. American officials already knew of the Japanese peace feelers, because U.S. military intelligence personnel had been intercepting and decoding Japanese messages. They also knew that Japanese army officers, controlling the government, meant to fight on.

After discussions with his advisers at Potsdam, Truman issued a final warning to Japan before dropping the bombs. The message urged Japan to surrender unconditionally, or face "the utter devastation of the Japanese homeland." It made no mention of atomic weapons. The divided Japanese government, rejecting the ultimatum as "unworthy of public notice," ignored it.

Interpreting their silence as rejection, Truman saw no need to rescind an order given on July 30 to proceed with the atomic bomb attack. Early on the morning of August 6, 1945, three B-29s lifted off the runway at Tinian, bound for Hiroshima, Japan's eighth largest city. The lead aircraft, the *Enola Gay,* carried a five-ton atomic bomb in its specially configured bomb bay. The other two planes were escorts; they carried cameras and assemblages of scientific recording instruments.

At 8:16 A.M. local time, the sky exploded over Hiroshima. The world's first atomic bomb struck with the force of 12,000 tons of TNT. It killed or seriously wounded about 80,000 people instantly, many of them vaporized by the intense heat that exceeded 50 million degrees Fahrenheit at the center of the huge fireball. By the end of the year, 60,000 more people had died a dog's death from burns, wounds, and radiation poisoning. A thriving city of 320,000 inhabitants was reduced to instant rubble. A few hours after the bombing, Truman announced to the world the existence and first use of the atomic bomb. He also warned the Japanese that, unless they surrendered unconditionally, immediately, "they may expect a rain of ruin from the air, the like of which has never before been seen on earth." The Japanese did not surrender. Military leaders urged death over defeat.

Bad weather delayed for a few days the dropping of the second bomb. On August 8, Red Army units invaded Manchuria and Korea. The day after the Soviet Union entered the Asian war, a second atomic bomb was dropped on Nagasaki, as previously planned. Originally the city of Kokura had been selected for the second bombing, but stormy weather made bombing that target impossible. Nagasaki was an alternative target. The bomb that devastated Nagasaki was a plutonium one that yielded about 20,000 tons of TNT. It destroyed large sections of the city and killed 26,000 people. It would have killed far more people and done far greater damage had it not fallen off target.

Even after the atomic bombings and Soviet entry into the war, Japanese military leaders wanted to fight on. Only the personal intercession of Emperor Hirohito induced them to surrender. On August 10, the Japanese offered to surrender if they could keep their emperor. Truman accepted surrender unconditionally on August 14, although he did offer veiled assurances that the Japanese could retain their emperor, providing that he was stripped of his status as a divinity. Surrender ceremonies occurred on September 2 aboard the battleship USS *Missouri,* anchored in Tokyo Bay, with General Douglas MacArthur presiding.

Most Americans have accepted President Truman's justification for using the atomic bomb: "We have used it in order to shorten the agony of war, in order to save the lives of thousands and thousands of young Americans." But since the 1960s, critics have contended that the Japanese, perceiving their cause as hopeless, would have surrendered soon, without the atomic bombings. They argue that Truman had other, more important motives for using nuclear weapons besides ending the war—he wanted to enhance American postwar diplomatic leverage against the Soviet Union. They accuse him of using "atomic diplomacy," of dropping the bombs on the already beaten Japanese to hasten their surrender to keep the Soviets from venturing too far into China and from sharing in the postwar occupation of Japan. Critics further contend that Truman also intended the bombings to make the USSR more agreeable to American solutions to postwar political problems.

It is impossible for any scholar, after examining the extensive available evidence, to determine, with any degree of certainty, Truman's exact motives for ordering the two atomic bombings. Truman never debated with his senior advisers over whether to use atomic weapons on the Japanese. The atomic bomb project, initiated by Franklin Roosevelt years earlier, was nearing completion at the time Truman assumed the presidency. FDR had understood that the bomb, when available, would be used on the Germans and the Japanese if the wars were still raging. Since Germany surrendered on May 8, 1945, Truman assumed that atomic bombs would be used on Japan as soon as they became available.

Truman and his advisers discussed where, when, and how to use atomic weapons; they did not debate over whether to use them or not to use them. No one in Truman's circle considered the morality, wisdom, or strategic necessity of using those incredibly destructive weapons. Truman's role in the decision-making process was essentially a decision not to interfere with existing plans for the bombs' uses. Truman himself said later, "I regarded the bomb as a military weapon and never had any doubt that it would be used." There were additional considerations. U.S. leaders feared *post hoc* criticisms if they did not use the weapons. Suppose it came out after the war that they had wasted $2 billion on a giant atomic boondoggle that was developed and never used? Suppose it came out that they had developed a powerful weapon that might have shortened the war and saved thousands of U.S. soldiers' lives and failed to use it?

Although there can be no certainty in discerning Truman's motivation, it appears that his primary concern was to try to shorten the war and save American soldiers' lives, just as he always claimed. He hoped to avoid a protracted, bloody campaign to conquer the Japanese home islands. Truman also hoped that American use of the powerful new weapon would make the Soviets more cooperative, that it would give the U.S. additional bargaining leverage with them. And he hoped that use of the bombs might induce Japanese surrender before the Soviet Union entered the war, but the Soviets intervened between the dropping of the bombs. Truman also was disappointed to discover that U.S. possession and use of atomic bombs did not soften Soviet diplomacy. Whenever the Americans brought up the matter of atomic bombs with the Soviets, Stalin's response was to become more intractable, not less.

American willingness to use the atomic bombs in war along with Washington's failure to keep Stalin informed of the progress of the Manhattan District Project and American refusal to share any broad scientific information about nuclear weaponry with the Soviets were contributing causes of the Cold War. At a reception one afternoon at the Potsdam conference, Truman told Stalin informally that the United States had recently tested an extremely powerful new weapon. He did not tell the Soviet dictator that it was a nuclear device. Stalin merely smiled and said that that was fine, and that he hoped that it would soon be used on Japan. Truman did not have to tell Stalin that the United States had developed an atomic bomb; the Soviet leader understood instantly what Truman was referring to. But when Truman walked away, Stalin hastily conferred with his aides and decided on the spot to speed up a Soviet atomic weapons project that had been curtailed in wartime. The nuclear arms race began at that moment at a garden party in Potsdam.

FBI files, subsequently made public, proved that a spy ring working for the Soviet Union, whose most prominent members included an English physicist Klaus Fuchs and Americans David Greenglass, Harry Gold, and Julius Rosenberg, had penetrated the Manhattan District Project. By the time Americans had atomic bombed two Japanese cities, the spy ring had already delivered about 10,000 pages of classified documents to their Soviet masters. These secret data significantly helped the Soviet atomic bomb project. Experts have estimated that espionage accelerated the Soviet bomb project by as much as two years. At war's end, Soviet scientists already understood much of the technology required to process fissionable materials; they would build their own bombs within four years.

At war's end, the United States was overwhelmingly the world's preeminent economic and military power. With about 5 percent of the world's population, the United States produced over 60 percent of the world's goods and controlled over half of the world's wealth. Its $14 billion in gold reserves stored at Fort Knox represented about 75 percent of the world's gold supply in 1945. Despite its great wealth and power, the United States could not prevent the growing division of Europe nor bring stability to the Far East.

When American, British, and Soviet foreign ministers met in London in September 1945, they quarreled bitterly over who threatened whom. Mutual suspicion and hostility rendered diplomacy impossible. The Western powers demanded that the Soviets ease their control of Eastern Europe. In response, the Soviet leaders accused the West of capitalist encirclement and atomic blackmail. The former allies appeared to be on a collision course: the Soviets were determined to dominate the lesser states of Eastern Europe to erect a security sphere around their nation; the United States was determined to break down international trade barriers and to rebuild Germany, policies that frightened the Soviet leaders. Further, American leaders shared a vision of national greatness and national mission. In the postwar era, America intended to build a prosperous new world order, one based on free governments and free trade. In the world's family of nations, given its great wealth and power, America would be *primus inter pares* (first among equals). Such arrogance, with an atomic holster hanging on its hip, frightened and angered Soviet leaders.

From the American perspective, neither its great wealth nor its atomic monopoly guaranteed U.S. security in the postwar era. The destruction of German and Japanese power had removed historic barriers to Soviet expansion in Europe and Northeastern Asia. Rising anticolonial rebellions against lingering Western imperialism also gave the Soviet Union opportunities to expand its influence. From the Soviet perspective, expanding American influence in Europe and Asia alarmed the Soviet leaders. They were skeptical that the capitalist West could work cooperatively with the Communists, and they were fearful of the vastly superior American wealth, technology, and military power. Instinctively, Stalin tried to isolate the Soviet Union and its newly acquired empire in Eastern Europe from contact with the Western powers.

In early 1946, both sides escalated their rhetoric. On March 5, 1946, former Prime Minister Winston Churchill, visiting in the United States, declared "From Stettin in the Baltic to Trieste in the Adriatic, an iron curtain has descended across the continent." He then called for a joint Anglo-American effort to roll back the Soviet Iron Curtain. Stalin promptly accused Churchill of calling for war against the Soviet Union. U.S. public opinion polls showed widespread disapproval for Soviet actions in Germany and Eastern Europe. Stalin had also given a speech previously in which he reasserted the Leninist doctrine of the incompatibility of capitalism and socialism, and the necessity of revolutionary conflict in the world. Following this angry exchange, the Soviets rejected an American offer to join the World Bank and the International Monetary Fund, the two principal agencies for promoting free trade and stable currencies in the postwar world. The Soviets refused to join because they saw the Bank and the Fund as instruments through which the United States intended to dominate the emergent world economy.

American possession and use of nuclear weapons had spurred the Soviets to accelerate their own nuclear weapons development projects. Scientists knew that the U.S. monopoly was temporary; it was only a matter of time until the Soviets produced a bomb. The scientists predicted that it would take the Soviets about five years. The world would then be at the mercy of a costly and dangerous arms race without precedent in human history. They urged political leaders to implement a system of international control of nuclear weapons technology to fend off the looming arms race.

In an atmosphere of growing hostility and suspicion, Truman and his advisers tried to work out a plan for the international control of nuclear weapons through the UN. Bernard Baruch, the American delegate, proposed a plan calling for the international control of atomic weapons to be achieved in stages, during which the United States would retain its nuclear monopoly. His plan called for inspections within the Soviet Union by a UN commission to ensure compliance. The Soviets, working feverishly to develop their own nuclear weapons, rejected on-site inspections within their territory. They proposed an alternative plan calling for the destruction of American nuclear weapons before any control system would be devised. The Americans rejected the Soviet plan. Each side insisted on its plan or nothing, and they got nothing. The United States then opted for its own internal control mechanisms. In 1946, Congress enacted the Atomic Energy Act, which empowered the newly created Atomic Energy Commission (AEC), a civilian agency, to control all atomic energy research and development in the nation under tight security restrictions.

Thus vanished the world's only chance, admittedly a slim one, to eliminate the nuclear arms race before it became a major feature of the Cold War. It was the nuclear arms race that added a terrifying dimension to the U.S.-USSR rivalry, making it unlike any previous great power conflict in history. By 1955, both sides possessed the technical capability to destroy the other, and much of the rest of the world. Ironically, nuclear weapons also functioned to keep the Cold War cold. Had it not been for nuclear weapons, the Americans and the Soviets would probably have had a war long ago, for there was enough provocation on both sides. But neither dared attack the other because it knew the other side would resort to nuclear weapons before it would accept defeat. Mutual terror deterred both sides from full-scale war during the Cold War.

The failure of Washington and the Kremlin to find a mutually acceptable formula for controlling nuclear weapons technology highlighted the dawn of the Atomic Age. At about the same time the UN was debating the weapons issue, the United States conducted a series of atomic bomb tests in the South Pacific at Bikini atoll. Radio accounts and dramatic photos of the tests forced Americans to the horrific realization that humankind had produced weapons of mass destruction that could destroy the world. Some jaunty folks tried to make light of the matter, to laugh it off. Later that year, a French designer brought out a new type of women's bathing suit, which he named the "bikini." It had an explosive impact on women's swimwear fashion, because the new-style swimsuits exposed much more of the female body than did any previous model. Despite these brave efforts to laugh it away, the fear of a nuclear holocaust had rooted itself in the popular imagination. The American imagination in the postwar era was haunted for decades by the twin symbols of catastrophe—the mushroom cloud and nuclear missiles striking America's great cities. The Atomic Age ushered in the age of anxiety that continuously undercut celebrations of the affluent society.

There were many other conflicts and misunderstandings arising in the period 1945–1946 that poisoned the postwar U.S.-USSR diplomatic atmosphere. The major conflicts—

Figure 2.2   The Atomic Age begins. The mushroom cloud became one of the haunting symbols of catastrophe, proving that the age of affluence also was the age of anxiety.   *Source:* Joint Army Navy Task Force One photo.

over the postwar political status of Eastern Europe, over occupation policy in Germany, and over international control of atomic weapons—drove the United States and the Soviet Union apart. They were the major causes of the Cold War.

These disputes between America and the Soviet Union grew out of the war and the power vacuum created by the smashing of German power, a vacuum into which rushed the two expansionist powers: the United States, a global power, its leaders motivated by a sense of righteous power based on America's prosperous economy and atomic monopoly, strong ideological convictions, and important economic interests; and the USSR, a strong regional power, its leaders motivated by a fervent Communist ideology, an urgent desire to protect vital security interests, and a pressing need to rebuild its shattered economy. The United States and the Soviet Union collided at many points in Central and Eastern Europe. Emotions flared as leaders on both sides struggled to solve challenging and frustrating problems. Given their fundamental differences, their differing beliefs and perceptions, the intrinsic difficulties of their many problems, the pressures and antagonisms inherent in their many disputes, and their clashing goals and ambitions, in retrospect, it appears that conflicts between the Americans and the Soviets were inevitable.

Perhaps the Cold War also was inevitable, but it is at least remotely possible that more adroit and patient diplomacy by leaders of both sides, especially by Truman and Stalin, might have prevented these disputes of the 1945–1946 period from hardening into the long-term conflicts of the Cold War. The Cold War occurred because of the tragic failure of the two most powerful nations emerging from World War II to resolve their major disputes through the traditional processes of diplomacy, by negotiations and compromise. Instead, the leaders of the two nations, ready to read the worst intentions into the actions of their rivals and to anticipate worst-case scenarios, believed themselves compelled to resort to over four decades of ideological warfare. They also felt compelled, "like two apes on a treadmill," in Paul Warnke's phrase, to engage in a costly and dangerous thermonuclear arms race without precedent in history. The Cold War evolved into an interlocking, reciprocal process, involving genuine differences of principle, clashes of interest, and a wide range of misperceptions and misunderstandings.

CONTAINING COMMUNISM

From the vantage point of Washington in early 1947, the world appeared to be sinking into chaos. A nearly bankrupt Great Britain prepared to abandon India, Palestine, and Greece. The Vietnamese refused to accept the return of French colonialism, and Indochina was engulfed in war. Likewise, the Indonesians refused to accept the return of the Dutch and ignited a war. In China, a civil war raged between the Nationalists and Communists. Amidst rubble-strewn cities and ruined economies, the Japanese and Germans struggled to avoid famine. American leaders feared that the Soviet Union would try to exploit the severe political and economic problems of Europe and Asia.

In 1947, crises arose in the Balkans involving Greece and Turkey. Greece was engulfed in a civil war that pitted Communist-led insurgents against a Rightist government backed by the British. Simultaneously, the Soviets were pressuring the Turkish government to grant them joint control of the Dardanelles, a strait between the Black Sea and the Mediterranean. Control of the strait had been a long-term Soviet foreign policy goal. Stalin viewed joint control of the strait as vital to Soviet security. The Turks rebuffed the Soviets, and Stalin threatened to take action against them. The British also were backing the Turks in their dispute with the Soviets over control of the waterway. On February 21, 1947, citing economic problems, the British government informed Washington that it could no longer support Greece and Turkey with economic and military aid.

TWO HALVES OF THE SAME WALNUT

President Truman wanted the United States to replace the British in the Mediterranean and to help the Greeks and Turks, but he had to convince the Republican-controlled and economy-minded 80th Congress that his initiative served the national interest. The principal architect of the American aid program to Greece and Turkey was Undersecretary of State Dean Acheson. Acheson evoked an early version of the "domino theory" to stress the need for American aid to the two countries. He stated that if Greece fell to the Communists and the Soviets gained control of the Dardanelles, North Africa and the Middle East would be endangered. Morale would sink in Italy, France, and Western Germany; all would then be more vulnerable to a Communist takeover. Three continents would be opened to Soviet penetration. Acheson's alarmist presentation persuaded Senator Arthur Vandenberg, chairman of the Senate Foreign Relations Committee, a former Republican isolationist turned internationalist, to support Truman's proposed aid bill for Greece and Turkey.

George Kennan, a brilliant State Department Soviet expert, also furnished arguments supporting Truman's interventionist policy. Back in February 1946, Kennan, at the time the number two man in the U.S. Embassy in Moscow, had written a long telegram to Secretary of State Byrnes, alerting his boss to the threat to U.S. interests posed by the expansionist Soviet system. In July 1947, an expanded version of Kennan's telegram appeared in the influential journal *Foreign Affairs,* under the pseudonym of "Mr. X." In the article, Kennan contended that the Soviet system had a built-in expansionist dynamic, a dynamic driven by ideology. Soviet leaders were "impervious to the logic of reason" (diplomacy), but they remained "highly sensitive to the logic of force." Instead of trying to negotiate with Stalin and the other Soviet leaders, Kennan advised President Truman and his senior advisers to respond with:

> a policy of firm containment, designed to confront the Russians with unalterable counter-force at every point where they show signs of encroaching upon the interests of a peaceful and stable world.[1]

Kennan's analysis coincided with Truman's views of Soviet behavior and his recommendations accorded with the president's desire to get tough with the Soviet leaders. Containment, stopping the spread of Communist influence in the world, soon became the chief operating principle of American foreign policy in the postwar era. It would remain the cornerstone of U.S. foreign policy for more than forty years.

Truman also actively promoted the proposed aid bill for Greece and Turkey. In a speech given at Baylor University on March 6, 1947, he said that the American system of free enterprise could survive only if it were part of a free world economic system. He contended that American aid to Greece and Turkey was part of his strategy for preserving economic freedom in the world. Only a peaceful and prosperous world ensured American security in the Cold War era. He warned his audience that the "seeds of totalitarian regimes are nurtured by misery and want."

Truman's Baylor University speech preceded his major address before a joint session of Congress on March 12 to ask Congress to appropriate $400 million for Greek and Turkish aid. In the most important foreign policy speech of his presidency, mostly written for him by Acheson, Truman told the American people that the Communist threat to Greece and Turkey was Hitler and World War II all over again. History appeared to be repeating itself in Southern Europe. Truman then spoke the famed words that soon became known as the Truman Doctrine. The anti-Communism of the Truman Doctrine became, in the words of historian Thomas G. Paterson, "the commanding guide to American foreign policy in the Cold War."

> At the present moment in world history, nearly every nation must choose between alternative ways of life.

[1]George Kennan, *American Diplomacy* (New York: New American Library, 1952), p. 104. (Reprinted with permission of the editor from *Foreign Affairs,* XXV, No. 4, July 1947, pp. 566–582.)

One way of life is based upon the will of the majority, and is distinguished by free institutions . . . and freedom from political oppression. The second way of life is based upon the will of a minority forcibly imposed on the majority . . . and the suppression of personal freedom.

I believe that it must be the policy of the United States to support free peoples who are resisting attempted subjugation by armed minorities or by outside pressures. . . . If we falter in our leadership, we may endanger the peace of the world—we shall surely endanger the welfare of our own nation.[2]

Truman's speech amounted to a declaration of ideological warfare against the Soviet Union. He depicted a world engaged in a struggle between the forces of freedom and the forces of tyranny. The political fate of mankind hung on the outcome. In this mortal struggle, American aid to Greece and Turkey would serve the American mission of preserving freedom in the world and preventing World War III. Senator Vandenberg had told Truman that if he wanted to get bipartisan support for his aid program, he would have to "scare hell out of the American people." Truman apparently did. The President also played to America's idealistic bent for moral crusades for universal causes. Polls, which had been negative before his speech, soon showed a large majority favoring the aid program.

Not everyone accepted Truman's eloquent invitation to join the anti-Communist crusade. Both liberal and conservative critics opposed aid to Greece and Turkey. Some liberal intellectuals questioned Truman's use of the adjective "free" to describe the authoritarian governments of Greece and Turkey. "Free," in Truman's usage, had referred to any government threatened by Communism, not to genuine democracies. Henry Wallace denounced the aid bill as a waste of money and provocative to the Soviets. Walter Lippmann, the nation's most influential political journalist, also opposed it, observing that the United States could not police the world. But after a brief debate, large bipartisan majorities in both houses of Congress supported the aid bill. Truman's powerful rhetoric had carried his cause.

The Truman Doctrine defined a new American postwar foreign policy. Isolationism had been abandoned and the United Nations bypassed. Truman had committed America to resist actively Soviet expansionism in Southern Europe. The Truman Doctrine proclaimed that the era of the containment of Communism had begun. Although the first application of the new containment policy was limited, the doctrine justifying it was unlimited. During the early 1950s, American foreign policy based on the containment of Communism would inevitably expand to become a global commitment.

Congress fashioned several new government agencies to implement the containment policy. The National Security Act (1947) created the Department of Defense and established the Joint Chiefs of Staff. The act also made the Air Force a separate branch of military service and put the administration of the Army, Navy, and Air Force under a single department. The first Secretary of Defense was a hard-line Cold Warrior, James Forrestal. The National Security Act also created the National Security Council (NSC), a Cabinet-level advisory body to coordinate military and foreign policy for the president. The creation of the NSC indicated the growing influence of strategic considerations in the conduct of American foreign policy. The National Security Act also created the Central Intelligence Agency (CIA)

---

[2]Taken from a printed copy of Truman's speech, found in Armin Rappaport, ed., *Sources in American Diplomacy* (New York: Macmillan, 1966), pp. 329–330.

as an agency directly under the authority of the National Security Council. The CIA, a child of the Cold War, became a covert arm of American foreign policy during the early 1950s. The National Security Act institutionalized the Cold War.

In 1947, European recovery from the devastation of war was flagging. Washington feared that continuing hardships could force cold and hungry Europeans to turn to Communism, particularly in France and Italy, which had strong and popular Communist parties. A prostrate Europe also endangered American prosperity because of a huge "dollar gap" that had emerged. The dollar gap, totaling about $8 billion in 1947, represented the difference between the value of U.S. exports and the amount of dollars that European customers had on hand to pay for them. The dollar gap threatened to undermine American overseas trade and to erode U.S. postwar economic growth and prosperity.

Europeans could not buy American products unless they received dollars from the United States. Short-term credits, extended by the American government and banks, were only stopgap measures that perpetuated the economic imbalance between rich Americans and poor Europeans. To offset the lure of Communism and the possibility of Soviet intervention in Western Europe and to pump dollars into the impoverished European economy, American officials drafted a comprehensive European recovery program. They agreed that containment of Communism in Europe required the reconstruction of European economies. The new Secretary of State George Marshall, speaking at Harvard University on June 5, 1947, formally announced the outlines of a European recovery plan that came to bear his name directed against "hunger, poverty, desperation, and chaos." Truman called upon Congress to back up the proposed Marshall Plan with a $27 billion appropriation. The president called the Truman Doctrine and the Marshall Plan "two halves of the same Walnut."

The Marshall Plan called for a cooperative approach in which Europeans would plan their recovery needs collectively and the United States would underwrite a long-term recovery program. All European nations were invited to participate in the Marshall Plan, including the Soviet Union and the East European nations. With the British and French leading the way, Europeans responded immediately and enthusiastically. A general planning conference convened in Paris on June 26, 1947, to formulate an European reply. But the Soviets walked out of the conference, denouncing the Marshall Plan as an American scheme to dominate Europe. Stalin also may have feared that American economic aid would undermine his control of Eastern Europe, so he forced these nations to abstain from the recovery program. On July 16, Europeans established a Committee on European Economic Cooperation, which drew up plans for a four-year recovery effort.

Within the United States, Senator Vandenberg led a bipartisan effort to get congressional approval for the plan. Support for the aid program increased when Americans learned of a Communist takeover in Czechoslovakia that occurred as Congress debated the bill. Stalin apparently ordered the Czech coup as a response to the increasing integration of the West German economy into the liberal capitalist order. Truman used the Communist takeover in Czechoslovakia to promote the passage of the Marshall Plan. He argued that the Czech coup proved the Soviets' intentions to dominate the remaining free nations of Europe. Congress passed a slimmed-down version of the aid plan. The legislators appropriated $5.3 billion to implement the Marshall Plan in the summer of 1948. Congress also appropriated billions of dollars to rebuild Japan's shattered economy. When the Marshall Plan ended in 1952, the United States had provided over $13 billion for European economic recovery.

The Marshall Plan worked. European industrial production increased 200 percent from 1948 to 1952. The foundations for the West's later affluence were firmly laid. The appeal of Communism in the West dropped sharply. The program worked mainly because of its planned, long-term, cooperative approach. It also succeeded because Europe possessed the industrial base and skilled manpower needed to use the aid funds effectively. European economic recovery restored a region of crucial importance to the United States. It also proved to be a major stimulus to American economic activity and was in accord with Cold War ideological goals. George Marshall expected American economic aid to permit the "emergence of political and social conditions in which free institutions can exist." The Marshall Plan gave the U.S. policy of containment of Communism in Europe a sound economic foundation.

NATO

While furnishing the means for Europe's economic reconstruction, America also concerned itself with rebuilding Western Germany. With the rise of Soviet power in Eastern Europe, there was a power vacuum in Central Europe that America wanted to fill with a democratic and capitalistic Germany. Near the end of 1946, the Americans and British merged their German occupation zones and began to assign administrative responsibilities to German officials. By mid-1947, the effort to rebuild Germany's industrial economy had begun.

The Soviets reacted to Western efforts to rebuild the German economy and incorporate it into the European recovery plan by tightening their control of Eastern Europe. Perceiving that he had failed to prevent the restoration of a West German state, Stalin also tried to squeeze the Western powers out of Berlin. In June 1948, the Soviets suddenly shut down all Western access routes to their Berlin sectors, which lay deep inside the Soviet zone. The Berlin Blockade confronted the Truman administration with a serious crisis. Choices, at first, appeared only to include surrender or to risk World War III. Truman ordered sixty U.S. strategic bombers with the capability of hauling nuclear weapons to fly to bases in England. The Western powers also devised an Anglo-American airlift that flew food and fuel to 2.5 million West Berliners. The Soviets, not wanting to start World War III, did not interfere with the airlift. Soviet aircraft never challenged the Anglo-American aerial lifeline to the beleaguered city. In May 1949, after 324 days, the Soviets canceled the blockade. It had failed to dislodge the Allies, and it had failed to prevent the integration of the West German economy into the European recovery program.

In American eyes, the airlift symbolized Western resolve to maintain an outpost of freedom in the heart of Soviet tyranny. Truman had outmaneuvered the Soviets and forced them to rescind the blockade. The airlift also confirmed George Kennan's contention that only force, or a credible threat of force, could contain Communist expansionism. The Western powers created the Federal Republic of Germany (West Germany) soon after the blockade ended. In retaliation, the Soviets erected the Democratic Socialist Republic of Germany (East Germany). The Berlin Blockade represented the first major American-Soviet conflict

Figure 2.3   Berlin airlift.   *Source:* Brown Brothers.

of the Cold War. It also was the paradigmatic conflict that established the pattern of U.S.-USSR confrontations that would continually recur until the Cold War ended during the period 1989–1991 with the collapse of European Communism and the demise of the Soviet Union.

The Czech coup, the Berlin Blockade, and other Soviet actions hostile to Western interests convinced Washington officials that containment required military as well as economic measures. The germ of the North Atlantic Treaty Organization (NATO) appeared in a Senate resolution passed in 1948, expressing America's resolve to defend itself through collective security if necessary. The Truman administration began planning for the defense of Western Europe.

NATO came to life on April 4, 1949; ten European nations, Canada, and the United States signed the treaty. The heart of the mutual security pact could be found in Article 5: "an armed attack against one or more members . . . shall be considered an attack against them all." Attack any NATO member and you have to fight them all. With the establishment of NATO, Soviet aggression against Western Europe would mean World War III. The Senate ratified the treaty 82 to 13 on July 21, 1949, with little debate. Most Americans believed that NATO was a necessary response to current Soviet actions and future threats. One of the few prominent figures to criticize NATO was Republican Party leader Senator Robert Taft. He denounced the pact as unnecessary, provocative to the Soviets, too expensive, and likely to accelerate the arms race. He also noted that NATO gave the president the power to commit U.S. soldiers to battle without the customary constitutional or congressional restraints. At the time, few heeded Taft's trenchant Right-Isolationist critique of NATO.

Congress followed its approval of American membership in NATO by voting to grant military aid to its allies and to contribute American troops to NATO defense forces. By early 1950, a NATO command structure had been created. American forces stationed in Europe would function as a "tripwire" in case of Soviet aggression, guaranteeing that U.S. strategic bombers would attack the Soviet Union if Western Europe were invaded. The Soviets responded to the creation of NATO by creating the Warsaw Pact among East European countries.

Because U.S. forces were not sent to Europe until 1952, the creation of NATO did not immediately alter the strategic balance of power in that critical region. At the time of NATO's creation, there was no imminent threat of war in Europe. Few senior American civilian or military advisers believed that the Red Army was poised to invade Western Europe. The United States appeared to be winning the Cold War in Western Europe and Japan. The Marshall Plan nations and the Japanese were both well on the road to economic recovery. The new state of West Germany, under the leadership of Konrad Adenauer, had been firmly established. Soviet efforts to keep Japan and Europe weak and divided and isolated from the United States had obviously failed. By 1949, Stalin was clearly on the defensive.

Given the geopolitical situation in Europe, it is evident that NATO had other uses besides giving containment of Communism in Europe military muscle. NATO was less about giving Europeans arms and more about giving them the confidence to combat internal subversion and the will to resist Communist aggression. NATO conveyed a sense of security that encouraged West European economic recovery under the Marshall Plan. NATO also served as a means to bind Western Europeans more tightly into an American sphere of influence and to discourage any tendencies to make deals with or to appease the Soviets. Ironically, NATO later proved useful in providing a way to rearm West Germany. By integrating the new West German military forces into NATO, the United States could allay French alarm at a rearmed Germany by "containing" the new Wehrmacht.

From 1947 to 1949, American leaders made many crucial decisions that shaped American Cold War policy for decades to follow. First came the formulation of containment ideology, the declaration of principles embodied in the Truman Doctrine. It represented a contemporary reformulation of the traditional doctrine of American mission: Americans had a special mission to protect free nations from expansionist Communism in the Cold War era. The Marshall Plan offered economic aid enabling Western Europeans to stay clear of the Iron Curtain and to rebuild their war-shattered economies. NATO added a strategic component. NATO also represented a historic departure for the United States: America joined its first binding military alliance in modern history. Foreign entanglements now appeared necessary to ensure U.S. security in the nuclear age.

Soon after Senate ratification of NATO came the alarming news that the Soviets had developed an atomic bomb. The American nuclear monopoly, which had functioned as a security blanket to dampen Cold War anxieties, had vanished. The atomic "genie" had escaped from its bottle. Soviet possession of nuclear weapons prompted President Truman to consider ordering the development of a hydrogen fusion weapon, a "superbomb" many times more powerful than atomic fission weapons. In January 1950, an intense secret debate occurred between scientific supporters of the H-bomb, led by Dr. Edward Teller, and its opponents, led by J. Robert Oppenheimer, the leader of the scientific team that had created nuclear weapons in 1945. Teller carried the debate with his argument that if the United States failed to develop the weapon and the Soviets did develop it, the Kremlin could blackmail the United States. Truman agreed with Teller and ordered the hydrogen bomb to be built.

After obtaining the go-ahead to build the new super-weapons, American scientists exploded a hydrogen bomb in November 1952. But the American technological edge in the spiraling arms race against the Soviet Union proved to be short lived. The Soviets tested their own hydrogen bomb in August 1953, less than a year later. These thermonuclear weapons were a thousand times more powerful than the bombs dropped on Hiroshima and Nagasaki in 1945. With the advent of the hydrogen bomb, an ominous threshold had been crossed; the potential thermonuclear threat to world survival had taken a quantum leap.

THE CHINESE REVOLUTION

Since the Cold War began, the Truman administration had pursued an Europe-oriented foreign policy. But the collapse of the Chinese Nationalist government in October 1949, after years of civil war between its forces and Communist troops, brought American Asian policy to the fore. As the Communist leader Mao Zedong established the People's Republic of China, the American people were disheartened at the loss of a favored ally, and conservative critics of the Truman administration went on the political warpath.

America's China policy had been in disarray since the end of World War II. The long civil war between the Nationalists and the Communists, suspended during the war against Japan, resumed soon after the Japanese surrendered. Between 1945 and 1949, the United States had given Jiang Jieshi's Nationalist government $2 billion in economic and military assistance. In 1946, Truman had sent General George C. Marshall to China to try to arrange a political compromise between the warring parties. But both sides, each believing that it could win a military victory over the other, refused to share power. Marshall gave up his futile efforts in January 1947, pronounced a plague on both of their houses, and returned to America.

In 1947, Nationalist leader Jiang Jieshi, using American logistical support, launched a major offensive designed to destroy his Communist foes. His armies captured the major cities of China, but in doing so, Jiang's forces spread themselves thin. The Communists controlled the countryside that contained over 85 percent of the vast Chinese population and provided food for the cities. The Maoist armies besieged the Nationalist troops in the cities. By the summer of 1949, Nationalist forces had lost their will to fight and surrendered en masse. As 1949 ended, Jiang, with a remnant of his army and government, sought refuge on the island of Formosa (Taiwan).

Figure 2.4   Division of Europe, 1945–1955.   *Source:* George D. Moss, *Moving On,* 1/e (Englewood Cliffs, N.J. Prentice Hall, 1994), p. 38. Public Domain Map.

Washington cut itself loose from the failing Nationalist government in August 1949, a few months before Jiang fled China. A State Department report, known as the China White Paper, condemned Mao for being a Soviet puppet, but the paper maintained that the United States had done all it could for the Nationalists; they had lost the civil war because they had not used U.S. assistance properly.

The Communist victory in China triggered an intense debate within the United States over foreign policy in general and Asian policy in particular. Bipartisanship, which had prevailed during the years of containing Communism in Europe, disintegrated as Republican leaders attacked Truman's Far Eastern policy. The Asia-first wing of the Republican Party and the China Lobby, led by Senator Styles Bridges and Congressman Walter Judd, charged the Democratic-controlled Congress and the Truman administration with responsibility for Jiang's fall. They argued that U.S. military involvement in the Chinese civil war could have saved Jiang's government. They asked the rhetorical question: If the essence of U.S. foreign policy was containing Communism without geographical limit, as stated in the Truman Doctrine, why did the United States not intervene in China? If Greece and Turkey, why not China?

But China was not America's to lose. Jiang and his corrupt and inept government lost China, not the Truman administration. The American failure in China was not providing insufficient aid or lack of concern. American leaders never understood the dynamic force of a peasant society ripe for change and the strong appeal of the Maoist land reform program among the Chinese peasants. The mistake the Truman administration made was to continue to cling to Jiang until it was much too late. As historian Barbara Tuchman observed, "There is little virtue in a client being anti-Communist if he is at the same time rotting from within."

However, millions of Americans believed the charges brought by the Asia firsters and the China Lobby. Such beliefs stemmed from a false assumption many Americans made about U.S. foreign policy during the early Cold War era—that the rich and mighty United States could control political events around the globe if only leaders took the right actions. They could see no limits to American power. If China had fallen to Communism, millions reasoned that such a catastrophe could occur only because U.S. leaders had blundered, or worse, as Senator Joseph McCarthy and others charged, because disloyal American officials, secretly favoring the Communist forces, had subverted America's China policy.

If the Chinese revolution could have been thwarted, it would have taken a massive, sustained American military intervention for years. In 1949, the United States lacked the ground troops to intervene in China. Had Truman confronted Congress and the American people with the hard choices of either a large-scale military intervention or a Communist victory in China, they probably would have opposed direct American involvement in an Asian civil war. The American people probably did not want to fight a major land war in Asia, but Truman tried to hide the declining status of the Nationalist regime until near the end, hence its collapse came as a sudden shock. Its own actions left the Truman administration vulnerable to Republican accusations that it had lost China. Whereas containment of Communism had worked in Europe and in Japan, it had failed in China. The Maoist victory in China was a devastating diplomatic defeat for the United States and a political disaster for the Truman administration.

After the Maoist victory, Secretary of State Dean Acheson wanted to grant diplomatic recognition to the Communist regime, but he changed his mind after Maoists seized American property, imprisoned American citizens, and signed a pact with the Soviet Union. Instead, the United States implemented a policy of nonrecognition and clamped a trade boycott on the world's most populous nation. American officials insisted that Jiang's government now ensconced in Formosa constituted the legitimate government of

China. Nonrecognition toward mainland China would represent official U.S. policy for the next twenty years, until Richard Nixon made his famous journey to Beijing in February 1972.

VIETNAM: THE BEGINNINGS

The success of the Chinese Communist revolution also had a major influence on U.S. foreign policy in Southeast Asia. Since 1946, the French had been trying to reimpose colonialism on the Vietnamese people. The Vietnamese, led by Ho Chi Minh and General Vo Nguyen Giap, leaders of a Nationalist front organization known to the West as the Viet Minh, refused to accept the return of their former imperial masters and waged a guerrilla war that the French could not suppress. American policy toward the war in Indochina had been ambivalent. Publicly, the United States took a neutral stance; the Americans did not wish to align themselves with European colonialism in Southeast Asia, and they were skeptical that the French could defeat the Vietnamese Nationalists. But since Ho and Giap and most of the other Vietnamese leaders were Communists, Americans strongly opposed the

Figure 2.5   In homage to Mao Tse Tung, crowds filled the streets of China's cities in 1949, celebrating the triumph of the Communist revolution.   *Source:* AP/Wide World Photos.

idea of another country joining the Communist world. Hence, Americans covertly supported the French effort in Vietnam. The United States also supported the French war in Vietnam because Washington feared that a French defeat in Indochina might weaken Paris's resolve to resist Soviet expansionism in Europe. In 1949, the French made their cause in Southeast Asia more palatable to the Americans when they set up a puppet government in Saigon under the nominal leadership of Bao Dai, a descendant of the last Vietnamese royal family. Now the French could claim, disingenuously, that they were fighting to preserve Vietnamese national independence from the threat of Communism.

The Communist victory in China had a major impact on the Indochinese war. Hitherto the Vietnamese had been fighting alone against the French. Now they had a powerful friend and ally in the Chinese Communists, with whom they shared a long common border. Soon Chinese economic and military aid flowed to the Viet Minh, and the war began to go badly for the French. In February 1950, China and the Soviet Union formally recognized Ho's revolutionary government. Alarmed, the French appealed to the United States for help. Dean Acheson, who had become Secretary of State in 1949, succeeding Marshall, responded by formally recognizing Bao Dai's pseudo-government. In May 1950, the United States began to send economic and military aid to the French forces fighting in Vietnam. A small group of U.S. military advisers arrived in Vietnam during the summer of 1950. On a modest scale, the Truman administration began an American involvement in Vietnam during the summer of 1950 that would last for twenty-five years, include a major war, and would ultimately end in disaster for the United States and the people in Southeast Asia whom it tried to help.

NSC-68

Truman's response to the news that the Soviets had developed atomic weapons and the fall of China was to direct Secretary of State Acheson to conduct a full-dress review of American foreign and strategic policy. Under Acheson's guidance, the review was conducted by the State and Defense Departments, coordinated by the National Security Council. Six months later, analysts produced National Security Council Document Number 68 (NSC-68), an important top-secret paper that shaped American foreign policy for the next twenty years. Truman received NSC-68 in April 1950. NSC-68 was mostly written by Paul Nitze at the direction of Acheson. Nitze and his fellow analysts assumed continual conflict in the world between the United States and the Soviet Union. It depicted this struggle in stark terms—what was at issue was no less than the survival of America, its free institutions, and its ideals. It assumed that the Soviets would achieve the nuclear capability to destroy the United States within a few years. Hence, NSC-68 called for a massive buildup of American military force to resist the Soviet menace anywhere in the world that it might arise. It recommended defense budgets of $50 billion a year, a fourfold increase over the $13 billion for 1950. NSC-68 called these huge expenditures "the necessary price of freedom." The outbreak of the Korean War would give President Truman the opportunity to implement many of the recommendations contained in NSC-68, which militarized containment and transformed it from a regional into a global policy.

KOREA

After the fall of China, the Administration forged a new Asian policy. Secretary of State Acheson delineated a new defense perimeter in the Far East, incorporating Japan, Okinawa, and the Philippines. It excluded Formosa, Korea, and Southeast Asia. The new line suggested that nations located within the excluded regions would have to defend themselves against Chinese aggression, or they would have to seek help from the United Nations. Republican leaders vigorously attacked Truman's Asian policy. Senator McCarthy said it proved that the State Department was riddled with Communists and their fellow travelers. Senator Robert Taft called it a policy that promoted Communism in China.

As partisan political controversy over American Asian policy continued, the Truman administration confronted another Far Eastern crisis—North Korea's invasion of South Korea. The invasion was rooted in divisions within the country stemming from World War II. As the war ended, Soviet and American troops had occupied the Korean peninsula, which had been a Japanese colony since 1910. The two nations arranged for Soviet soldiers to accept the surrender of Japanese troops north of the thirty-eighth parallel of north latitude and for American soldiers to accept the surrender of Japanese forces south of that line. Efforts to unify Korea failed, and the nation remained divided at the thirty-eighth parallel in the years after the war. North of the boundary, the Soviets created a Communist state and trained an army to defend it. South of the border, the United States supervised the creation of a government headed by Syngman Rhee. The Soviet Union and America removed their troops from the divided land in the late 1940s. Both Rhee and Kim Il-sung, the North Korean leader, sought to unify Korea—one under capitalism and the other under Communism.

Kim moved first. On June 25, 1950, North Korean forces invaded the South in an effort to unify Korea under Communist control. Kim expected to win an easy victory, having calculated that the United States would not intervene given the recent policy statements out of Washington that Korea lay outside of the boundary of U.S. vital interests. Kim evidently had received Stalin's permission to invade South Korea, and Mao Zedong concurred. They anticipated a quick victory for the North Koreans and saw the move as advancing their diplomatic interests in Northeastern Asia.

President Truman, surprised by the invasion, immediately conferred with his advisers. He understood that if the United States did not intervene quickly, North Korea would overrun the South. He quickly decided to send American troops to try to save South Korea from Communism. He called Korea "the Greece of the Far East." He compared Communist aggression in Korea to Fascist aggression during the 1930s. He said that if the United States let aggression go unchallenged, as the democracies had done in the 1930s, "it would mean a third world war." Truman viewed the conflict in global terms. He assumed that the Soviets had masterminded the attack, and he believed that U.S. national security and world peace were threatened. Truman also believed that the Soviets might be using the invasion as a feint to suck American troops into Korea, leaving Western Europe vulnerable to Soviet attack just at the time NATO was being implemented. He further shared a concern about Japanese security. The conquest of South Korea would give the Communists airfields within thirty minutes' flying time of Japanese cities. Finally, Truman responded to domestic political pressures. He dared not serve up the loss of Korea to the Republicans in an election year that followed so soon after the "loss" of China.

When Truman committed the U.S. Armed Forces to the Korean War, he did not seek a declaration of war from Congress. He and his advisers were concerned that Congressmen and Senators might engage in divisive debates that would delay military action and allow the Communists an easy victory. He claimed that he lacked time, and he relied on what he called his "inherent war-making powers" as commander-in-chief of the Armed Forces. But the United States did obtain UN endorsement for its Korean intervention. The Security Council approved American military intervention because the Soviet delegate was absent from its sessions. The Soviet representative had been boycotting the Security Council sessions to protest its refusal to replace the Chinese Nationalist delegate with a Communist delegate following Mao's victory. Officially, the Korean War was a United Nations "police action" to repel aggression against South Korea. In reality, the UN sanction furnished a legal cover for what was mainly an American unilateral effort. The United States provided 90 percent of the ground forces and all of the sea and air power aiding the South Koreans. All battlefield commanders came from the United States. General MacArthur, whom Truman appointed to head the Korean campaign, took orders from the American Joint Chiefs of Staff.

The war was nearly lost at its beginning. North Korean troops overran most of South Korea, except for a small area around Pusan, a seaport at the southern tip of the peninsula. For a time, Washington feared that the defenders would be pushed into the sea. But American and South Korean forces finally halted the invaders at Pusan in August 1950. General MacArthur then turned the war around with a brilliantly executed amphibious landing at Inchon 150 miles north of Pusan. American forces moved south from Inchon as other forces broke out at Pusan and headed north. They caught the North Koreans in a giant pincers, and a rout was on. By the end of September, the UN forces had pushed the retreating North Koreans back across the thirty-eighth parallel.

Within three months, the UN mission had been accomplished. The aggressors had been cleared from South Korea. With the North Korean army in disarray, and the USSR and China apparently not inclined to intervene, Truman decided to go north across the thirty-eighth parallel. General MacArthur enthusiastically approved. Truman's decision to cross the line transformed the war. Containment became rollback, an effort to liberate North Korea from Communism. UN forces set out to destroy a Communist satellite and to unify Korea under a pro-Western government. The Security Council obediently endorsed Truman's decision to transform the war.

At first, all went well. The U.S. forces drove their foes north. Meanwhile, the general American military buildup in accordance with NSC-68 continued. Conscription had been reinstated. Congress doubled the Pentagon's budget, from $13 billion to $26 billion. Additional troops were earmarked for NATO. The Seventh Fleet was stationed between the Chinese mainland and Formosa to shield Jiang's forces from a possible Communist attack. Both the rapid military buildup and the war in Korea enjoyed strong bipartisan support and broad popular approval. The UN forces appeared to be headed for victory. The North Korean army was on the verge of destruction.

As the UN forces advanced northward, Chinese leaders issued a series of warnings. When General MacArthur ignored their warnings, the Chinese stated publicly that if the

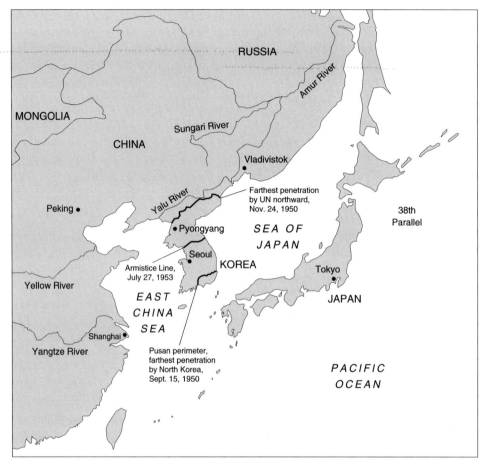

Figure 2.6   The Korean War, 1950–1953.   *Source:* Public Domain map.

U.S. forces continued their advance, they would intervene. On October 15, 1950, President Truman flew to Wake Island in the mid-Pacific to confer with General MacArthur. Sitting in a shack on the edge of the runway at Wake, the imperious MacArthur assured the President that the Chinese would not intervene, and if they did, they would be slaughtered. He also told Truman that he would win the Korean War and "have the boys home by Christmas." Truman accepted MacArthur's assessment and discounted the Chinese warnings. MacArthur launched what he thought would be the final offensive of the Korean War on November 24. UN forces advanced along two widely separated routes toward the Yalu River border with China and toward Pyongyang, the North Korean capital. Two days later, the Chinese sent more than 300,000 troops swarming across the frozen Yalu. Fighting in icy winter weather, the Chinese armies split the UN forces and sent them reeling backward. The rout was on. In two weeks they drove MacArthur's forces back across the thirty-eighth parallel and down the Korean peninsula.

American officials, who had walked into disaster together, were now divided over how to respond to it. General MacArthur, humiliated and angry, wanted to expand the war and strike at China. He was supported by many conservative Republicans and some Democrats, including a young Congressman from Massachusetts, John F. Kennedy. MacArthur believed that the Chinese made the decision to invade Korea on their own. Truman and Acheson assumed that the Chinese were carrying out "Russian colonial policy in Asia." If they were correct, going to war with China meant going to war with the Soviet Union in Asia. Washington was not prepared to fight World War III. Truman opted for a return to the original limited UN mission of restoring the prewar status quo in Korea and for continuing the U.S. military buildup in accordance with NSC-68.

In December, U.S. field commander General Matthew Ridgway brought in reinforcements and rallied the American forces, stemming the Communist tide. Heavy artillery slaughtered the Chinese forces that were advancing in massed formations. American naval and air forces helped blunt the Chinese drive. Ridgway's Eighth Army fought its way back to a point near the thirty-eighth parallel and held that line for the rest of the war. Truce negotiations began on July 10, 1951, but they were unproductive for a long time. A seesaw war of trenches and fortified hills would continue for two more years and claim thousands of American lives.

During the first months of 1951, as Ridgway's troops held the line in Korea, Truman continued his implementation of NSC-68. Annual military spending reached $50 billion. The United States committed additional forces to NATO and obtained additional overseas bases. The army expanded to 3.6 million men, six times its size when the Korean War began. Military aid was sent to Jiang's Nationalist forces on Formosa. The United States also increased the amount of military aid going to the French forces fighting in Indochina. Washington signed a peace treaty with Japan that ended the occupation and restored Japanese sovereignty. The treaty permitted America to maintain military bases in that country. The Truman administration embraced the general strategy of ringing China and the Soviet Union with U.S. military might. Containment had become a global commitment, and it now packed potent military muscle.

The huge military buildup did not satisfy Republican critics supporting General MacArthur's proposal to take the war to China. He did not want to hold the line at the thirty-eighth parallel and negotiate; MacArthur wanted a military victory over China and a unified, pro-Western Korea. Ordered by Truman to make no public statements, he defied his commander in chief. On April 5, House Republican leader Joseph Martin read a letter from MacArthur to Congress calling for an alternative foreign policy. If victory in Asia required bombing Manchurian bases, blockading Chinese ports, using nuclear weapons, and employing Nationalist forces from Taiwan, so be it: "In war there is no substitute for victory." MacArthur's letter also stated: "Here in Asia is where the Communist conspirators have elected to make their play for global conquest." MacArthur rejected Truman's Europe-first orientation, his effort to achieve limited political goals in Korea, and his containment policy. He had issued a fundamental challenge to the Administration's foreign policy. Truman responded to MacArthur's letter by dismissing him from his command and ordering the old general home. Truman's firing of General MacArthur provoked one of the great emotional events of recent American history. The White House was swamped with letters and phone

Figure 2.7   U.S. soldiers in the 2nd Infantry Division, fighting in Korea near the Chongchon River, December 1950. The Korean War was the first war in American history in which soldiers fought together in racially integrated combat units.   *Source:* Moss, *America in the Twentieth Century,* 3d ed. Corbis. Photo by Dept. of Defense/Acme/UPI.

calls, mostly supporting MacArthur. Polls showed that 75 percent of the people supported the general. Republican supporters of MacArthur heaped abuse upon the embattled Truman. Many newspaper and magazine editors called for his impeachment.

Much of the uproar over Truman's firing of MacArthur reflected popular disenchantment with the Korean War. Many Americans neither understood nor accepted the concept of limited war for particular political objectives. After all, when an easy military victory appeared possible, Truman himself had tried to take all of Korea, only to revert to the original, limited objective following Chinese intervention. The President wanted to avoid a major war that he feared could escalate into World War III, but MacArthur's contempt for half measures and his stirring call for victory appealed to a nation of impatient idealists. The United States obviously had the military power to destroy North Korea and China. Why not use it?

MacArthur returned to America to a hero's welcome. About 500,000 people turned out to greet him when he arrived in San Francisco on April 16, 1951. Three days later, he addressed a joint session of Congress. His moving speech was interrupted thirty times by applause. Millions of his fellow Americans who watched or heard General MacArthur's speech were equally moved.

As MacArthur basked in public acclaim, Congress investigated the circumstances of his removal. Hearings were held before the combined Senate Armed Services Committee and Foreign Relations Committee. At first, the senators favored MacArthur, but the testimony of the Joint Chiefs, particularly of General Omar Bradley, put the case for containment in Korea forcibly and clearly: the Soviet Union, not China, was America's main enemy; Europe, not Asia, was the most important region of American interest. General Bradley stated that fighting China in Asia "would be the wrong war in the wrong place at the wrong time against the wrong enemy." There also were the matters of MacArthur's refusal to follow orders and his efforts to make foreign policy over the President's head. The constitutional principle of civilian control of foreign policy and military strategy was at stake. Truman had fired an insubordinate general. Gradually, the tumult subsided, and MacArthur faded into quiet retirement.

Meanwhile in Korea the truce talks between the Americans on the one side and the North Koreans and Chinese on the other side dragged on inconclusively, and fighting continued. Fighting and talking would continue until July 1953. The main cause of the impasse at the talks was Chinese insistence that captured North Korean and Chinese soldiers be returned to them, even though these soldiers wanted to remain in South Korea. The United States refused to return them against their will. An armistice was finally reached on July 27, 1953, when President Eisenhower threatened the Chinese with an expansion of the war. The Chinese yielded, and the prisoners remained in the South. The thirty-eighth parallel was restored as the boundary between North and South Korea. To appease Syngman Rhee, who was unhappy with the settlement, the United States furnished his government with military aid and kept 50,000 American troops in South Korea.

Although it has been forgotten by many Americans, Korea was a major land war in Asia. It lasted for three years and involved over 3 million American military personnel. Its costs exceeded $100 billion; only World War II and the Vietnam War cost more. About

Figure 2.8   General Douglas MacArthur.   *Source:* National Archives.

54,000 Americans died in Korea, and another 150,000 were wounded. Millions of Koreans and Chinese perished during the war. Korea proved to be an unpopular, frustrating and confusing war that ended in a draw. No celebrations greeted its end. Returning Korean veterans melted into society to became part of the 1950s "silent generation."

The Korean War significantly influenced American foreign policy. In Korea, the Cold War suddenly turned hot. Containment was transformed from a regional policy to a general global stance. U.S. foreign policy shifted from its Eurocentric focus toward increasing involvement in the Pacific and the Far East. War with the People's Republic of China ensured that the United States and China would remain bitter Cold War adversaries for decades. The image of an aggressive Soviet Union commanding a centralized, worldwide Communist movement fastened itself on the American imagination. China was seen as an extension of Soviet power. Truman incorporated the defense of Formosa and French interests in Southeast Asia into the larger pattern of American containment of Communism in the Far East.

The Korean War transformed the Cold War from a political and an ideological conflict into a military struggle. Containment was militarized. Prior to the war in Korea, containment primarily represented an effort to eliminate the political and economic conditions that spawned Communism. After Korea, containment consisted of setting up military frontiers behind which free societies would have an opportunity to develop. The United States committed itself to maintaining a huge permanent military force in peacetime, although given the crisis atmosphere prevailing during much of the Cold War, the traditional distinction between peace and war was blurred. The military-industrial complex expanded rapidly as a major component of the permanent war economy. Foreign aid was militarized, and the power of the presidency to conduct foreign policy was expanded. Truman also extended the draft, raised taxes, and imposed wage and price controls during the Korean War. Although it failed to take hold of American emotions and imprint itself indelibly on the national memory, the Korean War transformed the Cold War and influenced American foreign policy for decades.

THE COLD WAR CONSENSUS

From the end of World War II to the spring of 1947, the Cold War between the United States and the Soviet Union emerged as the major reality shaping America's foreign policy in the postwar world. Containment of Communism evolved as the major American foreign policy response to the emergence of the Cold War. Beginning as a response to perceived Soviet threats to the security of small nations in Southern Europe, containment expanded to include the periphery of East and Southeast Asia in 1950 following the Maoist triumph in China, the U.S. decision to support the French in Indochina, and the outbreak of the Korean War.

As the world split between the former allies widened, most Americans came to support President Truman's "get tough" approach to the Soviet Union. Influenced by the media, Americans increasingly viewed the Soviet Union as the aggressive successor of the destroyed Third Reich. Communism was equated with Fascism, and Stalin was seen as a Red Hitler, a despotic ruler with megalomaniacal ambitions to dominate the new postwar world order. Soviet leaders were depicted as Marxist-Leninist zealots in the service of a master plan for imposing Communism on the world. The great lesson of World War II internalized by U.S. leaders was that aggressors could not be appeased. As the Soviet leaders came to be seen as the new Nazis in the world, American leaders vowed to contain them, to prevent aggression and ensure that there would be no World War III.

Some Americans dissented from Truman's new foreign policy approach. These critics did not embrace the pressures and pitfalls of the world leadership role that Truman and his senior advisers had designed for America in the postwar world. They balked at the enormous costs of rearmament and foreign aid, the new internal security controls clamped onto American life, the complexities and tensions of great power rivalries, and the domination of public life by foreign policy issues. Some idealistic Americans did not relish having to support reactionary governments just because they appeared to be threatened by Communism. Liberals such as Henry A. Wallace and conservatives such as Senator Robert Taft of Ohio were articulate critics of the Truman Doctrine, the Marshall Plan, and NATO.

But the dramatic events of the early Cold War years—the Soviet takeover of Eastern Europe, Soviet pressures on Turkey, the civil war in Greece, the Communist coup in Czechoslovakia, the Berlin Blockade, Soviet acquisition of nuclear weapons, the "fall" of China, and the Korean War—worked on the American public consciousness to create a consensus supporting the Truman administration's policy of containment. During World War II, cooperation with the Soviets had been a strategic necessity. By 1947, the world had changed dramatically. Containing the expansionist tendencies of the Soviet Union had become the new American strategic imperative. A revolution in world affairs brought about by World War II necessitated a revolution in U.S. attitudes and approaches to foreign policy.

Despite continuing criticism from both the Left and the Right, a bipartisan consensus in support of the main direction of U.S. foreign policy had emerged in this country by 1947. There was broad agreement spanning all but the fringes of the political spectrum that the major objective of American foreign policy would be the containment of Communism. The American bipartisan foreign policy consensus in support of the containment of Communism would remain intact until the Vietnam War cracked it during the late 1960s and provoked the first serious debates over American foreign policy goals in nearly twenty years.

BIBLIOGRAPHY

Dean Acheson's *Present at the Creation* is a superb account of the origins of the Cold War by a former high State Department official who was one of the principal architects of U.S. Cold War foreign policy. Recently, James Chace has written a fine biography, *Acheson: The Secretary of State Who Created the American World*. Stephen Ambrose's *Rise to Globalism: American Foreign Policy, 1938–1980* contains an excellent account of the origins of the Cold War. Another good study of the genesis of the Cold War is John L. Gaddis's *The United States and the Origins of the Cold War*. Gaddis, America's most imminent diplomatic historian, has recently written an important new study of the origins of the Cold War, *Now We Know: Rethinking Cold War History*. The book, based on materials recently accessed in Soviet archives, makes a convincing case that Stalin is primarily responsible for provoking the Cold War. See also Daniel Yergen's *A Shattered Peace: The Origins of the Cold War and the National Security State*. Walter LaFeber's *America, Russia, and the Cold War* is a classic account of the Cold War conflict between the United States and the Soviet Union. A fine, recent, interpretive study of the Cold War is Thomas J. McCormick's *America's Half-Century: United States Foreign Policy in the Cold War.* Another magisterial recent account of the Cold War is Melvyn Leffler's *A Preponderance of Power.* Problems in Germany that were the major causes of the Cold War are carefully analyzed in John Gimbel's *The American Occupation of Germany: Politics and the Military, 1945– 1949.* Thomas Parrish's *Berlin in the Balance, 1945–1949: The Blockade, the Airlift, the First Major Battle of the Cold War* is an excellent recent study of the first major U.S.-USSR confrontation of the evolving Cold War. John Gimbel's *The Origins of the Marshall Plan* and Robert E. Osgood's *NATO: Entangling Alliance* are two important studies of major American postwar foreign policy initiatives in Europe. Akira Iriye's *The Cold War in Asia* is a good account. See also Michael Schaller's *The American Occupation of Japan: The Origins of the Cold War in Asia.* Another fine study of the origins of the Cold War in Asia is Robert M. Blum's *Drawing the Line.* The best short history of the Korean War is Burton I. Kaufman's *The Korean War.* Robert H. Ferrell's *Harry S. Truman and the Modern Presidency* is a recent short biography of the American leader who presided over the rise of the Cold War.

3

Postwar America

As they emerged from the intense experiences of World War II, most Americans believed that they were entering a new era, that postwar America would be a very different nation from the one that had gone to war on December 7, 1941. At the same time that they looked ahead to new opportunities and new experiences, Americans yearned for a return to the normal routines and rhythms of everyday life. They wanted to put the disruptions and dangers of the wartime crisis behind them. But for many Americans, the road back to normality in the years immediately after the war proved rocky. The immediate postwar years were dominated by disorder, hyperinflation, bitter strikes, continuing shortages of housing and consumer goods, fierce partisan political divisions, and racial conflict. Compounding the many problems inherent in adapting to the new postwar world, the Cold War struck home with a special fury: the nation was convulsed by a Second Red Scare and the rise of the politics of anti-Communism that reached intense levels during the Korean War.

THE MAN FROM MISSOURI

Harry S Truman had come to the presidency on April 12, 1945, ill prepared and nearly unknown. Immediately he had to confront a host of momentous challenges at home and abroad. In fact, Truman's entire presidency of nearly eight years was spent grappling with difficult issues amidst a society often in turmoil and riven by bitter partisan divisions. The man who succeeded Franklin Roosevelt was a jaunty, feisty leader who never tried to avoid responsibility or duck a fight. He expressed his views openly and candidly, a trait that a later generation of Americans, sickened by the lies and evasions of Vietnam and Watergate era politicians, would admire in retrospect. But for most of his presidency, Truman's contemporaries viewed him as an ineffective, unpopular leader.

Truman was born on May 8, 1884, on his father's farm near Lamar, Missouri. He grew up in Independence, Missouri, graduating from high school there in 1902. (Truman was the only modern president never to attend college.) His boyhood ambition was to be a professional soldier, but poor eyesight prevented him from passing the physical examination for attending the U.S. Military Academy at West Point. He later joined the Missouri National Guard. During World War I, Truman shipped out to France as the commanding officer of an artillery battery. His unit saw heavy action, and Truman proved a courageous and an effective military leader under fire.

Returning to Independence after the war, Truman married his high school sweetheart, Elizabeth (Bess) Wallace. In 1921, with two partners, Truman opened a men's clothing store in Kansas City. The store failed within a year. Truman, approaching forty, with a wife and a daughter to support, found himself nearly bankrupt, without a job and without prospects. At that low point in his life, it would have astonished Truman, and no doubt anyone who knew him, to have been told that he was one day going to be president of the United States.

Truman's political career began in 1924, when he became a county judge, a minor functionary in a corrupt political machine, led by Tom Pendergast, which controlled Kansas

Figure 3.1   Harry Truman takes the oath of office on the evening of April 12, 1945, in the Cabinet Room at the White House. Swearing him into office is Chief Justice Harlan Fiske Stone. Standing between them is the new First Lady, Elizabeth "Bess" Wallace Truman. Standing behind Chief Justice Stone are, from left to right: Speaker of the House Sam Rayburn, Office of War Mobilization Director Fred Vinson, and House Minority Leader Joseph Martin.
Source: National Archives.

City and Jackson County politics. Truman soon proved himself an able and a popular administrator. Despite his affiliation with the Pendergast machine, Truman apparently remained an honest and a conscientious public official. In 1934, with the Pendergast machine's support, Truman was elected to the U.S. Senate. Although an energetic supporter of the New Deal, Truman did nothing to distinguish himself during his first term in the Senate. President Roosevelt, his fellow senators, and the press dismissed him as Pendergast's "errand boy" in Washington.

Narrowly reelected to the Senate in 1940, Truman performed effective service to the nation in wartime. From 1941 to 1944, he chaired a special committee that investigated the awarding of government contracts to businesses to supply the Pentagon with war material. Truman's committee saved the taxpayers billions of dollars by eliminating waste and fraud. The committee also expedited the delivery of vital war supplies and saw to it that small businesses received a larger share of government business. Truman left the Senate to assume his duties as Roosevelt's vice president in January 1945, and he ascended to the presidency following FDR's death three months later.

Truman appeared in many ways to be an ordinary man, a small-town, middle-class Midwesterner. He was unpretentious, a man of simple tastes and pleasures, and shared many of the values and attitudes of ordinary citizens. He thought of himself as an average guy who, by an extraordinary turn of events, found himself in the White House. He once observed that there were probably thousands of Americans who could perform the duties of the president's office as well as or better than he could. He cherished his family, he was loyal to his friends, and he was a fierce political partisan.

Although he never sought the presidency and had doubts about his abilities to do the job initially, Truman willingly assumed its awesome responsibilities. He soon demonstrated that he was a quick study and could act decisively. He grew confident, even cocky, in office. Truman became famous for placing a sign on his desk that read, "The buck stops here." He worked hard, he could withstand pressure, and he never feared unpopularity. He had great moral courage and a clear sense of duty. Truman's presidency, above all, served as an inspiring example of a leader responding to severe challenges, a man growing in the office. He was forced by the demands of the presidency during times of crisis to develop qualities that perhaps he did not know he had. Most presidents who have followed Truman, whether Democrats or Republicans, have admired him. In their eyes, he was a kind of president's president. Most historians rate Truman very highly, mainly for his foreign policy achievements as the principal architect of America's Cold War foreign policy based on the containment of Communism. They rank him among the top ten presidents in the nation's history.

POSTWAR POLITICS

Truman experienced difficulties early in his presidency because of his inexperience and because he inherited an administration, many of whose members viewed him as an inferior successor to Roosevelt. They lacked confidence in him, and he did not trust them. Prominent New Dealers departed, and Truman replaced them with more conservative advisers recruited from the ranks of big business, corporate law firms, Wall Street brokerage houses, and the senior ranks of the military. Honest and able himself, Truman tolerated a crowd of political hacks who had followed him to Washington. Most of these camp followers belonged to the "Missouri gang," led by obese politician Harry Vaughn. A liberal journalist, I. F. Stone, penned an enduring description of Vaughn and his cronies:

> the kind of men one was accustomed to meet in county courthouses . . . big-bellied, good-natured guys who knew a lot of dirty jokes, spent as little time in their offices as possible, saw Washington as a chance to make "useful" contacts, and were anxious to get what they could for themselves out of the experience.[1]

When the war ended, Truman's first major domestic issues involved demobilizing the armed forces and reconverting the war economy to peacetime production. The rush to disarm after the war was irresistible. The Armed Forces were quickly dismantled. When the Army and Navy could not bring servicemen home fast enough, they rioted overseas. A force that had numbered 12 million at its peak quickly shrank to 1.5 million, and the draft was canceled. As the Cold War heated up in 1946 and 1947, the United States had only a small arsenal of nuclear weapons with which to protect Europeans or Asians from Soviet expansion.

During his campaign for reelection in 1944, Roosevelt had promised the American people that after the war he would craft an economic bill of rights for all Americans, including jobs, decent housing, adequate health care, and a good education. Roosevelt's proposals convinced many of his liberal followers that the president planned to revive the New Deal reform tradition that had been placed on hold for the duration. Truman appeared to share his predecessor's reform commitments when he proposed to Congress in the fall of 1945 a sweeping program of social legislation. Truman called upon the legislators to enact a national housing program, to raise the minimum wage, to extend Social Security benefits, and to pass a full employment bill.

The proposed full employment bill was the centerpiece of Truman's reform package. It called for the federal government to assume responsibility for full employment by enhancing purchasing power and spending for public works. As the nation demobilized its military forces and shut down its war industries, most Americans shared a persistent fear that the American economy, no longer stimulated by war spending, would regress to massive unemployment and even depression. They feared that millions of suddenly released war workers and discharged veterans could not be absorbed by a peacetime economy.

But after making his bold proposals, Truman vacillated, allowing Congress to enact a measure in 1946 called the Employment Act. It called for "maximum employment" rather than full employment. It established the government's responsibility for maintaining prosperity without prescribing the means to achieve it. It was more a statement of principles than a program of action. The act's most significant reform was the creation of a Council of Economic Advisers to provide policy recommendations to the president and to assist in long-range economic planning. Congress failed to enact any of Truman's other reform pro-

---

[1]Quoted in Michael Schaller, Virginia Scharff, and Robert D. Schultzinger, *Present Tense: The United States Since 1945* (Boston: Houghton Mifflin Company, 1992), pp. 45–46.

posals. Truman's liberal rhetoric did not get translated into legislative action in the more conservative postwar era.

The economy shrank during the first year after the war, mainly because the government abruptly canceled $35 billion in war contracts. The gross domestic product (GDP) for 1946 was slightly smaller than for 1945, the last year of the war. Unemployment, which had vanished in wartime, rose to 4.5 percent in 1946. But the feared reversion to depression never happened; most war workers and veterans were absorbed into the postwar economy. Many factors accounted for the economy's unexpected resiliency. The GI Bill provided low-interest loans to help veterans buy homes, farms, and businesses. It granted billions of dollars of educational benefits, permitting millions of veterans, many with families, to attend colleges and trade schools. Tax cuts strengthened consumer purchasing power and stimulated business activity. Government also aided the business sector by transferring over $15 billion worth of government-owned plants to the private sector, adding some 20 percent to industrial capacity. Further, government spending, although much reduced from wartime levels, remained far higher than prewar levels. But the most important reason for the economy's transition from war to peace without recession or depression lay in an unforeseen powerful force. American consumers came out of the war with billions of dollars in savings and with long-frustrated desires to buy new clothes, homes, cars, radios, and appliances. Unleashed consumer spending kept factories humming and people working after the war ended, and it staved off recession or depression.

But unleashed consumer demand ignited hyperinflation as the economy was decontrolled. By early 1946, the Office of Price Administration had removed most rationing restrictions, but it had kept wage, price, and rent controls. Inflation soared. Desired goods like new cars and refrigerators remained scarce. Businessmen, farmers, and trade unionists demanded the removal of all remaining restrictions on their economic activity. A rash of strikes broke out in the auto, meat packing, electrical, and steel industries, idling productive capacity and delaying fulfillment of consumer demands. President Truman tried and failed to ensure a gradual, orderly phaseout of controls by restraining all interest groups.

In the spring of 1946, the bipartisan conservative coalition controlling Congress battled the President over extending the life of the OPA. Congress enacted a weak control measure that Truman vetoed, causing all controls to expire on July 1. There followed the worst surge of inflation since 1919. Congress, deluged with angry complaints, hastily passed another, even weaker bill, which Truman signed. Consumer prices continued to soar amidst the politics of confusion. Thereafter, the OPA lifted all remaining controls and faded away. The cost of living rose 20 percent in 1946, and acute shortages persisted.

LABOR TROUBLES

Organized labor had grown powerful during wartime. Union membership surpassed 15 million, as almost every major industry had been unionized. The CIO's political arm, the Political Action Committee (PAC), was committed to working with the liberal factions of the Democratic Party to institutionalize the welfare state in America. Some liberal labor leaders such as Walter Reuther, head of the United Auto Workers (UAW), and David Dubinski, leader of the International Ladies' Garment Workers' Union (ILGWU), hoped to forge new labor-management industrial partnerships in the postwar era: representatives from the unions and corporations would jointly determine workplace policies. But liberal labor aspirations soon foundered amidst economic dislocations and the conservative postwar political climate. Trade unions found themselves on the defensive, trying to preserve wartime gains. Real industrial wages and consumer purchasing power fell during 1945 and 1946 because of skyrocketing inflation.

As runaway inflation degraded their incomes and purchasing power, frustrated workers went on strike. Waves of strikes swept through important industrial sectors. Over 200,000 General Motors workers walked off the job on November 20, 1945. They were soon joined by striking electrical and steel workers. During the first year after the war, over 5 million men and women went on strike, tying up most of the nation's major industries. Reflecting their primary concern with inflation that was eroding incomes and living standards, strikers' demands focused on pay increases and job security.

Many of these strikes lasted for months, as management resisted union demands and workers refused to back down. Eventually most were settled on terms that resulted in significant pay increases for workers and substantial price increases for companies' products. Corporations passed their increased costs of production onto their customers, thereby retaining high profit margins but adding to the inflationary spiral. The settlement of the UAW strike against General Motors set the pattern for postwar industrial relations. After a bitter 113-day strike that hurt both sides, they agreed on a new contract, which granted workers substantial pay increases over the life of the contract and tied wage levels to increases in the cost of living. The new contract also strengthened job security for senior workers and contained more generous pension plans. In addition, the new agreements signaled that union leaders and management representatives in the postwar era would confine negotiations to the traditional issues of wages and hours, working conditions, fringe benefits, and job security. Union leaders quickly abandoned their social agenda for restructuring industrial relations or remaking society and focused henceforth on "bread-and-butter" issues.

Strikes also threatened in railroads and coal, two primary industries. Walkouts in both of these industries could have paralyzed the economy. The railroad strike was averted, but not before the President had asked Congress to grant him authority to draft striking railroad workers into the Army. Congress refused. John L. Lewis took his coal miners off of the job in April 1946 over wage and pension fund disputes with mine owners. Industrial production dropped. Efforts to settle the strike failed. On May 21, with the nation's supplies of coal exhausted, President Truman ordered the federal government to seize the mines. The coal mines were administered by Julius Krug, Secretary of the Interior, who promptly began negotiations with Lewis. They reached an agreement within two weeks, and the coal strike ended. The mines were returned to their owners. Truman's bold efforts to prevent the strikes hurt him politically; he and his party lost support among resentful workers, which affected the upcoming elections.

THE ELECTION OF 1946

As the 1946 midterm elections approached, Truman and his party faced serious political trouble. The Democrats split into their Northern and Southern wings, with Southern conservative Democrats often joining Northern Republicans to block liberal measures. Many liberal Democrats still yearned for Roosevelt, dismissing Truman as an inept successor. Truman and his party were damned both for shortages and for skyrocketing prices. Organized labor, sullen over Truman's threat to draft strikers, made only token efforts to support the Democrats.

Republican congressional candidates attacked the failures of Truman's price control program. They jeered "to err is Truman." When beef disappeared from meat markets, housewives rioted. When beef was back on the shelf a week later, they were shocked to discover that prices had doubled. "Had enough?" chorused Republicans. On the eve of the elections, polls showed that Truman's popularity had dropped to 32 percent. The election results mirrored the popular mood. Republicans scored substantial victories, winning control of the new House of Representatives by 246 to 188, and they would hold a 51 to 45 majority in the new Senate. For the first time since 1928, the first time since before the Great Depression, the Republicans won control of both houses of Congress. Many working-class voters deserted the Democrats, shattering the labor bloc that had been solidly Democratic since 1932. The election results also confirmed the new conservative mood of the electorate and doomed liberal hopes for a revival of the New Deal spirit or the enactment of social reforms in the postwar era.

THE 80TH CONGRESS

A lot of new faces appeared in Washington as members of the 80th Congress. Many were war veterans, representing a new generation of politicians that had come of age. This new breed of politico tended to be less idealistic, less liberal, and more pragmatic in its approach to public policy. One congressional rookie, Republican Richard Nixon, hailed from Southern California. Another, Democrat John F. Kennedy, represented a working-class district of southside Boston. A conservative Republican from Wisconsin, Joseph McCarthy, went to the Senate. McCarthy would soon propel himself into the center of the Communists-in-government controversy that rocked Washington and made his name a household word.

The Republicans took charge of the new Congress. So long out of power, the GOP set out to reassert the authority of Congress and to trim the executive branch. They proposed the Twenty-Second Amendment, which limited future presidents to two elected terms. They wanted to ensure there would be no more presidential reigns such as Franklin Roosevelt's. Ironically, the Twenty-Second Amendment, in place since 1951, has worked to prevent two popular Republican presidents, Dwight Eisenhower and Ronald Reagan, from considering a third term, while affecting no Democratic incumbents. The 80th Congress tore to shreds Truman's liberal domestic program to extend the welfare state and rejected all of his important proposals. Although it did not abolish basic New Deal programs, the 80th Congress certainly trimmed its edges.

Senator Robert Taft of Ohio, son of a former president and the intellectual leader of the GOP, spearheaded the Republican assault on the New Deal. Taft, who had been in the Senate since 1938, hoped to create a record that would vault him into the White House one day. Taft believed that the voters had given the Republicans a mandate to cut the New Deal. He stated that most Americans wanted lower taxes, less governmental interference in busi-

Figure 3.2   Class of 1946. A group of freshman Congressmen introduces them-selves in January 1947. Standing to the right rear of this gathering of rookies are two future presidents, John F. Kennedy and Richard M. Nixon.   *Source:* National Archives.

ness, and curbs on the power of organized labor. Twice in 1947, Congress enacted tax cuts. Truman vetoed both measures. A third tax cut was passed over his veto in 1948.

In 1947, Taft led the fight to enact a measure, passed over Truman's veto, modifying the National Labor Relations Act (Wagner Act), the nation's basic labor law and center-piece of the Second New Deal. The new law, the Labor Management Relations Act, popu-larly called the Taft-Hartley Act, made many changes in the Wagner Act. It extended the concept of "unfair labor practices," previously confined to management, to unions. Among forbidden union practices were the closed shop, which required a worker to join a union before working. It required unions to file annual financial statements with the Department of Labor. Cold War concerns could be seen in the requirement that all union officials file affidavits showing that they were not members of the Communist Party or any other sub-versive organization. It prohibited union contributions to national political campaigns, and it forbade strikes by federal employees. In cases of strikes that "affected the national wel-fare," the Taft-Hartley Act empowered the attorney general to seek a court injunction or-dering an eighty-day delay in the strike. During this eighty-day "cooling-off period," fed-eral mediators would try to settle the conflict. If, after eighty days, union members rejected the mediator's final offer, the strike could occur. One section of the new law, Section 14(b), permitted states to legalize the open shop, making union membership voluntary.

Organized labor vigorously attacked the Taft-Hartley Act. William Green, head of the AFL, charged that the bill was forged "in a spirit of vindictiveness against unions." Many workers condemned what they called the "slave labor law." President Truman claimed that it was both unworkable and unfair. In addition to general denunciations, labor leaders attacked particular provisions of the new law, such as the mandatory eighty-day strike delay feature. For years, repeal of the new law was the major political goal of organized labor.

The Taft-Hartley Act was the most important social legislation enacted during Truman's presidency. It did not undermine the basic strength of American trade unions that conservatives hoped and liberals feared might happen. The Communist registration requirement was nullified by the Supreme Court. Union membership increased from 15 million at the time of passage to 17 million five years later. During the 1950s, collective bargaining between teams of labor and management representatives generated wage increases and improved fringe benefits that made American industrial workers members of the most affluent working class in history. Later Congresses never repealed the Taft-Hartley law, nor even amended any of its major provisions.

WOMEN

The postwar era proved disappointing to millions of women who had hoped to consolidate and build upon their wartime achievements in the nation's workforce. Women were subjected to tremendous pressures from industry, government, and influential media to surrender their well-paying jobs and to return to their "rightful" places in the homes of America. Ads placed in mass circulation magazines implied that any woman who resisted the propaganda campaigns aimed at driving her out of the workplace and back to the kitchen was being selfish, greedy, and a poor wife and mother as well.

As factories converted from war to peacetime production, women by the hundreds of thousands were fired. Under the provisions of the Selective Service Act, returning veterans had priority over civilian war workers in competition for factory jobs. In the auto industry, which during the war years made jeeps, army trucks, and tanks, women had constituted 25 percent of the workforce in 1944. A year after the war, as automakers began producing new cars for civilian consumers for the first time since 1942, women comprised only 7 percent of auto workers. Sometimes, older married women workers ran afoul of newly imposed, or reimposed, age requirements or restrictions on the hiring of married women. In the immediate postwar years, as women were swept out of jobs in the mass production industries, the percentage of women members in many industrial unions also declined sharply.

Overall, female employment did not decline in the postwar years. By 1950, women made up 32 percent of the workforce, compared to 27 percent at war's end. But women had been forced out of high-paying jobs in manufacturing to resume work in occupations traditionally reserved for women such as waitresses, maids, and service jobs. Women welders and riveters now washed dishes and scrubbed floors for a lot less money. Women's median earnings had reached 66 percent of what men were paid in wartime manufacturing jobs. Studies in the postwar era showed women earning 53 percent of what men earned for comparable work. Although more women than ever before were working in the postwar era, most found themselves back in low-paying jobs, with little possibility of promotion. By 1950, for many a former Rosie, mired in a dead-end job at low pay, the glories of wartime work, of participating in a good cause at good pay, were only a fading memory.

Professional opportunities for middle-class women also deteriorated in postwar America. The number of women doctors, lawyers, and college professors declined. Medical schools and law schools imposed quotas on women's admissions, usually in the 5 to 10 percent range. The Equal Rights Amendment, which had been introduced in every congressional session since the 1920s, did not come close to garnering enough votes for passage. In fact, prominent women leaders continued to oppose the amendment on the grounds that retaining laws providing special protections for women in the workforce was more important than establishing a constitutional principle of equal rights. Organized feminism did not exist in postwar America; no one challenged traditional definitions of masculinity and femininity. Neither the Truman administration nor any government agency showed the slightest concern about declining opportunities for women in the job markets. Women's issues were simply not part of public policy debates in the postwar era. According to historian William Chafe, any changes in the status of women occurred "within a structure of assumptions and values that perpetuated massive inequality between the sexes."

CIVIL RIGHTS

African Americans emerged from the war years with an enhanced pride in themselves. Despite their encounters with racism and indifference, black soldiers had fought well and over 1 million African American men and women had worked in war industries to produce the ships, tanks, and guns that had enabled the Allied forces to triumph over their Axis foes. African American leaders sensed a new spirit of militancy in the land. Returning veterans would lead the assault on Jim Crow in the South; they would fight for full citizenship and equal access to housing, jobs, and schools.

Blacks achieved some successes in the postwar years. The number of African Americans eligible to vote rose slightly in some Southern states. Attorneys from the NAACP pushed court cases that chipped away at the judicial foundations of segregation. But everywhere in the postwar South, black insurgents encountered massive, and often violent, resistance to change. No Southern white political leader voiced any support for African American aspirations; most loudly asserted their unstinting support of black disfranchisement and systemic segregation, a kind of American apartheid that kept African Americans locked in separate and unequal statuses. Sometimes violence and intimidation were employed by Southern whites determined to confine African Americans to traditional subservient roles, but often more subtle methods worked just as effectively. Ninety-five percent of blacks in the South worked for white people. African Americans brave enough to show up on the voting rolls risked losing jobs, having insurance policies canceled, being evicted from rented farms or businesses, or having lines of credit revoked. Literacy requirements for voting, discriminatorily applied, meant that black college graduates sometimes failed to qualify for the vote, while ignorant whites happily signed on. Poll taxes continued to disqualify masses of poor Southern African Americans (and poor whites and Hispanic Americans) from the ballot.

A dramatic breakthrough occurred in 1947, when Branch Rickey, the general manager of the Brooklyn Dodgers, broke the color line of major league baseball by adding a gifted black athlete, Jackie Robinson, to his team's roster. Robinson quickly became an all-star player and future hall of famer on a team that won six National League pennants in the next ten years. His success paved the way for other gifted African American athletes, previously confined to segregated black leagues, to play major league ball, including Larry Doby, Henry (Hank) Aaron, and the legendary Satchel Paige.

The Cold War brought additional pressure for integrating African Americans and other nonwhite minorities into the mainstream of American life. The United States was now seeking the support of African and Asian nations whose leaders resented American mistreatment of its racial minorities. Jim Crow laws also made the United States vulnerable to Soviet propaganda that sought to highlight the inequities of American democracy and win influence among Third World people.

Truman was the first modern president to promote civil rights causes. His involvement came from both moral and political considerations. He passionately felt a strong need for justice for African Americans. He also was aware of the growing importance of the black vote in Northern cities, and he wanted to offset efforts by Republicans to regain African American support that they had enjoyed before the Great Depression. Truman had supported the creation of the Fair Employment Practices Commission (FEPC) in 1941, and he wanted to extend it after the war, but Congress refused to renew it.

Responding to the concerns of African American leaders, Truman created a Committee on Civil Rights in December 1946. The committee issued a report entitled "To Secure These Rights," in which it recommended a series of actions to eliminate racial inequality in America. Among its recommendations were: the creation of a civil rights division within the Justice Department, the creation of a Commission on Civil Rights, the abolition of the poll tax, the desegregation of all government agencies, the desegregation of the Armed Forces, and the enactment of a permanent FEPC. In a special message to Congress, Truman endorsed the committee's recommendations. Black leaders, delighted by Truman's statements, lavishly praised him.

But the President's rhetorical support for civil rights did not produce any positive legislative results. Congress rejected all of the committee's proposals, Republicans generally ignored them, and Southern Democrats denounced them. The Justice Department did not investigate Southern efforts to prevent African Americans from registering to vote, although Justice Department attorneys began to submit friends-of-the-court briefs on behalf of civil rights cases involving public schools and housing. Truman became the first president ever to address a civil rights organization when he spoke at an NAACP convention in 1948.

In February 1948, the president made an important contribution to the cause of racial equality when he issued an executive order barring discrimination in government bureaucracies. In July of that year, Truman also ordered the desegregation of the Armed Forces. At first progress was slow in desegregating the military, particularly the Army, which had more African Americans than the other branches of military service. Segregation persisted in the Army until the Korean War. Integration of the Army occurred during that conflict when Army officers discovered that African American soldiers fought more effectively in integrated units than in segregated ones. It was Truman's most important civil rights victory. Within a few years, the Army became the most integrated American institution, and many African Americans found opportunities in the military during the 1950s and 1960s that were not available to them in civilian life.

Truman used the presidency as a "bully pulpit" to dramatize civil rights as a moral issue that challenged Americans to align their political practices with their democratic professions. He played a major role in bringing civil rights issues to the center of the American political stage, his greatest domestic political achievement.

THE ELECTION OF 1948

As the 1948 election approached, Truman appeared to have no chance for reelection. At times he was discouraged by his inability to lead the country and by his low ratings in the polls. In the fall of 1947, he had even sent a member of his staff to talk to General Eisenhower, then Army Chief of Staff, to see if Ike might be interested in the Democratic nomination for 1948. Eisenhower was not. Truman then decided to seek reelection. At the Democratic Convention, held in Philadelphia in July, delegates, convinced that Truman could not win, tried to promote a boom for Eisenhower; it fizzled. Disappointed Democrats then held up signs that read, "I'm just mild about Harry."

To add to his political woes, the Democratic Party was fragmenting. Splinter groups formed on the Left and on the Right. At the convention, Northern liberals forced the adoption of a strong civil rights plank over the furious objections of Southern leaders. Fearing a party rupture, Truman's supporters had tried to soften the language of the civil rights plank. But when it passed unsoftened, Truman boldly endorsed it and praised the convention for adopting it.

With its adoption, delegates from Mississippi and Alabama marched out in protest. These renegade Southerners later formed their own party, the States' Rights, or "Dixiecrat" Party. At their convention, delegates from thirteen states nominated South Carolina Governor J. Strom Thurmond as their candidate for President, who ran on a segregationist platform. These Southern defections appeared to remove any remaining Democratic hopes for success. The Solid South, a Democratic stronghold since the end of Reconstruction, had vanished.

The liberal wing of the Democratic Party also threatened to split off. Back in 1946, Truman had fired his Secretary of Commerce Henry Wallace for publicly criticizing his "get tough" foreign policy toward the Soviet Union. In 1948, Wallace became the presidential candidate of a leftist third party, the Progressive Party. Many New Dealers considered Wallace, whom Truman had replaced as Roosevelt's vice president in 1944, the true heir to the Roosevelt legacy and supported his candidacy. Polls taken that summer showed that Wallace could cost Truman several Northern industrial states. It appeared that the remnants of his party had given Truman a worthless nomination. But the gutsy leader accepted their unenthusiastic endorsement in a fighting spirit. He told them, "I will win this election and make those Republicans like it—don't you forget that." Few believed him.

The confident Republicans, eager to regain the White House after a sixteen-year Democratic hold on the presidency, again nominated New York Governor Thomas E. Dewey and adopted a moderate program. Dewey, soundly beaten by Roosevelt in 1944, was determined to avenge that defeat this time around. Polls taken at the outset of the electoral campaign in September showed Dewey running far ahead of Truman. It appeared that Truman might get only about one-third of the popular vote, and that Dewey could coast to an easy landslide victory. Dewey opted for a safe, restrained strategy to carry him to the executive office. He spoke in platitudes and generalities, raised no controversial issues, and never mentioned his opponent by name. Dewey's manner conveyed an air of absolute confidence that he would soon be president of the United States.

But Truman, assisted by a young legislative aide, Clark Clifford, had devised an electoral strategy that he believed could win. Truman would stress his adherence to the New Deal tradition, advocating an advanced program of liberal reform to appeal to urban voters, unionized workers, and minorities. He would ignore the Dixiecrats, counting on party loyalty to keep many Southern whites within the Democratic fold. He would link the Wallacites to the Communists, and he would attack the Republicans as unreconstructed reactionaries. As soon as he got the nomination, he called the 80th Congress into special session and reintroduced all of his reform programs that Congress had failed to pass in regular sessions. Again, Congress rejected them. This bold move set the tone for the campaign.

Truman took off on a transcontinental train tour in search of an electorate. He traveled over 32,000 miles and made hundreds of speeches, talking directly to about 12 million people. He repeatedly blasted what he called the "do nothing, good for nothing" 80th Congress, blaming all of the ills of the nation on the Republican-controlled legislature. He called the Republicans "gluttons of privilege" who would destroy the New Deal if elected. He evoked dire images from the Great Depression and depicted Dewey as Hoover *redux*. He insisted that a Republican administration would bring back the grim days of depression. Speaking in an aggressive, choppy style, he delighted his crowds: "Give 'em hell, Harry!" they would yell. "I'm doin' it!" Truman would yell back. When he was not "depression-baiting" the Republicans, Truman was Red-baiting the Progressives: "I do not want and will not accept the political support of Henry Wallace and his Communists."

At times, Truman's campaign was so strapped for funds that supporters had to pass the hat at whistle-stop rallies to raise enough money to keep the train moving on to the next stop. Despite his strenuous campaign and his spirited attacks on his political opponents, Truman apparently faced certain defeat. As the election date neared, he continued to trail badly in the polls. Dewey was far ahead, and Wallace's support had dwindled to a few percentage points. Two weeks before the election, fifty political experts unanimously predicted that Dewey would win; most predicted that Dewey would score a landslide victory. Pollsters stopped interviewing a week before the election, assuming that Dewey already had it wrapped up.

On Election Day, Truman pulled off the biggest upset in American political history. He beat Dewey in the popular vote, 24.2 million to 22 million, and 303 to 189 in the electoral college. His party also regained control of Congress by a 54 to 42 margin in the Senate and a whopping 263 to 171 margin in the House. It was a significant victory for the party as well as for the man at the top of the ticket. Wallace's campaign fizzled. Most liberals ended up voting for Truman. The Dixiecrats carried only four Deep South states, enabling Truman and the Democrats to win most of the South.

How could Truman score such a surprising victory? How could the experts all be wrong? Republican complacency and overconfidence helped. Many Republicans, assuming victory, did not bother to vote. Truman's spirited, grassroots campaign effort was a factor, but mainly, Truman won because he was able to hold together enough of the old New Deal coalition of labor, Northern liberals, blacks, and farmers to win. Black voters provided Truman with his margin of victory in key states such as California, Ohio, and Illinois. Many independent voters opted for Truman, blaming an obstructionist Republican-controlled Congress rather than the President for the legislative gridlock. Many Southern whites, although offended by Truman's advocacy of civil rights, nevertheless voted for Truman out of party loyalty and perhaps because they did not want to waste their votes on a protest candidate who had no chance to win.

Truman successfully pinned an anti-New Deal label on the Republicans and identified them with depression memories. He effectively identified the Progressives with Communism and support for the Soviet Union at a time of rising Cold War tensions. A commentator suggested that "Roosevelt had won a fifth term." Ironically, the splits within his party worked to Truman's advantage. They sheared off the Democratic Left and Right and allowed Truman to concentrate on the political center, where most of the votes were. In fact, Truman's energetic centrist 1948 campaign became the model that most subsequent successful presidential candidates of either party would follow: ignore or denounce the extremes, stake out the center, and campaign where the voters are. In reality, a trend toward Truman had surfaced in the final week of the campaign, but the pollsters missed it, since they had already quit taking opinion samples.

Figure 3.3   How sweet is was! A jubilant Harry Truman holds up a Republican paper whose prediction of victory for Thomas Dewey was to say the least a bit premature.   *Source:* St. Louis Mercantile Library. Used with permission.

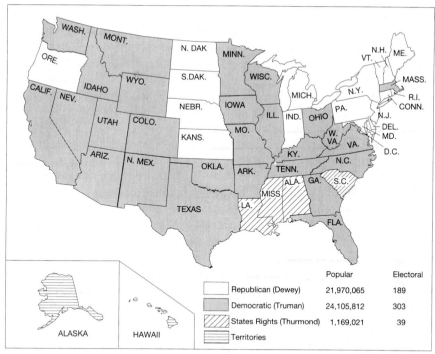

Figure 3.4   The election of 1948.   *Source:* Public Domain map.

THE FAIR DEAL

Now president in his own right, Truman moved to expand the New Deal as he had promised during his campaign. In the fall of 1945, he had sent an ambitious package of legislative proposals to Congress, only to see them shunted aside during the political scrambling over decontrol and inflation. His state of the union message on January 5, 1949, began: "Every segment of our population and every individual has a right to expect from our government a fair deal." Truman's Fair Deal proposals included price controls, tax increases, improving civil rights, expanding public housing, raising the minimum wage, expanding Social Security, repealing the Taft-Hartley law, supporting farm prices, providing federal aid to education, and implementing national health insurance.

The 81st and 82nd Congresses enacted only a small portion of the Fair Deal during Truman's second term. They rejected his proposals for tax hikes and price controls; refused to repeal the Taft-Hartley law; and refused to implement his agricultural program embodied in Secretary of Agriculture Charles F. Brannan's plan for high fixed supports for commodity prices. Truman's civil rights proposals were thwarted by the threat of a Southern filibuster in the Senate. Federal aid to education was opposed by the Catholic Church for not including funds for parochial schools. Truman's controversial proposal for national health insurance provoked opposition from the American Medical Association (AMA), a powerful doctor's lobby that successfully blocked what it called "socialized medicine."

There were many reasons for the defeat of the Fair Deal during the period 1949–1952. The informal bipartisan conservative coalition of Northern Republicans and Southern Democrats in both houses of Congress represented a potent force that could coalesce to block or water down any significant reform legislation that expanded the welfare state, raised taxes, or increased the role of the federal government in the lives of its citizens. Public opinion had drifted toward the center; there was no strong, broad-based popular support for Truman's Fair Deal proposals. Most of the nation's influential media opposed Fair Deal measures on the grounds that they were not needed, cost too much, and gave government bureaucrats too much power over the private sector. Truman's leadership also was ineffective. He failed to rally public opinion in support of his reform proposals, and he failed to work effectively with congressional leaders to get his proposals through the House and the Senate. In addition, Truman often gave top priority to foreign policy issues in the late 1940s and early 1950s, thus neglecting domestic reform politics.

Nevertheless, the president succeeded in getting some Fair Deal measures passed during his second term. The minimum wage was raised from forty cents to seventy-five cents an hour. Social Security coverage was extended to 10.5 million additional workers, and benefits were increased on an average of 77 percent. The most important Fair Deal measure to pass in 1949, with the help of Senator Taft, was the National Housing Act, which provided funds for slum clearance and for the construction of 810,000 units of low-income housing over a period of six years.

Truman's efforts to expand the boundaries of the welfare state were defeated by a combination of lobbyists, the congressional conservative coalition, an apathetic citizenry, and his own ineffective leadership. But he did succeed in updating and expanding many existing programs, and he thereby helped assimilate the New Deal into the vital center of American life. The Fair Deal was a centrist variant of liberal reformism that presaged the New Frontier and Great Society reforms of the 1960s.

During the midterm elections of 1950, the Republicans picked up twenty-eight seats in the House and gained five senators. Although still nominally controlled by the Democrats, the 82nd Congress saw the bipartisan conservative bloc grow more powerful than it had been in the 81st. The Fair Deal lost momentum, and no new social legislation of any consequence was enacted in 1951 or in 1952. Social reform was submerged by Cold War concerns and growing public complacency about domestic institutions. Truman spent much of the last two years of his presidency focused on foreign policy and the Korean War. He also was on the defensive much of the time, trying to defend his floundering government against mounting Republican charges that his administration had been infiltrated by Communists and was riddled with corruption.

Republican charges that corruption was rampant in the Truman administration stemmed from irregularities unearthed in several government agencies that involved minor officials. The "mess in Washington" never reached Truman personally, but one of the accused "influence peddlers" turned out to be Harry Vaughn, the head of the notorious Missouri gang and military aide to the president. Vaughn had been given a deep-freeze unit allegedly for using his influence on behalf of clients who had business with federal agencies. The wife of an official with the Reconstruction Finance Corporation (RFC), which loaned money to banks and insurance companies, was given a mink coat. The coat was a gift from an executive with a company that borrowed funds from the RFC on very favorable terms. The RFC also was reorganized in the wake of the mink coat scandal. Scandals in the Internal Revenue Service (IRS) forced several officials to resign from their positions and led to an administrative overhaul of the agency.

It may have been true that the Truman presidency was the most corrupt since Harding's, but the corruption infesting Truman's administration appeared to be confined to a handful of low-level officials at the periphery of power and influence. Nevertheless, when the wrongdoing was exposed, the American people were shocked and angry. Republicans got a lot of partisan political mileage out of the Truman scandals. In the wake of these damaging exposés, public support for the Truman administration, never very high, plummeted to historic lows. One Gallup Poll gave Truman an approval rating of only 23 percent, the lowest rating ever given to a sitting president. Truman's approval rating was even lower than Richard Nixon's had been on the eve of his resignation from office.

COLD WAR AT HOME

The Cold War hit home in early 1950, when millions of Americans were alarmed by charges that Communists had infiltrated their government and many other institutions. Fears of internal threats posed by Communists long preceded the Cold War era. They first surfaced in the decade of the 1850s and flared periodically during times of social tension and political upheaval. Following World War I, jittery Americans worried that a Bolshevik-style uprising would occur in America. The Red Scare of 1919 and 1920 had culminated in government raids on the homes and meeting places of suspected revolutionaries, followed by mass deportations of radical aliens. In 1938, Southern opponents of New Deal agricultural policies established the House Committee on Un-American Activities (HUAC), chaired by Martin Dies. Dies and his colleagues accused New Deal farm officials of marching to Moscow's beat. In 1940, Congress enacted the Smith Act, which made it a federal crime for anyone to advocate the overthrow of the government.

Neither the Palmer raids nor HUAC's accusations of the late 1930s were justified, but fears of Communist subversion arising after 1945 had a basis in reality. During the late 1930s and early 1940s, government security procedures had been lax. Communists had infiltrated government agencies, some of whom spied for the Soviets. Unfortunately, during this Second Red Scare, opportunistic politicians exploited the popular fear of Communism to enhance their power. They exaggerated the Communist menace, harmed innocent people, confused and divided Americans, and undermined basic political freedoms.

The drive to root Communists out of government agencies began in 1945. FBI agents discovered classified State Department documents in the offices of *Amerasia,* a left-wing journal of Asian affairs. Later that year, the Office of Strategic Services (OSS), a wartime intelligence agency, discovered that some of its classified documents had been delivered to Soviet agents. In February 1946, a Canadian investigating commission exposed the operation of Soviet spy rings within Canada and the United States that had given the Soviets military and atomic secrets.

These spy revelations, coming at a time when United States–Soviet relations were deteriorating, energized Washington. President Truman issued an executive order on March 21, 1947, establishing a loyalty program for federal employees. Truman also directed the Attorney General to publish a list of ninety organizations that were considered disloyal to the United States. The federal loyalty inquest was thorough. More than 4 million individuals were checked. Charges were eventually brought against 9,077 federal employees. Of those charged, about 2,900 resigned and 379 people were dismissed from various federal agencies. The people dismissed were considered "security risks," among them alcoholics, homosexuals, and debtors thought to be susceptible to blackmail. In most cases, there was no question of employee loyalty. Although federal investigators found no spies, the Truman loyalty program heightened rather than calmed public fears of subversion.

Congress also actively hunted subversives. In October 1947, HUAC, with Richard Nixon as its junior member, launched a sensational two-week-long investigation of Hollywood to see whether the film industry had been subverted by Reds. For anyone familiar with the ways of Hollywood, the notion that party members had inserted Communist propaganda into movies that brainwashed the children of America as they sat innocently in their corner neighbor theaters munching popcorn on Saturday afternoons was absurd. No doubt, a few Communists and fellow travelers were working in Hollywood during the 1940s, but they worked for studio heads, not for Moscow. As writer Murray Kempton observed, it was Hollywood that corrupted the Communists, not vice versa.

Nevertheless, HUAC's investigation of the movie colony made for great political theater, and it generated tremendous national attention. Actor Ronald Reagan, president of the Screen Actors' Guild (SAG), appeared before the committee to defend the loyalty of his industry. Although they found little evidence of celluloid Communism, HUAC subpoenaed a group of ten writers, directors, and actors who were or had been members of the Communist Party USA. They refused to answer any questions about their political beliefs and lectured committee members about civil liberties. Such political grandstanding proved to be poor tactics; the "Hollywood Ten's" confrontational tactics confirmed committee suspicions that they were disciplined Stalinists determined to disseminate agitprop through the movies. The studio heads, already worried about dropping box office receipts for their films, panicked. They considered the Congressional investigation and the performance of the Hollywood Ten a public relations disaster. The moguls blacklisted the ten radicals. No studios would hire them until they agreed to cooperate with HUAC. They refused, and all went to jail for contempt of Congress.

During the early 1950s, the blacklist grew dramatically and extended to Broadway, radio, and television. For several years, government investigators, private vigilantes groups, and political conservatives working within the entertainment industry continually accused various actors, writers, and directors of past membership in the Communist Party or in Communist front organizations. Fearing box-office disaster, loss of advertising revenue, and drops in audience ratings, Broadway producers and network executives were no more willing than the film bosses had been to resist political pressures and protect the accused performers.

Those who were accused came under tremendous pressures to repudiate their radical pasts. They confronted a Hobson's choice: they could defy the inquisitors and risk being blacklisted, or they could cooperate with the authorities by recanting their radical beliefs and naming names, that is, providing investigators with the names of individuals they had known from party or front activities. Some defied the committee and were blacklisted. Others named names and continued to work in the entertainment business. Altogether, about 250 people were blacklisted; many of these blacklistees never worked again in show business. They generally were younger or supporting actors, or were second- and third-rate writers and directors. A few big names were accused, but they survived. The most prominent were Edward R. Murrow and Lucille Ball. For big-name stars, accusations that they were Reds did not get them pink slips.

In the aftermath of Truman's loyalty program and HUAC's Hollywood investigations, a powerful fear of anyone thought to be disloyal spread across the land. Teachers and professors were fired for expressing dissenting views. Books were removed from library shelves. Parent-Teacher Association (PTA) leaders were attacked as subversives. Liberal ministers were harassed. Liberals, dissenters, and reformers of every stripe were criticized. Guilt-by-association tactics damaged the reputations and livelihoods of many men and women. School districts required teachers and administrators to sign loyalty oaths. Many states enacted legislation denying public employment to Communists or to anyone affiliated with any organization that showed up on the Attorney General's list.

Ironically, those who waged the domestic Cold War in the name of national security often undermined the democratic rights and intellectual freedoms for whose sake the United States waged the Cold War against the Soviet Union. The idea that an open society tolerant of rigorous criticisms of American institutions might be the best defense against the spread of Communism in the United States was an alien notion to those engaged in the urgent quest for internal security. During the early 1950s, to many an enthusiastic Red hunter of that era, it had become necessary to destroy freedom in order to save it.

The domestic Cold War also engulfed the American trade union movement. Within the ranks of the CIO, Communist Party members or individuals supportive of the Communist Party program held leadership positions in many of the affiliated unions. Often these Communist labor leaders had been skilled organizers who had helped build the CIO unions into strong institutions. The Communists had risen to positions of power within the ranks of labor because they were committed trade unionists. Most of the rank-and-file members of these Communist-led unions were either indifferent or hostile to Communism.

In 1948, Philip Murray, head of the CIO, fearing his organization's vulnerability to attack by powerful anti-union forces for having Communist leaders, began to purge the CIO of its Communist influences. Within a year, eleven unions had been expelled from the CIO. CIO membership fell from 5.2 million to about 3.7 million. In the aftermath of these expulsions, within some unions, leaders branded as Communists anyone who challenged or spoke out against them.

In 1948, the Truman administration went after the leadership of the American Communist Party. The Justice Department put the top leaders of the party on trial for violating the Smith Act. They were convicted, and the Supreme Court upheld the verdicts. After the Court had sustained the convictions of the top leaders, the Justice Department prosecuted dozens of lesser figures within the Communist movement over the next several years.

Truman's loyalty program and the actions of the Justice Department did not quiet popular fears of Communist subversion nor prevent Republicans from exploiting the Communists-in-government issue. One event severely damaged the reputation of the Truman administration and hurt liberal Democrats. In 1949, after the most famous political trial in American history, Alger Hiss was ostensibly convicted of perjury, but in the public mind, he had been convicted for having been a Communist spy. Hiss, allegedly a participant in a Soviet espionage ring during the late 1930s, had risen to become an assistant secretary of state. He had been an adviser at Yalta and had chaired the founding sessions of the United Nations in San Francisco. He left the State Department in 1947 to become director of the prestigious Carnegie Endowment for International Peace. Outwardly, Hiss's public career had been that of a model New Deal bureaucrat.

Hiss's downfall came in 1948, when Whittaker Chambers, a confessed former currier in a Communist spy ring, appeared before HUAC in a closed session to accuse Hiss of having been a member of that same spy ring. He accused Hiss of spying for the Soviets while working for the State Department in 1937 and 1938. Chambers offered no evidence to substantiate his charges. In a later closed HUAC session, Hiss confronted Chambers and threatened him with a libel suit if he dared make his accusations public. Chambers appeared on the television show *Face the Nation* and repeated his charge that Hiss was a former Communist spy. Hiss denied the charge and filed his libel suit. Many prominent public figures, including Secretary of State Dean Acheson, backed Hiss and dismissed the charges against him. Among HUAC members, only Richard Nixon, who believed that Hiss was lying, initially backed Chambers's unsubstantiated charges.

To defend himself against Hiss's libel suit, Chambers brought federal agents to his farm near Westminster, Maryland, where he showed them microfilm copies of government documents stored in a hollowed-out pumpkin. The "pumpkin papers" turned out to be evidence that helped implicate Hiss: microfilm copies of sixty-five classified State Department documents that Chambers claimed Hiss had passed to him in 1937 and 1938 to give to the Soviets. A federal grand jury could only indict Hiss for perjury, because the statute of limitations on espionage had expired. Hiss was tried twice, his first trial having ended with a hung jury. During the second trial, the prosecution established that many of the "pumpkin papers" had been copied in Hiss's handwriting and others had been typed on a typewriter that had belonged to Hiss at the time. Experts dated the microfilm as being from 1937 and 1938. Hiss was convicted and sentenced to five years in prison for perjury.

Hiss was HUAC's greatest catch and vaulted Richard Nixon into national prominence. Many liberals believed that Hiss was innocent, that he had been framed by a conspiracy of vindictive conservative political forces. But the Hiss conviction, more than any other event of the domestic Cold War, convinced millions of Americans that there was truth to the oft-made Republican charges that Roosevelt and Truman had not been sufficiently alert to the dangers of Communist infiltration, subversion, and espionage. Americans worried about other undetected Communist agents who might still be working at the State Department and other government agencies. The Hiss case boosted the anti-Communist crusade at home and legitimated the witch-hunts that followed.

Other events shook the Truman administration. In March 1949, the FBI caught Judith Coplon, a former political analyst at the Justice Department, with her Soviet lover, passing classified documents to a Soviet agent. In September 1949, the Soviets exploded an atomic device, ending the American nuclear monopoly. A month after this shock came the Communist victory in China. Over 600 million people passed behind the "bamboo curtain." The stage was set for the emergence of a demagogue—widespread fear of a hidden enemy thought to be everywhere, frustration that victory in the Second World War had brought not eternal peace but only the tensions and setbacks of the Cold War, and the nightmare possibility of a nuclear holocaust.

Enter Senator Joseph McCarthy. In 1950, casting about for an issue that might get him reelected, the first-term senator from Wisconsin decided to see if he could get any political mileage out of the Communists-in-government issue. He had previously used the issue effectively in Wisconsin political battles. McCarthy was by no means the only politician who practiced the politics of anti-Communism, in fact, he was something of a latecomer to the issue. But McCarthy quickly became the political star of the domestic Cold War, and he retained his top billing until his power was destroyed in 1954.

McCarthy opened his anti-Communist campaign on February 9, 1950, in Wheeling, West Virginia. He told the Ladies' Republican Club of Wheeling that the United States found itself in a weak position in the Cold War because of the actions of disloyal officials in the State Department. Holding up a piece of paper in his right hand, he told his fascinated

Figure 3.5   The Red Scare of the late 1940s gave Richard Nixon, a young Congressman from California, his chance to become nationally prominent. Here he is shown with Robert Stripling, chief investigator for the House Committee on Un-American Activities, examining some of the microfilm evidence that led to Alger Hiss's perjury convictions.   *Source:* Bettmann Archive.

audience that, "I have in my hand" a list of 205 names of Communists working at the State Department. Further, he charged that some of them were in policy-making positions and that their names were known to the Secretary of State. An unknown rookie Senator had dared accuse Dean Acheson of permitting known Communists to hold high-level positions in the State Department! McCarthy then took off on a whirlwind trip across the country, where he repeated his sensational charges. The Wisconsin senator's numbers were inconsistent, and he was difficult to pin down, but the media carried his charges of Communists in the State Department. Quickly this obscure, young politician had captured the limelight; the whole nation soon knew of his accusations.

The Democratic leadership in the Senate, responding to this Republican upstart's sensational charges, convened a subcommittee chaired by a distinguished Maryland Senator, Joseph Tydings, to investigate McCarthy's charges. The Tydings Committee quickly demonstrated that McCarthy not only did not have 205 names, he did not have even the name of one Communist employed in the State Department. Undaunted, McCarthy then accused Owen Lattimore, a prominent expert on Far Eastern affairs, of being the leader of "the espionage ring in the State Department." At the time McCarthy accused him, Lattimore did not work for the State Department. Lattimore denied under oath that he was or had ever been a Communist or had ever espoused the Communist line. The charges against Lattimore also collapsed. In a public report issued in July, the Tydings Committee dismissed McCarthy's charges as a "fraud and a hoax."

Such setbacks at the outset of his campaign might have derailed a less nervy politician, but McCarthy persisted. Most Republican members of Congress backed McCarthy. They sensed that the "Communists in government" issue could pay partisan political dividends. Frustrated and embittered by their losses in the 1948 elections, Republicans hoped that the politics of anti-Communism could be the vehicle that would carry them to power in 1950 and 1952. Conservative Democrats from the South and the West also took up the politics of anti-Communism.

Congress enacted the McCarran Internal Security Act in September 1950 over President Truman's veto. The act required that all Communist and Communist-front organizations register with the Attorney General's office. It also forbade Communists from working in defense factories and prohibited them from traveling abroad on an American passport. Congress enacted another strong anti-Communist measure in 1952, again, over Truman's veto, the McCarran-Walter Act, which forbade Communists and other "undesirables" from entering the United States.

The 1950 elections confirmed the Republicans' hunch that they had found a popular issue. In California, Richard Nixon won a seat in the Senate by calling his liberal Democratic opponent, Helen Gahaghan Douglas, "the pink lady." Several prominent liberal Democrats went down in defeat, including Senator Joseph Tydings. McCarthy quickly became one of his party's most popular campaigners.

McCarthy and his fellow practitioners of the politics of anti-Communism soon acquired a vast following among a public primed by the Hiss case and frustrated by the Korean War. McCarthy stayed on the political offensive. He kept making unsubstantiated charges and naming names. He implied guilt by association, and he told outright lies. It was impossible to keep up with his accusations or to pin him down. He could never be put on the defensive. If one set of charges was dismissed as bogus, he was soon back with another. He called Secretary of State Acheson the "Red Dean of the State Department." He denounced George Marshall, a man with a distinguished record of public service, as a liar and a traitor. McCarthy was always careful to make his charges when shielded by his senatorial cloak of immunity that prevented his victims from suing him for libel. His smear tactics and his use of the "big lie" technique added a new word to the American political lexicon—"McCarthyism."

Several factors accounted for McCarthy's spectacular success. The ground had been prepared by years of Cold War conflict with the Soviet Union, and by politicians who had dramatized the issue, frightening Americans with their accounts of the hidden enemy within. J. Howard Mcgrath, Truman's Attorney General, had alarmed the nation in 1949 with his vivid warning:

> Communists . . . are everywhere—in factories, offices, butcher shops, on street corners, in private business. . . . At this very moment (they are) busy at work—undermining your government, plotting to destroy the liberties of every citizen, and feverishly trying, in whatever way they can, to aid the Soviet Union.[2]

Alarms raised by politicians were seconded by prominent media editorials. McCarthy's sense of timing, his ruthless tactics, and his demagogic ability to voice the fears of many ordinary American citizens all strengthened his cause. He made skillful use of the news media. Radio and television newscasts carried his charges. Newspapers headlined his accusations. Millions of Americans, frightened by revelations of real espionage, found McCarthy's lies plausible. McCarthy's popularity also came from his being the man with a simple, plausible explanation for America's Cold War setbacks and defeats: Communists and liberals who secretly supported the Communists had undermined American foreign policy from within. Traitors working within the State Department and other government agencies were responsible for Communist Cold War triumphs.

Events also played into McCarthy's hands. Two weeks after his Wheeling speech, British intelligence agents discovered an Anglo-American spy ring that had penetrated the atomic bomb project in New Mexico. The key man in the ring had been a nuclear physicist, Dr. Klaus Fuchs, a German-born, naturalized British citizen assigned to the bomb project. He was arrested and confessed everything. He told the British that he had succeeded in delivering complete information on the bomb to Soviet agents between 1943 and 1947. Using information from Fuchs's confession, FBI agents arrested his American accomplices, Harry Gold and David Greenglass. Greenglass, in turn, implicated Julius and Ethel Rosenberg. The Rosenbergs were tried for espionage and were convicted and executed in 1953. The stalemated Korean War also aided McCarthy significantly. As American morale sagged, he attacked those whom he called "the traitors and bunglers in the State Department who were losing the Cold War to the Communists."

[2]Quoted in Athan Theoharis, *Seeds of Repression: Harry S Truman and the Origins of McCarthyism* (Chicago: Quadrangle Books, 1971), p. 136.

**Figure 3.6   The preeminent practitioner of the pol-
itics of anti-communism, Senator Joseph McCarthy
of Wisconsin. For a few years during the early
1950s, this ruthless and clever demagogue was the
second most powerful politician in Washington.**
Source: National Archives.

BIBLIOGRAPHY

Robert H. Ferrell's *Harry S. Truman and the Modern Presidency* is a fine short biography of
the American leader who presided over the first seven years of the postwar era. Alonzo L. Hamby's
Beyond the New Deal: Harry S. Truman and American Liberalism is the most comprehensive account
of postwar politics. Eric Goldman's *The Crucial Decade and After: America, 1945–1960* is a lively
account of the Truman and Eisenhower years. Samuel Lubell's *The Future of American Politics* remains an informative, interpretive account of changing postwar politics. A recent, well-written account of African Americans concerned with the postwar years is Nicholas Lemann's *The Promised
Land: The Great Black Migration and How It Changed America.* William Berman's *The Politics of
Civil Rights in the Truman Administration* is the most complete account of Truman's civil rights policies. David Brody's *Workers in Industrial Society* is the best account of postwar labor history. Two
good studies of Senator Joseph McCarthy are Richard Rovere's *Senator Joe McCarthy* and Robert
Griffith's *The Politics of Fear.* Allen Weinstein's *Perjury: The Hiss-Chambers Case* is a brilliant study
that argues persuasively that Hiss was a secret member of the Communist Party and was guilty of espionage. Richard Freeland's *The Truman Doctrine and the Origins of McCarthyism* is a good account
of the origins of the Second Red Scare. Richard Gid Powers's *Secrecy and Power* is an excellent biography of J. Edgar Hoover. Stephen J. Whitfield's *The Culture of the Cold War* recreates the atmosphere of the 1950s, when fear of international Communism pervaded American culture. The best account of the general issues of anti-Communism during the domestic Cold War is Earl Latham's *The
Communist Controversy in Washington.*

4

The American People at Mid-Century

At the middle of the twentieth century, a majority of Americans enthusiastically participated in a culture of abundance and leisure. The world's most productive economy generated a cornucopia of consumer goods that crowded the shelves and display racks of supermarkets and department stores everywhere. Millions of working-class families owned those twin symbols of American affluence—a home in the suburbs and a gleaming new automobile. Americans at mid-century were the most mobile people on the planet. By the millions, families moved from the cities to the suburbs. From the Northeast and the Upper Midwest, they moved to the dynamic states of the Sunbelt region.

Americans had evolved into an affluent middle-class society, based on consumerism fueled by credit buying on an unprecedented scale. The children of affluence created their own teen variant of the consumer culture, buying adolescent staples such as chewing gum, Cokes, hamburgers, clothes, and rock 'n' roll records. During the 1950s, television quickly established itself as the dominant mass medium, drastically reducing the sizes of audiences for radio and Hollywood movies. Television also quickly established itself as the most important advertising conduit for the producers of the myriad goods and services that constituted the living heart of the consumer economy. Religion enjoyed a major revival, as America remained the most religious nation in the Western world.

During the 1950s, legions of critics developed a scathing critique of the culture of affluence: millions of American families were mired in poverty amidst plenty. Many young people were growing up alienated and rebellious. They did not fit into the niches of the consumer society. As to the majority who did fit in, critics found them to be suffering from a herd mentality; America had reared a generation of mindless conformists. Looking through the picture windows of suburban homes, critics could see that millions of middle-class

Americans, displaying all of the outward trappings of affluence, found achieving the 1950s' version of the American Dream insufficient. Some of these troubled souls sought solace and meaning in religion; some sought escape in popular music, sports, alcohol, and a frenetic social life. Others worried about the possibility of nuclear war and continued to live lives of quiet desperation. For many Americans in the 1950s, the age of affluence also could be an age of anxiety.

DEMOGRAPHIC PATTERNS

The postwar "baby boom" caused a tremendous population increase, as returning veterans and their wives made up for lost time. The American population grew from 153 million in 1950 to 179 million in 1960, the largest decennial increase ever. In 1957, 4.3 million births were recorded, the highest one-year total in American history. That year, demographers discovered that over 50 million Americans were age fourteen or younger. These young baby boomers created powerful demands for new houses, appliances, bicycles, toys, and diapers. During the decade of the 1950s, the number of youngsters enrolled in schools from grades K–12 increased from 28 million to 42 million. More new schools were constructed during the 1950s, mostly in the burgeoning suburban communities surrounding central cities, than had been built during the first fifty years of the twentieth century. As the U.S. birthrate shot up, the death rate fell. Americans added five years to their life expectancy during the 1950s, and death rates among young people declined dramatically as well. New "miracle drugs" such as penicillin and cortisone took much of the pain and misery out of life. Polio vaccines tamed a cruel childhood disease that often left its victims crippled and helpless for life.

Suburban growth, underway in the late 1940s, exploded during the 1950s. Millions of families seeking new homes and jobs or just fleeing from myriad urban problems moved from metropolitan centers to outlying communities. By the end of the decade, the suburban population of 60 million equaled that of the rest of urban America. During the 1950s, most large cities within the United States lost population. Of cities with more than 1 million people, only Los Angeles grew significantly during the decade. The flight to the suburbs transformed living patterns for millions of middle-class families at mid-century.

During the 1950s, Americans were not only the richest and healthiest generation ever, they also were the most mobile. Regionally, the American population continued its shift west and south. Families poured into the South, the Southwest, and the West. California, Florida, and Texas added millions of new residents. Soon the Sunbelt encompassed most of the southern rim of the nation, from Southern California to Florida. Americans moved in search of better jobs and business opportunities and the more spacious lifestyles that were possible in Sunbelt suburbs. The economic foundations of the Sunbelt's spectacular population boom included agribusiness, aerospace, electronics, oil, real estate, and a large infusion of military spending. Low taxes and right-to-work laws also attracted industry to the Southern Rim. Rural America continued to lose population during the 1950s. The depopulation of the countryside, a demographic trend that had accelerated during the years of World War II, continued into the postwar era and the 1950s.

AN ECONOMY OF ABUNDANCE

War spending restored American prosperity in the early 1940s, ending a decade of depression and beginning an era of sustained economic expansion and rising living standards that stretched into the 1970s. Between 1945 and 1960, the GDP doubled. During the 1950s, the American economy grew at an average rate of 4.0 percent per year, despite enduring periodic recessions. Between 1946 and 1960, the American workforce grew from 54 million to 68 million jobholders. Median wages in manufacturing industries rose 60 percent, and median family income rose from $3,000 to $5,700 during that same period. Since the rate of inflation remained low, about 2 percent per annum for the decade of the 1950s, wage increases translated into significant gains in purchasing power and rising standards of living. Unemployment rates remained low, averaging around 4 percent in the 1950s. During this decade, millions of Americans could afford goods and services that would have been beyond their means previously. The rapidly growing American economy generated a widespread abundance that became the envy of the world. During the 1950s, the United States, with about 5 percent of the world's population, consumed over one-third of its goods and services.

Credit significantly enhanced consumer purchasing power. Short-term installment credit, mainly for new cars, increased fivefold from 1946 to 1960. A revolution in spending patterns got underway in 1950, when the Diners' Club introduced the general credit card, soon followed by American Express. During this decade, oil companies and department stores issued millions of revolving credit cards. Private debt within the affluent society climbed from $73 billion to $200 billion during the decade of the 1950s. Consumer demand stimulated huge private sector investment in new plant capacity and new technology, an average of $10 billion per year. Automation, the use of self-regulating machines to control manufacturing operations, enhanced the nation's industrial productivity and improved the quality of products.

Big business grew bigger during the postwar era. Another wave of mergers swept the industrial economy. By 1960, America's 200 largest industrial corporations owned over half of the nation's industrial assets. But unlike the merger waves of the 1890s and 1920s, which joined businesses within the same economic sectors, the 1950s' mergers brought together businesses in unrelated fields. Conglomerates such as International Telephone and Telegraph (ITT) linked a car rental company, a home construction company, a retail food outlet, a hotel chain, and an insurance company under the same corporate roof.

THE CAR CULTURE

Automobiles remained the most important American industry during the 1950s. New car and truck sales averaged 7 million units annually during the decade. By 1960, there were 70 million vehicles on the nation's roads and highways. Two-thirds of the nation's employees commuted to work by car. The number of service stations, garages, motels, and the size of the oil industry all expanded with autos.

The growth of suburbia and the automobile boom occurred together. Suburbia required automobiles. Mothers driving station wagons, piled full of kids on their way to school, shopping centers, or team practice, became the reigning symbol of the 1950s' suburban lifestyle. In the late 1950s, the federal government began constructing an interstate highway system funded mainly by gasoline taxes. Summer traveling vacations became the great American pastime. The huge highway building project also included the construction of thousands of miles of freeways connecting the new suburbs to the central cities. Government road building amounted to a subsidy for the American car culture that promoted suburban growth and urban decay.

As the numbers of cars on the roads multiplied, they became longer, wider, more powerful, and gaudier. Detroit reached its pinnacle in the late 1950s. Automakers outdid themselves, creating chromium ornaments, two- and three-tone color combinations, soaring tailfins, and gas-guzzling V-8 engines. The buying public was delighted with Detroit's offerings, which also included wrap-around windshields, power steering, automatic transmissions, air conditioning, and hi-fi radios. Advertisers stressed the power, the flashiness, and even the sex appeal of these elaborate machines. Popular entertainers such as Dinah Shore appeared on television to sing, "See the U.S.A. in your Chevrolet." Advertisers linked owning a new car to participating in the very essence of what it meant to be a successful American: what was more American than apple pie, mom, and your new Chevrolet? Domestic automakers had the American market all to themselves; imports accounted for less than 1 percent of sales in 1955. Gas was cheap and plentiful at twenty-five cents to thirty cents per gallon. A big, gleaming new car was one of the supreme status symbols of the affluent society, a shining testament to America's technological world supremacy. It would be left to later generations of urban planners to worry about the decay of mass transit, the decline of smog-choked inner cities, and freeway gridlock.

Figure 4.1   A big gleaming new car was one of the supreme status symbols of the affluent society. Here a 1954 Buick Super Riviera shines in all of its glory. *Source:* National Archives.

GROWTH INDUSTRIES

The chemical industry grew even faster than the auto business during the 1950s. Du Pont's slogan, "Better things for better living through chemistry," became known to every television viewer. Du Pont, Dow, and the other chemical giants turned out a never-ending feast of new synthetic products—aerosol spray cans, Dacron, and new plastics like vinyl and Teflon.

Electricity and electronics also grew rapidly in the postwar era. A horde of new electric appliances sprang forth—air conditioners, electric blankets, automatic clothes washers, clothes dryers, and hair dryers. The electronics industry expanded mainly because of the advent of television. By the early 1950s, dealers were selling 6 million new TV sets each year. Other popular electronic products enjoyed wide sales during the 1950s. Almost every one of the nearly 60 million new cars sold in the decade had a radio. Transistors made possible the development of new computer technologies. International Business Machines (IBM) marketed its first mainframe computers, inaugurating the postindustrial age. In 1960, the Xerox corporation marketed its 914 copier, thereby inaugurating a revolution in document copying. The aerospace industry kept pace with other growth industries, stimulated by multibillion dollar contracts to supply the Pentagon with sophisticated military hardware. Air travel increased rapidly after 1945 and took a quantum leap forward in 1958 with the introduction of regularly scheduled commercial jet travel.

Although postwar growth industries flourished, some traditional heavy industries and manufacturing declined such as railroads, coal mining, and textiles. Long-haul trucking and air travel cut heavily into railroad freight and passenger business. Coal could no longer compete with oil, natural gas, and electricity. Cotton and woolen manufacturers succumbed to synthetic fibers spun out by the chemical companies. Americans increasingly wore clothes made of nylon, orlon, and polyester. Industrial decline brought permanent depression to New England mill towns and to Appalachia, creating pockets of poverty amidst general affluence.

Agriculture changed drastically in the postwar years. Farmers produced more foodstuff than consumers could buy, and commodity prices dropped. Profits could be made in farming only by reducing unit costs of production through intensive use of fertilizers, pesticides, expensive farm machinery, and sophisticated managerial techniques. Larger farms prospered from a combination of greater efficiency and government subsidies. Small farmers got squeezed out and joined the rural exodus to the cities. The nation's farm population dropped from 25 million at the end of the war to 14 million in 1960. The number of agricultural workers dropped to just 6 percent of the workforce. In regions of Arizona, Florida, and California, huge corporate farms dominated many agricultural sectors. These "agribusiness" enterprises replaced the family farm.

THE MIXED ECONOMY

The federal government stimulated economic growth during the 1950s in many ways. Washington dispensed billions of dollars annually as welfare payments, Social Security

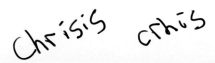

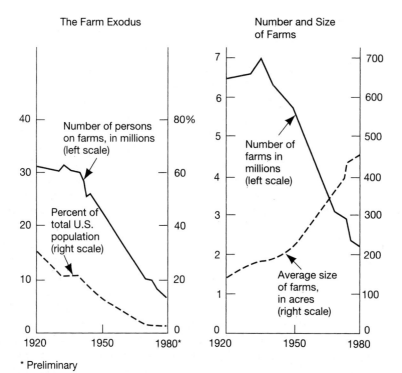

The Farm Exodus

Number and Size of Farms

Number of persons on farms, in millions (left scale)

Percent of total U.S. population (right scale)

Number of farms in millions (left scale)

Average size of farms, in acres (right scale)

* Preliminary

Figure 4.2   In the postwar period, the trends toward fewer but larger farms and a much smaller rural population accelerated. By 1980, three out of every four Americans lived in a metropolitan area.   *Source:* Public domain.

checks, and farm subsidies. Congress funded over half of the nation's industrial research and development and over half of all university scientific research. The Federal Reserve Board regulated the money supply and interest rates. Other government bureaucracies regulated the securities and communications industries, interstate transportation, and aviation. During the 1950s, military budgets pumped $40 billion to $50 billion a year into the economy, and government spending as a percentage of the gross national product (GDP) increased steadily. The number of Americans working for government at all levels increased by 50 percent during this decade. The prosperity of many locales became dependent on government purchases or government payrolls.

Americans at mid-century celebrated what they were fond of calling the "American free enterprise system." But economic reality was more complex and ambiguous than their simplistic rhetorical labels implied. Out of their efforts to battle the Great Depression and to produce the materials needed to win World War II, Americans had fashioned a mixed economy that blended public and private enterprise. Government spending and regulatory activities had become integral elements of the mixed economy. The mixed economy conformed to no economic model or theory. Most Americans did not understand its nature or how it worked, but they were delighted with its prime creation—the culture of abundance.

LABOR AT MID-CENTURY

Organized labor prospered during the 1950s, as trade unions won wage increases and new fringe benefits from corporate employers. The United Auto Workers and General Motors agreed to a clause in their contract calling for automatic annual cost-of-living adjustments in wages. That agreement set a pattern soon copied in other industries and occupations. Corporate managers discovered that it was more profitable to negotiate wage increases with union representatives and to pass their increased costs on to consumers rather than to engage in lengthy strikes with strong unions. Organized labor remained a powerful force within the Democratic Party that normally controlled Congress during the 1950s. George Meany declared in 1955, "American labor never had it so good." Labor's major achievement was to bring about the merger of the AFL and CIO in 1955. The creation of the AFL-CIO brought 90 percent of America's 18 million trade unionists into a single national labor federation, headed by George Meany.

Although unions generally prospered during the 1950s, they also faced serious problems. Corruption riddled several of them. Senator John McClellan of Arkansas chaired a Senate committee that investigated union racketeering in 1957. The McClellan committee exposed widespread corruption in the Teamster's Union. Robert "Bobby" Kennedy served as chief counsel for the committee and his brother Senator John F. Kennedy also served on the committee. They found that Teamster officials had involved themselves in a wide range of crooked activities, including the misappropriation of union funds, rigged elections, extortion, and association with members of organized crime. Committee investigations led to the enactment of the Landrum-Griffin Act in 1959. This moderate labor reform measure imposed new legal restrictions on unions, and expanded the list of union unfair labor practices. It also contained anti-corruption provisions to safeguard democratic election procedures within unions and to make misuse of union funds a federal crime.

Trade unions also confronted a more fundamental problem than racketeering during the late 1950s. Union membership peaked in 1956 at 18.6 million and declined thereafter. The proportion of the workforce that belonged to unions declined mainly because of the loss of jobs in heavy industry. The American economy continued to grow and prosper after 1958, but organized labor could not keep pace. Many industries moved to the South to take advantage of lower wage levels and non-union workers. But even where unions remained strong, workers were less inclined to join them than before, primarily because, without joining, they received the higher wages and benefits that union negotiators had obtained. Most important, the economy was shifting from a production-oriented to a service-oriented one, which meant a shift from blue-collar occupations to white-collar jobs.

Most of the new job growth in the 1950s economy occurred in the service, clerical, and managerial sectors. In 1956, for the first time in American economic history, white-collar workers outnumbered blue-collar workers in the workforce. White-collar workers generally resisted the efforts of union organizers in the 1950s. As white-collar jobs multiplied in the growth sectors of the economy, technological innovations eliminated jobs in mining, manufacturing, and transportation. A few unions did manage to organize categories of white-collar employees, the most successful being the American Federation of State,

County, and Municipal Employees (AFSCME), whose members worked for various state and local government agencies.

POVERTY AMIDST PLENTY

Although the large majority of American families were eager participants in the culture of abundance, millions of their fellow citizens were mired in poverty. In 1960, according to the Bureau of Labor Statistics, about 40 million Americans representing 25 percent of the population were poor. These data were computed at a time when the Bureau established the poverty line as an income of $2,500 a year or less for an urban family of four. The elderly, people over sixty-five, made up one-fourth of the poor. One-fifth were non-white, including 45 percent of the black population. Two-thirds of the poor inhabited households headed by a person with an eighth-grade education or less. One-fourth of poor people lived in a household headed by a single woman.

The poor congregated in the inner cities, as middle-class people fled to the suburbs. Between 1945 and 1960, over 3 million black people, most of them unskilled and many of them illiterate, moved to Northern and Western cities from the rural South. Poor whites from Appalachia joined blacks in this migration from the country to the cities. Many poor people also inhabited rural America in the 1950s. Both white and black tenant farmers and sharecroppers were trapped in a life cycle of poverty and hard work. A famous television documentary shown in 1960, *The Harvest of Shame,* narrated by Edward R. Murrow, depicted the poverty and hopelessness of migrant farm workers.

One of the major causes of poverty in America lay in the fact that wealth in America remained highly concentrated. In 1960, the richest 1 percent of the population owned one-third of the national wealth. The wealthiest 5 percent of America's families owned over half of the nation's wealth. At the same time, half of the nation's families had no savings. Some of the poverty in mid-century America could be attributed to the failure of the welfare state forged during the New Deal era to provide for poor people. Its benefits had gone to groups that were organized to make demands on Congress and the broker state. The Wagner Act did nothing for non-union workers. Minimum wage laws and Social Security benefits did not extend to millions of low-income workers in dozens of occupations. Welfare programs available to poor people maintained them at subsistence levels and perpetuated a demoralized lifestyle based on dependency.

Women made up a large percentage of poor Americans at mid-century. Few well-paying jobs were open to them in the 1950s. A greater portion of women's jobs than men's jobs was not covered by minimum wage or Social Security protection. Also, divorced women usually were saddled with major child-rearing responsibilities. Ex-husbands often failed to make child support payments, and many divorced women with children slipped into poverty.

Few government officials or anyone else showed much interest in the plight of poor Americans during the 1950s. Publicists focused on celebrating the achievements of the affluent majority. The poor themselves were silent. They lacked organizations and articulate leaders to call attention to their problems. They inhabited another America, neglected and suffering in silence, beyond the boundaries of affluence.

THE RISE OF SUBURBIA

America experienced the greatest internal population movement in its history in the fifteen years following World War II, when 40 million Americans fled the cities for the suburbs. Young, well-educated, white, middle-class people led the flight to the suburbs. Many factors combined to create this mighty exodus from the inner cities to the outlying areas. Families fled traffic jams, high taxes, contact with racial minorities, overcrowded schools, high real estate prices, and high crime rates. Suburbia beckoned for many reasons: the obvious attraction of open country where spacious houses could be built for a fraction of what big-city construction would cost. People wanted homes with yards where, as one father put it, a kid could "grow up with grass stains on his pants." Suburban homes also promised the privacy and quiet not found in crowded city apartments. Many suburbanites sought a community of like-minded people and accessible local government.

Government subsidies permitted millions of families to move into suburbia who otherwise could not have afforded to. Low-interest mortgages requiring little or no down payments and tax subsidies produced a postwar housing boom. During the 1950s, contractors built an average of 2 million new homes a year. Across the country, developers busily tossed up new housing tracts, replacing forests, bean fields, fruit orchards, and grazing lands. By 1960, over 60 percent of American families owned their homes, the most significant accomplishment of the affluent society. Businesses also moved to the suburbs in response to the growing demands of suburbanites. Suburban shopping centers multiplied; by 1960, there were 3,840 such centers sprawled across the nation, transforming shopping patterns throughout the nation. Suburban dwellers no longer needed to shop in the central cities; they bought whatever they needed in suburban stores. New freeways connected the suburbs to the central cities.

Some suburban developments were tossed up virtually overnight. Using mass production and merchandising techniques, William Levitt built Levittown, Long Island. Soon, a flourishing community of some 16,000 homes built on 1,100 streets existed where only a few months earlier farmers had raised potatoes. Other Levittowns soon appeared in Pennsylvania and New Jersey. Penn Kimball, a *New York Times Magazine* writer, vividly described the process of Levittown's instant community formation:

> Starting from scratch the Levitts have converted eight square miles of open farm country into a densely populated community of 70,000. Paved streets, sewer lines, school sites, baseball diamonds, shopping centers, parking lots, new railroad station, factory sidings, churches, trunk arteries, newspapers, garden clubs, swimming pools, doctors, dentists, and town hall   all conceived in advance, all previously planned in one of the most colossal acts ever of moral creation.[1]

The Levittowns were immediate successes; tens of thousands of young families, many of them headed by veterans, left their urban neighborhoods and joined the rush to the suburbs. But social critics made Levittown stand as a metaphor for the postwar failings of

[1]Quoted in Dewey W. Grantham, *Recent America: The United States Since 1945* (Arlington Heights, Ill.: Harlan Davidson Inc., 1987), pp. 160–161.

Figure 4.3   Levittown, Long Island, New York, USA, during the 1950s.
Source: National Archives.

suburban society. They condemned Levittown for its uniform houses lined up on uniform streets in a treeless communal waste. According to cultural critic Lewis Mumford, Levittown homes were inhabited by people of the same class, the same income, and the same age group, watching the same pallid fare on television and eating the same tasteless, prefabricated foods from the same home freezers. Both inwardly and outwardly, in every aspect of their lives, the denizens of Levittown conformed to a common mold.

Mumford's elitist indictment, although exaggerated, was not so much incorrect as it was beside the point. Levittown appealed to the mass of ordinary American families, precisely because it was safe and reassuring as well as affordable. Although suburbs tended to be internally homogeneous, they were typically differentiated along social and economic lines. Suburbs were identified as working class, middle class, or elite enclaves of upper-middle-class families. Analysts of suburban culture observed that ethnic identities attenuated in suburbia; in that sense, suburbs tended to make people more homogeneous. Suburban community identities were based more on shared styles of consumerism than on ethnic ancestry.

While ethnicity declined in mid-century America, suburbanization separated Americans racially. Most African American and Hispanic families remained in large cities as white families headed for the suburbs. The national metropolitan pattern became one of predominantly black cities encircled within white suburbs. The 1960 census showed that suburbia was 98 percent white; it also showed that some of the nation's larger cities—Washington, D.C., Newark, Richmond, and Atlanta—had black majorities. As the white middle classes moved out, the central cities declined. Urban tax bases shrunk, social services shriveled, and crime rates soared. A consequence of the white flight to suburbia that left black inner-city populations entrapped in deteriorating ghettos was the fiery urban riots during the summers of 1965 to 1968.

CLASS AND STATUS

Sustained postwar economic growth and prosperity allowed millions of Americans to increase their incomes, advance their occupational statuses, and improve their standards of living. During the 1950s, most Americans believed that their society offered the hard-working individual abundant opportunities—a better job, a higher income, more profitable business ventures, or a college education. They believed that enhanced occupational and social mobility operated to diminish social distinctions and to distribute income more equitably in mid-century America.

While it was undoubtedly true that 1950s' American society was highly mobile and that many people found opportunities to enhance their wealth, status, and influence, it also remained in many important ways a class society. Wealth remained concentrated in the hands of a relatively small number of families at the top. Below the wealthy elite classes, Americans aligned themselves in strata markedly differentiated by wealth, status, culture, ethno-racial identities, political clout, legal protections, education, health, and patterns of recreation and leisure. At the bottom rungs of American society were the masses of poor people. These 40 million of course had little money, status, power, and they had only meager opportunities to acquire them.

Champions of the affluent society believed that it provided the ultimate counter to the ideological challenge posed by Communism during the Cold War. These pundits believed that Americans had eliminated class conflict, that ancient problem that had driven capitalistic societies for centuries. In the America of the 1950s, they argued, everyone was middle class. Industrial workers were members in good standing of that vast middle class that constituted nearly the entire American society. By becoming a nation of middle-class families, Americans had attained social equality and had done so while maintaining an unprecedentedly high level of material well-being. Within America, it had not been necessary to dispossess the wealthy or to redistribute wealth, merely to let the solvents of economic growth and social mobility work their magic. The pie was so large that all could share in the abundance.

It was certainly true that unionized workers employed in the mass production industries made striking gains in job security and economic well-being during the 1950s. Many senior skilled workers earned larger incomes annually than many traditional middle-class office workers, teachers, and those in the service trades. Yet achieving middle-class incomes, buying a new car, and moving into Levittown did not mean that industrial workers adopted middle-class manners, attitudes, and values. The great American middle class remained split, if no longer along class lines, then along cultural lines. Working-class lifestyles in many instances remained distinct from middle-class suburban lifestyles based on consumerism.

THE CULTURE OF AFFLUENCE

A vast increase in the size of the middle classes was the most significant characteristic of the affluent society. The postwar class structure resembled a diamond instead of a pyramid, with the bulge of the diamond representing the 60 percent of the population that had joined the middle classes. A large increase in college enrollments accompanied the growth in numbers of middle-class households. A college education became accessible to young people from average American families. As the 1950s ended, nearly 4 million young people were enrolled at more than 2,000 colleges and universities across the land. Most individual members of this large college population sought the conventional goals of family, career, and a home in the suburbs. College campuses were quiet, businesslike places during the 1950s. Students shunned politics, radicalism of any kind, and intellectual adventure. Observers labeled these careful young men and women of the 1950s the "silent generation."

American teenagers often set popular cultural trends during the 1950s. A teen culture flourished with money to spend and clear consumer preferences. Merchandisers responded synergistically to these teenage consumers. Ray Kroc, a traveling salesman from Chicago, observed a drive-in restaurant in San Bernardino, California, that was doing a thriving business. It sold only hamburgers, french fries, and milk shakes, and it sold them fast. Its owners, Dick and Mac McDonald, had applied assembly-line, mass production technology to the preparation of food, and in the process they had invented the fast-food restaurant. With borrowed money, Kroc concluded a business arrangement with the McDonald brothers that permitted him to establish a chain of fast-food restaurants using their name and modeled on their format. The first McDonald's, complete with twin golden arches, sprang out of the prairie soil of Des Plaines, Illinois, a suburb of Chicago, on April 15, 1955. By the end of the decade, there were hundreds of McDonalds' restaurants spreading rapidly across the country selling hamburgers for fifteen cents, french fries for a dime, and milk shakes for twenty cents. Ray Kroc was fast becoming rich.

In the same year Ray Kroc opened the first McDonald's fast-food restaurant in the Midwestern heartland, Walt Disney offered Disneyland, the first theme park, to American consumers. Disney sponsored a lavish telecast the night before Disneyland opened to the public. One of the hosts of the telecast was a future president, screen actor and television personality Ronald Reagan. Disneyland, in Anaheim, California, a suburb that lies thirty miles southeast of Los Angeles, immediately attracted hordes of visitors, mostly families with children. It featured combinations of fairy tale images derived from Disney's earlier animated masterpieces and sanitized historical images from his live-action films.

The Autopia ride was meant to be the major magnet when the theme park first opened. Autopia was a miniature freeway with small cars for child drivers. Disney believed that it would not only be fun for kids but also would teach youngsters to be responsible adults behind the wheel. Within six weeks after opening, only six of the cars were drivable, the rest battered wrecks. Rather than drive safely and responsibly, young scofflaws had turned their vehicles into bumper cars, happily chasing and slamming into one another at high speeds. Autopia was shut down and redesigned. When it reopened, the cars could only go slow and were fastened to tracks.

Figure 4.4   Affluent Americans at mid-century had more money to spend and more leisure time to enjoy than any previous generation. Here people flock to the beach at Coney Island for a day of sun and surf.   *Source:* National Archives.

Some areas of the park—Main Street, Frontierland, and Adventureland—featured a vast display of the icons of Americana. Young people also could take a Jungle Cruise and conquer the "dark continent." They could take a cruise on the steamboat *Mark Twain* down a man-made river. They could enter the Enchanted Tiki Room, where mostly white visitors mingled with friendly ethnic stereotypes. And they could be inspired by a larger-than-life robotic Abraham Lincoln who, in a deep, rumbling voice, declaimed the virtues of constitutional democratic governance.

Much of the 1950s' popular culture can only be explained by recapitulating the American historical trajectory since the Great Depression of the 1930s. As Franklin Roosevelt famously observed, the dominant reaction to the financial collapse and severe economic down of the early 1930s was fear, "stark unreasoning terror." Add to that decade of depression the disruptions of the 1940s—the horrors of World War II and the rise of the Cold War. Americans had to endure nearly twenty years of frightening historical experiences before they could enjoy the prosperity and popular culture of the 1950s. Finally, Americans could once again believe that the conventional order of things could be relied upon and that American institutions and core values were fundamentally sound. Americans could now feel safe and secure. The awful fears caused by economic collapse, global war, and the rise of the Soviet menace could be banished as Americans took refuge in a culture of conformity and mass consumerism. Disneyland epitomized this popular culture of reassurance.

WOMEN: FAMILY LIFE AND WORK

The postwar years were a time of transition, frustration, and confusion for many American women. *Life* magazine ran a feature in 1947 entitled "The American Woman's Dilemma." Its author found that many women were torn between the traditional expectation of staying home and the desire to work outside of the realm of domesticity. Millions of women continued to work outside of the home, mostly because they had to. Whether they wanted to work or not, more and more women married and gave birth to children in the postwar era. During the late 1940s and the decade of the 1950s, the family was the most rapidly growing American social institution. These new families held down well-paying jobs, purchased suburban homes, reared children, and made the consumer purchases that kept the mighty U.S. economy growing and prospering.

American families became more child oriented after the war. Dr. Benjamin Spock published the first edition of his *Baby and Child Care* in 1946, which strongly influenced child-rearing practices in the postwar era. He advised women to make child rearing their most important task, to put their children's needs first. Early editions of Spock's book also advised women to stay at home and not to work outside of the home so that they would be available to meet all of their babies' needs.

Some psychiatrists, influenced by Sigmund Freud's writings, criticized working women. To these writers, the independent woman was an oxymoron. They considered women who held jobs outside of the home neurotic feminists trying to be "imitation men." They claimed that women could only be fulfilled and happy through domesticity. They argued that a woman's gender determined her role in life. Anatomy was destiny. At the core of this "feminine mystique" was the idea that women constituted the foundation of society. Women made the home a haven from the stress of the competitive business world. Women in their roles as wives and mothers did necessary and noble work, and in the process they fulfilled their feminine destinies.

In 1956, *Life* magazine published a special issue on American women. It profiled housewife Marjorie Sutton as a successful woman who fulfilled her feminine potential, epitomized the feminine mystique. She was mother, wife, home manager, and hostess. She was active in the PTA, the Campfire Girls, and charity work. Married at age sixteen, Sutton had four children, and she did all of the cooking, cleaning, and sewing for her family. She chauffeured her large brood of children wherever they needed to go. She also helped her husband's career by entertaining his business clients. Marjorie Sutton fulfilled the official feminine ideology of the 1950s, the suburban wifely counterpart to her husband, the organization man.

Films of the 1950s highlighted sex symbols such as Marilyn Monroe or wholesome heroines such as Doris Day. They became role models for women. Women's fashions stressed femininity at the expense of practicality or comfort. In *Modern Woman: The Lost Sex,* one of the authors called feminism a "deep illness." There were strong pressures on women to conform to the prevailing sexual stereotype. During the decade, no organized feminist movement existed to challenge the prevailing feminine mystique.

Mid-century women were caught in a dilemma. According to the prevalent ideology, the ideal role for women was found in the home. Her fulfillment lay in creating an island of love and security for her children and husband, with scant regard for her own needs. But studies of women, especially college-educated women, showed that many were unhappy with the constraints and lack of fulfillment in their lives, as defined by domesticity. They especially resented the lack of mental stimulation, the lack of any outlet for their academic skills and intellectual energies. The rise of social pathologies—of alcoholism, divorce rates, and anomie among women who supposedly had it all, who had fulfilled the cultural ideal of wife and mother—furnished additional evidence of their widespread stress and confusion.

Compounding the confusion over women's roles in mid-century society was the fact that millions of middle-class women had entered the job market. The female labor force expanded from 17 million in 1946 to 22 million in 1958. By 1960, 40 percent of women were employed full time or part time. During the decade of the 1950s, female employment increased at a rate four times faster than male employment. By 1960, 30 percent of married women worked outside of the home. Despite the burgeoning cult of motherhood, most new entrants to the female job market during the 1950s were married women with children. Most

Figure 4.5   An office in New York City. Women at work during the 1950s.   *Source:* Brown Brothers.

of these married women workers were not pursuing full-time careers, were not competing with men, and certainly were not seeking or finding equality in the workplace. Many worked part time, and most did "women's work," that is, they took positions in clerical and other white-collar fields traditionally reserved for women, where the pay was low and the prospects for promotion were slim.

In many instances, these married, middle-class women worked to supplement their families' incomes. Their contributions ensured a solid, middle-class status and lifestyle for their families that was not attainable from their husbands' earnings alone. A sizable proportion of middle-class family incomes in the $12,000 to 15,000 per annum range during the 1950s was made possible by having two income earners. The wife's income made possible the purchase of a split-level suburban home in a fashionable neighborhood and the purchase of a second car or station wagon. These hardworking 1950s' middle-class women did not see a conflict between working outside of the home and maintaining their duties as wives and mothers. Most worked for a few years until their children were born, then quit their jobs until their children had become teenagers. They then reentered the workforce. They were not careerists competing with their husbands or seeking independence; they were merely helping their families achieve a higher status and a better standard of living. These women, of course, deviated from the norms prescribe by the feminine mystique, from the roles played to perfection by the Marjorie Suttons of the 1950s, but, according to historian William Chafe, these working women "were carving out one of the only paths available within the existing culture for resolving the contradiction between traditional and modern definitions of women's 'place.'"

Another factor strongly influencing family life and the roles of women during the 1950s was a consequence of American social history. Millions of American families during the 1950s were headed by men and women who had grown up amidst the economic deprivations of the Great Depression of the 1930s. They had been young adults during World War II, experiencing the loneliness and physical separation from friends and family inherent in military service in wartime. After experiencing fifteen years of economic and emotional insecurity, they were determined to enjoy the material security of the affluent society, and they were equally determined to have the emotional security found in a cohesive family life. These men and women made the baby boom and championed "togetherness." The term *togetherness* first appeared in a 1954 *McCalls* article. It meant a happy family melded into a team, specifically the woman fusing herself with her husband and children. Family life was oriented around shared activities—television watching, backyard barbecues, outings to parks and beaches, and vacation trips.

RELIGION REVIVED

Religion enjoyed a revival during the 1950s. President Eisenhower tied religion to patriotism when he observed that recognition of God was "the first, the most basic, expression of Americanism." With America locked in a Cold War with godless Communists, religious worship became one of the defining characteristics of Americanism. Atheism was associated in the popular mind with Communism and disloyalty; a mix of religious worship, free enterprise, and political democracy epitomized the American way. Religion also was promoted as bonding family members together in worship: "The family that prays together stays together." The Bible topped the best-seller charts every year during the 1950s. Congress inserted the words "under God" in the Pledge of Allegiance to the American flag, recited in classrooms, and it put the motto "In God We Trust" on paper money.

Hundreds of new suburban churches appeared during the 1950s. From 1945 until 1960, church attendance in this country increased by 50 percent. Baptist evangelist Billy Graham emerged as the major leader of a mass movement back to Bible fundamentalism. Bishop Fulton Sheen became a prominent television personality, speaking to millions of people about ethical and spiritual issues; he also denounced Communism, collectivism, and atheism. A minister with training in psychology, Dr. Norman Vincent Peale was the most popular preacher of the 1950s. His book *The Power of Positive Thinking* sold millions of copies. Blending religion with pop psychology, Peale preached a gospel of reassurance. He told his anxious listeners that God watched over Americans, assuring individual success in careers and ultimately victory over Communism in the Cold War.

A public opinion poll taken in 1955 showed that 97 percent of Americans believed in God and that two-thirds of the population claimed to attend church regularly. America remained the most religious nation in the West. Religion played a serious role in the lives of millions of American families. Most Americans appeared unconcerned over doctrinal differences among the various religions or with serious theological issues. For most Americans, religious commitments had little intellectual content. Rather than reorient their lives to God, most Americans considered religious observances essentially a social activity. For others, religious belief got intermixed with patriotism, family togetherness, and Thursday night bingo. High school and college athletic events began with a prayer or a moment of meditation. Religion also could serve as a means of establishing one's social identity, of becoming a member of a suburban community. Religion in the 1950s suffused most American social and public affairs, adding a sense of goodness, appropriateness, and Americanism to these activities.

SOCIAL CRITICS

Although the decade of the 1950s is remembered mainly as a time of conformity and complacency, an era of pervasive intellectual blandness when Americans took a holiday from thinking to indulge in the pleasures of affluent consumerism, it also produced a number of independent thinkers who maintained a lively critical discourse about the foibles and failures of mid-century Americans. While most 1950s' social critics agreed that Americans had created an affluent society, that most Americans no longer needed to concern themselves with basic questions of economic survival, they also observed that pockets of poverty, concentrations of wealth and power, class distinctions, and social injustice persisted in mid-century America. Others raised questions about the quality and lack of meaning in lives based on work, consumerism, and social conformity.

William Whyte, author of the best-selling *Organization Man,* claimed that Americans no longer followed the traditional individual success ethic. They embraced what Whyte termed an *organizational ethic,* which stressed belonging to a group and being a team player. Corporations employed more and more Americans. Within these large companies, bureaucratic management styles prevailed. Businesses encouraged their employees to look, dress, and act alike. Each appeared to be *The Man in the Gray Flannel Suit,* the title of a best-selling 1950s' novel by Sloan Wilson. Whyte raised serious questions about the energy, drive, and productivity of corporate executives whose highest ambition was to belong to a group.

The urge to conform spread to the general society. A classic study of the postwar social character, sociologist David Riesman's *Lonely Crowd,* highlighted the lonely individual lost within mass society. Riesman observed that mobility had uprooted people from their traditional ethical moorings. Old values no longer offered guidance or meaning. People were cast adrift morally. Young people adapted to the new social environment by embracing peer group norms and turning to television for guidance. They consumed their values as they did their breakfast cereals. Unpopularity with peers was more to be feared than violations of personal standards, which often were confused. People valued success in the personality market more than retaining their integrity.

Riesman called this new American character type "other-directed" in contrast to the traditional "inner-directed" American who internalized individualistic success values early in life from his parents and thereafter followed his destiny. Other-directed men preferred to join the lonely crowd, not lead it. They would rather fit in than stand out. Other-directed workers were better adapted to fill the niches of the consumer economy. The American workforce at mid-century was predominantly white collar. New jobs were mostly generated in the service sectors—sales, advertising, customer service, clerical, accounting, and the like. Organization men, whose tickets to employment were high school diplomas or college degrees instead of union cards, proliferated.

Critics of the 1950s also attacked the rampant consumerism of the age; they questioned whether a fulfilling life could be based on earning money only to spend it on the proliferating goods and services churned out by the productive American economy. Other mid-century critics raised serious questions about the quality of suburban life. They wrote about hastily built, shoddy developments teeming with haggard men, frustrated women, and demanding children. Economist John Kenneth Galbraith, in *The Affluent Society,* while praising the triumphs of the private sector, wrote about the squalor of the public sector and the persistence of poverty. One radical critic of the 1950s, Columbia sociologist C. Wright Mills, argued in his book *The Power Elite* that American political democracy was a facade. In reality, a small group of powerful military, political, and corporate leaders controlled America within a political framework that left most Americans relatively powerless. Anarchist Paul Goodman, in *Growing Up Absurd,* leveled a withering criticism at public schools for stifling the individualism and creativity of America's children. Probing beneath the bland surface of 1950s' complacency about society, perceptive social critics understood that America's problems had not disappeared; they were simply being ignored by the nation's political leaders, influential mass media, and most of its people.

THE ADVENT OF TELEVISION

Americans not only fashioned an abundant economy and affluent society at mid-century, they also evolved a flourishing popular culture. Americans, especially young Americans, were vigorous participants in the 1950s' popular culture: they watched hours of television daily, went to movies, watched and participated in numerous sports and recreational activities, and listened to popular music.

The most remarkable aspect of television was how quickly it became a mass medium. Regularly scheduled telecasts began in this country in 1947. As late as 1948, fewer than 2 million households owned a television set. That year, most people watched television in bars and taverns, or perhaps stood in front of a department store window gazing in wonderment at the new electronic marvel that broadcast pictorial imagery. Some skeptics were unimpressed by the new electronic gadgetry called television. They dismissed it as "radio with pictures" and predicted it would be merely a passing fad. But within five years, half of America's households had a television set, and by 1960, 90 percent of homes had at least one black-and-white set. No new household technology had ever spread so wide or so fast nor acquired such a tight hold on the entire culture. By the mid-1950s, studies revealed that the average American spent more time watching television than he or she spent in school or on the job.

Prime-time evening television viewing became the social focus of family life during the 1950s. It displaced listening to the radio, attending movies, reading magazines and books, playing cards and board games, and conversation. A comedian joked that after-dinner conversation in the typical television-saturated American household of the 1950s consisted of two phrases: "What's on the tube tonight?" and "Good night."

As television fastened itself onto American popular culture during the early 1950s, programming was dominated by the "Big Two," NBC and CBS. The prime-time television fare that Americans watched during the 1950s was mostly dictated by a bicoastal duopoly: NBC's programs produced in New York and CBS's shows emanating from Television City in Los Angeles. Both national networks owned many of the nation's 240 television stations, especially those broadcasting in the larger metropolitan markets. By the mid-1950s, those stations earned a high return on their investments, often in the 30 percent to 35 percent per annum range. So lucrative had television broadcasting become by the mid-1950s that getting a license from the Federal Communications Commission (FCC) to operate a television station amounted to getting a government permit to print money.

Initially the producers of television shows borrowed from all established popular cultural forms for their programs, particularly vaudeville and radio. Many of the early television stars such as Jack Benny, Burns and Allen, Red Skelton, Groucho Marx, and Arthur Godfrey had previously been popular performers on radio. Some TV performers reached heights of stardom in the new visual medium, far surpassing anything that they had achieved in radio. Milton Berle, a second-rate nightclub comedian, became NBC's biggest TV star. As the star of the variety show *The Texaco Comedy Hour,* "Uncle Miltie," often appearing in drag, became known as Mr. Television. Another top variety show host, CBS's Ed Sullivan, could neither sing nor dance. A New York newspaper gossip columnist, Sullivan's awkward posture, mechanical gestures, and slurred speech became the standard fare of nightclub impressionists for twenty years.

As radio and Hollywood had done previously, 1950s' television programming relied on standard formats or genres. In addition to variety shows, popular TV genres included thirty-minute situation comedies (sitcoms), dramatic series, musicals, and Westerns. The most popular TV sitcom of the 1950s, *I Love Lucy,* starred Lucille Ball. She played Lucy Ricardo, the bubble-headed wife of Cuban-born band leader Ricky Ricardo, played by Desi Arnaz, Ball's real-life husband. Another popular situation comedy, *The Honeymooners,* starred Jackie Gleason as bus driver Ralph Cramden and his good buddy, sewer-pipe repairman Ed Norton, played by Art Carney. Other 1950s' sitcom stars included Phil Silvers as *Sergeant Bilko,* Eve Arden as the quick-witted schoolmarm in *Our Miss Brooks,* and Sid Caesar, Carl Reiner, and Imogeen Coca in *The Show of Shows.*

In the late 1950s, Westerns became the most popular television genre. At one time there were thirty-nine Westerns on each week. CBS showed most of these top-rated shows, including *Have Gun Will Travel,* which starred Richard Boone as "Palladin," a hired gunman from San Francisco who killed wicked men in the Old West. The most durable of the 1950s' television Westerns turned out to be *Gunsmoke,* starring James Arness as U.S. Marshall Matt Dillon, enforcing the law in Dodge City, Kansas.

Many factors accounted for the vast popularity of the 1950s' TV horse operas. Children, especially young boys, loved to watch them. They afforded viewers the opportunity to watch gunplay and violence. The charismatic actors who starred in the leading shows had vast appeal. More important, Westerns evoked the frontier myth of national origins. Each show recapitulated, in melodramatic style, a chapter in the saga of how the West was won— the taming of the wild frontier, the suppression of the Indians, and the triumph of law and order over villainy and anarchy. Westerns were a highly romanticized, didactic genre that celebrated the triumphalism of America's democratic national culture.

The appeal of Westerns also connected with America's Cold War contest with the Soviets that raged with great intensity during the 1950s. Westerns reaffirmed the American national identity in a time of ideological conflict with Communism. Just as Marshall Dillon's steady hand maintained the rule of law and morality in a violent frontier cattle town, so too would America's nuclear-carrying bombers maintain law and order in the violent world frontiers of the 1950s. Westerns reigned supreme in the late 1950s, while the Cold War consensus remained intact. The genre vanished precipitously amidst the cultural crisis attendant among the American disaster in Vietnam. As disillusioned Americans rejected the frontier as a viable national myth, Westerns disappeared from the nation's television screens.

In addition to the programs produced in studios, television covered many live events during the 1950s. Sporting events quickly became a staple of live television: professional wrestling, auto races, boxing, and roller derby were early favorites. Football, baseball, and basketball, all of which had been covered extensively on radio, also received television coverage. Initially, because of technological limitations, neither National Football League games nor major league baseball games telecast particularly well. An innovation that greatly increased the size of the audience for televised football games was the introduction in 1960 of instant replay. In the early years of TV, baseball was an especially difficult game to telecast. One camera stationed behind home plate tried to cover all of the action. The single camera gave a static, one-dimensional aspect to the game; it also foreshortened the distances that balls were hit and players had to run. Owners of professional sports franchises in the early years resisted television coverage. They claimed that it cut into their attendance. Many minor league baseball teams and entire leagues folded during the 1950s, in part the victims of the advent of television coverage of major professional sports.

During television's early years, many hours were devoted to live coverage of public affairs and news features. United Nations sessions at Lake Success, New York, received extensive live coverage. Starting with the 1948 conventions, television quickly established the tradition of live coverage of the major political parties' quadrennial presidential nominating conventions. Controversial Congressional hearings were telecast during the 1950s, the most famous being the Army-McCarthy hearings of 1954. The major networks all inaugurated nightly newscasts of a fifteen-minute duration. In retrospect, it appears that during the 1950s television had limited impact on American politics. There was no evidence that television altered political behavior in any significant way nor had any impact on voting patterns. Millions of Americans continued to rely on radio for political commentary, for news, and for listening to presidential speeches.

Serious scandals rocked the world of television in the late 1950s. During the mid-1950s, a few quiz shows that awarded winning contestants rich cash prizes became very popular. *The $64,000 Question* and *Twenty-One* were the two most popular shows. *Twenty-One* was especially dramatic. Contestants, sweating in isolation booths under the glare of studio lights, answered lengthy, complex, and very difficult questions about a wide range of topics. In 1956, Charles Van Doren, a young English instructor at Columbia, and the bearer of a distinguished literary pedigree, became a celebrity performer on *Twenty-One*. Week after week, Van Doren demonstrated encyclopedic knowledge, a phenomenal memory, and grace under pressure, winning a total of $129,000. He was celebrated in the media and became a role model. *Time* magazine featured him on its cover. Educators hailed Van Doren's inspiring example for young people and contrasted his influence with the supposedly baneful influence of rock 'n' roll stars such as Elvis Presley.

Alas, Van Doren turned out to be a fraud. One of the contestants that Van Doren had defeated complained that Van Doren had been fed answers to questions in advance. A congressional subcommittee investigated *Twenty-One* and other game shows. Van Doren admitted under oath that he had cheated. He claimed that he had been corrupted by the lure of wealth and fame. He also admitted that he had even been given acting lessons to appear more convincing as he feigned to struggle to answer questions. Disgraced, Van Doren lost his academic job and quickly faded from public view. The networks canceled the big-money quiz shows. A wave of angry disillusionment swept the nation. The print media devoted much space to soul-searching and to asking rhetorical questions about the sources of corruption in American life. Critics of television used the quiz show scandals to indict the new mass medium as a cultural wasteland and corrupter of youth.

Whether it was a corrupt wasteland, as its intellectual critics charged, television had surely become an all-encompassing cultural force as the 1950s ended. An estimated two-thirds of the nation's 60 million households watched television on an average of six hours a day. Art and culture came free, with an ease of accessibility never before available. Television had entered politics. Network executives aimed their fare at the largest possible audiences, treating their viewers as though they were an undifferentiated mass with identical tastes and preferences. In reality, the mass audience, "mass culture," was comprised of diverse, distinctive viewing groups, differentiated by age, lifestyle, gender, class, education, ethnicity, and race. Their particular preferences simply got overridden during the heyday of crude demographics and mass marketed national network shows.

Television programming during the 1950s generally reinforced official values and established hierarchies of power, wealth, and status. Popular programs such as *Father Knows Best* portrayed the warm inner life of a typical, middle-class, white suburban family. It celebrated togetherness and the domestic destinies of women. Television functioned as a conservative, hegemonic cultural instrument. It never challenged the powers that be nor their official views. Racial minorities hardly appeared on television; when they did, they were cast in traditional servile roles and depicted as demeaning stereotypes. Mostly television served up popular entertainment and commercials. It functioned primarily as a commercial instrument, an advertising conduit, the most intrusive yet invented. Television quickly became the vital center of the consumer culture. It was a vast educational enterprise teaching American consumers about the latest styles of mass consumerism and creating wants and needs for the multitudinous products of consumer civilization.

ROCK 'N' ROLL

American teenagers often set popular cultural trends during the 1950s. A teen culture flourished, with money to spend and clear consumer preferences, centered around fads and pop music. Affluent teenagers constituted a vast new market that the recording companies and record stores hastened to exploit.

Before rock music made its appearance in the mid-1950s, mainstream pop music was a diverse mélange of pleasant if somewhat bland musical styles. Novelty songs, ballads, waltzes, celebrations of teenage love, and an occasional significant song such as Les Paul's and Mary Ford's beautifully rendered *Vaya Con Dios* (Walk with God) topped the charts. African American music, although supercharged with religious and sexual energies, remained largely unknown to white audiences and off of the pop charts.

In the early 1950s, a white Cleveland disc jockey, Allen Freed, began playing African American music, which he called "rhythm-and-blues," on the air. In 1954, Freed moved to New York, where he continued to promote rhythm-and-blues recordings. That same year, a white band, Bill Haley and the Comets, recorded *Rock Around the Clock,* the first rock 'n' roll hit.

In 1956, a sullenly handsome nineteen-year-old truck driver from Tupelo, Mississippi, Elvis Presley, became the first rock 'n' roll superstar. Presley, who developed his unique blend of black rhythm-and-blues and country-and-western idioms, shot to the top of the hit parade in 1956 with a series of monster hits, including *Heartbreak Hotel, Blue Suede Shoes,* and *Hound Dog.* Crowds of teenage girls screamed hysterically at Presley's highly suggestive stage performances, particularly his gyrating hips keeping time with the frenetic chords he banged out on his acoustic guitar. He made a famous appearance on the *Ed Sullivan Show,* where the cameras focused discreetly on Presley's midsection to conceal his suggestive pelvic thrusts from the huge audience. Over the next two years, Presley released an amazing string

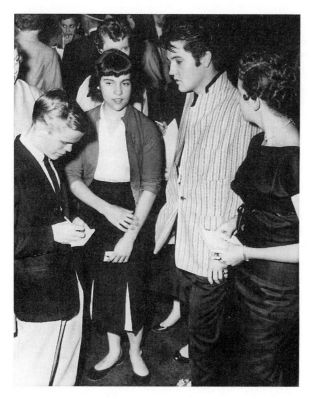

Figure 4.6   Elvis Presley with fans.
Source: St. Louis Mercantile Library. Used with permission.

of fourteen consecutive hit recordings. His incredible success helped bring African American music into the pop mainstream and also helped win white acceptance of African American recording artists such as Chuck Berry, Little Richard, Ray Charles, and Fats Domino.

Presley's performing style became a symbol of youthful rebellion. His concerts provoked criticism from parents, teachers, and ministers, who encouraged youngsters to listen to the recordings of Pat Boone, a devoutly religious, wholesome performer with a rich baritone voice. The Presley rebellion was implicit in his music, in its rhythms, which excited youngsters and provoked sexual fantasies. Presley himself was anything but a rebel. He was an artist and a showman, a champion of traditional values and a political conservative. When the Army drafted Presley in 1958, he dutifully served his two-year stint without fanfare or incident. Student radicals of the 1960s outraged him.

Controversy over the moral threat to young people posed by rock 'n' roll music in the late 1950s was closely linked to a taboo subject, sexual behavior. An Indiana biology professor, Dr. Alfred Kinsey, had published *Sexual Behavior in the Human Male* (1948) and its sequel *Sexual Behavior in the Human Female* (1955). Kinsey interviewed thousands of subjects and used statistical analyses to produce the first scientific study of American sexual behavior. Among his most important findings, Kinsey discovered that premarital sexual relations, adultery, and homosexuality were more widespread than previously thought. Subsequently, investigators would discredit many of Kinsey's findings, particularly his use of statistical data that significantly exaggerated the number of homosexuals inhabiting American society.

REBELS

Not everyone was caught up in the culture of conformity during the 1950s; rebels, especially young people, rejected the manners and mores of the affluent society. Juvenile delinquency increased, and violent gangs of brawling teenagers staged gang fights in the streets of New York and Chicago. Bands of motorcyclists roamed the streets and highways. Some middle-class youngsters dropped out of the college-career "rat race." They joined Bohemian enclaves in Greenwich Village and in San Francisco's North Beach district. Herb Caen, a San Francisco columnist, dubbed these dropouts "beatniks"; they preferred to call

Figure 4.7   A close-up of Jack Kerouac, ca. 1958. *Source:* Corbis.

themselves the "beat generation." "Beats" confronted the apathy and conformity of American society; they went out of their way to defy prevailing norms of respectability; they abandoned materialistic values to embrace poverty; and they lived in cheap flats, did not work or study, listened to jazz, smoked marijuana, and indulged in a casual sexuality. The Beats were harbingers of the hippie rebellion of the 1960s.

Beat writers wrote poems and novels espousing the values of their rebellious generation. Jack Kerouac wrote the best Beat novel, *On the Road* (1958), which told the tale of two young men, Sal Paradise and Dean Moriarty, who had no money, traveling across America and into Mexico in frantic search of emotionally engaging adventures, what Kerouac and his buddies called "kicks." Poet Allen Ginsberg wrote the most famous beat poem, *Howl,* which scathingly indicted a materialistic age that destroyed sensitive souls:

> I saw the best minds of my generation destroyed by madness, starving hysterical naked, dragging themselves through the negro streets looking for an angry fix, . . . burned alive in their innocent flannel suits on Madison Avenue amid blasts of leaden verse & the tanked-up clatter of the iron regiments of fashion.[2]

In addition to the Beat writers, individual authors expressed their alienation from the conformist culture. Novelist J. D. Salinger expressed the theme of personal alienation in one of the finest 1950s' novels, *Catcher in the Rye.* Salinger's hero, Holden Caulfield, was a schoolboy trapped in a world populated by adults with whom he could not communicate and who did not understand him. Caulfield rebelled, ran away, and had a weekend fling in New York, desperately trying to find an island of integrity amidst a sea of conformity. His efforts failed, and in the end, the system triumphed. Caulfield returned to home and school. Salinger's novel was especially popular among 1950s' college students, for he expressed their discontent with a culture that masked a painful reality—not everyone easily fit into the society of would-be organization men and women.

BIBLIOGRAPHY

There are many fine books written about American economic, social, and cultural history during the 1950s. John Kenneth Galbraith's *The Affluent Society* is a good analysis of postwar prosperity. John B. Rae's *The American Automobile* describes the car culture of the 1950s. Landon Y. Jones's *Great Expectations: America and the Baby Boom Generation* is the best study of the most important demographic development of postwar America. Two excellent studies of suburbia are Kenneth Jackson's *Crabgrass Frontier: The Suburbization of the United States* and John Keats's *The Crack in the Picture Window.* See also Herbert J. Gans's *The Levittowners.* For women's roles during the 1950s, see Betty Friedan's famed *Feminine Mystique.* Elaine T. May's *Homeward Bound: American Families in the Cold War Era* is a fine recent study. Will Herberg's *Catholic-Protestant-Jew* stresses the important role of religion in mid-century American society. The role of the church in suburbanization is well treated in Gibson Winter's *The Suburban Captivity of the Churches.* C. Wright Mills's *White Collar: The American Middle Class* and *The Power Elite* are two very good accounts of the affluent

---

[2]From George Donelson Moss, *America in the Twentieth Century, 1/E* (Englewood Cliffs, N.J.: Prentice Hall, 1987), p. 282.

society by a radical critic. For two classic studies of the social and cultural history of the 1950s, see *The Lonely Crowd: A Study of the Changing American Character,* by David Riesman et al. and *The Organization Man,* by William H. Whyte Jr. The mass culture of the 1950s is analyzed critically in *Mass Culture* by Bernard Rosenberg and D.M. White, eds. Myron Matlaw's *American Popular Entertainment* contains sections on the television, pop music, and films of the 1950s. Erik Barnouw's *Tube of Plenty* has become the classic study of television during its "golden age." Another good study of television during the 1950s is Alexander Kendrick's *Prime Time.* Bruce Cook, in *The Beat Generation,* writes about these writers who flourished in the late 1950s.

5

The Politics of Consensus

In the larger world, the Cold War conflict between the United States and the Soviet Union raged unrelentingly throughout the 1950s. During this decade, the focus of the U.S.-Soviet rivalry shifted to the Third World, to those nations of Africa and Asia emerging from long periods of colonial domination by fading European imperial powers. At home, a bipartisan consensus spanning the American political spectrum supported the American global commitment to contain Communism.

The domestic Cold War climaxed in 1954, when the Eisenhower administration combined with the Senate leadership to destroy the power of the preeminent Red hunter in Washington, Senator Joseph McCarthy. After 1954, the Cold War at home receded; fears and tensions calmed. As the domestic Cold War cooled, the drive by African Americans for full citizenship and dignity in America intensified. In a historic decision, the Supreme Court nullified school segregation and undermined the legal basis of the entire segregationist system. Heartened by the Court's decision, black people accelerated their drive for freedom and equality, and for inclusion in the mainstream of American life.

President Dwight D. "Ike" Eisenhower was the dominant political leader and appropriate symbol for the 1950s. He projected an image of confidence and optimism. Ike also was a determined anti-Communist, committed to maintaining American strength during continuing Cold War conflicts with the Soviets. British writer Godfrey Hodgson wrote that Americans in the 1950s were "confident to the verge of complacency about the perfectibility of American society, anxious to the point of paranoia about the threat of Communism." Americans embraced a consensus in the 1950s, that America was the greatest nation in the world, and they also agreed that the American Dream required thermonuclear defenses in the Cold War era.

THE ELECTION OF 1952

Eisenhower and the Republicans swept to power in 1952. The Korean War had boosted their chances. The Republicans also capitalized on many scandals unearthed within Truman's administration. As the Republican presidential race shaped up in 1952, Senator Robert Taft, leader of the conservative Midwestern heartland, appeared to have the inside track to the nomination. But the powerful Eastern internationalist wing of the party promoted the candidacy of popular war hero General Dwight Eisenhower, at the time the commander of NATO forces in Europe. At the Republican Convention, held in Chicago in July, Eisenhower won a close first ballot nomination. He chose thirty-nine-year-old Senator Richard Nixon, a fast-rising political star who had nailed Alger Hiss and raised Red-baiting to a high art, to be his running mate. When Truman declined to seek reelection, the Democrats chose Illinois governor Adlai Stevenson to challenge Eisenhower.

Eisenhower launched the Republican drive for the White House by announcing a "great crusade" for honest, efficient government at home and for freedom abroad. Republican campaign strategists devised what they called their winning formula: K_1C_2 = Korea, Communism, and Corruption. The 1952 Republican presidential campaign was the first in U.S. political history to be reduced to a chemical formula. Nixon and Senator Joseph McCarthy turned their rhetorical siege guns on the Democrats. They convinced millions of voters that Communist infiltration of government agencies posed a serious threat to internal security, for which the Democrats were mainly responsible. Eisenhower's genial smile caused crowds to shout, "We like Ike!" His Horatio Alger background offset the Republican image as an elite party. He proved to be an adroit campaigner. His most dramatic move came when he took up the Korean War, the chief issue of the campaign. In a speech given in Detroit, he declared that "an early and honorable" peace required a personal effort, and he pledged, "I shall go to Korea."

In September, a hitch developed that threatened briefly to derail the smoothly running Republican campaign machine. Reporters discovered that Richard Nixon had benefited from a secret fund raised by wealthy Southern California businessmen to pay his political expenses. The party that had been scoring points from its moral crusade against its scandal-plagued opposition suddenly had a scandal of its own. A wave of anti-Nixon sentiment swept the land. Stevenson had a glimmer of hope. Pundits raised the possibility that Eisenhower might have to dump Nixon from the GOP ticket.

But the Republican National Committee purchased air time and gave Nixon the opportunity to to go on television and radio to defend himself before the bar of public opinion. Nixon convinced most of his huge television audience that he had not broken the law or done anything wrong. The emotional high point of his speech came when he referred to a cocker spaniel puppy that a supporter had sent the family, which one of his daughters had named "Checkers."

> And you know the kids, like all kids, love the dog, and I just want to say this right now that regardless of what they say about it, we're going to keep it.[1]

The "Checkers" speech outmaneuvered the Democrats and turned a potential disaster for Nixon's party into political advantage. He stayed on the ticket, and the Republican campaign resumed its march toward victory.

[1]Quoted in Stephen E. Ambrose, *Nixon: The Education of a Politician, 1913–1962* (New York: Simon & Schuster, 1987), p. 289.

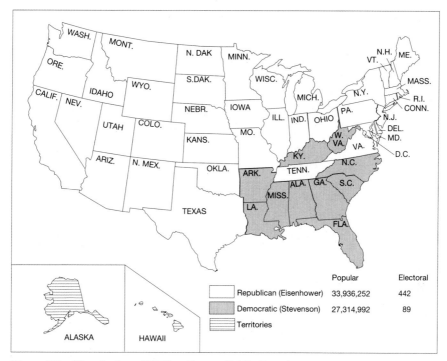

Figure 5.1   The election of 1952.   *Source:* Public Domain map.

On Election Day, Eisenhower scored a lopsided victory. Ike received 33,824,351 votes (55.4 percent) to Stevenson's 27,314,987 votes (44.4 percent). Eisenhower carried the electoral college, 442 to 89. Stevenson carried only nine Southern and border states. The Eisenhower-Nixon ticket lured millions of voters from the Democratic coalition that had given Truman his 1948 triumph—Catholics, ethnic, working-class voters, and Southerners. Victory was in large measure a personal triumph for the popular general. He ran far ahead of his party, despite Korea, Communism, and corruption. The Republicans also regained control of Congress, but only by narrow margins: 221 to 214 in the House, and 49 to 48 in the Senate, with Vice President Nixon voting. In defeat, the Democratic Party showed considerable strength, and election returns indicated that a majority of the electorate still thought of themselves as Democrats. The Democratic majority coalition had crumbled, but no new Republican majority emerged to replace it. Issue differences between the parties appeared slight. The politics of consensus prevailed.

THE WAR HERO

The thirty-fourth president brought a political style to office that served the nation well during the 1950s. He helped cool the partisan rivalries that had divided Americans. His basic decency and moderation took some of the mean-spiritedness out of national politics. He phased out the unpopular Korean War, helped destroy the demagogic Joseph McCarthy, and worked cooperatively with a Congress often controlled by the Democrats.

Born in 1890 in Denison, Texas, Dwight David Eisenhower spent his boyhood on his father's farm near Abilene, Kansas. He won an appointment to West Point, where he was a star running back with All-American potential until he suffered a career-ending knee injury. Following his graduation from West Point in 1915, he embarked on a military career that took him through a variety of assignments over the next twenty years. During the late 1930s, he served as an aide to General Douglas MacArthur, commander of the Army of the Philippines.

As World War II approached, Eisenhower caught the attention of Army Chief of Staff George C. Marshall. Marshall jumped Eisenhower over hundreds of more senior officers to assign him to command the Allied invasions of North Africa, Sicily, and Italy in 1942 and 1943. Following these assignments, Ike was then chosen to be the supreme commander of Allied forces in Europe. As supreme commander of Allied forces, Eisenhower directed the famed invasion of Normandy along the western coast of France in June 1944, which led to the final defeat of Nazi Germany eleven months later. Ike emerged from World War II as a five-star general, the nation's preeminent war hero, and a potential candidate for president.

Eisenhower's greatest talents were managerial and diplomatic; he was a skilled coordinator and conciliator. He was not a brilliant strategist or battlefield commander, but he had tremendous talents as an organizer and a director of vast military enterprises. He assumed awesome responsibilities and made the big decisions. He also had a keen grasp of international affairs and understood the interrelationship between diplomacy and grand strategy. Unlike most senior military leaders, Eisenhower was a strongly committed internationalist. His military career had prepared him well for the tasks of presidential leadership in the Cold War era.

Eisenhower's genial personality, warm smile, and unassuming modesty appealed to his fellow countrymen. Instinctively wary of generals with Caesarean attitudes, Americans found Ike to be homespun, informal, and democratic. He liked people, and people liked Ike. His rural roots and allegiance to traditional American values and virtues accorded with the 1950s' ethos.

Although unfamiliar with the ways of American domestic politics, he struck an above-politics pose, recruited able staffers, and left the details of governance to subordinates. He allowed Congress to take the initiative in most domestic legislative fields, reserving the conduct of foreign policy for himself. His approach was effective for most of his presidency. Eisenhower proved to be one of the nation's most popular and successful modern presidents. Although often criticized by contemporaneous liberal journalists, Eisenhower's reputation has grown with the passage of time. Historians consider Eisenhower to have been a "near great" president; a detailed poll of American historians conducted in 1983 ranked him ninth overall.

DYNAMIC CONSERVATISM

President Eisenhower projected an image of bland, moderate nonpartisanship. He came across as the amateur in politics, a disinterested leader serving the nation while relying heavily on subordinates. In reality, Ike embraced a strong conservative philosophy. He believed in fiscal restraint, balanced budgets, and devout anti-Communism. Beneath the bland mask was an able, effective politician who controlled his administration and its policies. Eisenhower also was a skilled, precise writer. Both his best-selling book, *Crusade in Europe,* which made him rich, and his memoirs, written after his presidency, show a talent capable of lucid, exact, and occasionally elegant prose. His writing stands in sharp contrast to the rambling, incoherent utterances characteristic of his press conference responses to reporters' questions. Liberal intellectuals made fun of Eisenhower's apparent muddleheadedness and ignorance without realizing that they had fallen for one of his ploys. Eisenhower often feigned ignorance or resorted to gobbledygook to avoid premature disclosures of information or policy decisions. His frequent hunting and fishing trips and his passion for golf masked a hard-driving, domineering chief executive.

Eisenhower began his presidency proclaiming a new "dynamic conservatism," which he said meant "conservative when it comes to money, liberal when it comes to human beings." Most of his leading advisers came from the ranks of business. Charles E. Wilson, the president of General Motors, became secretary of defense. The Treasury Department went to George Humphrey, a wealthy Ohio industrialist. Secretary of State John Foster Dulles was a wealthy corporation lawyer.

The new Administration tried to implement conservative policies in several important areas. Humphrey put conservative fiscal policies in place. Income taxes and federal spending were both cut by 10 percent. Interest rates were raised, and credit was tightened to reduce inflation, which had averaged 10 percent between 1950 and 1953. Republicans tried hard to balance the budget, but they usually failed. Republican efforts to reduce the role of the federal government and to strengthen local and state governments also failed. In addition, Eisenhower tried to reduce the role of the federal government in developing electrical power sites and offshore oil wells. On the electric power issue, his efforts usually failed. On the offshore oil issue, Congress enacted legislation giving states access to submerged coastal lands. For agriculture, the Administration pushed for more flexible and lower price supports for farmers. Crop production increased, farm income dropped, and farmers angrily protested the new policies.

But it soon became evident that "dynamic conservatism" was not an effort to repeal the New Deal. Although a fiscal conservative, Eisenhower accepted the expansion of several New Deal programs. Congress expanded Social Security coverage, raised the minimum wage, and extended unemployment insurance. It also created a new Department of Health, Education, and Welfare to coordinate government social programs. The size and scope of the authority of the federal government continued to expand during the Eisenhower years. State and local governments also grew rapidly throughout the years of Eisenhower's presidency.

Eisenhower proposed the largest domestic spending program in American history in 1955, a vast federal-state highway construction program. Congress enacted the Interstate Highway Act in 1956, setting in motion the largest public works project in U.S. history. The federal government provided 90 percent of the costs through the Highway Trust Fund, financed by users' taxes on cars, trucks, buses, gasoline, tires, lubricants, and auto parts. It projected a 42,000-mile network of freeways linking all major urban areas. Construction of mammoth freeway systems continued into the 1970s, and the government spent billions of dollars annually on them. These road-building projects had an enormous impact on American life. Annual driving mileage increased fourfold. Shopping centers, linked by the new roads, sprang up to serve rapidly growing suburban communities. By the 1970s, the new freeways covered as much land as the nation's central business districts. Every suburb had a highway strip mall with drive-in movies, bowling alleys, gas stations, and fast-food restaurants.

Eisenhower's moderation accorded with the public mood of the 1950s. Most Americans felt smugly complacent about their society. They believed that economic growth would solve all social problems, gradually enlarging the economic pie until poverty vanished. There was no need for higher taxes, special programs, or sacrifices by anyone. The 1950s were a time for holding the line against inflation, recession, and social disorder—of balancing liberty and security within a moderate framework acceptable to all.

The New Deal was legitimated during the reign of Ike. It became the status quo undergirding consensus politics. Despite its business orientation and its conservative ideology, the Eisenhower administration supported the welfare state and managed the economy much as Truman had done. The pragmatic accommodation that the conservative Eisenhower made by protecting and expanding the welfare state signaled the breakdown of traditional political categories. Politicians no longer battled one another over fundamental issues; they merely quarreled over which interest group got how much. Previously, big government had been linked to liberalism and limited government to conservatism. In the 1950s, except for a few traditional ideologues on the Left and the Right, the real issue was no longer whether government was large or small, but whose interests it served. Conservatives often voted for huge spending programs such as defense budgets, highway programs, and Social Security extensions. Liberals often voted for huge defense budgets in the name of Cold War bipartisanship and to protect national security in the nuclear age.

MCCARTHY: ZENITH AND RUIN

National alarm over Communist infiltration of government agencies persisted well into Eisenhower's presidency. Joseph McCarthy quickly resumed his investigations of alleged subversion in government. For eighteen months, McCarthy was the second most powerful politician in Washington. He dominated the news with his spectacular accusations. A 1954 poll showed that 50 percent of Americans approved of his activities, and only 29 percent opposed them. Many of his Senate colleagues, knowing that he was a fraud, despised him. But they feared him even more, and they refused to challenge him openly, having seen what McCarthy could do to an opponent at election time. Eisenhower also was personally contemptuous of McCarthy. He once said, "I will not get in the gutter with that guy." But Eisenhower also refused to confront him, not out of fear, but because he did not want a party rupture over the controversial demagogue.

The State Department continued to be McCarthy's favorite hunting ground, even though it was now controlled by Republicans. In 1953, McCarthy went after the State Department's overseas information service. Secretary of State John Foster Dulles ordered department personnel to cooperate fully with McCarthy's investigation. Supposedly subversive books were dutifully removed from the shelves by State Department functionaries, and some of the books were burned.

In 1954, McCarthy went after the U.S. Army. His subcommittee investigated alleged Communist subversion at Fort Monmouth, New Jersey, the site of sensitive communications technology. During the inquiry, McCarthy discovered that the Army had promoted a dentist, Irving Peress, to the rank of major and had then given him an honorable discharge when it learned that he had once invoked the Fifth Amendment when asked about Communist affiliations. An angry McCarthy bullied and humiliated General Ralph Zwicker, Peress's commanding officer, when he refused to give him Peress's file.

The Army mounted a counterattack against McCarthy, accusing him of trying to blackmail the Army into giving preferential treatment to G. David Schine, a former McCarthy staffer who had been assigned to Fort Monmouth. McCarthy retorted that the Army was holding Schine hostage to keep his committee from investigating the Army. McCarthy's subcommittee voted to hold hearings on the charges made by the two adversaries, with Senator Karl Mundt of South Dakota temporarily assuming the chairmanship. On April 22, 1954, the famed Army-McCarthy hearings began. For six weeks, they were telecast daily to 15 million viewers.

McCarthy himself starred in the televised political drama. He bullied and harried witnesses. He interrupted the proceedings frequently, made threats, and shouted "point of order, Mr. Chairman, point of order!" Some committee members, particularly Senator Stuart Symington of Missouri, gave as well as took from McCarthy. Symington was especially adept at making fun of McCarthy and of annoying him. The hearings also made a star out of Joseph Welch, a soft-spoken trial lawyer who was the Army's chief counsel. At one point, Welch left McCarthy temporarily speechless by asking rhetorically, "At long last, sir, at long last, have you left no sense of decency?" The hearings ended inconclusively. Neither the Army nor McCarthy won. It is not true that television exposure or Welch's dramatic remark undermined McCarthy's popularity. Polls taken shortly after the hearings showed that McCarthy still retained his 50 percent approval ratings.

It was McCarthy's methods, his unruly behavior, that provoked his downfall. He went too far when he attacked the Army; ironically, McCarthy himself was becoming a security risk. In August 1954, the Senate established a committee to study a set of censure charges brought against McCarthy by Republican Ralph Flanders of Vermont. Chairing the committee was conservative Republican Arthur Watkins of Utah. The committee recommended that the Senate censure McCarthy. After noisy hearings, the full Senate voted 67 to 22 to "condemn" McCarthy on two counts: for contempt of the Senate and for abuse of Watkins' committee members.

Senate condemnation, which amounted to censure, effectively destroyed McCarthy. He still made accusations, but his attacks no longer made headlines. He still called press conferences, but journalists no longer attended them; McCarthy was no longer newsworthy. He had lost the spotlight even faster than he had found it. His health failed, and he did not live out his Senate term. He died in May 1957, of infectious hepatitis, aggravated by heavy drinking, at age forty-seven. McCarthy could perform only as long as his Senate colleagues were willing to tolerate his behavior. The most significant fact about the career of the nation's premier Red hunter was that in four years of investigations, McCarthy never unearthed a single Communist working in the State Department or any other government agency.

CONSENSUS POLITICS

The 1954 midterm elections were the last ones in which the Communist-in-government issue had any force. Anti-Communism as a major issue in American domestic politics died with McCarthy. Americans became less obsessed with paranoid fantasies about Communist subversives threatening the nation's internal security. Supreme Court rulings in a number of cases strengthened the constitutional rights of radicals. But anti-Communism remained a staple of American political culture, far outliving its foremost practitioner. Intolerance, fear, and suspicion of dissent, of deviations from the reigning conformist orthodoxies, persisted. Most Americans regarded as axiomatic the notion that Communism was the embodiment of evil. In 1954, even as the Second Red Scare was waning, Congressional Democrats tried to enact legislation that would have outlawed the American Communist Party. They viewed the Soviet Union as the head of an international conspiracy that was unrelentingly hostile to the United States. The bipartisan Cold War consensus on the conduct of American foreign policy remained intact.

Political alignments during the 1950s remained unstable. Eisenhower's 1952 victory signaled the breakup of the Roosevelt coalition of labor, farmers, ethnics, and Southerners, forged during the 1930s, but the Republicans could not form a majority coalition to replace it. As traditional political allegiances declined during the 1950s, a large independent "swing" vote emerged, varying in size with each election. Millions of citizens voted a split ticket, supporting a man or an issue instead of a party, and shifted sides in response to particular situations. The two major parties attained a rough equality for the first time since the early 1890s. An unstable equilibrium prevailed.

National elections held during the 1950s reflected the unstable balance of political forces. Except for 1952, the Democrats won the Congressional elections and the Republicans the presidential elections. The 1956 election was a dull replay of 1952. Ike was at the peak of his popularity and almost immune to criticism. Stevenson campaigned tentatively, groping for an issue and never finding one. He tried to make issues of Ike's age and health. Eisenhower had suffered a serious heart attack in September 1955 and had been incapacitated for weeks. But he recovered, and in 1956 the sixty-five-year-old leader enjoyed good health and was obviously fit to run again. In 1956, the Democratic arsenal contained no political weapons to match the Republican slogan of "four more years of peace and prosperity."

Eisenhower won reelection by a larger margin than his 1952 landslide victory. He received 35.6 million votes (58 percent) to 26 million (42 percent) for Stevenson. Ike received 457 electoral votes to Stevenson's 73. The Democrats carried only seven states. Eisenhower ran well everywhere and cut deeply into traditional Democratic votes. But, as in 1952, 1956 was much more a personal victory for the popular president than it was a Republican Party victory. In fact, the Democrats regained control of both houses of Congress—234 to 201 in the House, and 49 to 47 in the Senate. Eisenhower was the first president in modern political history to begin a term with Congress controlled by the opposition.

But the nominal Democratic congressional majorities were undercut by the conservative bipartisan coalition of Southern Democrats and Northern Republicans who could gut or block most liberal legislation. During the 1950s, moderate Texas politicians led the Democrats in Congress. Speaker Sam Rayburn led the House, and his protege Lyndon Johnson led the Senate. Both leaders pursued a strategy of compromise and cooperation with the Republican White House.

CIVIL RIGHTS

Soon after taking office, President Eisenhower appointed Governor Earl Warren of California as Chief Justice of the Supreme Court. The Court had been chipping away at the constitutional foundations of racial discrimination since the 1940s in two areas—denial of voting rights and school segregation. It was in the realm of education that the Court chose to nullify the "separate but equal" principle that had provided the constitutional basis of Jim Crow.

Several cases challenging school segregation came before the Court. With Warren providing the leadership that spurred his associates to action, the justices decided a representative case, *Brown v. the Board of Education of Topeka,* on May 17, 1954. A unanimous Court ruled that public school segregation was unconstitutional under the Fourteenth Amendment, reversing the "separate but equal" doctrine established in *Plessy v. Ferguson* (1896). The Court's decision incorporated much of the legal brief filed by Thurgood Marshall, chief counsel for the NAACP:

> In the field of public education, the doctrine of "separate but equal" has no place. Separate educational facilities are inherently unequal.[2]

A year later, the Supreme Court instructed federal district courts to order school desegregation to begin in their areas and to require "good faith compliance with all deliberate speed." Having destroyed the legal basis of school segregation, the courts proceeded to undermine Jim Crow everywhere. Federal court decisions nullified segregation in public housing, recreational facilities, and interstate commerce. The *Brown* decision was the most important Supreme Court decision of modern times.

White Southerners defied the *Brown* decision and refused to implement it for many years. In 1956, a group of 101 Congressmen and Senators from eleven Southern states that had comprised the Confederacy almost a century before signed the Southern Manifesto. It pledged to "use all lawful means to bring about a reversal of this decision which is contrary to the Constitution." The Southern Manifesto also encouraged Southern officials to try to prevent implementing the law. A confrontation between federal and state authorities over

[2]Quoted in Anthony Lewis, *Portrait of a Decade: The Second American Revolution* (New York: Bantam Books, 1965), p. 26.

school desegregation came at Little Rock, Arkansas, where Eisenhower faced the most serious domestic crisis of his presidency.

In September 1957, Central High in Little Rock planned to enroll nine African-American students under court order. But Arkansas Governor Orville Faubus prevented integration by ordering National Guardsmen to block the school entrance. A federal court ordered the troops to leave, and the African-American students enrolled. But white students threatened them, and school officials, fearing for their safety, removed them from the school. Faced with clear defiance of the law, Eisenhower acted. For the first time since Reconstruction, a president sent federal troops into the South to protect the rights of African Americans. Paratroopers entered Central High, and the National Guardsmen were placed under federal command. Guarded by soldiers with fixed bayonets, the nine teenagers enrolled again at Central High.

As the Court struck down the legal foundations of segregation, African Americans stepped up their attacks on racial injustice. Eighteen months after the *Brown* decision, in Montgomery, Alabama, Rosa Parks refused to surrender her seat at the front of a bus to a white man and ignited the modern civil rights movement. Her action brought to prominence a young Baptist minister who, for the rest of his tragically short life, would be the foremost leader of the civil rights revolution. He was Dr. Martin Luther King Jr., and he declared:

> Integration is the great issue of our age, the great issue of our nation and the great issue of our community. We are in the midst of a great struggle, the consequences of which will be world-shaking.[3]

Under Dr. King's visionary leadership, Montgomery African Americans organized a boycott of the city's bus lines. Helped by a Supreme Court decision declaring bus segregation unconstitutional, they eventually forced the city to integrate its bus service and to hire African-American drivers and mechanics.

At the same time, the NAACP mounted an intensive legal campaign against segregation. Victorious in forty-two of forty-six appeals to the Supreme Court, the NAACP advanced voting rights and integrated housing, transportation, public accommodations, and schools in many parts of the South. While the NAACP fought its civil rights battles in the courts, Dr. King and his followers fought theirs in the streets of Southern cities.

A drive to guarantee African-American voting rights also began. A civil rights bill moved through Congress, mainly because of the leadership of Eisenhower and Texas Senator Lyndon Johnson. The Civil Rights Act of 1957, the first since Reconstruction, created a Civil Rights Commission and gave the Attorney General power to take local officials to court in cases where they denied African Americans the right to vote. Johnson also was instrumental in getting a stronger civil rights law enacted in 1960, which provided legal penalties against anyone interfering with the right to vote. The civil rights movement made a powerful beginning during the 1950s. Most progress came from the efforts of African Americans themselves, aided by Supreme Court decisions that nullified the legal foundations of segregation and by Congressional legislation that strengthened the gathering forces of the black revolution.

[3]Quoted in ibid., p. 62.

Figure 5.2   The Montgomery, Alabama, bus boycott ignited the modern civil rights movement in the South. The boycott began in December 1955 when Rosa Parks, here shown sitting in the front of a city bus, refused to surrender her seat to a white man and return to the back of the bus.   *Source:* National Archives.

THE NEW LOOK

During the 1952 presidential campaign, Republicans charged that the Truman-Acheson policy of containing Communism had failed, especially in Asia with the loss of China and the stalemate in the Korean War. John Foster Dulles insisted that the United States, instead of pursuing containment, should make it "publicly known that it wants and expects liberation to occur." Despite their campaign rhetoric, Eisenhower and Dulles, once in office, continued the containment policies, with some minor alterations, which they had condemned during the 1952 campaign. Accepting the foreign policy premises of the Truman administration, Eisenhower and Dulles supported and at times expanded American Cold War commitments and goals. In reality, they had no choice. The logic of liberation led inescapably to one conclusion—Americans would have to fight to free the captive nations, because the Communists would never voluntarily set them free. Freedom for Eastern Europe meant war with the Soviet Union. Further, Eisenhower had committed himself to cutting military expenditures. Liberation, far more costly than containment, could never be carried out by fiscal conservatives. Republicans hid their failure to liberate anyone from Communism behind tough talk.

Republicans called their foreign policy the New Look. It relied on strategic air power to destroy the Soviet Union with nuclear bombs if Communist aggression occurred anywhere in the world. Dulles believed that the threat to obliterate the Soviets would "deter" them from hostile actions. The New Look strategy allowed the Administration to reduce outlays for conventional forces. Dulles described their approach as "massive retaliation."

Figure 5.3   John Foster Dulles and Dwight D. Eisenhower.   *Source:* Dwight D. Eisenhower
Presidential Library-Museum.

Secretary of Defense Wilson observed that the New Look provided "more bang for the
buck." President Eisenhower insisted that cuts in defense spending were necessary to preserve the American way of life. In a speech given on April 16, 1953, he said,

> Every gun that is made, every warship launched, every rocket fired signifies, in the final sense,
> a theft from those who hunger and are not fed, those who are cold and are not clothed.[4]

Critics of the New Look strategy charged that "massive retaliation" locked America
into an all-or-nothing response to Communist aggression. A Communist-led uprising in a
small country would not warrant an attack on the Soviet Union, hence the revolution would
probably succeed. The Soviets also could see the limitations of massive retaliation and
would not be deterred from promoting small-scale insurrections in Third World countries.
Freedom would be nibbled away at the periphery.

[4]Charles C. Alexander, *Holding the Line: The Eisenhower Era, 1952–1961* (Bloomington, Ind.: Indiana
University Press, 1975), p. 164.

Ike defended his New Look foreign policy by contending that the United States could not afford to police the entire world, that it must concentrate on defending its vital interests. If NATO nations or Japan were attacked, the United States' response would be swift and overwhelming. Dulles also tried to compensate for the limitations of the New Look strategy by forging regional security pacts with allies in which the United States would furnish the military hardware and the allies the troops if the Communists attacked. By 1960, as a result of "pactomania," the United States had committed itself to defend forty-three countries.

VIETNAM: GETTING IN DEEPER

Dulles described his diplomatic method as the willingness to go to the brink of war to achieve peace. "Brinkmanship" was more threatening as rhetoric than as action. Dulles never used brinkmanship on the Soviets, nor did the United States become embroiled in any major wars during the Eisenhower-Dulles tenure. Brinkmanship was tried mainly in Asia, with mixed results. It worked in Korea to phase out a war. The President told Dulles to warn the Chinese that if they did not accept a settlement, the United States might use nuclear weapons in the war. That threat broke a two-year-old deadlock and ended the conflict on American terms.

Dulles then applied brinkmanship to Southeast Asia, where, since 1946, the French had been fighting to reimpose colonialism in Indochina. In 1950, the Truman administration had incorporated supporting the French effort in Indochina as part of the larger U.S. strategy of containing Communism in Asia following the Maoist triumph in China. Eisenhower expanded American aid to the French; by 1954, the United States was paying 78 percent of the cost of the war. Eisenhower, like Truman before him, applied Cold War ideology to this struggle between Asian nationalists and European imperialists. Washington viewed the Indochina War as part of the global conflict between Free World forces and Communism. They viewed Ho Chi Minh as an advance agent of Beijing and Moscow.

Despite American help, the French were losing the war. By 1954, Viet Minh forces held most of Vietnam. French generals tried to retrieve the military initiative. They put 11,000 of their best troops in a remote fortress deep within guerrilla-held territory at Dien Bien Phu and dared them to fight an open battle. The French believed that Asians could not defeat European forces in a conventional battle. They proved to be mistaken. Superior Vietnamese forces besieged the garrison. Within weeks, it was on the verge of surrender. With war weariness strong in France after eight years of war, the fall of Dien Bien Phu would mean victory for the Vietnamese Nationalists and the end of French Indochina.

Facing imminent ruin in Southeast Asia, the French appealed to the Americans to save them. President Eisenhower considered air strikes to relieve the siege around Dien Bien Phu, but he insisted that American allies join the effort and that Congress support it. Prime Minister Winston Churchill rebuffed Dulles's efforts to enlist British support. Senate leaders told the President that without British involvement, the Senate would not approve U.S. military intervention. Lacking support from allies or Congress, Eisenhower rejected the French request. On May 7, 1954, Dien Bien Phu fell to the Communists.

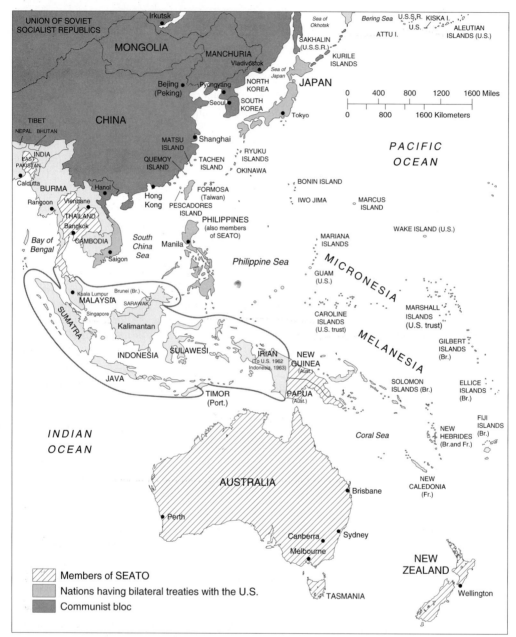

Figure 5.4   The Alliance System in the Far East.   *Source:* Moss, *Moving On,* 1/e, p. 119.

Meanwhile, an international conference previously convened in Geneva sought to find a political solution to the Indochina War. Conferees worked out a settlement in July 1954. By its terms, the French and Viet Minh agreed to a cease-fire and a temporary partition of Vietnam at the seventeenth parallel of north latitude, with French forces withdrawing south of that line and Viet Minh forces withdrawing to the north. Free elections were to be held within two years to unify the country. During the interim, the French were to help prepare Southern Vietnam for independence and then leave.

The United States opposed the Geneva Accords but could not prevent the conferees from approving them. The American delegate refused to sign them, but he agreed to accept them and pledged not to use force to upset the arrangements. But at the time, President Eisenhower announced that the United States "has not been party to or is bound by the decisions taken by the conference." Ho Chi Minh, whose forces verged on taking all of Vietnam, settled for just the northern half of the country at Geneva, because he was confident of winning the forthcoming elections over the French-backed regime in the south and because he was pressured by his allies, the Soviets and the Chinese, who wanted an end to the fighting in Vietnam.

After Geneva, Dulles salvaged what he could from what Washington regarded as a major Communist victory that threatened all of Southeast Asia. In September 1954, Dulles arranged for Great Britain, France, Australia, New Zealand, Thailand, Pakistan, and the Philippines to create the Southeast Asia Treaty Organization (SEATO). It was not a mutual security pact like NATO. SEATO members agreed only to "meet and confer" if one of them were attacked. A separate agreement covered Laos, Cambodia, and "South Vietnam," that is, Vietnam south of the seventeenth parallel. SEATO tried to project American power into Indochina in the aftermath of the French defeat and to provide a legal basis for subsequent American interventions in Southeast Asia.

The United States also supported a new government emerging in Southern Vietnam, headed by Ngo Dinh Diem. Americans trained and equipped Diem's army and security forces. The Eisenhower administration promoted the diplomatic fiction that the seventeenth parallel had become a national boundary separating two states, "South Vietnam" and "North Vietnam." America also backed Diem when he subverted the Geneva Accords by refusing to allow the scheduled elections to unify the country to take place in 1956.

Eisenhower believed that if Southern Vietnam fell to the Communists, all of Southeast Asia would be imperiled. He compared the nations of Southeast Asia to a row of dominoes: knock one over, and the rest would fall quickly. After Geneva, the United States committed its resources and prestige to creating a new nation in Southern Vietnam that would "serve as a proving ground for democracy in Asia." The survival of the new South Vietnam would sabotage the Geneva settlement that had assumed the emergence of a unified, Communist-controlled Vietnam following the elections, which were never held.

With United States' backing during the late 1950s, Diem attempted to suppress all opposition to his regime among religious sects, Viet Minh remnants, and other groups of dissidents. His repressive actions provoked violent opposition. Local officials and Diem informers were assassinated by Communist and non-Communist opponents, all of whom Diem called "Viet Cong," meaning Vietnamese who are Communists. The Viet Minh infiltrated men and supplies south of the seventeenth parallel to take control of the anti-Diem

Figure 5.5   In the dense jungle terrain of Vietnam, South Vietnamese nationalist forces were unable to defeat the Viet Minh.   *Source:* National Archives.

insurgency. Small-scale civil war had begun. By 1959, the Second Indochina War was underway; in time, that conflict would become the American Vietnam War. Without intending to, the Americans and the North Vietnamese had launched themselves on collision courses.

THE CHINA CRISIS

While Americans were trying to build a nation in Southeast Asia, they faced a confrontation with mainland China over Formosa (Taiwan). The question of the two Chinas was a dilemma that preoccupied the Eisenhower administration for its entirety. Nationalist Chinese pilots, flying from Formosan bases in U.S. planes, had bombed mainland shipping and ports since 1953. The U.S. Seventh Fleet patrolled the waters between China and Formosa, protecting the Nationalists from Communist reprisals. In 1955, Communist Chinese artillery began shelling Nationalist defenders of Quemoy and Matsu, two small islands sitting in the mouths of two mainland ports about 100 miles from Formosa.

Eisenhower was determined to hold these islands that he believed were essential to the defense of Formosa. The United States prepared for nuclear air strikes against China. If the Communist Chinese had invaded the islands, the United States probably would have bombed Chinese targets. The Soviets, alarmed by the threat of war between China and the

United States, intervened to help relieve the crisis. The Chinese reduced the shelling and offered to negotiate "a relaxation of tensions." The United States, which did not recognize the mainland Chinese government, refused to negotiate with the Communist Chinese, but it stopped its war preparations, and the situation calmed.

American problems in Asia highlighted the emergence of Third World nations as a major force in world affairs during the 1950s. These nations, many of them recently independent former European colonies, increasingly became the focus of the Cold War conflict between the USSR and the United States. Third World nations were sources of raw materials, they attracted foreign investment, and they provided markets, particularly for American exports. Many Third World nations wanted to remain neutral in the Cold War. But to U.S. Secretary of State Dulles, neutralism in a bipolar world dominated by two superpowers, one of which was "immoral," was wrong. He opposed a conference of twenty-nine African and Asian nations held at Bandung, Indonesia, in April 1955, during the height of the Quemoy-Matsu crisis. Leaders of the Afro-Asian nations called for these nations to form an alternative to the two superpowers and their alliance systems. Chinese Premier Jou En-lai played a prominent role at Bandung; China moved to assert leadership of the emerging Third World nations.

AT THE SUMMIT

When the United States considered using nuclear weapons during the Formosan crisis, it highlighted a frightening world reality. Thermonuclear weapons of the mid-1950s were 1,000 times more powerful than the two bombs that had devastated Hiroshima and Nagasaki in 1945. A lone U.S. strategic bomber in 1955 carried more destructive power than all of the explosives previously detonated in world history. Both the Soviets and Americans possessed hydrogen bombs, and both were developing intercontinental missiles. Both sides had to face the possibility of a nuclear exchange if they went to war. They agreed to hold a "summit conference" to try to reduce the possibility of nuclear catastrophe.

The conference convened at Geneva on July 18, 1955. President Eisenhower, Premier Nikolai Bulganin of the Soviet Union, Prime Minister Anthony Eden of England, and Premier Edgar Faure of France attended. Geneva signaled a turning point in the Cold War. Both sides conceded in effect that the Cold War could not be won militarily. The atmosphere at the summit was cordial. A "spirit of Geneva" emerged, symbolized by a photograph of Eisenhower shaking hands with Bulganin. Eisenhower told the Soviet leaders that the United States would never participate in an aggressive war. He also proposed new initiatives to solve the perennial German problem and made some suggestions for disarmament. Ike also scored a propaganda victory when he offered, and the Soviets rejected, his "Open Skies" proposal that would permit aerial surveillance of both countries' nuclear development and testing facilities.

The summit brought little progress toward concrete solutions to the problems dividing the East and the West. The Soviets rejected Eisenhower's proposals for German reunification and its right to join NATO. The Americans, in turn, rejected the Soviet proposal of a general European security pact that would have required the withdrawal of U.S. troops from Europe. The thermonuclear arms race roared on after the summit ended. But a thermonuclear stalemate had forced the superpowers to a relaxation of tensions. The Cold War thawed a little. Both sides agreed to begin arms control negotiations and later suspended atmospheric testing of nuclear weapons.

THE CIA AT WORK

In 1953, Ike appointed Allen Dulles, younger brother of the Secretary of State, as director of the Central Intelligence Agency (CIA). Dulles recruited Cold Warriors eager to fight Communism. Under his leadership, paramilitary covert operations became a secret arm of U.S. foreign policy. The CIA's first major triumph came in Iran in 1953. A Nationalist government, led by Mohammed Mossadegh, had nationalized oil fields controlled by the British and forced the young Shah of Iran into exile. The United States, fearing that Mossadegh might sell oil to the Soviets and align himself with Iranian Communists, sent CIA operatives to Iran. Working with the British and Iranian army officials, they helped overthrow Mossadegh and restored the Shah to power. Iran then made a deal that gave U.S. oil companies 40 percent of Iranian oil production, the British 40 percent, and the Dutch 20 percent. The CIA significantly advanced American interests in the Middle East by helping subvert a government hostile to the United States and helping the United States to acquire a major share of Iranian oil production.

The CIA also helped overthrow a Leftist government in Central America. Jacob Arbenz Guzman had been elected president of Guatemala in 1951. Arbenz was not a Communist, but Communists supported his government and held offices within it. In 1953, the government expropriated 234,000 acres of land belonging to an American corporation, the United Fruit Company, Guatemala's largest landowner, for a land reform program. The company claimed that Latin America was being threatened with Communism.

The United States cut off economic aid and sent CIA forces to Guatemala to overthrow Arbenz. CIA officials recruited an army of exiles in neighboring Honduras, led by Colonel Carlos Castillo Armas. Faced with a military threat to his power, Arbenz turned to the Soviet Union for weapons. When Armas's forces were ready for attack, CIA pilots airlifted their supplies and bombed the Guatemalan capital. Arbenz, facing military defeat, fled into exile. Armas established a military dictatorship and returned the expropriated lands to the United Fruit Company. The U.S. intervention in Guatemala intensified resentment toward U.S. foreign policy throughout Latin America. When Vice President Nixon traveled to Venezuela in 1958 as part of a goodwill tour of Latin America, he was met in the streets of Caracas by angry mobs who stoned his car.

TROUBLE IN SUEZ

During the 1950s, the Cold War spread to the Middle East, deeply involving the United States in a strategically significant region that had previously been of only peripheral interest. Long dominated by Western colonial powers, the Middle East was a compound of many parts: Arab nationalism, regional rivalries, weak and unstable governments, the world's richest oil reserves, masses of poor peasants, feudal societies, religious extremism, superpower penetration, and most of all, the intractable Arab-Israeli conflict. It is the presence of a Jewish state on land that was formerly Palestine that lies at the core of many Middle East conflicts.

The modern Arab-Israeli conflict dates from the end of World War II. Most of the European Jews who survived the Holocaust wanted to go to Palestine, where a sizable Jewish population had been built up since 1900. Palestine was administered by the British, who tried to prevent Zionist refugees from entering Palestine in order to safeguard their Anglo-Arabian oil interests. But the British, weakened by losses in World War II, withdrew from Palestine in 1947, turning its problems over to the United Nations. At that time, the United States and the Soviet Union cooperated to carve an Israeli homeland out of the western portion of Palestine. The United Nations partitioned Palestine to create a Jewish state, Israel, along the Mediterranean coast. On May 14, 1948, Israel proclaimed its independence. America recognized Israel immediately and the Soviet Union soon afterward.

Instantly, Arab armies attacked, determined to drive the Jews into the Mediterranean Sea, to destroy the new Jewish state, and to preserve all of Palestine for the Palestinian Arabs. At first, the outnumbered Israelis were driven back. They asked for a truce, and the Soviets and Americans imposed one. During the cease-fire, with tacit American approval, the Soviets flew in quantities of heavy arms, violating the truce. When fighting resumed, the well-armed Israelis routed the Arab forces. Israeli forces also advanced far beyond the original boundaries assigned by the UN partition. The beaten Arabs sued for peace in 1949.

African American diplomat Ralph Bunche arranged an armistice ending the first Arab-Israeli war. Israel's inflated borders included thousands of Palestinians. Another 700,000 Palestinians fled or were driven from their homes by the advancing Israeli forces, creating a Palestinian refugee problem that has never been resolved. The Soviets supported Israel until 1955, when they switched to the Arab side. The United States has continued to be Israel's major supporter, while trying to maintain friendly relations with moderate Arab nations.

With U.S. assistance, Gamal Abdul Nasser came to power in Egypt in 1952, the first of a new generation of Arab Nationalist leaders. America offered him $270 million to build a dam on the Upper Nile to control flooding and to generate hydroelectric power. The aid money for the Aswan Dam represented an American effort to tilt its Middle East policy in a more pro-Arab direction. In 1955, Dulles arranged the signing of the Baghdad Pact, linking Britain, Turkey, Iran, Iraq, and Pakistan in an agreement to strengthen the Middle East against Soviet penetration. The pact angered Nasser, who viewed it as an effort to bring the Cold War to the Middle East and to strengthen Iraq, Egypt's chief rival for Arab leadership. The Soviet Union reacted to the signing of the Baghdad Pact by becoming more active in Arab affairs, particularly in Egypt and Syria.

Egyptian and Israeli forces clashed along the Gaza Strip, territory that both nations claimed, inhabited mainly by Palestinian refugees. The Israelis suddenly attacked in force in 1955, inflicting a major defeat on the Egyptians. Nasser, angry and humiliated, asked the

United States for arms. Washington refused him. Nasser then turned to the Soviet bloc and concluded an arms deal with the Communists. Dulles, fearing that Egypt might become a Soviet client, withdrew American aid for the Aswan Dam. Nasser responded by nationalizing the Suez Canal, owned by an Anglo-French consortium. He used its $30 million of annual revenues to finance the Aswan Dam, and also closed the canal to Israeli shipping. The Soviets supported Nasser's actions.

Britain and France, dependent on Persian Gulf oil shipped through the Suez Canal, proposed overthrowing Nasser and returning the canal to its former owners. The United States, afraid such actions could bring the Soviets into the fray and even lead to World War III, rejected the Anglo-French proposal. Despite the American rejection, the British and French decided to overthrow Nasser, and they incorporated the Israelis into their plans. On October 29, 1956, Israel invaded Egypt. A week later, the French and British landed troops in Egypt to seize the canal. The United States condemned the Anglo-French-Israeli actions before the United Nations. America also cut off oil shipments to France and Britain and threatened to wage financial war against the British pound sterling. The French and British, reeling from a combination of U.S. and UN opposition, Soviet threats to intervene, and an Arab oil boycott, withdrew without occupying the canal. The invasion proved to be a fiasco. It was a humiliating defeat for the two fading European imperial powers. The Soviets used the occasion to provide funds for the Aswan project in return for which the Egyptians granted the Soviets use of a former British military base at Suez.

American efforts to avoid war in the Middle East had mostly negative consequences for American foreign policy interests. Administration efforts weakened NATO, humiliated America's major European allies, alienated Nasser, angered the Israelis, helped the Soviets get a military base in Egypt, and failed to improve relations with other Arab countries. But Nasser eventually paid the French and British $81 million for the Suez Canal, and Middle Eastern oil supplies remained in Western hands. Most important, the United States had supplanted the French and British as the dominant Western power in the Middle East arena.

While the Suez crisis raged, crises erupted in Eastern Europe. Early in 1956, the new Soviet leader, Nikita Khrushchev, promised to ease Soviet restrictions in satellite countries. Ferment spread quickly throughout Eastern Europe. Riots in Poland forced the Soviets to grant the Poles substantial concessions. Hungarian students and workers overthrew a Stalinist puppet. He was replaced by Imre Nagy. Nagy demanded the removal of Red Army forces and the implementation of democracy; the Soviets acceded to both of these demands. Dulles promised the Hungarians economic aid if they broke with the Soviets. On October 31, Hungary announced that it was leaving the Warsaw Pact. Liberation appeared to be at hand; a captive people were freeing themselves from Communist tyranny.

The Soviet Union, unwilling to let the Warsaw Pact disintegrate, invaded Hungary. 200,000 Soviet troops and hundreds of Soviet tanks crushed the Hungarian revolution and killed 30,000 Hungarians. Radio Budapest pleaded for help, but none came from America or elsewhere. Eisenhower had never considered sending troops, nor would he have had there not been a Suez crisis. Neither he nor any other U.S. president would ever risk World War III to help liberate an East European country. American talk of liberation for Eastern Europe had always been a sham. American forces were not strong enough to defeat the Red Army in Hungary, except with the use of nuclear weapons that would have ruined the country and killed millions of people. Hungarians learned the hard way that East European nations would have to go on making deals with their Soviet masters, while Americans would go on mouthing pious rhetoric about the evils of Communist imperialism.

After the Suez incident, at the request of the Eisenhower administration, Congress enacted a joint resolution authorizing the extension of economic and military assistance to any Middle Eastern nation resisting armed aggression from the Soviet Union or its satellites. This resolution announced the Eisenhower Doctrine to try to offset Soviet influence and militant Arab nationalism in the Middle East. The Eisenhower Doctrine extended containment to the Middle East. Twice it was implemented. In the spring of 1957, King Hussein of Jordan faced an Egyptian-backed revolt. Eisenhower sent the U.S. Sixth Fleet to the eastern Mediterranean and granted Hussein a $20 million credit. With American support, Hussein managed to survive. A year later, a more serious crisis erupted in Lebanon. Lebanon's Christian, pro-Western government was threatened by Nasserite forces. At the same time, a pro-Western government in Iraq was overthrown by Nationalist forces backed by Egypt.

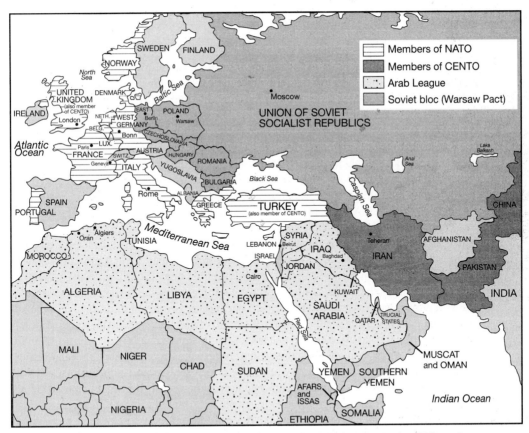

Figure 5.6   Postwar alliances: Europe, North Africa, and the Middle East in the 1950s.   *Source:* Litwack & Jordan, *The United States: Becoming a World Power,* Vol. 2, Seventh ed. (Prentice Hall, Englewood Cliffs, N.J.), p. 416.

Fearing a similar outcome in Lebanon, Eisenhower, in July 1958, sent 14,000 marines to that country. Lebanon's pro-Western government survived. The Eisenhower doctrine, which provided a rationale for American military interventions in the Middle East, was used sparingly, with limited success.

As the 1950s ended, America enjoyed good relations with traditional Arab states such as Saudi Arabia, the region's major oil producer, which had become a U.S. client through economic aid and arms sales. Middle Eastern oil continued its flow through the Suez Canal. But U.S. influence in the Middle East was declining. Arab nationalism and Soviet influence were growing. Egyptian and Syrian armies were equipped with Soviet weapons, and the Soviets were financing the Aswan project. Arab hostility toward Israel combined with the American commitment to the survival of the Jewish state allowed the Soviets to champion Arab nationalism. American efforts to balance Arab and Israeli interests largely failed. No conceivable diplomatic formula promised a long-term solution to Middle East conflicts unless the Arab-Israeli impasse was overcome.

SPUTNIK

After the Suez crisis, the military balance appeared to shift toward the Soviet Union. In September 1957, the Soviets test fired an intercontinental ballistics missile (ICBM) more than one year ahead of the United States. One month later, they launched the first space satellite, a 184-pound vehicle that they called *Sputnik*. One month after that, the Soviets launched *Sputnik II,* a much larger space vehicle carrying a live dog, Laika, on board. In addition to their tremendous propaganda victories, the two *Sputniks* carried ominous strategic implications. They proved that the Soviets had powerful rockets and had solved guidance problems essential to delivering a thermonuclear warhead to its target. They also suggested that the Soviets could soon launch human beings on space travels. Soviet military and space technology surpassed American efforts in these crucial areas. The United States appeared to face both a missile "gap" and a space "lag" with the Soviets.

At first, President Eisenhower played down the Soviets' achievements, trying to reassure anxious Americans. But he was not convincing. He offered no new programs to catch the Soviets in either the arms or space race. For the first time, Ike was vigorously attacked in Congress and in the media. The attacks were reinforced by the sluggish performance of the economy, which had slipped into recession, and the revelation of a scandal in the administration. Eisenhower's chief of staff, Sherman Adams, was forced to resign for accepting favors from a businessman who needed a favor from the federal government. The Soviets had scored a tremendous ideological victory over their rivals. American technological superiority over the supposedly backward Soviets, a source of security during the Cold War, was wiped away. Senator Lyndon Johnson conducted a thorough investigation of the nation's missile and space programs, thereby establishing the Democrats as favoring stronger national defense and space efforts than the Administration.

Critics faulted American public schools for not demanding excellence from students and for stinting on basic education, math, and science training. There had been persistent criticisms of public schools preceding *Sputnik*. Dr. Rudolf Flesch, in his best-selling *Why*

Johnny Can't Read (1955), had attacked overcrowded schools that used obsolete teaching methods and offered diverse, aimless curricula to bored students. After the launching of the *Sputniks,* educational shortcomings became a national security issue. Educators insisted that Americans must put greater emphasis on mathematics, foreign language study, and science to regain its technological edge over the Soviets. Eisenhower and Congress responded in 1958 by enacting the National Defense Education Act (NDEA), which funded high school math, language, and science programs, and offered fellowships and loans to college students entering these fields.

Initial American efforts to match Soviet rocketry embarrassed the nation. Two months after *Sputnik II's* launching, an American rocket blew up on its launch pad; a U.S. journalist promptly dubbed it "kaputnik." Not until January 1958 did an Army rocket team manage to get a small American satellite into orbit. But the Soviets then hurled aloft a 3,000-pound satellite. Khrushchev claimed that Soviet leadership in rocketry demonstrated the superiority of socialism over capitalism. He boasted to alarmed Americans that "we will bury you," meaning that Soviet Communism would outlast American capitalism.

CUBA AND CASTRO

Eisenhower, preoccupied with the arms race with the Soviets and conducting Cold War diplomacy in Europe, Asia, and the Middle East, usually gave relations with Latin America a low priority. Nevertheless, Cold War concerns extended to the Western Hemisphere in 1954 with the U.S. intervention in Guatemala to overthrow a government that displayed Communist sympathies. Latin American politics during the 1950s swung between the extremes of Leftist democracies and Rightist military dictatorships. Washington, while paying lip service to democracy, preferred military regimes that maintained order, protected private property, supported U.S. foreign policy, and suppressed Communists. Latin Americans envied U.S. wealth, feared U.S. power, and resented U.S. diplomacy.

In the 1950s, U.S. economic interests dominated the Cuban economy, a result of the neocolonial relationship between the countries that had evolved since the Spanish-American War. American companies owned Cuba's oil industry, 90 percent of its mines, 80 percent of its utilities, 50 percent of its railroads, 40 percent of its sugar plantations, and 40 percent of its cattle ranches. Most of Cuba's major export crop, sugar, was sold on U.S. markets, and two-thirds of Cuban imports came from the United States.

At the end of 1958, Fidel Castro overthrew Fulgencio Batista, a corrupt dictator who had protected U.S. economic interests in Cuba. Castro immediately began a social revolution in Cuba. He broke up the large cattle ranches and sugar plantations and distributed the land to peasants. He established summary courts that condemned former Batista supporters, thousands of whom were shot or imprisoned. Communists took over Cuban trade unions and infiltrated Castro's army.

Although alarmed by Castro's radical actions, the United States quickly recognized his regime. Castro had considerable popular support within the United States; he was viewed as a liberal reformer who would restore Cuban democracy. He visited the United States in April 1959. In meetings with American officials, he spoke reassuringly about fu-

Figure 5.7   Cuban President Fidel Castro jabs two fingers together during a lengthy address before the United National General Assembly on September 26, 1960.   *Source:* AP/ Wide World Photos.

ture relations with the United States. He promised that any future expropriations of American property would be legal and the owners compensated, but these were pledges that he failed to keep. He tried to borrow money from U.S. bankers but rejected their terms because they conflicted with his plans for Cuban economic development. He then returned to Cuba and began nationalizing more U.S. property.

Relations between the United States and Cuba continued to deteriorate as Castro's revolution continued its left-wing tack. Cuban liberals, many of them former Castro supporters, fled Cuba for Florida. Castro, who had come to power with only vague notions about implementing an economic program once in power, joined the Communists in mid-1959. By the end of the year, his government had confiscated about $1 billion in U.S. properties. In February 1960, Castro signed an agreement with the Soviet Union in which the Soviets traded oil and machinery for sugar, and they also loaned Cuba $100 million. Khrushchev pronounced the Monroe Doctrine dead and said that Soviet rockets would defend Cuba from U.S. "aggression." Washington responded by ending all economic aid to Cuba and by sharply cutting the import quota on Cuba's sugar.

Eisenhower decided by mid-1960 that Castro would have to be removed from power by whatever means necessary. The President preferred to work through the Organization of American States (OAS), but that route proved ineffective. Castro had supporters among OAS members; they admired him as a Nationalist who had defied the United States. Others feared to oppose Castro, lest he foment unrest among their people. Frustrated by OAS inaction, Ike approved a CIA project to train Cuban exiles for an invasion of Cuba to overthrow Castro. The CIA established a training site in a remote mountainous region in Guatemala and began preparations. The United States then embargoed all trade with Cuba and severed diplomatic relations.

Cuban agents meanwhile spread Castroism elsewhere in Latin America, and Washington tried to blunt Castro's appeal by promoting social reform. Administration officials, working through the OAS, promoted a reform agenda including tax reform, improved housing and schools, land reform, and economic development. Congress appropriated $500 million to launch the ambitious program. President John Kennedy, upon assuming office, endorsed the effort, increased the funding, and supplied an upbeat title, "The Alliance for Progress." The Eisenhower administration's Latin American aid program failed to get off the ground. Administered by corrupt officials, opposed by ruling elites in every country, it also was too closely tied to the status quo to be effective.

CONTROVERSY IN EUROPE

During the late 1950s, the Cold War in Europe intensified, erasing any lingering "spirit of Geneva." The Soviets used the psychological advantage gained by their space exploits to put pressure on the United States. In November 1958, Khrushchev, unhappy with the integration of West Germany into NATO and the unresolved German question, announced that within six months he would sign a separate peace treaty with East Germany, thereby ending Western occupation rights in West Berlin. Another Cold War crisis was at hand.

Ike stood firm. He refused to abandon West Berlin, but he also used diplomacy to avoid a confrontation with the Soviets. Khrushchev extended the Berlin deadline following Eisenhower's invitation to him to visit the United States. Khrushchev spent two weeks in the United States in the summer of 1959, the first Soviet leader ever to set foot in America. Following meetings with Eisenhower at Camp David, an ebullient Khrushchev announced the cancellation of his Berlin ultimatum. At the same time, Eisenhower suggested that the troubling question of West Berlin ought to be speedily resolved. Once again, a Cold War crisis over Berlin receded. One month after Khrushchev's American tour, Eisenhower announced that there would be another summit meeting in Paris scheduled for May 1960, and he invited the Soviet leader to attend. Khrushchev accepted and invited the President to visit the Soviet Union following the summit. Ike accepted Khrushchev's invitation. The Cold War appeared to be thawing once again.

But the Paris summit never occurred. Two weeks before its scheduled opening, the Soviets shot down an American U-2 spy plane over Soviet soil. Initially the United States stated that a weather reconnaissance plane had flown off course and had inadvertently violated Soviet air space. An angry Khrushchev then revealed that the aircraft had been shot

Figure 5.8   On July 7, 1959, Vice President Richard Nixon, accompanied by Soviet leader Nikita Khrushchev, made an official visit to the American pavilion at an exhibit in Moscow. Moments later, the two leaders staged their famous "kitchen debate," arguing over the merits of their respective systems of government. The debate was one of the dramatic moments of the Cold War.
Source: National Archives.

down 1,200 miles into the Soviet Union and that the Soviets had captured the pilot who admitted that he had been on a spy mission. When President Eisenhower took full responsibility for the flight and refused to repudiate it, Khrushchev angrily denounced Eisenhower, canceled the summit, and withdrew Ike's invitation to visit the Soviet Union. Eisenhower deeply regretted the breakup of the summit, seeing all of his efforts for peace dashed because of the U-2 incident. Khrushchev refused to have any more dealings with Eisenhower; he bided his time, waiting for the Americans to select a new president.

END OF AN ERA

The U-2 incident, the launching of *Sputnik,* and the seemingly endless crises of the Cold War took their toll on the American people in the late 1950s. American prestige and power in the world declined. This sense of declining power to control events in the world spurred a rising debate in this country over national purpose. Social critics wondered if Americans retained the same drive to achieve goals that had motivated previous generations. Did Americans still want to be great? Did they have the will to face future Soviet challenges? Had Americans gone soft from technology and affluence? Adlai Stevenson said that the nation suffered from a "paralysis of will"; Americans appeared committed only to "pleasure and profit" and the "pursuit of ease."

In the spring of 1960, both *Life* and the *New York Times* published a series of commentaries on the national purpose written by prominent authors. All agreed that something was lacking in the national spirit. President Eisenhower established a National Goals Commission to develop national objectives. The Commission brought out a book, *Goals for*

Americans, in which it recommended an increase in military spending to meet the Soviet challenge, a government commitment to an expanding economy, a college education for all, the promotion of scientific research and the arts, and a guaranteed right to vote for all citizens. The commission's suggested goals expressed a need felt by many Americans to restate the meaning of national existence; to reaffirm the American identity in a dangerous world; and to point the direction in which American society should be heading. John Kennedy later added many of the National Goals Commission's recommendations to his New Frontier agenda.

As Eisenhower prepared to leave office, the United States faced crises in Cuba, Berlin, and Southeast Asia. All were bequeathed to his young successor. On January 17, 1961, Ike spoke to the American people for the last time as president. His Farewell Address consisted of a series of warnings to his countrymen, as had George Washington's famed address of 1797. Eisenhower warned of the Communist menace, of squandering the nation's resources, and of spending too much on either welfare or warfare. The most famous part of Ike's valedictory warned about the power of the military establishment and its corporate clients:

> we must guard against the acquisition of unwarranted influence, whether sought or unsought, by the military-industrial complex.[5]

Ike asserted that the military-industrial complex could endanger basic liberties and democratic processes. In light of Vietnam and Watergate, the old general's caveats proved prophetic. He understood more clearly than any other modern president the dangers that the Cold War posed to his nation's wealth and freedom.

Eisenhower presided over a peaceful and prosperous interlude in American history. But as he exited public life, the nation faced many foreign crises and unsolved domestic problems. The civil rights movement was gathering momentum, and other disadvantaged groups would soon challenge the status quo. Although the United States remained the world's wealthiest, most powerful nation, its prosperity and power had suffered relative decline in the late 1950s. Western Europe and Japan prospered. The Soviet Union's military power and diplomatic influence were expanding. Anti-Western nationalism intensified among Middle Eastern and Latin American nations. Eisenhower's successors in the 1960s would increase American military power and intensify the Cold War. They also would propose a broad range of social reforms. Troubled times lay ahead.

BIBLIOGRAPHY

There exists a sizable bibliography on domestic politics and foreign policy in the 1950s. The best biographies of Eisenhower are by Herbert S. Parmet, in *Eisenhower and the American Crusades,* and the second volume of Stephen E. Ambrose's *Eisenhower: The President, 1952–1969.* Eisenhower himself has left two volumes of memoirs: *The White House Years: Mandate for Change, 1953–1956* and *The White House Years: Waging Peace, 1956–1961.* There is a good collection of contemporary

[5]Quoted in ibid., p. 289.

appraisals of the Eisenhower presidency by Dean Albertson, ed., *Eisenhower as President.* Some of Eisenhower's former staffers have written accounts of his presidency. One of the best is by Emmet John Hughes, *The Ordeal of Power: A Political Memoir of the Eisenhower Years.* An important work is Fred I. Greenstein's *The Hidden Hand Presidency: Eisenhower as Leader.* Greenstein persuasively argued that Eisenhower was a strong and an effective leader on both domestic and foreign policy issues who "hid his hand" to achieve his goals. The best general political history of the 1950s is Charles C. Alexander's *Holding the Line: the Eisenhower Era, 1952–1961.* Juan Williams' *Eyes on the Prize: America's Civil Rights Years, 1954–1965* is a stirring account of the civil rights movement. Robert A. Divine's *Eisenhower and the Cold War* is the best diplomatic history of the Eisenhower years. H. W. Brands Jr.'s *Cold Warriors* also is excellent. Samuel P. Huntington's *The Common Defense: Strategic Programs in National Politics* is the best study of Eisenhower's strategic policies. Michael A. Guhin's *John Foster Dulles: A Statesman and His Times* offers the fullest treatment of Eisenhower's energetic Secretary of State. Using recently released documents and records, Keith Kyle, in *Suez,* has written a good account of that crucial episode in American Middle Eastern diplomatic history. Richard H. Immerman's *The CIA in Guatemala* is a well-done account of the CIA's subversion of the Arbenz government.

6

New Frontiers

In the early 1960s, Americans regained the confidence in their national destiny that had faltered in the late 1950s, when the economy went slack and the Soviets appeared to have gained a strategic advantage in the Cold War. The economy revived. Most middle-class American families enjoyed unprecedented affluence, and their children's prospects never looked brighter. An energetic, articulate young president kindled this resurgent optimism. John Fitzgerald Kennedy voiced national goals in language that Americans, particularly young Americans, could understand and accept. He told Americans that they could face the challenges of mid-century life, hold their own in world affairs, beat the Soviets in the space race, and solve nagging social problems at home. A new activist spirit surged across the land. For a few years, a spirit of "Camelot" reigned, a belief that anything was possible, that nothing was beyond the grasp of Americans.

A PATH TO THE PRESIDENCY

John F. "Jack" Kennedy inherited a rich political legacy. Both of his grandfathers, second-generation Irish immigrants, had been prominent ethnic politicians in Boston. His father, Joseph P. "Joe" Kennedy, a Harvard graduate, made a fortune estimated at $150 million in banking, real estate, and other enterprises. Joe Kennedy, a conservative Democratic supporter of Franklin D. Roosevelt, served as the Security and Exchange Commission's first chairman and later as ambassador to Great Britain. Jack's political career began successfully when he was elected to Congress in 1946, representing a heavily ethnic working-class section of Boston. His father played a major behind-the-scenes role, providing both money and clout to help his son win. During Jack's congressional career, he represented his constituents' interests and remained popular in his "safe" Democratic district.

While in Congress, Kennedy introduced no important legislation nor identified himself with any major issue. He usually took liberal positions on domestic issues. He worked to purge Communists from union ranks and opposed the Taft-Hartley Act. On foreign policy, he sometimes aligned himself with conservative Republican critics of Truman's Far Eastern policy. He supported General MacArthur's call for war against China in 1951, and Truman's firing of the old general outraged him. He formed political friendships with two rising Republican stars, Congressman Richard Nixon and Senator Joseph McCarthy.

Jack sought to move up to the Senate in 1952, even though it was clearly a Republican year. The GOP ran popular war hero General Dwight Eisenhower for president. Richard Nixon and Joe McCarthy drew blood with their supercharged attacks on corruption and Communism in the Truman administration. Jack Kennedy faced a formidable challenge and began his campaign as the underdog against incumbent Henry Cabot Lodge Jr. He ran as a moderate Democrat and dissociated himself from the Democratic national ticket, which obviously was losing that year. In a close race, his father's money and Kennedy's superb campaign organization, led by his younger brother Robert, proved to be the decisive factors. His election to the Senate in November 1952 signaled the arrival of a new-style Democratic politician. Kennedy was the leader of an emergent generation of postwar Democrats who were less ideological and less partisan than the traditional New Deal–Fair Dealers who had rallied to Adlai Stevenson's failed presidential bid.

The election also represented a major turning point in Jack Kennedy's political journey. In the Senate, Kennedy could devote more attention to foreign affairs, always his major interest. He consistently advocated a strong Cold War policy and called for increased defense spending. He became a critic of the Eisenhower-Dulles New Look foreign policy. Kennedy thought their cuts in defense spending were unwise, and he criticized their approach to the emerging nations of the Third World. He opposed giving aid to the French in Southeast Asia unless Washington prodded them to grant the people of Indochina independence. Senator Kennedy also became more partisan and liberal, and he held ambitions for higher office.

Early in his Senate career, Kennedy had to confront his relationship with Senator Joseph McCarthy. He was caught in several binds when the Senate moved to censure McCarthy in late 1954. At the time, Kennedy was recovering from back surgery and a postoperative infection that had nearly killed him. He was living at his parent's mansion in West Palm Beach, Florida, when the vote was taken that ruined McCarthy. Kennedy faced a dilemma. Nearly all Democrats, President Eisenhower, and many Republican senators favored censuring the irresponsible demagogue. Yet McCarthy was his friend, and Jack had supported some of his earlier investigations of Communism. McCarthy also was a friend of his father's, and Joe Kennedy had contributed money to McCarthy's electoral campaigns. Jack's younger brother Robert had worked for a time on McCarthy's staff. His former congressional district was McCarthyite, and McCarthy had a strong following in Massachusetts. Even though he was ill and absent from the Senate when the vote was taken, Kennedy could have voted to condemn McCarthy. Instead, he used his illness as an excuse to abstain. He was the only Northern Democrat who did not vote to condemn McCarthy, an evasion that caused him trouble with the Democratic Party's liberal elders when he sought the presidency in 1960.

At the 1956 Democratic Convention, Jack Kennedy made a strong bid for the Democratic vice-presidential nomination. He lost narrowly to Senator Estes Kefauver of Tennessee. Many Americans got their first look at Kennedy during his spirited fight for the vice presidency, and they liked what they saw. As it turned out, Kennedy's defeat at the convention was to his political advantage. Had he received the vice-presidential nomination and run with Adlai Stevenson, he would have shared the humiliation of another lopsided electoral defeat at the hands of popular incumbents Eisenhower and Nixon. Such an outcome might have derailed his future presidential bid.

THE ELECTION OF 1960

A Democratic resurgence began with the 1958 midterm elections. A series of events had shaken public confidence in the Eisenhower administration: *Sputnik* and the apparent missile and space race gaps, crises in the Middle East, and a sharp recession at home, which had driven unemployment above 7 percent, the highest level since 1941. Also, the Sherman Adams scandal tarnished the antiseptic image that the Republicans had enjoyed since coming to office. The Democrats increased their majorities in the Senate, 64 to 34, and in the House, 283 to 153. These were their largest majorities since the New Deal heyday of 1936. In Massachusetts, John Kennedy won a lopsided reelection victory. His impressive performance made him the Democratic front-runner for 1960.

Many Democratic leaders entered the race for their party's 1960 presidential nomination. With the popular Ike forced to resign because of the Twenty-Second Amendment, prospects for a Democratic victory looked better than anytime since the glory days of FDR. Other candidates included Senators Hubert Humphrey and Stuart Symington and Senate Majority Leader Lyndon Johnson. Adlai Stevenson was still a contender, even though he had lost twice to Eisenhower.

Two obstacles blocked Kennedy's path to his party's presidential nomination. First, he would have to dispel the myth that a Catholic could never be elected president. The second obstacle was the candidacies of his powerful rivals, all of whom had longer, more distinguished political careers than he. Kennedy was an upstart among seasoned veterans of the political wars. Many informed observers believed that Kennedy lacked the experience, confidence, and stature necessary to run the country in the 1960s.

Victories in the early primaries gave him momentum that carried him to the nomination. Only Humphrey challenged him in these popularity contests. Symington and Johnson took the organizational route to the nomination, seeking delegates from the thirty-four states that did not hold primaries. Stevenson did not campaign, relying on his liberal followers to orchestrate his nomination at the convention if Kennedy's bid fell short. Jack eliminated Humphrey early; he beat him decisively in New Hampshire, Wisconsin, and West Virginia. Kennedy demonstrated that he could win and put the Catholic issue to rest. His organization contained a Stevenson boom that developed at the convention, and Kennedy won a close first-ballot nomination. Kennedy chose Lyndon Johnson, who had come in second to

Jack in the convention balloting for president, to be his vice-presidential running mate. He needed Johnson to win Texas and to hold the South if he were to have any chance of winning the presidency in November.

In his acceptance speech, Kennedy attacked the Eisenhower administration's handling of Cold War issues; he claimed that the Republicans had been too soft in responding to Communist threats, and he pledged a stronger approach. He set forth an agenda of unfinished business facing the nation in the 1960s and exhorted his fellow Americans to meet the challenges of new frontiers.

When the Republicans gathered in Chicago a week later, Richard Nixon had the nomination sewn up. The nearest thing to a challenge came from Nelson Rockefeller, governor of New York. He had no chance and withdrew long before the convention. But Rockefeller influenced the drafting of the party platform. Two days before the convention opened, Nixon accepted Rockefeller's proposals, calling for stronger defense programs, a faster buildup of missiles, stronger civil rights measures, and government stimulation of the economy to promote economic growth. The Republican platform came out similar to the Democratic one and amounted to an implicit indictment of Eisenhower administration policies. Conservative Republicans reacted angrily to the Rockefeller platform. Arizona Senator Barry Goldwater called it "the Munich of the Republican Party." Nixon had to use all of his political skill to keep the unhappy conservatives in the party fold.

The 1960 presidential campaign broke all records for money spent and miles traveled by the candidates. Nixon campaigned in all fifty states. Kennedy traveled over 100,000 miles in a jet airplane leased by his family for the campaign. It was the toughest, closest presidential election in modern American political history. The jousting of two able and energetic political leaders generated tremendous interest among the electorate.

Despite the candidates' dramatically different backgrounds—Nixon, the poor boy from rural southern California who had fought his way up the political ladder and Kennedy, the child of privilege whose political career depended largely on his father's wealth and influence—they shared similar political views. Nixon was a moderate conservative with liberal tendencies. Kennedy was a moderate liberal with conservative tendencies. Both were Cold Warriors. Both accepted the basic structure of the New Deal welfare state. Both advocated civil rights and believed in a strong presidency. Both were young men, Nixon, forty-seven, and Kennedy, forty-three. Because they shared similar political views, the campaign featured few substantial debates over the issues. The two candidates quarreled over details and means. Each challenged the other's capacity to govern, and each insisted that he was the better man to get tough with the Soviets. Because the electorate perceived their views to be so similar, the outcome of the election turned on personal image and the voter's feel for one or the other, not on the issues.

Even though he was only a few years older than Kennedy, Nixon portrayed his opponent as immature and inexperienced, a dangerous man to have at the helm in the nuclear age. Kennedy linked Nixon to what he called "the horse-and-buggy" policies of Eisenhower that had let the nation fall behind the Soviets in missile and space technology and had allowed the economy to stagnate. Kennedy promised "to get the country moving again" by providing strong leadership. He reminded audiences that although Richard Nixon might act the role of statesman in 1960, behind that facade lurked the real Nixon, the mudslinger of the early 1950s, the man who belonged to the party of Lincoln, but unlike Lincoln, showed "charity to none and malice toward all."

Nixon began the campaign with some liabilities. The sagging economy was the most serious. The Cold War setbacks that the Eisenhower administration suffered also hurt the candidate's chances. Eisenhower gave Nixon only lukewarm support. Ike made matters temporarily worse for the candidate when a reporter asked him what decisions Nixon had helped him make and the old general quipped, "If you give me a week, I might think of one." Even so, the early advantage clearly lay with Nixon. He was far better known to the American people because of his active role in Eisenhower's administration, and he used this role to make his point that he was better qualified for presidential leadership than Kennedy, Eisenhower's quip notwithstanding. September public opinion polls gave Nixon the lead. The election appeared to be Nixon's to lose.

Kennedy's religious affiliation was an important campaign issue, and he met his detractors forthrightly. He clearly stated his views: there was nothing in his religion that would prevent him from obeying his constitutional oath and governing the nation; he supported the First Amendment's separation of church and state; he opposed federal aid to parochial schools; and he favored birth control. He appeared before a gathering of prominent Protestant leaders in Houston, and he told the ministers, "I am not the Catholic candidate for president, I am the Democratic party's candidate for president, who also happens to be a Catholic." As he neared the end of his short speech, he told the assembled divines:

> If this election is decided on the basis that 40 million Americans lost their chance of being president on the day they were baptized, then it is the whole nation that will be the loser in the eyes of history, and in the eyes of our own people.[1]

Kennedy won his audience. When he finished, the ministers gave him a warm, standing ovation. His performance could not remove anti-Catholicism from the campaign, but it defused the religious issue and freed Kennedy to concentrate on attacking Nixon and the Republican record.

The highlight of the campaign occurred when the candidates staged four nationally televised debates between September 26 and October 21. They were the first televised debates between presidential candidates, and they reflected the growing influence that television was now playing in the nation's political life. The first debate was decisive, and Kennedy won it. Nixon looked haggard; he was weakened by a knee infection and tired from a long day of campaigning. He was victimized by a poor makeup job that did not hide his dark stubble. On camera, under hot lights, the makeup powder streaked as Nixon sweated noticeably. He faltered in answering some of the questions. Kennedy, in contrast, was fresh and primed for the encounter. He had rested that day, pouring over his notes like a college student cramming for an examination. He exuded cool, cheerful confidence, dis-

---

[1]Quoted in Herbert Parmet, *JFK: The Presidency of John F. Kennedy* (New York: Penguin Books, 1984) p. 31.

played a sure grasp of the issues, an agile intelligence, and a sharp wit; Kennedy dispelled any lingering doubts about his maturity or ability to be president. Nixon did much better in the three subsequent debates and had a slight advantage overall, but he could not completely overcome the disadvantage of his appearance and performance during that crucial first debate.

In none of the televised debates did the candidates explore issues in depth, and no clear issue distinctions between them surfaced. The debates were essentially popularity contests, whose outcomes depended on the cosmetic factors of personality and appearance. Kennedy won the one that counted most. October polls showed him taking the lead for the first time. In the final month of campaigning, Kennedy attracted large, excited crowds. He appeared along a beach in Southern California and was mobbed by excited followers who were behaving like rock 'n' roll or movie star fans. Kennedy had momentum, and the Democrats could smell victory.

But in the final week of the campaign, the Republicans almost pulled it out. Nixon strongly defended the Eisenhower record and hammered away at Kennedy's inexperience in international affairs. Republicans staged a media blitz across the nation. Eisenhower entered the fray. He campaigned energetically for Nixon in those final days. On Election Day, Ike went on national television to exhort the American people to elect Nixon and to reject Kennedy. The old campaigner nearly eliminated Jack's lead.

Kennedy's 303 to 219 edge in electoral votes masked the closest presidential election in American history. In some states, the outcome was in doubt for days. Kennedy, by nar-

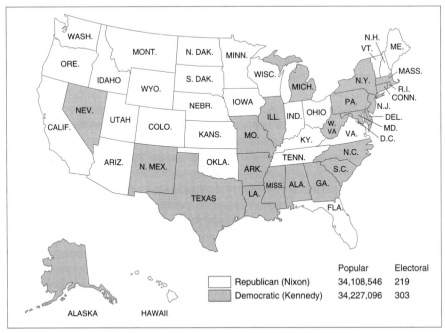

		Popular	Electoral
☐	Republican (Nixon)	34,108,546	219
▨	Democratic (Kennedy)	34,227,096	303

Figure 6.1   The election of 1960.   *Source:* Public Domain map.

rowly winning populous states such as New York, Pennsylvania, Michigan, and Texas, squeezed out victory. The close, exciting contest between two able candidates brought out 64 percent of the electorate, the highest since 1920. Out of a record 68 million votes cast, Kennedy's margin of victory was 118,574. Kennedy received 49.7 percent of the popular vote to Nixon's 49.5 percent. In congressional elections, Republicans picked up twenty-two seats in the House and two seats in the Senate, leaving the Democrats with large majorities in both. Most Democratic candidates ran better than Kennedy. His party was more popular than he. There were no presidential coattails in 1960.

It is impossible to say precisely what factor determined Kennedy's hairline victory. In such a close election, many variables could have determined the outcome, and there are too many imponderables involved. Suppose Eisenhower had entered the campaign a week earlier? Kennedy's religious affiliation cut both ways: in rural Protestant areas of the South, Southwest, and West, it cost him votes, but in Northeastern, Midwestern, and Western urban states, it gained him votes. On balance, he may have gained more votes than he lost because of his religion, for the states where people voted for him because of his religious affiliation contained the largest clusters of electoral votes. Kennedy benefited from the televised debates, particularly the first. A poll showed that 57 percent of voters felt that the debates had affected their choice, and of these, 75 percent voted for Kennedy. Kennedy himself said, "It was TV more than anything else which won it." The winner also ran well among black voters, getting more of them than Stevenson had in 1956. Kennedy had followed a bold strategy during the campaign of relying on Johnson to hold white Southerners while he appealed for black voters. He responded to an appeal to help Dr. Martin Luther King Jr. gain release from a Georgia jail, where his wife feared he would be killed. Kennedy also promised to sign an executive order forbidding segregation in federally subsidized housing. Black votes provided his winning margin in Texas and North Carolina, and he received most of the Northern black inner-city vote.

The 1960 election signaled the end of the Solid South. Nixon received about half of the Southern vote in 1960. After the race, Nixon noted that if he had concentrated his efforts on the South in the final week, he might have won the election. He would put that knowledge to good use in his winning campaign of 1968. Kennedy did well in traditional Republican strongholds in New England, the Midwest, and the suburbs everywhere. Sectional, class, and party loyalties continued to erode. Many voters split their tickets in 1960. Millions of Republicans, many of them Catholics, voted for Kennedy. Millions of Democrats, mostly Protestants, voted for Nixon. The 1960 election further blurred the distinctions between the major parties and their candidates. The politics of consensus still prevailed.

THE KENNEDY STYLE

Kennedy's inauguration occurred on a clear, cold day in Washington on January 20, 1961. The inaugural ceremony vividly expressed the fresh start that his administration intended to make. Consciously emulating Franklin Roosevelt, who had roused the country from depression torpor in 1933, Kennedy intended to "get the country moving again." Black contralto Marian Anderson sang the national anthem. Poet Robert Frost read a work that he had written for the occasion. Kennedy's speech stirred the nation:

> Let the word go forth from this time and place, to friend and foe alike, that the torch has been passed to a new generation of Americans.[2]

He called for a global alliance against the common enemies of mankind, "tyranny, poverty, disease, and war itself." It was high noon in the Cold War, and Kennedy welcomed the challenge: "In the long history of the world, only a few generations have been granted the role of defending freedom in its hour of maximum danger. I do not shrink from this responsibility, I welcome it." He sent a warning to the Kremlin: "Let every nation know, whether it wishes us well or ill, that we shall pay any price, bear any burden, meet any hardship, support any friend, oppose any foe to assure the survival and the success of liberty." As he approached the end of his short (eleven minutes), splendid speech, he spoke his most famous line. He appealed to his countrymen, especially to young Americans, to:

> ask not what your country can do for you—ask what you can do for your country.[3]

The new administration accented youth, physical fitness, brains, action, and glamour. Kennedy and his beautiful young wife Jacqueline exuded stylish charm. Intellectuals were frequent visitors to the White House. Kennedy hosted a dinner for Nobel Prize winners. Distinguished musicians often performed at the White House. The Kennedys and their friends played touch football on the White House lawn, expressive of the youthful energy and exuberance characterizing the new government. One of Kennedy's earliest presidential acts was to create the President's Council on Physical Fitness to encourage schoolchildren, military personnel, and indeed all Americans to raise their levels of physical fitness, to "get in shape." Kennedy's salient presidential traits included energy, enthusiasm, confidence, and intelligence. His speeches, punctuated with apt quotations from a wide range of literary and historical sources, revealed a leader with unusual depth and learning. He was the author of two books. He represented himself as a man of action, comfortable in the world of ideas.

Kennedy believed in a strong, centralized presidency that operated free of the restraints of Congress, public opinion, and the media. He also believed that managerial competence was more important than dedication to a cause or commitment to dogma. He thought that the major problems he had inherited from the outgoing administration—a sluggish economy at home and Cold War crises abroad—stemmed from Eisenhower's failure to assert his power and to streamline the executive office for action. Kennedy was determined to energize the presidency. He would be at the center of action. The young leader told reporter Hugh Sidey of *Time* magazine that the main reason he had sought the presidency was so he could be on center stage, so he could be in the vortex of history.

Kennedy recruited his top advisers from a far wider talent pool than had his prede-

---

[2]Quoted in Arthur M. Schlesinger Jr., *A Thousand Days* (Greenwich, Conn.: Fawcett Publications, 1965), p. 16.

[3]Quoted in ibid., p. 14.

Figure 6.2   John and Jacqueline Kennedy. Photo by Peskin HY.
Source: FPG International LLC.

cessor, who had drawn most of his senior advisers from the world of business. Secretary of State Dean Rusk came from the Rockefeller Foundation. For Secretary of Defense, Kennedy chose Robert S. McNamara, the president of Ford Motor Company. McGeorge Bundy, an administrator from Harvard, was appointed National Security Adviser, managing foreign policy. Kennedy's talented young staffer who had served with him in the Senate, Theodore Sorensen, took charge of domestic issues and wrote many of his speeches. Kennedy's younger brother Robert became Attorney General. When critics complained that "Bobby" was too young and inexperienced for the job, the president quipped, "I thought my brother might as well get some experience before beginning the practice of law." He appointed several Republicans to be his top advisers and administrators, among them McNamara and Bundy, to try to reassure the business community that his administration would not be antibusiness nor inflationary spenders.

THE COLD WARRIOR

Kennedy gave top priority to the conduct of American foreign and military policy that centered on America's global rivalry with the Soviets. His administration sought to contain the Soviet Union and prevent revolutionary change in the Third World. Cold War ideology shaped Kennedy's view of the world. He viewed the Communist system itself as the Free World's main enemy:

> . . . implacable, insatiable, unceasing in its drive for world domination. For this is not a struggle for supremacy of arms alone—it is also a struggle for supremacy between two conflicting ideologies: Freedom under God versus ruthless, godless tyranny.[4]

Kennedy and his advisers made their major foreign policy goal the development of policies and means to restore American primacy in world affairs. They would reverse the decline that they believed had occurred under the cautious leadership of Eisenhower. They viewed the Third World as the primary arena and the key to winning the Cold War. It was among the underdeveloped countries of Asia, Africa, and Latin America where the battle against Communism would be joined and won. Kennedy told an audience at the University of California in Berkeley that "freedom and diversity," the essence of the American way, would prevail in the "lands of the rising people" over the Communist monolith. He had a bold vision, rooted in a deep faith in the American system, confident that American technology and expertise could prevail in the long, twilight struggle with the Soviet menace.

THE BAY OF PIGS

The new administration encountered its first Cold War crisis in Cuba. Kennedy no more than his predecessor could tolerate the existence of a Communist state in the Caribbean that expropriated American property, developed close ties with the Soviet Union, and tried to foment revolution throughout Latin America. The CIA project to overthrow Castro, begun by Eisenhower six months earlier, readied for action. Anti-Castro Cuban exiles, many of them former liberal supporters of the Cuban dictator, had been trained for an amphibious assault on Cuba at a secret camp set up in the Guatemalan Mountains. CIA officials believed that an invasion of Cuba would activate a general uprising within Cuba that would overthrow Castro. Kennedy, after consultations with senior advisers, all of whom assured him that the planned invasion would succeed, gave the operation the green light. The invasion would be risky, but Kennedy and his New Frontiersmen were eager to strike the Communists.

About 1,450 invaders, debarking from a Nicaraguan port in ships provided by the CIA, landed before dawn at the Bay of Pigs, a remote area on the southern Cuban coast. Castro quickly deployed his army to meet them. Cuban gunners sank many of the landing craft. Attackers who made it ashore were hit by tanks and tactical aircraft. Lacking adequate

---

[4]Quoted in Herbert Parmet, *Jack: The Struggles of John F. Kennedy* (New York: Dial Press, 1980), p. 301.

artillery support and air cover, the invaders were quickly overwhelmed. Within three days, the Cuban Army had captured 1,189 of the invaders and killed 114. (About 150 were able to escape.) The invaders never made contact with Cuban underground elements, and the expected anti-Castro uprising never occurred.

The Bay of Pigs disaster humiliated the Kennedy administration. The United States' European allies sharply criticized its actions, and Third World spokesmen took turns condemning the United States at the United Nations. Within the United States, liberals attacked Kennedy for undertaking the invasion, and conservatives condemned him for failing to overthrow Castro. The United States stood before the world exposed as both imperialistic and inept, a pathetic combination of wickedness and weakness.

The U.S.-backed invasion had violated the OAS's charter that prohibited any Western Hemispheric nation from intervening in another's affairs. Latin American nations, resenting the thinly disguised American reversion to gunboat diplomacy, refused the U.S. request to quarantine Cuba from inter-American affairs. Castro and Khrushchev enjoyed a propaganda harvest. Both Soviet aid to Cuba and the pace of Cuban socialization accelerated in the aftermath of the failed invasion.

The invasion project had been ill conceived and mismanaged from the start. The CIA victimized itself with faulty intelligence data and wishful thinking. It underestimated Castro's military strength and exaggerated the extent of anti-Castro sentiment in Cuba. Kennedy ensured the mission's failure when he curtailed CIA air strikes preceding the landings and then refused all requests for naval air support as Castro's forces overwhelmed the invaders. Kennedy had concluded that the invasion had failed within the first twenty-four hours and that air cover could not save it, so he decided to cut his losses. He also did not want a war with Cuba, and he tried to preserve the fiction that the invasion was an all-Cuban affair.

Kennedy received a rough baptism of fire and his first serious criticism as president. He assumed full responsibility for the fiasco, but afterward he ordered an investigation of the CIA. He forced its aging director, Allen Dulles, who had assured him that the Bay of Pigs operation would succeed, into retirement, and he replaced him with John McCone, a conservative California oilman. Kennedy also made an aggressive speech before a convention of newspaper editors in which he made it clear that he remained determined to get rid of Castro despite the spectacular failure of the invasion.

According to the findings of a special Senate investigating committee that later examined CIA covert operations, Kennedy ordered the CIA to eliminate Castro following the failure of the Bay of Pigs invasion. Robert Kennedy took charge of Operation Mongoose, which included efforts to disrupt the Cuban economy and to support anti-Castro elements. During 1961 and 1962, CIA operatives tried various schemes to kill the Cuban dictator. These efforts included cigars laced with explosives and deadly poison and an attempt to spear him with a harpoon while he was snorkeling at a Caribbean resort. CIA agents even plotted with Mafia elements to get rid of Castro, but they had to abandon the project because of opposition from FBI Director J. Edgar Hoover. Castro knew about Operation Mongoose and was aware of some of the CIA plots to assassinate him. He appealed to his allies in Moscow for help. The Soviets responded by sending troops. Later they would try to station nuclear-capable, intermediate-range missiles in Cuba, which provoked the most dangerous crisis of the Cold War.

THE THIRD WORLD

During his campaign for the presidency, Kennedy had repeatedly criticized the Eisenhower administration for failing to promote economic development and the growth of political democracy among the nations of Latin America, Asia, and Africa. He insisted that such neglect had given the Soviet Union opportunities to get ahead of the United States in the race for influence among the strategically important developing nations of the Third World. Kennedy pledged to help these nations modernize their societies and restore American influence among them.

For Latin America, the Kennedy administration developed a multifaceted assistance program called the Alliance for Progress. Kennedy proposed the alliance in a dramatic speech given in Mexico City in May 1961. The alliance built upon and expanded Eisenhower's previously announced aid program for Latin America. Congress appropriated $500 million to start the program, which was designed to eradicate poverty and social injustice in the Western Hemisphere. Over the life of the program, billions of dollars in loans and grants from both public and private sources were fed into the Alliance for Progress. In most Latin American countries, the results were disappointing. Conservative governments refused to reform their tax systems, grant land reform, or democratize their politics. Economic growth was sluggish throughout the 1960s in the region. Unemployment rates, mortality rates, literacy rates, and levels of education did not improve in most Latin American countries. Perhaps the elite classes who held power in these lands feared Castroism as much as Kennedy, but they preferred to rely on repression rather than take their chances with social reform. If the Alliance for Progress could have succeeded, it would have required far more funds than were made available, and mechanisms would have to have been created to bypass the governing elites and get money directly to the poor people most in need.

In the summer of 1961, the Kennedy administration launched the Peace Corps, a much more successful initiative to help people in Third World countries. The Peace Corps derived from the same Cold War concern to involve the United States more directly in Third World countries and to give idealistic young Americans an opportunity for public service. Over the next two years, about 7,500 mostly young Peace Corps volunteers were sent to forty-four nations in Asia, Africa, and Latin America. Most worked as teachers; others found jobs in health care, agricultural reform, and community development. For many of the young people who served in the Peace Corps, they not only found an opportunity to help poor people, but they also returned to America with a greater appreciation of the diversity of the world's cultures. Most recipients of Peace Corps assistance were grateful and admired the young Americans they got to know.

Although Africa remained a relatively low priority for the Kennedy administration, the United States did intervene in Zaire, formerly the Belgian Congo, in 1961, to support an anti-Communist leader as head of the government. The CIA maneuvered to block more radical candidates whom Washington feared might have the backing of the Soviet Union from coming to power. Amidst chaotic conditions, civil war broke out. The United States pulled out. Washington then backed a successful United Nations effort to end the civil war and to prevent Zaire from disintegrating.

BERLIN

At the beginning of his presidency, Kennedy and Secretary of Defense McNamara began a crash program to expand and diversify America's military forces. They believed that Eisenhower's reliance on massive retaliation and his refusal to engage the Soviets in a missile race had set dangerous limits on the American ability to counter Soviet-backed insurgencies in Third World countries. The United States rapidly increased its strategic nuclear forces, which included ICBMs, missile-launching Polaris submarines, and long-range bombers. They also built up conventional war capabilities, adding a Kennedy favorite, counterinsurgency forces. The president sought strategic versatility, which he termed "flexible response"—the ability to intervene anywhere in the world with flexible force levels in response to Soviet or Soviet-backed initiatives.

The Kennedy military buildup had broad bipartisan congressional and popular support. At the same time the United States expanded its military capacities, Kennedy repeatedly urged the Soviets to join in arms limitation talks aimed at reducing the arms race. But Khrushchev responded by increasing Soviet military spending for more ICBMs, the backbone of the Soviet strategic system. The American arms buildup had triggered another upward spiral in the nuclear arms race.

Having been burned badly by the Bay of Pigs fiasco, Kennedy was more determined than ever to respond strongly to Communist threats. He worried lest his administration appear weak willed and lose prestige in the eyes of the world and its own people. Three months after the invasion, he met for a series of private talks with Khrushchev in Vienna in June 1961. The two leaders exchanged views on a wide range of issues and used the occasion to size each other up. Kennedy was calm, rational, and polite in these conversations. Khrushchev's moods varied. At times he talked warmly of peaceful coexistence between Communism and capitalism. At other times he became angry, even threatening. He turned into an ideologue, asserting the inevitable triumph of socialism in the world. He bullied the young president, coming away from these meetings with the mistaken impression that Kennedy could be pressured. Khrushchev misread Kennedy's civility as weakness. His misjudgment would later contribute to the most dangerous moment in modern history.

The major issue discussed in Vienna was the long-standing problem of Berlin. The German question had never been formally settled after World War II because of Cold War conflicts. At war's end, Germany had been divided into occupation zones by the victorious nations. In 1948 and 1949, the Western zones were merged into one zone, which became the Federal Republic of Germany (West Germany), a Western liberal state. The Soviet zone in Eastern Germany became the Socialist Democratic Republic of Germany (East Germany), on which the Soviets imposed a Communist system. By 1950, there existed two de facto German states. Neither state accepted the other as legitimate, but most Germans clung to the hope that someday Germany would again be a unified nation.

Berlin, lying deep within East Germany, also remained divided between East and West, causing periodic crises during the Cold War. Tensions had flared in 1948, when the Soviets had tried to drive the Western nations out of Berlin and Truman had thwarted them with the Berlin Airlift. Khrushchev had pressured Eisenhower in 1958 about Berlin and then backed off when Ike stood firm. Now, with Kennedy in office, the Soviet leader pressed for a peace treaty between the two German states that would legitimate the de facto division of the country, remove the possibility of reunion, and deprive the West of any legal basis for its occupation of West Berlin. Khrushchev told Kennedy that he wanted the Berlin issue settled by year's end; if it was not settled, he threatened to conclude a separate peace treaty with East Germany, forcing the West to negotiate with a government that none of the Western states recognized. Khrushchev and the East German rulers also wanted to stop the flow of East Germans into West Berlin. Thousands of East Germans fled poverty and tyranny each month to enter free and prosperous West Germany through West Berlin.

Kennedy rebuffed Khrushchev's proposals and reaffirmed the Western presence in West Berlin. Kennedy told the American people on July 25: "We cannot and will not permit the Communists to drive us out of Berlin." He also asked Congress to increase military appropriations by $3 billion, tripled draft calls, called up reserves, and extended enlistments of military personnel on active duty. He also asked for $207 million from Congress to expand civil defense fallout shelters, dramatizing the terrifying implications of the Berlin crisis.

The Soviet response came on August 13, when East German workers suddenly erected a concrete, barbed wire wall across Berlin, imprisoning East Germans in their own country and stanching the flow of refugees into West Berlin. Before the wall, nearly 3 million East Germans had escaped to the West since 1945. During the first twelve days of August 1961, about 46,000 had fled Communism. The Soviet action caught the Americans by complete surprise. Some of Kennedy's hawkish advisers urged him to tear down the wall. Kennedy never considered doing that, because he did not want to risk war. To reassure West Berliners that accepting the wall did not presage eventual Allied withdrawal from the divided city, Kennedy sent an additional 1,500 combat troops to West Berlin. In June 1963, he visited West Berlin and told a huge crowd, "Ich bin ein Berliner" ("I am a Berliner") to dramatize the United States' determination to stay.

Months of tension followed the building of the Berlin Wall. East Germans tried to escape over the barrier and were shot by East German military police. The Berlin Wall quickly became a potent Cold War symbol of the impasse between East and West, and of the division of Germany and its major city. It also was a stark admission of Communism's failure to win the hearts and minds of East Germans.

But the Wall also provided a practical solution to the Berlin question. It stopped the flow of refugees, which was Khrushchev's immediate goal, and it allowed West Berlin to remain in the Western orbit, which was Kennedy's main goal. German reunification was deferred to the indefinite future. Khrushchev announced in October that he would no longer insist on Western withdrawal from West Berlin. The crisis ended, and Berlin was never again a major source of Cold War conflict. But the Wall endured for nearly thirty years as the most vivid symbol of European Cold War divisions—until the people of East Germany themselves breached the wall in November 1989 as they began the process of dismantling the Communist system imposed on them after World War II.

THE MISSILE CRISIS

Following the Bay of Pigs, the Soviets sent soldiers and weapons to Cuba to protect that Communist satellite from U.S. hostility. By the summer of 1962, U.S. intelligence sources estimated that there were from 10,000 to 40,000 Soviet troops stationed in Cuba. Castro also supported guerrilla actions and subversion in other Latin American countries. Republicans, looking for election-year issues, attacked the Kennedy administration for allowing the Soviet arms buildup in Cuba. Kennedy opposed attacking or invading Cuba as long as the Soviets placed only defensive weapons in Cuba that posed no threat to the United States or any other hemispheric nation. But Khrushchev and Castro decided on a daring move to deter any further U.S. action against Cuba and to score a Cold War coup. The Soviet Union secretly tried to install medium-range and intermediate-range nuclear missiles and bombers in Cuba. These missiles and bombers were offensive weapons capable of carrying nuclear payloads to U.S. cities and military installations.

On October 14, 1962, a U-2 reconnaissance plane photographed a launching site for an intermediate-range missile nearing completion in western Cuba. Kennedy immediately determined that the missiles and bombers must be removed from the island. His sense of strategic and political reality told him that they had to go. But how to get the missiles out of Cuba? How without triggering a nuclear war? The most dangerous Cold War crisis ever had begun.

Kennedy convened a special executive committee consisting of thirteen senior advisers to find a way to remove the missiles and planes. The committee met secretly for the

Figure 6.3   Medium-range ballistic missile base in Cuba. The United States detected Soviet efforts to install missiles in Cuba when reconnaissance aircraft photographed missile bases under construction on the island. Here is an example of the photographic evidence shown to President Kennedy in October 1962. *Source:* U.S. Air Force.

next twelve days. Their assignment was to propose tactics that would force the Soviets to remove the missiles from Cuba without igniting World War III. The president's brother and closest adviser, Robert, chaired the committee sessions.

Beginning with their initial session, all members of the committee agreed that the missiles had to be removed, but they disagreed on tactics. Some members, led by the chairman of the Joint Chiefs of Staff, Army General Maxwell Taylor, wanted to take the missile sites out with surprise air strikes that were likely to kill both Soviet technicians and Cuban soldiers. Robert Kennedy, who proved to be the most influential member of the executive committee, rejected that idea, saying he wanted "no Pearl Harbors on his brother's record." The Taylor-led faction then proposed an invasion to get rid of both the offensive weapons and the Castro regime. The president rejected this suggestion as being too risky; it could involve a prolonged war with Cuba, provoke a Soviet attack on West Berlin, or even bring nuclear war. Secretary of Defense McNamara proposed a naval blockade to prevent further shipments of weapons to Cuba. The blockade would allow both sides some freedom of maneuver. The United States could decide to attack or negotiate later, depending on the Soviet response to the blockade. A majority of the committee members endorsed McNamara's proposal. The president accepted the blockade tactic.

President Kennedy attended few of the committee sessions, and when he did attend, he said little to allow free deliberations by the committee members. With the 1962 midterm elections only three weeks away, he was on the campaign trail, acting as though everything was normal. He campaigned mostly about domestic issues, trying to build support for his New Frontier reform programs that were stalled in Congress. Neither the media nor the public had any inkling of the serious crisis that was building. The Soviets did not know that the missile sites had been detected, nor that Kennedy and the Executive Committee were planning the U.S. response.

On Monday morning, October 22, the blockade began. That evening, Kennedy went on television to inform the nation and the Soviets about the missile crisis. He bluntly told his audience around the world; "unmistakable evidence has established the fact that a series of offensive missile sites is now in preparation on that imprisoned island." He spoke of the naval blockade, which he called a "quarantine," that was in place around Cuba. He demanded that the Soviets dismantle and remove all missile bases and bombers from Cuba immediately, and he stated that the quarantine would remain in place until all offensive weapons had been removed. Then he spoke these chilling words:

> It shall be the policy of this nation to regard any nuclear missile launched from Cuba against any nation in the Western Hemisphere as an attack by the Soviet Union on the United States, requiring a full retaliatory response upon the Soviet Union.[5]

Kennedy confronted Khrushchev with the risk of nuclear war if he did not remove the missiles. For the next five days, the world hovered at the brink of catastrophe. Khrushchev denounced the United States and denied that he was installing offensive weapons in Cuba. Meanwhile, work on the missile sites continued. The first sites would be operational

---

[5]Quoted in Elie Abel, *The Missile Crisis* (New York: Bantam Books, 1966), p. 106.

in a few days. The Air Force prepared strikes to take them out before they could be used to fire missiles at targets in the United States. Soviet merchant ships hauling more weapons continued to steam toward Cuba. The U.S. Navy positioned its blockade fleet to intercept them. American invasion forces gathered in Florida. B-52 strategic bombers took to the air with nuclear bombs on board. U.S. strategic missiles went to maximum alert. The moment of supreme danger would come if a Soviet ship tried to run the blockade, for American ship commanders had orders to stop them.

The first break came on October 24. Soviet ships hauling offensive weapons turned back. Two other Soviet freighters, hauling no offensive weapons, submitted to searches and were permitted to steam on to Cuba. Two days later, Khrushchev sent a letter to President Kennedy offering to remove all offensive weapons from Cuba in exchange for a U.S. pledge not to invade Cuba. Kennedy accepted the offer, but before he could send his reply, Khrushchev sent a second letter raising the stakes: America would have to give a no-invasion of Cuba pledge plus remove its Jupiter missiles that were stationed in Turkey, which were targeted at the Soviet Union. Kennedy refused to bargain. It was his view that Khrushchev's reckless initiative had threatened world peace, and it was the Soviet leader's responsibility to remove the missiles from Cuba quickly.

As the point of no return neared, Kennedy, heeding the advice of his brother, made one last try to avoid the looming cataclysm. The president sent a cable to Khrushchev accepting the offer in the first letter and ignoring the second letter. The next night, on October 27, Robert Kennedy met with the Soviet ambassador to the United States, Anatoly Dobrynin, to warn him that the United States had to have "a commitment by tomorrow that those bases would be removed." He told Dobrynin this was the Soviets' last chance to avoid war: if the Soviets "did not remove those bases, we would remove them." He also indicated to Dobrynin that the American missiles in Turkey, although not part of any quid pro quo, would be removed soon after the Cuban missiles were removed.

While these tense negotiations were in progress, a U-2 spy plane was shot down over Cuba and the pilot, U.S. Air Force Major Rudolph Anderson, was killed. Angry hawks on the executive committee wanted to launch air strikes and invade Cuba, not only to destroy the missile sites but to overthrow Castro's regime and send the Soviet troops back home. Robert Kennedy, McNamara, and others restrained them, pleading that a few more days were needed to allow the president to work out a diplomatic solution to the crisis.

U.S. officials learned years later that their restraint may have avoided nuclear war with the Soviet Union. Unbeknownst to Washington at the time, the Soviet field commander in Cuba had six tactical nuclear surface-to-surface missiles in his arsenal. He is on record as having stated that if the Americans had invaded, he would have used the nuclear missiles on them. Secretary of Defense McNamara has stated that if any American troops had been killed by Soviet nuclear missiles, "It is a 100 percent certainty" that the United States would have retaliated with their own nuclear weapons.

The next morning, on October 28, Khrushchev agreed to remove the missiles and bombers in return for the president's promise not to invade Cuba. He claimed that he had achieved his goal of protecting Cuba from American attacks. The United States suspended its blockade. The United Nations supervised the dismantling and removal of the Cuban bases. American missiles were removed from Turkey a few weeks later. The missile crisis had been resolved, without war. Kennedy received high praise for his actions. The Democrats gained in the fall elections. Kennedy's standing in the polls soared to new heights. Americans, who had been on the defensive in the Cold War for years, were elated. National pride soared, along with Kennedy's popularity. America had stood up to the Soviets and had forced them to back down.

Although Kennedy was showered with praise for his handling of the missile crisis, it proved humiliating to Khrushchev. The Russian leader fell from power within a year, and his actions during the crisis contributed to his demise. The missile crisis had exposed the Soviets as strategic inferiors to the Americans. An angry Soviet official told his American counterpart, "Never will we be caught like this again." The Soviets embarked on a crash program to expand their navy and to bring their missile forces up to parity with the United States.

Foreign policy analysts have raised serious questions about the missile crisis. Why had Khrushchev tried to put the missiles in Cuba? Had he really believed that Washington would acquiesce in the stationing of nuclear missiles ninety miles from U.S. territory? Surely Khrushchev and his colleagues on the Politburo would not expose the Soviet Union to nuclear obliteration just to protect Castro's regime. Historians who have examined documents found in Soviet archives recently made accessible to Western scholars state that what Khrushchev hoped to achieve by placing the missiles on Cuban soil was to use them as bargaining chips. He would offer to withdraw them in exchange for U.S. concessions on Berlin. He hoped to extract a German peace treaty from the West and possibly an Allied withdrawal from Berlin.

This ploy was blocked by the discovery of the missile sites on October 14 and Kennedy's proclamation of a "quarantine" on Cuba, effective October 22. Khrushchev had not anticipated Kennedy's strong response, having previously sized him up as being weak under pressure. Kennedy's behavior in previous crises had fed Khrushchev's suspicions that he lacked courage. From Krushchev's vantage point, it appeared that during the Bay of Pigs invasion, Kennedy had backed off from a war with Cuba, let the invasion fail, and allowed Castro to consolidate a Communist revolution right in the United States' backyard. He had let the Berlin Wall stand rather than risk a confrontation with the Soviets. These acts of restraint had sent the wrong signals to the adventurous Soviet ideologue. Khrushchev was not looking for a confrontation with the United States when he tried to put the missiles in Cuba, and he certainly did not want a war. He also may have been trying to appease Kremlin hawks and silence Chinese Communist criticisms that Soviet foreign policy was not doing enough to protect Third World countries from the ravages of U.S. imperialism.

The missile crisis forced both sides to tone down their Cold War rivalry. Khrushchev shifted back to emphasizing peaceful coexistence. Kennedy stressed the need for arms reductions. Direct communication, a "hot line," was established between Moscow and Washington so that the two leaders could talk to each other in time of crisis to reduce the chances of miscalculation and war. A mutual desire to control nuclear testing gave the two leaders an opportunity to improve relations.

President Kennedy, hoping to move arms negotiations forward, spoke at American University on June 10, 1963. He called upon Americans to reexamine their attitudes toward the Soviet Union and the Cold War. He called peace between the superpowers "the necessary end of rational men." He spoke of "making the world safe for diversity," conceding that every world problem did not require an American solution. Following the speech, he sent Undersecretary of State Averill Harriman to Moscow to negotiate an agreement. The Soviets proved eager to conclude a treaty. The agreement, signed on July 25, banned all atmospheric and underwater testing of nuclear weapons. The Senate promptly ratified the treaty. The Nuclear Test Ban Treaty was the first agreement that imposed a measure of control on the nuclear arms race. Soon after signing the treaty, the United States and the Soviet Union concluded an agreement for Soviet purchases of U.S. wheat. A year after the showdown in Cuba, Americans and Soviets enjoyed friendlier relations than at any other time since World War II.

VIETNAM: RAISING THE STAKES

Throughout the Kennedy years, the United States continued its involvement in Indochina. The president first turned his attention in that region to Laos, which had been the scene of conflict for years. Neutral under the terms of the 1954 Geneva Accords, Laos was engulfed in a three-way civil war among pro-Western, pro-Communist, and neutralist forces. Kennedy, inheriting the conflict from Eisenhower, sought a political solution involving the Soviets that guaranteed a "neutral and independent Laos." Another Geneva conference worked out a settlement. On June 12, 1961, the leaders of the three Laotian factions formed a neutralist coalition government. But in South Vietnam, Kennedy significantly escalated U.S. involvement in response to the Communists' stepped-up efforts to topple the American-backed government of Ngo Dinh Diem.

Kennedy viewed the civil war in South Vietnam as a crucial part of the global Cold War struggle between the United States and Soviet Union. Ironically, Kennedy, when he had been a senator, often criticized the Eisenhower administration's Third World foreign policy for failing to understand the powerful appeal of nationalism in countries emerging from long periods of colonial domination by Western imperial powers. Kennedy had criticized American backing of French efforts to reimpose colonialism in Indochina by suppressing a Nationalist revolution. But as president, Kennedy apparently failed to understand that Ho Chi Minh, although a Communist revolutionary ideologue, for millions of Vietnamese personified their nationalism and their desire to be free of all Western domination. He also did not understand that millions of Vietnamese citizens viewed the U.S. presence in Vietnam supporting Diem as a continuation of Western imperialism. Kennedy also applied the domino theory to Vietnam:

> Vietnam represents the cornerstone of the Free World in Southeast Asia, . . . Burma, Thailand, India, Japan, the Philippines and obviously, Laos and Cambodia are among those whose security would be threatened if the Red tide of communism overflowed into Vietnam.[6]

Kennedy and his leading foreign policy advisers all shared with Eisenhower and Truman the ideological fundaments of the Cold War. They believed that it was imperative to

---

[6]Quoted in George C. Herring, *America's Longest War,* 2d ed. (New York: Knopf, 1986), p. 43.

Figure 6.4   President Kennedy inherited the conflicts in Indochina from the Eisenhower administration. Here, at a press conference held in April 1961, he tells the American people about his policy for Laos, which was then engulfed in civil war.   *Source:* National Archives.

contain Communist expansionism in Southeast Asia. The legacy of McCarthyism also stalked the Democrats in power. Since the early 1950s, they had been politically vulnerable to charges that they were "soft on Communism," at home and abroad. Kennedy dared not appear irresolute in Southeast Asia, lest his administration suffer political reprisals at the hands of Republican critics in subsequent elections.

Further, the Kennedy team shared a faith in American power, technical expertise, and national goals. They believed that the Americans would succeed in southern Vietnam where the French had failed. To them, Vietnam furnished a bright opportunity for nation building. They believed that aid programs, military support, and the use of America's counterinsurgency forces would show the world that Moscow-backed wars of national liberation could not succeed. Kennedy also deployed the U.S. Army Special Forces, the Green Berets, in Southeast Asia. They represented a key component of the flexible response capability to counter Communist insurgencies in peripheral regions without risking confrontations with China or the Soviet Union. Kennedy believed that the Special Forces, using counterinsurgency techniques, would neutralize the Communist threat and win the hearts and minds of the Vietnamese people for Diem and the United States.

In 1961, there were about 600 U.S. military advisers in South Vietnam assisting Diem's forces. Kennedy sent Vice President Lyndon Johnson to Saigon to emphasize the American commitment to Diem and to assess his needs. Johnson called Diem "the Winston Churchill of Southeast Asia." Upon his return, Johnson advised Kennedy to increase American aid to South Vietnam. He told the president that the United States had to "help these countries to the best of our ability or throw in the towel and pull back our defenses to San Francisco." During the next eighteen months, Kennedy sent some 16,000 American troops to South Vietnam. Even though the soldiers went officially as advisers, some units occasionally engaged Viet Cong forces in combat.

Despite the huge increase in American support, Diemist forces were losing the civil war to the Viet Cong insurgents and their North Vietnamese backers in 1962 and 1963. U.S. officials tried to persuade Diem to implement social reforms, including land reform, and to curb his repressive police forces. Diem refused to do either. Diem's decline stemmed mainly from the inability of his military forces to fight effectively and his failure to win the loyalty of the peasants, who constituted 85 percent of the South Vietnamese population. At the "rice roots" level, Diem was losing the battle for hearts and minds.

Diem provoked a political crisis in June 1963 that led to his downfall when he ordered Buddhists to obey Catholic religious laws. When they refused and took to the streets of Hue to protest, Diem's police, led by his brother Nhu, brutally crushed their rebellion. In response to this repression, an elderly Buddhist monk immolated himself by fire at a busy intersection in downtown Saigon. Other monks followed suit as opposition to Diem's government mounted. Observing that Diem's political base had been reduced to family members and a few loyal generals and bureaucrats, and fearing that his army was losing the civil war, Washington decided that Diem had to go. On November 1, an army coup, acting with the foreknowledge and support of the CIA, overthrew Diem. U.S. officials backed a directorate of generals who formed a new government and continued the war. Three weeks later, Kennedy was assassinated.

At the time of Kennedy's death, U.S. Vietnam policy was in disarray, and his advisers were divided over what to do. Although he had increased the U.S. stake in Indochina significantly, Kennedy hinted that he might reappraise his commitment to South Vietnam because of Diem's political failures. In September 1963, Kennedy had attempted to warn Diem:

> I don't think that unless a greater effort is made to win popular support the war can be won out there. In the final analysis it is their war. They are the ones who have to win it or lose it.[7]

But in that same speech, Kennedy also reaffirmed the American commitment:

> For us to withdraw from that effort would mean a collapse not only of South Vietnam but Southeast Asia, . . . so we are going to stay there.[8]

Kennedy had inherited a deteriorating situation in Southeast Asia; his actions ensured that the United States would remain there a long time. Had Kennedy lived and been reelected in 1964, he probably would have reacted as Lyndon Johnson did in 1965 and committed the United States to war in Vietnam.

The pattern of Kennedy's foreign policy fitted that of an orthodox Cold Warrior striving to fulfill the extravagant rhetorical claims of his inaugural address. Undeniably,

---

[7]From a transcript of a televised interview with Walter Cronkite, broadcast on CBS News on September 2, 1963.

[8]Ibid.

Kennedy had the intelligence and the insight to see that the world was changing, that Third World independence movements were redrawing the map of the world. He also understood that the old bipolar world was being replaced by a more polycentric one. He understood that the American-Soviet rivalry had to be replaced by détente. But the main thrust of his foreign policies was to escalate the arms race, sustain a tense relation with the Soviet Union for most of his presidency, and, at one terrifying point, push the world perilously close to nuclear disaster. He built up the American presence in Vietnam, assuring the debacle that followed. In the summer of 1963, he improved relations with the Soviets, and the two powers signed a nuclear test ban treaty.

THE SPACE RACE

In mid-April 1961, at the time that the United States was being humiliated at the Bay of Pigs, a Soviet cosmonaut, Yuri Gagarin, became the first human to orbit the earth. Once again the Soviets boasted of their accomplishments in space technology; the rest of the world was impressed, and Americans were dismayed. Even though National Aeronautics and Space Administration (NASA) scientists assured the president that American space science was superior to Soviet efforts, it had been the popular perception in this country since *Sputnik* that the United States trailed the Soviets. Media editorialists fretted that the United States had fallen behind in the Cold War and was losing the ideological battle to the Soviets. Maybe the Soviets were right: the world would go to sleep under a Communist moon.

Not according to President Kennedy. He was determined to beat the Soviets in the space race; he also was determined to rally the American people to face a Cold War challenge that he believed America could win. He put Vice President Lyndon Johnson in charge of the Space Council and told him to do whatever had to be done to defeat the Soviets. Kennedy also persuaded Congress to vote for a large increase in NASA's budget to develop a space program "to put a man on the moon in ten years." He went before Congress in May 1961 to push the moon project:

> No single space project in this period will be more impressive to mankind or more important for the long-range exploration of space . . . than putting a man on the moon.[9]

To fulfill Kennedy's vision, NASA created the Apollo program. Soon, complexes of aerospace facilities mushroomed from Southern California to Texas to Florida. NASA employed thousands of technicians, engineers, and scientists. Private-sector subcontractors hired thousands more. Within five years, upwards of a half-million people were employed on the vast multibillion-dollar Apollo project.

As scientists worked toward the goal of putting a man on the moon, they also tried to match the Soviet Union's space achievements. Seven military test pilots were recruited for

[9]Quoted in Tom Wolfe, *The Right Stuff* (New York: Bantam Books, 1979), pp. 228–229.

**Figure 6.5   Three American heroes. Proj-
ect Mercury astronauts John Glenn (left),
Gus Grissom (center), and Alan Shepard
(right) are shown during their training for
manned space flights.**   *Source:* NASA
Headquarters.

Project MERCURY, and they became the nation's first astronauts. After months of rigorous
training, the astronauts readied for their flights. On May 5, 1961, a cocky, wise-cracking
Navy Commander, Alan B. Shepard Jr., strapped into a space capsule fastened to the nose
of an Army Redstone rocket, was fired from a launch pad at Cape Canaveral, Florida, into
a fifteen-minute suborbital flight 116 miles aloft. On February 20, 1962, nearly a year after the Soviets had put a man in space, Marine Colonel John H. Glenn Jr. was blasted into
orbit aboard his space capsule *Friendship 7*. During his five-hour flight, Glenn orbited the
earth three times. Americans were delighted by Glenn's remarkable achievement. Spirits
were lifted: maybe Americans could win the space race with the Soviets. Glenn made an attractive hero. He was a much-decorated jet fighter pilot from the Korean War, an All-American boy who grew up to become the first American to reach outer space. After his epic
flight, President Kennedy invited Glenn to the White House. Glenn also addressed a joint
session of Congress and later received a frenzied ticker tape parade down Manhattan's
famed Broadway. Following Glenn's flight, other astronauts rocketed into space and orbited
the earth. At the time of Kennedy's death, the American space program was gaining momentum, the seven MERCURY astronauts had all become national heroes, and Project APOLLO
was ahead of schedule.

SOCIAL REFORM

President Kennedy had more successes in the diplomatic arena than in the realm of domestic reform legislation. Although espousing liberal goals and calling for social justice for all Americans, he failed to persuade Congress to enact most of his ambitious New Frontier program of medical care for the elderly, tax reform, federal aid to education, housing reform, aid to cities, and immigration reform. His New Frontier program faced many political obstacles. In Congress, the bipartisan conservative coalition could block any effort to expand the welfare state and could often dilute measures designed to broaden existing programs. Kennedy's thin electoral victory in 1960 carried with it no mandate whatsoever for social reform. The Democrats had lost seats in both the House and the Senate.

Two years later, Kennedy tried to focus the 1962 midterm elections on New Frontier issues, but the dangerous Cuban missile crisis forced him to curtail his campaign efforts. The new Congress of 1962 was similar to its predecessor. Public opinion in the early 1960s reflected the complacency toward unsolved social problems that had been characteristic of the 1950s. Kennedy's efforts to make most Americans share his sense of urgency for social reform through televised speeches and remarks at press conferences failed. Most New Frontier proposals never made it it out of committee. The few that did were either defeated on the floor of the House or cleared Congress in diluted form.

Kennedy also failed to assert effective legislative leadership. Congress questioned the depth of his commitment to social reform, understanding that he gave higher priority to foreign policy, military matters, world trade, and strengthening the economy. In addition, Kennedy wanted to maintain bipartisan support for American foreign policy initiatives, and he was reluctant to strain the unity of Congress with divisive battles over reform measures. Kennedy was not given to rhetorical speeches and making excessive demands on Congress in the name of high-flown principles. He disliked using political muscle, and he disliked losing political battles. He could see that the votes simply were not there for many New Frontier measures, and he thought it was unreasonable to battle for a losing cause: "There is no sense in raising hell and not being successful."

A major defeat came early when Congress rejected Kennedy's $2.3 billion education bill. It foundered over the issue of federal aid to parochial schools. A Catholic himself, Kennedy knew that he would be accused of showing favoritism toward his co-religionists if he favored federal aid to Catholic schools. His bill excluded federal aid for private schools with a religious affiliation. He claimed that such aid would violate the First Amendment principle of separation of church and state. Opposition to the bill from the Catholic lobby was intense. The education bill never got out of the House Rules Committee. Members of Congress, observing that Kennedy had little leverage with its members, understood that they could go their own political ways on important White House measures without fear of reprisal. The failure of the education bill foreshadowed the defeat of the rest of the New Frontier agendum.

Although Kennedy failed to achieve his broad program of social reform, he scored some victories. Congress enacted an Area Redevelopment Act in 1961 to provide funds for economically depressed areas. The Manpower Retraining Act of 1962 provided $435 million over three years to train unemployed workers in new job skills. Congress raised the minimum wage from $1.00 to $1.25 per hour and extended coverage to 3.6 million more workers.

THE ECONOMY

When Kennedy took office, the American economy was stagnating, suffering from a lingering recession. The new president tried to work with the business community to restore prosperity. He consulted with several of his cabinet advisers recruited from the business world. He held meetings with corporate leaders to obtain their policy suggestions. He tried to reassure them that he was not a reckless spender nor a liberal ideologue, and that he was committed to a stable price structure. And he told them that the age of ideology had ended and the time had come for government, business, labor, and academic leaders to combine their expertise in seeking solutions to complex technical problems that afflicted the economy. Corporate leaders, apparently wedded to a Republican approach, refused their cooperation, angering the president. They insisted on blaming the Kennedy administration for all of their problems, and they rejected his technocratic approach to problem solving.

A major confrontation with business came in the spring of 1962. Earlier in the year, a strike in the steel industry had been averted when Secretary of Labor Arthur Goldberg had persuaded the steel workers to accept a modest pay increase that eliminated the need for a steel price rise. At the time, the president had praised both labor and management for their "industrial statesmanship." Ten days later, Roger Blough, the chief executive officer of United States Steel, announced that his company was raising the price of steel by six dollars a ton. Other major steel producers promptly announced identical increases.

Kennedy, feeling betrayed, denounced the steel companies. At a press conference, he said he was shocked that "a tiny handful of steel executives, can show such utter contempt for the interests of 185 million Americans." He promptly mobilized all of the considerable powers of the federal government to force the steel companies to rescind their price hikes. The Federal Trade Commission (FTC) announced that it would investigate the steel industry for possible price fixing. Robert Kennedy hinted that he might open antitrust proceedings against the steel industry. Secretary of Defense McNamara announced that the military would buy steel only from companies that had not raised their prices. Under an all-out assault from the White House, the steel companies quickly surrendered. U.S. Steel and the other companies canceled their price increases. Kennedy had won, and his was a popular victory. But he paid a political price for winning: the business community remained intensely hostile toward his administration.

Kennedy proposed innovative economic policies to end the business slump of the early 1960s. Aware that huge budget deficits during World War II had promoted prosperity, he reasoned that deficit financing also would work in peacetime. In June 1962, he proposed a deliberately unbalanced budget to promote economic growth. Six months later, he asked Congress to enact a $13.5 billion cut in corporate and personal income taxes over the next three years. The tax cuts, coupled with increases in spending for military and space programs already in place, would guarantee budget deficits. Kennedy insisted that these applied Keynesian economic strategies would generate capital spending that would stimulate economic growth, create new jobs, and provide increased tax revenues—all without rampant inflation. But Kennedy's tax bill never cleared Congress.

Even though Kennedy failed to get his new economic policy enacted, the economy recovered from recession in 1962 and 1963 and began an extended period of growth. Recovery mainly occurred because the Kennedy administration sharply increased military and aerospace spending. Kennedy's first defense budget called for spending $48 billion, a 20 percent increase over Eisenhower's final budget. Kennedy's foreign economic policies also contributed to the economic rebound of 1962 and 1963. Most of his foreign aid requests were approved, including increased spending for technical assistance and economic development for Third World countries. The Senate ratified a treaty in 1961, making the United States a member of the newly created Organization of Economic Cooperation and Development (OECD), made up of the United States, Canada, and eighteen European nations. Congress also enacted Kennedy's proposed Trade Expansion Act in 1962, his most important legislative victory, which established closer ties with European Common Market countries, America's most important trading partners. The Trade Expansion Act allowed the President to reduce tariffs on commodities in which the United States and European nations accounted for most of the world's trade. American overseas trade increased significantly during the years of Kennedy's presidency.

LET FREEDOM RING

During the 1960 presidential campaign, Kennedy came out strongly for civil rights to prevent Nixon's siphoning of African-American voters, but at the same time he also had sought the votes of Southern whites. His campaign rhetoric was bold: "If the president himself does not wage the struggle for equal rights, then the battle will inevitably be lost." He promised to issue an executive order ending racial segregation in federally funded housing. During the campaign, he helped get Dr. Martin Luther King Jr. released from jail. African Americans appreciated these gestures from the candidate and gave Kennedy a large black majority in 1960, which helped him win his narrow victory.

But Kennedy in office proved to be a cautious leader on civil rights for much of his presidency. He delayed introducing civil rights legislation, fearing that it would fail and also alienate Southern Democrats, whose votes he needed on other measures. He appointed some African Americans to federal offices, the first president to do so. Robert Weaver became head of the Housing and Home Finance Agency, and Thurgood Marshall became a circuit court judge. But Kennedy also appointed many segregationist judges to Southern courts, and he delayed issuing his promised housing desegregation order for nearly two years.

At the beginning of his administration, the official lead in civil rights was taken by the president's brother, Attorney General Robert Kennedy. The Justice Department worked to end discrimination in interstate transportation and supported the voting rights of African Americans in the South. President Kennedy believed that the best civil rights policy would be a gradual achievement of integration over the years, without disruption and violence. Dr. Martin Luther King Jr., the foremost civil rights leader, pointedly observed: "If tokenism were our goal, this administration has moved us adroitly towards its accomplishment."

But from the outset of his presidency, Kennedy had to respond to pressures created by civil rights activists and their segregationist foes. In the spring of 1961, the Congress of Racial Equality (CORE) sponsored "freedom rides." Groups of black and white travelers rode through the South deliberately entering segregated bus terminals and restaurants. Local mobs often attacked the "freedom riders." In Anniston, Alabama, the Greyhound bus in which one group had been riding was burned. In Mississippi, "freedom riders" were jailed en masse. Responding to the "freedom riders" and their violent encounters with segregationists, the Interstate Commerce Commission (ICC) ordered bus companies to desegregate all of their interstate routes and facilities. The companies complied, and black passengers soon began entering previously "whites-only" restaurants, waiting rooms, and restrooms. The Justice Department persuaded thirteen of the nation's fifteen segregated airports to desegregate and filed suit against the two holdouts.

The following year, Mississippi became a civil rights battleground. In September 1962, an African American Air Force veteran, James Meredith, attempted to enroll at the all-white University of Mississippi. Although he met their entrance requirements, university officials refused to admit him. Meredith then obtained a court order from Supreme Court Justice Hugo Black, enjoining the university to admit him, whereupon Mississippi Governor Ross Barnett personally intervened to prevent his enrolling. President Kennedy responded to Barnett's defiance of federal authority by sending federal marshals and troops to the university. They were met by a mob, who treated them as though they were foreign invaders. Violence ensued, in which vehicles were burned and destroyed. Tear gas covered the campus, and it took several thousand troops to restore order. During the mayhem, two men were killed and hundreds were injured.

Another confrontation occurred on Good Friday, on April 12, 1963, when Martin Luther King Jr. led a demonstration into the heart of white supremacy, Birmingham, Alabama, whose leaders boasted that it was the most segregated city in the South. Dr. King and his followers sought to end discrimination against African-American customers in shops and restaurants, and in employment and hiring policies. Their protests were nonviolent; the city's response was not. City officials declared that the marches violated city regulations against parading without a permit, which they had previously refused to grant to the protesters. During the next month, Birmingham police arrested over 2,000 African-American demonstrators, many of them schoolchildren. The police commissioner ordered his police to use high-pressure fire hoses, electric cattle prods, and police dogs to break up the demonstrations. Newspapers and television news broadcasts conveyed the brutal police assaults on African Americans to the nation, which watched in horror. King was jailed. During his stay in jail, he composed his famed "Letter from Birmingham Jail," an eloquent defense of the tactic of nonviolent civil disobedience.

The Justice Department intervened during the Birmingham demonstrations. Government officials and city leaders worked out an agreement calling for the desegregation of municipal facilities, the hiring of African Americans, and the creation of a biracial committee to keep the channels of communication open between the races. President Kennedy called the African-American quest for equal rights a "moral issue."

Figure 6.6   Dr. Martin Luther King Jr. led demonstrations into the heart of the segregated South—Birmingham, Alabama—in April 1963. Local authorities fought back hard. Here, firemen use high-pressure fire hoses to disperse civil rights demonstrators.   *Source:* AP/ Wide World photo.

A few months after the Birmingham encounter, two young African Americans, Vivian Malone and James Hood, tried to enroll at the University of Alabama. Governor George Wallace stood at the entrance to Carmichael Hall on the campus of the university. With television cameras rolling and over 200 reporters looking on, Wallace raised his hand and refused to allow the two black students to enter the building. Two hours later, the crisis was over. President Kennedy, hoping to avoid a replay of the Mississippi violence, federalized the Alabama National Guard. He confronted Wallace with an overwhelming show of force, using native Alabama white and black soldiers. Wallace stood in the doorway only long enough to have his picture taken for the papers and to ensure that his actions made the nightly TV news. He then stepped aside. Malone and Hood enrolled peacefully.

That night, June 11, 1963, President Kennedy gave the first civil rights speech ever delivered by a president. Part of his speech was extemporaneous, and he conveyed a sense of moral urgency, an emotional concern for civil rights:

> If an American, because his skin is black, cannot eat lunch in a restaurant open to the public; if he cannot send his children to the best public school available; if he cannot vote for the public officials who represent him; if, in short, he cannot enjoy the full and free life which all of us want, then who among us would be content to have the color of his skin changed and stand in his place?

One hundred years of delay have passed since President Lincoln freed the slaves, yet their heirs, their grandsons, are not fully free. They are not yet free from the bonds of injustice; they are not yet free from social and economic oppression. And this nation will not be fully free until all its citizens are free.[10]

A week later, the President, stating "the time has come for this nation to fulfill its promise," proposed the most comprehensive civil rights bill in American history. It called for the desegregation of all public accommodations, the protection of voting rights for African Americans, and the end of job discrimination. Congress did not show a similar enthusiasm and gave no indication that it would enact the measure any time soon.

To show support for the pending legislation, civil rights leaders organized a march on Washington. Over 200,000 people gathered in front of the Washington Monument on August 28. Black and white people joined in a peaceful, festive occasion. Adults chatted and sang songs. Children played, got lost, and were usually found. Dogs barked and chased Frisbees. The highlight of the gathering came when Dr. King, the leader of the growing civil rights movement, passionately affirmed his faith in the decency of man and in the ultimate victory for his cause:

I have a dream that one day this nation will rise up and live out the true meaning of its creed: We hold these truths to be self-evident; that all men are created equal. I have a dream that one day on the red hills of Georgia, the sons of former slaves and the sons of former slaveowners will be able to sit together at the table of brotherhood.[11]

The crowd was caught up in the power of his fervent rhetoric. Each time he shouted, "I have a dream," the massive crowd roared in support. Dr. King concluded his stirring speech with a magnificent peroration:

When we let freedom ring, when we let it ring from every village and every hamlet, from every state and every city, we will be able to speed up that day when all of God's children, black men and white men, Jews and Gentiles, Protestants and Catholics, will be able to join hands and sing in the words of the old Negro spiritual, "Free at last! Free at last! Thank God Almighty, we are free at last!"[12]

Immediately following the demonstration, Dr. King and other civil rights leaders met with President Kennedy. But Congress continued to stall; Southern Senators threatened to filibuster any civil rights bill to death. Three weeks after the march on Washington, Ku Klux Klan terrorists bombed an African American Sunday school in Birmingham, killing four little girls. Two months later, President Kennedy was assassinated, his civil rights legislation still pending. The South remained segregated; Dr. King's dream remained unrealized.

[10]From the transcript of Kennedy's televised speech over the three major networks on June 11, 1963.
[11]Quoted in Anthony Lewis, *Portrait of a Decade* (New York: Bantam Books, 1965), pp. 218–219.
[12]Ibid.

Figure 6.7   On August 28, 1963, supporters of the pending civil rights bill staged a march on Washington to show their support. Over 200,000 people rallied in front of the stately Washington Monument to sing songs and hear speeches.   *Source:* National Archives.

TRAGEDY IN DALLAS

In the fall of 1963, President Kennedy was giving much thought to next year's election. He traveled to Texas in late November to mend some political fences. With the help of Vice President Johnson, who accompanied him on that fateful rendezvous, he came to unify warring factions of Texas Democrats who had feuded over policies and patronage. Texas was a populous state with a large bloc of electoral votes that Kennedy and Johnson had carried narrowly in 1960 and hoped to win again in 1964. Kennedy arrived at the Dallas airport on the morning of November 22. Governor John Connally and his wife Nellie joined the president and his wife Jacqueline in an open-air limousine for the trip into the city. The presidential motorcade proceeded from the airport into downtown Dallas. The motorcade route had been published for days in the local papers to ensure a large turnout. Thousands of people lined the motorcade route, most of them smiling, waving, and cheering the president as he passed by. Kennedy responded warmly to their enthusiasm, waving, frequently flashing his million-dollar smile, and stopping the motorcade twice to shake hands with well-wishers.

At 12:30 P.M., the motorcade turned onto Elm Street and drove by the Texas Book depository building. At 12:33 P.M., three shots rang out. The president clutched his neck with

Figure 6.8   Dr. Martin Luther King Jr. delivered his most famous speech at the rally in front of the Washington Monument in August 1963. He inspired the huge crowd with his vision of one day achieving an integrated America: "I have a dream . . . "
Source: National Archives.

both hands and slumped downward. One bullet had passed through his throat and another struck the back of his head, blowing off part of his skull. Texas Governor John Connally, sitting beside the president, also had been hit. The president's limousine quickly pulled out of the motorcade and raced the mortally wounded leader to nearby Parkland Hospital, where, in its emergency room, Kennedy was pronounced dead at 1:00 P.M.

Within two hours of the shooting, police captured the apparent assassin, twenty-four-year-old Lee Harvey Oswald, who worked in the book depository building. Oswald was a drifter with a troubled, confused past. He had recently moved to Dallas after spending two years working in the Soviet Union. He had a wife Marina, a Russian woman whom he had met and married while living in the Soviet Union. He had previously served in the Marine Corps. He held Leftist political views and was a Marxist sympathizer. Earlier in the year, he had tried to go to Cuba, but the Cuban Embassy in Mexico City, after consultations with Soviet officials, had refused to grant Oswald a visa.

Aboard the presidential plane, still on the ground at Dallas's Love Airport, ninety-nine minutes after Kennedy's death, Lyndon B. Johnson was sworn in as the thirty-sixth president of the United States. The former president's widow, Jacqueline, stood at Johnson's side. Two days later, a Dallas nightclub owner, Jack Ruby, shot and killed Oswald at pointblank range in the basement of the Dallas police station in full view of a national television audience. Ruby's murder of Oswald eliminated the possibility of ever discerning Oswald's political beliefs, his motives for killing the president, and whether he was part of a conspiracy.

From the moment of Kennedy's death, many people doubted that Lee Harvey Oswald had acted alone. A public opinion poll, taken within a week of the president's murder, showed that only 29 percent of Americans believed that Oswald was a lone killer. Within two weeks of Kennedy's murder, President Johnson appointed a special commission, headed by Chief Justice Earl Warren, to investigate the assassination and to report its findings to the American people. Ten months later, the commission published its conclusion: "The Commission has found no evidence that anyone assisted Oswald in planning or carrying out the assassination."

The commission's findings failed to satisfy those who felt others had to be involved in a plot to murder the president. Critics undermined the credibility of the Warren Commission's analysis of evidence and its findings, which were seriously flawed and limited. Many people have proposed conspiracy theories to account for Kennedy's death, and millions of people have found them credible. These theories have implicated both pro- and anti-Castro Cubans, Leftists, Rightists, Texas oilmen, segregationists, Vietnamese, rogue elements within the Pentagon, the FBI and the CIA, the Mafia, the KGB, and even Lyndon Johnson. The few responsible journalists and scholars who believe that it is at least possible that a conspiracy was involved in the assassination of the President think that Cubans and elements within organized crime were involved.

The most important critique of the Warren Commission came in 1979, when a special congressional investigating committee released the results of a two-and-one-half year examination of the deaths of both President Kennedy and Dr. Martin Luther King Jr. Its key finding: "The scientific evidence available to the committee indicated that it is probable that more than one person was involved in the president's murder." But FBI experts demonstrated that the committee's evidence was flawed.

In all of the time that has passed since Kennedy's murder, no tangible evidence has been found that proves that the Warren Commission's conclusion was incorrect, despite its flawed and limited investigation of the murder. Nor has any evidence turned up that links any particular group to the assassination. If a group of conspirators killed the President, which is doubtful, their identities remain unknown and probably will never be known.

The persistence of the belief, especially among young people, that a conspiracy killed Kennedy, mainly represents an effort to make sense out of a horrific act that frightened Americans and shook their faith in the decency and viability of American political institutions. The notion that a sociopath, an utterly insignificant wretch acting alone, could bring down a great leader and wreak such havoc made the crime appear senseless and devoid of any political meaning. Novelist Norman Mailer has suggested that many Americans cling to conspiracies to explain the president's death because they cannot recognize the irrationality, the absurdity of some historical events. The belief that a great and good man had been destroyed by powerful evil forces lurking within the dark underside of the American political system made sense in a bleak, rueful sort of way to many people: the man was too good, therefore the evil "theys," who really run things in this country, indeed the world, had to get him.

In the years following Kennedy's death, Americans watched other leaders die at the hands of assassins—Malcolm X, Martin Luther King Jr., and Robert Kennedy. These assassinations reinforced a growing sense among Americans in the 1960s that they inhabited a violent, dangerous country where criminal conspirators thought nothing of snuffing out the lives of idealistic leaders. For many Americans, the age of innocence ended on November 22, 1963, and they have found it difficult to trust and support government leaders since then.

The young president's murder gouged a deep wound in the nation's psyche. People around the world wept openly at the horrid news. A weeping woman on a Moscow street grabbed an American reporter by the arm and shouted, "How could you let it happen? He was so young, so beautiful!" Explorers, hiking in a Colombian rain forest, came upon a little makeshift shrine honoring the murdered president's memory. A stricken nation watched numbly the solemn aftermath of the absurd tragedy. The president's body lay in state on the rotunda of the Capitol on the same catafalque that had held the body of Lincoln. Kennedy's funeral was held on November 25, on a clear, cold day in Washington. At St. Matthews Cathedral, Kennedy's friend, Richard Cardinal Cushing, archbishop of Boston, said the funeral Mass. The funeral train slowly wound its way past national monuments to Arlington Cemetery. There, on a grassy knoll overlooking the capital of the nation, John Fitzgerald Kennedy was buried. Adlai Stevenson, in a moving eulogy, observed that:

> Today we mourn him, tomorrow we shall miss him. . . . No one will ever know what this blazing political talent might have accomplished had he been permitted to live and labor long in the cause of freedom.[13]

THE LEGACY OF CAMELOT

Kennedy's violent death instantly transformed the man into a myth. After conversations with Kennedy's widow, Theodore White wrote an essay in which he compared Kennedy's presidency to "Camelot." Camelot had recently been popularized in this country by the successful Broadway run of a musical of that same name. Kennedy had seen *Camelot,* and he loved to listen to the sound track. Camelot referred to the Arthurian legend, to the mythical kingdom of Arthur and the Knights of the Round Table. Because America, soon after Kennedy's death, got caught up in a full-scale war in Southeast Asia and in violent domestic rebellions, followed a few years later by the sordid Watergate scandal, people viewed the Kennedy years as a brief "golden age." Those who came of age during his reign felt an especially painful loss. For them, the Kennedy years had been a glorious interlude between the dull days of Eisenhower and the dark days of Johnson and Nixon. It had been a time when talent, chivalry, and idealism reigned, when the world appeared young and all things seemed possible.

For those who believed in Camelot, Kennedy had been the democratic prince whose achievements symbolized the American dream of success, both personal and national. His family history had been a saga of upward mobility from humble immigrant origins to the upper reaches of wealth, power, and fame. Then, in an instant, a loser's bullets had turned spectacular achievement into tragic loss. The death of the president shattered their dreams of glory.

The historical record belies the myth. Kennedy's record of accomplishment is mixed. Much of his New Frontier agenda failed to pass in his lifetime. He was usually a cautious leader on civil rights issues. He only belatedly sensed the moral passion that motivated civil rights activists such as Martin Luther King Jr. He got only a portion of his economic program enacted. Posthumous revelations about his extramarital affairs, drug use, serious health problems, and other Kennedy family scandals have tarnished his moral stature and diminished his reputation. The book *Profiles in Courage,* which established his credentials as a scholar in politics, was mostly written by his aide Theodore Sorensen.

---

[13]Quoted from the documentary film *The Age of Kennedy, Part 4.*

Figure 6.9   Jacqueline Kennedy, dressed in black mourning attire, holds Caroline and John Jr.'s hands as they prepare to descend a flight of stairs during President Kennedy's funeral, Washington, D.C., November 26, 1963.   *Source:* Archive Photos.

His foreign policy achievements were more significant. America's putting a man on the moon in 1969 was a belated triumph. The Peace Corps and the Trade Expansion Act succeeded. But the Alliance for Progress flopped, neither undercutting the appeal of Castro nor promoting democracy and economic growth in most Latin American countries. Kennedy's "crisis managing" in Cuba was a disaster at the Bay of Pigs, and he risked nuclear war to pry Russian missiles out of Cuba. The Berlin issue was defused after years of tension, but its resolution owed more to Khrushchev's Berlin Wall than to any initiatives taken by Kennedy. The test ban treaty and détente with the Soviets in 1963 decreased the danger of nuclear war, but Kennedy had previously ordered major increases in American military spending, particularly for strategic thermonuclear weapons, which had escalated the arms race. Kennedy also significantly expanded American involvement in Vietnam, putting the country on course for war in Southeast Asia.

Kennedy's best speeches proved that he had the imagination and courage to see beyond the confines of the Cold War, but he spent the greatest part of his presidency fighting it. The man who could see the need for developing new relations with Third World people nevertheless applied counterrevolutionary Cold War ideologies to all nationalistic insurgencies. He remained a Cold Warrior at heart to the end.

Any full and fair accounting of his leadership must include intangible dimensions. He was a superb politician. His intelligence, wit, and immense personal charm contributed to his personal style and set a high tone for his presidency. Many of his countrymen felt great admiration and affection for him, viewing Kennedy as a fine symbol of the nation that he had been elected to lead. He was devoted to the ideal of national service. His administration cultivated the arts. He paid high tribute to science and scholarship. He sought always to bring out the best in Americans, to challenge them to seek excellence in all things, especially young people, with whom he felt a special bond. Whatever the failings of the private man, the public image that Kennedy cultivated was positive, energetic, and effective. Always there must be the rueful speculation, what if he had lived? Any fair historical judgment must take into account the brutal fact of his abruptly abbreviated career, a young man in his prime cut down before he could make his full mark on history.

BIBLIOGRAPHY

There is a vast literature on John Fitzgerald Kennedy, his family, and all facets of his political career. The best and most balanced biography is Herbert Parmet's two-volume study, *Jack: The Struggles of John F. Kennedy* and *JFK: The Presidency of John F. Kennedy.* The best recent scholarly history of the Kennedy presidency is James N. Giglio's *The Presidency of John F. Kennedy.* Two highly favorable insider accounts of his presidency are Arthur M. Schlesinger Jr.'s *A Thousand Days* and Theodore C. Sorensen's *Kennedy.* Kenneth P. O'Donnel and David F. Powers, two political associates of Kennedy's, have left an affectionate account in *Johnny, We Hardly Knew Ye.* Bruce Miroff's *Pragmatic Illusions: The Presidential Politics of John Kennedy* and Garry Wills's *The Kennedy Imprisonment* are both negative assessments of his presidency. A controversial recent work by investigative reporter Seymour M. Hersh, *The Dark Side of Camelot,* amounts to a lengthy catalogue of the sins of the president. The best account of the exciting and significant election of 1960 is found in Theodore H. White's *The Making of the President, 1960.* The best account of Kennedy's World War II career is Robert J. Donovan's *PT 109: John F. Kennedy in World War II.* For civil rights literature during Kennedy's years, see the relevant chapters in Taylor Branch's magisterial *Parting the Waters: America in the King Years, 1954–1963.* Carl M. Brauer's *John F. Kennedy and the Second Reconstruction* is a favorable assessment of the president as civil rights leader. See also Peter Wyden's *Bay of Pigs: The Untold Story,* the best account of Kennedy's most embarrassing foreign policy venture. The best short account of the Cuban missile crisis is Elie Abel's *The Missile Crisis. The Kennedy Tapes: Inside the White House during the Cuban Missile Crisis,* edited by Ernest R. May and Philip D. Zeilkow, allows the reader access to history as it was being made by the Executive Committee. Two critical accounts of Kennedy's conduct of foreign policy include Richard J. Walton's *Cold War and Counterrevolution* and David Halberstam's *The Best and the Brightest.* A fine, recent study of Kennedy's foreign policy is Michael R. Beschloss's *The Crisis Years: Kennedy and Khrushchev,*

1960–1963. A first-rate diplomatic historian, Thomas Paterson, has edited a fine collection of critical essays on Kennedy's foreign policy, *Kennedy's Quest for Victory: American Foreign Policy, 1961–1963.* For Kennedy's space policy, see Walter A. McDougall's *The Heavens and the Earth: A Political History of the Space Age.* Anyone who cares to know about Kennedy's assassination must start by reading the *Report of the Warren Commission on the Assassination of John F. Kennedy.* Readers also might want to read one of the responsible accounts of the assassination, such as Michael L. Kurtz's *Crime of the Century: The Kennedy Assassination from a Historian's Perspective.* Gerald Posner's *Case Closed: Lee Harvey Oswald and the Assassination of JFK* does an effective job of demolishing the leading conspiracy theories and providing plausible answers to the lingering questions about the assassination.

7

Great Society and Vietnam

Lyndon Johnson deftly took charge of the nation's political life following President Kennedy's shocking assassination. He skillfully steered stalled New Frontier legislation through Congress. Following his landslide election victory in November 1964, he presided over the flowering of the Great Society, a multidimensional reform program that promised to fulfill the social vision of the New Deal and improve the quality of life for all Americans. For a time, Great Society programs worked, and President Johnson was an admired and a powerful leader.

At the same time that Johnson asserted effective leadership as a domestic reform leader, he had to manage America's far-flung international commitments. Johnson was neither well informed nor experienced in foreign policy realms. The knowledge and skill that made him an effective domestic legislative leader could not be applied to the conduct of foreign policy. Johnson inherited a series of difficult world situations: the NATO alliance showed signs of strain, pressures for social and political change were rising in many Latin American nations, and the Middle East remained a powder keg that could blow at any time. Most of all, Johnson inherited a growing U.S. involvement in the Vietnam War. President Johnson met his nemesis in Vietnam. Vietnam undermined his credibility, strangled his beloved Great Society, and eventually forced him from office. The triumphs of the Great Society would be overwhelmed by the tragic losses of the Vietnam catastrophe.

THE TALL TEXAN

Lyndon Baines Johnson, the thirty-sixth president of the United States, was the eighth vice president to ascend to office following either the death or murder of a sitting chief executive. The new president was a brilliant politician.

Johnson was born on August 27, 1908, near the village of Stonewall, in a cabin on his daddy's ranch. His family, long-time residents of the hard-scrabble southwest Texas hill country, was poor but prominent. Lyndon's father and grandfather had both served in the state legislature. Politics appear to have been bred into Lyndon Johnson's bones, plus a driving ambition to someday become rich and famous. He attended Southwest Texas State Teachers College at San Marcos. Following graduation, he taught elementary school for a couple of years in a one-room schoolhouse where most of his students were the children of Mexican farm workers. From all accounts, Johnson was a dedicated teacher who tried very hard to help the children assigned to his classes. Always, one of Johnson's top priorities after he became a powerful politician was to improve the quality of public education available to the children of low-income families.

Johnson's political career began in 1932, when he joined the staff of his district's Congressman. In 1935, the young politician became state director of the National Youth Administration (NYA), an important New Deal agency whose prime mission was to help young people finish high school and attend college during hard times. At a time when it was politically risky to do so, Johnson saw to it that NYA funds were made available to African-American students, schools, and colleges. He was elected to Congress in 1937 and quickly made a name for himself in Washington as an ardent populist and a New Dealer. He came to President Roosevelt's attention as a fund-raiser and future leader of the Democratic Party. In 1948, Johnson moved up to the Senate, winning a bitter, hard-fought, and corrupt election by a scant eighty-seven votes. His squeaky-thin margin of victory coupled with charges of voting irregularities earned him his Senate sobriquet of "landslide Lyndon."

Johnson's rise in the Senate was meteoric. He quickly made himself indispensable to senior Democratic leaders such as Richard Russell of Georgia. Russell and his colleagues saw to it that Johnson became Senate minority leader in 1953. When the Democrats regained control of the Senate in 1955, Johnson became majority leader. From 1955 to 1960, as Senate majority leader, Johnson was the second most powerful politician in Washington. He inhabited the center of the political spectrum. He sometimes supported liberal measures, but more often he took a moderate stance on issues. Johnson worked cooperatively with the Eisenhower administration. The key to his power was his mastery of the Senate legislative process. He did his best work behind the scenes; he was a skilled negotiator and deal maker. He always seemed to know just the right mix of carrots and sticks required to put together winning coalitions of diverse groups in support of important legislation.

Johnson was in his element in the Senate. He was the consummate professional politician. Although a Southerner, he transcended his regional roots by identifying with the West. As he became more prominent and ambitious for the presidency, he increasingly took national positions on important issues. In 1958, he took the lead in responding to the Soviet challenge, becoming a strong advocate of increased spending for defense and aerospace projects. In 1960, he made a bid for the presidency, finishing second to Kennedy in the balloting at Los Angeles. During his vice presidency, he had an active and a visible role in governance. He and President Kennedy both liked and respected each other. When Kennedy was gunned down, Johnson was ready to take his place.

JOHNSON TAKES COMMAND

The new president assumed office under horrendous circumstances. The nation's papers all carried the photograph of a somber Lyndon Johnson being sworn into office by a federal judge on board Air Force One, parked at the Dallas airport less than two hours after John Kennedy was murdered. Also on board, in the back of the plane, was Kennedy's body, awaiting its mournful flight back to Washington.

Johnson's immediate duty was to preside over an orderly transition of power that ensured continuity in government and restored the people's shattered confidence in the political order. He handled this delicate task with great skill and remarkable sensitivity. He persuaded almost all of Kennedy's key White House staff and cabinet officials to remain at their jobs. His first speech to Congress and to the American people, given five days after the assassination and probably the most important speech of his presidency, demonstrated that a sure hand was at the helm. The words that counted most in his speech were the following: "Today, in this moment of new resolve, I would say to my fellow Americans, let us continue." Johnson pledged to continue what Kennedy had started. He made it clear that stalled New Frontier legislation would be the top priority on his domestic agenda. He called specifically for Congress to enact swiftly the stalled civil rights act and tax reduction bill.

Johnson possessed tremendous political talents. He was driven by an intense ambi-

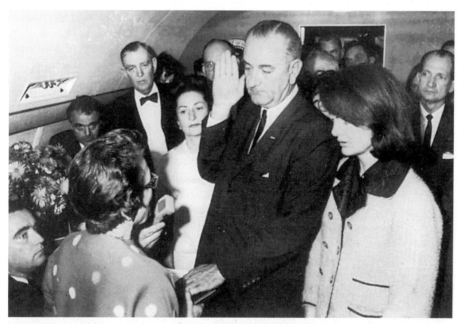

Figure 7.1   Less than two hours after President Kennedy's death, a somber Lyndon Johnson was sworn into office aboard *Air Force One,* **still parked on the ground at Dallas Airport. He is flanked by Kennedy's widow Jacqueline and his wife Lady Bird.**   *Source:* AP/Wide World photo.

tion to succeed. A highly intelligent man, he was brighter than most of the Harvard intellectuals who trailed Kennedy to Washington. But Johnson always felt inferior to these
poised and articulate men because of his lowly social origins, crude manners, and second-
rate education. He never read anything except newspapers, and he had no interests outside
of politics. He knew nothing about sports, art, music, or even popular culture. He acquired
his intricate knowledge of government from experience, shrewd observation, conversation,
and picking the brains of associates, much as Franklin Roosevelt had mined his advisers for
ideas and programs.

During his first six months in office, President Johnson had a passionate concern for the welfare of poor people, the elderly, and minorities, especially African Americans. Considering his essentially Southern origins, he was
remarkably free of racial prejudices. He believed that the federal government could be a
major instrument for improving the lot of America's disadvantaged citizens, and he was determined to use its resources on their behalf. Much more than his patrician predecessor, Lyndon Johnson was the inheritor of the New Deal commitment to achieving social justice for
all Americans.

During his first six months in office, President Johnson used a successful strategy for
getting Congress to enact much previously blocked New Frontier legislation. He evoked
memories of the deceased Kennedy as a moral lever to pry bills out of congressional committees. He also sought to overcome conservative resistance to social reform by insisting
on balanced budgets and reducing government expenditures. Johnson was both a liberal social reformer and a fiscal conservative. He obtained congressional passage of Kennedy's
long-stalled tax cuts, which reduced personal and corporate income taxes about 5 percent
across the board. Enactment of these tax cuts represented the first deliberate use of Keynesian fiscal policy to stimulate demand and to promote investment to keep the economy prosperous and expanding, thereby generating the tax revenues to pay for proposed reforms.
President Johnson also persuaded Congress to enact the most comprehensive civil rights
bill in American history.

The civil rights bill passed in the House in February 1964, but it ran into a Southern filibuster in the Senate that delayed its passage until June 1964, when a bipartisan effort broke
the filibuster and passed the measure by a vote of 77 to 18. The Civil Rights Bill of 1964 went
far beyond Kennedy's original proposal. It was the most sweeping affirmation of equal rights
and the strongest commitment to their enforcement ever made by Congress. Its key provision
guaranteed equal access to all public accommodations such as restaurants, bars, hotels, theaters, and casinos. Other provisions strengthened federal machinery for combatting discrimination in hiring and promotions. The bill also empowered the federal government to file
school desegregation suits, and it further strengthened voting rights. In addition, it required
corporations and trade unions to ensure equal employment opportunities to all applicants.

In addition to promoting tax cuts and civil rights, Kennedy was considering an antipoverty program at the time of his death. He had ordered his chief economic adviser, Walter Heller, to draft a plan for an assault on poverty. Heller informed Johnson of the plan, and
the new president eagerly adopted it. In his first State of the Union address delivered in January 1964, Johnson declared "unconditional war on poverty in America." Congress, a few
months later, enacted the Economic Opportunity Act, authorizing the spending of $1 bil-
lion over three years, beginning in 1965. The act created an umbrella agency called the Of-

fice of Economic Opportunity (OEO) to administer the various antipoverty programs. Johnson appointed Sargent Shriver, former director of the Peace Corps, to run the OEO. The most radical feature of the new antipoverty law created a "community action program" (CAP) that involved the poor themselves in devising the kinds of programs that they wanted in their communities. The CAP quickly generated controversy as poverty advocates fought with local politicians for control of OEO funds and programs.

THE ELECTION OF 1964

As Lyndon Johnson established himself as an effective president during the first six months of 1964, the Republicans sought a candidate to run against him. Within Republican ranks, conservatives, unhappy with their party's tendency, ever since the New Deal, to nominate nonideological centrists for the presidency, were determined this time to nominate one of their own. Conservatives represented diverse groups: Midwesterners, Southerners, Westerners, far-right groups such as the John Birch Society, and New Right newcomers to the GOP, such as former screen actor Ronald Reagan and an activist attorney from Illinois, Phyllis Schlafly. These aggressive conservatives supported the candidacy of Arizona Senator Barry Goldwater. Goldwater's political philosophy blended traditional conservatism with New Right ideological discontent with the restraints imposed on the American system by the welfare state and the Cold War. Goldwater, a product of Sunbelt politics, favored both free enterprise and unilateral military action against the Communists.

Moderate Eastern Republicans mounted an all-out effort to stall Goldwater's drive for their party's nomination in the California primary in June. Nelson Rockefeller, dynast, vastly rich, the quintessential establishmentarian, challenged Goldwater in a bruising battle that split the California Republican Party. Goldwater scored a narrow victory, and with it he secured his party's nomination.

At the Republican nominating convention, held in the Cow Palace near San Francisco in August, moderates hoped to tone down Goldwater's strident rhetoric and to persuade the party to adopt a moderate platform. But Goldwater's people were in no mood to compromise with the hated moderates, especially now that they had them on the run. Goldwater's acceptance speech was a New Right manifesto. He denounced government, especially the federal government. In memorable words, he read the moderates out of the GOP:

> Those who do not care for our cause, we don't expect to enter our ranks. . . . Extremism in the defense of liberty is no vice! Moderation in the pursuit of justice is no virtue![1]

The election campaign between President Johnson and his challenger was a dull, one-sided affair. Goldwater never had a chance. From its outset, pollsters predicted an overwhelming victory for the Democrats. Early in the campaign, Goldwater urged that NATO field commanders be given control of tactical nuclear weapons. His proposal frightened most

[1]Quoted in Michael Schaller, Virginia Scharff, and Robert D. Schulzinger, *Present Tense: The United States Since 1945* (Boston: Houghton Mifflin, 1992), p. 250.

Americans, who thought it made nuclear war more likely. The Democrats hired an ad agency that ran a television commercial showing a little girl picking petals from a daisy; then the image of the little girl faded as an ominous voice counted down from ten. As the voice reached one, the screen suddenly filled with a mushroom cloud. Johnson is then heard in a voice-over saying, "These are the stakes. We must learn to love one another, or surely we shall die." The ad ran only once; Republican complaints forced the Democrats to pull it. But it probably damaged Goldwater's election prospects, which were not good to begin with.

Goldwater often did not need Democratic help to drive away voters, as he insisted on waging an ideological rather than a pragmatic campaign. He told an audience of elderly people in Florida that he favored Social Security voluntary. He chose Memphis, Tennessee, the cotton capital, to attack farm subsidy programs. He then journeyed to Knoxville, located in the center of a region made prosperous by the Tennessee Valley Authority (TVA), to tell voters that the TVA must be sold to private power companies. In Charleston, West Virginia, located at the edge of Appalachia, one of the poorest regions in the nation, he announced that the impending war on poverty was unnecessary.

Johnson refused to debate Goldwater on television. Because all of the polls showed him holding a big lead, Johnson did not bother campaigning until the final month. When he did enter the fray in October, he campaigned as a unifier. He forged a broad electoral consensus, including much of the business community, trade unions, farmers, most middle-class voters, liberals, intellectuals, the elderly, the poor, blacks, and other minorities. A sizable part of Johnson's support came from Republican voters who were fleeing Goldwater's extremist campaign. Goldwater showed strength among white Southerners, his true-believer followers, and hard-core Republicans.

On Election Day, Johnson won his predicted landslide. In the popular vote, he received 43 million votes to Goldwater's 27 million, and 486 electoral votes to Goldwater's 52. Johnson carried forty-four states and received 60.7 percent of the popular vote. Democrats added thirty-seven House seats and two more seats in the Senate. The new House of Representatives would have 295 Democrats to 140 Republicans. The new Senate would have 68 Democrats to only 32 Republicans.

In the aftermath of the Goldwater debacle, some analysts spoke of the impending demise of the Republican Party as a major political force. Such epitaphs proved premature; it turned out that Goldwater was merely ahead of his time. Ronald Reagan, inheriting Goldwater's cause, would ride it to the White House in 1980. While celebrating their landslide victories, some Democratic Party leaders nervously took note of the fact that five of the six states carried by Goldwater were Southern. The Solid South was disintegrating as white voters, perceiving the Democratic Party to be increasingly identified with the drive by African Americans for full participation in American public life, abandoned their historic political allegiances and voted Republican.

GREAT SOCIETY

Soon after his overwhelming victory, Johnson, backed by the most liberal Congress since 1936, set out to complete what New Dealers had begun during the 1930s. He organized task forces made up of his staffers, social scientists, bureaucrats, and activists to draft legislative proposals to send to Congress. Johnson and his liaison people also worked closely with Congress during all stages of the legislative process to pass the programs that became the Great Society. Dozens of programs poured from the most cooperative Congress since the First Hundred Days of FDR's administration. Among the most important measures enacted during 1965 was the Appalachian Regional Development Act. Appalachia, a mountainous region extending from Pennsylvania to northern Alabama, contained 17 million people and was a vast pocket of poverty. The act provided over $1 billion in subsidies for a variety of projects stressing economic development of the region.

Congress also attacked the problem of America's decaying central cities. The Housing and Urban Development Act of 1965 provided funding for 240,000 units of low-rent housing. It also authorized spending $2.9 billion over four years for urban renewal projects. Federal rent supplements for low-income families were added in 1966. Congress also created a new Cabinet-level Department of Housing and Urban Development (HUD). President Johnson appointed Robert Weaver to head the new agency; Weaver became the first African-American Cabinet member.

In addition to attacking urban problems, Congress enacted both the Medicare and the Medicaid programs in 1965. Medicare provided health care for people age sixty-five and over, while Medicaid provided health care for low-income people not eligible for Medicare. Both programs would be funded through Social Security. At the time of the passage of these programs, the United States was the only industrial democracy in the world without some form of national health insurance. Organized physicians, working through their powerful lobby the American Medical Association (AMA), had blocked all efforts to enact national health insurance since Truman had first proposed it in 1945. President Johnson, determined to add medical insurance in some form to the Great Society, overcame the opposition of the AMA and conservative legislators by limiting the insurance program to the elderly and to the poor, and by funding it through the Social Security system.

One of the most important achievements of Great Society was the enactment of federal aid to education. The Elementary and Secondary Education Act of 1965 ended a long debate in Congress over the use of federal funds to support public schools. President Kennedy had made federal aid to public schools a top New Frontier priority and had suffered a serious defeat because of Catholic opposition to his bill, which did not fund parochial schools. On the other hand, Protestant and Jewish leaders strongly opposed funding parochial schools. Kennedy could never resolve the impasse. President Johnson, believing that education was the primary way in which the federal government could promote equality of opportunity in America, overcame the religious roadblock. He convinced Cardinal Spellman, the Reverend Billy Graham, and Jewish leaders to accept an aid program that provided federal funds for states based on the number of low-income students enrolled in their schools. The funds would be distributed to both private and public schools to benefit all children in need.

Johnson rescued another stalled New Frontier reform when he secured congressional passage of the Immigration Act of 1965, the first comprehensive overhaul of U.S. immigration policy in forty years. The new law abolished the discriminatory national origins quota system implemented during the 1920s, which had restricted immigration to this country on the basis of ethno-racial descent and national origins. Under the new legislation, each country would have an annual quota of about 20,000 immigrant slots. Eligibility to fill these slots would be based upon the skills and education of the individual immigrant and his family ties to people living in the United States.

Additional civil rights legislation joined the Great Society agenda in 1965. Many African Americans could not yet vote in the Deep South states, despite the enactment of three previous civil rights bills and voter registration drives by civil rights groups. Hundreds of student volunteers working in Mississippi in the summer of 1964 to register African-American voters encountered stubborn, and often violent, opposition from white segregationists. The Mississippi "Freedom Summer" dramatized the continuing disfranchisement of Southern African Americans. In the spring of 1965, Martin Luther King Jr. prepared to lead a fifty-mile march of demonstrators from Selma, Alabama, to the state capitol in Montgomery to publicize continuing denial of African-American voting rights. A few days before the march was scheduled to begin, President Johnson made a nationally televised speech to a joint session of Congress calling for a voting rights bill that would close all remaining loopholes in civil rights laws. Near the end of his speech, Johnson raised his arms in the style of a country preacher and recited the words from an old black spiritual that had become the anthem of the civil rights movement: "And . . . we . . . shall . . . overcome." The demonstrators in Selma, poised to begin their march, listened to his speech through tears of joy.

As the demonstrators began their march for the right to vote, they were attacked by Alabama state troopers who gassed, clubbed, and whipped them. These vicious attacks on nonviolent protesters marching on behalf of a fundamental democratic right were televised nationally to a shocked nation. An angry president, viewing the attacks, federalized the Alabama National Guard and ordered it to provide protection for the marchers all the way to Montgomery. Johnson then used all of his political skill to maneuver the voting rights bill through Congress. The Voting Rights Act of 1965 gave the Attorney General the power to appoint federal registrars to register voters in districts where historic patterns of disfranchisement prevailed. Empowered by the new law, federal officials registered hundreds of thousands of African-American and Hispanic voters in six Southern states during the next three years. As a result of these actions, the 1966 election was the first one held in this country in which most adult Southern African Americans could vote.

In addition to voting rights for African Americans, the Great Society also was committed to the cause of conservation. Congress enacted the National Wilderness Preservation Act in 1964, which incorporated all federally owned wilderness areas into a national wilderness system. It also established a program for meeting the nation's future wilderness preservation and recreation needs. Conservation and wildlife preservation laws were enacted. In early 1965, Congress passed the Highway Beautification Act, a cause pushed by First Lady Claudia "Lady Bird" Johnson. It also enacted the Water Quality Act and the Clean Air Act; these important measures provided federal funds for assisting state and local governments to set up air and water purification programs.

There were many more Great Society measures enacted in 1965 and 1966. The first session of the 89th Congress approved ninety administration-sponsored reform bills. The legislative pace slowed in 1966, but more measures continued to flow from the congressional hopper. Two important pieces of consumer protection legislation passed, a "truth-in-packaging" bill and a "truth-in-lending" act. The former required sellers to label accurately the contents of packages sold for household use; the latter required detailed information about the true rate of interest charged on bank loans and credit purchases. Congress added a new Cabinet-level Department of Transportation in 1966 and enacted a series of highway safety laws. Consumer advocate Ralph Nader did more than anyone to secure the passage of these new safety laws. His book, *Unsafe at Any Speed* (1966), documented hazardous design defects in Detroit-made automobiles, promoting public awareness of these problems.

Great Society measures enacted between 1964 and 1966 represented the most far-reaching assault ever mounted on a vast array of social problems by the federal government. Reform measures left over from the New Deal and Fair Deal eras were enacted during the mid-1960s. Most of the problems Great Society tried to solve had been around for years. They were challenged during the mid-1960s because of a confluence of circumstances that gave reformers opportunities normally unavailable within the American political system. The nation was prosperous, and there existed a widespread sense that Americans could afford the costs of social reform. Large liberal majorities prevailed in both houses of Congress, breaking the bipartisan conservative bloc's power to veto or water down reform legislation. Johnson's smashing victory in the 1964 election had given the activist liberal reform leader a mandate for social change. Most of all, Johnson's special political skills made the Great Society a reality. He formed broad-based coalitions supporting reform, and he used his remarkable abilities to steer complex legislation through congressional "minefields" of special interest groups. President Lyndon Johnson ranks along with Franklin Roosevelt and Woodrow Wilson as one of the great reform leaders of modern American history.

For a time, many Great Society programs worked. In part stimulated by tax cuts, the economy grew rapidly. The GDP increased by 25 percent from 1964 to 1966, providing billions of dollars of additional tax revenues to fund the new programs without incurring budget deficits, raising interest rates, or igniting inflation. Unemployment dropped below 4 percent in 1965, the lowest rate since World World II. The number of poor people declined by millions; this reduction came from both antipoverty programs and new jobs generated by the strong economy. Medicare and Medicaid improved the quality of health care available to the elderly and to the poor. Students at all educational levels benefited from federal programs. African Americans in the South at long last had the vote.

But the Great Society immediately incurred a flurry of criticism from both the Left and the Right. Conservatives assailed its high costs, its centralization of government authority, and its proliferation of new federal bureaucracies. Conservative critics insisted that social problems could not be solved by creating new federal bureaucracies and by throwing money at the problems. A small group of articulate Leftist radicals charged that most Great Society programs were woefully inadequate. A young militant, Tom Hayden, observed that "the welfare state is more machinery than substance."

Johnson's war on poverty, which was launched in 1965 with much fanfare, came under heavy fire. Some of its programs worked well, particularly those that helped prepare poor minority youngsters for school and those that furnished job training for disadvantaged young men and women. But radical critics insisted that if government officials were serious about eradicating poverty in America, then a few billion dollars could not begin to meet the needs of the nation's 40 million poor people. In their view, the poverty program was both oversold and underfunded. It generated unrealistic expectations among poor African

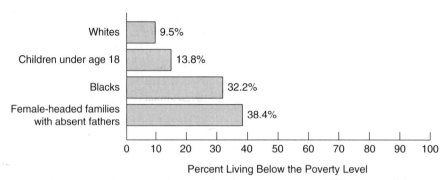

Figure 7.2   Poverty, 1969.   *Source:* U.S. Bureau of the Census, Current Population Reports, Series P-60, No. 194, and unpublished data.

Americans and fierce resentments among working-class whites, who perceived antipoverty programs as favoring militant protesters over hard-working people who kept quiet, obeyed the law, and got nothing from the government except higher taxes. Michael Harrington, whose book *The Other America* (1962) had helped President Kennedy discover poverty in America, observed sadly: "What was supposed to be a social war turned out to be a skirmish, and in any case, poverty won."

After 1966, Congress, concerned about rising crime rates, violence, and inflation, was reluctant to vote more funds for reform and social programs. Johnson had expected to finance the Great Society from increased tax revenues derived from an expanding economy. He believed that affluent Americans could continue to prosper without having to make any sacrifices to help the poor. He believed that the Great Society would enable the one-fourth of Americans who were disadvantaged to join the affluent three-fourths without requiring any tax increases or redistribution of wealth. He promised more than the Great Society could deliver. He both exaggerated American wealth and underestimated the profound structural barriers to achieving affluence for all.

He further believed that America could both fight a costly, large-scale war in Vietnam and continue to build the Great Society at home. Ironically, the leader who wanted to achieve his place in history as the man who fulfilled the social vision of the New Deal, escalated the war in Vietnam, thereby strangling his beloved Great Society. Liberal reformers lamented the fact that by 1967, except for token gestures, the Great Society was dead. The fight for civil rights, the struggle to save the cities, and the efforts to improve the public schools—all of these and other programs were starved for the sake of the escalating war in Southeast Asia. Great Society proved to be the last major reform spasm of social liberalism in modern times.

THE WARREN COURT

Led by energetic Chief Justice Earl Warren, the activist liberal majority controlling the Supreme Court during the 1960s rendered a series of landmark decisions that struck down the last remnants of the segregation system. The Court also protected the right of dissent, expanded the freedom of the press, regulated obscene materials, and restricted the role of religion in public schools. It further altered criminal legal procedures, expanded the right to privacy, and made the American political system more nearly representative of all of the people.

In *Bond v. Floyd* (1966), the Court ordered the Georgia House of Representatives to admit an elected representative, civil rights activist Julian Bond, who had been denied his seat because of his opposition to the Vietnam War and the conscription system that sustained it.

In *The New York Times v. Sullivan* (1964), the Court ruled that people in the public eye—elected officials and celebrities—could not win a libel suit against a publication solely because its editors had published untrue statements. Under the Court's reading of libel laws, plaintiffs had to prove that the statements were "recklessly false" and made with "malice aforethought." Since motivation was extremely difficult to establish within a court of law, the practical effect of *The New York Times v. Sullivan* was to make it unlikely that a public figure could win a libel suit against a newspaper or a magazine publisher.

In *Roth v. United States* (1957), the Court defined obscenity as material "without any redeeming social importance." The Court also defined as obscene material that "the average person, applying community standards, regarded as appealing to prurient interests." However, the Court found it impossible to come up with objective criteria to determine what materials were obscene under its definitions. The problems were twofold: community standards varied, and any definition of obscenity involved inherently subjective judgments. Associate Justice Potter Stewart acknowledged the Court's dilemma when he asserted that while he could not define obscenity, he knew it when he saw it.

The Court also broadened the First Amendment's ban on the establishment of religion as a part of the state. In *Engel v. Vitale* (1962), the Court banned prayer in public schools. In a later decision, the Court banned Bible readings from public school classrooms. The Court also nullified an Arkansas law mandating the teaching of "creation science" as an alternative to Darwinian evolutionary theory. The cumulative effect over the years of these decisions was to remove religious observances from public schools.

Figure 7.3   The Warren Court. Photo taken on November 22, 1965. (L-R) (Standing): Byron White, William Brennan, Potter Stewart, and Abe Fortas. (Seated): Tom Clark, Hugo Black, Earl Warren, William Douglas, and John Marshall Harlan.   *Source:* National Archives.

Figure 7.4   Clarence Earl Gideon.   *Source:* Corbis.

In two controversial 5 to 4 decisions, the Supreme Court also enhanced the procedural rights of citizens accused of crimes. In the first case, *Gideon v. Wainwright* (1963), the Court ruled that Clarence Gideon, a professional criminal, had never gotten a fair trial because he had never had an attorney to defend him in court. The Court, in effect, ruled that the right to a fair trial included the right to be represented in court by a lawyer. As a consequence of the Court's rulings in *Gideon v. Wainwright,* all cases in the country where defendants had been convicted of felonies without the benefit of attorneys to represent them had to be retried. If the defendant could not afford an attorney, the state, that is, the tax-payers, had to furnish one. In the second case, *Miranda v. Arizona* (1966), the Court enhanced citizens' Fifth Amendment rights against self-incrimination. In this case, the Court ruled that Ernesto Miranda, a suspect charged with burglary, had been coerced by the Phoenix, Arizona, police into confessing. The police questioning Miranda had told him that if he did not confess, the judge would give him a longer sentence. According to the new rules implemented in *Miranda v. Arizona,* police were required to inform suspects of their rights at the time of arrest: their right to remain silent and that anything they said could and would be used in a court of law to convict them; their right to have an attorney represent them in court; and, in the event that they could not afford a lawyer, their right to have the state provide them one free.

In 1965, the Warren Court struck down a Connecticut law that forbade the sale or use of contraceptives. In *Griswald v. Connecticut,* Associate Justice William O. Douglas, writing for the majority, found the law an unwarranted invasion of privacy. Nowhere in the Bill of Rights is there delineated a specific right to privacy; Douglas apparently inferred a right of privacy. Years later, another Supreme Court justice, Harry Blackmun, would ground the right of women to have an abortion on demand during the first trimester of pregnancy on that same inferred right of privacy.

Warren Court rulings also affected political practices in this country. In *Baker v. Carr* (1962), the Court declared that it could determine whether state legislative districts had been fairly drawn. The principle that the courts used during the 1960s to determine whether state legislative districts had been fairly drawn was "one person, one vote," derived from the equal protections clause of the Fourteenth Amendment. During the 1960s, as a consequence of *Baker v. Carr,* several states in which rural voters were overrepresented in state legislatures at the expense of urban residents had to redraw the boundaries of their legislative districts to make them equal in population.

The cumulative effects of these landmark court decisions were to enhance significantly the rights of individuals, curtail the arbitrary powers of government, and make the political system more democratic. Ironically, the least democratic branch of the federal government, and the only one beyond the reach of the voting majority, had done much to strengthen American democracy and to validate the growing pluralism of the political culture. In the process, the Warren Court provoked many powerful enemies. Conservatives were enraged by what they considered judicial usurpations of the lawmaking process. Law enforcement officials complained that Court decisions made their jobs more difficult, allowed obviously guilty people to avoid punishment, and seemed to place the law on the side of criminals rather than on the side of law-abiding victims. Devoutly religious people were often offended by the Court's proscriptions of religious observances in public schools. Loud calls to impeach Earl Warren resounded across the South and the Midwest. As the conservative revolt gathered momentum in this country during the 1970s, one of their salient issues was curtailing the judicial activism of the Supreme Court.

LYNDON JOHNSON AND THE WORLD

Johnson tried to conduct foreign policy using the same methods and skills that worked so well for him in domestic affairs. But he was handicapped by inexperience, and he lacked the depth of knowledge of world affairs required for effective diplomacy. His early ventures in world affairs met with mixed results. In time, his efforts to achieve a U.S. military victory in Vietnam would destroy his presidency and bring his nation, and those whom he had tried to help in Southeast Asia, to disaster.

In Europe, Johnson could not prevent relations with NATO allies from deteriorating. His chief difficulties came with Charles de Gaulle, who wanted France and Western Europe to rid themselves of U.S. domination. The French leader spurned Johnson's offer to create a multilateral nuclear force and directed France to accelerate development of its own nuclear forces. In early 1966, the French withdrew their forces from NATO and ordered the United States to remove all of its military installations and personnel from France. They also expelled the NATO headquarters. France's dramatic actions signaled that de Gaulle believed that the Cold War in Europe was waning. Prosperous European countries no longer feared Soviet aggression, hence they no longer felt dependent on U.S. support, nor were they inclined to passively support all American foreign policy initiatives.

As de Gaulle challenged American influence in Europe, tensions in the Middle East caused Johnson persistent problems. The president perceived Egyptian leader Gamal Abdul Nasser's efforts to promote Arab nationalism to be the chief threat to American Middle Eastern interests. The Soviet Union, backing Nasser, was gaining influence in the region. Then came another Arab-Israeli war. It occurred in June 1967, following border clashes between the Israelis and Syrians in the Golan Heights area between Syria and Israel. Nasser, backing Syria, mobilized his forces and blockaded Israel's Red Sea port of Elath.

Egypt also worked out an agreement with Jordan that placed its forces under Egyptian command. The Israelis, concluding that an Arab attack was imminent, launched an offensive on June 5. Israeli forces quickly destroyed the Egyptian air force, decimated Jordan's army, and defeated Syrian forces. Israeli tanks routed the Egyptian army. Israel won the war in six days. When a UN-proposed cease-fire went into effect, Israel occupied the Sinai and that part of Jordan west of the River Jordan (the West Bank). Israeli forces also held Syrian territory in the Golan Heights. Egyptian military power was shattered, Nasser was humiliated, and Soviet interests were set back. Israel, now a major power in the region, kept all occupied territories, determined to use them to enhance its territory and to guarantee its security. Israeli imperialism intensified already-powerful Arab anti-Zionist animosities.

Nasser survived the debacle of the Six Day War. He remained popular with the Egyptian people, and the Soviets quickly rebuilt his military forces. The Soviets also expanded their naval forces in the Eastern Mediterranean to challenge the U.S. Sixth Fleet. The United States remained Israel's chief supporter. As Johnson's presidency ended, the danger of another Arab-Israeli war remained great. It now carried with it the ominous potential of an American-Soviet confrontation.

Aware of the dangers inherent in the U.S.–USSR competition for influence and strategic advantage in the Middle East and elsewhere in the Third World, President Johnson invited Soviet Premier Alexei Kosygin to the United States for another summit conference. The two leaders made limited progress toward controlling the spiraling thermonuclear arms race. Johnson and Kosygin agreed that negotiations would begin soon on limiting the number of strategic bombers that each side possessed. They also announced plans to hold regu-

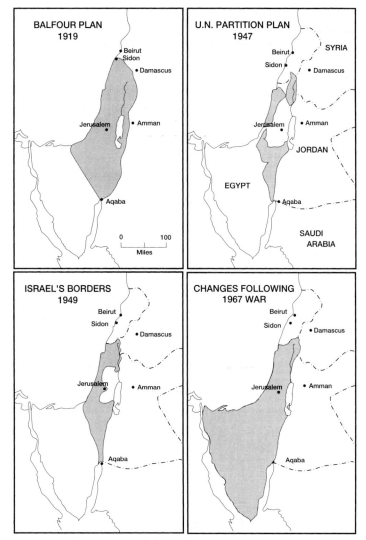

Figure 7.5   Israeli expansion.   *Source:* Yahya Armajani, *Middle East: Past and Present,* 1970, p. 323. Reprinted with permission of Prentice Hall, Englewood Cliffs, N.J.

lar summit meetings to discuss arms control and other issues of paramount importance to both. Unfortunately, there were no more summits during Johnson's presidency. Johnson had planned to go to Moscow in the fall of 1968, but the Soviet Union sent its tanks into Czechoslovakia on August 20, 1968, to crush efforts by the Czechs to establish a social democratic government. Johnson canceled the impending meeting. His presidency ended without any additional diplomatic accomplishments that might have eased tensions with the Soviets.

During his presidency, Johnson faced crises in the Caribbean, where he made preventing further Castro-like insurgencies his top priority. His first crisis came in Panama, which had long been an American protectorate. Violent conflicts erupted between Panamanians and American citizens living in the Canal Zone in January 1964. The violence began when Panamanian students demanded that their national flag be flown alongside the American flag at a high school located in the Canal Zone. American authorities rejected the students' demand. U.S. soldiers killed twenty-one Panamanians, and three Americans died during several days of rioting. Panama severed diplomatic relations with the United States. The OAS mediated the dispute. Normal relations between the two countries were quickly restored. American and Panamanian negotiators then produced a series of agreements, allowing Panamanian participation in the management of the Panama Canal and granting Panama a share of canal revenues.

A more serious crisis occurred in the Dominican Republic, which also had a long history of American domination. A right-wing dictator, Rafael Trujillo, was overthrown in 1961 by a military coup, ushering in years of political instability in that impoverished island country. President Kennedy, delighted to see Trujillo go, sought free elections. The elections brought Juan Bosch to power in 1962. Bosch, a social democrat, was overthrown by another military coup seven months later. In early 1965, a coalition of liberals, radicals, and young army officers launched a revolution to restore Bosch to power.

President Johnson, fearful that pro-Castro elements might come to power and turn the country into another Cuba, sent U.S. troops to suppress the insurgency. U.S. Marines and Army infantrymen prevented Bosch's return to power. Administration spokesmen announced that U.S. intervention had prevented a Communist takeover of the Dominican Republic. An occupation force was set up to maintain order. Elections were held in 1966, and Joaquin Balaguer defeated Bosch. Balaguer established a government that protected U.S. interests, and Johnson withdrew the American forces.

But the Bosch movement was an independent, nationalistic movement, not a Communist conspiracy. U.S. intervention violated the OAS charter and canceled the U.S. pledge not to intervene militarily in the internal affairs of other Western Hemisphere countries. U.S. public opinion supported Johnson's military intervention. Liberals and foreign critics attacked his actions, but he ignored them. The campaign was limited in duration, and few American lives were lost. Johnson quickly accomplished his objectives, and his success silenced his critics. Success in the Dominican operation encouraged Johnson to try more of the same in Vietnam, expecting U.S. military success there to also silence any domestic or foreign detractors who might emerge.

VIETNAM: GOING TO WAR

The roots of U.S. intervention in Southeast Asia could be traced back to Truman's presidency, but it was not until the Kennedy years that the United States became inextricably involved in a war in Vietnam. At the time Johnson replaced Kennedy, the political situation in South Vietnam was deteriorating. A succession of inept military governments had followed Diem, none of which governed or fought effectively. National Liberation Front forces, the "Vietcong," supported by arms, supplies, and troops from North Vietnam, extended their control over the territory and the people of southern Vietnam.

Johnson did not concern himself greatly with Vietnam during his first year in office, meanwhile continuing Kennedy's policy of supplying economic and military assistance to the South Vietnamese government. He retained Kennedy's top advisers, sharing their commitment to contain the spread of Chinese Communism into Southeast Asia. Johnson, as Kennedy had before him, dismissed any possibility of an American withdrawal from Vietnam or any political solution that did not guarantee the survival of an independent, non-Communist government in southern Vietnam. He increased both the number of American advisers in Vietnam and the level of economic aid. He also approved a series of covert operations against North Vietnam, including commando raids along the North Vietnamese coast and the infiltration of CIA operatives into the North. This subtle shift of military action toward the North opened the way to a wider war.

In the summer of 1964, as the presidential campaign was getting underway in the United States, there occurred a relatively minor event in the developing Vietnam War that had major consequences. On August 1, while engaged in electronic espionage off the coast of North Vietnam, the American destroyer USS *Maddox* was attacked by North Vietnamese torpedo boats. The *Maddox* returned the fire and repulsed the attackers with the aid of U.S. naval aircraft. The *Maddox* resumed its spy operations and was joined by another destroyer, *Turner Joy*. On the night of August 4, as they operated in heavy seas about fifty miles from the coast of North Vietnam in the Gulf of Tonkin, both ships reported that they were under attack. No one on either ship sighted any attackers; their initial reports were based on radar and sonar contacts. Later, the *Maddox's* captain reported that weather effects and a misreading of sonar data may have been responsible for the reported attacks.

Even though evidence of a second attack was not certain, President Johnson authorized retaliatory air strikes against North Vietnamese naval bases. Johnson also asked Congress to approve a resolution authorizing him to take "all necessary measures to repel any armed attack against the forces of the United States and to prevent further aggression." Johnson's use of force coupled with his appeal for public support silenced his Republican challenger Barry Goldwater, who earlier had called for the bombing of North Vietnam. In presenting the Johnson administration's case for the resolution, Secretary of Defense Robert S. McNamara misled Congress. He did not tell the Congressmen and Senators that the *Maddox* was on a spy mission when it was attacked, or that the second attack may not have occurred. McNamara characterized both incidents as mindless acts of aggression against American ships on routine patrol in international waters. Congress quickly gave the president what he wanted, without serious debate. The House passed the resolution unanimously, and the Senate enacted it by a vote of 88 to 2.

During the final months of the 1964 presidential campaign, Johnson said little about the war in Vietnam. Goldwater did not make an issue of it, and most Americans did not concern themselves much about a dirty little war in a faraway place. Vietnam was not in the news much, nor was it a major public issue at the time. At times during his electoral campaign, Johnson appeared to be telling the American people that he did not want to get involved in a war in Vietnam and that Americans would not be sent to fight there. At Akron, Ohio, on October 21, he stated, "We are not about to send American boys nine or ten thousand miles away from home to do what Asian boys ought to be doing for them-selves."

At the time that he made those remarks, Johnson had not yet committed himself to further bombing of North Vietnam, nor had he decided to send American ground combat troops there. But he knew the situation in southern Vietnam was deteriorating, despite his own public assurances to the contrary. He also was involved with advisers who had devel-oped contingency plans that could be implemented in the future, including bombing the North and sending American combat troops to South Vietnam. During his reelection cam-paign, he deliberately misled the American people, conveying the impression that he would limit American efforts in Vietnam to helping one side in a civil war. He offered himself as a peace candidate who did not seek a wider war, in contrast to the hawkish Goldwater, who called for an unlimited American military effort in Vietnam. Voters who thought that they were voting for peaceful restraint in November 1964 soon got war.

As the new year began, the South Vietnamese government verged on defeat, and John-son confronted a dilemma that was largely of his own making. Since he had ruled out Amer-ican withdrawal from Southeast Asia, there remained only the options of negotiation or es-calation. But negotiations with Hanoi in early 1965, given military realities in southern Vietnam, could only mean having to accept a neutral coalition government for South Viet-nam with National Liberation Front (NLF) participation. Johnson feared that such a gov-ernment would soon be dominated by the NLF, since South Vietnam could only survive with strong U.S. support. He therefore ruled out negotiations until the military situation was more favorable, and he made his decisions to escalate the war.

Johnson authorized a sustained, gradually expanding bombing campaign called Op-eration Rolling Thunder against North Vietnam beginning on February 13, and he signifi-cantly expanded the much larger air war in southern Vietnam. There was a direct connec-tion between the air war against North Vietnam and Johnson's decision to send combat forces to South Vietnam. Within two weeks, General William Westmoreland, the U.S. com-mander in Vietnam, requested Marine combat units to defend a large U.S. Air Force base at Danang, because he could not rely on South Vietnamese security forces. Johnson quickly approved his request. On March 8, two Marine battalions in full battle gear waded ashore at beaches just south of Danang.

In July 1965, Johnson and his advisers made a series of fateful decisions that set the United States on a course in Vietnam from which it did not deviate for nearly three years, and from which also began over seven years of war. They approved General Westmore-land's requests for saturation bombing in southern Vietnam and for expanding the air war against North Vietnam. They also authorized sending an additional 100,000 combat troops to South Vietnam. Most important, President Johnson gave General Westmoreland a free hand to assume the major burden of fighting in the South. These decisions, made during the last week of July, represented a conscious decision by Johnson and his senior civilian and military advisers to conduct an American war in Vietnam.

When he committed the United States to war in Southeast Asia, President Johnson re-fused to tell the American people what he had done, and he refused to seek a formal decla-ration of war against North Vietnam. He claimed that the Gulf of Tonkin resolution granted him authority to wage war in Vietnam. Since the Supreme Court never ruled on the matter,

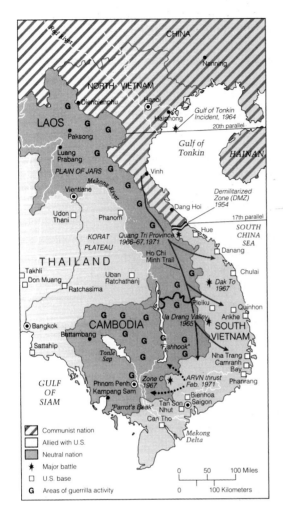

Figure 7.6   South Vietnam and Cambodia.
Source: Public Domain map.

it remains a moot question whether the resolution amounted to a declaration of war against North Vietnam. Senator Fulbright, along with other legislators who later turned against the war, believed that Johnson had tricked them into supporting a war. At the time, Johnson felt confident that he could win the war and persuade Congress and most Americans to support it.

The Johnson administration's decisions for war were based on two fundamental errors in judgment. First, they seriously underestimated the capacity of the NLF and the North Vietnamese to resist large-scale applications of American military power over a long period of time. Johnson and his advisers assumed that within a year or two, North Vietnam would "break" from the ever-increasing punishment inflicted by American bombers, and that they would abandon their support of the revolution in the South. Johnson could not conceive of a poor, underdeveloped Asian country about the size of New Mexico standing up to the military power of the United States. The second error was to underestimate drastically the cost of the war in both lives and dollars, and thus to overestimate the willingness of Americans to go on passively paying those costs year after year.

THE AMERICAN WAY OF WAR

The United States relied heavily on air power to win the war. Air Force and Navy pilots had two primary missions—to check the infiltration of men, equipment, and supplies coming south from North Vietnam along the Ho Chi Minh Trail, and to punish the North Vietnamese from the air until they abandoned the insurgency in the South and came to the bargaining table on American terms. Bombing failed to achieve either objective, even though the Americans waged the largest aerial war in history. The bombing slowed the rate of infiltration down the Ho Chi Minh Trail, although never enough to seriously hamper the NLF war effort. Bombing disrupted North Vietnam's agriculture, destroyed its industry, and damaged some of its cities. Thousands of civilians were killed or wounded. But bombing never appreciably reduced North Vietnam's war-making ability, nor broke the morale of its people.

Although it failed to achieve its objectives, the air war proved very costly for the United States. Between 1965 and 1968, America lost nearly 1,000 fixed-wing aircraft worth an estimated $6 billion. Hundreds of flyers were killed or captured. The bombing also handed the Communists a propaganda weapon. Foreign and domestic foes of the war denounced the air war. To them, the bombing of a small, poor Asian country was immoral as well as costly and relatively ineffective. "Stop the bombing" became a rallying cry for antiwar activists.

American ground combat operations also escalated drastically between July 1965 and the end of 1967, when the United States had deployed nearly 500,000 troops. General Westmoreland used a strategy of attrition against the enemy. The American commander believed that "search-and-destroy" operations would eradicate the enemy and force them to the negotiating table. American troops tried to use their technological superiority to counter the enemy's guerrilla warfare tactics. Herbicides were used on a wide scale to deprive the Vietcong of forest cover and food crops. These chemicals caused widespread ecological devastation and posed health hazards within southern Vietnam. Americans also relied on artillery, helicopter gunships, and bombing to destroy enemy bases and to drive the guerrillas into open country. Since all of South Vietnam became a combat zone, American soldiers found themselves fighting an unconventional war without fronts or territorial objectives. The only measure of progress toward victory in a war of attrition was the amount of enemy supplies captured or destroyed, the amount of enemy weapons and ammunition captured or destroyed, and most of all, the number of enemy soldiers captured, wounded, or killed.

The American takeover of the war in early 1965 had prevented certain South Vietnamese defeat. But the United States could only achieve a stalemate, not a victory. General Westmoreland's attrition strategy was based on the assumption that U.S. forces using their superior firepower could inflict irreplaceable losses on the enemy while keeping their own casualties low. Even though the Americans inflicted heavy casualties, both the NLF and the North Vietnamese replaced their losses and matched each American escalation with one of

Figure 7.7   Vietnam was primarily a small unit war in which squads of American troops engaged the NLF forces in jungles, swamps, and rice paddies. Here a wounded U.S. soldier is being evacuated.   *Source:* U.S. Army photo.

their own during the years 1965 to 1967. They retained the strategic initiative, and the NLF political structure in the South remained intact.

American artillery and bombing campaigns below the seventeenth parallel disrupted the southern Vietnamese economy. Large numbers of civilians were killed; millions more were driven into the arms of the Vietcong or became refugees. The violent American assault undermined the social fabric of a fragile nation and alienated villagers from the South Vietnamese regime, which had never enjoyed much support from the rural population. The American takeover of the war further weakened the resolve of the South Vietnamese forces, who became more dependent than ever on American combat forces. The South Vietnamese forces were more than happy to let the Americans take over much of the fighting and dying.

In 1967, with firm prodding from Washington, the South Vietnamese government, headed by General Nguyen Van Thieu, attempted to build popular support among the rural population. It focused on pacification and rural development. Government cadres moved into villages, providing medical supplies and social services. They tried to insulate the villagers from both Vietcong appeals and reprisals. They sought to promote a national rebirth, while American forces tried to defeat the Communists militarily. These pacification efforts sometimes succeeded, but they more often failed, for many reasons. Americans occasionally bombed or shelled pacified villages by mistake. Vietcong terrorists assassinated many rural development leaders. Often the cadres were inept or corrupt. Progress in the crucial area of nation building was slow and always secondary to the war effort. The inability of

Figure 7.8   The helicopter war: The Vietnam War was the first in which helicopters were used extensively to airlift men into combat. Here, riflemen of the 25th Infantry Division prepare to board a squadron of "Hueys" (Bell UH-1Ds) for an assault on Communist positions.   *Source:* U.S. Army photo.

the South Vietnamese military government to win mass allegiance or to solve its country's massive social problems were major reasons for the eventual failure of the U.S. effort in Vietnam.

The Thieu government survived, not because it was strong, because it was popular with most South Vietnamese, or because its soldiers fought well, but because it was backed by massive American economic support and firepower. But relations between American advisers and their Vietnamese clients often were ambivalent. The Vietnamese resented American arrogance and American inability to understand them. The Americans were frustrated by pervasive Vietnamese corruption and inefficiency. U.S. soldiers, fighting in the steamy jungles and swamps of an alien land, and not always able to tell a friendly Vietnamese from a deadly enemy, often expressed hostility and mistrust toward the people that they were defending. Many American soldiers felt that they were risking their lives fighting to save a people that did not deserve to be saved.

The steady escalation of the war between 1965 and 1967 generated both international and domestic pressures for a negotiated settlement. But the continuing stalemate on the battlefields ensured that neither side wanted negotiations. For political reasons, both sides had to appear responsive to peace initiatives, but neither side would make the concessions that were necessary to negotiations. Hanoi's strategy was to get maximum propaganda value out of peace initiatives, while matching U.S. escalations until the Americans wearied of the war and pulled out. President Johnson continued to believe that the steadily expanding American military effort would eventually break Hanoi's will to support the revolution in South Vietnam and force them to accept an American solution.

Hanoi maintained that the American military presence in South Vietnam violated the 1954 Geneva Accords, and that the bombing of North Vietnam was unprovoked criminal aggression. The North Vietnamese refused to negotiate until the United States ceased all acts of war against their country and withdrew its forces. Hanoi also insisted that the government in Saigon would have to be replaced by a coalition government including the NLF. The United States refused to withdraw its forces until a political solution could be reached in the South that excluded the Vietcong. It also refused to stop the bombing, which it maintained was necessary to keep the Communists from overrunning the South. The United States remained committed to achieving a non-Communist South Vietnam. So the war went on, and numerous peace initiatives from various sources failed in 1966 and 1967.

WAR AT HOME

While the expanding military stalemate continued, within the United States, supporters and opponents of the war engaged in debates of rising intensity. On one side were the Hawks, mostly conservative Republicans and Democrats, but also included were some Cold War liberals, who wanted to expand the U.S. war effort. On the other side were the Doves, challenging both the effectiveness and the morality of the war. The Doves represented a more diverse group: old-line pacifists, student radicals, civil rights leaders, some college professors, and liberal politicians. The most prominent Dove was Senator Fulbright. Initially a supporter of the war, Fulbright had turned against it by early 1966.

Opposition to the war took many forms. Senator Fulbright held hearings on the conduct of the war before his Senate Foreign Relations Committee, providing a forum for war critics and helping to legitimatize opposition to the war. The Doves staged many rallies and protest demonstrations during 1967, the first year of extensive antiwar activity. On October 21, about 50,000 opponents of war demonstrated in front of the main entrance to the Pentagon. Thousands of young men resisted or evaded the draft, and thousands fled the United States and its war for Canada or Sweden.

Most Americans in 1967 were neither Hawks nor Doves. Nearly all citizens had supported the initial escalations that had Americanized the Vietnam War. Confident of quick victory, they had rallied around the flag. But after two years of rising costs and casualties, with military victory still elusive, popular frustration with the Vietnam War had mounted. Polls taken in August 1967 showed for the first time that a majority of Americans believed that sending American combat troops to Vietnam had been a mistake. But opponents of Johnson's war policy in 1967 formed no consensus on Vietnam. They were divided over whether to escalate the war drastically and win it, or to negotiate an American withdrawal. But the growing divisiveness, coupled with declining confidence in the integrity and competence of government officials, strained the social fabric. A housewife in Iowa summed up the dilemma facing the average American: "I want to get out, but I don't want to give up." Meanwhile, the war went on.

The president, trying to dampen growing criticism within Congress of his war policy, brought General Westmoreland to Washington in November. Speaking before the National Press Club on November 21, Westmoreland gave an optimistic appraisal of the war. He said that the Vietcong could no longer replace their losses. Pacification was going so well that they could no longer mount a major offensive anywhere in South Vietnam. He stated, "We have reached an important point where the end begins to come into view." Johnson and other administration spokesmen stressed the theme of impending military victory in Vietnam and exhorted Americans to stay the course just a little longer. The president's public relations campaign worked; popular support for the war increased as the year ended.

TET-68 AND ITS CONSEQUENCES

Then came the Tet Offensive. On January 30, 1968, choosing the Lunar New Year, the most important Vietnamese holiday, as a time to strike in order to catch their opponents by surprise, about 80,000 NLF and North Vietnamese troops suddenly brought the war to the cities and towns of South Vietnam. They simultaneously attacked provincial capitals, district towns, and a dozen major American military facilities all over the country. At most attack sites, the Vietcong were beaten back within a few hours or a few days and sustained heavy losses. Within a month, they had lost all of the cities that they had originally taken in the offensive.

Hanoi had planned the Tet Offensive carefully; it was designed to give them a smashing victory over the Americans, to demoralize the Army of the Republic of Vietnam (ARVN) forces, and to bring the urban population of South Vietnam over to their side. They would show the urban populations of South Vietnam that neither the Americans nor the South Vietnamese forces could protect them. The Communists hoped that their assaults would provoke popular uprisings against the South Vietnamese government, forcing Americans to leave and hastening the end of the war. But Tet turned out to be a major tactical defeat for the Communists; they failed to achieve most of their goals and suffered heavy losses. Most Vietcong military forces were decimated, and much of their political infrastructure was exposed and eliminated.

Within the United States, the Tet Offensive had a tremendous impact. Tet turned out to be a crucial psychological and political victory for the Communists. It had caught the South Vietnamese and Americans by surprise, although they had responded quickly to counteract it. President Johnson too was surprised and confused by the ability of an enemy that he had been told was verging on defeat to stage coordinated attacks against supposedly secure sites all over South Vietnam.

Although General Westmoreland talked confidently of having anticipated and suppressed the Tet Offensive, while inflicting heavy losses on the enemy, he shortly thereafter requested an additional 206,000 combat troops to be able to follow up and win the war. The chairman of the Joint Chiefs, General Earle Wheeler, gave the president the first pessimistic appraisal of the war that the president had ever heard from a military adviser. Wheeler hinted that Tet had "been a very near thing" and that the Americans could lose the war unless the requested reinforcements were sent. Johnson, confused by events and conflicting military opinions, asked his new Secretary of Defense Clark Clifford to conduct a thorough review

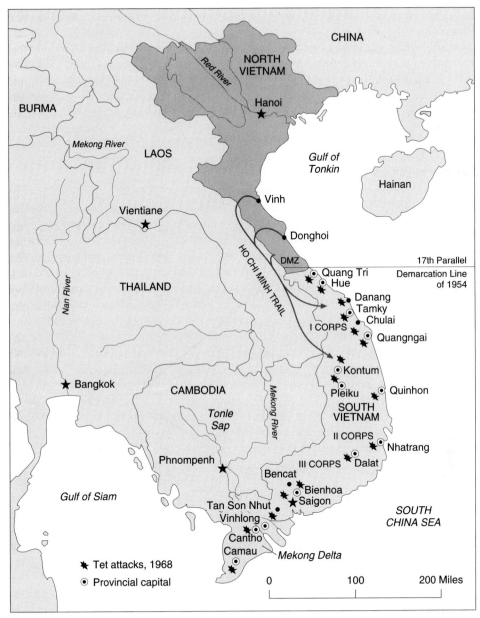

Figure 7.9   *Source:* U.S. Army map.

of the troop request before the administration responded to the military's request for more troops.

Clifford formed a task force of senior civilian and military officials, whose investigations ranged far beyond the troop request issue; they conducted the first full-scale review of the U.S. war effort in Vietnam. Clifford demanded precise answers to fundamental questions: What were the ultimate objectives of the United States in Vietnam? How would additional forces contribute to attaining these goals? What would be the impact of a major escalation of the war on the public and on the economy? Was there a definable limit to the American commitment to Vietnam? Was there a point at which the price became too high? How would General Westmoreland deploy these troops, and exactly what results could be expected from this additional manpower?

The answers he received from the Pentagon discouraged Clifford. To provide 206,000 more troops for Vietnam required further reductions of U.S. military commitments elsewhere, which were already stretched dangerously thin. America's ability to meet its major strategic commitments in other parts of the world and its capability to respond to challenges to its vital interests elsewhere would be compromised. Meeting these troop requests would require calling up reserves, increasing draft calls, and raising taxes. Casualties would rise, and domestic opposition would intensify. Civilian analysts in the Pentagon told Clifford that the current war strategy could not bring victory, even with the proposed escalation; they recommended that the United States start phasing back its military involvement and trying for a negotiated settlement. They also proposed turning over more of the fighting to the South Vietnamese forces. After his careful reappraisal of the entire war effort, Clifford recommended to President Johnson that he reject Westmoreland's request for additional troops, assign the ARVN a greater fighting role, and seek a negotiated settlement.

The Tet Offensive also influenced the way in which the media, particularly television news, covered the Vietnam War. Previously, television had usually presented a well-ordered vision of the war—on-the-scene reports of combat operations that were usually reported as American victories, along with periodic analytical reports of the war's progress and of pacification programs. With Tet, viewers for the first time saw the results of a major Communist offensive striking all over South Vietnam. A rush of violent, confusing images flooded television—fighting in the streets of Saigon and Hue. The chaos in Vietnam viewed on television appeared to contradict all of the official reports and media coverage of the past three years that had conveyed the idea of steady progress toward military victory. That the enemy could stage surprise attacks all over South Vietnam caused a growing number of Americans to wonder if all that three years of escalating war had achieved in Vietnam was an unending stalemate with ever-rising costs and casualties. In the months following the Tet Offensive, public opinion polls recorded increases in the number of people expressing dovish sentiments.

Congressional opposition to the war also escalated after Tet. Antiwar sentiment on Capitol Hill boosted the candidacy of an obscure Minnesota Senator Eugene McCarthy, who had announced in December 1967 that he would challenge Lyndon Johnson for the presidency as an antiwar candidate. In the New Hampshire primary on March 12, 1968, McCarthy received 42 percent of the vote, almost as many as Johnson, indicating more widespread opposition to Johnson's war policy than previously thought. Johnson appeared unpopular and politically vulnerable. Four days after the New Hampshire primary, a more formidable antiwar candidate, Robert Kennedy, announced that he too would seek the Democratic nomination.

At the White House, Johnson struggled with his failing Vietnam policy. He convened a panel of distinguished civilian and military advisers who had previously endorsed his war policy. But in March, these "wise men" told the president that the Vietnam War could not be won, "save at unacceptable risk" to national interests at home and abroad. Their advice influenced Johnson. He accepted Clark Clifford's recommendations to scale back the war. On March 31, 1968, Johnson told the American people that he would not grant the army's request for another 206,000 troops. He also announced that he would reduce the bombing of North Vietnam in an effort to get negotiations underway. As he neared the end of his speech, he stunned the nation by stating, "I shall not seek, nor will I accept, the nomination of my party for another term as your president." To restore unity to America, he would remove himself from politics and seek peace in Vietnam. To end the war that was tearing the nation apart at home, he would abandon the strategy of gradual escalation in Vietnam that he had begun three years earlier. Vietnam had claimed its most prominent victim.

BIBLIOGRAPHY

Robert Caro has completed two volumes of his massive biographical study of Lyndon Johnson, *The Path to Power* and *Means of Ascent.* Caro's research has given him encyclopedic knowledge of the details of Johnson's life, and he writes well. His books are marred by his remorseless hostility to his subject. Robert Dallek has written a substantial two-volume biography of Johnson, *Lone Star Rising: Lyndon Johnson and His Times, 1908–1960* and *Flawed Giant: Lyndon Johnson and His Times, 1961–1973.* Dallek's work is balanced and more sophisticated than Caro's. Doris Kearns's *Lyndon Johnson and the American Dream* is an insightful study of Johnson's political career. Eric Goldman's *The Tragedy of Lyndon Johnson* is a sympathetic account of his presidency. James M. Sundquist's *Politics and Policy: The Eisenhower, Kennedy, and Johnson Years* offers a good account of the Great Society programs. Michael Harrington's analysis of poverty in the United States, *The Other America,* helped start the war on poverty. James C. Harvey's *Black Civil Rights during the Johnson Administration* is a good account of this important issue. Bernard Schwartz, in *Super Chief: Earl Warren and His Supreme Court,* offers a good study of the many landmark decisions of the Warren Court and of the man who led it. Johnson's foreign policy is studied by Philip L. Geyelin in *Lyndon B. Johnson and the World.* A good general military and diplomatic history of U.S. involvement in Vietnam is my *Vietnam: An American Ordeal,* 3d ed. George C. Herring's *America's Longest War: The United States and Vietnam, 1950–1975,* 3d ed., is a concise diplomatic history of the war. Larry Berman's *Planning a Tragedy* is an acute study of the Johnson administration's decision to go to war in Vietnam. Neil Sheehan, in *A Bright Shining Lie: John Paul Vann and America in Vietnam,* offers a fine study of a capable official who gave ten years and finally his life to the American cause in Vietnam. It also is a finely crafted history of American involvement in Vietnam.

8

Rebellion and Reaction

The 1960s had begun with President Kennedy's appeal for national renewal. He had urged young people to channel their energy and idealism into community service at home and the Peace Corps abroad. Thousands followed his lead. But after his assassination, the national scenario that unfolded for the rest of the decade featured sit-ins, marches, riots, bombings, the burning of cities, and more assassinations. Hopes for peace, prosperity, and justice for all vanished in the face of political conflict, cultural crisis, and the Vietnam War. Some Americans were temporarily radicalized by their experiences; far more Americans turned conservative or simply abandoned politics. The liberal consensus that had been forged during the 1930s, 1940s, and 1950s as a consequence of fighting the Great Depression, World War II, and the Cold War disintegrated during the 1960s.

During the early 1960s, the economy was strong, the federal budget was balanced, inflation was low, and the nation was at peace. Most Americans were happy, better off materially than they had ever been, and optimistic about a future in which conditions, already good, could only get better. Social tranquility prevailed everywhere. Prospects had never looked better for the children of affluence. By 1968, inflation riddled the economy, the people were divided over a stalemated, controversial war, and race riots tore apart major cities. Political assassinations agonized everyone; students protested on college campuses and in the streets. Other radical insurgents protested historical exclusions and injustices and demanded their fair share of the American Dream. Drugs and crime had become major concerns.

As civility was drained from American public life, many thoughtful Americans feared that the dark forces unleashed by protest and war might rip the social fabric apart and undermine the political order. Amidst the worst backdrop of violence and disorder since the

Civil War, Americans conducted the 1968 election. Amidst a complex, chaotic campaign, Richard Nixon emerged as the candidate pledged to end a controversial war abroad, to uphold traditional values, and to restore peace and unity at home.

YOUNG RADICALS

The insurgencies that characterized the middle and late 1960s began on the campuses of some of America's leading universities, the prestigious Ivy League schools, and the great public universities such as the Berkeley campus of the University of California and the University of Michigan at Ann Arbor. A new generation of politically committed young people had already become involved in the civil rights movement and had also tried to organize poor people at the community level. After 1965, many of these youthful insurgents, most of them from affluent middle-class families, became involved in protesting the Vietnam War. In 1960, a group of young activists organized Students for a Democratic Society (SDS). In 1962, one of its leaders, Tom Hayden, wrote a manifesto for the new organization, the *Port Huron Statement.* Hayden criticized the apolitical apathy of college students and attacked the military-industrial complex as a threat to democracy. He called for an end to poverty in America and for the creation of "a democracy of individual participation," in which all members subject to the authority of a government institution would participate in its decision-making processes. Until it disintegrated in 1969, the SDS led the emergent New Left.

The first student uprising occurred on the Berkeley campus of the University of California in the fall of 1964. A group of students, many of them civil rights activists who had spent the previous summer registering voters in Mississippi, protested university efforts to prevent their using a campus area for rallying support for off-campus political activities. Student leaders Mario Savio and Jack Weinberg, both veterans of the Mississippi "Freedom Summer," formed the Free Speech Movement (FSM) to lead the resistance. When university officials attempted to discipline leaders of the FSM, about 600 students and nonstudents occupied Sproul Hall, the university administration building. After university efforts to persuade the protesters to leave failed, Governor Edmund G. "Pat" Brown ordered state police to remove and arrest them. The forced removal of the demonstrators provoked a student strike, which was supported by a large majority of the faculty. After two months of turmoil on campus, university officials rescinded the order and permitted "free speech" on campus.

Leaders of the FSM aimed their attacks at the university itself. They saw it as a willing servant of a corporate order that controlled society and maintained an economic system that oppressed blacks and poor people. In their view, Berkeley had become an "impersonal machine," serving the established power structure and preparing students for careers as corporate functionaries. Cards designed by IBM and used to classify and identify students became for young radicals symbols of an educational system that had lost sight of its primary humanistic goals of making people better and improving society.

The rebellion that began at Berkeley soon spread to other campuses around the country. Insurgents attacked university complicity with racial injustice and the Vietnam War.

Figure 8.1   Columbia 1968: Young people occupy an area of Hamilton Hall on the Morningside Heights campus in New York City. *Source:* AP/Wide World Photos.

They also attacked the universities themselves. They rebelled against receiving "assembly line educations." Protesters demanded the right to sit on governing boards with the power to veto faculty appointments. Curricula and methods of instruction came under fire. Students objected to taking "irrelevant" courses, mostly required science and language classes. They called for fewer required courses, more electives, and fewer tests and grades. Other campus protests arose over issues concerning the personal lives of students. Protesters demanded the elimination of college parietal rules, which set curfews, imposed dress codes, and regulated visiting hours for university housing.

The SDS became prominent on many college campuses, as it took the lead organizing opposition to the expanding war in Vietnam. By the mid-1960s, the stalemated Vietnam War had become the main student protest issue. Since the military draft was the prime way the war could reach young people, opposition to the draft brought thousands of new recruits into protest politics. When the SDS launched a national draft resistance program, new chapters proliferated as thousands of recruits rushed to join. The SDS organized a Stop the Draft Week for October 16 to 21, 1967. It staged sit-ins at army induction centers, held meetings for draft card burnings, opposed campus ROTC programs, demonstrated against corporations known to be prime Defense Department contractors, and harassed military recruiters. Thousands of protesters besieged the Oakland, California, Army Induction Center; hundreds sat in the street blocking buses hauling in draftees. Between 1965 and 1968, the SDS led or joined hundreds of demonstrations at over 100 colleges and universities involving about 50,000 students. As the Vietnam War grew larger, the protest tactics employed by the SDS and other antiwar war groups grew more militant. The SDS also joined other groups opposed to the continuing war. The SDS participated in the march on the Pentagon, staged on October 21, 1967. About 50,000 protesters participated in the largest antiwar demonstration to date.

The SDS also joined in one of the most violent student uprisings of the turbulent 1960s, which occurred at Columbia University during the first six months of 1968. The issues that sparked the conflict were two potent catalysts of student militancy—civil rights and Vietnam. Antiwar radicals and civil rights activists joined forces to attack one of the nation's most prestigious universities. The SDS sought an end to university ties with a military research institute on campus. The Black Student Union opposed university plans to construct a gymnasium on land adjacent to Harlem. Both groups occupied campus buildings to force the university to sever its ties with the military and to abandon the gym project. When negotiations between administration officials and students failed, police stormed the buildings to remove the protesters, who had barricaded doors and windows. Hundreds of students were injured, and about 700 were arrested. Following the arrests, the SDS organized a campus strike that forced the university to close early that spring.

American student protests in 1968 were part of a larger web of student and worker militant actions around the world. While students barricaded buildings at Columbia, 10 million French workers went on strike, and students battled police in the streets of Paris. Mass demonstrations occurred in Sao Paulo, Brazil; the most violent street fighting in decades occurred in Italy. In London, 25,000 people protested the Vietnam War. Radical political movements of every kind convulsed the planet during one of the most transformative years of the twentieth century.

At its 1969 annual meeting, the New Left collapsed, splitting into warring factions. Its left-wing faction, calling itself the "Weathermen," went off on its own. In October, hundreds of Weathermen staged "the days of rage" in Chicago, which they intended to be the opening campaign of a new American revolution. They broke windows in buildings and smashed automobile windshields. Police arrested and jailed most of them. About 100 Weathermen went underground, forming terrorist bands that carried out sporadic bombings of public buildings and corporate headquarters during the early 1970s.

The New Left radicalized only a small portion of the millions of young people attending college during the 1960s. Most students attended class, pursued their social lives, worked part time, and sought conventional goals. They never participated in radical protests on or off campus. Student rebels were mostly clustered on the campuses of major metropolitan universities such as Berkeley and Columbia. Because they were a highly visible, articulate group that received extensive media coverage, especially television news coverage, the public perception was that student radicalism was much more extensive than demographic data confirmed. Most of the nation's 2,300 community colleges, state universities, private liberal arts colleges, and campuses with religious affiliations, which educated the vast majority of the nation's collegians, remained quiet, orderly, businesslike places during the 1960s. The young radicals of the 1960s came mostly from upper middle-class backgrounds; they were mostly the children of college-educated, liberal, affluent, and often influential parents. They formed a politicized radical elite that rebelled against some of the institutions and practices of the affluent society. But these comparatively few privileged insurgents provoked a rebellion that spread beyond politics to challenge the entire culture. This cultural rebellion posed a more fundamental challenge to the values and mores of the consumerist culture than did the New Left, and it had a far wider appeal to young people of the 1960s.

THE GREENING OF AMERICA

Far more young people who felt alienated and frustrated by the affluent society of the 1960s fled from it rather than radically confronted it. These "hippies" took a path previously traveled by Bohemians during the Roaring Twenties and the Beats during the 1950s. In fact, the best of the Beat poets, Allen Ginsberg, was a prominent member of the 1960s' counterculture. The hippies embraced a new youth culture that ran counter to much that was cherished by middle-class Americans—affluence, economic growth, high technology, and, according to historian William Leuchtenburg,

> the institutions and value systems associated with the Protestant ethic of self-denial and sexual repression and more modern premises of the consumer culture and the meritocracy.[1]

The discipline of parents, schools, and jobs was abandoned for a free-flowing antinomian existence expressed by the hippie motto, "Do your own thing."

Hippies grew long hair and donned a uniform of jeans, tank tops, and sandals. These refugees from the "uptight, straight" world of parents, schools, and eight-to-five jobs flocked to havens in the Haight-Ashbury section of San Francisco, the Sunset Strip in Hollywood, and New York's East Village. They "dropped out" of straight society to join communes that cropped up in both urban neighborhoods and rural retreats. Communes varied considerably in their creeds and customs, but most were founded on hippie notions of extended family and collective property ownership. The appeal of the commune movement lay in a romantic urge to return to the land: to take up a simpler lifestyle, to regain physical and mental health, and to seek spiritual renewal. Most communes turned out to be short-lived experiments in communal living. They foundered on the inexperience of their members, practical problems of organization and financing, and personal conflicts and jealousies among the participants. Some communes were successful, but those that worked were usually organized along hierarchic lines, often assigned women traditional subordinate domestic roles, and were usually held together by strong religious commitments. Whether these latter-day communitarians were aware of it or not, their communes resembled the utopian communities that dotted the American rural landscape in the first three decades of the nineteenth century.

[1]William E. Leuchtenburg, *A Troubled Feast,* updated ed. (Boston: Little, Brown, 1983), p. 179.

One commune turned pathological. A deranged ex-con, Charles Manson, who drifted into the Haight-Ashbury *demimonde* after his release from prison, gained control over a small Haight-Ashbury commune of nine young women and five young men. Manson, who was a paranoid psychopath, relocated his "family" in an arid mountainous region north of Los Angeles. In April 1969, upon Mason's orders, four members of his family murdered actress Sharon Tate and four of her jet-set friends at her expensive Bel-Air home. Manson was convicted of several counts of first degree murder and sentenced to life imprisonment. Several other members of the Manson family also served time in prison for murder and for conspiracy to commit murder. No coherent motives for the mass murders were ever established. Manson appears to have had some absurd notion of starting a race war between black people and white people that could lead to anarchy and revolution, because he had directed the murderous members of his family to scribble slogans on mirrors in the homes of their victims that were supposed to make it appear that black militants had killed rich white people, simply because they hated them for being rich and white.

The counterculture repudiated science, systematic knowledge, and rationalism. It embraced a notion of organic, mystical consciousness in which the Self merged seamlessly with Community and Nature. Infinite being supplanted linear boundaries of time and space. Feeling and intuition replaced thought and knowing. Hippies explored ancient mystical Asian and African religions. Saffron-robed skinheads on San Francisco street corners chanted the "Hare Krishna." Others found the Age of Aquarius in astrology. Some hippies turned to witchcraft and demonology. They also flocked to religious revivals and joined fundamentalist churches to participate in the emotional exaltations of passionate worship. Nature was valued as being superior to society and technology. A wide array of synthetic consumer products were rejected as artificial, "plastic." Hippies prized being natural, using nature's products, and eating natural foods. The hippie ideal was authenticity, to live a life free of conflict, exploitation, and alienation; a life in harmony with society, nature, and one's true self.

Hippies also repudiated the restrictive sexual practices of "Puritan" America. Although Dr. Kinsey's studies had shown that sexual behavior in this country had become more liberal, hippies moved far beyond middle-class proprieties and inhibitions. The freer sexuality of the hippie lifestyle became one of its main attractions and also provoked the wrath of elders. Casual sex often tied into countercultural music, as flocks of teenage "groupies" sought out rock musicians. English groups, especially the Beatles and the Rolling Stones, expressed the central themes and ideals of the hippie worldview. Folk singers Joan Baez and Bob Dylan were the main American countercultural icons. Dylan sang "The Times They are A-Changin" and "Blowing in the Wind."

Rock 'n' roll music evolved from the sweet and sentimental love songs of the Beatles to the overt sexuality of the Rolling Stones and the Doors. In San Francisco, "acid rock" appeared. Promoter Bill Graham staged concerts at the Fillmore West, featuring the psychedelic sounds of San Francisco's homegrown bands, the Grateful Dead and Jefferson Airplane. A young white blues singer from Port Arthur, Texas, Janis Joplin, became the queen of San Francisco's psychedelic music scene. Drugs intertwined with music to form the vital center of the counterculture. "Tune in, turn on, and drop out" urged the high priest of LSD, Timothy Leary, a former Harvard psychologist who had been fired for conducting

Figure 8.2   The Beatles. (L-R): John Lennon, Paul McCartney, George Harrison, and Ringo Starr. *Source:* St. Louis Mercantile Library. Used with permission.

psychedelic drug experiments on his students. Song lyrics such as the Beatles' "Lucy in the Sky with Diamonds" spelled out LSD. Steppenwolf sang "Magic Carpet Ride," celebrating drug tripping. Many of the prominent musical stars of the counterculture were heavy drug users, and several died of drug overdoses, including Joplin and Jimmy Hendrix. Authorities found Joplin dead of a heroin overdose at age twenty-seven in a seedy Hollywood hotel room.

Drugs reached into the countercultural literary scene, continuing a Beat Generation tradition. A gifted young writer, Ken Kesey, wrote part of his best-selling first novel *One Flew Over the Cuckoo's Nest* under the influence of LSD. With money earned from its sales, he purchased a bus and named it "Further." He painted it in psychedelic Day-Glo colors, wired it for stereo, and he and his friends, who called themselves the Merry Pranksters, toured up and down the West Coast. Everywhere they went they conducted "acid tests," wild parties featuring LSD-spiked Kool-Aid, loud rock music, and light shows. Kesey and the Merry Pranksters also joined forces with rock impresario Bill Graham to stage a Tripps Festival at the Fillmore, starring the Grateful Dead and Big Brother and the Holding Company, whose lead singer at the time was Janis Joplin.

Marijuana use was far more widespread than LSD. "Pot" became the common currency of the counterculture and spread into mainstream society. Marijuana turned up at high school and college parties during the 1960s. Older people, with a yen for experimenting or a desire to be "with it," also tried marijuana. As the counterculture moved out of its enclaves in San Francisco, Los Angeles, and New York and began to spring up in other towns and cities in the late 1960s, it evolved into a kind of youth mass movement. Each community appeared to have its coterie of long-haired, drug-using rock devotees. Hippies also experimented with other drugs, including mescaline and methedrine. Countercultural drug use provoked a pathetic debate over whether smoking marijuana was less harmful than smoking cigarettes or drinking alcoholic beverages. All of these substances could be harmful, but that fact was beside the point, because the debate was really about values and lifestyles, not the pharmacological properties of marijuana, tobacco, and alcohol.

One of the major events in the life of the counterculture, "the summer of love," occurred in the summer of 1967 in San Francisco's Haight-Ashbury district. Hippies sought a cultural counterpart to the SDS's proclaimed summer of protest against the Vietnam War. Young people would flock to "the Haight" from all over the country; just as radical politics was transforming American political life, the summer of love would transform society by creating a community of young dropouts uninhibitedly enjoying the pleasures of the flesh. The reality of what occurred was dismal. Thousands of youngsters showed up, most of them runaways from troubled homes, utterly unprepared to support themselves. Many were poorly educated and lacked any job skills; they often were reduced to panhandling, drug dealing, and prostitution to survive. Sexual promiscuity and rampant drug use led to epidemics of venereal disease and drug overdoses. Far from fleeing the social problems of the larger society, the runaways brought these problems with them. Racial tensions between hippies living in the Haight-Ashbury and a nearby African-American community in the Fillmore district added a hateful dimension to the summer of love. Writer Joan Didion, who visited the Haight-Ashbury during the summer of 1967, wrote a famous essay, *Slouching toward Bethlehem,* in which she recorded the squalor, pain, and aimless drifting of hippie existence. Didion found the summer of love to be

> the desperate attempt of a handful of pathetically unequipped children to create a community in a social vacuum. . . . They are less in rebellion against society than ignorant of it.[2]

The hippie triad of drugs, sex, and rock music came together at rock festivals, the most important ritual of the countercultural community. The greatest of these "happenings" occurred at Woodstock, New York, in August 1969. At a site near the village of Woodstock in New York's Hudson River valley, between 300,000 and 400,000 young people gathered to hear music, enjoy drugs, and engage in casual sex. In time, the Woodstock festival assumed mythic proportions; it was remembered as the highpoint of the counterculture. The following summer, another rock festival held at Altamont Speedway, located in a rural area sixty miles east of San Francisco, turned violent. The headline rock band, the Rolling Stones, hired an outlaw motorcycle club, the Hell's Angels, to provide security for the Altamont festival. The Hell's Angels, high on dope and drunk on beer, killed one participant, severely injured scores of others, and succeeded in terrorizing the entire gathering. If Woodstock was the alpha of the counterculture, Altamont was its omega.

Intellectuals fashioned ideologies for the counterculture. Charles Reich wrote in *Greening of America* about a new consciousness that would renew America, forming the basis of another American revolution, one without tears or violence. The new order would just happen. But the counterculture's expected new utopia never arrived. Instead, it turned sour and disintegrated. In the Haight-Ashbury, tough street hustlers drove out the hippies and took over the drug traffic. Hard drugs replaced marijuana. Violence, most of it con-

[2]Joan Didion, *Slouching toward Bethlehem* (New York: Washington Square Press, 1968), p. 127.

Figure 8.3   Cheerful Hippies at Woodstock.   *Source:* Corbis.

nected with illegal drug traffic, destroyed much of what had been attractive in the hippie culture, particularly its gentleness and openness.

The counterculture lasted half a decade, then it simply evaporated, quickly becoming only an exotic memory. It had sprung to life because of some special circumstances prevailing during the 1960s. The postwar baby boom had created a large population cluster of young people between the ages of fourteen and twenty-five. Such a huge youth population created, for a moment, a consciousness of a separate culture. Permissive child-rearing practices also contributed to the formation of the counterculture. These children of abundance confronted a complex, affluent, and mobile world of protracted education, large-scale corporate and government bureaucracies, an intricate, powerful technology, severe social conflicts and inequities, and most of all, the military draft and a controversial war in Vietnam. Young people recoiled in fear and loathing over a world that they never made and became "flower children" who urged others "to make love not war."

Although it held far greater attractions for young people than radical politics, it remains true that only a minority of young people ever joined the counterculture. Most youngsters went about the difficult enterprise of growing up and entering the adult world without visible alienation or protest. The greatest gap in the 1960s social fabric was not a generation gap between children and parents but between different segments of the youth population. The more significant gap was intragenerational, not intergenerational. Value conflicts between middle-class and working-class young people were profound and occasionally violent. Middle-class campus radicals scoffed at bourgeois sensibilities and burned their draft cards. Young workers, for whom middle-class respectability remained a cherished ambition, defended their ways of life and patriotically supported the Vietnam War. Long-haired hippies and antiwar demonstrators infuriated working-class youth who regarded them as effete cowards and traitors. One of the most violent riots of the era occurred in New York, when construction workers attacked a crowd of antiwar demonstrators.

Although short-lived and engaging only a small fraction of young people during the 1960s, both the New Left and the counterculture left their marks. They heightened consciousness of imperialism, war, poverty, and racial injustice. They called attention to the negative ecological and human consequences of modern technology. And they forced some people to confront the disparities between their professed ideals and the lives that they lived. The most enduring impact of the counterculture came in lifestyle realms—diet, dress, decorative art, music, and sexual practices. People became more concerned about developing their inner selves, achieving their human potential, rather than seeking the external trappings of success. The transient young rebels of the 1960s triggered a host of insurgencies that brought about a fundamental reappraisal of American values and goals during the late 1960s.

THE FIRE THIS TIME

The civil rights movement crested in 1965 when Martin Luther King Jr. led the Selma march and Congress passed the Voting Rights Act. Five days after President Johnson signed that historic measure, the Watts section of Los Angeles went up in flames. It ushered in the first of several successive "long, hot summers." The Watts riot, a week-long orgy of burning and looting, claimed thirty-four lives, injured 1,100 people, and destroyed $40 million worth of property. The Watts explosion dismayed civil rights reformers, because the residents of Watts generally lived much better than most African-American slum dwellers in America. Watts was not physically a ghetto, since families did not live in crowded, dilapidated tenements; they lived in single, detached houses with lawns located along palm-shaded boulevards. Three African Americans sat on the Los Angeles City Council; Watts was represented by a black Congressman and two black state assemblymen. Economically, African Americans living in Watts were better off than blacks in any other large American city.

Watts revealed a depth of antiwhite bitterness and alienation that few civil rights workers of either race even knew existed. African-American progress in recent years and the promise of more to come had only raised exaggerated expectations and intensified the rage of many Watts residents. A special commission investigating the Watts upheaval warned that if the breach between the races was not healed, the riot might be a curtain-raiser for future racial blowups. The commission's warning proved prophetic. Between 1965 and 1968, hundreds of inner cities exploded into major riots.

The worst violence occurred in Newark and Detroit within the same week of July 1967. In Newark, twenty-six people died and 1,200 were injured. In Detroit, forty-three people died and another 2,000 were hurt. Fires burned out the center of the nation's fifth largest city. For two weeks that summer, Detroit was a war zone with tanks rolling through the streets and the sound of machine-gun fire piercing the air.

Detroit's riot was the most alarming, not only because of the extensive destruction of life and property, but also because it occurred in a city governed by a coalition that included extensive African-American participation. Great Society reformers had lavished extensive antipoverty and urban renewal programs on the Motor City. One-fourth of all workers employed in the automobile industry, Detroit's major business, was black; the UAW was a progressive, integrated union. About 45 percent of Detroit's African-American families owned their own homes. Analysts of the Detroit riot drew a portrait of the typical rioter—a young adult black male, a high school graduate, employed, often an auto worker and a union member, a veteran, married, and an annual income slightly below the national median for his age group. This data suggests that the typical Detroit rioters were neither juveniles out on a spree nor despairing members of a black underclass. The rioting did not occur in the worst neighborhoods but in black working-class neighborhoods containing a high percentage of owner-occupied homes and intact families. African-American rage and violence in Detroit were apparently provoked more by insensitive police tactics than by deprivation and despair.

Nearly all major race riots started from minor episodes, often from incidents growing out of white police arresting African Americans. Watts blew up when a crowd gathered to protest the arrest of a drunken motorist. Newark exploded after police arrested an African American taxicab driver, John Smith, for following a police car too closely. Smith protested and was beaten by the arresting officers; news of the beating provoked the riot. Detroit erupted when police raided an after-hours bar hosting a party for two returning Vietnam veterans.

Studies revealed a general pattern prevailing in the major urban riots. Most rioting occurred within ghetto confines; most of the destruction was inflicted upon ghetto homes and businesses; and most of the violence occurred between rioters and law enforcement personnel. Over 80 percent of the fatalities were rioters, shot either by the police or by soldiers. Studies of all major riots also suggested that the underlying causes of the uprisings were chronic slum conditions, aggravated by rough police tactics and hot, humid weather. Frustration with the slow pace of black economic progress, despite years of civil rights agitation, Great Society reforms, and the war on poverty, also fueled the rioting. The National Advisory Commission on Civil Disorders called attention to a crucial reality about the black ghetto: "White institutions created it, white institutions maintain it, and white society condones it."

BLACK POWER

The slogan "black power" made its appearance in 1966, when James Meredith attempted to march from Memphis, Tennessee, to Jackson, Mississippi, to inspire African Americans of his native state to assert their rights. He got only ten miles into Mississippi when a sniper severely wounded him. Dr. King and other civil rights leaders quickly arrived to complete his march. Two of the marchers, young leaders of the Student Non-Violent Coordinating Committee (SNCC), began chanting "black power." Soon, most of the marchers were chanting it. Initially, black power was a cry of outrage and defiance. It later became political doctrine, although remaining diffuse, meaning different things to different people. For SNCC leader Stokely Carmichael, black power meant that African Americans should take control of the civil rights movement, developing their own tactics and instruments of power. Implicit in these actions was a rejection of integration, of "black and white together." At the extremes, black power became an expression of African-American separatism and nationalism.

Black militants scorned white allies and approved of self-defensive violence. In 1968 and 1969, the Black Panthers, based in Oakland, California, replaced the SNCC as the vanguard black militant organization. Led by Huey Newton, Bobby Seale, and Eldridge Cleaver, the Black Panthers wore black leather jackets and brandished weapons, taking on a paramilitary cast. They espoused a Marxist rhetoric and declared war on capitalist institutions that they insisted kept black people enslaved. They also promised to liberate the black community from police harassment and intimidation, and they established some community-based programs. The Black Panthers did not succeed in establishing a broad base of community support, and they were repudiated by most responsible black political leaders. They came under FBI and police surveillance, and they were involved in shootouts with police that left several Black Panthers dead and wounded. It became fashionable, a statement of radical chic, among groups of affluent liberal whites to support the Panthers.

Black power also expressed African-American pride; it became a celebration of African-American history and culture, of "blackness itself." African-American students in high schools and colleges demanded that courses be added to established curricula in African-American history, literature, and languages. Black hair and dress styles appeared. Black power encouraged young blacks to seek success and to avoid emulating white role models. The popular soul singer James Brown sang, "Say it loud, I'm black and I'm proud."

MALCOLM X

The Nation of Islam, popularly known as the Black Muslims, articulated the most important expression of 1960s' black nationalism. Founded during the 1930s in Detroit by Elijah Poole, who called himself the Prophet Elijah Muhammad, it remained a small, obscure religious sect with about 100,000 members until the 1960s. Black Muslim ideology included hateful doctrines. Elijah Muhammad taught that all white people were evil, and that they were members of a satanic race sent by Allah to persecute black people. The Prophet also taught that the U.S. government ought to give African Americans a state of their own, as reparations for centuries of slavery and segregation. The Nation of Islam had recruited many of its followers from the bottom ranks of ghetto society—street hustlers, drug addicts, and ex-cons. Its most famous recruit was world heavyweight boxing champion Cassius Clay, who changed his name to Muhammad Ali following his conversion in 1965 to the Black Muslim sect.

The most articulate Nation of Islam spokesman was Malcolm Little, an ex-con who took the name Malcolm X. During the early 1960s, he offered a separatist alternative to Martin Luther King Jr.'s nonviolent tactics and goal of an integrated society.

Malcolm Little was born in 1925 in Nebraska, the son of an impoverished Baptist preacher, who had formerly worked as an organizer for Marcus Garvey. When Malcolm was six, his father was murdered, probably by members of the Ku Klux Klan. His mother had a nervous breakdown soon afterward, and Malcolm and his siblings were placed in foster homes. He dropped out of school during the eighth grade. As a teenager living in Boston, he got involved in a life of petty crime. The tall, light-skinned, red-haired man became known as "Detroit Red." Sent to jail for burglary in 1946, he spent the next five years in prison. While in prison, he converted to the Nation of Islam. A bright, intense man, he completely turned his life around. Abandoning his "slave name," he took the Black Muslim name of Malcolm X. Following his release from prison, he became an evangelist for the Nation of Islam. Gradually, Malcolm X emerged as the most eloquent and popular Black Muslim preacher.

He regularly denounced and ridiculed white people. He also jeered at Dr. King's tactics of nonviolent Christian love: "You need somebody who is going to fight, you don't need any kneeling in and crawling in." He both angered and frightened whites with his tirades against integration with "white devils." He preached both the doctrines of racial separation and self-defensive violence. He was suspended from the Nation of Islam by Elijah Muhammad after appearing to gloat over John Kennedy's assassination.

Following a pilgrimage to Mecca in 1964, Malcolm X's ideology began to evolve. He traveled to Africa, where he spoke in support of the efforts of black African nations to reclaim their sovereignty after a long period of European colonial domination. He returned to this country and founded his own movement—one that was more secular and political than the Nation of Islam's. He met with Dr. King and spoke to the people gathered in Selma, Alabama, for their march for voting rights. He warned the American people that if they did not accommodate moderates like Dr. King, they would have to deal with him. He acknowledged that the idea that all whites were devils was wrong. His political ideas were still evolving in the spring of 1965; he appeared to be groping for a radical integrationist

Figure 8.4   Malcolm X emerged during the early 1960s as the most militant voice of black nationalism. *Source:* Bettmann Archive.

strategy when he was murdered. Apparently his assassination had been ordered by Elijah Muhammad, or by leaders close to him. His book *The Autobiography of Malcolm X,* written with Alex Haley, became a posthumous best-seller. The book established Malcolm X as one of the foremost prophets of black liberation. Film actor Ossie Davis paid high tribute to Malcolm X when he said, "Malcolm expressed what was in all our hearts; he redeemed our manhood."

FREEDOM'S MARTYR

During the late 1960s, as the civil rights movement became radicalized and fragmented, Dr. King, who remained committed to the tactic of nonviolence and the goal of an integrated, color-blind society, remained the foremost black leader. But he found that his methods did not work in the North. He tried and failed to desegregate Chicago. Tactics that had been effective against the *de jure* segregation of Southern towns could not overcome the *de facto* segregation of Northern cities. Dr. King also became increasingly involved in protesting the Vietnam War, because it drained away funds for civil rights and the war on poverty. His attacks on the Vietnam War alienated President Johnson and cost him the support of the NAACP and the Urban League.

The civil rights movement, politically successful in the South but an economic failure in the North, was faltering by 1967. In the spring of 1968, trying to regain momentum,

Dr. King prepared to lead a poor people's march on Washington. He also took time to go to Memphis to lend support to a garbage workers' strike. While standing on a Memphis motel balcony, he was shot by James Earl Ray, a white drifter and an ex-con. News of King's murder provoked race riots across the land. The worst occurred in the nation's capital. Buildings burned within a few blocks of the White House, and soldiers mounted machine guns on the Capitol's steps.

RED AND BROWN POWER

Other minorities, spurred by the example of African-American insurgents, rebelled during the 1960s. Hispanic militants made their presence felt. Latinos living within the United States were diverse. They shared a common heritage based on the Spanish language and culture, but their families had come from Mexico, Puerto Rico, Cuba, Nicaragua, El Salvador, and a dozen other nations. It was impossible to form a pan-Hispanic organization or to articulate goals that all Latinos shared. Puerto Rican students in New York demanded that courses in Puerto Rican studies be added to high school and college curricula. Mexican-American militants also waged campaigns for recognition and self-assertion. Brown power militants began calling themselves "Chicanos," turning a term of opprobrium into a badge of pride and an assertion of ethnic identity that did not depend on a relationship with the "Anglo" world.

The most prominent Chicano militant of the 1960s was labor leader Cesar Chavez. A migrant farm worker turned labor organizer, Chavez founded the National Farm Workers Association (NFWA) in 1963. The NFWA joined other farm worker unions to form the United Farm Workers Organizing Committee (UFWOC), affiliated with the AFL-CIO. Chavez organized lettuce workers and grape pickers, using techniques developed by civil rights organizers, including marches, rallies, songs, and symbols that stressed the Chicano cultural heritage. Chavez led successful strikes in California's San Joaquin Valley in the 1960s. His movement obtained crucial assistance from urban, liberal, middle-class support

Figure 8.5   Cesar Chavez (checked shirt, right) leads striking grape pickers. Most of the pickers working the grape fields of California in the 1960s and 1970s were of Mexican descent.   *Source:* National Archives.

groups that raised funds for the strikers and staged consumer boycotts, making table grapes picked by "scab" (non-union) labor forbidden fruit.

Native American militants demanded respect for their cultural traditions and called attention to their severe economic needs, particularly repayment for their ancestral lands that had been illegally taken from them by Europeans and their descendants. Red power militant Vine Deloria Jr. wrote *Custer Died for Your Sins,* emphasizing the historical injustices European settlers in the New World had committed against Native Americans. A group of attorneys, including Native American lawyers, formed the Native American Rights Fund to seek the return of tribal lands illegally taken from Indians and to obtain compensation for other properties confiscated by whites.

GAY-LESBIAN LIBERATION

Another expression of the 1960s' insurgent spirit was the open avowal of homosexuality by formerly closeted gays and lesbians. If people could mobilize for political action around the issues of race, ethnicity, and gender, so too could they fight for their sexual identities and preferences. A dramatic event ignited the gay liberation movement: on June 29, 1969, police raided the Stonewall Inn, a gay bar located in Greenwich Village. Instead of meekly submitting to arrest, patrons defiantly hurled bottles at the police. They sent a message: there was a new militancy and pride growing among members of the gay community; they were no longer willing to passively accept police harassment and society's condemnations.

Gay and lesbian intellectuals developed ideologies that defined homosexuality as a legitimate sexual preference; they insisted that it was not abnormal, it was not sick, and it was not perverse. Gay and lesbian theorists attacked the psychoanalytic establishment for diagnosing homosexuality as a form of mental illness. Within gay-lesbian communities, a debate occurred over whether homosexuality was innate or a consequence of socialization. Essentialists argued that individuals were born gay or lesbian; others argued that gay and lesbian identities were socially constructed. Although gays and lesbians could not resolve the debate over nature versus nurture, the gay liberation movement enabled millions of homosexuals to come out of the closet and to make their claim for acceptance into the larger society. Militant homosexuals marched in gay liberation parades chanting, "Say it loud, gay is proud." Gay and lesbian activists organized for political action, seeking an end to legislative and job discrimination against homosexuals and a diminution of massive homophobic prejudices and violent assaults.

THE REBIRTH OF FEMINISM

The social and cultural ground was being prepared during the 1950s for a rebirth of feminism. By 1960, it had become the norm for middle-class white married women to perform paid work outside of the home. By 1962, married women accounted for nearly two-thirds of the female workforce. At the same time that they were entering the paid workforce in ever-greater numbers, more and more women were going to college and earning degrees. In 1961, women received over 40 percent of all baccalaureate degrees awarded by the nation's colleges and universities.

Despite such progress, women still entered a sex-segregated job market. They mostly took "women's jobs," such as nursing, clerical work, teaching, and domestic service—jobs that paid less than men's jobs and offered few prospects for promotion. In 1960, the median compensation for women working in full-time, year-round employment was 61 percent of men's earnings. Traditional assumptions about the proper roles of men and women in the society remained deeply ingrained. There was no organized feminist alternative to challenge the established order or male hegemony. The wife who worked was perceived to be helping her family achieve a middle-class status and lifestyle, not pursuing a career of her own. As the 1960s began, there existed an ideological lag; feminine consciousness lagged behind social reality. Even though cultural norms remained unquestioned, there was increasing ev-

Figure 8.6   Betty Friedan, founder of the modern women's movement and author of the best-selling *Feminine Mystique* (1963).   *Source:* AP/Wide World Photos.

idence that many college-educated, middle-class women were restive, frustrated, and un-fulfilled by lives that increasingly diverged from prescribed roles.

Because women, as women, did not share a common social experience, they tended to view their problems as individual rather than as socially derived. It was left to the founder of the modern women's movement, Betty Friedan, author of the best-selling *Feminine Mystique* (1963), to show women that what they had previously understood to be their individual problems were in fact women's problems. They were caused not by personal inadequacies but by deeply rooted attitudes that would have to be changed before women could achieve equality and fulfillment. Friedan, giving eloquent voice to the discontents of middle-class women, called the suburban split-level home "a comfortable concentration camp." She called attention to the "problem which has no name": feelings of emptiness, of being incomplete, of wondering who am I? She asked: "What is the cause of the identity problems which bothers so many women who have ostensibly fulfilled the American dream?" She urged women to listen to that still-small voice within that demands "something more than my husband and my children and my home."

The civil rights movement of the early 1960s catalyzed a sense of grievance among women. Women witnessed, and often joined, civil rights demonstrations. The civil rights movement also offered a model for political activity. Women made connections between African-American demands for freedom, equality, and dignity and their own lives; they saw possibilities for acting for themselves, of mobilizing for group political action. Women perceived that the same society that oppressed blacks also oppressed women; both groups had been assigned separate and unequal spheres and had been told to stay in their respective places. Any efforts at self-assertion or challenges to the status quo were considered deviant and were punished. Women reasoned that if it was wrong to deny opportunity to one group because of skin color, it was wrong to deny it to another group because of gender.

The Great Society inadvertently helped the cause of women's rights. When the bill that eventually became the Civil Rights Act of 1964 was being drafted in committee, conservatives tried to kill it. Title VII of the Act contained a provision banning discrimination in hiring and promotion on the basis of race. Howard Smith, a powerful conservative Democrat from Virginia, introduced an amendment to Title VII, banning job discrimination on the basis of sex. Smith believed that his amendment would defeat the proposed Title VII by reducing the whole matter of civil rights to an unenforceable absurdity. He and his conservative colleagues were mistaken. Supporters of Title VII pushed it through along with Smith's amendment, and it became the law of the land.

Initially the Equal Opportunity Employment Commission (EOEC), which had responsibility for enforcing Title VII of the Civil Rights Act, did not enforce the provision against sex discrimination. In response to EOEC's failure to enforce Title VII on behalf of women workers, Betty Friedan and other women activists formed the National Organization for Women (NOW) in 1966 to pressure the commission to take seriously sex discrimination in hiring. Other groups soon mobilized, and the women's rights movement was reborn. Initially these feminist organizations were pressure groups that sought to mobilize public opinion and obtain litigation on behalf of their cause. They sought change from within the existing structure. In part, the new feminism was a species of liberal reform. It called for equal pay for equal work and demanded that women have equal access to all pro-

fessional schools and middle-class occupations. Feminists noted that women college graduates earned only about half of the median income of men with similar credentials. To allow women to compete equally in the job market with men, feminists demanded publicly
funded child care centers for women with pre-school-age children, and they sought legislation ending all forms of gender discrimination.

WOMEN'S LIBERATION

There also was a radical dimension to the emerging feminism of the 1960s that grew out
of the experiences of young women in the New Left, in SNCC and SDS. Mary King and
Casey Hayden, both civil rights activists within SNCC, had come to resent the arrogance
of male activists who expected the women to work hard, to take responsibilities and
risks, and yet to leave leadership and policy making to the men. When they raised these
issues at a SNCC convention, the male leaders responded by laughing at them. SNCC
Chairman Stokely Carmichael quipped, "The position of women in our movement is
prone."

These radical women gradually evolved a language to express their grievances. They
defined the problem as "sexism" or "male chauvinism." Having diagnosed the illness, they
proposed a cure—"women's liberation." While liberal feminist reformers in NOW fought
for equal pay for equal work, radical feminists such as King and Hayden demanded control
over their own bodies. They called for wider distribution of birth control literature, tougher
enforcement of rape laws, the sharing of housework and child-rearing duties with husbands,
and the right to abortion on demand. They met in small groups for intense "consciousness-
raising" sessions. These sessions also allowed women to understand that their personal
problems were connected to the larger realms of social power, of "sexual politics." Feminist writer Robin Morgan contributed the defining slogan of the women's liberation movement: "The personal is political." Some radical feminists such as Ti-Grace Atkinson and
Susan Brownmiller expressed hostility toward men, considering the sexual act a form of
male domination. They rejected such revered institutions as family and home, spurned
childbirth, and advised women to seek lesbian relationships.

The reborn feminist movement encountered a formidable array of obstacles from the
beginning. Many women as well as men rejected radical feminist demands. A 1970 Gallup
Poll showed that 70 percent of American women believed that they were treated fairly by
men. Feminist leader Gloria Steinem acknowledged that she spoke for only a minority of
women, but she attributed that reality to cultural conditioning. She asserted that women had
been brainwashed to accept their oppression; they required consciousness-raising sessions
to ignite a sense of grievance. Many men worried about the loss of male prerogatives that
had long been givens in the culture. Many women feared that men would respond to their
new assertiveness by abandoning their roles as providers and protectors. Fundamentalist
Christians were incensed, because feminist demands violated biblically ordained roles for
women.

The most serious obstacle faced by feminists trying to build a movement based on
women's common problems and concerns was the diversity of women the movement was

trying to organize. Women were differentiated on the basis of ethno-racial descent, class, age, education, occupation, and sexuality. Feminists quickly discovered that they had sharp differences among themselves on many matters. There were disagreements over priorities, over long- and short-term goals, and over methods and tactics. Was the most pressing problem economic—a capitalist system that oppressed women? Or was it cultural—male chauvinism? Because of the diversity prevailing among women activists, the reborn feminist movement of the 1960s spawned a proliferation of organizations, tactics, ideologies, and goals.

BACKLASH

By 1967, it seemed as though some unspoken signal had been sent coursing through the culture; the message had been received by SDS radicals, by black, brown, and red militants, and by activist women. Those who perceived themselves as oppressed, disadvantaged—to have been denied their full measure of freedom, equality, opportunity, and dignity—rose in rebellion. To borrow a phrase from the days of trade union organizing, these people vowed that, "We're not going to take it anymore!" Perhaps they sensed that their time had come, that the system was vulnerable, that it would be more responsive to their claims for justice and inclusion in the American Dream, that it would not, perhaps could not, strike them down, repress them, or deny them their due. These militants were no longer willing to play the game by the old rules. Never in the history of the Republic had so many groups mounted such a radical assault on cherished national values, mores, and institutions.

The radical insurgencies of the late 1960s provoked a furious response from the middle-class majority of Americans determined to uphold traditional American values and ways of life. The media dubbed their response the "backlash." Millions of citizens had raised their families, attended church, voted, paid taxes, obeyed the law, accumulated a modest estate, and sent their sons to fight the Vietnam War. The militant minority of blacks who rioted in the cities, of students who opposed the Vietnam War and carried Vietcong flags, and of long-haired hippies who openly flaunted their sexuality infuriated the middle-class majority.

The emergence of black power advocates provoked a response from hitherto passive groups. White, working-class ethnics felt especially threatened by African-American militants and were galvanized into action. These people had worked hard to achieve a modest piece of the American Dream: a decent home, a secure job, and perhaps a chance to see a bright son or daughter graduate from college. To them, it appeared as though militant blacks were demanding that the government give them these same things without working and without a struggle. White ethnics resented especially the antipoverty programs that appeared to reward black militants who threatened violent reprisals if they did not receive grants and jobs immediately, while law-abiding whites got nothing except higher tax bills. "Middle" Americans, those earning between $8,000 and $15,000 a year, who constituted the rank-and-file blue-collar and white-collar workforces of the country, generally opposed and resented the challenges posed by the insurgents.

Analysts have discerned a mix of forces driving the backlashers. In part, it was simply residual antiblack racism. Many Northern white ethnics and Southern white working-class people had been taught to hate and fear black people and to consider them inferior. They did not want to associate with them, they did not want their children attending school with them, and they surely did not want to have to compete with them in the workplace. Economic insecurities also drove the backlash. By the late 1960s, many Middle Americans were feeling the effects of inflation, indebtedness, and declining real income. A lot of Middle Americans, while not poor, enjoyed at best a marginal prosperity. Black demands for employment, rising taxes, and expensive governmental programs appeared to be direct threats to the economic well-being of increasingly hard-pressed Middle Americans.

Most important, it was a sense of cultural crisis that activated the backlash response. The demands of the militants—antiwar protesters, black power advocates, and feminist radicals, all magnified by extensive media coverage and commentary—represented an attack on the American way and its most cherished values and institutions: patriotism, the work ethic, mobility, family, and religion. While the sons of Middle America were fighting and dying in Vietnam, the sons of upper-middle-class families were opposing the war from the safe havens of prestigious university campuses and denouncing American society into the bargain. To many parents of soldiers, and to the soldiers themselves, these antiwar protesters appeared to be a privileged corps of impudent cowards and traitors.

The rise of the backlash was another important indicator of the conservative drift underway in the American political culture. By the late 1960s, working-class white families had come to distrust, and even to despise, what they had held in high regard since the 1930s: centralized governmental power. During the 1930s, New Dealers had used the power of the federal government to establish a lifeline for millions of American families left impoverished and bewildered by the Great Depression. By the 1960s, decades of prosperity had created a new middle class that included millions of working-class families that opposed higher taxes and many of the social programs that they funded. These Middle Americans also embraced traditional values and were unhappy when liberal Democratic leaders did not denounce immorality and social disorder. It also appeared to them that liberals were much too attentive to the needs of the dispossessed—the poor, minorities, and radicals, and they were neglecting the needs of hardworking, patriotic, God-fearing folks like themselves. The backlash was the most visible phenomenon feeding the growing anti-government mood of the late 1960s. But it was only part of a larger revolt in motion, a profound disillusionment with liberal government and those politicians and pundits who championed it.

THE ELECTION OF 1968

The radical insurgencies loose in the land, coupled with the intense backlash that they provoked, guaranteed that the 1968 election would occur against a backdrop of the worst conflict and violence within American society since the Civil War. The Democratic Party, closer to the social pulse than the Republican Party, was splintered by divisions seething within the deeply troubled nation. The antiwar candidacies of Senators Eugene McCarthy and Robert Kennedy gained momentum in the spring primaries. Party regulars backed Vice President Hubert Humphrey, a Cold War liberal supporting Johnson's Vietnam policy. It was a wide open race, with public opinion polls giving Kennedy an edge over Humphrey and McCarthy.

Although Robert Kennedy focused his presidential bid on opposing Johnson's Vietnam War policy, he appears to have also been searching for a new political vision for his troubled nation. Sensing that the liberal consensus of social reform at home and containing Communism abroad had collapsed, Kennedy groped for an alternative. He visited Native Americans on reservations, and he broke bread with Cesar Chavez in California. Robert Kennedy was the only established white politician with any credibility among black people following the assassination of Martin Luther King Jr. Kennedy also reached out to white, working-class backlashers. He stressed the importance of self-government, of citizen participation in the civic life of the nation. He urged people to get involved in community affairs. He sought a new community, more inclusive and more involved in the process of self-government. For the most part, he sought to revitalize and reshape liberalism, but he also picked up the growing conservatism of Middle Americans and sounded some of its themes. He criticized welfare programs because they created a class of dependents who existed on government handouts. He proposed job programs and community development programs involving local people and the private sector. His was a brave, lonely, and ultimately doomed voice, trying desperately to refashion a vision of the American nation that included everyone and thereby heal the cultural and class divisions that had set class against class, race against race, and fathers against sons during those terrible years.

In the California primary, Kennedy and McCarthy waged a decisive showdown battle. Kennedy, cashing in on his remarkable ability to attract black, Hispanic, and white working-class voters, narrowly defeated McCarthy. With his California victory, Kennedy appeared to have the Democratic nomination within his grasp. But on victory night, he was shot and fatally wounded in Los Angeles. His assassin was Sirhan Sirhan, an Arab Nationalist who apparently hated Kennedy for his strong support of Israel. Once again, a senseless act of violence had destroyed another popular leader. Kennedy's murder appeared to remove what little civility and restraint remained in the American political culture. Once more the nation paused, hurt and saddened, to pay their final respects to a second Kennedy who had fallen while trying to redeem his nation.

Robert Kennedy's murder removed any chance that antiwar forces could win at the Democratic Party's Chicago convention. The convention was a bitter affair. Humphrey won an easy first-ballot nomination. Convention delegates, after a lengthy, angry debate, adopted a pro-administration plank on the Vietnam War. The rest of the platform focused on domestic issues and reflected traditional liberal stands: consumer protection, increasing farmers' incomes, and supporting trade unions. Humphrey chose Senator Edmund Muskie of Maine, a respected party leader, as his running mate.

As the Democratic delegates gathered in Chicago to nominate a presidential candidate, some 10,000 to 12,000 antiwar radicals gathered in the Windy City to protest the war. Most came to support the efforts of antiwar Democratic politicians. More militant groups came to disrupt the convention and to provoke confrontations with the police. The demonstrators came up against Mayor Richard Daley, the convention host, who had vowed that there would be no disruptions. His forces cordoned off the convention site, and Daley deployed his police in the parks of Chicago, where protesters had gathered. He also had thousands of National Guardsmen and federal troops available if he felt they were needed. The total number of police, guardsmen, and federal troops probably outnumbered the protesters.

**Figure 8.7   War in the streets of Chicago. Police battle demonstrators outside of the De-
mocratic Convention on the night that Hubert Humphrey was nominated.**   *Source:*
Bettmann Archive.

The night that Hubert Humphrey was nominated, violence reigned in the streets of
Chicago. Protesters, attempting to march on the convention, were blocked by police. They
taunted them, shouted obscenities at them, and threw rocks and bottles at them. As some of
the demonstrators attempted to break through police cordons, the police attacked in force.
In a frenzy of violence, some of the police, chanting "Kill! Kill!" indiscriminately clubbed
and gassed demonstrators, newsmen, and bystanders. Television cameramen brought the violence into millions of living rooms. Many liberal Democrats were everlastingly horrified
by the actions of the Chicago police. But millions of other Democrats in white-collar suburbs and blue-collar neighborhoods cheered the police, seeing in the radical politics and
countercultural lifestyles of the youthful protesters an intolerable threat to order and traditional values. The different reactions to the televised violence reflected the profound divisions seething within the American political culture created by Vietnam, race riots, and domestic insurgencies. Hubert Humphrey emerged from the political ruins as the candidate of
a profoundly divided party.

   The divisive Democratic Convention and the violence in the streets of Chicago played
into the hands of the Republicans, who had previously held an orderly convention in Miami. They had nominated Richard Nixon, who had made a remarkable comeback. Nixon
had retired from politics following a disastrous defeat in the 1962 California gubernatorial
election, but he had worked hard for Republican candidates in 1964 and 1966, building support among party regulars. He had won a series of primary victories and gathered hundreds
of delegates from nonprimary states. He came to Miami the front-runner and easily repelled
his only remaining serious challenger, California Governor Ronald Reagan, who was mak-

ing the first of his several runs at the presidency. Nixon chose Spiro T. Agnew, the governor of Maryland, who had a reputation for talking tough on law and order issues, to be his running mate. The Republican platform called for an all-out war on crime, reform of the welfare laws, an end to inflation, and a buildup of defense forces. On the crucial Vietnam War issue, the Republicans promised to end the American war through purposeful negotiations but not to accept "camouflaged surrender." The Republicans pledged peace in Vietnam but not peace at any price.

Behind the Republican platform rhetoric and the choice of Agnew for vice president lay a shrewd political strategy. Nixon perceived that Southerners had become a power within his party. He also understood that Americans had become more conservative since 1964, when Johnson had scored his landslide victory over the hapless Goldwater. Nixon cut his ties with declining Northeastern liberal Republicans to forge an alliance with conservative Southerners led by Strom Thurmond. Nixon promised Thurmond that he would never abandon the South Vietnamese government and that he would slow the pace of school desegregation. He also promised to crack down hard on demonstrators who broke the law. Nixon's "Southern strategy" stopped Ronald Reagan's bid for the presidency, which had counted on winning the votes of Southern delegates. The only reason the Southern strategy did not give Nixon the entire South was because a popular third-party candidate who had a Southern base entered the campaign.

George Wallace, governor of Alabama and leader of the American Independence Party (AIP), mounted a presidential campaign with popular appeal in all sections of the nation. Wallace, formerly a Southern populist Democrat, had become increasingly unhappy with the Democratic national policies. He left the party, formed the AIP, and chose General Curtis Lemay, formerly the chief of the Strategic Air Command, as his vice-presidential running mate.

A small, combative man with a quick wit and a folksy speaking style, Wallace articulated the frustrations and resentments of his followers, who were upset by radical disruptions in the land and by liberal politicians and intellectuals who appeared to sanction them. Wallacites could be found in the greatest numbers within the ranks of Northern blue-collar workers and Southern lower-middle-class whites. Many of these people had also lost faith in the leadership offered by the two major political parties. Wallace told his followers that there was not "a dime's worth of difference" between the Democrats and Republicans. His main issue was playing to white antipathy toward civil rights and antipoverty programs. He was the first important political leader to sense and then exploit the changes in social attitudes that the pundits labeled the backlash. Wallace possessed a remarkable talent for voicing the fears and resentments of working-class whites, especially young men. He chiefly attacked liberal intellectuals, black militants, antiwar protesters, and hippies. Although his message was never a purely racist one, most of his appeal derived from white anxieties about integration and black progress. Opposition to race-related federal initiatives was always at the heart of Wallace's message to his supporters. But he learned to soften his language; he replaced the crass, racist venom spewed by extremists with a set of coded phrases such as "law and order" and "welfare chiselers" that ignited raw racial anger without making his supporters appear or feel racist.

Wallace also championed free enterprise capitalism and traditional moral values and took a more hawkish stance on the Vietnam War than either Humphrey or Nixon. Polls showed that Wallace was a political force to be reckoned with. A mid-September survey gave him 21 percent of the vote, almost as many as supported Humphrey. Had he held that 21 percent to November, he would have denied any candidate an electoral college majority and thrown the election into the House of Representatives. That was his strategy and goal—to play the role of "spoiler" and to force Nixon and Humphrey to bargain for his support to win the presidency.

Meanwhile, Nixon mounted the most expensive, sophisticated presidential campaign in American political history. His acceptance speech had sounded his principal theme, a promise to heed the voice of "the great, quiet forgotten majority—the nonshouters and the nondemonstrators." He called for unity and a lowering of voices. He pledged "peace with honor" in Vietnam. His appeal reached millions of voters yearning for an end to years of discord. It was a smooth, professional campaign. Nixon campaigned at a deliberate, dignified pace. He projected an image of maturity and inner tranquility; commentators spoke of a "new Nixon" who had replaced the fiery Red-baiter of the 1950s. His campaign featured slick television commercials and short speeches filled will patriotic generalities. Admen packaged and sold his candidacy to the electorate.

While Nixon played the role of unifier and harmonizer, his vice-presidential running mate Spiro Agnew took the offensive. His task was to battle Wallace for the backlash vote. Agnew attacked the media for promoting radicalism, and he took a hard law-and-order line. Journalists dubbed Agnew "Nixon's Nixon." Polls taken in early October showed Nixon well ahead of both Humphrey and Wallace.

Humphrey's campaign floundered along, disorganized, short of both money and campaign workers. McCarthy's followers initially refused to support Humphrey. He was hurt badly by his identification with an unpopular administration and its unpopular war. Reflecting the growing conservatism of the electorate, millions of nominally Democratic voters were turning to Nixon and Wallace.

But in October, Humphrey's campaign suddenly came to life. He distanced himself from Johnson's war policy by calling for a bombing halt. Union leaders campaigned hard for Humphrey, and many antiwar activists drifted back into his fold, preferring a flawed liberal to the hated Nixon and the populist demagogue Wallace. McCarthy finally endorsed Humphrey on October 29, and Johnson helped his chances by halting all bombing of North Vietnam and talking as though the war were about to end. Humphrey sliced into Nixon's lead. Wallace's popularity declined. On election eve, pollsters said that the election was too close to call.

But Humphrey's late surge fell just short. Nixon held on for a narrow victory. He received 31.7 million votes to Humphrey's 31.2 million and Wallace's 9.9 million. Nixon received 43.4 percent of the popular vote to Humphrey's 42.7 percent and Wallace's 13.4 percent. Nixon carried thirty-two states with 301 electoral votes. Humphrey carried thirteen states with 191 electoral votes, and Wallace carried five Southern states with 46 electoral votes. The Democrats retained control of Congress with sizable majorities in both Houses.

On the surface, the electorate appeared to speak in many voices, reflecting the acute political divisions within the country. Many young, idealistic citizens and older liberals did not vote. The old Democratic coalition had fractured, split by civil rights issues and divisions over the war. The huge majority of 16 million votes that Johnson had rolled up only four years ago had simply vanished. Humphrey retained urban and union voters, although in reduced strength, and he got most of the African-American vote. But his appeal was confined largely to the Northeastern industrial states. The rest of the country voted for Nixon, except for five Deep South states that went for Wallace. The 1968 election revealed that the Democratic Solid South had vanished. Humphrey received only 31 percent of the Deep South vote, mostly from newly enfranchised African Americans. About 90 percent of Southern whites voted either for Nixon or Wallace. Racial attitudes were significant vote determiners in 1968, the year of the backlash. Election results also signaled that the American electorate was moving toward the Right.

Although they cannot be certain in such a close election, most analysts believe that the Vietnam War probably gave Nixon his narrow win. In the final weeks of the campaign, Nixon attracted support with his talk of a plan to end the war, the details of which he refused to divulge because he said its prospects for success depended on its remaining secret until after the election. Analysts have suggested that Humphrey could have won had he disavowed Johnson's war policy sooner. Nixon's centrist-rightist appeal had worked. He won, liberalism was weakened, and radicalism was contained. The large "silent majority" of American voters, as political analyst Richard Scammon observed, constituted "the unyoung, the unblack, and the unpoor," and they had voted for Nixon. During an election year that had featured the worst violence and turmoil since the Civil War, Middle Americans had

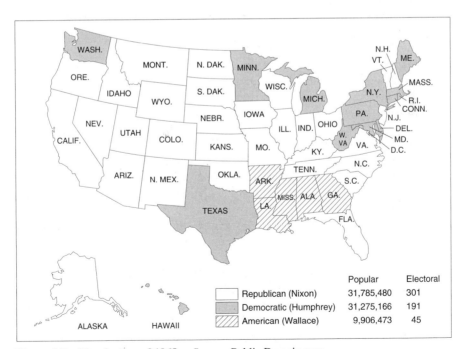

Figure 8.8   The election of 1968.   *Source:* Public Domain map.

opted for the center. American political institutions had faced their most severe test in over 100 years and had survived.

SUMMING UP THE 1960S

Forces that had been building for years in this country climaxed in 1968 in political polarization and a full-blown cultural crisis. The Cold War consensus was fractured beyond repair. The forces of reform liberalism achieved their greatest victories with Johnson's smashing electoral victory in 1964 and the subsequent enactment of stalled New Frontier legislation, and most of all, the enactment of Great Society, the most important social reform agenda since the days of the Second New Deal. Ironically, at its moment of triumph, Great Society unraveled. The liberal reform coalition fragmented over the controversial Vietnam War and black power militancy. Congress, faced with the mounting costs of the war, rising crime and disorder at home, and growing opposition to liberal reforms, was loath to expand the boundaries of the welfare state. Great Society died in 1967.

By 1967, many civil rights leaders, militant students, and radical women, despairing of ever achieving the kinds of fundamental reforms that they sought within existing political structures, chose to challenge the established order and to build radical movements outside of the mainstream. These various political insurgencies provoked a counterresponse led by Northern working-class ethnics and lower-middle-class white Southerners. Beneath the surface of polarized politics, a profound cultural crisis gripped the nation in 1967 and 1968. A relatively small number of articulate radicals challenged not only established political processes, but they also attacked traditional American institutions, mores, and values. The far more numerous backlashers vociferously and sometimes violently defended those same political processes and traditional values. The majority of Americans got caught in the middle of this political and cultural warfare during the election of 1968.

Both the political and cultural crises peaked during the election of 1968. With the murders of Martin Luther King and Robert Kennedy, left-wing radicals were denied access to established political processes; they could only sit on the sidelines in despair or try futilely to disrupt proceedings at the Democratic Convention in Chicago. The backlashers found a tribune to champion their cause in Alabama's Governor George Wallace. The two major party candidates were men of the center. The Democrats chose Hubert Humphrey, a traditional Cold War liberal, and the Republicans nominated the reborn Richard Nixon, who returned Phoenix-like from the political ashes. In one of the closest elections in American political history, characterized by a low voter turnout, Nixon bested Humphrey, with backlasher George Wallace finishing a distant third. The radical Left was simply not a political factor. The election revealed above all else the strength of American political institutions and the centrist instincts of the voting majority of the American people in a time of political and cultural crisis. The centrifugal forces were contained, radicalism was defeated, and liberal reformism was weakened.

The legacies of the 1960s are various, and different people draw different lessons from those turbulent times. How one remembers the 1960s turns on questions of age, gender, race, ethnicity, class, education, and above all, political ideology. A sizable number of today's scholars in the social sciences and humanities were participants in one or more of the radical insurgencies of the late 1960s, most likely the antiwar movement. For these nostalgic academics, they remember the 1960s as a time when it appeared possible that a community of progressive forces could be forged that could bring about fundamental reforms through the established political system, reforms that would bring forth peace, prosperity, and genuine social equality for all. But these utopian dreams were smashed by violence, assassinations, backlash, and most of all by the determination of the middle-aged, middle-class voting majority to turn to centrist candidates in a time of crisis.

Most radical insurgencies did not survive the 1960s. The most important one that endured has been the women's movement. The New Left fragmented in 1969, and a small faction functioned as a terrorist underground for a few more years. The counterculture simply evaporated, much of it co-opted by the mainstream culture. The civil rights movement also fragmented. Some of its most militant leaders fled into exile or were killed. Some leaders such as Jesse Jackson moved into the political mainstream and became powers within the Democratic Party. Environmentalism, a cause that would become much more important in the 1970s and 1980s, derived in part from the 1960s' upheavals. Former hippies often became environmentalist advocates, as did some former antiwar activists.

The year 1968 can also be read as a turning point in American politics. It marked the end of a period dominated by the forces of liberal reformism and the beginning of a conservative resurgence. The rise of black militants, radical students, and hippies and the spread of crime provoked a popular backlash against what was perceived as permissive and ineffectual liberalism, a liberalism that coddled rebels and criminals and neglected the interests of the middle-class majority. The stalemated war in Vietnam that was inflating the economy and undermining U.S. power in the world also discredited liberalism, as did what many perceived to be the excessive costs and expansion of governmental power associated with Great Society reforms. The spreading perception that liberalism was a prescription for dysfunctional policies at home and abroad fueled a rising conservatism. Conservative forces would steadily gather strength during the 1970s and would come to power in 1980 with the election of Ronald Reagan. The upheavals of the late 1960s left liberalism discredited and in decline. These disruptions also destroyed left-wing radicalism as a viable alternative, if it ever had been one for more than a handful of visionaries. The destruction of the Left and the decline of liberalism opened the political door to the growing legions of conservatives who had first surfaced in the 1964 election as fervent supporters of Barry Goldwater and who then turned to either Nixon or Wallace in 1968.

BIBLIOGRAPHY

Scholars have found the political and cultural protest movements of the 1960s and their impact on American society fascinating subjects to study. There is already a large, generally excellent literature on these important topics. Clayborn Carson, in *In Struggle: SNCC and the Black Awakening of the 1960s*, shows how black power militancy grew out of the experiences of civil rights activists working in the South during the early 1960s. See also William H. Chafe's *Civilities and Civil Rights: Greensboro, North Carolina, and the Black Struggle for Freedom*. The best biography we have of Dr. Martin Luther King Jr. is Stephen Oates's *Let the Trumpet Sound: The Life of Martin Luther King Jr.*

A reading of *The Autobiography of Malcolm X* (co-written with Alex Haley) will provide an understanding of the sources of black nationalism during the 1960s. For student radicalism during the 1960s, see Irwin Unger's *The Movement: A History of the American New Left, 1959–1972.* Todd Gitlin's *The Sixties: Years of Hope: Days of Rage* is a thoughtful meditation on the 1960s by a former leader of the SDS. Another fine account of the student radicalism of the 1960s is James Miller's *Democracy Is in the Streets: From Port Huron to the Siege of Chicago.* On the counterculture, see Charles Perry's *The Haight-Ashbury.* Theodore Roszak's *The Making of a Counter Culture* is a stylish, sympathetic account of the hippie movement. Julian Messner's *The Superstars of Rock: Their Lives and Their Music* contains insight into the pop music of the 1960s. Tom Wolfe's *The Electric Kool-Aid Acid Test* has captured Ken Kesey's adventures and the whole "acid rock" scene in psychedelic prose. Barbara Deckard, in *The Women's Movement,* offers a fine account of the revived feminist movement. See also the relevant chapters of William H. Chafe's *The American Woman: Her Changing Social, Economic, and Political Role, 1920–1970.* Alfredo Mirande's *The Chicano Experience* documents militancy in the Mexican-American world. Vine Deloria Jr.'s *Custer Died for Your Sins* records centuries of white mistreatment of Native Americans. Richard Krickus, in *Pursuing the American Dream: White Ethnics and the New Populism,* features a fascinating study of blue-collar culture and its resentment of liberal welfarism, student radicals, hippies, and black militants. A lively account of the crucial 1968 election is Theodore White's *The Making of the President, 1968.*

9

Calming Down

The disorders and violence that had been building during the mid-1960s climaxed in 1968. First came the surprise Tet Offensive in Vietnam, which convinced many Americans that the United States was not winning the war. On March 31, President Johnson surprised the nation with his terse announcement that he would not seek reelection. A week later, a white assassin gunned down Dr. Martin Luther King Jr. King's murder set off riots in 168 cities and towns in which black rioters attacked white businesses and properties. Terror on the streets in the spring of 1968 provoked a white backlash against African Americans. Student protests multiplied in 1968, both in America and around the world. As New Left militants led a strike that forced Columbia University to close down, revolutionary students and striking workers in Paris nearly overthrew the government. In June, Robert Kennedy, a contender for his party's presidential nomination, was murdered while celebrating his victory in the California primary. In late August, the Chicago police attacked antiwar protesters in the streets, while the Democrats meeting in that city were nominating Hubert H. Humphrey as their candidate for president. In October, in Mexico, thousands of young people protested their country's staging of the 1968 Olympic Games. Police shot and killed scores of demonstrators gathered in a plaza in Mexico City. Throughout 1968, millions of Americans watching the nightly news felt threatened by the electronic images of war, rebellion, and violent social conflict that were beamed into their living rooms from around the world and from their own divided society.

Richard M. Nixon was elected president by a narrow margin amidst the worst domestic violence and disorder in nearly 100 years. He made his top priorities restoring national unity and phasing out the American war in Vietnam. He partially succeeded in calming the country, although the American Vietnam War continued for four more years.

Reelected by a landslide margin in November 1972, President Nixon was never able to exercise the full powers of the presidency and to achieve all of his political goals because of the developing Watergate scandals. Watergate became a public issue early in 1973, when the men caught burglarizing Democratic Party headquarters the previous summer went on trial. Public concern about the growing scandals was heightened when a Senate committee began holding televised hearings in May. Thereafter, the remainder of Nixon's presidency was increasingly preoccupied by his efforts to contain and survive Watergate. Ultimately the president and his men were overwhelmed by media investigations, federal grand jury probes, special prosecutors, congressional investigations, the courts, and public opinion. Richard Nixon resigned from the presidency in disgrace on August 9, 1974, mainly to avoid impeachment, trial, and probable conviction for "high crimes and misdemeanors" that he had committed while president.

THE POLITICIAN

Richard Nixon's national political career began with his election to Congress in 1946. His role in exposing Alger Hiss quickly brought him to prominence, which he parlayed into a Senate seat in 1950 and the vice presidency in 1952. After eight years as Eisenhower's active vice president, Nixon was narrowly beaten by John Kennedy in the 1960 presidential election. Apparently destined for the political scrap heap following his 1962 loss in the California gubernatorial campaign, Nixon rose from the ashes in 1968 to beat Hubert Humphrey and gain the White House.

Nixon's political career was characterized by a relentless ambition and sustained effort to achieve his goals. He combined incisive intelligence with hard work to master the art of politics. But Nixon was in many ways ill-suited for the public career that he chose. Shy, introverted, and a loner, he lacked the easy charm and affability characteristic of most American politicians. The enduring image of Nixon the politician is of a man working alone in his office well into the night—writing memos, reading a bill, or perhaps simply thinking about political strategy or the answer to a hard question of public policy. Although he chose the profession of politics, Nixon did not always enjoy being a politician or performing many of the activities associated with a public career. He armored himself for the stresses and pressures of politics by imposing a tight discipline on his personal behavior and emotions. Many people intuitively regarded Nixon's public personality as a fabrication; they wondered who the "real Nixon" was, what the inner man was really like.

The real Nixon was a fascinating, complex, and conflicted personality. He was a devout patriot who prized hard work, tenacity, self-reliance, and seriousness of purpose. He possessed a soaring ambition. He was determined to be a great leader of a great nation. But Nixon also had used smear tactics to identify his political opponents with Communism in order to win elections in 1946 and 1950. He furiously Red-baited his hapless Democratic opponents during the bitter 1952 campaign, which helped bring a Republican president to the White House for the first time in twenty years. Often, Nixon's ruthless political tactics appeared to serve no larger political cause than partisan advantage or furthering his own ca-

Figure 9.1   In contrast to his often stormy and controversial public career, Richard Nixon enjoyed a warm family life. Here he shares a joyous moment with (from left to right) son-in-law David Eisenhower, wife Pat, and daughters Julia and Tricia. *Source:* Bettmann Archive.

reer. He held a cynical view of politics, seeing it as a process in which all politicians advocated principles and ideals as a cover for self-interest. Nixon viewed politics as a tough game, one in which winners played hardball. Victory went to the gutsy players who could make the big plays when they had to, whether it was winning an election or opening up China. Nixon often compared politics to his favorite sport, professional football. He agreed with Vince Lombardi, the famed coach of the Green Bay Packers, the winners of the first two Super Bowls, who said, "Winning isn't everything; it's the only thing." Nixon's political opponents were not rivals to be defeated but enemies to be destroyed. He perceived them as obstacles in the way of his climb up the political ladder—to be removed by any means necessary.

Nixon's blend of moral self-righteousness and dirty campaign tactics accounts for his most singular quality—his ability to inspire strong loyalty among Republican supporters and intense loathing among liberal Democratic opponents. He was a complete partisan who divided everyone into two political groups—"us against them." He was the foremost modern practitioner of the politics of division. Nixon combined in one complex personality an unusual mix of admirable and despicable traits. His tragedy was rooted in a paradox—the qualities that enabled him to win the presidency and made him a bold, innovative world statesman also rendered him arrogant, insensitive to the American preoccupation with political means, and susceptible to the corruptions of power. These character flaws ultimately destroyed his presidency and deprived him of an honored place in national history.

PRAGMATIC CENTRISM

Nixon came to the presidency determined to restore the consensus politics that had prevailed in this country during the 1950s and early 1960s before being shattered by the Vietnam War, the civil rights movement, and other domestic insurgencies. In many ways, Nixon's domestic political strategy resembled that of Eisenhower's during the 1950s, when the Republican president brought much of his party toward making a pragmatic accommodation with the New Deal-Fair Deal tradition. During the 1968 campaign, Nixon had attacked the Great Society at the same time he endorsed its goals of ending poverty and racial discrimination. He was especially critical of the war on poverty, which he said had been lost because of corruption and mismanagement by incompetent federal bureaucrats.

To achieve his goals, he moved in different policy directions simultaneously. His general thrust was toward the center, but he also struck out in conservative directions in pursuit of his Southern strategy, and he proposed far-reaching reforms to co-opt liberal causes. He failed to restore the lost consensus during his first term because he could not end the American war in Vietnam, because pursuit of his Southern strategy perpetuated the divisions he hoped to end, and because various activists and reformers continued to press their causes despite his efforts to co-opt or suppress them.

Nixon's Cabinet selections and choices for leading advisory positions represented a mix of conservatives, moderates, and liberals recruited from business, academia, and politics. The key men in Nixon's administration included the moderate Attorney General John Mitchell, a former law partner and his chief political adviser. Nixon's Chief of Staff Harry R. "Bob" Haldeman, a conservative, came from the world of advertising. A liberal attorney, John Erlichman, became Nixon's chief domestic affairs adviser. Nixon appointed liberal Democrat Daniel Patrick Moynihan, a long-time Harvard professor, head of the newly created Urban Affairs Council.

Like Kennedy had before him, Nixon always considered domestic affairs secondary to foreign policy concerns. His own lack of enthusiasm, the fact that 57 percent of the voters in 1968 preferred another candidate to him for president, and Democratic control of Congress all diminished his influence over domestic affairs. Liberal Democrats in control of Congress extended the Voting Rights Act of 1965, increased spending for food stamps, increased Social Security benefits, and increased federal aid to education. Congress also proposed the Twenty-Sixth Amendment, ratified in 1971, enfranchising eighteen year olds. The new amendment added 12 million potential voters to the rolls. Nixon was not enthusiastic about any of these measures, but he did not oppose them.

Nixon proposed policies reflecting the growing conservatism of voters opposed to solving social problems by expanding the powers of the federal government and by spending more money on them. A major target was the welfare system. After consultations with Moynihan, Nixon proposed a work incentive program to replace the Aid to Dependent Children Program (ADFC), a welfare program dating from the New Deal era. The proposed program was called the Family Assistance Plan (FAP). It guaranteed to a family of four with no income $1,600 a year plus food stamps and Medicaid. It further required all heads of households on welfare, except for single mothers with pre-school-age children, to register for job training. The FAP would supplant the existing welfare schedules set by the states,

Figure 9.2   President Nixon confers with his top aides in the Oval Office. Standing in front of Nixon is Henry Kissinger, national security adviser. Sitting to Kissinger's right is Harry R. "Bob" Haldeman, chief of staff. To Kissinger's left is John Erlichman, chief adviser for domestic affairs.   *Source:* National Archives.

most of which were lower than $1,600 a family, with a single national schedule of payments. The innovative proposal proved controversial, and it was rejected by an unusual alliance of congressional liberals and conservatives. Liberals rejected the FAP because they did not like the work requirements, and they thought the proposed payment schedules were too small. Conservatives opposed the FAP because they did not like the idea of a federally guaranteed annual income for poor people. Welfare reform, a top priority on Nixon's domestic agendum, failed.

In 1972, Congress belatedly passed the "Workfare" feature of the FAP, requiring heads of households to register for job training. That same year, Congress also enacted a new program called Supplemental Security Income (SSI), which provided monthly income for the elderly and disabled. It also authorized automatic annual cost-of-living increases for all Social Security recipients. These increases were tied to annual increases in the Consumer Price Index, as recorded by the Bureau of Labor Statistics. If the cost of living rose 5 percent during a calendar year, the following year all Social Security recipients would receive a 5 percent increase in payments.

Nixon's other innovative proposal, revenue sharing, was part of what he called the "New Federalism," designed to reduce the power of the federal government and to strengthen state and local governmental agencies. Congress enacted a revenue-sharing program to begin in 1972, when $30 billion in federal funds would be split over five years on a basis of two-thirds to local governments and one-third to the state. The money was awarded to state and local agencies as "block grants" to be used in programs such as education, mass transit, job training, and law enforcement. To ensure that some of the money funneled through the revenue-sharing pipeline went to poor people, Congress, in 1973, enacted the Comprehensive Employment Training Act (CETA) to provide job training for low-income people.

NIXONOMICS

Nixon had to spend much of the time that he devoted to domestic affairs trying to manage an increasingly erratic American economy. The economic difficulties stemmed mainly from the Vietnam War, former president Johnson's fiscal irresponsibility, and increasing competition from prosperous foreign economies such as West Germany and Japan. Johnson had drastically increased spending for the war in the midst of a booming economy without raising taxes. Prices rose 5 percent in 1968, the highest inflation rate since the Korean War. Nixon initially applied the monetarist theorists of economist Milton Friedman, who claimed that prices could be lowered by reducing the money supply. The results were disastrous. In 1969, the stock market suffered its worst crash since 1929. The federal deficit increased, and the GDP declined for the first time since 1958. Unemployment doubled, from 3 percent to 6 percent, and prices continued to rise. Monetarism generated both inflation and recession, creating stagflation. Stagflation signaled that the American economy no longer operated according to the old rules. Historically, when unemployment rose, prices fell, or least did not rise. Experts on the president's Council of Economic Advisers could describe stagflation, but they could neither explain it nor cure it.

Appalled by its disastrous results, Nixon abandoned monetarism for a new economic approach, "jawboning," which amounted to pressuring both business and trade unions to keep down prices and wage demands. Jawboning produced only continuing stagflation. Nixon then decided that economic decline was a greater evil than inflation. He also decided not to pay much attention to his economic advisers. Announcing his sudden conversion to Keynesian economics, he deliberately unbalanced the budget to stimulate demand and increase employment. These efforts also failed. Stagflation stubbornly persisted, as unemployment and inflation both remained high. In 1970, the U.S. economy also ran its first trade deficit since 1893.

The President announced a New Economic Policy (NEP) on August 15, 1971. The NEP represented the most stunning turnabout in economic policy since the New Deal era. The new policy entailed freezing wages, prices, and rents for ninety days. Nixon also asked Congress for tax cuts to promote business expansion. He clamped a 10 percent tax on imports and devalued the dollar. At the end of ninety days, he replaced the freeze with more flexible guidelines, allowing annual price increases of 2.5 percent and wage increases of up to 5.5 percent. Devaluation took the form of cutting the dollar loose from gold, that is, Nixon announced that the U.S. Treasury would no longer exchange dollars held by foreigners or foreign governments for gold at the thirty-five-dollar rate. In effect, Nixon's actions, taken upon the advice of Assistant Secretary of the Treasury Paul Volcker, destroyed the international monetary system based on fixed rates of currency exchange pegged to the dollar, which in turn was based on gold valued at thirty-five dollars an ounce, the system that had been created by U.S. bankers in 1944 at Bretton Wood. From now on, currency exchange rates would float, that is, they would fluctuate daily in the world's exchanges.

In the short run, the drastic measures constituting the New Economic Policy worked. The trade deficit vanished, and inflation was halved. The economy snapped out of recession, and the GDP rose sharply. Polls showed that the American public generally approved of Nixon's bold, unorthodox methods of fighting stagflation. He proved a resourceful, pragmatic economic manager, not bound by tradition or conventional wisdom. Good times returned briefly in 1972 and contributed to Nixon's landslide reelection victory in November. But by early 1973, pressures from business and labor undermined the controls, and the inflation rate soared. The OPEC (Organization of Petroleum Exporting Countries) oil embargo ruined the NEP's efforts to restrain inflation in 1973 and 1974. The price of oil quadrupled, and the inflation rate soared to 7 percent during those two years. The international monetary system nearly collapsed, and the American economy plunged into a deep recession. Some economists have contended that Nixon's decision to let the dollar's value float on international exchange markets probably slowed the rate of growth of the U.S. economy. A slow rate of growth was one of the most serious structural weaknesses of the U.S. economy throughout the 1970s and into the 1980s.

THE SOUTHERN STRATEGY

Despite his appeals for unity and peace, Nixon had only partial success in reuniting and quieting the American people. Discords inherited from the Johnson years continued and at times intensified. A rash of terrorist bombings damaged public and corporate buildings in various cities. The bloodiest prison riot in U.S. history occurred in September 1971 in Attica, New York, when militant prisoners organized a large-scale rebellion, taking thirty-nine hostages, mostly guards. When the warden refused their demands, they threatened to kill the hostages. Governor Nelson Rockefeller then ordered an army of police to assault the prison barricades. Thirty prisoners and ten guards died in the ensuing violence; the ten guards were all killed by friendly fire.

Nixon's most divisive actions occurred when he implemented his "Southern strategy," which aimed to outflank George Wallace and secure the Middle American vote, comprising Southern whites, Northern ethnics, blue-collar workers, and conservative suburbanites. He also sought to attract the vote of the Sunbelt, the most dynamic region of the country. Middle America and the Sunbelt composed what political theorist Kevin Phillips called the new Republican majority. According to Phillips, these voters were "in motion between a Democratic past and a Republican future." The Southern strategy involved stressing "law and order," phasing out most antipoverty programs, and slowing the rate of school desegregation in the South.

Nixon's efforts to slow the pace of school desegregation involved his administration in a controversy over busing to achieve school integration. The Justice Department filed suits prohibiting transporting children to desegregate public schools. The busing issue had arisen in 1971, when the Supreme Court had ordered the Charlotte-Mecklenburg school system in North Carolina to use busing to achieve school integration after its efforts at voluntary desegregation had failed. Soon, many other Southern school districts were under court orders to bus children to achieve school integration. It was effective, and within a few years, the Southern public school system was largely desegregated. Ironically, the South soon achieved a more integrated public school system than the North. By 1971, 44 percent of African-American children in the South attended integrated schools, whereas only 28 percent of African-American children in the rest of the nation attended integrated schools.

Figure 9.3   The inmates at Attica State prison raise their hands in clenched fists in a show of unity. They are observing the third anniversary of the Attica uprising, which took the lives of 40 persons during September 1971.   *Source:* AP/Wide World Photos.

Court-ordered busing spread to the North, where resistance was often fierce and occasionally violent. The worst incidents occurred in South Boston, Massachusetts, in 1974, when a federal judge ordered busing to integrate its public school system. Over half of the public schools in Boston had student bodies that were 90 percent black. White pupils boycotted South Boston High School rather than accept integration. Buses hauling in African-American students were stoned, injuring several youngsters. Racial conflict in South Boston and other Northern cities led to a flight of white students from the public school system.

Administration efforts to thwart busing in order to slow the pace of school integration infuriated civil rights leaders. But the Supreme Court upheld busing, which infuriated Nixon and Attorney General John Mitchell. Despite Nixon and Mitchell's efforts, many Northern and Southern cities used busing to achieve desegregation. Far more schools integrated during Nixon's presidency than during the administrations of Johnson and Kennedy. African Americans progressed in other areas as well. The size of the African-American middle class increased rapidly, black college enrollment nearly doubled between 1968 and 1972, and African American political leaders emerged—thirteen black Congressmen and eighty-one black mayors held office in 1971. Nixon tried to steer a middle course between what he termed "instant integration and segregation forever." He also wanted to gain the votes of his growing Middle American and white Southern supporters. Despite the progress that black people were making during Nixon's presidency, most African American leaders and their white liberal allies viewed Nixon as an enemy of their cause.

Nixon used Vice President Agnew to implement part of the Southern strategy. Agnew campaigned extensively during the 1970 elections on behalf of Republican congressional candidates. During the elections, he tried to link his Democratic opponents to campus upheavals, race riots, bombings, rising crime rates, drug use, and pornography. His verbal onslaughts had little noticeable impact on the elections. Republicans gained two Senate seats but lost nine in the House. Nixon's Southern strategy had yielded meager political dividends, and Agnew's inflammatory rhetoric perpetuated divisions within the nation.

As part of its law and order campaign, Nixon's Justice Department prosecuted antiwar activists. The most famous trial occurred in Chicago in 1971. It involved a group of radicals that became known as the "Chicago Eight." The trial turned into a farce because of the disruptive antics of the defendants and the extreme bias against them of Judge Julius Hoffmann. Seven of the activists were convicted of various charges stemming from their roles in demonstrations at the 1968 Democratic Party Convention in Chicago. But all of the convictions were overturned on appeal because of Judge Hoffmann's procedural errors and patent bias against the defendants.

Along with its efforts to prosecute antiwar activists, the Nixon administration also took a hard line on crime and drug use. During his 1968 presidential campaign, Nixon had blamed the rise in street crime and drug use on "liberal permissiveness" and had promised a crackdown on both if elected. In both 1969 and 1970, Nixon proposed tough anticrime legal reforms. The Democrat-controlled Congress responded by enacting anticrime laws in 1970. The general effect of the new laws was to increase penalties for federal crimes. In 1972, the Nixon administration declared war on drugs, particularly on heroin. The President created a new agency called the Office for Drug Abuse and Law Enforcement (ODALE) to spearhead the assault on heroin dealers. Celebrities joined the war on drugs, including Sammy Davis Jr., who had become a Nixon supporter, and Elvis Presley. Neither crime rates nor drug use showed appreciable drops during Nixon's presidency, but his strenuous efforts in these areas paid political dividends. He could campaign for reelection in 1972 as a champion of law and order and as a leader concerned with diminishing the contagion of violence and drug use in America.

THE BURGER COURT

Nixon's Southern strategy also influenced his choices to fill Supreme Court vacancies, four of which opened up during his first term. He tried to appoint a Deep South conservative, but the Senate rejected both of his choices. His four appointees, Associate Justices Harry Blackmun, Lewis Powell, William Rehnquist, and new Chief Justice Warren Burger, who replaced the retired Earl Warren in 1969, all had reputations as strict constructionist conservatives. Nixon expected that the Burger Court would reverse some of the Warren Court's decisions on civil rights, civil liberties, and the rights of criminal defendants. But the more conservative "Nixon Court" did not overturn any of the controversial decisions of its liberal activist predecessor. In fact, many of its decisions went against the grain of the Nixon administration. The Burger court upheld busing, the right of women to have an abortion on demand,

and the publication of the *Pentagon Papers.* It struck down death penalty laws and limited Justice Department efforts at electronic surveillance. It did sustain laws banning pornography, where those statutes reflected "community standards." The Nixon Court proved an unpredictable, politically independent agency whose decisions often angered conservatives.

In the area of civil rights litigation, the Burger Court consolidated and sometimes expanded on the gains made by African Americans during the Warren Court years. Supreme Court rulings strengthened the provisions of the Civil Rights Act of 1964. In two important cases, the Burger Court upheld lower court rulings that mandated busing to achieve integration of public schools.

In one important civil rights area, the Burger Court moved far beyond its more liberal predecessor; that area involved discrimination based on gender. Frequently using the provisions of the Civil Rights Act of 1964 that prohibited gender-based segregation, the Court struck down many laws that had in various ways made women subordinate to men. In *Phillips v. Martin Marietta* (1971), the Burger Court nullified corporate hiring practices that discriminated against women with small children. In an important 1973 decision, *Frontero v. Richardson,* the Court ruled that the U.S. armed forces had to provide the same fringe benefits and pensions for female veterans as they did for males.

In 1973, the Supreme Court went far beyond questions of equal pay and employment rights for women. In *Roe v. Wade,* by a 7 to 2 vote, the justices struck down all state laws restricting abortions. Feminist attorneys had challenged a Texas law that made any abortion a felony, on behalf of a poor single woman, Norma McCorvey, who could not afford to raise the impending child properly. Associate Justice Harry Blackmun, who wrote the majority decision, anchored the right of a woman to have an abortion in a right to privacy, which, while not explicitly stated in the Constitution, according to Blackmun's reading of that document, could be inferred. The decision granted women an absolute right to obtain an abortion during the first trimester of pregnancy, because medical experts all agreed that the fetus was not viable during that phase of pregnancy. During the second trimester, when fetus viability was possible, states could regulate abortions. During the third trimester, according to *Roe v. Wade,* states could prohibit abortions.

Roe v. Wade was the most controversial Supreme Court decision since the Warren Court's famed 1954 *Brown* decision that had outlawed segregation in public schools. *Roe v. Wade* immediately provoked an angry outcry from Catholics, from the Protestant religious Right, from prominent conservative politicians, and from many others. For the next twenty years, the waters of public life in this country would be frequently roiled by controversy over *Roe v. Wade.* The issue proved impossible to compromise politically, because it involved two absolutist moral views that flatly contradicted each other. As conservative political forces steadily built up their strength during the 1970s, attacking *Roe v. Wade* became one of their most powerful rallying points.

ACTIVISTS AND REFORMERS

One of the insurgencies that had arisen during the 1960s continued into the 1970s. The women's movement gained momentum as more women changed their perceptions about

Figure 9.4   Norma McCorvey, 35, the Dallas mother whose desire to have an abortion was the basis for a landmark Supreme Court decision a decade ago, takes time from her job as a house painter to pose for a photograph in Terrel, Texas. To legal scholars, she is simply "Jane Roe," the fictitious name McCorvey used when her two attorneys filed her historic lawsuit. Photo by Bill Jenscha.   *Source:* AP/Wide World Photos.

themselves and their roles in society. Women opted for many new career choices. The number of American women in medical schools, law schools, and graduate business programs doubled between 1970 and 1974. New magazines devoted to women's issues emerged. The most successful of these publications was *Ms.*, edited by Gloria Steinem. *Ms.* focused on the emotional and political needs of women, explored the frustrations of working women, and gave liberated women a forum of their own. The women's movement of the 1970s continued to be divided between reformers in the National Organization for Women (NOW) who sought equality before the law, no-fault divorces, equal pay for equal work, child care centers, and abortion rights and radical feminists who sought to achieve women's liberation through fundamental changes in the structure of society and changes in sexual identity.

Political opposition to feminism in the 1970s came from an antifeminist conservative leader, Phyllis Schlafly, head of the Eagle Forum. Schlafly led an effort to defeat the Equal Rights Amendment (ERA). She insisted that its passage would not help women and would take away rights that they already had, such as the right to be supported by a husband, the right to be exempted from conscription, and the right to special job protections. Schlafly succeeded when the ERA fell three votes short of the thirty-eight needed for ratification.

While feminists organized for action, so did Native Americans. Militant Indians occupied Alcatrez Island in San Francisco Bay in November 1969. The protesters wanted to highlight their demand that the Bureau of Indian Affairs respond more effectively to a myriad of Native American social problems. One of the prominent supporters of the Indian cause was popular movie actress Jane Fonda, who soon moved on to become involved in radical anti-Vietnam War activities. In 1973, the most important militant Native American group, the American Indian Movement (AIM), seized the South Dakota town of Wounded Knee, the site of an 1890 massacre of Lakota Sioux Indians by U.S. soldiers. AIM activists wanted to call attention to the misery of the poverty-stricken Native American inhabitants of Wounded Knee and to the hundreds of Indian treaties broken by the federal government. Armed federal agents reclaimed the town, killing an AIM member in the process. In negotiations that followed, government officials agreed to examine conditions among the Indians and their treaty rights. The Second Battle of Wounded Knee signaled that a new era of Indian activism had arrived.

Hispanic organizations also were active in the early 1970s. Young Chicanos formed a militant organization that called itself the Brown Berets. The Brown Berets were active

Figure 9.5   Indians standing guard at Wounded Knee.   *Source:* Corbis.

in the Midwest and Southwest. Some Chicano activists also joined the antiwar movement. Spokesmen called attention to Chicano casualty rates in Vietnam that were proportionally higher than those of the Anglo population. Aware of the political activity of some Mexican Americans, President Nixon set out to win their support, offering them political appointments and programs. The effort paid off; in the 1972 election, Nixon received 31 percent of the Chicano vote, which helped him carry California and Texas. In 1974, the Supreme Court responded to another Chicano concern when it ruled that public schools had to meet the learning requirements of youngsters with limited English language skills. That decision led to the federal funding of bilingual education programs.

ECOLOGY AND CONSUMERISM

Environmentalism was another movement that emerged during the 1960s and grew rapidly during the early 1970s. The origins of the modern ecology movement lay in a book written by Rachel Carson called *Silent Spring* (1962). When there was almost no concern about ecological issues, Carson wrote about environmental damage caused by chemical pesticides, particularly DDT. Her writings spawned a cause. The Great Society contained an important environmentalist component. By 1970, a broad-based, diverse environmentalist movement was active on a variety of fronts.

During the Nixon presidency, Congress responded to growing environmental concerns. Legislators enacted the Water Quality Improvement Act in 1970, tightening existing safeguards against threats to water quality. The National Air Quality Standards Act required automakers to reduce exhaust emission pollutants significantly by 1975 and the federal government to establish air quality standards. The Resource Recovery Act provided $453 million for resource recovery and recycling systems.

In 1971, Congress created the Environmental Protection Agency (EPA), which combined federal agencies concerned with pesticides, nuclear radiation, auto exhaust emissions, air and water quality, and waste disposal under a single Cabinet-level department. Nixon appointed William Ruckelshaus to head the new agency; Ruckelshaus proved an energetic director. The EPA quickly initiated action on several fronts. It provoked a reaction from Detroit automakers, who insisted that EPA emission and safety standards were too expensive and beyond their technological capabilities. Nixon's Secretary of the Interior Walter Hickel, a conservative, self-made oil millionaire, also turned out to be an energetic environmentalist who protected the public domain.

Ecology was not a major Nixon priority, and at times he opposed the environmentalists. Nixon vetoed a mammoth $24.7 billion measure to clean up America's polluted rivers and lakes. He claimed that it was much too costly, but Congress enacted the law over his veto. Environmentalism was a political issue that cut across party, class, and ideological lines. Most everyone endorsed in principle the need for clean air and clean water and the protection of natural resources, scenic landscapes, and wilderness areas. But not everyone was willing to pay the high costs of environmental safeguards. At times, environmentalists clashed with vested economic interests.

Related to the ecology movement and sometimes overlapping with it, a strong consumer movement developed during the early 1970s that concerned itself with protecting consumers from unsafe, shoddy products and with making the business community more responsive to consumers' interests. Ralph Nader, whose attacks on the auto industry during the mid-1960s had led to the enactment of federal safety laws, headed the consumer movement of the 1970s. Operating out of a small office in the nation's capital, Nader organized task forces of volunteers called "Nader's Raiders," who examined many industries and governmental agencies and followed up these investigations with critical reports and with proposals for their reform.

Nader's Raiders attacked governmental regulatory agencies for being more protective of the businesses that they were supposed to regulate than of the consumers who used the products made by these businesses. These latter-day Muckrakers also attacked the multibillion-dollar processed food industry, accusing it of serving American consumers a "chemical feast" of harmful food additives. They also attacked agribusiness for its use of chemical fertilizers and pesticides that harmed the environment and put toxic substances into the nation's food supplies. In their most radical finding, they reported on the adverse economic impact of land-use monopoly in some states. As a consequence of the consumer movement, millions of Americans became much more concerned about product safety and quality, and more assertive of their rights as consumers.

THE ELECTION OF 1972

The president and his men prepared carefully for his 1972 reelection campaign. Attorney General John Mitchell resigned from his office to devote his full attention to directing the newly formed Committee to Reelect the President (CREEP). CREEP fund-raisers accumulated a $60 million war chest to finance his campaign. CREEP also recruited men who were fiercely loyal to the president and who shared his siege mentality of politics as war, as "us against them." These men appeared ready to do anything to ensure Nixon's reelection, including breaking laws and violating the ethical norms of democratic electoral practices. Nixon had always campaigned with a fierce determination to win. He remembered his narrow loss to John Kennedy in 1960 and that he had barely beaten Humphrey in 1968. The 1970 midterm election results had shown strong continuing support for congressional Democrats. Polls taken early in the 1972 primary campaigns showed that several Democratic contenders would make strong challenges against the president's bid for a second term. Nixon was determined to leave nothing to chance to secure his reelection.

The Democratic Party was still in disarray from the upheavals of 1968, and its members remained deeply divided over emotional issues such as the war, busing, and "law and order." Nevertheless, many Democrats sought their party's nomination at the outset of the 1972 campaign. They included Senators Edmund Muskie, impressive as the vice-presidential candidate in 1968; Hubert Humphrey, around for another go; and George McGovern, an outspoken critic of the Vietnam War. After them came two formidable possibilities, Senator Edward "Ted" Kennedy and George Wallace. Kennedy's appeal had been tarnished by his irresponsible behavior following an auto accident in 1969 in which a young woman riding in his car had been killed, but he still retained the vote-getting magic of the Kennedy name. Kennedy insisted that he was not an active candidate, however, he indicated that he could accept a convention draft. George Wallace, now returned to the Democratic fold, also remained a major player in the Democratic presidential candidate sweepstakes.

Muskie flamed out early, in part the victim of Watergate "dirty tricks," as the nation would discover a year later. A would-be assassin eliminated Wallace by wounding him severely and forcing him out of the campaign in May. With Muskie and Wallace eliminated, McGovern moved strongly ahead. He won a series of primary victories, including California, where he beat Humphrey, and he rolled on to a first-ballot nomination. As a result of new rules implemented by the Democratic Party following its bitter 1968 convention, state delegations at the 1972 convention in Miami contained high proportions of women, blacks, and young, antiwar activists. These insurgent practitioners of a "new politics" replaced party regulars. They took control of the convention and forged McGovern's victory.

McGovern had pulled off a major political upset. His victory was largely a triumph of an organization that took advantage of the new rules. He had borrowed savvy political professionals from the Kennedy organization, and his aides had enlisted young enthusiasts who rallied to McGovern's call for ending the war in Vietnam. He chose Thomas Eagleton, a young liberal senator from Missouri, as his running mate. His supporters drafted a platform calling for an "immediate total withdrawal of all American forces in Southeast Asia" and supported busing to achieve school integration, full employment, tax reform, and various social reforms. McGovern's acceptance speech stirred his followers when he sounded the neoisolationist theme of "come home America": get out of Vietnam and attend to the nation's unfinished social agenda. His campaign began on a high note of enthusiasm and moral principle.

Meeting in Miami after the Democrats, the Republicans unanimously chose Nixon and Agnew to run again. The Republican platform staked out a clear strategy. It called for a "new American majority" to repudiate the "far-out goals of the far left," meaning McGovern's program. It also called for arms limitations with the Soviets, full employment,

Figure 9.6   George McGovern on the campaign trail in 1972.   *Source:* National Archives.

and tax reform. It opposed busing. On the crucial war issue, Republicans insisted that America could not withdraw from Vietnam until all of the prisoners of war had been returned.

The presidential campaign proved boring and one-sided, reminiscent of the election of 1964. McGovern never had a chance, and most Americans quickly lost interest in the contest. The Democrats remained divided. Most Wallace supporters and about half of Humphrey's followers voted for Nixon. Organized labor, the strongest power bloc within the party, refused to support McGovern.

McGovern's campaign suffered serious damage at the outset when the public learned that Senator Eagleton had undergone psychiatric care in the past. At first, McGovern stood behind Eagleton, but after a week's adverse publicity, he panicked and forced Eagleton off of the ticket. McGovern then began a search for a substitute and suffered six embarrassing turndowns before finally persuading Sargent Shriver, former director of the war on poverty and the Peace Corps, to accept. McGovern's inept, expediential handling of the Eagleton affair managed to alienate both young idealists and party regulars. To many of the new political enthusiasts, McGovern appeared to be just another pragmatic politician; to the regulars, he appeared to be an incompetent bungler.

The qualities that brought McGovern the Democratic Party nomination proved to be political liabilities in the contest against Nixon. McGovern's left-of-center appeal to the new politics cost him the political center inhabited by most voters. Republicans put McGovern on the defensive early in the campaign by depicting him as a radical, even though he was a mild-mannered preacher's son, a World War II hero, and a former college professor. McGovern was a Midwestern liberal in the New Deal–Fair Deal–Great Society mold with perhaps a whiff of 1930s' Prairie Populism. But in the conservative political atmosphere of 1972, his advocacy of traditional liberal reforms sounded radical to the ears of many voters. He alienated far more voters than he attracted with his stands on emotion-laden issues such as his calls for amnesty for Vietnam draft resisters and for liberalizing abortion and marijuana laws.

Borrowing a page from Lyndon Johnson's successful 1964 campaign, Nixon campaigned very little. He stayed in Washington and concentrated on appearing presidential, while the hapless McGovern futilely struggled to get the monkey of radicalism off of his back. Nixon refused to consider appearing in any televised debates with McGovern. He never mentioned his opponent by name. Nixon possessed formidable political assets that made him practically unbeatable, even if the Democrats had run their strongest possible ticket of Ted Kennedy and George Wallace. The president had achieved impressive diplomatic victories, capped by *détente* with the Soviets and the opening to China. The American war in Vietnam was winding down, and most U.S. troops had been withdrawn. At home, the economy was reasonably strong, and the society had calmed. Nixon also stood four square against all of those features of American life that so upset Middle Americans and gave liberalism a bad name—busing, hippies, the coddling of criminals and welfare chiselers, antiwar activists, drug use, and sexual permissiveness. He also employed, it came out later, an undercover army of political hirelings, using their capacious arsenal of "dirty tricks" to sabotage the Democratic campaign.

There was a potential chink in Nixon's political armor—corruption. McGovern attacked it hard, calling Nixon's administration "the most morally corrupt in history." He cited several seamy deals where corporations and trade associations had given the GOP large campaign donations in exchange for political favors. The most blatant case of corruption involved a break-in at Democratic Party National Headquarters at Watergate Towers in Washington on June 17, 1972. Seven men, including two former White House aides and a member of CREEP, had been caught trying to photograph and steal documents and to install electronic bugging equipment. It appeared that members of the Republican campaign organization and even members of the president's staff had engaged in burglary and espionage against their opponents.

But news of the burglary excited little public concern at the time, and the prominent mass media exhibited little sustained interest in the bizarre event after a day or two of sensational headlines. Republicans denied all of McGovern's charges and dismissed the Watergate break-in. Nixon categorically denied that any member of his administration was involved. Even though he had tried, McGovern failed to generate much voter interest in Watergate or the corruption issue. He sounded like a desperate loser trying to find an issue, any issue. Within less than a year, it would turn out that McGovern had barely touched the tip of the corruption iceberg.

Nixon scored a landslide victory in November. He carried forty-nine of fifty states and rolled up an electoral vote of 521 to 17. He received 61 percent of the vote, 45.6 million votes, the most ever by a presidential candidate. Nixon tore huge holes in the Democratic coalition. The Southern strategy paid off in the 1972 election results. Nixon swept the South, getting 75 percent of the 1968 Wallace vote. Nixon even got a majority of the urban vote. The "silent majority" whom the president had courted—middle- and lower-middle-class whites, blue-collar voters, ethnics, Sunbelt inhabitants, and Westerners—all voted for him. He got a majority of the Catholic vote, the first Republican candidate to carry that important constituency. The 1972 election was the first in which newly enfranchised eighteen to twenty-one year olds could vote. McGovern spent much of his time campaigning for their vote, considering the youth vote his secret weapon. Only one-third of them voted, and half of these opted for Nixon when he announced during the campaign that he would soon end the draft.

Despite Nixon's sweep, Democrats retained control of Congress, even gaining two seats in the Senate while losing twelve in the House. Such ticket splitting suggested that millions of voters had cast their ballots for Nixon because they could not abide McGovern, not because they wanted to endorse the President or his party. Voter turnouts were lower than for any election since 1948. Except for the South, results gave no indication that political realignment was occurring or that a new Republican majority was emerging. American voters mainly repudiated a candidate whom they saw as lacking in leadership qualities and taking stands on many issues with which they strongly disagreed. They opted to keep the incumbent, whom they perceived to be a strong, successful leader. A strongly performing economy during the summer and fall of 1972 was another factor that contributed to the Nixon landslide victory.

WATERGATE

President Nixon began his second term in January 1973, convinced that his landslide victory was a mandate for moving in more conservative directions. His new budget cut spending for welfare and education. He removed all remaining controls from the economy and impounded billions of dollars appropriated by Congress for purposes he opposed. Nixon also began reorganizing the federal government to make the bureaucracies more efficient and more responsive to his authority. His attitude toward the Democratic Congress was belligerent and contemptuous. He believed that the large majority of American citizens supported him and his agenda; he also believed that the tides of history were flowing in the direction he wanted to take the country. Richard Nixon was riding high that spring of 1973. Then his administration began to self-destruct. A process of disintegration was set in motion that ultimately brought him down.

Watergate, latent since the break-in, suddenly erupted with a rash of disclosures and confessions that made it one of the most serious political scandals in American history. Watergate activities fell into two categories—those occurring before the June 17, 1972, break-in and those following. The break-in turned out to be only one event in an extensive dirty-tricks campaign developed by CREEP and White House staffers to prevent news leaks, to spy on radicals, and to ensure Nixon's reelection. Investigators eventually unearthed an astonishing web of criminal activities and abuses of power that had begun early in Nixon's presidency. These activities included illegal wiretaps placed on government bureaucrats and journalists suspected of leaking embarrassing information about administration policies to the press, using the Internal Revenue Service (IRS) to harass political opponents, raising millions of dollars in illegal campaign funds, and ordering a break-in of Daniel Ellsberg's psychiatrist's office.

The burglars caught inside of Democratic Party National Headquarters had previously tried unsuccessfully to break into McGovern's campaign headquarters. Other dirty tricksters circulated literature slandering Democratic candidates and disrupted their meetings. All dirty tricks were cleared with the president's top advisers. Nixon's defenders argued that many of the dirty tricks had been used by previous administrations and were traditional parts of the American political process. That contention was true, but the extent of Nixonian dirty tricks vastly exceeded any previous administration's efforts. More seriously, these practices flowed from a mind-set that was contemptuous of law and fair play, viewed politics as war, and saw political opponents as enemies to be destroyed.

Dirty tricks proved to be only the beginning. The Watergate burglars had been caught red-handed. CREEP officials and White House staffers who sent them in could have confessed and resigned. Such actions would have embarrassed the Nixon administration, but the president would still have been reelected easily. But White House officials instead chose to cover up its and CREEP's complicity; the cover-up began immediately following the Watergate arrests. White House aides moved to destroy all evidentiary links between the burglary, themselves, and CREEP, and to concoct denials and alibis. An FBI investigation of the break-in and testimony before a federal grand jury were carefully limited so that they could not uncover any tracks leading to CREEP or the White House. The cover-up began immediately after White House officials learned that the burglars had been caught. President Nixon was directly involved in the cover-up activities from the start. He put White House Counsel John Dean in charge; at times, Nixon himself directed the cover-up activities. From the moment the cover-up efforts began, a process was set in motion that would strain the constitutional system of government, cause many American citizens a great deal of anguish, provide some of the most bizarre political theater in American history, and eventually destroy Nixon's presidency.

The cover-up orchestrated by Nixon, Dean, and other top White House aides succeeded for a time. In September 1972, the federal grand jury indicted only the seven men involved in the burglary. The cover-up also held through the November election, in which Nixon won his landslide reelection victory. The cover-up was still holding as the trial of the seven burglars began in March 1973. Meanwhile, it was business as usual for the president and his men, who were confident that they had contained the incident and remained in the clear.

Theirs proved a foolish confidence. Too many people were involved in the cover-up. Too many connections among the burglars, CREEP, and White House survived. Too many investigators were looking for answers to puzzling questions. The *Washington Post* had assigned two young reporters, Carl Bernstein and Bob Woodward, to find answers. They were able to trace some of the illegal campaign funds to CREEP. The Senate created a Select Committee on Presidential Campaign Activities, soon to be known as the Watergate Committee, chaired by Senator Sam J. Ervin, to investigate the burglary and other dirty tricks that may have influenced the outcome of the 1972 election. Federal prosecutors, continuing the federal grand jury probe, continuously investigated the burglary, other dirty tricks, violations of campaign spending laws, and the cover-up. The Watergate trial judge, John J. Sirica, who did not believe the burglars when they told him that they alone had planned the break-in, pressured them to tell the truth.

The cover-up began to come unglued when one of the convicted burglars, James McCord, hoping to avoid a long prison term, wrote a letter to Judge Sirica implicating CREEP and prominent White House officials in the planning of the Watergate burglary. After McCord cracked, the whole cover-up edifice crumbled. The accused officials hired lawyers and promptly implicated other prominent officials in the hope of getting immunity from prosecution or a lighter sentence. Federal prosecutors often entered into plea bargaining arrangements with accused lesser officials to gather evidence against the ringleaders, including President Nixon.

In April, Nixon was forced to fire several key advisers implicated in the cover-up—L. Patrick Gray III, acting director of the FBI, and Erlichman, Haldeman, and Mitchell. Nixon also fired John Dean for telling the Watergate Committee staffers that the president had been involved in the cover-up from the beginning. President Nixon maintained publicly that he had only learned about the cover-up from Dean in March 1973, and since then he had done everything he could to cooperate with investigators, get out the truth about Watergate, and punish wrongdoers. Nixon tried to discredit Dean by suggesting that he had directed the cover-up without the president's knowledge. To reinforce the image of a president concerned with getting to the bottom of the scandal, Nixon appointed a Special Prosecutor, Harvard law professor Archibald Cox, a liberal Democrat, to continue the Justice Department's investigation of the Watergate cover-up.

On May 17, 1973, public interest in the scandal picked up when the Senate Watergate Committee began holding televised hearings that ran through the summer. The committee started with low-level hirelings, CREEP minions who did the dirty work and delivered illegal payments. Gradually they worked their way up the chain-of-command in CREEP and in the Nixon White House. On the way up, the millions of American citizens who watched the proceedings daily got a fascinating, appalling tour through the dark underside of American politics. They learned about political dirty tricks and the details of the cover-up and about shredding documents, blackmail, bribery, forgery, perjury, and "laundered money." They also learned about the misuse of government agencies, including the FBI and the IRS. And they learned about fund-raising techniques that violated election laws and often amounted to blackmail. The televised hearings made a folk hero out of the committee's chairman, seventy-nine-year-old Sam Ervin. Ervin's folksy manner and good humor cloaked a keen intellect and a fierce moral outrage at the steady parade of criminals and crooked politicians who appeared before his committee.

By mid-June, as a result of the committee's investigations, the key question had become whether President Nixon had been involved in the Watergate cover-up: in the words of the committee's vice chairman, Tennessee Republican Howard Baker, "What did the president know and when did he know it?" On June 25, John Dean appeared before the committee. For two days he read a lengthy 250-page statement describing the details of the cover-up. He detailed President Nixon's role in the cover-up: Nixon knew all about it, had approved it, and indeed had played a central role in it from the outset. Despite efforts by the White House to discredit Dean's testimony, the fired counselor came across as credible to members of the committee and to the large television audience. He displayed a phenomenal memory. He knew too much; he had too many details at his command. The testimony of Nixon loyalists before the committee further damaged the president's position. Men such

Figure 9.7   In May 1973, the Senate Watergate Committee began holding televised hearings. For months, fascinated television audiences were treated to exposures of corrupt political practices that pervaded the Nixon presidency.
Source: Bettmann Archive.

as Haldeman, Erlichman, and Mitchell often gave rambling, incoherent, evasive answers to direct questions.

But Dean's testimony, while sounding plausible and authentic, was legally inconclusive. It depended entirely on his ability to recall the events and conversations that he described before the Committee. He had no corroborative evidence or documents to substantiate his testimony. Only Dean had implicated President Nixon in the cover-up activities. The President had denied all of Dean's accusations and fired him. Dean himself was a suspect source. He was deeply involved in the cover-up. All of the Nixon loyalists who had appeared before the committee had insisted on the President's innocence, and they all accused John Dean of being the evil mastermind of the cover-up. They also accused Dean of wickedly trying to pin the blame on an innocent President in order to save his own skin.

THE DECLINE AND FALL OF RICHARD NIXON

A sensational discovery came on July 16. The chief counsel for the Watergate committee, Sam Dash, found out from Alexander Butterfield, an assistant to Haldeman, that President Nixon had recorded White House conversations and phone calls on a secret tape-recording system installed in the Oval Office in 1970. It turned out that the last tape was recorded on July 12, 1973, the day before Dash made his astounding discovery. If the disputed conversations between Dean and Nixon were on tape, it would be possible to find out which one of them was telling the truth and if the president had been involved in the cover-up. From that date on, the Watergate drama focused on the tapes and the prosecution's efforts to obtain them from the President, who was determined not to surrender them.

Immediately both the Watergate Committee and the Special Prosecutor subpoenaed the tapes of the Nixon–Dean conversations. Nixon rejected both subpoenas. Both investigators then asked Judge Sirica to force Nixon to honor their subpoenas. Nixon's attorneys defended his right to refuse to surrender the tapes on the grounds of "executive privilege." Judge Sirica rejected the argument and ordered Nixon to release the tapes. Nixon's attorneys appealed his ruling. The appeals court upheld the ruling, saying that "The president is not above the law's commands."

While the battle for control of the tapes was raging, another White House scandal surfaced, unrelated to Watergate, involving Vice President Agnew. Justice Department investigators learned that Agnew, when governor of Maryland during the 1960s, had taken bribes from construction companies in return for favorable rulings on their bids. He had continued to receive payments while serving as vice president. In August 1973, Agnew was charged with bribery, extortion, conspiracy, and income tax evasion. Nixon, convinced of his guilt, pressured Agnew to resign. To get rid of him, Nixon offered him a deal: resign and plead "no contest" to a single count of tax evasion for not reporting or paying taxes on the bribes, and the other charges would be dropped. The other charges and evidence sustaining them would be published so people would know why Agnew resigned. Knowing that the federal prosecutors had hard evidence against him, Agnew accepted the offer. Otherwise, he knew that he would go to prison. He resigned, was fined $10,000, and was given three years' unsupervised probation. The evidence released to the public showed that the case against Agnew amounted to fifty indictable offenses. Even so, Agnew, displaying considerable gall, toured the country, making speeches and appearing on talk shows. Everywhere he insisted on his innocence, and he argued that he only resigned to avoid embarrassing the embattled president.

Shortly after Agnew's forced resignation, President Nixon chose House minority leader Gerald R. Ford of Michigan to succeed the fallen vice president. Ford was a conservative, a Nixon loyalist, and was popular with his colleagues. Further, there were no political or personal scandals in his life. This last factor was crucial, because many Senators who voted to confirm Ford knew that if the tapes substantiated Dean's charges, Nixon was not only selecting a Vice President, he was choosing his successor. Ford had to be squeaky clean.

Meanwhile, Archibald Cox and the Watergate Committee were pressing the Nixon administration for tapes of key conversations with his top aides on the Watergate cover-up. The release of these tapes posed a mortal danger to the president, which he knew better than anyone. Nixon decided on a bold move to avoid surrendering them: unless a compromise was arranged, permitting the president to keep custody of the tapes, Nixon would dismiss Cox and prepare his own summaries of the tapes for Judge Sirica. Efforts to forge a compromise failed. On Saturday evening, October 20, Nixon ordered Attorney General Elliot Richardson to fire Cox. The attorney general refused and resigned. Nixon then directed Deputy Attorney General William Ruckelshaus to fire Cox. Ruckleshaus also refused, and Nixon dismissed him from office. Finally, the third-ranking officer at the Justice Department, Robert Bork, dismissed Cox. Nixon also abolished the Special Prosecutor's office and ordered the FBI to seal all of the office files.

Journalists dubbed these resignations and the firing of Cox the "Saturday Night Massacre." The firings provoked a dramatic outpouring of public protest. During the next forty-eight hours, over 1 million letters, telegrams, and phone calls poured into Senate and Congressional offices, nearly all of them denouncing the Saturday Night Massacre. Eight resolutions of impeachment were introduced into the House of Representatives. Nixon's approval rating in the polls dropped to 27 percent. Polls also revealed that most Americans suspected that the President was trying to hide his involvement in criminal activities. In addition to his Watergate actions, Nixon also came under attack for questionable financial dealings involving his real estate holdings in California and Florida. He was accused of charging the government for making improvements to both properties (which were primarily for his personal use) that enhanced their value considerably. The IRS also investigated Nixon for tax evasion.

Nixon tried hard to repair the largely self-inflicted damage with a public relations campaign. He agreed to release the original tapes ordered by Judge Sirica. He replaced Cox with another Special Prosecutor, Leon Jaworski, a Houston corporation lawyer. Nixon met with Congressmen and Senators to reassure them of his innocence. He released a detailed financial statement to dispel doubts about his personal finances. He went on a national speaking tour to reclaim his lost reputation. Before an audience of newspaper publishers, he insisted that he was "not a crook." His efforts failed. Except for hard-core loyalists, the public, the media, and Congress remained skeptical of Nixon's efforts at reassurance. The president's lingering credibility was further undermined when White House officials admitted that two of the nine subpoenaed tapes, covering important conversations with Dean, did not exist. Even worse, an eighteen-and-one-half-minute segment of a crucial conversation between Nixon and Haldeman, held three days after the break-in, had been erased. Calls for Nixon's impeachment grew louder.

With the failure of his public relations campaign, Nixon grew defiant. He refused Jaworski's requests for more tapes. On March 1, 1974, the grand jury indicted several key players in the cover-up, including Erlichman, Haldeman, and Mitchell. It would have indicted Nixon as well if Jaworski had not told them that under the law a sitting president was not indictable. At about the same time the grand jury issued its indictments, the House Judiciary Committee began impeachment proceedings against the president. When its staff sought tapes and documents from the White House, Nixon refused its requests as well. Both Jaworski and the House Judiciary Committee then issued subpoenas to obtain the desired evidence and to overcome the president's "stonewalling" tactics.

Nixon was caught in a serious bind. He knew that refusal to comply with subpoenas would not work; the courts would not sustain his efforts. He also knew that conversations on several of the requested tapes would ruin him if released. He came up with one more big play to try to escape the trap. He decided to release edited transcripts of the requested tapes. In a speech to the American people, delivered on April 29, dubbed by the media "Checkers II," he made a final effort to retrieve his political reputation. He told his audience of his intent to release the transcripts. "These materials will tell all," he said. The next day, the transcripts were published in full.

The public response to Nixon's ploy was again emphatically negative. House Judiciary Committee members, comparing the edited versions with tapes already released, discovered many discrepancies. They refused to accept the edited versions and told the president that as far as they were concerned, he had refused to comply with the committee's subpoena for the tapes. The contents of the edited tapes were even more damning to the President's cause because of the impression they conveyed of Nixon's conduct of the presidency: crude, vulgar language; the voicing of racial and ethnic stereotypes; wheeling and dealing; and the complete lack of scruples or morality. Nixon evidently failed to understand that the inner workings of his government could not stand public exposure. Conservatives as well as liberals were appalled by Nixon's way of governing. Senate Republican leader Hugh Scott said that the transcripts revealed a "deplorable, disgusting, shabby, and immoral performance" by everyone recorded on the tapes. House Republican leader John Rhodes of Ohio called upon Nixon to resign. Both the House Judiciary Committee and Jaworski continued their demands for more tapes from the White House. Nixon refused all of their requests. Jaworski subpoenaed sixty-four additional tapes. Nixon tried to quash the subpoena, but Judge Sirica upheld it and ordered Nixon to release the tapes.

When the White House announced that it would appeal the ruling, Jaworski asked the Supreme Court to decide the matter. It agreed to do so. The question before the Court was clear: who had the final authority to decide whether a president had to obey a subpoena, the subpoenaed president himself or the courts? The Court heard arguments by both sides in July. Nixon's attorneys argued that the president had the right to decide; the only way the law could be applied to the president was through the impeachment process. Jaworski countered with the argument that if the president decides what the Constitution means, "if he is wrong, who is there to tell him so?"

In the case of *United States of America v. Richard M. Nixon,* the Supreme Court, by an 8 to 0 vote, ruled unanimously that Nixon had to surrender the subpoenaed tapes to Judge Sirica. On the same day the Court announced its verdict, the House Judiciary Committee began voting on articles of impeachment against the president. Within a week, it voted to send three articles of impeachment to the full House. Article I accused the president of obstructing justice for his involvement in the cover-up of the Watergate break-in. Article II accused the president of abusing power by his involvement in efforts to harass his political opponents. Article III accused the president of unconstitutionally refusing to honor the Committee's subpoenas. Two other proposed impeachment articles were defeated. If the full House of Representatives adopted at least one of the three approved articles, Richard Nixon would become the second president in U.S. history to be impeached. (Andrew Johnson had been the first, in 1868.) Nixon would then go on trial before the Senate, who would sit as a jury of 100 members. The Senators would decide whether Nixon would be removed from office for "high crimes and misdemeanors" or be allowed to continue serving as president.

The evidence that destroyed Nixon's presidency was a tape released on August 5, 1974, of a conversation between Nixon and Haldeman, held on July 23, 1972, six weeks after the Watergate burglars had been caught: Nixon can be heard ordering Haldeman to tell the CIA to fabricate a national security operation to keep the FBI from pursuing its investigation of the burglary. Here was the "smoking gun," clear proof of a criminal act—conspiring to obstruct justice. The taped conversation also proved that Nixon had been lying about his Watergate involvement. He had known of the cover-up and had been involved in it from the beginning. Nixon, in a written statement, conceded that the tape was "at variance with certain of my previous statements." With the release of the "smoking gun" tape, remaining congressional support for the president collapsed.

For several days, Nixon wavered between resigning and fighting the impeachment process. On August 7, Republican Congressional leaders called on Nixon at the White House. They told the President that he faced certain impeachment, conviction, and removal from office. Some of the president's advisers worried about his mental health; they felt that he had been broken by the stresses and strains of the long Watergate ordeal. Both Secretary of Defense James Schlesinger and White House Chief of Staff Alexander Haig informed all American military commanders around the world to check with them before carrying out any unusual orders that might come from President Nixon. Henry Kissinger urged a distraught Nixon to resign before the crisis damaged American foreign policy. That night, the President decided to resign.

On the evening of August 8, President Nixon spoke to the American people for the last time. He told the nation that everything he had done he believed had been done with the best interests of the country in mind. He expressed regret for any harm that he might have done others. He admitted to making "errors in judgment." He did not admit to breaking the law or to any wrongdoing. He claimed that he was resigning only because he had lost his political base and could no longer govern effectively. On the morning of August 9, he made a rambling, incoherent, and often emotional farewell speech to his White House staff. His resignation became effective at 12:00 noon that day. At that point in time, Nixon was aboard the Spirit of '76, flying over "Middle America" en route to "exile" in Southern California. At 12:00 noon, Gerald R. Ford took the oath of office as the thirty-eighth president of the United States. The new president began his short acceptance speech by saying "our long national nightmare is over."

Ford was right; Watergate had been a long national nightmare, its impact accentuated by extensive media coverage for over a year. Americans reacted differently to the Watergate scandals. For well-educated, well-informed citizens who understood that the integrity of the American system of constitutional governance was at stake, the events of Watergate were the stuff of high drama. For less well-informed people, the revelations of Watergate appeared confusing and perhaps much ado about not very much. For millions of Middle Americans who had voted for Nixon in 1972 in good faith, Watergate was a series of painful disillusionments. For young people especially, Watergate was traumatic. Many of these youngsters sought refuge in a pathetic cynicism. They shrilly insisted that Watergate was what all politicians did; Nixon and his minions merely got nailed. And even to the bitter end, Nixon retained many defenders. These stalwarts insisted that the only mistake Nixon made was to not burn the tapes. It was the tapes that had ruined him, because they made him vulnerable. The tapes had given his enemies among the liberal political and media establishments, the people who hated Nixon because he had proven them wrong so often, the opportunity to destroy him. And then there were the professional Nixon haters. These liberals rejoiced in their long-time political adversary's humiliation and fall from power. For them, his disgrace was richly deserved and poetic justice. They pointedly observed that Watergate only revealed aspects of the man that they had known were there all along.

Thoughtful analysts searched out the multiple causes of the Watergate scandals. Some found the springs of Watergate within the personality and approach to politics of Richard M. Nixon. Relentlessly ambitious, intensely partisan, insecure, and perhaps even paranoid, Nixon was willing to use or countenance ruthless, even criminal, means to advance his career, to achieve his policy goals and destroy his enemies. Some analysts located Watergate in the institution of the presidency itself, in the rise of an "imperial presidency" since the 1940s. The presidency dominated the federal government, particularly in the realms of national security and foreign policy. All modern presidents wielded awesome powers and came to be regarded as special people, as a kind of royalty, above the restraints of the Constitution and the claims of morality. Other analysts saw the rise of a Cold War mentality as contributing to the Watergate syndrome. In a struggle for survival against ruthless and powerful adversaries, it is sometimes necessary to employ the same ruthless methods that the Communists used, and to employ them more extensively than they. It was necessary to enter an Orwellian world where undemocratic methods were required to preserve democracy. Still others saw the Watergate scandals as deriving from an ethic that held that winning was so important that there were no limits on what could be done to achieve victory. This do-whatever-it-takes-to-win attitude also reflected the political ethics of the many nouveau-riche Sunbelt politicians who rode to power on Nixon's coattails. Nixon was the leader of this dangerous new political class that did not play the game of politics by the traditional establishmentarian rules. It therefore had to be destroyed.

George McGovern was right when he labeled Nixon's administration the most corrupt in U.S. history. But the corruption of the Nixon White House, Agnew excepted, was not the commonplace corruption of crooks, thieves, bribers, grafters, chiselers, and influence peddlers that infested past presidencies. It was a more dangerous kind of corruption that threatened the integrity of the American system of government. It threatened to replace a government based on constitutional law with the rule of a powerful leader heading a staff of fanatical loyalists, whose highest calling was to do his bidding and vanquish his enemies. His list of enemies included Democratic Party leaders, prominent journalists, bureaucrats, antiwar protesters, black militants, celebrities, and hippies, who posed threats to the leader's personal authority, which he equated with national security. Their threat would be contained by any means necessary, including wiretapping, surveillance, burglary, blackmail, political sabotage, and intimidation. President Nixon and his men, for a time, posed the most serious threat to constitutional governance and democratic political processes, in American history.

But they failed. A constitutional crisis was resolved. Arbitrary power was thwarted. Eventually due process ran its course. Three hundred seventy-eight officials, including three former Cabinet members and several top-level White House aides, either pleaded guilty or were convicted of Watergate-related offenses. Thirty-one went to prison. It is probable that only President Ford's pardon kept Nixon from prison. Assisted by some good fortune, the system of checks and balances established by the Founding Fathers eventually worked. The system met its gravest challenge. A free press sounded alarm bells. Various investigations exposed the culprits. The Supreme Court firmly established the principle that no one, including the President, is above the law. Congress, spearheaded by the Senate Watergate Committee and the House Judiciary Committee, overrode efforts at executive usurpation. The forces of democracy united to purge a would-be tyrant and his lackeys from office.

Watergate left a mixed legacy. Paradoxically, it revealed both the terrible vulnerability and the underlying strength and resiliency of the American democratic political system. The abuses of power by the president and the president's men were finally checked. But it took an agonizingly long time for the mainstream media to get involved, for the public to become aroused, and for Congress to take action. Suppose the tapes had not been discovered? Or suppose that Nixon had ordered them destroyed? Watergate's outcome provided no guarantee that the system would be able to contain a subsequent president's abuses of power. Watergate, along with the Vietnam War, made Americans skeptical, even cynical, about politics and politicians. Watergate reminded thoughtful Americans of what the Founding Fathers knew to be the chief threat to republican government: that power can corrupt fallible leaders. Within the psyches of political leaders, the grubby demons of greed and lust for power compete with desires to serve and to do good. And sometimes the demons prevail. Above all, Watergate reaffirmed the oldest lesson of our political heritage: eternal vigilance is the price of liberty.

POSTMORTEM

Henry Kissinger has written that Richard Nixon's biographer will require the skills of a historian and the literary talents of a dramatist. It is exceedingly difficult to render balanced judgments of Richard Nixon's presidency and public career. This complex, divided man rendered both great service and great harm to his nation. His was a long, distinguished public career. His presidency was perhaps the most significant since the great Franklin Roosevelt's. He was a bold, innovative diplomat with major achievements: the historic opening to China, stabilizing relations with the Soviet Union, and reducing the threat of nuclear war. He also eventually ended the disastrous war in Southeast Asia and placed U.S. foreign policy worldwide on a sound, realistic basis. He ensured that the United States would continue to occupy the central role in world affairs. In the process of bringing about these historic accomplishments, Nixon achieved the stature of world statesman. His accomplishments in domestic policy are less impressive, but he restored a measure of social peace, wrestled energetically with economic problems, and supported some ecological causes. He also proposed innovative solutions to welfare problems and arrested the decline of local government.

But, in the ultimate crisis of his political career, he strained the American system of constitutional government that he had sworn to defend, damaged the presidency, harmed the Republican Party, destroyed his public career, and ruined his historical reputation. He was forced to resign in disgrace, and he fled into "exile" within his own country. Ironically, Nixon's forced resignation probably did more to unite the country, to bring Americans together, than any other act of his presidency. The leader who tried to dominate the government and intimidate his foes provoked a counterassault that overwhelmed him and his allies. Americans breathed a collective sigh of relief and congratulated themselves for having saved their democratic system. Justice and the rule of law under the Constitution prevailed.

In the 1980s and 1990s, the American people's anger at Nixon had diminished. He achieved a partial rehabilitation. He had acquired the stature of an elder statesman; presidents occasionally sought his advice on matters of foreign policy. He achieved respect and became rich as the author of several substantial books about politics and foreign policy. His memoir is the best and most revealing of any president. Upon his death in June 1994, he was honored with a splendid state funeral in front of the magnificent Nixon presidential library in Yorba Linda, California. Nearby stood the modest wood frame house that his father had built, in which Richard M. Nixon had been born in 1913. All who came could see how high in the world the shy Quaker boy had risen. Thousands of his fellow citizens braved driving rains to pay their final respects. All of the prominent people who spoke at his funeral praised his patriotic service to his nation, especially his foreign policy accomplishments. No one mentioned Watergate or the fact that his presidency had ended in failure and disgrace.

BIBLIOGRAPHY

James T. Patterson's *Grand Expectations: The United States, 1945–1974* is a comprehensive survey of the first three decades of post-World War II U.S. history that includes virtually every major development that marked American life during those years. Several major studies of Richard Nixon have been undertaken in recent years. The best of these works is Stephen E. Ambrose's three-volume biography: Volume 1 is entitled *Nixon: The Education of a Politician, 1913–1962;* Volume 2 is entitled *Nixon: The Triumph of a Politician, 1962–1972;* and Volume 3 is entitled *Nixon: Ruin and Recovery.* Roger Morris, a scholar who worked for the National Security Council staff under both Johnson and Nixon, has written a major study of Nixon covering the years of his life and political career up to 1952, entitled *Richard Milhous Nixon: The Rise of an American Politician.* Another fine study is Garry Wills's *Nixon Agonistes.* The former president is himself the author of several books, the best of which is his autobiography, *RN: The Memoirs of Richard Nixon,* one of the finest presidential memoirs ever done. The best historical study of the Watergate crisis is Stanley I. Kutler's *The Wars of Watergate.* Kutler sees Watergate as a reflection of the essence of Nixon's political career and presidency. Kutler has also edited *Abuse of Power: The New Nixon Tapes.* These newly released tapes fill in some of the remaining gaps in the Watergate story and provide more evidence of criminal behavior by the president and the president's men. See also the two books by *Washington Post* reporters Carl Berstein and Bob Woodward, *All the President's Men* and *The Final Days.* The two best of many books written by men involved in the Watergate scandals are Harry R. Haldeman's *The Ends of Power* and John Dean's *Blind Ambition.* Theodore H. White, in *Breach of Faith: The Fall of Richard Nixon,* attempts to explain the causes of the Watergate scandals. Kevin B. Phillips's *The Emerging Republican Majority* is an important theoretical tract that influenced Richard Nixon's domestic political strategies. Leonard Silk, in *Nixonomics,* illuminates Nixon's unorthodox approaches to economic policy. Allen J. Matusow's *Nixon's Economy: Booms, Busts, Dollars, and Votes* is a recent study of Nixonomics. The author charges Mr. Nixon with pursuing economic policies primarily to win reelection in 1972 that did serious harm to both the U.S. economy and the developing world economy. Melvin Urofsky's *The Continuity of Change: The Supreme Court and Individual Liberties, 1953–1986* offers a good section on the Burger Court.

10

The World and Richard Nixon

Richard Nixon assumed office amidst the gravest political and cultural crises in modern American history. He had won a narrow plurality of votes, in part by appealing to the vast unhappiness of millions of citizens with the costs and consequences of America's global foreign policy, particularly the seemingly interminable Vietnam War, which the Johnson administration could neither win nor terminate.

Aware that America's Vietnam entanglement was dividing the nation, sapping its strength, and diverting it from full pursuit of its global rivalry with the Soviet Union, the new president made phasing out the Vietnam War his top foreign policy priority. Aware also that the world was rapidly changing in the early 1970s, Nixon, aided by his most prominent foreign policy adviser, Henry Kissinger, sought to change American relations with the major Communist powers, with the turbulent nations of the Middle East, and with America's major allies in Western Europe. As they forged and implemented the nation's foreign policy, Nixon and Kissinger sought three major goals: to bring America's foreign policy commitments in line with the nation's ability to meet them more effectively; to ensure that the United States continued to play the central role in world affairs; and to erect a structure of peace that would last a generation. During Nixon's presidency, significant changes occurred in all facets of American diplomacy, including a dramatic opening to China, the relaxation of tensions with the Soviet Union, and the eventual phaseout of the Vietnam War. Nixon proved a bold, innovative diplomatist who achieved the respect of other world leaders. However, many of his and Kissinger's foreign policy achievements turned out to be short lived. Relations between the Soviet Union and the United States deteriorated in the late 1970s, as the Cold War heated up.

NIXON AND KISSINGER

At first glance, the foreign policy tandem of Richard Nixon and Henry Kissinger appeared a highly improbable mismatch. Nixon had been the anti-Communist firebrand who had incurred the enmity of the Eastern establishment, which viewed him as a cynical opportunist whose prime political goals appeared to be partisan advantage and career advancement. Given his reputation as a vintage Cold Warrior, Nixon's foreign policy views were believed to turn on a reflexive anti-Communism. Until the Communist Tet-68 Offensive undermined popular support for the Vietnam War, Nixon had been one of the nation's most prominent hawks.

Kissinger, a German Jew whose family had fled Nazi tyranny during the late 1930s, had become a respected member of the American intelligentsia. He had been a Harvard professor of international relations. His politics were liberal, and he had acquired a reputation as a sophisticated analyst of foreign policy and national security issues. Before joining Nixon's administration, Kissinger had served as an adviser to President Kennedy and New York Governor Nelson Rockefeller. Kissinger believed that it had been a grave error of statecraft to intervene militarily in Vietnam. He thought the United States should have sought a political solution to Vietnam's problems.

After holding a series of conversations, Nixon and Kissinger discovered that they shared similar goals, priorities, and strategies concerning the kinds of foreign policies America required in the early 1970s. Nixon brought Kissinger aboard to head the National Security Council. Both men agreed that Lyndon Johnson's method of seeking a foreign policy based on a consensus among his senior civilian and military advisers was cumbrous and ineffective, a prescription for either inaction or disaster. To streamline the process, Nixon and Kissinger sought to concentrate in their hands the power to make and direct foreign policy, bypassing the bureaucracies at the State and Defense departments. Both men believed that effective diplomacy required a great deal of maneuvering, bold actions, secret contacts with foreign leaders using back channel communications, and keeping the media and the public out of the process until decisions were made or goals accomplished. The two leaders considered themselves realists; they had little use for doctrine, philosophy, idealism, or moralizing about relations among nations. For them, great power diplomacy was a high-stakes game played with both friends and foes. It was about getting and using power to protect and enhance the national interest as they conceived it within a shifting, dangerous world.

DÉTENTE

Nixon, who had built his political reputation as a hard-line Cold Warrior during the most intense phases of the Cold War, with help from Kissinger, launched a new era of détente with the Soviet Union, built on a relaxation of tensions and realistic diplomacy. The development of new relations with the Soviets reversed the direction that American foreign policy had taken since 1945. A glimmer of détente had surfaced in 1963 in the aftermath of the Cuban Missile Crisis with the signing of the Nuclear Test Ban Treaty, but Lyndon Johnson had been unable to sustain it. Because of the Vietnam War and Arab-Israeli conflicts in the Middle East, relations between the United States and the Soviet Union were strained at the time of Nixon's accession to office, and ongoing efforts at arms control negotiations were unproductive.

Since the beginning of the Cold War, U.S. foreign policy had been premised on the need to respond to threats to U.S. interests posed by expansionist Communist states. Both Nixon and Kissinger knew that by the time they acceded to power, the model of a world dominated by a bipolar struggle between Communism and the Free World had been rendered obsolete by world developments. They could see that other power centers had arisen. Power now flowed along a pentagonal axis representing the United States, Western Europe, the Soviet empire, China, and Japan.

The two leaders also understood that American power had suffered relative decline since the late 1950s. The United States no longer dominated its major allies. They also observed that the unity of the Communist world had been fatally sundered. In early 1969, the most serious international conflict pitted the two major Communist states, the Soviet Union and the People's Republic of China, against each other. Kissinger and Nixon perceived that, in the case of the quarreling Communist giants, questions of conflicting national interests often overrode their ideological kinship. The Soviets and Chinese engaged in skirmishes along border territories long claimed by both, and the two nations prepared for a major war. Nixon and Kissinger set out to use this rift between the two Communist powers, if they could, to improve American relations with both and to enhance American power in the world.

Nixon and Kissinger had many reasons for seeking détente with the Soviets. They hoped to persuade the Soviets to help them achieve a satisfactory peace in Indochina by linking Soviet willingness to persuade the North Vietnamese to accept American terms with improved relations between the two superpowers. The American diplomatists also expected détente to enable the United States to maintain control over its NATO allies, who had recently shown a distressing tendency to make deals of their own with the Soviets and with the Eastern bloc countries. Prosperous and no longer fearful of Soviet aggression, the French and West Germans had been pursuing their own détentes with the Communists and were no longer automatically supportive of U.S. foreign policy initiatives such as the Vietnam War. The West Germans, led by its new Chancellor, Social Democrat Willy Brandt, had loaned the Soviets money and had concluded a series of joint business ventures with them potentially worth billions of dollars. Another powerful motive for détente was the desire of American industrial and financial interests to move into Soviet and Eastern European markets. Powerful U.S. agricultural interests saw the Soviets as major customers for their wheat and other commodities. Of utmost importance, Nixon and Kissinger had to be concerned by the ever-present danger of nuclear war arising from the spiraling arms race. Both sides felt an urgent need to bring a measure of control to the arms race that would significantly reduce the threat of nuclear catastrophe engulfing both nations and much of the rest of the world.

In 1969, Nixon signed the Nuclear Non-Proliferation Treaty with the Soviets. At Nixon's initiative, American and Soviet delegates began strategic arms limitation talks (SALT) in April 1970 at two sites, Helsinki and Vienna. At the same time, Kissinger began a series of conversations with the Soviet Ambassador to the United States, Anatoly Dobrynin. Nixon wanted nuclear weapons agreements with the Russians to be the key to détente and the foundational arrangements for an expanding network of agreements with the Soviets.

As he pushed for SALT to begin, Nixon expanded America's nuclear arsenal, believing that the United States must always negotiate with the Soviets from a position of strength. At the time, both nations possessed roughly equal nuclear arsenals, and both were working hard to refine and expand their nuclear weapons systems. Nixon wanted to add two new weapons systems to the U.S. arsenal, an anti-ballistic missile (ABM), which would protect American strategic ICBM missiles from a possible first strike, and what in military jargon were known as multiple, independently targeted reentry vehicles (MIRV). MIRV technology would make it possible for multiple nuclear warheads to be fired from a single ICBM missile in flight at several targets simultaneously. The Soviets also were at work on ABMs and MIRV missiles in the late 1960s.

Nixon also began a phased reduction of U.S. conventional military forces. These military cutbacks coincided with a general scaling back of American global commitments. In August 1969, the president proclaimed a new Asian policy, called the Nixon Doctrine. According to this new strategic doctrine, America would no longer provide direct military protection in the Far East. Asian nations must henceforth assume greater responsibility for their own strategic security. The United States could furnish economic and technical assistance, and logistical support, but not troops. The clear implication of the Nixon Doctrine was that there would be no more Vietnams or Koreas. The Nixon Doctrine also had implications and applications for other regions and other conflicts outside of Southeast Asia. The new doctrine also signaled that a new dynamic U.S. policy of negotiation and maneuver was supplanting the essentially static policy based on military containment of Communism. Active and resourceful diplomacy would supplant drawing lines on maps and daring the Communist powers to cross them.

While SALT negotiators representing both sides grappled with the intricate and technical questions involved in controlling the asymmetric nuclear weapons systems of the United States and the Soviet Union, other negotiators concluded a series of important economic agreements. In November 1971, representatives of both governments signed agreements whereby the United States would sell the Soviets $136 million of wheat and $125 million of oil drilling equipment. New agreements with the Soviets also included a joint venture, the building of a large truck factory. These and many other smaller deals led to a threefold increase in American–Soviet trade over the next three years. These expanding economic arrangements with the Soviets also reflected another element in the Nixon–Kissinger approach to foreign policy. Washington wanted to give the Soviet leaders a greater stake in the world status quo. They were convinced that the more comfortable the Soviets became with their status in the world, the less likely they would feel the need to aid revolutionary forces such as the Communists in Vietnam or compete with the Chinese to disrupt Western relations with Third World nations. The Soviets would develop a realistic sense of national interests that would override their ideological zeal.

In March 1972, Nixon sent Kissinger to Moscow to make preparations for a summit meeting between the American president and his Soviet counterpart Leonid Brezhnev, General Secretary of the Soviet Communist Party. Nixon later journeyed to Moscow, where he and Leonid Brezhnev met for a series of talks. In May 1972, out of these extraordinarily productive talks came three uniquely significant, groundbreaking agreements. The first agreement limited each country to two ABM sites, and it also set a ceiling on the number of ABMs per site. The second agreement, an interim agreement called SALT I, froze the number of strategic missiles in both arsenals at 1972 levels for five years. However, it placed no limits on the number of MIRVs that each side could retain, and both nations continued to build them. Neither the ABM treaty nor SALT I ended the thermonuclear arms race, but the arms agreement did bring a measure of stability and control welcomed by both powers. The third agreement formally acknowledged what had long been a strategic reality—known as Basic Principles of U.S.–Soviet Relations, the agreement officially committed both sides to accept strategic parity as the basic premise for future arms control negotiations. By assenting to the new agreement, Americans officially announced that they would no longer seek to attain nuclear superiority over the Soviets; they had accepted sufficiency. Congress subsequently approved all three agreements. These breakthrough agreements fundamentally altered American–Soviet relations in the world and constituted the bedrock of the new superpower relationship founded on détente, a relaxation of tensions. These new treaties were the most important diplomatic accomplishments of the Cold War era.

Other significant diplomatic agreements between the United States and the Soviet Union were concluded. The Berlin question, a recurring flash point in the Cold War, was once and for all resolved. Both sides signed the Berlin Agreement of 1971, which defined clearly the political status of Berlin and created mechanisms for peaceful resolution of any conflicts that might arise in the future. The next year, the two German states normalized relations, and the United States recognized East Germany as a legitimate state, thus terminating at last the strained and anomalous relationships between the two superpowers that had arisen from the outcome of World War II. The United States and the Soviet Union even managed to settle the long-standing question of the Soviet Lend-Lease debt left over from that war. The Soviets agreed to pay a portion of a scaled-down debt annually for the next twenty years.

All of these significant agreements forged during the most productive era in U.S.–USSR relations since World War II did not make the two superpowers allies. The United States and the Soviet Union remained political and ideological adversaries. But détente had at least created the opportunity for realistic agreements between the two countries, which stabilized the arms race, reduced tensions, significantly reduced the risk of nuclear war, and resolved several long-standing political problems that had divided the two superpowers. Competition and rivalry between the superpowers would continue, especially in the Third World, but "peaceful coexistence" had become an acknowledged official reality.

The Nixon and Kissinger policy of détente with the Soviet Union came under attack from the liberal Democratic Cold Warriors who controlled Congress. Senator Henry "Scoop" Jackson, from the state of Washington, emerged as the leader of the Democratic opposition to détente. Jackson attacked SALT I. He insisted that it gave the Soviets a dangerous advantage over the United States, because it allowed them to keep more land-based ICBMs than America. Jackson's criticism missed the mark in that he ignored the fact that the United States relied for strategic deterrence on a triad of strategic weapons comprised of land-based missiles, submarine-launched missiles, and strategic bombers. The Soviets, lacking equivalent submarine and strategic bomber forces, required additional ICBMs to offset the American advantage.

Senator Jackson also criticized the Nixon administration for its toleration of Soviet human rights violations, particularly Moscow's refusal to let all Soviet Jews who wanted to exit the Soviet Union emigrate. Jackson's criticism was valid, although the Soviets had liberalized their emigration policy. They permitted 30,000 Jews to leave the country during 1973, the largest number ever. Jackson, who harbored presidential ambitions, helped push the Jackson–Vanik amendment through Congress, which denied the Soviet Union "most favored nation" trading status with the United States, until it stopped human rights abuses and allowed unlimited emigration. The Jackson–Vanik amendment that effectively prevented Washington from granting equal trading rights to the Soviet Union hindered the developing commerce between the two nations, undermined détente, enraged President Nixon, and disappointed Brezhnev.

THE CHINA OPENING

Nixon's most dramatic foreign policy achievement was the famed opening to China. Since the Chinese Communist revolution in 1949, the United States had insisted that Jiang Jieshi's regime on Taiwan was the true government of China and had refused to recognize the Communist government in Beijing. For twenty years, America and China had had no commercial, diplomatic, or cultural relations, and the United States had successfully prevented China from joining the United Nations. Americans, even those of Chinese ancestry, were forbidden to travel to China. The United States also had maintained a trade boycott and loan ban against China and had attempted to prevent other nations from trading with the Chinese. When Nixon took office in 1969, China was emerging from years of internal upheaval caused by Mao Zedong's "Cultural Revolution," and Chinese leaders, worried about threats to China's security posed by conflicts with the Soviets, sought contacts in the West. Mao was hopeful that friendly relations could be developed with the United States, a country that he had long admired.

Beijing sent friendly signals to Western nations. Nixon, sensing possibilities for rapprochement with the People's Republic, responded. Trade and travel restrictions between the two countries were eased. In April 1971, the Chinese invited an American table tennis team to visit China to play Chinese athletes. This "ping pong gambit" preceded the major breakthrough that came in July, when Henry Kissinger secretly visited China. Nixon then stunned the American people when he suddenly announced on July 15 that Kissinger had made arrangements for him to visit China in early 1972. By deploying their secretive style of diplomacy, Nixon and Kissinger were positioned to stage one of the most significant diplomatic transformations of modern times.

Nixon sought to improve relations with China for several reasons. He knew that the American policy of nonrecognition was unrealistic. China was an established major power in world affairs. He also knew that pressures were mounting within the United Nations to evict Taiwan and to seat China in its stead. Further, Nixon expected to use friendly relations with China as a diplomatic weapon against the Soviets; he wanted to be able to play the "China card" in order to make the Soviet leaders more inclined to conclude arms control and other agreements with the Americans. Improved relations with China also were part of Nixon's and Kissinger's strategy of extricating the United States from its Vietnam entanglement. They expected Beijing to be helpful in persuading Hanoi to negotiate a settlement of the Vietnam War on terms that the Americans could accept. A relationship with China also would help the United States reassert its power in Southeast Asia and develop a wider network of interests in that important region. Most of America's European allies had long since normalized relations with China; the current U.S. ban obviously had failed. Domestic politics also figured in Nixon's decision to go to China. He knew his impeccable anti-Communist credentials protected him from attacks about his being soft on Communism. Nixon also knew that television coverage of the dramatic trip would boost his political stock at home during an election year.

The announcement that Nixon was going to China was greeted with tremendous enthusiasm and support by just about all Americans, regardless of their political leanings. Media commentary was overwhelmingly favorable, even ecstatic. Many Democratic political leaders put aside their usual criticisms of Nixon's and Kissinger's diplomacy to praise both men effusively. Kissinger returned to China in November 1971 to finalize the arrangements. While he was in Beijing, the United Nations expelled Taiwan and awarded its seat on the Security Council to China. There was no protest from President Nixon, who was willing to sacrifice the Taiwanese on the altar of détente with the major Communist powers. Some critical voices, mostly on the Republican Right, remnants of the old China Lobby, were raised in protest over Washington's quick abandonment of its longtime ally and friend.

President Nixon arrived in China on February 22, 1972, accompanied by advisers and a host of U.S. journalists. Back in the United States, millions of fascinated Americans

Figure 10.1 Nixon's greatest diplomatic feat was the opening to China, achieved when he journeyed to that great country in 1972. Here he greets Mao Zedong at the latter's apartment. *Source:* National Archives.

watched spectacular live television coverage of Nixon's arrival at the Beijing airport, his journey into the Forbidden City, and many other highlights of his five-day visit. Nixon's party and the journalists were the first Americans officially to go to China in over twenty years. The video images beamed back to America through a communications satellite were the first live U.S. television pictures ever shot in China. Nixon met with Premier Jou En-lai several times for hours of discussion. Nixon and Kissinger also had a lengthy meeting with the legendary Mao Zedong. The American delegation was the guest of honor at a huge banquet hosted by the Chinese leaders inside of the Great Hall of the People. Later, Nixon and his wife Pat were photographed at the Great Wall of China. The entire visit seemed to consist of a series of dazzling photo opportunities for the President.

At the conclusion of the historic visit, President Nixon and Premier Jou En-lai issued a joint statement, known as the Shanghai Communique, which defined the terms of the new U.S.–Chinese relationship. Each country agreed to open a legation in the other's capital, offices that could evolve into embassies in time. The United States removed its restrictions on trade and travel to China. The United States acknowledged that Taiwan was part of China. Both sides were critical of what they referred to as "Soviet hegemonism." There was no agreement on the Vietnam War, and both China and the United States reaffirmed support for their respective sides in that ongoing conflict. But the joint communique itself, the fact that it was being promulgated jointly by former adversaries, signaled that the United States had moved beyond Vietnam, beyond the war, toward a larger role in Southeast Asia. U.S.–Chinese relations would go forward, regardless of the Indochina War. Both China and the United States affirmed a commitment to work toward normalizing relations. Within a year of Nixon's visit, American travelers flocked to China. Trade between the two nations increased rapidly. Both countries exchanged diplomatic missions. The China opening was

Figure 10.2   Richard Nixon and First Lady "Pat" Nixon visit the Great Wall of China.   *Source:* National Archives.

the high point of Nixon's presidency and perhaps the most significant diplomatic achievement of any modern American president. *Time* magazine named President Nixon and Henry Kissinger as "Men of the Year for 1972."

VIETNAM: A WAR TO END A WAR

The most pressing international problem confronting Nixon was extricating America from Vietnam. Nixon tried new approaches to end the war, including implementing the so-called secret plan announced during his presidential campaign. But his policies suffered from the same flaw as President Johnson's. Nixon still sought to achieve an independent, non-Communist South Vietnamese government, which the North Vietnamese absolutely refused to accept. Therefore, the war went on.

Even though Hanoi had consistently rejected any settlement that would leave a non-Communist government in the South, Nixon and Kissinger believed that they could compel Hanoi to accept one. They planned to use the improved relationship between the United States and the USSR by linking increased trade and arms agreements with the USSR to the Soviet's willingness to pressure Hanoi into accepting U.S. terms in Vietnam. Nixon also escalated the war by removing the limits that Johnson had placed on the use of military force in Southeast Asia. In the spring of 1969, Nixon ordered a bombing campaign to begin against the Vietcong and North Vietnamese sanctuaries in Cambodia. Since Cambodia was a neutral nation, the bombing was illegal and kept secret from Congress and the American people. Nixon also ordered an expansion of U.S. bombing of Laos. In addition, Nixon, through Soviet intermediaries, offered the North Vietnamese more realistic peace terms. He proposed withdrawing both American and North Vietnamese troops from the South and re-instituting the demilitarized zone as the boundary between North and South Vietnam. At the same time, to appease American public opinion that had turned against the war, Nixon announced a phased withdrawal of American combat troops from Vietnam.

But Hanoi was neither intimidated by threats nor lured by concessions into changing its basic terms. Hanoi continued to demand the unilateral withdrawal of all U.S. forces from South Vietnam and the creation of a coalition government in the South, excluding General Thieu. The Paris talks remained deadlocked. Nor did the Soviets cooperate. The linkage strategy proved a failure in 1969. With the failure of his plan, Nixon faced a dilemma. Unable to extract the slightest concession from Hanoi, he had to choose between a major escalation of the war or a humiliating withdrawal.

Unwilling to make concessions and unable to use greater force because he did not want to arouse domestic opponents of the war and because of doubts about its effectiveness, Nixon offered what he called "Vietnamization"—the United States would gradually continue to withdraw its troops while building up South Vietnamese forces in order to enable them to defend themselves against a Communist takeover following the U.S. pullout. At the time Nixon announced his Vietnamization plan, it had already been in place for a year. He had inherited it from the outgoing Johnson administration and had given it a new label. While U.S. Marines and Army infantry battled the North Vietnamese and Vietcong, American advisers built up the South Vietnamese forces. Pacification and rural development programs accelerated. The first troop withdrawals were announced in June 1969. In March 1970, President Nixon announced that an additional 150,000 U.S. combat troops would be withdrawn that year.

In March 1970, in neighboring Cambodia, neutralist leader Prince Sihanouk was suddenly overthrown by his pro-American Prime Minister Lon Nol. Nixon, fearing that the North Vietnamese might take over Cambodia following the coup and responding to a long-standing U.S. Army request to attack North Vietnamese sanctuaries in that country, ordered American troops into an area of Cambodia, about fifty miles northwest of Saigon. The Cambodian incursion produced mixed results. It relieved pressure on Saigon and bought more time for Vietnamization. It also widened the war and provoked Hanoi into full-scale support of Cambodian insurgents fighting Lon Nol's forces. The United States now had two fragile client states in Southeast Asia to defend against insurgents backed by North Vietnam. The Vietnam War had been widened; it had become an Indochina War. The Cambodian campaign also proved to be the last major campaign of the Indochina War involving American ground combat forces.

Nixon did not anticipate the furious domestic reaction to the Cambodian invasion. College campuses across the land exploded at the news of an unexpected widening of a war that the president had promised to phase out. At Kent State University, tragedy occurred when Ohio National Guardsmen opened fire into a crowd of student protesters, killing four of them and wounding nine others. Following these shootings, hundreds of student strikes

Figure 10.3   Tragedy struck at Kent State University on May 4, 1970. Troops of the Ohio National Guard fired into a crowd of student protesters, killing four. In this photo, students attend to one of their fallen classmates.   *Source:* National Archives.

forced many colleges to shut down. More than 100,000 demonstrators gathered in Washington to protest the Cambodian invasion and the "Kent State massacre." The Cambodian initiative also caused the most serious congressional challenge to presidential authority to conduct the war. The Senate repealed the Gulf of Tonkin resolution and voted to cut off all funds for military actions in Cambodia. But the fund cutoff failed to clear the House and never went into effect. Both the North Vietnamese and the Vietcong broke off negotiations in protest, confident that domestic and international pressures would eventually force American withdrawal from both Cambodia and South Vietnam.

To appease dovish critics at home, the president accelerated his timetable for troop withdrawals in 1971. He also expanded the air war by ordering more bombing missions into Cambodia and along the Laotian panhandle. He also authorized an ARVN raid into Laos to disrupt enemy supply routes and staging areas, but the raid failed to achieve most of its objective. The South Vietnamese forces retreated after taking heavy casualties. President Nixon claimed that the Laotian campaign had been a success and that it demonstrated that Vietnamization was on schedule and working. Neither assertion was true. The American viewing public watched television images of beaten, terrified South Vietnamese forces streaming back into South Vietnam. The South Vietnamese government, its army, and its people knew that they had been defeated. Within America, Doves attacked another widening of the war that Washington was supposedly winding down.

During the spring and summer of 1971, two events at home shocked an increasingly war-weary nation. First, on March 29, a military court convicted Lieutenant William Calley of multiple murders and sentenced him to life imprisonment for ordering his infantry platoon to kill over 200 Vietnamese civilians at a hamlet called My Lai-4 in South Vietnam. Calley's men had been brought in to destroy the hamlet, which had been suspected of harboring Vietcong. But instead of evacuating the population beforehand or eliminating the village with long-range artillery and bombs, Calley's men had massacred the villagers at close range with machine-gun and automatic rifle fire.

Calley claimed that he only followed orders. Army attorneys insisted that Calley had misunderstood his orders. No one else was convicted of war crimes. Many Americans felt sympathy for Calley and his men; a public opinion poll showed that a majority of Americans blamed the media for reporting the incident, which had exposed Army efforts to cover up the affair. Hawks denounced the verdict, arguing that no soldier should ever be convicted in wartime for doing his duty. Some Doves condemned the verdict, because they believed a junior officer was being scapegoated while his superiors got off free. Responding to the angry outcry over Calley's conviction, President Nixon reduced Calley's sentence.

Some Americans wondered how many other My Lai-type massacres had gone undetected, although there was no hard evidence that there were any other massacres in which U.S. soldiers had deliberately murdered hundreds of unarmed civilians. Others found cold comfort in the fact that Vietcong and NVA (North Vietnam Army) forces were guilty of systematic atrocities and mass murder. There also was the troubling inconsistency of convicting one young junior officer for mass murder in a war where long-range artillery fire and aerial bombing had killed thousands of villagers since the Americanization of the war in 1965. What My Lai revealed above all was that the hellish circumstances of combat, which could generate intense confusion, fear, rage, and hate, sometimes brought out the worst in men.

On June 13, 1971, not long after the uproar over Calley's conviction had subsided, the *New York Times* began publishing excerpts from the *Pentagon Papers*. These were top-secret government documents stolen from the files of the Rand Corporation by former employee Daniel Ellsberg, who turned them over to his friend Neil Sheehan, a reporter for the *Times*. Ellsberg, formerly a Marine officer who had served in Vietnam and as a Defense Department analyst, had become disillusioned with the American war effort. He believed that President Nixon intended to prolong the war indefinitely in search of an American victory, and he hoped that the publication of the papers might generate a groundswell of popular protest that would force an end to the war.

The papers revealed that American leaders had deliberately escalated the war, violated international law, ignored peace offers, and often lied to Congress and the American people about their actions. Documents also showed that American leaders had often manipulated the Saigon governments, and that President Kennedy had been aware of and supported the military coup that had overthrown and murdered Ngo Dinh Diem. These revelations further undermined the credibility of government officials and weakened support for the war. Publication of the *Pentagon Papers* brought some people, whose support of the war had been wavering, into the opposition camp.

An increasingly frustrated president fought back against the mounting opposition to his war policy. He ordered wiretaps placed on National Security Council staffers and journalists suspected of leaking secret information to the media. He ordered illegal surveillance of antiwar groups by both the FBI and the CIA. He accused congressional Doves of encouraging the enemy and prolonging the war. The Nixon administration tried to prevent the *New York Times* from publishing the *Pentagon Papers* by securing a court injunction against their publication on the grounds that their release compromised national security. An appellate judge quashed the injunction, and the Supreme Court sustained his ruling, finding only the reputation of some public officials compromised by publication. Blocked by the Supreme Court, the president approved the creation of a special White House undercover unit, the "Plumbers," to prevent leaks from within the government and to discredit Ellsberg. Under stress, Nixon developed a siege mentality, feeling beset by enemies in Congress, in the media, in the bureaucracies, and in the streets—all of whom, he believed, were working to undermine his authority to govern. These paranoid attitudes, which drove him to order his men to commit illegal acts, were one of the prime causes of the Watergate scandal.

By the summer of 1971, polls showed that public support for Nixon's policies had dropped to 31 percent. Another survey revealed that two-thirds of Americans approved of the withdrawal of all American troops from Vietnam by the end of the year, even if that meant a Communist takeover in South Vietnam. The Senate twice passed resolutions setting a deadline for withdrawal of all troops as soon as North Vietnam had released U.S. prisoners of war. Nixon had responded to those signs of growing war weariness by making new, secret peace proposals to Hanoi: in exchange for the release of the American prisoners, the United States would withdraw all of its troops within six months and would no longer insist that Hanoi withdraw its troops. These new American concessions started the first serious negotiations since talks had begun in 1968. But deadlock continued, because the United States still insisted that Thieu remain in power in the South, whereas Hanoi insisted that his removal was a precondition of any settlement.

The American Vietnam War entered its final phase in 1972. Knowing there were only 6,000 American combat troops remaining in the South, North Vietnam launched its largest offensive of the war. About 120,000 North Vietnamese regulars struck directly at ARVN forces across several fronts. Simultaneously, Vietcong guerrillas resumed their attacks in rural areas to disrupt pacification efforts. The United States retaliated with massive B-52 bombing raids against targets in the Hanoi–Haiphong area. U.S. bombers also pounded the North Vietnamese invaders and their supply lines. The North Vietnamese and Vietcong continued to press their attacks. Nixon then carried out his boldest escalation of the war, ordering a naval blockade of North Vietnam, the mining of Haiphong harbor, and the expansion of the bombing campaigns. In addition to his military responses, Nixon also again approached the Soviets about persuading Hanoi to accept a diplomatic settlement of the war.

Nixon's decisive response to the North Vietnamese assault received strong support at home. Congress, and most Americans, supported Nixon's moves. The bombing and blockade disrupted North Vietnamese supply lines sufficiently to enable the hard-pressed ARVN forces to stabilize their lines around Hue and Saigon. Suffering heavy losses, the North Vietnamese offensive was stalled by summer. South Vietnam managed to survive the assaults, due to the strong response of the United States and its own determined resistance in some of the battles. By the end of the summer, the South Vietnamese, with strong tactical air and logistical support from the Americans, had retaken all major towns and cities that had been captured by the Communists during the early phases of the offensive. Both the Soviets and the Chinese, while publicly condemning the American response, privately exerted pressure on Hanoi to end its war with the United States. Détente with the two Communist powers at last paid dividends and helped Nixon bring the U.S. war in Southeast Asia to a belated conclusion.

With the onset of the summer rains in 1972, the war stalemated once more. The North Vietnamese had expected its spring offensive, combined with the approaching American election, to force Nixon to accept their terms and remove Thieu. But the president's powerful response had neutralized their assault and inflicted heavy losses. Soviet pressure on Hanoi also pushed them toward a diplomatic settlement. George McGovern, the Democratic challenger for the presidency in 1972, proved to be a weak candidate who posed no threat to Nixon or his war policy. A combination of military losses, economic strains, and diplomatic isolation finally forced Hanoi to seek a settlement with the United States, as long as it did not conflict with its long-range goal of achieving a unified Vietnam under Communist control.

Secret negotiations resumed in Paris. Hanoi dropped its demand that Thieu must go before any settlement could be reached. Kissinger and the North Vietnamese emissary, Le Duc Tho, bargained intensively. By October 11, 1972, they had forged an agreement: within sixty days after a cease-fire, the United States would remove all of its remaining troops, and North Vietnam would release the American POWs. The Thieu government would remain in power, pending a political settlement in the South. North Vietnamese troops would remain in the South, and the National Liberation Front, now calling itself the People's Revolutionary Government (PRG), would be accorded political status in southern Vietnam. Kissinger held a special press conference on October 26 to announce that "peace is at hand."

But General Thieu, who had the most to lose from these arrangements, refused to accept them. President Nixon, who shared some of Thieu's reservations about the proposed settlement, supported Thieu. The North Vietnamese, believing that the Americans were using Thieu to stall an agreement that they really did not want to accept, proposed some changes of their own. The October agreement was placed on indefinite hold, and the war went on. President Nixon, reelected by a landslide, decided that the North Vietnamese were not really trying to reach a settlement, and he directed Kissinger to break off the talks. The president ordered unlimited air attacks on North Vietnamese targets in the vicinity of Hanoi and Haiphong. There ensued against North Vietnam the most powerful attack in the history of aerial warfare. This "Christmas Bombing" lasted from December 18 to 29. Nixon was determined to pound Hanoi into resuming negotiations, and perhaps he hoped to achieve more favorable terms that would ensure the long-term survival of South Vietnam. At the same time that he turned the Air Force loose on the North, Nixon significantly increased U.S. aid to South Vietnam and bluntly told General Thieu to accept U.S. peace terms or the United States would settle without him. Nixon, in effect, was pressuring both sides into signing a peace agreement that would allow the United States to extract itself from a war that most Americans no longer believed in or supported.

The Christmas Bombing provoked worldwide criticism and a storm of protest at home. Congress moved to cut off all funding for the war. With time running out on his options, Nixon told the North Vietnamese that if they agreed to resume negotiations, he would halt the bombing. The battered North Vietnamese accepted his offer, and the talks resumed. Kissinger and Tho reached an agreement signed by all parties on January 27. The January agreement was similar in all major provisions to the suspended agreement of October 11. The bombing had not forced any major concessions from the North Vietnamese. This time Nixon imposed the agreement on Thieu, who signed reluctantly. To make the treaty more palatable to Thieu, Nixon pledged in writing that the United States "would respond in full force" if North Vietnam violated the agreement. The United States also significantly increased its military and economic aid to Thieu's government.

Although President Nixon insisted that the peace agreement had brought "peace with honor" to Indochina, in truth, the Paris Accords of January 1973 represented a disguised defeat for the United States, which permitted the Americans to extricate themselves from a war that they could not win and to retrieve their POWs. It also permitted North Vietnamese forces to remain in the South, and it granted the PRG political legitimacy. It allowed the Thieu regime to survive in the South for a time. The treaty was essentially a deal between Washington and Hanoi. The major question over which the war had been fought for nearly a decade—who would govern in the South—was deferred, to be resolved, according to treaty language, by "political means" in the future. The treaty did not resolve the fundamental issue of the war: was Vietnam one country or two? That question would be finally settled by force of arms in two years. For the Communists, the Paris Accords represented merely another delay in their thirty-year-long crusade to retrieve their sovereignty from Western colonialism and to unify their nation under their control.

The war went on, even as Kissinger and Tho signed the agreements; there was never an effective cease-fire, because neither the Communists nor the South Vietnamese made a sincere effort to stop fighting or to resolve their differences through negotiations. President Nixon continued to support the Thieu government after the American withdrawal, but his efforts were limited by the terms of the Paris Accords, by a lack of public and congressional support and by his own deepening involvement in Watergate. After the Paris Accords were signed and the POWs came home to heroes' welcomes, Vietnam faded from the American scene. Vietnam no longer dominated the television nightly news, or even received much coverage at all. When Watergate revelations forced Nixon to resign from the presidency in disgrace in August 1974, the wars in Vietnam and Cambodia were raging violently, the scale of casualties higher than ever. But now only Asians killed Asians, and most Americans were unconcerned. Their attention was turned elsewhere.

THE MIDDLE EASTERN DILEMMA

As they maneuvered to realign American relations with the major Communist powers and sought to extract the United States from the stalemated Indochina War, Nixon and Kissinger had to cope with another crisis in the Middle East, with another Arab-Israeli war. Since the 1967 Six Day War, a state of simmering hostility between Arabs and the Jewish state had prevailed; no progress toward resolving their serious differences had been made. Israel refused to surrender any of the Arab territories that it had seized during the Six Day War— East Jerusalem, the West Bank, the Golan Heights, and the Sinai. The Arabs, for their part, adamantly refused even to meet with Israeli representatives or to accord the Jewish state the right to exist. Sporadic border skirmishes between Israeli and Egyptian troops occurred in 1969 and 1970, reflecting a kind of war of nerves between two bitter enemies. In the fall of 1970, Gamal Abdul Nasser, the Arab Nationalist leader, suddenly died, to be replaced by his key assistant Anwar Sadat. Sadat, in time, found the tense state of relations between his country and Israel intolerable; he plotted with his ally Syria to stage another attack on Israel. The ground was prepared for another bloody Middle Eastern war.

On October 6, 1973, the fourth Arab–Israeli war commenced. Choosing Yom Kippur, the holiest day of the year for Jews, the Egyptians and Syrians launched surprise attacks on Israeli positions in the Sinai and along the Golan Heights. Egyptian forces captured hundreds of Israeli soldiers. To the north, Syrian forces regained territory in the Golan Heights region and threatened to slice Israel in two. Caught off guard by the surprise Arab attacks, Israeli Prime Minister Golda Meir appealed to Washington to send the Israelis more planes, tanks, and ammunition. The United States responded promptly with an airlift of war materiel to their beleaguered ally.

Washington's decision to resupply the Israelis had unanticipated economic consequences for the American people, because it provoked Saudi Arabia to cut back sharply on its oil production and to impose an oil embargo against the United States as reprisal for its support of Israel. The oil embargo, although it proved to be of brief duration, destabilized world oil markets. It also created the first of a series of "energy crises" in the United States, an energy crunch that had devastating impacts and far-reaching consequences. Unemployment rose, as did the rate of inflation. The stock market dropped sharply and the U.S. economy went into a steep recession. "Stagflation," a condition of high unemployment, stagnant economic growth, and a high rate of inflation, worsened.

Amply resupplied by their American patrons, Israeli armor counterattacked in force both in the Sinai and Golan Heights regions. They drove the Syrians from the Golan Heights and chased them back towards Damascus, the Syrian capital. In the Sinai, Israeli tanks stemmed the Egyptian offensive and drove them back toward the Suez Canal. A frightened Sadat now turned to his ally, the Soviet Union, for help, a move that alarmed Washington because it appeared to threaten détente. On October 20, Nixon dispatched Kissinger, now Secretary of State as well as National Security Adviser, to Moscow to meet with Brezhnev. The American envoy told the Soviet leader not to send forces to the Middle East. Kissinger also rejected a Soviet proposal that the United States and the Soviet Union jointly impose a cease-fire. Meanwhile, Israeli armor crossed the Suez, enveloped large numbers of Egyptian troops, and placed troops on Egyptian soil. Egypt's situation was growing desperate, and the Soviets were growing more nervous as Sadat's situation deteriorated.

The anxious Soviets warned the Israelis not to continue their war or else risk Soviet military reprisals. On October 25, Nixon responded to the Soviet threat to Israel by ordering U.S. forces around the world to go on full military alert. The next day, the President announced that intelligence sources had evidence that the Soviets were preparing to airlift combat forces to the Middle East. The worst crisis in U.S.–Soviet relations since the Cuban Missile Crisis was at hand. Another eyeball-to-eyeball confrontation between the two superpowers appeared a distinct possibility.

But the crisis passed quickly. The Soviets, if they had ever intended to send troops, quickly made it clear that they would not. A United Nations peacekeeping force that excluded both U.S. and Soviet troops was dispatched to the region. Kissinger, shuttling back and forth between Cairo and Jerusalem, persuaded the Egyptians and Israelis to accept a cease-fire that left the Israelis in control of more territory than when the Yom Kippur War had begun, but it permitted the Sadat regime to survive. The cease-fire was the first of a series of Middle Eastern agreements facilitated by Kissinger's "shuttle diplomacy." Subsequently, the Suez Canal was reopened, and the Arabs lifted their oil embargo. Egypt and Syria resumed diplomatic relations with the United States. In June 1974, not long before he was forced to resign the presidency, President Nixon traveled to the Middle East. He went both to Cairo, where he was cheered by huge throngs, and to Jerusalem, where he received a more restrained reception by the Israelis, who were still recovering from the effects of the Yom Kippur War. The junket to the Middle East was President Nixon's last hurrah as world leader and peacemaker.

Paralleling their fervid diplomacy vis-à-vis the seemingly intractable Arab–Israeli conflict, Nixon and Kissinger sought to strengthen American relations with Iran. Washington wanted to involve Iran in U.S. efforts to contain Soviet expansionism into the Middle East. More important, Nixon and Kissinger intended to use Iran as a stabilizing force within that turbulent region to enable the United States to distance itself from the chronic Arab–Israeli disputes. Washington tapped Iran, led by the Shah, whom the CIA had helped reclaim his throne in 1953, to become the major U.S. ally in the Persian Gulf region.

The United States began importing more oil from Iran, and in May 1972, in effect, it gave Iran a blank check to buy conventional weaponry from American arms manufacturers. Iran quickly became the preeminent military power in the region and the leading purchaser of U.S. arms. With help from Washington, relations improved between Saudi Arabia and Iran, who historically had been rivals. The rapprochement between the Saudis and

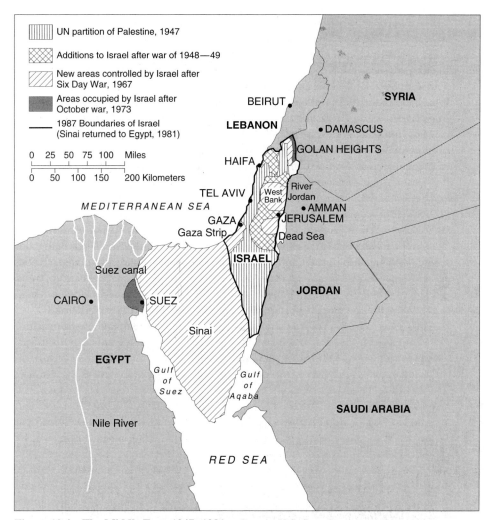

Figure 10.4   The Middle East, 1947–1981.   *Source:* U.S. State Department.

Iranians strengthened OPEC, an emerging consortium of leading oil exporters that challenged the power of the Western oil companies that had hitherto controlled the world's oil markets. Washington's opening to Iran had sacrificed the interests of the major oil companies to the larger goals of Nixon's and Kissinger's Middle East diplomacy. These goals included keeping the Soviets out, stabilizing the region, ensuring Israel's security, maintaining good relations with moderate Arab regimes, and neutralizing the effects of (if not eliminating) the zero-sum game known as the Arab–Israeli conflict. Nixon's and Kissinger's grand design for the Middle East would come a cropper in 1978, when the Shah of Iran was overthrown by anti-Western Islamic fundamentalists.

Further to the east, the United States became embroiled in a regional dispute between India and Pakistan. The cause of the conflict was Pakistani efforts to suppress a Nationalist rebellion in its East Bengal territory. India intervened in the civil war on behalf of the Bengali rebels. Nixon and Kissinger decided to support Pakistan to prevent the Indians from going to war against the Pakistanis. The Soviets backed the Indians and the rebels; the Chinese, fearful of a Soviet–Indian alliance, supported the Pakistanis, making the Americans and the Chinese, in effect, allies. The United States suffered a diplomatic setback when the Bengalis, assisted by the Indians and Soviets, won their independence from Pakistan and became the new state of Bangladesh. The Soviets gained enhanced prestige and influence in the region, strengthening their ties with the Indians and the new country of Bangladesh.

CHAOS IN CHILE

Nixon's and Kissinger's foreign policy focused on the nations of the northern tier; they were relatively unconcerned about the affairs of most Pacific island, African, and Latin American countries that constituted the Southern Hemisphere of the planet. One significant exception to this general pattern of neglect of much of the Third World was Chile. In 1970, Chile's national congress elected a Marxist, Salvador Allende Gossens, as Chile's president. The CIA had tried to prevent Allende from coming to power, but its efforts had failed.

Upon his election to office, Allende quickly moved to nationalize U.S.-owned enterprises in Chile, including two copper mining companies and telephone companies. He also established friendly relations with China, the Soviet Union, and Cuba. Under Allende's leadership, Chile was traveling the road to socialism. In response to Allende's socialist agendum, Washington declared economic war on Chile. U.S. banks no longer loaned Chile money. Washington also prevented international agencies such as the International Monetary Fund and the World Bank from providing Chile with financial assistance. All military assistance programs to Chile's armed forces were suspended. According to a 1975 report, issued by a Senate committee that investigated CIA activities in Chile during the early 1970s, the agency worked to destabilize Chilean politics and plotted to overthrow Allende. It bankrolled the opposition press and the main opposition party, the Christian Democrats. It also supported a teamsters strike that paralyzed the nation's economy and deprived the urban populations of food.

By the summer of 1973, the Chilean economy was in ruins and the newly impoverished middle classes were in revolt. With the CIA's support, on September 11, 1973, a junta of disgruntled army officers, led by General Augusto Pinochet, overthrew Allende, who was killed or who committed suicide during the coup d'etat. Pinochet instituted a reign of terror that resulted in the deaths of hundreds of Allende supporters, the torture and imprisonment of thousands more, and the forced exile of additional thousands. Soon after taking power, Pinochet restored the American properties that had been nationalized to their former owners. The United States quickly lifted all restrictions on economic and military assistance to Chile. Pinochet established a military dictatorship and ruled Chile for the next sixteen years. The CIA did not overthrow the Allende regime, perhaps his government would have been overthrown without U.S. involvement; but the hostile actions of the Nixon administration, coupled with the activities of the CIA, helped to create the economic and political conditions within Chile that provoked the coup.

TROUBLES IN EUROPE

At the time Nixon came to the presidency, a number of political, strategic, and economic factors were creating serious strains between the United States and the three major powers of Western Europe—Great Britain, France, and West Germany. All three nations were asserting greater autonomy from the United States. Both Nixon and Kissinger perceived the danger in this West European trend to their carefully crafted strategy of détente with the Soviet Union. Détente could never realize its full potential unless the NATO nations as well as the Eastern bloc nations remained subservient to their respective superpower patrons.

In response to the growing assertiveness of the Western European nations, Washington sought a new relation with its major allies, one that superseded the costly commitments assumed early in the Cold War to provide for Western Europe's defense and its economic reconstruction. At the same time, they hoped to hold the evolving new relationship somewhat short of full autonomy for Great Britain, France, and West Germany. Washington wanted the new relationship to be characterized by limited autonomy within the Atlantic community, which was still firmly tied to the United States. It hoped to find ways to use Western Europe's new power and wealth globally but at the same time to keep the major Western nations from asserting their independence from American world leadership. But Washington failed to achieve most of its goals in Western Europe during Nixon's tenure. It was perhaps Nixon's and Kissinger's greatest diplomatic failure. NATO retained its traditional structure, organization, and strategic goals, but West Germany, France, and Great Britain continued to draw away from the United States.

By 1970, West Germany was beginning to reassert its traditional national identity. The nation lay at the economic heart of a prospering Western Europe. In 1969, Social Democrat Willy Brandt became Chancellor, the leader of a coalition of the Social Democratic Party (SDP) and the Free Democratic Party (FDP), a liberal party committed to policies promoting the interests of big business and free enterprise. Quickly Brandt implemented his *Ostpolitik,* the most serious challenge to U.S. hegemony in Western Europe since the end of World War II. At its core, *Ostpolitik* was an economic strategy that entailed opening up the markets of Eastern Europe and the Soviet Union to West German high-tech exports. *Ostpolitik* also entailed investments, loans, and joint ventures with East bloc nations and the Soviets and served as a kind of West German détente with the Soviets, breaking through the barriers of traditional anti-Communism that had dominated West German foreign policy for twenty years. Finally, *Ostpolitik* represented an assertion of Germany's sovereignty that ran counter to Washington's "grand design" goals for the nations of Western Europe.

The British and French also began a series of collaborations that ran counter to American expectations and interests. First, the French, under the leadership of Georges Pompidou, dropped their long-standing opposition to British membership in the European Economic Community (EEC), also known as the Common Market. The French apparently were alarmed by the growing economic power of the Germans and sought closer ties with the

British to offset it. The British, for their part, now appeared ready to join the EEC. Reduced tariffs would enable them to sell their exports on the lucrative continental market, and a recent devaluation of the pound sterling made their goods more competitive. After a bruising debate in the House of Commons in September 1971, the British Parliament voted by a large majority to join the EEC.

The British and French also began a series of military and technological collaborations. The most spectacular achievement of the new Anglo-French togetherness was to form a consortium to construct a new supersonic airplane capable of flying across the Atlantic Ocean at twice the speed of sound. It was designed to compete with a planned American supersonic aircraft called the Supersonic Transport (SST). The new French–British plane, called the Concorde, had British engines and a French air frame. It flew its maiden transatlantic flight in 1976. Meanwhile, the Democratic-controlled Congress had killed the SST project, despite intense pressure from the Nixon White House to go ahead with it, because congressional leaders viewed it as too expensive and too noisy. The United States has never built a supersonic civilian airliner.

THE EMERGENCE OF JAPAN

By the early 1970s, Japan was the most important nation in the American Far Eastern economic and strategic system. It also was increasingly a major player in the growing world economy of the 1970s. Yet, from Washington's perspective, Japan posed some serious problems. Like the prosperous nations of Western Europe, Japan exhibited some of the same tendencies to take a foreign policy tack more independent of Big Brother in Washington. The Japanese also contributed a minimal amount, a minuscule fraction of their gross domestic product, to their own national defense. They happily continued to rely on the American nuclear umbrella for their strategic security. Washington had been annoyed that the Japanese had not supported the American effort in Vietnam with any enthusiasm, even though one of the reasons the Americans had intervened in the Indochina War was to protect Japanese economic and strategic interests in that region. Further, the Japanese, with their rebuilt modern supercharged economy, were increasingly selling cars, television sets, and cameras on American markets during the early 1970s, hurting U.S. domestic industries in these crucial high-tech fields.

Nixon and Kissinger hoped to rein in the high-flying Japanese and make them pay more of the costs of their own defense. Washington also wanted to slow the penetration of American markets by Japanese exporters. In 1971, Nixon erected a 10 percent surcharge on all imports from Japan, which was aimed primarily at Japanese automakers. In addition, the OPEC oil embargo engineered during the fall of 1973 by the Saudis badly hurt the Japanese economy, because it was 100 percent dependent on imported oil, having no domestic petroleum sources.

NIXONIAN DIPLOMACY IN PERSPECTIVE

Nixon and Kissinger's diplomacy was a complex congeries of policies that had many successes and also knew many failures. During the years that Nixon and Kissinger worked together to forge and implement American foreign policy, journalists and other analysts tended to write favorably about Kissinger's diplomatic performances. Kisssinger was skilled at cultivating the media and often appeared on talk shows. He sometimes implied that he had provided most of the ideas that composed the grand design of American foreign policy; his concepts seemed to determine its structure and shape. Foreign policy analysts often assumed that this was so. Such views were unwarranted and unfounded. Nixon conceived America's foreign policy during his presidency. He was a bright, shrewd, and an experienced statesman, in charge conceptually as well as officially. It was Nixon's grand design that unfolded during his presidency. Kissinger was, in the last analysis, sophisticated hired help and an errand boy. Capable, intelligent, learned, and shrewd— Kissinger was adviser, envoy, and confidante to the president. Together they forged and implemented the most successful U.S. foreign policy since Harry Truman had initiated the policies that contained Soviet expansionism in Europe during the formative years of the Cold War.

Nixon's greatest success, of course, came with changing U.S. relations with the major Communist powers, the Soviet Union and the People's Republic of China. Nixon and Kissinger were less successful in Indochina. It took considerably longer than they had expected to phase out the U.S. Indochina War. The 1973 Paris Accords that they managed to arrange after four years of effort failed to save South Vietnam from a Communist takeover two years later. But in the aftermath of the failed Vietnam enterprise, America made important gains in its East Asian and Southeast Asian relations. Outside of Indochina, no more dominoes fell to Communist "wars of national liberation." Since 1975, most of the nations of Southeast and East Asia, such as Thailand, Malaysia, and South Korea, have become more stable, strong, and prosperous, enjoying friendly ties and strong commercial relations with the United States.

Foreign policy analyst Franz Schurman has written about the development of a world economic system during the 1970s, by which he means the emergence of an international economic system within which the national economies of most countries are inextricably interlinked in numerous ways. Trade has been integrated, a global monetary system has arisen, and capital markets are interdependent. Political links have likewise arisen through networks of political leaders, civil servants, and senior military officials. The appearance of a world economy suggests, among other things, that the traditional distinctions between foreign policy and domestic affairs have been breaking down. During the Nixon administration, foreign and domestic policy, especially economic policy, became inseparable. Nixon's frequent efforts to try to fix the American economy involved changing U.S. foreign economic policies that were influencing trade, tariff rates, and exchange rates. Nixon's foreign policy, by reducing the threat of war with the major Communist powers and by bringing them, at least to a limited extent, into the evolving world economic system, which is essentially a world capitalist system, ensured the further development of the world system. His grand design also ensured that the United States would continue to occupy the central place in that world system, because the prosperous Western European nations accepted America's central role, perceiving that their own future prosperity was inextricably linked to the United States. Nixon and Kissinger had managed a fairly smooth transition in the fundamental role of America in world affairs, from hegemon to the central power within an evolving world economy. In broad historical perspective, Nixonian diplomacy is best understood as capping the end of a thirty-year era that began with Truman in 1945 rather than viewed as a guide to future U.S. foreign relations of the 1980s and 1990s.

But there were many failures in Nixonian diplomacy during the early 1970s. The Iranian revolution, in time, destroyed all of his plans for the Middle East. His neglect of the poor nations of the Southern Hemisphere in Africa and Latin America ensured political instability and mass immiseration in those important parts of the world during the 1980s. The Nixon Doctrine, which was supposed to be a post-Vietnam politico-military strategy for dealing with insurgencies in the Third World, failed to work effectively. Most of all, Nixon's grand goal, a generation of peace, proved unattainable. Much of his foreign policy demonstrated a short-term brilliance, but it lacked staying power. By the late 1970s, détente was discredited, and Jimmy Carter felt compelled to revive the Cold War. If one of the purposes of Nixon's foreign policy was ultimately conservative and counterrevolutionary, that is, as an effort to stem the Marxist revolutionary tide in the Third World, it also must be counted as mostly a failure. True, Communism did ultimately fail, but its failure did not derive from any clever diplomatic, strategic, or economic maneuvers by Nixon and Kissinger. Ironically, Communism's demise stemmed from its own internal contradictions and failures. Communism did not work; it failed economically and politically, and it was rejected by the masses that it supposedly served.

BIBLIOGRAPHY

There have been several major studies of Richard Nixon undertaken in recent years. Most helpful in understanding Nixon's conduct of foreign policy are the relevant chapters in the second volume of Stephen E. Ambrose's magisterial three-volume biography entitled *Nixon: The Triumph of a Politician, 1962–1972.* Since his forced retirement from the presidency, Mr. Nixon has written several books about world affairs. The best of these books was his first, his memoirs, entitled *RN: The Memoirs of Richard Nixon.* This book contains extensive treatments of his foreign policies. The Nixon administration's foreign policy is analyzed by several authors, including Henry Brandon's *The Retreat of American Power.* A critical view of Nixon's and Kissinger's foreign policies can be found in Tad Szulc's *The Illusion of Peace: Foreign Policy in the Nixon Years.* See also Herbert Parmet's *The World and Richard Nixon* for a friendlier treatment of Nixon's foreign policy. Franz Schurman, in *The Foreign Politics of Richard Nixon,* offers an original analysis of the politics of Nixon's and Kissinger's diplomacy. For détente with the Soviet Union, see the relevant chapters of William G. Hyland's *Mortal Rivals: Superpower Relations from Nixon to Reagan.* The first book-length scholarly study of Nixon's Vietnam policies, Jeffrey Kimball's *Nixon's Vietnam War,* promises to become the definitive account. Also see Arnold Isaacs's *Without Honor: Defeat in Vietnam and Cambodia,* a scathing critique of Nixon's and Kissinger's Indochina policy. For Nixon's Middle Eastern diplomacy, see the relevant portions of Daniel Yergin's *The Prize.* Henry Kissinger, Nixon's able foreign policy adviser, has analyzed their foreign policies in two important books: *The White House Years* and *Years of Upheaval.* Seymour Hersh, in *The Price of Power: Kissinger in the Nixon White House,* has written an extremely negative critique of Kissinger's foreign policy role.

11

Era of Limits

Vietnam and Watergate ushered in a time of trouble for Americans. They experienced ineffective presidential leadership, partisan squabbling, continuing social divisions, severe economic dislocations, energy crises, and international disorders. All of these difficult problems were compounded by a massive loss of faith in politics and politicians, especially among young people. They feared that the American system would not be able to maintain affluence at home, and they worried about declining American influence in the world. A social malaise settled over the land. Americans experienced a crisis of confidence, fearful that their leaders and institutions could not find solutions to their many, complex, and often interrelated problems. Many lost faith in themselves, in their institutions, and in the future.

A FORD, NOT A LINCOLN

Personally, the new president stood in dramatic contrast to his deposed predecessor. Gerald Ford was open and outgoing. A nation weary of war and political scandal appreciated his personal charm, modesty, and integrity as he reminded his fellow citizens, "I am a Ford, not a Lincoln." He came from the Midwest. He had represented Michigan's Fifth District for thirteen consecutive terms until appointed vice president in 1973. He had risen through the ranks of the seniority system to become House Minority Leader in 1965. As president, Ford retained many of Nixon's advisers and tried to continue his policies both at home and abroad.

Sensing the malaise of the nation in the wake of war and Watergate, Ford made "binding up the nation's wounds" and restoring national confidence his top priorities. On September 8, 1974, a month after he took office, Ford astonished the nation by granting former President Nixon a "full, free, and absolute pardon" for any crimes he may have committed while in office. Ford granted the pardon to spare the nation the divisive spectacle of putting a former president on trial. He insisted that there was no advance understanding between himself and Nixon. Whatever his intent, Ford's decision to pardon Nixon backfired. His approval rating in the polls plummeted from 72 percent to 49 percent. The pardon ruined his chances for getting bipartisan support for his policies from the Democrat-controlled Congress. Despite his denials, many Americans suspected that Ford and Nixon had made a deal—Nixon had chosen Ford to replace Agnew with the understanding that if Nixon resigned or was removed from office, Ford would pardon him. Further, it was patently unfair to send underlings to jail for their parts in Watergate, while the leader whose directives they followed went free. Most Americans believed that if Nixon had broken the law, he should have to face trial like any other citizen. Ford appeared to be endorsing the dubious principle that the greater the power, the less the accountability. Ford's pardon of Nixon, however well intentioned, was a serious error in political judgment that perpetuated the suspicions and resentments of Watergate the new leader was trying to dispel; it tied his presidency to that of his despised predecessor. It hurt his party in the 1974 elections, and it may have cost him the 1976 election.

Ford generated further controversy when he established an amnesty program for the thousands of young men who had violated draft laws or had deserted from the military during the Vietnam era. If they agreed to perform public service for one to two years, their

Figure 11.1   Gerald R. Ford succeeded to the presidency in August 1974 following Richard Nixon's forced resignation. Here he acknowledges the cheers of his supporters during a 1976 campaign speech. *Source:* Bettmann Archive.

prison terms were waived or reduced. Hawks condemned the plan as being too lenient; Doves denounced it as being punitive. Another of Ford's efforts to bind up national wounds had the opposite effect of reopening them.

The President also provoked another uproar when he selected Nelson Rockefeller as his Vice President. During Rockefeller's Senate confirmation hearings, it was learned that he had given some of his vast personal wealth to officials prominent in Ford's administration, including Secretary of State Henry Kissinger, formerly a Rockefeller aide. These gifts and loans gave the appearance that a rich man was trying to buy the vice presidency. Rockefeller's confirmation was delayed for months, and the credibility of the new administration was tarnished.

The 1974 midterm elections took place amidst an atmosphere of continuing political controversy and public mistrust, much of which had been perpetuated by Ford's own actions. The Democrats gained forty-six seats in the House and four seats in the Senate, increasing their margins to 291 to 144 in the House and 61 to 38 in the Senate. The Democrats also won most of the state and gubernatorial elections. More voters than ever before called themselves Independents and split their tickets, and only 38 percent of those eligible to vote went to the polls.

Shortly after the midterm elections, a Senate committee investigating CIA operations discovered that over the years the CIA had been involved in numerous assassinations or attempted murders of foreign leaders, including Fidel Castro in Cuba and a Marxist political leader who had been elected president of Chile in 1973, Salvador Allende. A commission headed by Vice President Rockefeller found that the CIA had routinely kept citizens under surveillance and had conducted drug experiments on unwitting victims. The CIA also had engaged in illegal domestic espionage and compiled files on dissenters. Other investigations revealed that the FBI also had engaged in a variety of lawless actions, including wiretapping, spying, burglary, blackmail, and sabotage. Former FBI director J. Edgar Hoover had conducted a personal vendetta against civil rights leader Dr. Martin Luther King Jr. FBI agents had harassed King, had spied on him and his associates, and had read his mail. They also had tapped his phones, bugged his hotel rooms, blackmailed him, and sent him poison-pen letters.

These discoveries of official lawlessness, most occurring during Nixon's presidency, confirmed that the CIA and the FBI, in their obsessive pursuit of internal security, had repeatedly violated the constitutional rights of many American citizens. In response, President Ford issued new directives providing for greater congressional oversight of CIA activities and restricting its covert operations. The Justice Department issued new guidelines for the FBI. The new FBI director, Clarence Kelly, publicly apologized to the American people for the past sins of the Bureau and pledged that they would never recur.

ECONOMIC AND ENERGY WOES

While Americans learned more about official wrongdoing in Washington, their economy deteriorated. The inflation rate soared beyond 10 percent in 1974, spurred by wage hikes, increased consumer demand, budget deficits, and competition from the surging Japanese and Western European economies. The Ford administration, resorting to traditional con-servative economic policy, attacked inflation by slowing down the economy with tight money. Tight money brought the worst downturn in the economy since the Great Depres-sion of the 1930s. Some traditional American mass production industries with inefficient methods of production, poor quality control, and high payroll costs struggled to compete with manufacturers in Europe and the Pacific Rim. American multinational corporations moved their manufacturing facilities overseas to take advantage of lower costs and cheap labor. The primary manufacturing industry of the American economy, automobiles, lost a sizable portion of its domestic market to Japanese and German imports. Unemployment climbed to 7 percent by year's end and reached 9 percent in 1975, the highest since before World War II. Two years later, the inflation rate had dropped to 5 percent, but at the painful price of having 8 million workers unemployed.

In October 1973, an alarming new factor disrupted American economic life, an en-ergy crisis, adding to both inflation and recession. It appeared suddenly when OPEC em-bargoed oil shipments to the United States. The oil cutoff was initiated by Saudi Arabia and other Arab members of OPEC to protest U.S. support of Israel in its recent war with Egypt and Syria and to force a settlement of the war favoring the Arabs. Americans experienced shortages of heating oil and power "brownouts." Impatient motorists formed long lines at gas pumps for the first time since World War II.

The energy crisis had been building for years; the OPEC embargo had triggered it. American postwar growth and prosperity had been founded on cheap energy, increasingly derived from petroleum. American domestic oil production began declining in 1969, while demand had continued to rise. By 1970, the United States, with only 6 percent of the world's population, used over one-third of the world's energy. To meet the ever-increasing demand for oil, U.S. oil companies bought more and more imported oil. Daily consumption of im-ported oil rose from 12 percent in 1968 to 36 percent in 1973. A steadily increasing propor-tion of imported oil came from OPEC nations, and two-thirds of OPEC oil came from Middle Eastern sources. Oil companies became the mechanisms for maintaining the OPEC cartel, since they refined the oil for American markets. When OPEC shut off the oil spigot in October 1973, these companies made huge profits from the accompanying rise in oil prices.

The OPEC embargo was short lived; the Arab countries removed it after a few months, and oil supplies returned to normal. But gasoline prices rose from thirty cents to seventy cents a gallon during that period and stayed there. Much higher energy prices be-came a permanent, painful fact of American economic life. Higher oil prices sent a large in-flationary jolt coursing through all facets of the U.S. economy, because oil had seeped into the very fabric of American life. Oil heated homes; it was synthesized into fibers and plas-tics; farmers used it for fertilizer, pesticides, and fuel; and it was crucial to all forms of trans-portation. Rising energy prices struck hardest at the older industrial centers of the North-east and the Great Lakes region, which had to import most of their energy. Housing and plants constructed during the days of cheap energy proved wasteful and inefficient. In ad-dition, cutbacks in federal spending during the Nixon and Ford administrations fell hardest on cities in these same regions, given their shrinking tax bases, declining industries, and expensive social services. The severity of the fiscal crisis of the "rust belt" cities revealed itself in 1975, when New York City verged on bankruptcy.

Figure 11.2   Energy crisis USA. Motorists line up to get gas at a service station in Los Angeles.   *Source:* National Archives.

Before he was forced from office, President Nixon had tried to combat the energy crisis. He created the Federal Energy Office to formulate a national energy policy and to promote conservation. He proposed a plan called Project Independence to make the United States energy independent by 1980. It called for increasing domestic oil production by tapping Alaskan oil fields; accelerating offshore drilling; producing more natural gas, coal, and nuclear energy; extracting oil from shale deposits; and developing renewable energy sources. Project Independence made little progress. With the lifting of the OPEC embargo and the return of normal supplies of oil, most people quickly forgot about the energy crisis, although they complained about the high price of gasoline for their cars. As Ford took office, the United States continued to import one-third of its daily oil requirements.

President Ford tried to continue Nixon's energy program, but he encountered much opposition. Environmentalists opposed many features. Antinuclear groups opposed building additional nuclear power plants. Ford tried to deregulate domestic oil and natural gas prices, only to be blocked by congressional Democrats who believed that deregulation would hurt low-income families and aggravate inflation. Congress enacted legislation in 1975, giving the president standby authority to ration gasoline, create a strategic petroleum reserve, and set mandatory fuel economy standards for new cars. Three years later, the United States imported 40 percent of its daily oil requirements.

Partisan conflicts between the conservative Republican president and the Democratic Congress hampered government's effectiveness during Ford's tenure. He vetoed sixty-six bills enacted by Congress, including federal aid for education, a health care measure, a housing measure, and a bill to control strip mining. Congress enacted a few important measures, among them extending the Voting Rights Act of 1965 and increasing Social Security benefits. It also enacted several measures over Ford's vetoes, including a $3 billion public service jobs bill to combat the recession.

FORD, KISSINGER, AND THE WORLD

Henry Kissinger, whom Ford inherited from former President Nixon, doubled as Secretary of State and head of the National Security Council, and had a major part in shaping U.S. foreign policy. The new President, who had no background in foreign policy, was happy to give the experienced, capable Kissinger the leading role in conducting his administration's foreign policy. Ford and Kissinger tried to improve relations with China and the Soviet Union, but they had little success. Ford visited China in 1975, but Washington's support of Taiwan prevented him from forging closer ties. At the time, China's leadership was changing. Rival factions of pragmatists and radicals vied for power, as China's aged revolutionary leaders, Jou En-lai and Mao Zedong, passed from the scene. Any significant new diplomatic initiatives had to wait for a new leadership to establish control.

Efforts to extend détente and to forge additional arms control agreements with the Soviets failed. Negotiators got bogged down in technical details as advances in nuclear weapon technologies outstripped their efforts to impose political controls. In November 1974, Ford met Soviet President Leonid Brezhnev in the Siberian port of Vladivostok. There the two leaders signed an agreement for an arms control treaty that would be known as SALT-II, but the agreement never evolved into a full-fledged treaty. SALT-II never happened, because American domestic opponents of détente, led by Senator Henry Jackson, refused to accept any agreement that allowed the Soviets to maintain a large advantage in land-based ICBMs, even though the United States had more manned bombers and missile-launching nuclear submarines.

Another effort to extend détente brought Ford and Soviet leader Leonid Brezhnev together with European leaders at the Conference on Security and Cooperation in Europe, held in Helsinki, Finland, in August 1975. Both sides agreed to recognize the political boundaries dividing Eastern and Western Europe since the end of World War II. For the first time, the United States officially recognized the legitimacy of Communist rule in Eastern Europe. The Helsinki conference brought forth a declaration of human rights supporting basic freedoms, such as the right to emigrate, free speech, and religious freedom. For his part, Brezhnev agreed to ease restrictions on the right of Soviet Jews to emigrate. Kissinger's overtures to the Communists outraged conservatives within the Republican Party, such as presidential hopeful Ronald Reagan, who denounced both détente and Kissinger for trafficking with the Reds.

VIETNAM: DENOUEMENT

Between 1973 and 1975, Congress restricted the president's power to involve the United States in the continuing Indochina War. Congress also reduced the amount of aid going to Saigon. The War Powers Act, which was passed over President Nixon's veto in 1973, required that the president consult with Congress before sending American forces into a foreign war. When North Vietnam mounted a spring offensive in 1975, South Vietnam suddenly collapsed. The invaders overran its territory. President Ford wanted to honor U.S. commitments to intervene, but given the lack of Congressional and popular support, he could do nothing. On April 23, President Ford told a cheering audience at Tulane University that the Vietnam War "is finished as far as America is concerned," thereby making U.S. abandonment of the South Vietnamese government official. Saigon fell to the Communists six days later. About a month after the fall of Saigon, Cambodian Communists seized an American merchant ship, the *Mayaguez,* which was cruising near the Cambodian coast. On May 12, Ford sent in a detachment of 350 marines to rescue the ship and crew. Most Americans applauded the president's determined show of force at a time when Americans were feeling pushed around in Southeast Asia.

The twenty-five-year-long American effort to prevent a Communist takeover in southern Vietnam had ended in disaster for the United States and the people it had tried so hard for so long to help. The Indochina War had been the longest, least popular war in U.S. history. It had divided Americans more than any other conflict since their own Civil War. It was the first major war that Americans had ever lost. Its aftermath refuted every Cold War assumption upon which American involvement had been based. American security was not threatened. American alliances elsewhere were not weakened, nor were American allies disheartened by the outcome. American power and prestige in the world community was not significantly diminished.

There was no unified Communist takeover of Southeast Asia, because the victorious Communist states fell to warring among themselves. A vicious Marxist regime, which overthrew Lon Nol in Cambodia at about the same time the North Vietnamese conquered Saigon, was responsible for the death of at least 1 million of its own people. Communist Vietnam invaded Cambodia, now called Kampuchea. China, supporting the Kampuchean regime, attacked Vietnam. The Soviet Union backed Vietnam in these intramural Communist wars. The United States, which had gone to war in Southeast Asia, ostensibly to stop the spread of Chinese Communism, found itself quietly backing Chinese efforts to contain Vietnamese expansionism. Southeast Asian national interests turned out to be a stronger force than Marxist ideology in determining their behavior. There was no bitter "who lost Vietnam" debate in the United States and no resurgence of McCarthyite Red-baiting. Instead, amnesia set in; no one wanted to talk about Vietnam for years, much less indulge in recriminations over it.

The harm done to the United States and Vietnam by the long, losing war was severe and lasting. George Kennan, the principal theorist of containment, called the Vietnam War "the most disastrous of all America's undertakings over the whole 200 years of its history." The war killed perhaps 2 million Vietnamese and turned one-fourth of its population into refugees. It left 58,000 Americans dead and another 300,000 seriously wounded. There were few parades for returning Vietnam veterans. Except for the POWs, they were not welcomed home. A people who had carelessly sent them off to fight in Vietnam for a cause they no longer believed in were embarrassed by their presence and sought to ignore them, or worse, to denounce them.

The war experience for many veterans had been an ordeal. In addition to facing the ravages of war, many soldiers returned home disillusioned over their combat experiences. To these veterans, the war appeared futile and pointless. The rejection of the war by the civilian population made it more difficult for many soldiers to justify their efforts or to derive any meaning from them. Most returning veterans were neither war criminals nor victims. They did not suffer from drug or alcohol addiction nor did they have acute psychological or physical disabilities. But many veterans struggled to come to terms with their war experiences, to readjust to civilian routines, and to reintegrate into American life. Most succeeded; the typical Vietnam veteran has been more successful in life than his (or her) nonveteran counterpart. The stereotype of the typical Vietnam veteran as a loser or a drugged-out violent wacko is demonstrably false, a product of sensational television shows and motion pictures. Whatever their politics or view of the U.S. war policy, most Vietnam veterans served with pride. They went to Vietnam, did their duty, and returned home to get on with their lives, just as most soldiers who have fought in previous U.S. foreign wars have done.

In addition to the human costs of the war, the economic costs also were high. The Vietnam War cost $167 billion, more than any other war in U.S. history except World War II. President Johnson's efforts to finance both the Great Society and the war ignited inflation. His refusal to trim domestic spending, to raise taxes, or to apply economic controls because he was trying to hide the costs of war from the American people brought economic decline to millions of American households. The Vietnam War was both a symbol and a major cause of the relative decline of U.S. power and prestige in the world.

There were other costs of the Vietnam War. A bitter controversy erupted over whether hundreds of thousands of draft evaders and deserters should be granted amnesty or be severely punished. This nasty debate perpetuated the war-sown divisions between the Doves and Hawks. The war also undermined public faith in the competence and honesty of elected officials. Military service was discredited for years. The war shattered the bipartisan ideological consensus that had guided U.S. foreign policy since the late 1940s. The losing war also proved that American technology and wealth could not defeat a poor Third World nation determined to prevail, nor could the United States support forever an ineffective regime. Americans discovered that there were limits to U.S. power, and that there were limits to the burdens that Americans were willing to bear in pursuit of Cold War foreign policy aims. For the first time since the Cold War began, many Americans questioned the validity of their global mission to contain Communism. The ordeal of Vietnam also marred the American spirit. The ultimate domino was America's vision of itself as a powerful, benevolent nation. That lofty self-image perished in the jungles, swamps, and rice paddies of Vietnam.

THE ELECTION OF 1976

As the 1976 election approached, Ford appeared politically vulnerable. President only by the grace of Nixon's appointment, he had proven to be an ineffective caretaker during his two years of office. He faced a powerful challenge from within the Republican ranks from Ronald Reagan, former governor of California and leader of a resurgent conservative movement. Reagan accused Ford of becoming part of the Washington establishment, of being out of touch with ordinary Americans. The jaunty former actor voiced a litany of New Right grievances: too much governmental interference into the affairs of American citizens, busing to achieve school integration, the legalization of abortion, student radicalism, rampant sexual promiscuity, and the decline of the family. He attacked the Ford–Kissinger foreign policy based on détente with the Soviet Union and the opening to China. Reagan called for deep tax cuts, prayer in public schools, and a military buildup to offset Soviet gains in the aftermath of the Vietnam debacle.

As election-time approached, the Democrats were confident that they could beat either man. A large field of Democratic contenders sought their party's nomination. It looked as though it would be a wide-open race. Candidates included Senators Henry Jackson and Frank Church, Governors George Wallace and Jerry Brown, and Congressman Morris Udall from Arizona. The surprise of the 1976 Democratic race turned out to be the sudden emergence of James Earl Carter Jr., who called himself "Jimmy." Carter beat them all to capture the Democratic nomination. He was unknown outside of his native Georgia, where he had served one term as governor. Carter had decided to run for president following the Democratic debacle of 1972. As he sized up the Democrats most likely to seek the party nomination for 1976, the liberal Ted Kennedy and the conservative George Wallace, he saw that both men had liabilities and turned off large blocs of Democratic voters. He planned a moderate campaign that would fill the gaps and reunite a party that had been badly factionalized by the Vietnam War and domestic insurgencies, particularly the civil rights movement.

Carter and a small group of supporters quietly toured the country in 1975 and 1976 to meet people and raise funds. Carter burst upon the national political scene and gained media exposure with a victory in the Iowa caucus in January 1976, and he won the crucial New Hampshire primary in February. When he entered the New Hampshire race, few observers took his candidacy seriously. "Jimmy who?" the voters asked. Carter captured New Hampshire and was off and running. He waged a skillful primary campaign, capitalizing on the national backlash from Watergate and Vietnam, and from widespread popular disillusionment with Washington politics and politicians.

Carter's political style was earnest and folksy. His major pitch was the need for a leader untainted by residence in Washington, an outsider who could restore integrity to government. Carter, assisted by an able group of pollsters and political operatives, appeared to sense what people were feeling and thinking about politics in the wake of Vietnam, Watergate, and other revelations of official corruption and wrongdoing. People responded to the man and his message. When forced to take a stand on a specific issue, Carter usually sought the middle ground. For example, on abortion, Carter expressed his personal repugnance to abortion but said that he supported *Roe v. Wade.* On the issue of amnesty for Vietnam-era draft evaders, Carter supported pardons for draft evaders, but he did not favor amnesty because that might imply approval. Voters liked Carter less for his moderate political stances than for his honesty.

He scored a series of primary victories, and by April he was clearly the front-runner. Party liberals, unhappy with the moderate Southerner, tried to stop Carter. In May and June, Governor Jerry Brown of California and Senator Frank Church of Idaho beat Carter in a series of primaries in the West. But Brown and Church could not stop Carter's drive for the nomination. Although Carter won no more primaries after April, he continued to gather delegates. He had the nomination sewn up by mid-June. A month later, the Democratic Convention opened in New York. A unified, harmonious convention chose Carter on the first ballot. As a gesture to the traditional liberal wing of his party, Carter chose Senator Walter

Mondale of Minnesota as his vice-presidential running mate. They ran on a platform attacking Ford's "government by veto" and Kissinger's "manipulative" foreign policy. Carter's capturing of the Democratic Party nomination in 1976 had to be one of the most remarkable achievements in modern American political history. Victory by this obscure Southerner with scant political experience could only have happened within the context of the American peoples' post–Vietnam, post–Watergate massive disillusionment with politics as usual.

Meanwhile, Jerry Ford was locked in a fierce struggle with Ronald Reagan for the Republican nomination. Ford adopted a centrist stance, projecting an image of a moderate leader healing the nation's wounds, promoting economic recovery, and keeping the nation at peace. His strategy worked initially. He beat Reagan decisively in the early primaries. But the former California governor kept hammering away. When the Sunbelt primaries came up in the spring, Reagan ran off a string of victories, surging ahead of Ford in the delegate count. Ford rallied with victories in several Northern industrial states. Reagan countered with a big win in California. When the Republican Convention assembled in Kansas City, the two candidates were so close that the winner would be the one who captured a majority of the few uncommitted delegates. Ford managed to win a close first-ballot nomination, but Reagan forced Ford to move to the Right in order to survive. Reagan also influenced the drafting of a conservative platform that incorporated many Reaganite issues. Ford also discarded the liberal Nelson Rockefeller, replacing him with a sharp-tongued, conservative vice-presidential running mate, Kansas Senator Robert Dole. Although Reagan endorsed Ford, many of his supporters did not. Ford led a divided party into battle against a Democratic Party united behind Jimmy Carter.

The presidential campaign turned out to be rather dull and unenlightening. Neither man made much impact on a wary electorate or stood out in a series of three televised debates in what became a virtually issueless campaign. Both men trafficked in generalities. Carter appeared especially fuzzy on the issues. Ford made a serious gaffe during the second debate, when he insisted that the Soviet Union did not dominate Eastern Europe, but it is not clear whether that remark cost him many votes. Ford ran on his record, which was unimpressive. Carter, a Baptist Sunday school teacher and "born-again" Christian, conducted a populistic, highly moralistic campaign. He ran against the federal government, promising to tame Washington's "bloated, unmanageable bureaucracy." He promised that he would never lie to the American people, and he pledged a government that is "as good and honest as are the American people." Perhaps making an effort to appear more secular or "with it," Carter told journalist Robert Scheer during an interview printed in *Playboy* magazine that he had "committed adultery in my heart many times" and that he had lusted after women other than his wife. Such comments from the pious, square presidential candidate provoked mostly laughter rather than outrage from the media and from the general public.

When the contest started, the polls gave Carter a huge early lead. One poll showed Carter leading Ford 62 percent to 29 percent! Within six weeks, Carter's waffling on the issues and Ford's sharp attacks had eliminated it. Many voters found neither candidate impressive. Liberal historian Arthur Meier Schlesinger Jr. grumbled that voters had a choice between the "weirdness" of Carter and the "dumbness" of Ford. On election eve, pollsters termed it too close to call.

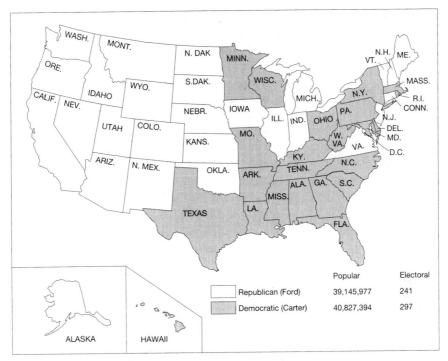

Figure 11.3   The election of 1976.   *Source:* Dubofsky & Theoharis, *Imperial Democracy: The United States Since 1945,* 2d ed., p. 22.

Carter managed a narrow victory. He took 50.1 percent of the vote to Ford's 48 percent. Carter garnered 41 million votes to Ford's 39 million. His winning margin in the electoral vote was 297 to 241. Ford carried twenty-seven states; Carter carried twenty-three states, plus Washington, D.C. Carter carried the South, several border states, and some Northern industrial states. He lost most of the Midwest and carried no states west of the Mississippi. Ford received a majority of the white vote nationally. Black votes provided Carter's margin of victory in the South. Carter also did well among traditional Democratic voters—those who made up labor, urban, Jewish, liberal, and intellectual constituencies. Although the race for the White House was close, the Congressional races were not. Carter's party ran much better than he. Democrats retained their large majorities in both houses of Congress. Voter turnout continued to be low—only 53 percent of the electorate cast ballots.

Carter's victory suggested that a majority of voters shared his revulsion over abuses of power by Washington-based professional politicians. He was viewed by his supporters as a man of character who was smarter than the incumbent. They were willing to suspend their misgivings about his lack of experience, his lack of specific views on issues, and his failure to develop a coherent political program. They were willing to entrust the reins of government to an outsider from a Southern village. Given a choice between "fear of the known and fear of the unknown," the citizenry opted for someone new who promised to tell the truth and bend Washington officials to the popular will.

Carter's winning the Democratic nomination before the convention signaled the advent of an important new political reality: most states were now holding presidential primaries. The primaries opened up the nominating process to the mass of voters and reduced the power and importance of political parties. It also lengthened the presidential campaigns, greatly increased their costs, enhanced the role of television, and made enormous demands on the candidates. Ford and Carter both accepted $22 million in federal funds to finance their fall campaigns, and both renounced private fund-raising. They were the first presidential candidates to use new federal election funds that had been provided by laws enacted following the Watergate disclosures of fund-raising abuses.

MR. CARTER GOES TO WASHINGTON

The thirty-ninth president came to the White House through an improbable route. He grew up on a farm in the southwest Georgia village of Plains. His first career choice was the Navy. He graduated from the U.S. Naval Academy in 1946 and spent seven years in the nuclear submarine program. When his father died, in 1953, Carter gave up his naval career and returned to Plains to take over the family business. By 1970, he had built up a prosperous agricultural conglomerate based on raising and processing peanuts. Elected governor of Georgia in 1970, Carter proved an able administrator and a moderate reformer. His chief accomplishment was to boldly announce the end of racial discrimination in Georgia. He brought about a marked increase in the number of black state employees. From this modest political base, he forged the political strategies that brought him to the presidency in 1976.

Carter possessed a keen intelligence, rigorous self-discipline, a capacity for sustained hard work, deep religious beliefs, and intense patriotism. He was one of the most conscientious, hardworking chief executives that the nation ever had. He was a reflective, well-read man who had a steely glint to his soft blue eyes. Behind the ready smile and informal manner lay a grimly serious personality. A private man, aloof, and somewhat shy, he was driven by a powerful ambition to succeed, to make a contribution, and to leave his mark on the national scene.

One of Carter's most valuable political assets proved to be his wife Rosalyn; she was attractive, strong, and politically shrewd. She made a dynamic First Lady, going well beyond the usual roles of hostess, ornament, and goodwill ambassador. She was her husband's principal adviser on many issues, a member of his inner circle. Not since Eleanor Roosevelt had a First Lady played such important political roles or achieved such power in her own right.

Jimmy Carter came to office knowing that millions of Americans were still deeply suspicious of the political system. He strove from the outset to "deimperialize" the White House, to bring his presidency closer to the people, and to restore popular faith in national politics. He accepted phone calls from ordinary citizens, hosted radio call-in shows, appeared at town meetings, and even stayed overnight in ordinary citizens' homes. He also

Figure 11.4   Jimmy Carter.   *Source:* National Archives.

wanted to bring previously excluded people into government. Of his 1,195 full-time federal appointments, 12 percent were women, 12 percent were black, and 4 percent were Hispanic. Far more of his appointments came from these historically disadvantaged backgrounds than in any previous presidential administration.

But Carter's populistic campaign style contradicted his managerial and technocratic approach to governing. As Bert Lance, his close friend and first budget director said, Carter "campaigns liberal, but he governs conservative." Carter was the most conservative Democratic president since Grover Cleveland. His top priorities became slashing the size and cost of government. He relied for advice on a handful of pollsters and political operatives that had orchestrated his electoral victory in 1976. He emphasized his outsider status and never did establish a good working relationship with Democratic congressional leaders, most of whom were more liberal than he. Failure to work closely with the legislators precluded Carter's having an effective presidency. Because his leadership relied on skillful management rather than emphasizing a few basic principles and proposing programs, the public and Congress had difficulty discerning what his goals and purposes were and where he was trying to take the nation. And when his presidency proved unproductive and his leadership ineffective, he lost the trust and support of many of his fellow citizens.

Carter's party was riven by factionalism. On the surface, the old New Deal coalition appeared to hold, but in truth the Democratic Party had become home to a host of competing interest groups that could not agree on a common program: white Southerners, African Americans, urban ethnics, organized labor, feminists, neo-isolationists, Cold Warriors, consumerists, environmentalists, bureaucrats, liberals, and conservatives. The Democratic Party was little more than a broad tent housing a multitude of conflicting interest groups increasingly divided by gender, race, ethnicity, class, and ideology.

In part, Carter's policies reflected the conservative mood that increasingly gripped the country by the late 1970s. More and more Americans repudiated 1960s' style liberalism, which they associated with foreign policy failures, inflationary domestic policies, oversized government, domestic rebellions, a decline of patriotism, a breakdown of the traditional family, a loss of community, high taxes, rising crime rates, drug abuse, and a generalized permissiveness and moral decline. For millions of American families, liberalism no longer worked at home or abroad. Elitist liberal politicians pushing a social agenda alien to the values and aspirations of the American middle-class majority had become a major problem. The antigovernment, antispending inclinations of voters were expressed dramatically in California's 1978 election. An elderly real estate lobbyist, Howard Jarvis, led a successful taxpayer's revolt that slashed homeowners' property taxes by two-thirds. National polls showed that a large majority of Americans supported cuts in the costs of government. A 1978 poll revealed that conservatives outnumbered liberals by a ratio of more than 2 to 1. That same poll showed that only about 15 percent of Americans were still willing to call themselves liberals.

When Carter took office, the inflation rate stood at 6 percent and the unemployment rate at 8 percent. Carter had gotten political mileage during his campaign against Ford by attacking the incumbent's failure to solve these serious economic problems, labeling the combined total of the inflation and unemployment rates as the "misery index." Carter pronounced the misery index of 14 intolerable and promised to reduce it. He first tried stimulating the economy to reduce unemployment by implementing traditional liberal Keynesian "pump-priming" programs. Congress enacted a $6 billion local public works bill, an $8 billion public service jobs bill, a bill cutting taxes, and an increase in the minimum wage. Unemployment declined to 6 percent in two years.

But simultaneously the inflation rate rocketed upward, to 7 percent in 1977 and 10 percent in 1978. It zoomed to 12 percent in 1979 and 13 percent in 1980, the worst two years since World War I. Confronted with hyperinflation, Carter radically shifted his economic focus. He concentrated on attacking inflation, adopting fiscal restraints similar to his conservative predecessor. In 1979, he appointed Paul Volcker chairman of the Federal Reserve Board. Volcker immediately imposed severe monetary restrictions on the economy that drove interest rates to historic highs, pulling the economy into recession without immediately curbing inflation. The ensuing "stagflation" of 1979 and 1980 was far worse than it had ever been under either Nixon or Ford. In 1980, the misery index had reached 21, a figure that Carter's Republican opponent, Ronald Reagan, would use against him with devastating effectiveness during the electoral campaign.

Declining American productivity signaled that another kind of economic rot had set in. Productivity (output per man-hour) had increased an average of 3 percent a year between 1945 and 1965. During the 1970s, productivity only rose at an annual rate of 1.3 percent. As late as 1968, the U.S. economy had been the most productive in the world; by 1980, it had slipped to twentieth. Energy problems added to America's economic difficulties. Despite the 1973 energy crisis, warnings from leaders, and new conservation laws, Americans continued to use more oil and to import a higher proportion of their daily requirements throughout the 1970s. Domestic oil production continued to decline.

In April 1977, President Carter developed a comprehensive energy plan that he termed "the moral equivalent of war" (MEOW). The energy plan tried to package a variety of conflicting regional and economic interests. It called for tax incentives and penalties to encourage consumers to conserve energy and to entice domestic producers to drill more oil and natural gas wells. Politicians representing particular interest groups hammered Carter's proposals. Conservatives attacked the proposed tax increases and government involvement

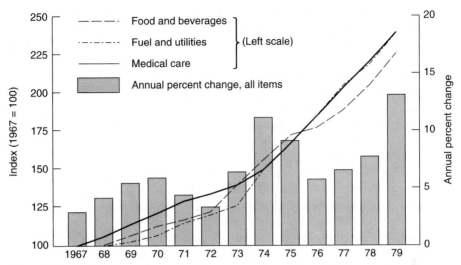

Figure 11.5   Inflation was the most serious economic problem afflicting the American people during the 1970s. Note that the cost of living, as measured by the Consumer Price Index, increased nearly 250 percent between 1967 and 1979.   *Source:* Statistical Abstract of the United States.

in the operations of important energy industries. Liberals opposed it as favoring producers at the expense of consumers and the rich at the expense of the poor. Carter's energy plan failed to clear Congress, and the MEOW soon faded from memory.

In 1979, a second oil crisis hit the deteriorating American economy when Iran cut off its oil exports soon after the fall of the Shah. Gasoline shortages again forced angry motorists to line up at the pumps. Carter responded to this second crisis with a phased deregulation of domestic oil prices to spur production. Oil deregulation immediately raised gasoline prices by 50 percent (from seventy cents to over one dollar per gallon) and increased oil company profits, some of which the government siphoned off as excise taxes. Again, there was bitter public outcry and a blizzard of attacks from both sides of the political spectrum at Carter's ineffective handling of a serious crisis that had an immediate pocketbook impact on virtually all Americans.

In July 1979, President Carter, baffled by the failures of Americans to solve their serious economic and energy problems, invited 130 leaders from all walks of life to Camp David for ten days of meetings with top government officials to determine what was wrong with the nation. From these intensive discussions, the president concluded that the nation was facing "a crisis of the spirit." Following the conference, Carter addressed the nation. In what proved to be his finest speech, he told Americans that they faced a crisis of confidence that posed a fundamental threat to American democracy—they had lost faith in themselves and in their institutions, and they had lost faith in the future. Americans faced their mounting economic and energy difficulties with uncharacteristic passivity and pessimism. Where was the old American optimism and "can-do" spirit? Carter pleaded with his fellow citizens to regain confidence in themselves and in their government, to reclaim the American future. To show good faith with the American people, Carter apologized for the mistakes and failures of his presidency, fired many of his Cabinet members, and promised a fresh start.

Critics of the Carter Administration suggested that the nation faced a different problem than the loss of national spirit. They said that the real problem was the failure of presidential leadership. Carter had never been able to outgrow his outsider status. He relied for advice and policy proposals on his small circle of Georgia loyalists. He never firmly grasped the reins of government, never asserted control over executive bureaucracies, and never established an effective liaison with Congress. He failed to develop a consistent approach to public policy. He mastered the details of problems, but he could never project a broad national vision or a sense of direction. He never learned to communicate effectively with the press or with the American people. His speaking style often took on a whiny quality; the President sounded like an old-fashioned schoolmarm scolding her students. His was a perpetually floundering, rudderless government that ultimately lost the trust and respect of most of the citizenry. At the time he made his "malaise" speech, his approval rating in the polls had dipped to 26 percent. (Richard Nixon's rating had been higher on the day he was forced to resign from the presidency.) Neither the American people nor Democratic leaders in Congress believed that President Carter could solve the difficult economic problems plaguing Americans, nor provide the kind of leadership that might solve the national malaise and restore confidence. By July 1979, most of his fellow citizens regarded the president as an incompetent bumbler and perhaps something of a fool, a little man unable to handle the job that he had coveted and won. *New York Times* columnist Tom Wicker called Carter's administration the greatest failure since Herbert Hoover's lackluster performance during the Great Depression.

CARTER AND THE WORLD

Carter came to office with almost no background in foreign affairs. His only previous international experience came from his having served on the Trilateral Commission, an association of businessmen, bankers, politicians, and intellectuals gathered from the United States, Japan, and European countries, committed to strengthening economic ties among major Free World nations. Carter recruited his two top foreign policy advisers from the commission, his Secretary of State Cyrus Vance, a Wall Street lawyer, and his National Security Adviser Zbigniew Brzezinski, a professor of international relations at Columbia.

Carter initially tried to steer U.S. foreign policy in new directions. He announced at the outset of his administration that he would make human rights the distinctive theme of his foreign policy; he said that human rights would be "the soul of our foreign policy." The new President's emphasis on human rights expressed both his Wilsonian idealism and his desire to move beyond the realm of Nixon–Kissinger realism. He wanted to reclaim the ideological high ground in the ongoing Cold War competition with the Soviet Union. Human rights espoused traditional American ideals and a noble cause but proved in practice to be a difficult program to implement.

Carter's greatest diplomatic triumph occurred in the Middle East, where he played a major role in achieving peace between Egypt and Israel. He built upon a foundation laid by Kissinger's shuttle diplomacy and the extraordinary actions taken by Egyptian leader Anwar Sadat. Sadat, perceiving that Egyptians could never dislodge the Israelis from the Sinai by force, offered them peace in exchange for the return of Egyptian lands. Sadat electrified the world when he went to Jerusalem in the fall of 1977. He told Israelis that any permanent agreement between Egypt and Israel must include an Israeli withdrawal from the West Bank and the Golan Heights, a homeland for Palestinian Arabs, and a recognition of the Palestine Liberation Organization (PLO) as the government of the Palestinians.

Israeli Prime Minister Menachem Begin was willing to strike a bargain with Egypt on the Sinai, but he balked at the Palestinian issues. Negotiations between the two countries reached an impasse after six months. President Carter then invited both leaders to Camp David for conferences. After two weeks of intense negotiations in which Carter was fully engaged, they achieved what he called "a framework of peace for the Middle East." Egypt agreed to a separate peace with Israel, and the Israelis agreed to return the Sinai region to Egypt. The Palestinian issues were left vague. Both sides agreed to a "self-governing" authority for the people inhabiting the West Bank, with their specific political status to be worked out in subsequent negotiations. Sadat and Begin signed the historic peace agreement, which ended more than thirty years of war between their countries, on March 26, 1979, in Washington. Egypt and Israel then proceeded to normalize their relations.

President Carter hoped that these Camp David Accords would launch a new era of peace in the Middle East, but insurmountable obstacles persisted. No other Arab nation followed Egypt's lead. Negotiations on the Palestine question went nowhere. Israel refused to recognize the PLO or any other Palestinian political organization, and these groups all refused to recognize the results of any negotiations excluding them. The Palestine issue was

Figure 11.6   The signing of the Camp David Accords. President Carter looks on as Israeli Prime Minister Menachem Begin (to Carter's left) and Egyptian President Anwar Sadat (to Carter's right) sign the historic pact on March 26, 1979, at a formal ceremony held on the North lawn of the White House. *Source:* National Archives.

further complicated by the outbreak of civil war in Lebanon between Muslim and Christian factions over PLO camps in southern Lebanon. These camps served both as staging areas for terrorist raids into Israel and as targets of Israeli reprisals.

Carter also acheived diplomatic successes in Latin America. In April 1978, he persuaded the Senate to ratify two treaties turning the Panama Canal over to Panama by 2000. These treaties permitted the gradual phasing out of the last vestiges of U.S. colonialism in Central America. The United States reserved the right to intervene to keep the canal open, and it also retained priority of passage in the event of a foreign crisis. The treaties protected U.S. interests and removed a source of resentment for Panamanians and other Central American Nationalists. The treaties proved popular in Panama and elsewhere in Latin America; they were taken as a sign that the Carter administration genuinely wanted to treat Latin American people as equals. Within this country, the Panama treaties drew fire from outraged conservatives. Senator S. I. Hayakawa said that the United States should never return the Canal Zone to Panama because "we stole it fair and square."

Elsewhere in Latin America, Carter changed U.S. policies, usually in the name of human rights. He withdrew support for the tyrannical Pinochet dictatorship in Chile, which Ford and Kissinger had backed. In February 1978, he cut off military and economic aid to Nicaraguan dictator Anastasio Somoza. Deprived of aid, Somoza was soon overthrown by revolutionaries calling themselves Sandinistas. The United States promptly extended a $75 million aid package to the new Sandinista government, which included Marxist elements. In El Salvador, Marxist guerrillas, assisted by the Sandinistas, began a civil war against the government. The Rightist government fought back brutally. The United States suspended aid to the Salvadoran government after government troops murdered of three American nuns.

In the Far East, Carter completed the process that Nixon had begun with his historic opening to China in 1972. Since Nixon's visit, both the United States and China had been moving toward normalizing relations. Carter, trying to continue the strategies of Nixon and Kissinger, wanted to use good relations with China as a lever to pry cooperation out of the Soviet Union. American businessmen eagerly anticipated tapping into China's consumer economy of 1 billion people. The two nations established normal relations with an exchange of ambassadors in 1979.

United States relations with sub-Sahara Africa improved during Carter's tenure. He appointed Andrew Young, a black minister and former civil rights activist, as the U.S. Ambassador to the United Nations. Young was able to dampen much of the rhetorical fire that Third World delegates to the UN routinely directed at the United States. President Carter made a successful trip to Liberia and Nigeria in 1978. Good relations with Nigeria were especially important. It was the richest, most populous black African nation and the second largest foreign supplier of oil to the United States.

THE DECLINE OF DÉTENTE

Détente had already begun to decline under Ford and Kissinger, and it continued to decline during Carter's presidency. Carter's diplomatic efforts toward the Soviet Union were hindered badly by his inexperience. He was influenced initially by Secretary of State Vance, who took a conciliatory approach to the Soviets. Carter sent what he intended to be a friendly signal to the Soviets when he announced his intention to withdraw U.S. troops from South Korea. Far from responding in kind, the Soviets took Carter's friendly words and gestures as signs of weakness; the Soviets became more aggressive. Escalating their arms buildup, they extended their influence in Africa, using Cuban soldiers as proxies, and they increased their military forces stationed in Cuba.

The president had hoped to achieve quick ratification of SALT II, but he surprised and angered the Soviet leaders at the outset of his presidency by proposing additional deep cuts in the two nations' strategic arsenals. His talk of human rights and his granting of full diplomatic recognition to China further annoyed the Soviets. It took more than two years before SALT II negotiators could complete their work. When finished, the treaty limited both sides to 2,400 nuclear launchers and 1,320 MIRVs. If implemented, it would have further stabilized the arms race.

But when the SALT II treaty was finally sent to the Senate in 1979, it encountered strong opposition. The chief senatorial critic was Nixon and Kissinger's old opponent, the nemesis of détente, Henry "Scoop" Jackson. Jackson insisted that the proposed agreement allowed the Soviets to retain strategic superiority in several categories of weapons. He also was upset by the expansion of the Soviet presence in Africa. More moderate critics of SALT II were uncomfortable with the fact that the treaty acknowledged that the Soviets had achieved nuclear parity with the United States, a reality that they interpreted as symbolizing the relative decline of U.S. strategic power. Some liberal senators were unhappy with SALT II because it did not eliminate key weapons systems, such as the huge Soviet land-based ICBMs and the new American cruise missiles.

Carter himself lost faith in SALT II and withdrew it from consideration before the Senate could vote it down. Instead, he took a tougher stance toward the Soviet Union. He accepted a controversial West German request to station new intermediate-range Pershing II missiles in Western Europe to counter the SS-20 missiles that the Soviets were installing in Eastern Europe. Carter also pressured all NATO members to significantly increase their military spending. Installing these weapons in Europe represented a major escalation of the nuclear arms race. As Carter made the transition from conciliation to a tougher stance vis-à-vis the Soviets, he relied more and more on foreign policy advice from the hawkish Zbigniew Brzezinski, and he no longer paid much attention to the dovish Vance.

Suddenly, in December 1979, 85,000 Soviet troops invaded Afghanistan to suppress a Muslim rebellion against a faltering Marxist regime. Alarmed, President Carter reacted strongly, calling the Soviet invasion "the most serious threat to world peace since the Second World War." Carter canceled grain shipments to the USSR, suspended the sale of high-level technology to the Soviets, and ordered American athletes to boycott the summer Olympic games, scheduled to be held in Moscow during the summer of 1980. The President also increased American military spending and removed restrictions on CIA covert operations. He proclaimed the Carter Doctrine for Southwest Asia. Calling the Persian Gulf a vital U.S. interest, he declared that the United States would repel "by any means necessary" an attack in that region by outside forces. Carter's reaction to Soviet aggression and his adoption of a hard line toward Moscow reversed U.S. policies toward the Soviet Union that went back to the Kennedy years. Ironically, the man who began his presidency espousing kind words for the Soviets killed détente and revived the Cold War.

DISASTER IN IRAN

It was in the Persian Gulf region that the United States suffered a major foreign policy disaster that humiliated President Carter and contributed to his defeat in the 1980 election. Nixon and Kissinger had made Iran America's major ally in the Persian Gulf area. It had played a key role in containing the Soviet Union. It was a major supplier of top-grade oil, and Iranians annually purchased billions of dollars worth of American arms. The Shah, whom a CIA covert operation had helped restore to power in 1953, permitted the intelligence agency to station electronic surveillance equipment along Iran's border with the Soviet Union. Tens of thousands of Iranian students attended American colleges and universities. American oil companies supplied the state-owned Iranian oil industry with equipment and technicians and shared in its profits. Iran was a vital U.S. interest, much more important than Korea or Vietnam had ever been. On the surface, Iran and America were best friends when Carter took office.

But beneath the surface, Iran in the late 1970s seethed with anti-Shah and anti-American fervor. Only the Shah and a powerful ruling elite were genuinely pro-American. Carter, in contradiction of his human rights policy and unaware of the tensions in Iran, traveled to Iran in late 1977 to pay tribute to the Shah. At a state banquet held in his honor, President Carter toasted the Shah for "the admiration and love your people give to you." He called Iran "an island of stability in one of the most troubled areas of the world." The CIA station chief in Teheran issued a report in 1978 stating that Iran was not even near a revolutionary situation. American intelligence operatives were blind to the faults of the Shah's corrupt, oppressive regime, and equally blind to the existence of revolutionary forces poised to destroy it.

The assault on the Shah was led by fundamentalist Islamic clergy intent on replacing Iran's modern, Westernized state with an Islamic republic. The revolutionaries were led by aged religious leader, Ayatollah Ruholla Khomeini. From exile in France in 1978, Khomeini ordered his legions to demonstrate, to disrupt the economy, to do anything to create chaos—to force the Shah to abdicate. Carter initially dismissed Khomeini's revolution, assuming that the Shah would suppress it. Carter watched in disbelief as Iran's oil production stopped and its economy ground to a halt. The Iranian army, forbidden by the Shah to fire upon the rioters for fear that it would ruin the chances of his son succeeding him, was demoralized. On January 16, 1979, the Shah fled his country. Khomeini returned to Iran to a frenzied hero's welcome from revolutionary crowds. One of the most bizarre events of modern times had occurred. A virtually unarmed people led by clergymen had overthrown one of the world's most powerful rulers and defeated one of the world's largest, best-equipped military forces, without firing a shot!

American leaders, thinking in conventional Cold War terms, did not know how to deal with a man who denounced both the United States and the Soviet Union with equal vehemence. Fearing Soviet intrusion into Iran and the loss of a crucial source of Western oil,

Carter tried to establish normal relations with the new Iranian government, which proved impossible. Khomeini, who called the United States the "Great Satan," refused all American overtures.

Meanwhile, President Carter allowed the Shah, who was suffering from terminal cancer, to enter the United States for medical treatment. On November 4, 1979, Iranian militants overran the U.S. Embassy in Teheran and took fifty-three Americans hostage. Khomeini approved the action, which violated the principle of diplomatic immunity observed by all nations. Carter retaliated for this outlaw act by ordering the 50,000 Iranian students within the United States to report to the nearest immigration office. Any students found to be in violation of their visas were deported. He also froze billions of dollars worth of Iranian assets in the United States. He further suspended arms sales and placed a boycott on all U.S. trade with Iran.

Carter made the return of the hostages his number one priority, which it remained for the rest of his presidency. The hostage crisis dominated American foreign policy for the next fourteen months. The crisis also dominated American television screens. Each night, when the most popular news program, the *CBS Evening News with Walter Cronkite,* would sign off, the viewing public would be reminded of just how many days of captivity the hostages had endured. The popular late-night television news show *Nightline* originated as a series of special reports on the Iranian hostage crisis. As the crisis wore on, day after day, Carter had to watch his own popularity plummet to new lows. For months, U.S. officials negotiated futilely for release of the hostages with a series of Iranian governments,

Figure 11.7   Carter's most serious setback and the nation's greatest humiliation occurred in 1979 when Iranian militants occupied the U.S. Embassy in Iran and took Americans hostage. Here their captors put the blindfolded hostages on display soon after taking them prisoner. *Source:* Bettmann Archive.

but no Iranian leader could acquire the necessary stable authority to make an agreement that would stick.

Six months after the hostages were taken, Carter severed diplomatic relations with Iran and authorized a military operation to attempt a rescue. He had previously resisted any suggestions to use force to attempt a rescue, because he feared that the hostages would be killed. On the night of August 24, 1980, three helicopters transporting the rescue team suffered mechanical failures. At a staging area in an Iranian desert north of Teheran, a fourth chopper crashed into a C-130 transport plane, killing eight soldiers and severely burning five more. For days following these accidents, the news media bombarded Americans with sickening pictures of the wreckage and charred corpses. Each photo and television image reinforced the notion that America was not what it used to be. They also reinforced the popular image of Carter as an irresolute bumbler. The failed rescue attempt also symbolized the impotence of the United States; a once-powerful and feared power, now apparently unable to protect its citizens against terrorism from revolutionary outlaws.

Prospects for resolving the hostage crisis improved in late 1980. The ailing Shah died in July. On September 22, Iraq suddenly invaded Iran, intending to take advantage of Iranian political instability to annex territories, and provoked a full-scale war between the two nations. In October, President Carter offered to release frozen Iranian assets and to resume normal relations and trade with Iran in exchange for the release of the hostages. On November 4, Ronald Reagan was elected President. Khomeini was responsive to the American offer. He needed money for the war with Iraq, and he now had another cause around which to rally support for the revolution. He also feared that the new president might take stronger action against his regime. On January 21, 1981, Carter's last day in office, Iran agreed to release the hostages in exchange for the return of $8 billion of Iranian assets. The hostages finally came home after 444 days in captivity.

THE ELECTION OF 1980

As the 1980 election approached, Carter was clearly in serious political trouble. His misery index, the sum of the rate of inflation plus the unemployment rate, was much higher than when he had run against Ford in 1976. He had failed to fulfill most of his campaign promises. He had been unable to develop and adhere to any consistent policies or programs. And above all, there was the daily embarrassment of the hostages.

Carter had to fight off a primary challenge from Senator Edward "Ted" Kennedy. At the outset of his bid, Kennedy had a big lead over Carter in the polls. But once the battle began, his popularity nosedived. His automobile accident in Chappaquidick on Martha's Vineyard, Massachusetts, in 1969, in which a young woman riding in his car drowned, continued to dog Kennedy, reviving old doubts about his character and judgment. His old-fashioned liberal philosophy did not inspire most Democratic voters in 1980. Carter refused to enter the primaries, claiming that his presence was required in Washington. This "rose garden" strategy worked, and Carter deflected Kennedy's challenge without ever leaving Washington. He was renominated easily on the first ballot.

The Republicans entered the 1980 presidential race brimming with confidence. Many

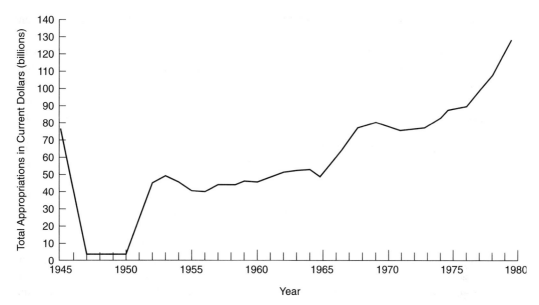

Figure 11.8   National defense outlays, 1945–1980. During the 1980 election, Ronald Reagan scored political points by accusing Carter of neglecting the nation's defenses and allowing the Soviets to forge ahead of the United States. Actually defense spending increased considerably during Carter's presidency.   *Sources: Historical Statistics of the United States: Colonial Times to 1970,* and *Statistical Abstract of the United States, 1980.*

candidates entered the race for the Republican nomination, but from the outset the clear choice of most of the party faithful was the old right-wing war horse Ronald Reagan. Of the others, only George Bush showed any strength in the primaries. Reaganites controlled the Republican Convention and pushed through a conservative platform calling for deep tax cuts, a balanced budget, large increases in defense spending, constitutional amendments banning abortions and restoring prayer in public schools, and opposition to the Equal Rights Amendment. Reagan chose Bush for the vice-presidential slot after failing to get his first choice, former President Ford, for the position.

A third party candidate joined the race, John Anderson, a former Goldwaterite, now running as a born-again Independent. He had no organization and no constituency, nor did he have many issues that set him apart from the major candidates. He offered the electorate his self-proclaimed integrity and competence. Anderson showed considerable strength early in the campaign, polling as high as 15 percent of the vote. He qualified for federal election funds, and his campaign received extensive media coverage. As the election date approached, Anderson's popularity declined markedly. He attracted mainly Democratic voters who were turned off by Carter's performance. Even so, his candidacy had no bearing on the outcome of the election.

Reagan was favored to win when the presidential campaign began in August. But he made several incorrect statements concerning important issues that conveyed the impression that he was dangerously out of touch. Within a month, Carter had caught up. Sensing an advantage, Carter attacked Reagan personally. He accused Reagan of racism and war-mongering, and he raised the question of Reagan's age. At sixty-nine, Reagan was the oldest major party candidate ever to seek the presidency. But Carter's personal attacks on the elderly candidate backfired; voters resented them. Polls taken at the end of September showed that Reagan had regained the lead.

Reagan attacked Carter's handling of the economy at a time of historically high "stagflation." He attacked Carter's handling of foreign policy at a time when the world was especially unstable, when the Soviets were expanding their influence around the world, and when the hostages were in Iranian hands. Carter, hoping to salvage his campaign, challenged Reagan to debate him on television. Carter was confident that his detailed knowledge of the issues would expose Reagan as a windy fraud. Reagan agreed to one debate, which took place in Cleveland's Convention Center on Sunday evening, October 28.

It was the best of the televised presidential debates. The panelists chose excellent questions about major issues. The candidates were evenly matched through the early rounds of questioning. Then Carter, responding to a question about nuclear arms control, said that he had consulted with his thirteen-year-old daughter Amy about the important issues of the campaign. His answer unintentionally suggested to the vast television audience that the president of the United States relied on the advice of a child when considering important policy matters. Reagan scored impressively when he responded to Carter's attacks on his record on Medicare. Using his actor's skills, Reagan shook his head ruefully, saying, "There you go again," then, in the manner of a parent correcting an erring child, he firmly set the record straight.

In terms of content, the debate was a draw. On image and personality, Reagan won decisively. In ninety minutes, Reagan had erased the image that Carter had been trying to stick on him throughout the campaign, that of a combination scrooge and a mad bomber. In the debate, Reagan came across as a firm, genial leader who would never push the nuclear button in panic or anger. He sealed Carter's fate when he closed the debate by looking the huge television audience squarely in its collective eye and asking a series of rhetorical questions: Are you better off than you were four years ago? Is America as respected throughout the world as it was four years ago? Are we as strong as we were four years ago?

Reagan's skillful performance during the debate had turned a close electoral contest into a rout. He received 44 million votes to Carter's 35 million and Anderson's 5.7 million. Reagan swept the election with 489 electoral votes to Carter's 49, with zero for Anderson. The Republicans gained thirty-three seats in the House. The most surprising outcome of the 1980 election was the Republican reconquest of the Senate for the first time since 1954. Republicans gained twelve senatorial seats, giving them fifty-three, the largest Republican total since 1928. Reagan shattered the Democratic coalition that had elected Carter in 1976. He received nearly half of the labor vote. He carried blue-collar voters, middle-income voters, the Catholic vote, the ethnic vote, and the Southern vote. He carried all of the populous Northern industrial states. He split the Jewish vote and got one-third of the Hispanic vote. Only African-American voters remained faithful to the hapless Carter.

The vote revealed two significant cleavages among voters. African Americans voted 90 percent for Carter; whites voted 56 percent for Reagan. This stark racial division sug-

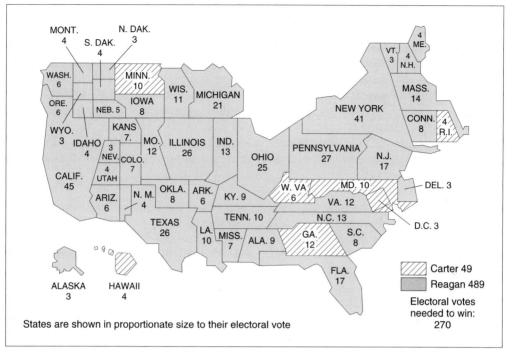

Figure 11.9   The electoral vote, 1980.   *Source:* Public Domain map.

gested that politics during Reagan's presidency could become racially polarized. There was another division among voters. For the first time in the sixty years since women got the vote, a significant gender gap appeared in the electoral results. Whereas 56 percent of men voted for Reagan and only 36 percent for Carter, only 47 percent of women voted for Reagan and 45 percent for Carter. Reagan's opposition to abortion and the ERA, plus his aggressive foreign policy rhetoric, alienated women voters. Many working women, struggling to cope with precarious economic circumstances to provide for their children, perceived that Reagan did not represent their interests and feared that he might call for Congress to eliminate governmental programs upon which they and their families depended.

Some analysts read the 1980 election as a harbinger of a new conservative Republican majority coalition. More saw it as the rejection of an ineffective leader who could not control inflation or retrieve the hostages. Voters were bored and put off by Carter's hand-wringing moralizing, ineffective leadership, and tiresome calls for sacrifice. The main issue apparently was Reagan himself. Could he be a safe replacement for the discredited incumbent? Many people had their doubts. They thought Reagan was too old, too uninformed, too conservative, and too dangerous—until the debate. Reagan's adept performance in that forum turned a close election into a landslide. Reassured, people voted for Reagan by the millions.

The 1980 election also showed that the traditional liberal agenda was bankrupt, a victim of both its past successes and its exhaustion. The old New Deal–Fair Deal majority coalition had disintegrated. Liberalism had lost its mass constituency. People no longer looked to liberal Democrats for leadership on issues concerning natural security, the functioning of the economy, or matters pertaining to social welfare. Above all, the results suggested continuing voter fragmentation, party decline, and citizen apathy. The dominant political trend could more accurately be described as political dealignment rather than realignment. Only 52 percent of the electorate bothered to vote. The electorate continued to shrink and increasingly consisted of political blocs bound together by class interest, ethno-racial descent, gender, and ideology pursuing a single set of interests. More and more Americans, particularly young people, repudiated politics as simply irrelevant to anything important in their lives.

Jimmy Carter was not a particularly successful or popular president, and he suffered a humiliating reelection defeat at the hands of Ronald Reagan in November 1980. Most historians and journalists who have assessed his presidency do not rate him very highly. His most impressive achievement came in the foreign policy area when he brokered the Camp David Accords, but overall, he had far more failures than triumphs in his conduct of foreign affairs. His bumbling reignited the Cold War with the Soviet Union. However, since the end of his presidency, after nearly two decades of tireless work as a patriot, practicing Christian, and elder statesman, Jimmy Carter achieved a stature and respect from his fellow citizens that he had never attained while in the White House. He taught Sunday school at an interracial church and worked with an organization that built homes for poor people. He established the Carter Center near his presidential library in Atlanta as a place where the parties to the world's most stubborn political conflicts could come together to try to find solutions. Most important, he set himself up as a kind of private-enterprise crusader for world peace. He supervised elections and guaranteed their legitimacy in Panama and Nicaragua. He inserted himself into dangerous confrontations in Haiti and North Korea to head off conflict. His religious commitments inclined him to side with underdogs and outsiders, and his conduct of personal diplomacy sometimes put him at odds with the reigning orthodoxies of U.S. foreign policy. Carter was far from a great president, but he became a great ex-president.

A TIME OF TROUBLES

In the aftermath of the upheavals of the late 1960s, the disastrous outcome of the Vietnam War, the Watergate scandals, and the revelations of wrongdoing by the CIA and FBI, millions of Americans lost faith in politicians and in political institutions. During the era of limits, both Gerald Ford and Jimmy Carter proved incapable of effective leadership; they confronted challenges, conditions, and problems beyond their capacities to control or master. Ford never had a realistic chance to lead. An unelected president who lacked a political base, he was chosen to serve out the unfinished term of the disgraced Nixon. He never rose above the level of interim caretaker. Carter, elected on a wave of public disenchantment with politics as usual, appeared initially to represent the aspirations of millions of ordinary citizens who wanted to make a clean, fresh start in politics. He was a tribune of all of those who yearned for simple honesty and decency in politics. But the inexperienced Carter could never transcend his outsider status and take hold of the levers of power. Within a few years, his bumbling, directionless presidency demonstrated that good intentions were insufficient for governing a complex society in the throes of major crises.

Serious economic problems appeared greater than the leaders who tried to solve them. Soaring inflation coupled with high unemployment, "stagflation," did not yield to Ford's and Carter's efforts to manage them, and the misery index continued to rise. Purchasing power and living standards for millions of families were eroded. Productivity declined. Major manufacturing industries lost large market shares to efficient foreign competitors. Periodic energy crises exacerbated economic woes and added an element of uncertainty to an already clouded future. In the larger world outside of American boundaries, the United States appeared to be a spent force, a declining entity. An aggressive Soviet Union appeared to be winning the Cold War. Prosperous West European nations increasingly asserted their independence from American initiatives, and the Japanese had become formidable commercial rivals. America and Americans were no longer respected in the world. The Iranian hostage crisis was a stark, humiliating, daily reminder of bumbling ineptitude in the White House and of American fecklessness in world affairs.

By the time of the 1980 election, many pundits, reflecting views widely shared by millions of Americans, were writing that America had become an ungovernable nation of dysfunctional institutions and demoralized citizens. They feared that the presidency had grown too large and too complex for any one person to control. They feared that America no longer worked; its economy was in decline, its society was fragmented, and its political system was controlled by incompetent leaders who lacked both vision and practical solutions to pressing problems. Americans turned, perhaps in desperation, to an aging former actor who promised to revitalize the American system, to reassert American primacy in the world, and to restore the American Dream. A large majority of Americans believed that Reagan could hardly do worse than his predecessors, and they hoped, he might do better.

BIBLIOGRAPHY

One of the most important general studies of American history from 1945 to the mid-1970s has been done by Godfrey Hodgson in *America in Our Time*. Peter N. Carroll, in *It Seemed Like Nothing Happened,* offers a general political and social history of the 1970s. Both President Ford and President Carter have written their memoirs. Ford's is called *A Time to Heal;* Carter's is entitled *Keeping Faith: Memoirs of a President.* John Osborne has the best account of the Ford presidency, *White House Watch: The Ford Years.* See also Robert T. Hartmann's *Palace Politics: An Insider Account of the Ford Years.* A. James Reichley, in *Conservatives in an Age of Change,* features an interesting account of the rising conservative cause throughout the 1970s. Peter Steinfels's *The Neo-Conservatives* is a critical account of the emergence of a neo-conservative intelligentsia, many of them formerly Leftist radicals, during the 1970s. A lively account of the rise of the Sunbelt region to political prominence is Kirkpatrick Sale's *Power Shift: The Rise of the Southern Rim and Its Challenge to the Eastern Establishment.* Stanley Hoffmann's *Primacy and World Order* is a critical assessment of the Ford administration's foreign policy. A critical study of the Carter presidency has been done by Clark Mollenkoff in *The President Who Failed: Carter Out of Control.* Barry Rubin, in *Paved with Good Intentions: The American Experience in Iran,* has the best study of the Iranian fiasco. A good study of the energy crises of the 1970s is Richard Victor's *Energy Policy in America Since 1945.* CIA abuses of power are portrayed in Victor Marchetti's and John D. Marks's *The CIA and the Cult of Intelligence.* David Halberstam, in *The Reckoning,* offers a good account of the decline of the American auto industry during the 1970s.

12

The American People in the 1970s

The decade of the 1970s was characterized by a series of significant social and cultural transformations that confirmed both the pluralism and volatility of American life. These changes often reflected and paralleled underlying technological, economic, and demographic developments that rapidly altered the contours of American society and changed the ways most Americans lived and worked. New attitudes toward sex, family, and work changed the nature of many important American institutions. Many members of two important groups, African Americans and women, maintaining the momentum generated by the movements of the 1960s, made dramatic gains during the 1970s in education and income. But at the same time that thousands of women and African Americans were taking advantage of new opportunities to achieve middle-class status, many other women and blacks remained locked into low-paying, low-status jobs, or slipped even further into the ranks of welfare dependency and poverty.

The most important development of the 1970s represented a historic shift in the direction of the American economy. The longest boom in American history, which had kicked in during World War II and had continued, with occasional recessions, for thirty years, came to a halt during the early 1970s. The seemingly perpetual American prosperity—fueled by a high growth rate, job creation, federal spending, innovative technology, and most of all, consumerism—stalled. The boom was replaced in the economic cycle by the double whammy of "stagflation," business stagnation and inflation, which eroded purchasing power and lowered living standards for millions of American families. The apparent end of economic progress frustrated and bewildered Americans. Stagflation undermined their morale and robbed them of their sense of control over their destinies.

A DEMOGRAPHIC PROFILE

The U.S. Census Bureau reported that there were 205 million Americans in 1970, 215 million in 1975, and 227 million in 1980. Regionally, Southern and Western states accounted for 90 percent of that population increase. Many Northeastern and Midwestern states showed little or no growth, and several lost population during the 1970s. Population trends that had first appeared in this country after World War II continued. The Sunbelt regions, stretching from South Carolina to Southern California, contained the dynamic centers of the nation's technological innovation, economic growth, and population increase. The expanding population, productivity, and wealth of the Sunbelt led to its increased political clout in Washington. Political leaders, including Senator Barry Goldwater and Presidents Lyndon Johnson and Richard Nixon, were products of Sunbelt politics. Ronald Reagan, the leader of the conservative revival, elected president in 1980, also was a product of Sunbelt politics.

Two additional demographic shifts with profound social implications occurred during the 1970s—the birthrate fell, and human longevity increased. Twentieth-century birthrates peaked in 1947 at 26.6 live births per 1,000 and tumbled to 18.1 per 1,000 in 1975. Low birthrates meant that adults were not bearing enough children to replace themselves, and only expanded immigration prevented long-term U.S. population decline. The steep drop in birthrates reflected several factors at work. The most important of these included the development of the birth control pill, the legalization of abortions, and the changing attitudes and values among women toward having children. Increasing longevity derived from advances in medicine and nutrition. Doctors perfected cures for some forms of degenerative diseases, such as heart disease and some types of cancer. But the most important causes of rising longevity rates were reductions in the infant mortality rate and the childhood death rate. By 1975, average longevity in America had reached 73.1 years. The fastest-growing age group was comprised of people age seventy-five and older. Declining birthrates and expanding longevity combined to produce an aging American population. The median age of the U.S. population reached 30.8 in 1978, making America one of the

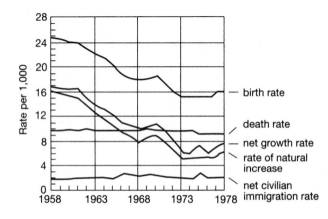

Figure 12.1   Population change.
Source: U.S. Department of Commerce, Bureau of the Census, Current Population Reports.

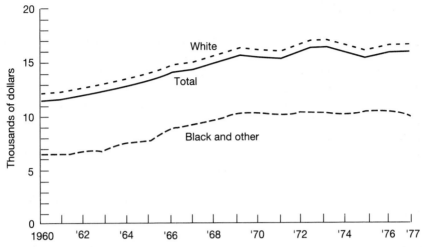

Figure 12.2   Median annual money income of families, by race, in constant 1977 dollars, 1960 to 1977.   *Source: U.S. Statistical Abstract, 1979,* p. 436.

oldest societies in the world. (In contrast, America's neighbor to the south, Mexico, had a median age of seventeen in 1980.)

Census data also showed that the number of traditional American households, composed of a nuclear family of four, declined during the 1970s. Nearly half of the households added in the 1970s consisted of persons living alone or with nonrelatives. Declining birthrates, declining marriage rates, high divorce rates, households occupied by unmarried couples, households occupied by single-parent families, and the existence of millions of men and women living alone all suggested that household arrangements in America increasingly reflected the social diversity that had become America's most salient characteristic. No longer could it be said that a nuclear family of one father, one mother, and two or three children was either typical or desirable.

By the late 1970s, one of the most rapidly growing population segments constituted the "thirty-somethings," the advance wave of baby boomers. This group received much media attention, particularly the better-educated "yuppies" among them. Yuppies were upwardly mobile, affluent young Americans earning $40,000 or more a year. Having few or no children, yuppie couples often held two high-paying jobs. Merchants and advertisers catered to their large disposable incomes and lifestyle preferences, based on buying expensive homes, cars, and clothes, taking costly vacations, and dining in expensive restaurants. Yuppies tended to embrace fashionably conservative politics and the ethics of Social Darwinism. Sometimes Yuppies supported trendy movements such as moderate environmentalist causes, and Yuppie women tended to embrace at least some feminist concerns. Yuppies generally were unconcerned about the struggles of disadvantaged Americans and absorbed in their careers and personal lives. Their lives could be defined in two words: careerism and consumerism.

But yuppies did not represent the norm. According to census data, of the 78 million baby boomers, only 5 percent had incomes of $40,000 or more in the late 1970s. The median income for baby boomers in 1977 was $16,000, well below the national average. The fundamental problem baby boomers faced was one of demographics: too many people chasing too few opportunities. Opportunities for baby boomers also were curtailed by the energy crisis and by the high inflation of the late 1970s and early 1980s. Most important, the slow rate of economic growth meant that the economy simply could not generate new jobs fast enough to meet the demands of boomers as they finished their schooling and entered the job market. Long-term unemployment rates during the 1970s were the highest since the 1930s. Baby boomers as a whole were less upwardly mobile than their parents, the first such group in America since the generation that came of age during the Great Depression of the 1930s. Not for a long time had a generation of young Americans worked so hard for so little. Baby boomers could be characterized as victims—victims of advertisers, of their parents' and their own unrealistic expectations, of demographic trends, of energy crises, and most of all, of the slow rate of economic growth during the 1970s.

ECONOMIC STASIS

During the thirty-year boom lasting from the early 1940s to the early 1970s, Americans had enjoyed unprecedented prosperity. Real per capita family income doubled, and the GDP more than doubled during those three decades of strong economic growth. The steadily expanding economy and rising living standards over a long period of time convinced most Americans that prosperity was perpetual. Americans also believed that economic progress would in time eradicate poverty from the land. But during the early 1970s, stagflation replaced perpetual growth, creating a set of economic circumstances that threatened to undermine national prosperity and imperil the living standards of millions of American families.

Signs of decline had first appeared in 1968. President Johnson's failure to raise taxes to pay for the Vietnam War while continuing to fund expensive Great Society reform measures at home increased government deficits and jacked up the inflation rate. During Nixon's presidency, both the deficits and the rate of inflation increased. In 1973, the national deficit reached $40 billion, and the rate of inflation soared to 8 percent.

During the early 1970s, the declining U.S. economy also was showing the effects of strong foreign competition. Rebuilt after having been destroyed during World War II, the industrial economies of West Germany and Japan were more productive than the older American industries. American shares of many world markets declined. Within the United States, many industries lost large shares of the domestic market to more efficient foreign competitors. In 1970, about 10 percent of new cars sold in America were imported; by 1980, that figure had reached 30 percent.

Inflation, deficits, and loss of both domestic and export markets combined by 1972 to create a serious balance of payment problem, which threatened to undermine the value of the dollar. When the Nixon administration devalued the dollar by severing it from gold, this action unleashed an orgy of gold speculation in the world that drove the price of gold from $35 an ounce to over $800 and added to the inflationary burden of American consumers. When the Nixon administration increased wheat sales to the Soviet Union to reduce the American trade deficit, food prices in this country rose sharply.

In geopolitical terms, the American defeat in Vietnam signaled that U.S. hegemony in the world had ended. In economic and financial terms, the declining American position in the world economy likewise signaled that the era of American dominance had ended. The OPEC embargo that kicked in during October 1973 compounded American economic difficulties, added to the inflation rate, and highlighted the dangers of continued dependency on foreign sources of oil. Yet during the 1970s, America became even more dependent on foreign sources of oil. The bill for oil imports in 1970 was $5 billion. By 1980, it was in excess of $90 billion! The huge rise in the cost of imported oil was another dramatic sign of U.S. economic decline in the world. It also served as a potent reminder that America no longer controlled its own economic destiny. The American economy had become increasingly connected to the emerging global economy. Americans could no longer control their economic future.

Economic woes continued throughout the 1970s for the national economy and for millions of American families. Industrial productivity stagnated, and living standards declined. During the 1950s, American living standards had been the wonder of the modern world, but during the 1970s, they fell below those of several European countries. Stagflation became an integral part of the American way of life, eroding both living standards and the confidence of Americans in their economic system.

The struggles of millions of American families for economic survival during the 1970s were exacerbated by structural trends that threatened the economic foundations of American middle-class society. As the economy became increasingly based on high-tech service and information-oriented industries, the number of jobs that provided middle-class incomes declined relatively. The 1970s' service economy employed millions of clerical workers, sales clerks, waiters, bartenders, cashiers, and messengers. Wages for these jobs were comparatively low. While millions of new service-sector jobs were created during the 1970s, the number of higher paying manufacturing jobs decreased.

During the 1970s, millions of factory jobs disappeared because of declining productivity, cutbacks in capital spending, and the increasing automation of production work. Jobs also disappeared in America, because U.S.-based multinational corporations exported jobs to Third World countries to take advantage of lower wages and taxes. Trade unions lost hundreds of thousands of members to automation and to declines caused by foreign competition in the steel, rubber, auto, and other manufacturing industries. The manufacturing jobs that disappeared during the 1970s tended to be skilled jobs from the middle-income spectra of employment. These displaced workers usually could not find alternative employment that offered comparable pay and fringe benefits. Their options were early retirement, if they could afford it, or taking jobs in the rapidly expanding service sectors of the economy. But many of these service jobs were low-skill, low-paying jobs with minimal opportunities for advancement or a career. In any case, most of these new service-sector jobs went to women, minorities, and youngsters. The fastest growing sector of the service economy in the 1970s, which carried into the 1980s, was the fast food industry. McDonald's became the nation's largest employer and established the largest job-training facilities in the country. During the

1970s, the fast food industry added workers faster than manufacturing lost them, but at wages that averaged about one-third as much.

There were other signs of economic decline during the 1970s. Real income declined by 15 percent from 1973 to 1980 in this country. By 1980, working-class family purchasing power had fallen back to 1960 levels. Meanwhile, inflation drove housing and new car prices ever upward. The median price of new single-family homes doubled during the decade. In this era of limits, stagflation was pricing the American Dream increasingly out of reach for young, working-class, and lower-middle-class families. The 1970s appeared to reverse the social and economic trends of the 1950s. There was a wholesale loss of faith in economic progress, in the notion that the next generation of Americans inevitably would be better off than their parents. During the 1970s, millions of families faced what they had been led to believe could never happen—economic retrogression, the first since the grim days of the Great Depression of the 1930s.

For generations, Americans had been sustained by their belief in economic individualism: talent, initiative, and hard work generated upward mobility and economic security. It enabled men (and women) to provide for their families and ensured that their children would have a better life than they. But during the era of limits, faith in the Protestant ethic was eroded. The question for millions of young people became how many could share in the dream, and for how many would America be more of a nightmare than a dream? Old men evoked the promise of American life; young people had to struggle harder than ever to achieve it. Millions of Americans could not find steady work in the 1970s. Millions who worked found not affluence but subsistence.

The American myth of success asserted that anyone could make it to the top if he or she tried hard enough. Statistical reality suggested something else in postindustrial America. Where abilities were about equal, the chance of a child from an upper-income family making it to the top of his or her profession was twenty-seven times more likely than for a child from a low-income family. For millions of young people, the struggle was to not reach the top but to not fall any lower. Millions of middle-class youngsters could not realistically expect to earn as much, to own as much, and to be as successful in material terms as their parents. Ironically, at a time when racist and sexist barriers to advancement were shrinking and the American Dream was open to all Americans for the first time, there was declining mobility. In an era of limits, declining economic opportunity diminished the American Dream.

CARS AND COMPUTERS

Despite stagflation and energy crises, Americans during the 1970s continued their love affair with the automobile. The car culture was alive and well in America during the era of limits. Automobile registrations reached 90 million in 1970 and 118 million in 1980 (Americans accounted for about one-third of all of the cars owned in the world in 1975.) Millions of Americans purchased automobiles manufactured in Europe and, especially, in Japan during the 1970s. High performance sports cars, pickups, and vans became more popular. Consumers became more value conscious and safety conscious; manufacturers responded by offering their customers a far greater choice of vehicles than had been previously available. The application of new technologies meant that 1970s' automobiles were more aerodynamically designed, more fuel efficient, safer, and much easier to handle than the cars of the 1950s and 1960s had been. Automobiles of the 1970s also were much more expensive and, especially the American-made cars, much more prone to breakdown and costly repairs.

Automobiles continued to be the primary means of intercity travel in the United States during the 1970s, although commercial airlines did increase their share of the travelers' market, from about 5 percent to 10 percent. Despite sizable increases in their business, most domestic airlines found themselves in serious financial difficulties during the late 1970s. Most of these difficulties derived from the deregulation of the airline industry, implemented during the Carter presidency. Several well-known airlines went out of business, including Eastern and Braniff.

Deregulation of the airlines probably created more problems than it solved. In the short term, passengers obviously benefited from the far greater variety of flights offered at lower prices generated by a new era of cutthroat competition. In the long run, deregulation created conditions in the airline industry that were reminiscent of the era of cutthroat competition in the railroad industry of 100 years ago: weaker competitors were driven to bankruptcy and either forced to shut down or be absorbed by the stronger airlines. Serious questions of reliability and safety also arose. As a result, as happened in railroading, a cry went up from customers and consumer advocates for a return to at least a measure of regulation to the airlines.

The most dramatic technological innovations of the 1970s were all connected to the computer revolution. America was computerized during the 1970s. There were approximately 6,000 computers in use in this country in 1972; by 1980, there were millions. The agent of revolution was the microcomputer. The use of microcomputers vastly enhanced the abilities of individuals working in a wide variety of fields to calculate and retrieve information. Individuals using computers also could build statistical models and process words. The key invention that brought forth the microcomputer was the microprocessor, or computer chip, perfected by Ted Hoff in 1972. Hoff was a young engineer on the staff at Intel Corporation when he designed the world's first microprocessor, which started the revolution in electronic technology. The computer revolution made possible the information revolution of the 1970s and 1980s, which transformed the way America worked.

The first personal computers were marketed in the mid-1970s. In California's "Silicon Valley," a suburban area located about fifty miles south of San Francisco, dozens of small computer companies found themselves on the cutting edge of technological revolution. In 1976, two young men, Steven Wozniak, a computer genius, and Steve Jobs, who possessed great entrepreneurial talents, opened a small business in a garage they had rented for fifty dollars a month. Wozniak designed, and Jobs sold small, inexpensive personal computers. They called their fledgling company Apple. Sales were slow at first; no one appeared to be interested in a small, cheap personal computer. However, sales picked up in the late 1970s, and in 1985, Americans bought 6 million of these machines. By the mid-1980s, Apple had become a multibillion dollar business; Wozniak and Jobs had become rich beyond their wildest dreams. The editors of *Time,* catching the spirit of the times, instead of desig-

Figure 12.3   Computer Science Professor Leonard Kleinrock, points out, Thursday, September 2, 1999, that the microprocessor in his watch is more powerful than that of the IMP (Interface Message Processor), left, the first network switch. Kleinrock, whose research into "packet switching" provided the technological foundation upon which the internet was built, is on hand to celebrate the 30th anniversary of the Internet, which began with IMP on September 2, 1969. The IMP's processor is the item that is pulled out below. Photo by Mark J. Terrill.   *Source:* AP/Wide World Photos.

nating a "Man of the Year," as they had done annually for decades, in 1982 designated the computer as "Machine of the Year."

NEW IMMIGRANTS

Because the Immigration Act of 1965 abolished the discriminatory national origins system of immigration dating back to the 1920s, there occurred both a large increase in immigration and a significant shift in the sources of immigrants coming to America during the 1970s. Most of the millions of immigrants who came to the United States in the 1970s were Asians and Latin Americans. Mexico furnished the most immigrants. Along with Mexicans came Cubans, Puerto Ricans, and Central Americans, particularly people from El Salvador and Nicaragua. Some of these new arrivals were fleeing religious and political oppression, but most of them came for the same reasons that have always attracted newcomers to America—opportunities for a better job and a better life for their families than they perceived possible in their homelands.

The United States, true to its ancient heritage, remained one of the few countries in the world to freely welcome millions of newcomers from foreign lands. But many native-born Americans were alarmed by the flood of poor immigrants arriving annually, especially the "illegals," who came mostly from Mexico through a porous membrane called the U.S.–Mexico border. They feared that these people would take away jobs from American workers, lower wages and living standards, overload welfare and school systems, and become an underclass of poor people without political or civil rights amidst an affluent society. Their fears were exaggerated and rested upon dubious assumptions and misperceptions. Studies showed that immigrants mostly took jobs at pay levels that most native-born Americans scorned, and that they payed more in taxes than they ever collected in government services. They also often became law-abiding, hardworking, productive citizens.

Another problem posed by elements in the Hispanic-American population, which, fueled by large-scale immigration from Mexico and other Hispanic countries, was growing at more than twice the rate of the general population, was the ancient question of assimilation. This demographic trend worries many native-born Americans, who focus on the fact that Hispanics often have formed their own communities, or "barrios," where they can get along quite well without having to speak or write English. Some Hispanics also have insisted that their children be taught in Spanish-speaking or at least bilingual schools. The Supreme Court has authorized bilingual instruction in public schools.

Spokesmen for the native-born population argued that the existence of large, Spanish-speaking populations—clustered in Southern California, Southern Florida, the Southwest, and sections of New York and Chicago—poses a threat to national unity and to the political cohesiveness of the American system. Hispanic spokesmen insist on their rights to have their children educated as they see fit. They also insist on retaining their language and identity as a distinct ethnic group within a pluralistic society. But an articulate Mexican American, Richard Rodriguez, has written of the need for Mexican Americans and all other Spanish-speaking citizens of the United States to learn English in order to realize their full opportunities, and he accepts as a painful necessity the loss of some parts of the tradi-

tional Hispanic culture and the comfort it provided. It is the price exacted for full participation in American life, a price Rodriguez believes that individuals from all immigrant
groups must pay.

After Hispanics, Asians and Pacific Islanders have furnished the largest supply of
newcomers. They have come mainly from Hong Kong, Taiwan, China, Vietnam, Korea,
Japan, and the Philippines. Their numbers boosted by large-scale immigration, the Asian-
American population grew rapidly during the 1970s. Asians were among the most upwardly
mobile population groups within American society, often outperforming native-born whites
in education levels attained and per capita annual income earned. In 1980, 75 percent of
Asian Americans had graduated from high school, compared to 68 percent for whites. One-
third of Asian-American adults had four or more years of college, twice the rate for whites.
Bright, ambitious Asian students had become so successful, especially in mathematics and
some of the sciences, that Asian spokesmen voiced the concern that elite American universities had imposed unofficial quotas in various departments in order to reduce the number
of Asians and to preserve places for less qualified white students. In the economic sphere,
data from the 1980 census shows that the Asian American median annual income was more
than $2,000 above the white median annual income.

Success did not come easy for Asian Americans. Historically, they have been the victims of exclusion, prejudice, discrimination in various forms, and even violent assaults. And
not all have achieved success. Many recent Asian immigrants remain mired in poverty,
alienated from the mainstream of American life and tempted by vice and crime. Many struggle to fathom a mysterious language and culture that is neither open nor friendly to them.
Incidents of violence against Asian immigrants have abounded.

One of the few positive consequences of the Vietnam War was the advent of major
new groups of immigrants to the United States. The first wave of Vietnamese immigrants,
about 130,000 strong, arrived in the United States in 1975, soon after the final collapse of
the South Vietnamese government. This largely middle-class, educated, and skilled population assimilated into the American mainstream fairly quickly. But the people arriving in
1979 and 1980, between 500,000 to 600,000 refugees from Vietnam, Cambodia, and Laos,
the "boat people," fleeing poverty, oppression, and genocide in their homelands, often encountered only alienation and failure in this country.

There also was the saga of Jean Nguyen. Miss Nguyen, at age eleven, escaped from
Vietnam with her family by boat when Saigon fell to the Communists in 1975. She spoke
no English upon her arrival in the United States that same year. In 1981, she graduated number one in her high school class, and in May 1985, she graduated from West Point, receiving a commission as a second lieutenant in the U.S. Army. President Reagan paid tribute to
Miss Nguyen in his 1985 state of the union address, calling her "an American hero."

The arrival of millions of non-European immigrants to the United States during the
1970s created a much more diverse, pluralistic, and multicultural American society. On the
whole, the economic benefits of the new immigration outweighed the liabilities. Asian immigrants opened small businesses in New York City and Los Angeles. Cubans did likewise
in Miami and elsewhere in Southern Florida. But they came during a time of economic sta-
sis, during an era of limits. They activated ancient nativist resentments and prejudices, exacerbated by hard times. As has happened in the past to nonwhite immigrants, they suffered

Figure 12.4   Mr. and Mrs. Van Ngo Vu stocking shelves in their family grocery store. Vu's Market opened in 1987.
Source: National Archives.

beatings and their properties were vandalized. The cry went up from native-born Americans for more restrictive immigration laws, both to stem the overall immigration flow and to curb the entry of undocumented aliens.

AFRICAN AMERICANS: A DUAL SOCIETY

For millions of African-American families, the decade of the 1970s was one of significant progress. Institutionalized racism and other obstacles to black achievement crumbled. Affirmative action programs, spawned by the civil rights movements of the 1960s, paid off for middle-class African Americans in the 1970s and carried into the 1980s. The greatest progress for African Americans came in education. By 1980, more than 1 million black people had enrolled in colleges, and thousands attended the finest universities and professional schools in the country. Thousands of young African American men and women became doctors, lawyers, college professors, government bureaucrats, and business executives. The size of the African American middle class increased rapidly, and black per capita income rose appreciably. African American couples married, had children, and bought homes in the suburbs, their lifestyles much like that of their white counterparts in similar circumstances. Many young black professionals, reared and educated in the North, flocked to the Sunbelt cities to live and work. Many black Americans found urban life in Atlanta, Houston, and New Orleans more congenial and nearly integrated, offering more opportunities for ambitious careerists than the supposedly more liberal Northern cities. African American political participation in Southern states also far outstripped that in the North.

Despite significant gains for some, millions of African Americans lost ground during the 1970s. Affirmative action admissions programs were challenged by the *Bakke* case. Allen Bakke, a white applicant to the University of California at Davis Medical School, sued the university when his application was rejected. He showed that his qualifications were superior to several minority candidates who were admitted as "disadvantaged students" under a special quota reserved for them. The state supreme court ruled in his favor, as did the U.S. Supreme Court in a 1978 5 to 4 decision. The Supreme Court held that Bakke's rights to equal protection under the Fourteenth Amendment had been violated, and it nullified the school's affirmative action program based on racial quotas. But by a similar 5 to 4 decision, the Court upheld the right of the university to use race as "one element" in its effort to recruit medical students. Meanwhile, Davis had admitted Bakke to its medical school, and he went on to become a physician. The university also continued a limited affirmative action admissions program without explicit quotas for minority group students. The Supreme Court, despite its confusions and ambiguities, appeared to be saying that limited affirmative action policies could continue if they did not rely on numbers or if they did not try to do too much too fast.

But the plight of poor inner-city blacks worsened during the 1970s. Unemployment among African Americans remained high, about twice the national average, averaging 14 percent to 15 percent. Unemployment among African-American teenagers skyrocketed to the 40 percent to 50 percent range by 1980. Black median family income was $12,800 in 1980, only about half that of whites. Ironically, African American income was proportionately higher in 1950, when Jim Crow was still intact and antiblack racism was nearly universal and before the modern civil rights movement, civil rights legislation, and affirmative action programs had appeared.

Among poor urban African Americans, statistics revealed a frightening pattern of intertwined social pathologies—rising drug usage, delinquency, vice, and crime; rising school dropout rates and unemployment rates; and rising numbers of illegitimate births and households headed by an unmarried female parent. A permanent underclass was being forged within black America, without the possibility of its integration into the American mainstream. People within the underclass had no chance of personally fulfilling lives.

According to sociologist William J. Wilson, one of the nation's most influential scholars, the fundamental cause of the social misery and disorganization afflicting the black inner city was economic. Factories and businesses providing good jobs at good wages have disappeared from most of the black inner cities of America. Most prosperous black working-class and middle-class families have long since exited once-thriving neighborhood communities. Without the prospect of good jobs and without positive role models to set good examples, many of the inner-city dwellers were deprived of opportunities to seek productive, and meaningful lives. Wilson believed that without the economic and moral anchor of respectable employment, there was little chance of solving the serious interrelated, nearly intractable social problems of the black inner cities.

Within America, African Americans have forged a dual society—on the one hand, a thriving middle class that has achieved a place for itself in recent years that is roughly equal to white America—and on the other hand, a declining underclass rotting on the mean streets of inner cities.

Figure 12.5   Boys play in a garbage-strewn vacant lot. Photo by Bayer.   *Source:* Monkmeyer Press.

WOMEN: CHANGING ATTITUDES AND ROLES

Of all of the movements born during the upheavals of the 1960s, the one that retained its momentum most effectively and had the greatest impact during the 1970s was the women's movement. Feminists challenged men and women to refashion their identities, to abandon traditional notions of masculinity and femininity. Women exhorted their "sisters" to demand an end to second-class citizenship, to class discrimination, and to sexual exploitation. Other activists encouraged women to no longer confine themselves to domesticity, to seek fulfillment in new roles and statuses beyond those of mother, wife, and homemaker.

Because the women's movement in this country during the 1970s was so diverse and decentralized, it suffered from serious internal conflicts. Lesbian and straight women often discovered that they did not share the same goals and priorities. Radical feminists called for fundamental changes in the social and political structures; liberal reformers sought to achieve their goals by working within the system. Feminist intellectuals often engaged in ideological controversies that divided women into hostile camps. More serious conflicts of interest often divided women along the fault lines of class and race. Middle-class white women found, for example, that they had little in common with black working women, nor did they share the same perceptions, beliefs, and values.

The women's movement also encountered much opposition and resistance from groups within the larger society. Women antifeminists like Phyllis Schlafly and Anita Bryant successfully campaigned against the Equal Rights Amendment. They also attacked the gay rights movement and fought to repeal the right of women to have an abortion on demand, as sanctioned by the Supreme Court. Antifeminists won an important victory in 1980, when the Supreme Court upheld the constitutionality of a congressional law prohibiting federal funding of abortions for poor women. Antifeminists also charged the women's movement with being responsible for the spiraling divorce rate and the breakdown of family life in America.

Many men felt threatened by the women's movement. They perceived that their power and privileges were under assault, that many women expressed hostility toward men qua men. Some men responded negatively to the women's movement and abandoned their traditional roles as financial providers and authority figures for their families. Many women who had devoted their lives to being good mothers, wives, and homemakers felt that feminists judged them as victims and failures.

Despite its internal conflicts and weaknesses, and despite encountering powerful and widespread opposition, the women's movement of the 1970s helped bring about major social and cultural changes. Attitudes toward gender roles in this country changed dramatically during the 1970s. When a Gallup Poll in 1962 asked women if they believed they were discriminated against, two-thirds said no. In 1974, two-thirds of women responded yes to the same question, and they also indicated that they favored efforts to improve their status. The women's movement probably had its greatest influence on young college-educated women during the 1970s, many of whom were movement activists. Surveys showed that a majority of women graduating from college during the 1970s believed that a career was as important to a fulfilling life as a good marriage. These women believed that women and men were born with the same talents and potentials. These same women also stated that they expected equality in their sexual relations. Surveys revealed that three-fourths of college women had engaged in premarital sex, and that college women were appreciably more active sexually than college men.

Such attitudinal changes were reflected in the accelerated pace of women's entry into the workplaces of America during the 1970s. Since 1945, the rate of employment for women had risen steadily. By 1970, over half of women with children over age six worked full time or part time outside of the home. But during the 1970s, a major change occurred in women's employment patterns. The proportion of younger women with children who worked increased dramatically. By 1980, more than half of the mothers with children under age six found themselves in the labor force. For many women, the notion of work had been redefined during the 1970s. Work for women had become a life vocation. Women expected to work for most of their lives, with a few years off for childbearing and child rearing. They expected to have careers of their own. This new concept of work as career for young women of the 1970s contrasted dramatically with their mothers' concept. For the older generation of women, work came after child rearing; it was defined primarily as helping the family enjoy a more affluent lifestyle, not as an opportunity to have a career.

Female enrollment in colleges, graduate schools, and professional schools expanded rapidly during the 1970s. The proportion of women entering law school increased fivefold. Some entering classes at medical schools were 30 percent to 40 percent women. Women earned 25 percent of all doctoral degrees awarded during the 1970s. Women also entered the corporate world in ever-increasing numbers. Working-class women continued to join unions, to enter the skilled trades, and to increase their numbers in previously all-male occupations. Both federal and state laws were enacted that helped women obtain credit, start their own businesses, and buy homes. Other women made their way in politics. Several were elected state governors and U.S. Senators. At the same time women flooded into profes-

Figure 12.6   Office staff talking at desk. Photo by Richard Hutchings.   *Source:* Photo Researchers, Inc.

sional fields hitherto exclusively or overwhelmingly male, the proportion of women entering the traditionally feminine fields of nursing, library work, and elementary school teaching declined sharply.

But despite their many impressive successes, women continued to encounter barriers in their struggle to overcome historical disadvantages and to achieve genuine equality in contemporary American society. "No-fault divorces," initially hailed as a great
victory for women, proved to be a two-edged sword, because equality before the law did
not bring equality in the marketplace. Compounding their economic difficulties, many
divorced women, who had obtained custody of their children, found that their former
husbands defaulted on child support payments. The courts were often lax in forcing ex-
husbands to pay.

Sophisticated postfeminist analysts faulted the liberal leaders of the women's movement for being too concerned with achieving legal and political equality and thereby neglecting fundamental economic pressures that women faced in a society where male economic domination remained a continuing reality. They also criticized feminists who were
obsessed with getting middle-class women into previously all-male professions and occupations, while neglecting the interests of the more numerous working-class women mired
in low-paying occupations traditionally reserved for women.

Harsh economic realities during the 1970s limited opportunities for women. For every
glittering career success scored by ambitious, capable, upwardly mobile women, many
more women worked in low-paying jobs, which offered few opportunities for promotion or
substantial pay increases. Occupational segregation, in which women remained concentrated in low-paying positions while men earned much higher incomes for their work, remained a persistent problem for women during the 1970s. Most of the new jobs created in
the service sectors of the economy were taken by women, and these jobs invariably paid
less than manufacturing or professional jobs. In the mid-1970s, women earned only sixty
cents for every dollar earned by men. The sixty cents represented an improvement over previous decades, but it fell far short of economic parity with men. Women also were the victims of the "superwoman syndrome." Early feminist leaders proffered an idealized image
of the woman who could have it all—career, home, husband, and family—a life of perfect
equality and complete fulfillment. In practice, having it all often meant doing it all: women
worked full time all day outside of the home, just like men, then they came home to continue working—doing all of the cleaning, cooking, and caring for their children, while men
watched "Monday Night Football" with their neighbors, drank beer, and played with the
family dog.

During the 1970s, the divorce rate rocketed upward. By 1980, more than 40 percent
of marriages ended in divorce. The median length of a first marriage fell to seven years. The
median length of a second marriage fell to four years. The number of households headed
by a single parent, almost always a female, climbed rapidly during the 1970s. The large majority of women entering the workforce during the 1970s did so because they had to support themselves or because they headed a single-parent household. They were not college-
educated professionals choosing a career; they were working women who had to find work
to survive within the American system. Inflationary pressures during the 1970s also drove
many women into the workforce to ensure that their families could still enjoy a middle-class

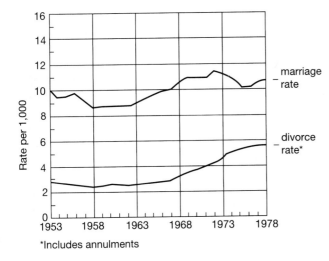

Figure 12.7   **Marriage and divorce rates.**   *Source:* U.S. Department of Health, Education, and Welfare, Public Health Service, Monthly Vital Statistics Report.

*Includes annulments

lifestyle no longer affordable on a single income. Many women slipped into the ranks of the working poor during the 1970s as a result of being divorced and saddled with child-rearing duties. The feminization of poverty and the fact that millions of American children were growing up poor were two ominous socioeconomic realities directly affecting the status of women that first surfaced during the 1970s.

EDUCATION

Most American colleges and universities continued to thrive in the 1970s. In 1975, an estimated 10 million students were enrolled full time or part time in the nation's 2,500 institutions of higher learning. Americans continued to spend far more on post–high school education than any other people, and America possessed 100 of the world's finest universities. Distinguished university faculty members continued to do important research and to publish their findings. American scholars led the world in many disciplines, especially the sciences. Each year, several U.S. scientists usually won Nobel Prizes in physics, chemistry, medical research, and economics. America's great universities were the vital centers of the nation's flourishing intellectual life.

In contrast to the turbulent 1960s, college campuses were mostly tranquil places in the 1970s. Students, reverting to historical norms, were much more interested in preparing for well-paying careers than they were in protesting public issues or trying to make society better. Yet some students could still respond to issues of conscience. Thousands of students joined protests against the nuclear arms race and called for universities to divest themselves of securities issued by companies doing business with the repressive apartheid regime in South Africa. Others continued to express concern about ecological and social issues. But for most students, it was business as usual—attending classes, perhaps working part time, and enjoying an active social life. College students of the 1970s were much less interested in the humanities and social sciences than they had been a generation earlier. Students of the 1970s flocked to majors in math, economics, finance, business, engineering, and computer science. Many students, including the bright ones, demonstrated deficiencies in verbal skills, ignorance of history and literature, and a general decline in cultural literacy. A generation of technocratic "wanna-bes" had no time to pursue the traditional goal of a broad liberal arts education.

While colleges flourished, in many cities, American public schools deteriorated. Scholastic aptitude scores declined during the 1970s, and the high school dropout rate increased. About one in three eighteen year olds in this country were declared functionally illiterate in 1980. At a time when competition for jobs and all of the accoutrements of the American-style good life were intensifying, when the economic and social life of the nation was becoming more complex and demanding, and when employers were demanding brighter and better educated employees, the public school system increasingly failed to meet individual and national needs. In May 1983, the National Commission on Excellence in Education reported that

> if an unfriendly foreign power had attempted to impose on America the mediocre educational performance that exists today, we might well have viewed it as an act of war.[1]

Many culprits were blamed for the dismal performance of the public schools during the 1970s. Television has been cited for keeping youngsters from reading books and for fostering boredom in the classroom. Indifferent and incompetent parents, who neither set a good example nor encouraged their children to do well in school, were part of the problem. Popular entertainers and professional athletes whose riches and fame derived from talent rather than study in schools were accused of setting bad examples and of leading youngsters astray. In addition, the best and brightest college graduates rarely went into elementary and secondary teaching. Entry-level salaries were low, and teaching commanded little prestige as a profession. Americans once believed that education could solve all social problems; by the 1970s, to many social critics, the schools had become a social problem. One study found that 10 percent of teachers were incompetent; they could neither teach nor keep order in the classroom. Another 20 percent were considered only marginally qualified to teach youngsters in any subject.

There were signs in the early 1980s that educators were trying to turn their public schools in the direction of excellence. Polls showed that people were willing to pay more taxes to improve their schools. California and other states implemented legislation lengthening the school day and year, strengthening the curriculum, raising teachers' salaries, and requiring new teachers to pass competency tests. The fundamental question raised by the public school issue is one of cultural value. How highly does the nation prize learning? How highly do parents prize learning, and how much are they willing to pay for good schools? Do many students care about becoming educated, or are they only interested in careers and money?

[1]Quote is taken from *Report of the National Commission on Excellence in Education*, May 1963, p. 1.

RELIGION

The United States in the 1970s remained the most religious nation in the Western world. Nearly all Americans espoused a belief in God, and 60 percent of the population claimed membership in a church in 1976. Members of the more liberal Protestant churches and Reformed Jews became more accepting of divorce, homosexuality, birth control, and women clergy. The ministers and rabbis of these groups often urged their congregants to work for a more humane and just social order. American Catholics in the 1970s and 1980s were concerned with the continuing consequences of Vatican II, the Church Council that had met in the early 1960s to bring the Church more into accord with modern life. After Vatican II, the liturgy was given in English, and the laity sang hymns during services. Priests were allowed more latitude in their interpretations of the Bible, and they sought ecumenical dialogues with Protestant ministers and rabbis. Catholics recognized the legitimacy of non-Catholic and non-Christian faiths and condemned anti-Semitism.

Church leaders spoke out on issues. In 1983, American Catholic bishops condemned nuclear war and urged the superpowers to disarm. In 1985, the bishops criticized the American capitalist economy for not meeting the needs of the millions of disadvantaged Americans. Many educated, liberal, middle-class Catholics welcomed the changes induced by Vatican II. But many traditionalists felt betrayed and were disturbed by these changes. They continued to adhere to the Church's traditional teachings on sex, birth control, abortion, homosexuality, and a celibate, male priesthood.

THE RISE OF THE RELIGIOUS RIGHT

Evangelical Christians formed one of the most powerful elements within the ranks of the growing conservative movement of the late 1970s and early 1980s. These fervent souls emphasized the personal responsibility of each individual believer. A sinner could be redeemed only by being "born again," that is, by confessing his or her sins, accepting Jesus Christ as a personal savior, and thereafter living a righteous life. Books by evangelical authors became best-sellers. "Christian Yellow Pages" appeared in many large cities. Millions of schoolchildren attended Christian elementary, middle, and high schools, where subjects were taught from an evangelical perspective. In Christian nightclubs, patrons could order fruit juice cocktails and listen to gospel singers. As the 1970s ended, over 1,500 radio stations were owned by evangelical Christians.

Television quickly became the prime conduit for spreading the evangelical message and promoting its conservative social and political agenda. Pat Robertson started the *700 Club,* aired over his Christian Broadcasting network. One of the regulars on his show, Jim Bakker, spun off to create his own program, the PTL (Praise the Lord) Club, starring his wife Tammy Faye Bakker, formerly a country-and-western singer. Bakker's show combined sermons, faith healing, inspirational stories, and musical entertainment, often featuring his wife joining the choir or doing a solo number. The PTL Club quickly became the most widely viewed television program on the planet. By 1980, Bakker's organization was taking in $25 million a year in contributions.

Born-again Christians frequently attacked what they called "secular humanism," the view that all truths were relative, all moral values situational, and all ethical judgments necessarily tentative. They supported the "right to life" movement, denounced *Roe v. Wade,* and condemned abortion as murder. They opposed most feminist demands and the Equal Rights Amendment. They declared war on pornography and insisted that homosexuality was sinful. Evangelical Christians sought to reintroduce school prayer and to have "creation science" taught in public schools as an alternative to the theory of evolution.

An evangelical leader, Jerry Falwell, became a prominent political activist. Falwell, for many years the pastor of the Thomas Road Baptist Church in Lynchburg, Virginia, had attracted a constituency of thousands. He also had his own television show *The Old Time Gospel Hour.* In July 1979, Falwell formed the Moral Majority. Combining old-time religion with the latest computer-age technology, Falwell's organization targeted potential contributors and kept scorecards on how politicians voted on key issues such as the ERA, school prayer, and public funding for abortions.

For the 1980 elections, Falwell's Moral Majority activists developed a "hit list" of liberal Senators and Congressmen, then they mailed out more than 1 billion pieces of campaign literature to selected voters gleaned from their computerized mailing lists. Falwell's organization played a major role in bringing about the Republican takeover of the Senate in January 1981. The Moral Majority also threw all of its considerable resources into campaigning for Ronald Reagan. Reagan consolidated his hold on the religious Right when he appointed Robert Billings, Executive Director of the Moral Majority, as his campaign's religious adviser. Reagan also incorporated the Moral Majority's social and political agenda into his successful campaign for the presidency in 1980.

In 1987, Pat Robertson announced that he would seek the Republican nomination for president in 1988. He was instantly a serious candidate with a potential electorate of millions. That same year, scandal rocked the Fundamentalist world when Jim Bakker was forced to resign his ministry because of sexual improprieties and financial irregularities.

THE "ME" DECADE

While some Americans carried the activist reform spirit of the 1960s into the 1970s, many more turned inward. They wanted to change themselves, not the external world of politics and society. They incorporated many of the elements from the hippie countercultural rebellion into their lifestyles—drug use, permissive sexuality, and above all, the "consciousness revolution." Participants included mostly young, middle-class professionals who prized affluence and professional attainment but who defined success primarily in psychological rather than material terms. It was more important to them to fulfill their "human potential" than to accumulate as much wealth as possible.

The cutting edge of the consciousness revolution could be found in California, home of the new lifestyles based on developing one's inner resources. Facilities like the Esalen Institute at Big Sur offered weekend encounter sessions for seekers wanting to "get in touch with themselves." Another entrepreneur of the human potential movement offered Erhard Seminars Training (est), built around marathon encounter sessions in which participants

Figure 12.8   Rev. Pat Robertson.   *Source:* AP/Wide World Photos.

were encouraged to confront their most powerful inner feelings. Journalist Tom Wolfe labeled these people "psychonauts of inner space," the "Me" generation, and he compared their movement to a religious revival. According to Wolfe, the whole effort was aimed at remaking "one's very self," to strip away the artificial elements of personality that had been added by society "in order to find the Real Me."

As millions of Americans joined the consciousness revolution to seek salvation in narcissistic self-absorption, others sought refuge from the stresses of secular society by joining religious cults. Some of these religious orders embraced Eastern mystical religious practices such as Transcendental Meditation (TM) or Zen Buddhism. One cult, led by Indian holy man Bhagwan Rajneesh Mahareshi Yogi, established a flourishing colony near Antelope, Oregon. Thousands of people, attracted by the Bhagwan's message of spiritual rebirth combined with permissive sexuality, lived and worked in apparently joyous harmony for a time. But the cult disintegrated in 1986 because of internal dissension among its leaders. The Rajneesh fled Oregon for India to avoid prosecution on several federal charges.

The most prominent of these religious cults was the Unification Church, founded by

Korean businessman and preacher Sun Myung Moon, who relocated to the United States. Moon, trained as a Presbyterian minister, developed his own brand of religion. He claimed to be the son of God and to receive divine revelations. His movement was controversial. His disciples were accused of kidnapping and brainwashing some of their teenage recruits. Reverend Moon also ran afoul of the law and was convicted on several counts of income tax evasion. Another cult came to a horrible end in November 1978, when its insane leader, Jim Jones, led the cult members from California to Guyana and later convinced more than 700 members to engage in a ghastly ritual mass suicide by poisoning.

POPULAR CULTURE

America calmed in the early 1970s; the era of limits also was an era of comparative civic and social tranquility. No more fiery urban riots or militant campus protests convulsed the nation. Gone was the strident rhetoric of youthful radicals denouncing government policies at home and abroad and challenging traditional American values, mores, and institutions. Gone were the calls for a new American revolution. Several factors accounted for the calming down of America during the 1970s. The end of the Vietnam War removed the single most powerful source of dissidence. The decline of the economy, stagflation, and energy crises shifted attention away from political troubles to more fundamental economic and financial dysfunctions. Young people abandoned politics to focus on getting college degrees and finding good jobs. The successes, or at least the partial victories, of many of the 1960s' movements led some of their participants to cease their activism in the 1970s with a sense of having accomplished their missions. Some radicals, suffering from moral and political exhaustion, abandoned their futile efforts to refashion American politics and society in accordance with their utopian visions. They retreated into a sullen personalism and quietism. Some joined the Me Generation, redirecting their reformist energies away from the world and toward their own personalities. Others, reaching adulthood, prepared to make an accommodation to the system that they had previously rejected. Many hippies and campus radicals abandoned their countercultural ways. Men shaved their beards, cut their hair, put on three-piece suits, and became yuppies. Radical rebellion for many, while no doubt sincere and serious, turned out to be evanescent growing pains during a time of troubles and significant transformations. In the words of historian John Wiltz, in America during the 1970s, "the national society became more mellow."

As society calmed in the 1970s, Americans, retreating into private realms, embraced an odd assortment of fads and strange activities. One such curious custom was "streaking." Naked youths, mostly young men, but also young women, streaked across college campuses, along busy streets and highways, and through malls. Sometimes more creative streakers invaded public buildings or disrupted important public events. The annual "Oscar" awards ceremony, sponsored by the Academy of Motion Picture Arts and Sciences, was streaked. Some Americans were bemused, some were angered, but most were amused by the antics of streakers. Streaking came and went fairly quickly during the early 1970s, and the Republic appeared to survive it.

While a few young people embraced streaking, millions more turned to disco dancing. Disco music appealed mainly because of its strong, rhythmic beat accompanied by simple, repetitious lyrics. Couples danced the night away beneath pulsating lights in one of the hundreds of nightclubs that sprung up across America in the mid-1970s. Attractive African-American soul singer Donna Summer became the "Queen of Discoland," her records selling millions of copies during the years of the disco craze. Many, mostly young, people went to discos to listen to Summer's sound as well as other disco artists. Many more learned to dance the "hustle" and "bus stop" or other new disco dance styles that proliferated.

Pets became more popular than ever in America during the 1970s. A pet census taken in 1974 found that the national pet population included over 100 million cats and dogs, with

Figure 12.9   Modern dancers, late 1970s or early 1980s.   *Source:* Archive Photos.

dogs slightly outnumbering cats. There also were 350 million fish and at least 22 million birds as well as over 1 million pet snakes. An estimated 10,000 bold pet owners had exotic pets such as lions, tigers, leopards, wildcats, and even a few aardvarks and elephants. Pet owners spent more money feeding and caring for their pets than the U.S. government did on the space race with the Soviet Union. During the mid-1970s, the money that American pet owners spent on food for their pets probably would have provided the one-third of the world's population that was malnourished with an adequate diet.

During the 1970s, millions of Americans became more diet conscious than ever before. Many diet books, including some written by people with dubious credentials, became best-sellers. People reduced their salt and cholesterol intake. Others stopped drinking alcoholic beverages and drinks that contained caffeine. And still others rejected processed sugar, sucrose, as though it were poison. Closely related to dieting and part of the new health consciousness, millions of people embraced the so-called fitness revolution. They became avid weight lifters as well as weight watchers. They swam, they jogged, they rowed, and they rode bicycles; they joined health clubs, played racquetball, and performed aerobic exercises. In addition, as another indicator of growing health consciousness during the 1970s, millions of people abandoned smoking cigarettes. Far fewer young people took up smoking as they reached adulthood than had been the case with previous generations. By the end of the 1970s, approximately 30 percent of the adult population smoked, the lowest percentage since the 1920s. Unfortunately, a higher percentage of teenage women took up

Figure 12.10   An aerobics class.   *Source:* Monkmeyer Press.

smoking in the 1970s than ever before, perhaps as a decadent manifestation of women's liberation or youthful rebellion.

If Americans were smoking fewer cigarettes during the 1970s, they were drinking more alcoholic beverages, especially beer. Per capita alcoholic beverage consumption increased from twenty-two gallons in 1970 to twenty-seven gallons in 1980. Two causes of the increased drinking could be found in the growing secularization of American life and in the increasing amounts of money that the major breweries were spending on television advertising. Televised sporting events invariably featured numerous beer commercials, which associated good times with their products. Directing their ads mainly toward single young men, breweries strove to link beer drinking with male fantasies about sexy young women.

During the late 1970s, alcohol abuse among teenagers and college students became a serious national issue. Studies found that thousands of high school students were teenage alcoholics. Binge drinking in fraternities and sororities on or near college campuses was on the rise. In 1975, of the approximately 45,000 Americans killed in traffic accidents, more than half died in accidents in which at least one of the drivers had been drinking. Fatal auto accidents were one of the leading killers of young people between the ages of fifteen and twenty-five. Another survey found that at least 10 million Americans were alcohol abusers. Alcoholism was by far the nation's number one drug problem during the 1970s, as it always had been.

Americans used other drugs besides alcohol in increasing amounts during the 1970s. The use of marijuana ("pot"), which had become a potent symbol of the youth revolt during the turbulent 1960s, expanded in the 1970s. Pot farming became a major underground industry in many parts of the country. Surveys showed that nearly half of the nation's college students during the 1970s used marijuana. Because marijuana use was so widespread and because most experts believed that the effects of the drug were comparatively mild if used in moderation, the federal government and most states reduced possessing a small amount of pot from a felony to a misdemeanor. A far more serious drug problem arose in the early 1970s, when there occurred a surge in heroin addiction. The nation discovered that it had nearly 1 million heroin addicts on its hands by 1975. In the 1980s, a potent new drug, cocaine, would join marijuana and heroin to create a crisis of drug abuse in this country.

Americans, during the 1970s, discovered the microwave oven, and they consumed a record number of TV dinners annually. American families also dined out much more often than ever before—at delicatessens, restaurants, pizza parlors, and especially fast-food franchises. The single most important reason for the 1970s' eating-out phenomenon was that more than 50 percent of married women with children now worked full time outside of the home. Many of these working mothers had little inclination or energy to fix dinner after spending long days in factories or offices. As the 1970s ended, Americans were spending forty cents out of every dollar they spent for food at restaurants. Sales of mustard and catsup soared to new records; the supermarket industry reported that business was down. The new dining out patterns attested to a major cultural change that had occurred: the great American dinner was being redefined for families with children. Dinner was no longer a private familial activity; it had become a public activity. Going out for dinner became as normal for kids as sitting down with mom and dad in the dining room at home.

The movie industry flourished during the 1970s. Hollywood turned out many fine films, some of which set box office records. In 1972, a brilliant young director Francis Ford Coppola made *The Godfather,* starring Al Pacino, Marlon Brando, and Diane Keaton. Based on a novel by Mario Puzo, the film told an epic story of a powerful Mafia family making it in America. In 1973 came the occult classic *The Exorcist,* starring a talented child actress, Linda Blair. Based on a novel by William Blatty, the film dealt in dramatic fashion with demonic possession and the valiant efforts of a Catholic priest to exorcise the devil from the body of the child. In 1975 came the techno-thriller *Jaws,* produced by a brilliant young filmmaker Stephen Spielberg, a terrifying account of a killer great white shark attacking swimmers. The star of the film turned out to be Jaws himself, the technological monster that terrorized a New England town; Jaws was shown devouring swimmers in gruesome detail. The movie had the largest box office gross of any film ever made.

Jaws' record take at the box office was broken in 1977 by *Star Wars,* the first of a brilliant series of original science-fiction films by George Lucas, another major filmmaking talent who burst onto the Hollywood scene in the 1970s. *Star Wars* was essentially a child's fantasy, a fairy tale about high-tech adventures in space, starring Mark Hamill as "Luke Skywalker," Harrison Ford as "Hans Solo," and Carrie Fisher as "Princess Leia," supported by a charming cast of bizarre-looking but gentle aliens and humanlike machines called androids. The plot was a simple morality tale of the good guys triumphing over the bad guys who controlled the evil Galactic Empire and banished freedom from the universe. Much of the appeal of *Star Wars* lay in the fact that it had no message, no sex, and only the mildest violence. It could be enjoyed by kids of all ages. It relied on a dazzling array of special effects and technological wizardry to mesmerize its audience. One critic called it a Wild West adventure in outer space. Other critics, pondering the symbolism and deeper meaning of *Star Wars,* suggested that it pointed the way toward a new American mythology in the wake of the disillusionment with the Vietnam War that had destroyed the American frontier myth. *Star Wars* represented a creative effort to reclaim lost American innocence.

Surveys showed that more Americans watched more television shows than ever before during the 1970s. New technologies significantly enhanced the range and capabilities of the dominant electronic medium. Communication satellites in stationary orbits hundreds of miles in space enabled television to provide live, instantaneous coverage of news events from anywhere on the planet. The 1970s also featured the advent of cable television. Viewers were freed from having to rely on the three major networks that controlled prime-time programming and the few shows worth watching generated by local independent stations. By the late 1970s, due to the advent of cable TV companies utilizing the VHF channels, viewers who signed on for their services had a choice of twenty to thirty stations to watch. During the 1980s, cable television grew exponentially, and viewers could receive up to eighty channels. One social critic, concerned about the same old drab fare and pabulum served up by all television stations, joked that even though he had eighty channels, he could find nothing to watch. The most important new television technology of the 1970s was the introduction in 1975 of the videocassette recorder, or VCR. Early versions of VCRs were difficult to use and rather expensive; they were slow to catch on. But sales boomed in the 1980s and wrought another revolution in the nation's television and movie-viewing habits.

Because so many sporting events were televised during the 1970s, big-time commercial spectator sports became a more important part of popular culture than ever before. Major professional spectator sports flourished, especially the National Football League (NFL), the National Basketball Association (NBA), and major league baseball. Due in large part to television, the big business of professional football became the most popular national sport. "Pro" football was a fast-paced, complex, highly competitive, violent game played by tough, smart, and highly skilled athletes. Some analysts linked its powerful hold on fans to the fact that pro football was a microcosm of the corporatist economy that America had become in the 1970s.

College sports, particularly football and basketball, grew rapidly in popularity. The growth of these major college sports was tinged with scandals. Some schools recruited so-called student athletes who were simply not equipped to succeed academically. Unless they were among the very few elite athletes who went on to successful careers as professional athletes, most of these college athletes left school after their athletic eligibility was expended without degrees and without the prospect of professional careers of any kind.

Other scandals plaguing college football and basketball programs included illegal payments to "amateur" athletes by alumni boosters and drug use and criminal behavior by some athletes. The National Collegiate Athletic Association (NCAA) exercised a rather ineffectual policing function over intercollegiate athletics. From time to time, it would investigate collegiate athletic programs, find illegalities, and impose penalties. One had a sense that the NCAA sporadically discovered the tip of a scandalous iceberg. Amidst the commercialism and scandals of collegiate sports was one positive innovation. Women athletes demanded, and eventually achieved, greater recognition and support from the nation's colleges and universities. These breakthroughs for women athletes represented another victory for the powerful women's movement of the 1970s.

A DISMAL DECADE

The 1970s was a dismal decade for millions of American families. The economic growth that had sustained the affluent society for thirty years had stalled. American power and prestige in the world had diminished. Politicians failed to provide effective leadership at home or abroad. The failure of the American war in Vietnam filled most Americans with shame. The revelations of the Watergate scandals filled most Americans with disgust. Revelations of wrongdoing by the agencies of the national security apparatus, the CIA and the FBI, frightened and angered most Americans. The Iranian hostage crisis humiliated most Americans.

For many citizens, the America of the 1970s no longer worked, or it did not work in accordance with traditional ideals and expectations. Young people coming of age during the 1970s enjoyed fewer opportunities and less mobility than did their parents. Double-digit inflation undermined real per capita income. For the first time in over 100 years, the average work week lengthened, reversing a long-running historical trend. Millions of Americans had to work harder for less during the 1970s. With more and more married women with children having to work or choosing to work, family life often deteriorated. People had less leisure time and fewer satisfying or fulfilling ways of using it. Those with disposable incomes threw themselves into a mindless, frantic consumerism. They often bought trendy new technologies, only to discard them after a short period of involvement. Many a personal computer sat idle or perhaps found use as an expensive planter.

Americans in the 1970s had to face a plethora of troubling, divisive problems, many of which proved interrelated and intractable. Abortion, legalized by the Supreme Court in 1973 in *Roe v. Wade,* generated enormous strife and anguish. The country's growing dependence on increasingly expensive foreign oil remained a worrisome issue. The decline of America's manufacturing industries in the face of fierce foreign competition and the decisions of American-based multinational corporations to export manufacturing operations presaged a bleak economic future for millions of American workers. Rising deficits in international trade balances and the federal budget made America one of the world's leading debtor nations. The deteriorating public school system suggested that young people would be poorly prepared for good jobs that were becoming scarce. Social problems abounded: medical care that was too expensive for millions of working-class families that did not have adequate health coverage, or any health coverage; serious shortcomings in the care available for the handicapped, the very elderly, and the terminally ill; the epidemic of drug use that swept the nation in the 1970s; the rising tide of crime, especially serious and violent crime; continuing massive poverty; continuing discrimination against racial minorities, women, and gay and lesbian people, despite the impressive gains that these groups had made during the 1960s; and continuing serious ecological problems that fouled the air and poisoned the environment.

It is little wonder that the American people turned to an aging former film actor in 1980 who promised to restore American primacy in world affairs and to revitalize the American economy. Even more important, Ronald Reagan promised to restore the American Dream and to make Americans feel good about themselves and their country again.

BIBLIOGRAPHY

There are several very good studies about the problems Americans faced during the 1970s. The implications of recent demographic shifts are discussed in Joseph J. Spengler's *Population and America's Future.* Several economists have written important books on the 1970s' economic crises. See Robert L. Heilbroner's *An Inquiry into the Human Prospect;* Lester Thurow's *The Zero Sum Game;* and Robert Reich's *The New American Frontier.* U.S. economic decline during the 1970s is charted in Barry Bluestone's and Bennett Harrison's *The Deindustrialization of America.* A fine recent study, edited by Michael A. Bernstein and David E. Adler, *Understanding American Economic Decline,* is the best analysis that we have of the economic downturn that began in the early 1970s. A good study of the impact of computer technology on American society and culture is Tracy Kidder's *The Soul of a New Machine.* For a study of African Americans in the 1970s, read Ken Auletta's *The Underclass* and William J. Wilson's *The Declining Significance of Race.* Wilson, one of the nation's most imminent scholars, recently published another important study, *When Work Disappears: The World of the New Urban Poor. Today's Immigrants: Their Stories* is a recent study by Thomas Kessner and Betty Caroli. There is an extensive and generally excellent literature on women during the 1970s and 1980s. See Winifred D. Wandersee's *On the Move: American Women in the 1970s.* Mary Ann Mason, in *The Equality Trap,* offers a perceptive study of the limitations of liberal feminism and its failure to cope with the economic plight of divorced working women. Christopher Lasch's *The Culture of Narcissism: American Life in the Age of Diminishing Expectations* catches many of the anxieties and discontents of the American people during the era of limits. Gillian Peele, in *Revival and Reaction: The Right in Contemporary America,* offers a study of current religious and political conservatism. Current education trends are analyzed in Sanford W. Reitman's *Education, Society, and Change.*

13

Conservatives Resurgent

When President Ronald Wilson Reagan addressed the nation on Inauguration Day on January 20, 1981, it marked the coming to power of a resurgent conservatism. Left for dead in the wake of the Goldwater debacle of 1964, conservatism had revived, gathered momentum during the 1970s, and captured the White House in 1980, when Reagan easily defeated the discredited Democratic incumbent Jimmy Carter. Resurgent conservatives did not form a monolithic political movement. Rather, they represented a diverse collection of people unhappy with the results of what they regarded as nearly fifty years of liberal governance or, more precisely, fifty years of liberal mismanagement of government. Conservatives did not embrace a unitary worldview. There was no essential conservative political philosophy embraced by all politicians who labeled themselves conservative. They formed no consensus and often bickered among themselves over issues and priorities. Libertarians and religious Rightists often locked horns over fundamental principles and the use of governmental power. In reality, a hodgepodge of ideas, beliefs, policy proposals, and critiques of liberalism was melded together under the marketing label "conservative."

In the early 1970s, conservatives of various stripes began to speak out forcibly on many issues. These resurgent conservatives voiced their vehement opposition to many public policies that they believed were bringing about too much social change much too quickly. Many conservatives, both North and South, attacked what they called "forced busing" to integrate the public schools. They also denounced affirmative action programs that guaranteed minorities, particularly African Americans, equal opportunity in their quest for schooling and employment. Antifeminists opposed the Equal Rights Amendment and helped defeat it. They also opposed efforts to protect the rights of gays and lesbians. Most conservatives opposed all gun control measures, and they favored the restoration of capital punishment. Most conservatives were outraged when the Supreme Court issued its controversial decision in *Roe v. Wade* (1973), which granted women the right to an abortion on demand during the first trimester of pregnancy. Many conservatives also attacked other Supreme Court rulings made during the 1970s that outlawed prayer in the public schools and strengthened the rights of criminals. Evangelical Christians stressed the cruciality of religion, private property, and family values. Most conservatives attacked what they regarded as unnecessary welfare programs, high taxes, and many wasteful and corrupt federal bureaucracies. Conservatives deplored the erosion of traditional family values and the decline of wave-the-flag patriotism. Conservatives from the business community championed free enterprise capitalism, criticized government regulation of economic activity, and attacked trade unions.

New Right conservatives, whose most prominent national leaders were Barry Goldwater and Ronald Reagan, believed that the Soviet Union's Communist leaders were the personification of evil and responsible for all that had gone wrong in the world since 1945. They insisted that America must maintain a strong arsenal of thermonuclear and conventional weapons to contain the aggressive tendencies of the Kremlin and its clients. Conservatives lamented the decline of U.S. power and influence in the world symbolized by the Vietnam debacle and the Iranian hostage crisis.

The diverse groups that called themselves conservatives, led by Ronald Reagan, within a few years brought about a remarkable transformation in the way most Americans viewed conservative political programs and conservative causes generally. Since the New Deal Era of the 1930s, the term *conservative* had been a political epithet; conservatism connoted selfishness, antiintellectualism, and, most of all, a mindless, desperate clinging to traditional ways in the face of unprecedented challenges and dangers. But since the 1970s, with the Democratic Party, and especially its liberal wing under siege as icons of discredited and dysfunctional policies, conservatives have stepped forward as dynamic agents of change.

During the 1980 presidential electoral campaign, Jimmy Carter appeared to be the inept defender of the status quo in the face of Reagan's dynamism and call for a new beginning. It may have been difficult for liberal Democrats to understand, and even harder for them to accept, but during the election of 1980, to a large majority of voters, the winning conservative coalition that embraced evangelical Christianity, family values, supply-side economics, calls for cuts in social spending and simultaneously a rapid buildup of U.S. military forces looked very much like a much-needed reform program to revitalize and redeem America. Ironically, given the political situation prevailing in 1980, the Democrats, historically the party of reform politics, had become defenders of the status quo, and the Republicans, historically the party of tradition, had been transformed into the party of reformers that mounted a withering, broad-based attack on the status quo.

THE MEDIA MAN

By the 1970s, Ronald Reagan had become the most articulate, persuasive champion of conservative causes. His career followed the classic Horatio Alger pattern of a poor boy who grew up to become rich and famous. He spent his boyhood living in rented apartments and houses in a series of small Midwestern towns, where his alcoholic father made an inconstant living as a shoe salesman. Reagan worked his way through college, graduating in 1932 during the depths of the Great Depression. Despite the hard times, Reagan managed to find work in radio, and within a few years, he had become a popular Midwestern sportscaster. In 1937, he came to Hollywood. He took a screen test at Warner Brothers and won a film contract. By 1941, Reagan had become a movie star, earning $5,000 a picture. Although he made a few serious films, the studio generally cast Reagan as the lead in "B" movies, usually as an All-American action hero. He spent World War II in Hollywood as a U.S. Army Air Corps officer making training films and documentaries for the Armed Forces.

After the war, Reagan's film career faded, and he became more active in Hollywood politics. His first marriage to screen actress Jane Wyman failed. He had embraced New Deal liberalism during the 1930s and early 1940s. Active in left-wing Democratic politics, he served two terms as president of the Screen Actors Guild. As his film career declined, he moved into television. As he was changing media, he married another screen actress, Nancy Davis, the adopted daughter of a wealthy, Chicago neurosurgeon.

Reagan drifted to the Right politically during the 1950s. He became a devout anti-Communist and cooperated with studio heads and the FBI to ferret out and blacklist writers, directors, and actors suspected of Communist affiliations. General Electric (GE) hired Reagan to host its popular television program *General Electric Theater.* He made speeches for General Electric, becoming comfortable espousing the company's conservative philosophy at business lunches and employee meetings. While making speeches for GE, Reagan developed the philosophy and refined the rhetoric that would propel him to leadership of the conservative cause and one day make him president of the United States. He left GE in 1962 and became active in right-wing Republican politics in Southern California. He continued to make speeches and to flesh out his conservative political philosophy.

Reagan emerged nationally in 1964, when he made a televised fund-raising speech on behalf of Barry Goldwater's faltering conservative crusade. "The Speech," as it came to be called, had a powerful impact on his audience and launched Reagan's political career. In his first try for public office in 1966, at age fifty-five, Ronald Reagan was elected governor of California. Quickly, the middle-aged former television host, screen actor, and radio sportscaster assumed national leadership of the rising conservative cause. He made his first bid for the presidency in 1968 but was stymied by Nixon's Southern strategy in Miami. He tried again in 1976, narrowly losing to Ford, but at age sixty-nine he won the office in 1980 on his third try.

Reagan had been an evangelical Christian since childhood, and his religious beliefs strongly influenced his life and thoughts. A large, handsome man of sunny disposition, Reagan's essential traits included a kind of "aw shucks" modesty that voters found irresistible. He also had a sense of himself as destiny's child, a blessed man fated for distinction. Reagan possessed a lively sense of humor and a limitless fund of stories and anecdotes that he used with great political skill. He believed in the frontier myth of heroic individualism, and he believed that anyone who wanted to could rise up and succeed as he did. For Reagan, America was still a land of innocence and unlimited possibilities. He harbored a profound hatred of Communism and was deeply suspicious of the Soviet Union. The private man differed from the affable public persona that Reagan consistently projected. He was an aloof, shy man, emotionally reticent. He had no close friends, no one to whom he ever confided his innermost thoughts, hopes, and fears. He was never close to any of his four children, none of whom could ever remember having an intimate conversation with their famous father. No one, except possibly his second wife Nancy Davis, ever got close to him or really knew him.

He mastered the art of media politics. Reagan's ability to deliver prepared remarks rivaled that of Franklin Roosevelt's, the new president's idol and role model. Nicknamed the Great Communicator, Reagan used television to sell himself and his conservative programs to the electorate. He showed great political skill by appealing to all varieties of conservatives and by keeping these disparate constituencies united, as well as attracting a broad spectrum of disaffected Democrats, many of whom were working-class voters who had supported George Wallace in 1968 and Richard Nixon in 1972. The outcome of the 1980 election and the subsequent popularity that he sustained for most of his long presidency convinced Reagan that most Americans shared his conservative vision and that they repudiated the goals and values of what he termed the *liberal special interest groups.*

THE ADVENT OF REAGANOMICS

When Reagan took office in January 1981, runaway inflation had ravaged the American economy for years. The average family's purchasing power was about $1,000 less than it had been a decade earlier. The value of the dollar had declined by 50 percent in five years. The new president called upon his fellow Americans to join him "in a new beginning" to clean up "the worst economic mess since the Great Depression." He blamed "the mess" on high levels of government spending and taxation. He said, "Government is not the solution to our problems; government is the problem."

Influenced by economist Arthur Laffer on the faculty of the University of Southern California, Reagan grounded his program for economic recovery in "supply-side" economic theory. Contradicting the long-prevailing Keynesian theory, which relied on government spending and tax cuts to boost consumer demand, supply siders favored cutting both federal spending and taxes at the same time. According to supply siders, high taxes siphoned off capital that would otherwise be invested in productive enterprises. They believed that the private sector, freed from the shackles imposed by government regulation, government spending, and high taxes would increase its investment in productive enterprises, thereby generating economic growth and creating millions of new jobs. Economic growth also would cut inflation and generate tax revenues that would more than offset losses from the reduced tax rates. Government expenditures would be trimmed by shrinking government benefits, especially entitlement programs, some of which had begun during the New Deal of the 1930s. Spending cuts coupled with the projected economic expansion would bring a balanced budget. To many skeptics, "Reaganomics" sounded almost too good to be true. When George Bush had campaigned for the Republican presidential nomination during the 1980 primaries, he had called Reagan's supply-side notions "voodoo economics."

The new president brought a mixed group of advisers to Washington. In a shrewd

Figure 13.1   President Ronald Reagan taking the oath of office from Supreme Court Chief Justice Warren Earl Burger. At the new president's side stands the new First Lady, Nancy Davis Reagan. Photo by Bill Fitz-Patrick.   *Source:* The White House Photo Office.

move, he appointed James A. Baker III, a close friend of Bush's, as his chief of staff. Baker, a savvy Washington insider, told Reagan to move quickly on his key issues—tax cuts and the military buildup. At the Treasury Department, the new president installed Donald Regan, a Wall Street securities broker and a conventional conservative Republican. David Stockman became director of the Office of Management and Budget. Stockman, a supply-side zealot, carried to Congress Reagan's program of cutting spending and reducing taxes. A brilliant workaholic and a missionary for cost and tax cuts, Stockman mastered the intricacies of the congressional budgetary process. He was the point man for Reaganomics. While Stockman overhauled the federal budgetary process, Paul Volcker, a Carter holdover and chairman of the Federal Reserve Board, kept a tight rein on the money supply by imposing historically high interest rates.

Stockman made cutting federal spending the Reagan administration's top priority. He slashed $41 billion in social spending for food stamps, public service jobs, student loans, school lunches, urban mass transit, and welfare payments. Middle-class entitlements such as Social Security were exempted, and Reagan also left what he called a "safety net for the truly needy." At the same time that he was cutting back social spending, Reagan significantly increased military spending.

The president exhibited great political skill and powers of persuasion by convincing many Sunbelt Democratic Congressmen to support his programs. These "boll weevils," led by Representative Phil Gramm of Texas, were crucial in getting his program through the Democrat-controlled House. Reagan made a dramatic personal appearance before a joint session of Congress to plead for his budget only a few weeks after being seriously wounded during an assassin's attempt on his life. His performance was dazzling and made for great political theater. Even liberal Democrats who opposed his budget and could not abide Reagan's conservative political philosophy were on their feet applauding the gallant old actor. He built up a strong bipartisan coalition in the House and won a commanding 253 to 176 victory. His winning margin in the Senate was even more impressive, 78 to 20. Many liberal Democrats were skeptical that supply-side economics could work as its disciples insisted it must, but they lacked an alternative program that commanded public support.

Congress enacted the key element within Reagan's economic program—tax cuts. The Economic Recovery Tax Act of 1981 was the most significant legislation of the Reagan era. Based on a proposal by Senator William Roth of Delaware and Congressman Jack Kemp, the across-the-board tax cuts reduced basic personal income rates by 25 percent over three years. It also indexed tax brackets, which kept tax rates constant when incomes increased solely because of inflation. The House accepted the 25 percent tax cuts, and the Senate approved them overwhelmingly. Congress wrote additional tax concessions into an omnibus bill. The top income tax rate was slashed from 70 percent to 50 percent. Capital gains, inheritance tax, and gift taxes also were reduced. Business tax write-offs were enhanced as well. The Reagan tax cuts, with congressional sanction, amounted to the largest, most generous tax reductions in the nation's history.

Reagan also sought to achieve his goal of restricting government activity by reducing federal regulation of the economy. He appointed to federal regulatory agencies men and women who shared his views that markets, not government agencies, ought to direct the national economy. He appointed Anne Gorsuch Burford, who opposed air quality and toxic waste regulations, to head the Environmental Protection Agency (EPA). During her tenure, the EPA budget was slashed, and all of its enforcement efforts were weakened. Reagan's most controversial appointment was James Watt to head the Department of the Interior. Watt was a conservative ideologue who had headed an antienvironmentalist legal action group before his appointment to the department. He supported strip mining and the opening up of public lands to private developers, including offshore oil-drilling sites. Reagan tried to eliminate the Department of Energy; failing that, he settled for severe cuts in its budget and operations. He also persuaded Congress to cut spending for elementary and secondary education. Much of the responsibility and costs of regulatory activity were shifted from the national government to state governments.

Drew Lewis, Reagan's secretary of transportation, removed many of the regulations to reduce pollution and to increase driver safety that had been imposed on the U.S. auto industry during the 1970s. He also persuaded the Japanese to voluntarily restrict automobile imports to the United States. Lewis opposed an illegal strike by an air traffic controller's union (PATCO) in the summer of 1981. President Reagan fired the 11,500 striking workers, decertified the union, and ordered Lewis to train and hire thousands of new air traffic controllers to replace them. The destruction of the air traffic controller's union was the most devastating defeat for organized labor in modern times. It had a demoralizing, paralyzing effect on a labor movement already reeling from the decline in American manufacturing industries and loss of political clout.

By the end of the summer of 1981, Reaganomics was in place. The new leader had moved most of his legislative program through Congress, wielding executive power with great skill and effectiveness. His efforts represented the greatest feat of presidential legislative leadership since the heyday of Lyndon Johnson's Great Society programs of 1964 and 1965. Reagan had asserted a popular mandate, seized the political initiative, manipulated the mass media, redefined the public agenda, and implemented most of his programs. *Time* magazine observed that, "No president since FDR had done so much of such magnitude so quickly to change the economic direction of the country." Reaganomics amounted to a radical assault on the welfare state erected during the previous fifty years, which all administrations, Democratic or Republican, had accepted in practice.

Aware that few African Americans had voted Republican, the Reagan administration was unresponsive to blacks' concerns. Federal support for civil rights weakened. Reagan opposed affirmative action hiring programs, which he said amounted to reverse discrimination. His Attorney General Edwin Meese opposed busing to achieve school desegregation. The number of African-American officials appointed to major government positions declined sharply. The budgets for federal agencies responsible for enforcing civil rights programs were curtailed. Both the staff and budget of the Civil Rights Division of the Justice Department were cut. The Justice Department filed few school desegregation and fair housing suits during Reagan's first term as president.

Reagan's record on female appointments was better than his record for African Americans. He appointed a few highly visible women to important government positions. He fulfilled a campaign pledge and made a major symbolic gesture to women when he appointed Sandra Day O'Connor to the Supreme Court, the first woman jurist ever chosen. He appointed Georgetown University political science professor Jeane Kirkpatrick as the U.S. ambassador to the United Nations. Several women served in the Reagan Cabinet, and women achieved leadership roles in the Republican Party. Feminists, however, pointed out that Reagan appointed far fewer women to federal offices and judgeships than had his Democratic predecessor. Reagan opposed the Equal Rights Amendment, plus he was an outspoken foe of abortion and denounced *Roe v. Wade*.

RECESSION AND RECOVERY

After a year, it was evident that Reaganomics had not brought forth the promised economic revival. In January 1982, unemployment exceeded 9 percent, the highest since 1941. Business bankruptcies rose to Great Depression levels. Steep interest rates priced homes and cars beyond the reach of millions of families and plunged those two major industries into depression. One year after Reagan's promised new beginning, the nation was mired in its worst business slump since the Great Depression. During 1982, the GDP shrank 2.5 percent, manufacturing output declined, and the construction industry slumped. Large cities fared the worst. In Detroit, unemployment reached 20 percent. Bewildered and angry work-

**Figure 13.2   Sandra Day O'Connor, the first woman to be appointed to the
U.S. Supreme Court.**   *Source:* Supreme Court Historical Society.

ers, many of them "Reagan Democrats," lined up to receive their unemployment checks. A
class of "new poor," not seen since the 1930s, appeared on the streets: homeless, unemployed workers and their families. The short-term consequences of the first application of
Reaganomics were the bitter fruit of hard times for millions of working-class and middle-
class families.

In the short run, supply-side economics did not work as advertised, and the promised
increase in tax revenues from economic growth never materialized. A combination of deep
tax cuts, steep hikes in military spending, and drastic economic shrinkage drove the federal
budget deficit over $100 billion for the fiscal year of 1981, the highest ever. The one bright

Figure 13.3   Pro-life demonstrator and a pro-choice demonstrator exchange barbs outside Faneuil Hall in Boston, where pro-life held their 11th annual Assembly for Life. About 1500 people attended a rally inside while pro abortion people numbering about 150 demonstrated outside the hall. No arrests were made as the two groups engaged in a shouting match. Photo by Paul Iglesias.   *Source:* Corbis.

spot in a dark economic picture was declining inflation, which dropped from 13 percent in 1980 to 9 percent in 1981 to 5 percent in 1982. The failure of Reaganomics in the short run derived from two fiscal realities: the failure of the tax cuts to stimulate increased business investment and production, and continuing high interest rates that curbed both business spending and consumer purchases. President Reagan, confronting a declining economy and rising criticism, pleaded for more time for his program to take hold. He insisted that Reaganomics did not cause the downturn, that it came from the accumulated mismanagement and mistaken policies of his Democratic predecessors. Reagan promised that prosperity would come but that it would have protracted birthing pains. The recession worsened all through 1982. Toward the end of the year, unemployment reached 10 percent; over 11 million Americans were out of work.

The 1982 midterm elections took place amidst the worst economic conditions that this country had seen in over forty years. Undaunted, Reagan campaigned hard for his program and for Republican candidates. The election amounted to a referendum on Reaganomics. The Democrats picked up twenty-five House seats, but the Republicans held on to the Senate. When the new Congress convened in January 1983, Reagan lost his bipartisan majority coalition in the House that had pushed through Reaganomics. House Speaker Thomas "Tip" O'Neill, the leader of the opposition to Reaganomics, forced the president to accept budget compromises in 1983. Cuts in social spending were lessened, and increases in military spending were reduced.

The economy recovered strongly in 1983, and the surge continued in 1984. The gross national product rose by 6.8 percent in 1984, the largest one-year gain since the Korean War. Unemployment and interest rates declined. Housing starts and new car sales picked up; domestic automakers reported strong sales and record profits in mid-1984. The rate of inflation dropped to 4 percent for both years, the lowest since the early 1970s. Personal income rose, and consumer and business confidence soared. Abundant world oil supplies were an important cause of the drop in the rate of inflation. By the end of 1984 the OPEC cartel was in disarray and world oil prices were falling. The economic expansion that began in 1983 lasted through that decade; it proved to be the longest sustained period of prosperity in modern American history. Eighteen million new jobs were added to the economy, productivity was significantly enhanced, and the prices of stocks had trebled by 1990.

Despite the strong rebound, serious problems continued to plague the American economy. Tax cuts combined with large increases in military spending to generate record federal deficits—$195 billion in 1983 and $175 billion in 1984. The nation's international trade deficit reached $58 billion in 1983 and a record $108 billion in 1984. The main causes of the soaring international debt were the nation's continuing thirst for foreign oil and imported manufactures such as autos, stereos, cameras, and clothes. By the end of his first term, Reagan, with help from Congress, had managed to double the national debt, from $1 trillion to $2 trillion! All talk of balanced budgets had been replaced by a frenzied concern to staunch the massive flow of red ink. Amidst the economic boom, over 7.5 million Americans remained out of work. The U.S. Census Bureau reported that the nation's poverty rate had reached 15.2 percent in 1983, the highest since 1965. A 15.2 percent poverty rate meant that there were about 35 million poor people in America, 6 million more than when Reagan assumed office.

THE COLD WAR REVIVED

Reagan came to office with even less background in foreign policy than did Carter. He also made reviving the American economy his first priority. Because of his lack of experience and because his main interests lay in domestic affairs, he relied heavily on advisers for both forging and implementing American foreign policy. The new president inhabited a foreign policy world of myths and symbols rather than programs and policies. For Reagan, the traditional verities of the Cold War still prevailed: America and its allies were locked in a life-or-death struggle for survival with a ruthless, expansionist Soviet empire. Reagan repudiated Washington's previous efforts at détente and announced his intention to challenge Soviet interests around the globe. He launched a rapid buildup of American military power to give the United States the muscle and confidence it needed to prevail in the long twilight struggle with its global rival. He announced what came to be known as the Reagan Doctrine: the United States would help anti-Communist resistance movements anywhere in the world.

He also made clear that he intended to make major use of the CIA as an instrument of U.S. foreign policy, especially its covert paramilitary operations. He freed American arms sales from the restrictions imposed by the Carter administration and scrapped Carter's human rights policies, which he believed had been used to weaken anti-Communist Rightist governments that served U.S. interests in the Cold War. Reagan appointed his campaign manager and good friend William Casey to head the restored CIA. The new President viewed the Cold War between the United States and the Soviet Union as a fundamentally moral conflict. Perhaps borrowing from his Hollywood days as a wholesome action hero, Reagan saw himself as the leader of the "good guys" against the "bad guys" who lurked in the Kremlin. He denounced the Soviet Union in a speech before the United Nations in 1982, charging that Soviet agents were working everywhere in the world "violating human rights and unnerving the world with violence." Addressing a convention of evangelical Christians in Orlando, Florida, in May 1983, he called the Soviet Union "an evil empire" and declared that the Soviet leaders were "the focus of evil in the modern world."

Ironically, Reagan was only continuing a trend begun under Carter in 1979. After the Iranian revolution and the Soviet invasion of Afghanistan, Carter had abandoned détente and had taken a tougher stance toward the Soviets that had reignited the Cold War. Influenced by his hard-liner foreign policy adviser Zbigniew Brzezinski, Carter had dropped the proposed SALT II treaty, canceled trade with the Soviets, significantly increased American military spending, and sought to put intermediate-range missiles in Europe. Whether he acknowledged it or was even aware of it, some of Reagan's hard-line, anti-Soviet policies often built upon Carter's initiatives.

Under Reagan, the U.S. military flourished. Secretary of Defense Caspar Weinberger proposed a $1.2 trillion defense buildup, which Reagan supported strongly. It called for doubling U.S. military spending over five years, from $171 billion in 1981 to over $360 billion in 1986. This huge increase in military spending fulfilled Reagan's campaign pledge to "make America Number One again." Weinberger insisted that during Carter's presidency the Soviets had achieved strategic superiority over the United States. A "window of vulnerability" existed for American land-based missiles that could tempt the Soviets to try a "first strike" nuclear attack. An expensive crash buildup of new strategic weapons systems was a crucial strategic priority. Weinberger ordered the building of a new strategic bomber, a new strategic missile, and an expanded navy from 450 to 600 ships. Reagan, determined to keep America the preeminent power in the world and to challenge the Soviet Union, strongly supported all of Weinberger's proposals for the military buildup. When David Stockman attempted to whittle military outlays by a few hundred million dollars, Reagan interceded to back Weinberger and to block Stockman's efforts. Chief of Staff James Baker then pushed Weinberger's military budget through Congress. During Reagan's presidency, the defense budgets were the largest in peacetime history.

Reagan, Weinberger, George Bush, and other administration officials spoke of being able "to prevail" in the event of a nuclear war with the Soviets. Such rhetoric, yoked to the gigantic increases in military spending, frightened millions of Americans, who feared that

Reagan was preparing for a nuclear war with the Soviets. The antinuclear peace movement expanded rapidly.

The Reagan administration had difficulty in achieving a unified approach to foreign policy because of internal feuding among key personnel. Reagan's administrative methods were lax, and he was careless about the details of particular policies. There were hazards entailed in Reagan's habit of deferring to his foreign policy advisers because they often disagreed among themselves. His first Secretary of State, General Alexander Haig, who was expected to be the strongman in orchestrating Reagan's foreign policy, ran afoul of Reagan's inner circle of Californians. He was replaced by George Shultz, an economist with extensive experience in government service, however, Shultz frequently worked at cross-purposes with Weinberger and Reagan's ambassador to the United Nations, Jeane Kirkpatrick.

Despite his tough anti-Communist rhetoric and the expensive military buildup, Reagan found it difficult to assert pressure on Communist states. In late 1981, the Soviet Union forced Poland to impose martial law in order to crush a trade union movement that was pushing Poland toward Democratic Socialism and away from Soviet Communism. Reagan, outraged, found his options limited. He could not risk nuclear war with the Soviet Union, nor could he persuade NATO allies to impose economic blockades on the USSR or Poland. He imposed an American boycott on the nearly bankrupt Polish economy that only caused additional hardship on the Polish people without saving the trade union movement. The Polish crisis demonstrated once again the determination of the Soviets to hold on to their Eastern European empire, no matter what U.S. presidents said or did. Reagan also discovered that sovereign and prosperous NATO countries felt no compunctions about resisting some of the U.S. anti-Communist initiatives.

Reagan met with frustration again in Europe in 1982, when he tried to block a major economic arrangement between the Soviet Union and Western European nations. The Soviets agreed to sell natural gas to the West Europeans if they would build a pipeline to transport the gas. The West Europeans had then agreed to purchase the natural gas from Siberia and to build the pipeline to transport it. The pipeline required American technology supplied by European corporations. Reagan tried and failed to stop the deal by imposing sanctions against these companies, some of which were partly government owned.

The Reaganauts had more success in stymieing the Soviets' efforts to crush Afghanistan's *mujahidin* rebels during the early 1980s. The CIA set up a clandestine arms supply operation. Arms were shipped to Islamabad in Pakistan, an American ally, and then funneled across rugged mountain passes into Afghanistan. The Soviets soon found themselves bogged down in a Vietnam-like quagmire. They unleashed a fearsome arsenal of modern high-tech weaponry against the rebels, including the Soviet air force. Soviet aircraft carpet bombed Afghan villages in an effort to destroy the guerrillas' popular base of support. Soviet infantry battalions, supported by armor, artillery, and helicopter gunships, tried to sweep the rebels from strategic valleys. The Soviets also tried to interdict the movement of arms and supplies from Pakistan and threatened the Pakistanis if they did not desist, all to no avail. The *mujahidin,* despite absorbing heavy casualties, maintained a determined resistance to the Soviets' efforts to pacify them. The application of the Reagan Doctrine in Afghanistan succeeded. One curious inconsistency was that many young Americans who had vigorously protested U.S. bombing in Vietnam appeared not to be concerned about Soviet bombing of Afghan villages, nor did they support Reagan's efforts to help the people of Afghanistan resist Soviet imperialism.

Reagan succeeded in implementing Carter's 1979 initiative to place 572 intermediate-range cruise missiles and Pershing II missiles in Western Europe that could strike targets in the western regions of the Soviet Union. These missiles would counter Soviet SS-20 missiles already deployed and aimed at NATO countries. This initiative provoked an angry response from the Soviets, who tried to stop it. It also aroused opposition from Leftist political leaders and peace groups in Europe and from a "nuclear freeze" movement in the United States. In the spring of 1982, nearly 1 million nuclear freeze supporters gathered in Central Park, the largest political rally in American history.

To offset European and widespread domestic opposition to his plan, Reagan offered two new arms control initiatives. The first, called the "zero option," offered to cancel the proposed deployment of cruise missiles and Pershing missiles in exchange for the Soviets' removal of their SS-20 missiles. Second, at a new series of arms talks between American and Soviet negotiators in Geneva, called START, the United States proposed that both sides scrap one-third of their nuclear warheads and permit land-based missiles to have no more than half of the remaining warheads. The Soviets did not take these proposals seriously and quickly rejected both of them. They had no incentive to remove missiles already in place in exchange for the cancellation of weapons not yet deployed. They rejected the second offer because 70 percent of their warheads were on land-based missiles, compared to about one-third for the United States. However, these U.S. arms control proposals reassured nervous Europeans and slowed the nuclear freeze movement at home. When the new missiles began arriving in Great Britain and West Germany in 1983, the Soviets broke off the START talks.

The United States escalated the arms race in 1983, when President Reagan ordered the Pentagon to develop a Strategic Defense Initiative (SDI). The SDI was an immensely complex antimissile defense system that would use high-powered lasers to destroy enemy missiles in space. The SDI was quickly dubbed "Star Wars" by its critics who sought to discredit the project. Many scientific and defense specialists expressed skepticism that the SDI could work. If it could be built, they estimated that it would take twenty years and would cost $1 trillion. If it proved successful, the new defense system also posed the danger of destabilizing the arms race, because it would force the Soviets to build more missiles and to develop an SDI of their own. President Reagan strongly backed the SDI, assuming that it could be built and that it would free the world from the deadly trap of deterrence based on mutually assured destruction. He clung to his vision of a world free from the threat posed by the nuclear arms race. Despite his hard-line anti-Communism and despite pushing for a powerful arms buildup and the SDI, Ronald Reagan was at heart a passionate antinuclear idealist. His overriding goal was to allow humanity to escape the awful dilemma posed by Mutually Assured Destruction (MAD), which kept both sides feverishly building increasingly efficient weapons of mass destruction and which also kept the people of both countries in a state of perpetual angst.

Thus the costly and dangerous nuclear arms race between the two superpowers roared on. Both sides continued to develop and deploy new weapons systems and to refine existing ones. Although both sides informally observed the unratified SALT II agreement, it placed few curbs on their activities. Arms control negotiations were suspended. The death of Russian leader Leonid Brezhnev, followed by two short tenures of old and sick successors, created a succession crisis for the Soviets. It also made any efforts at negotiations between the Soviets and the United States difficult. In March 1985, a dynamic new ruler, Mikhail Gorbachev, emerged in the Soviet Union. Gorbachev quickly established himself as a strong leader. Future negotiations on arms control between the United States and the Soviet Union once again became possible.

Even though he had only a few measurable diplomatic successes against the Soviets, had escalated the arms race, and had intensified the Cold War, Reagan's vigorous efforts against the Soviets did restore a measure of American pride and self-confidence. Reagan showed his fellow citizens that he had no fear of the Soviets, and he exuded a sublime confidence that the United States would eventually win the long Cold War with its Communist rival. Reagan's key insight, which he held at a time when almost none of the U.S. defense experts and Sovietologists shared his views, was that the Soviet Union was both evil and economically and technologically weak. He intuitively sensed that the Soviet Union could be beaten if Americans kept faith and jacked up military spending.

THE PACIFIC RIM

The Reagan administration also gave much attention to U.S. foreign policy interests in the Far East. Asia comprises a vast region of diverse nation-states which, many experts believe, is destined to become the center of American diplomatic concerns by the dawn of the twenty-first century. The most important nations were China, home to one-quarter of the planet's nearly 6 billion inhabitants, and Japan, a nation that rose from the ashes of total defeat at the end of World War II and became an economic powerhouse by the 1970s. The economies of South Korea, Taiwan, Hong Kong, Malaysia, and Singapore also were thriving in the early 1980s, their prosperity in large measure fueled, like Japan's, by the sale of manufactures to the United States and Western Europe.

Washington did not have good relations with China initially, mainly because of Reagan's efforts to bolster the military forces of Taiwan, which the Chinese considered an integral part of their country. In 1984, Sino–American relations improved when Premier Zhao Zivang of the People's Republic of China (PRC) visited the United States and signed agreements pledging cooperation between China and the United States in the crucial areas of industry, science, and technology. President Reagan later visited China and signed pacts pledging renewed cultural exchanges between the two countries. Relations between China and the United States were cordial by the end of Reagan's first term.

Diplomacy with Japan, a nation whose gross national product was more than five times the size of China's, was the Reagan administration's central Asian concern. Two major problems strained Japanese–American relations in 1981. The first concerned efforts by the Reagan administration to get Japan to pay a far larger share of its defense costs rather than continue to sit comfortably behind the nuclear shield provided by American taxpayers. The Japanese subsequently increased their defense outlays, to about 0.75 of 1 percent of GDP, far less than what the Americans wanted and far lower than the 6 percent of their own GDP that Americans spent annually for defense.

The second, more serious problem concerned the growing imbalance in U.S.–Japanese trade that increasingly favored the Japanese. The imbalance had reached $10 billion in 1980 and $16 billion in 1981. The largest part of the imbalance derived from the sale of Japanese cars to U.S. consumers. In 1981, Japanese automakers sold almost 2 million cars to eager American buyers, hurting domestic automakers who had lost 25 percent of their market to the Japanese in a decade. U.S. negotiators persuaded the Japanese to voluntarily reduce auto shipments to America for 1982, and they also convinced the Japanese to reduce barriers to the importation of U.S. agricultural commodities, particularly beef and citrus fruit. Despite these Japanese concessions, the trade imbalance continued to grow in favor of Japan. It reached $20 billion in 1983 and shot up to $35 billion in 1984. Although the Japanese consistently refused to open their markets to U.S. goods, the fundamental cause of the trade imbalance between the two nations was rooted in a reality of modern international economic life: Japanese manufacturers were far more adept at producing quality goods that American consumers strongly desired than Americans were at producing goods that Japanese consumers wanted to buy.

In Southeast Asia, the Vietnamese people endured a life of poverty and oppression. Their Communist leaders were far better equipped to fight American imperialism than they were to provide good government and a prosperous economy for their people. Soviet subsidies kept the backward Vietnamese economy going. Each year thousands of Vietnamese fled the country, willing to endure terrible risks and hardships to seek a better life for themselves and their families in Taiwan, Hong Kong, France, the United States, or wherever else they could find haven. Despite its impoverished state, Vietnam also maintained 200,000 troops in Kampuchea to support a puppet regime that the Vietnamese had installed there in 1979. The Reagan administration indicated its displeasure with Vietnamese imperialism and also sought an accounting from the Hanoi government about the fate of thousands of U.S. servicemen still missing in action (MIAs) from the Vietnam War. Reagan officials made it clear to the Vietnamese leaders that there could be no improvement in official American–Vietnamese relations until Vietnam pulled its troops out of Kampuchea and settled the MIA issue to the satisfaction of the concerned families.

DISASTER IN LEBANON

In the Middle East, the Reagan administration tried to continue the peace process established by Carter, that of providing Israel with strategic security and also giving the Palestinians a homeland on the West Bank. The larger goal of U.S. Middle Eastern policy continued to be containing Soviet influence in that strategic region. While trying to implement its policies, the United States became embroiled in the civil war going on in Lebanon. Israel continued its policy of gradual annexation of the West Bank, ignoring the national aspirations of the Palestinians. In June 1982, in an effort to destroy the PLO, Israeli forces invaded Lebanon and besieged West Beirut, where refugee camps contained thousands of Palestinians and provided a base for PLO fighters. The PLO and other Muslim factions in

Lebanon turned to Syria to contain the Israeli forces. American policy in Lebanon was contradictory. Even as it supported the Israeli invasion, the Reagan administration employed an envoy of Lebanese descent, Philip Habib, who arranged for the Israelis to lift their siege while a UN force supervised the removal of PLO forces. Following the removal of the PLO, the Israelis reoccupied West Beirut. On September 17, 1982, Lebanese Christian militia, working closely with Israeli forces, entered two Palestinian refugee camps and slaughtered hundreds of people in reprisal for the murder three days earlier of a Lebanese Christian leader. Following the massacre, the United States sent in troops to try to restore peace in Beirut.

But the U.S. forces proved unable to influence events and came under siege themselves as civil war raged in the streets of Beirut between Christian and Muslim militias. Syrian forces, aided by the Soviets, occupied eastern Lebanon and controlled most of the Muslim factions. Israeli troops remained in southern Lebanon. The 1,500 U.S. Marines, isolated at the Beirut airport, without a clear-cut mission nor possessing sufficient force to maintain order, were perceived by the Muslims and their Syrian supporters to be aligned with the Christians.

The United States tried unsuccessfully to restore order to Lebanon and to arrange for a Syrian and an Israeli withdrawal. Early on the morning of October 23, 1983, a yellow Mercedes truck loaded with explosives, driven by a Muslim terrorist, slammed into the U.S. Marine compound near the Beirut airport and killed 241 Marines who were sleeping inside. Following the slaughter of the Marines, Reagan was forced to withdraw the remaining U.S. forces in February 1984, ending the U.S. military presence in Lebanon. The civil war went on. Syria remained the controlling force in Lebanese affairs. Lebanon became a fertile source of kidnappings and terrorist attacks on American citizens. Moderate Arab states refused to support U.S. Middle East policy, and the peace process appeared hopelessly stalled. Lebanon was a humiliating defeat for the Reagan administration, and the killing of the U.S. Marines constituted the worst U.S. military disaster since Vietnam. Lebanon's agony continued.

POLICING THE WESTERN HEMISPHERE

Even though Reagan administration officials were quite involved with events in Europe, Asia, and the Middle East, they also gave high priority to affairs in the Western Hemisphere, where the United States had been the hegemonic power for over a century. Canada and the United States had long been each other's principal trading partner, and the two democratic nations shared the longest unfortified international boundary in the world. Canada also was the chief supplier of foreign oil to the United States. Even so, relations between the two countries had not been warm in recent years. Canadian Nationalists had long feared and resented U.S. domination of many sectors of their economic life. The two countries also were often at odds over trade policies, NATO affairs, fishing rights, disarmament policies, and pollution. Relations between Canada and the United States improved after a new conservative Canadian government, headed by Brian Mulroney, came to power in 1984. Mulroney and Reagan soon established a warm, personal relationship; both men were of Irish descent, and both were committed to the same free enterprise philosophy. Together they brought about a historic agreement: a treaty removing all barriers to trade between their two countries. The agreement went into effect in December 1988, making the Canadian–U.S. market the largest international free trade zone in the world (worth $125 billion in trade in 1988). The achievement of free trade with the Canadians was one of the major diplomatic accomplishments of the Reagan presidency.

In addition to Canada, the Reagan administration involved itself in the internal affairs of Central American countries. Hard-line Cold Warriors, including President Reagan, were obsessed with stopping the spread of Communism in that region. Washington made over-throwing the Sandinista government in Nicaragua its top regional priority. The Sandinistas were Leftists, and they were friendly with Marxist leaders in Cuba and the Soviet Union, but they were not Communists. Reagan accused the new Sandinista government of suppressing democratic elements within Nicaragua and aiding Marxist rebels in nearby El Salvador. Reagan viewed the Sandinista regime as a serious threat in Central America that must be contained, otherwise it could become another Cuba, allowing the Cubans and Soviets to export Marxist–Leninist revolution to neighboring countries, using Nicaraguan military bases as staging areas.

At the time Reagan assumed the presidency, the CIA estimated that there were about 500 Cuban, Soviet, and East European military advisors, technicians, and intelligence operatives in Nicaragua, performing various functions in support of the Sandinista regime in Central America. In the spring of 1982, Reagan approved the use of CIA political and para-military operations to interdict arms shipments from Nicaragua to El Salvador and to over-throw the Sandinista regime. Washington's chosen instrument for deposing the Sandinistas was to be a Contra military force recruited from various groups of anti-Sandinista Nicaraguans, including former supporters of deposed dictator Anastasio Somoza Debayle.

Congress, skeptical of Reagan's Central American policy, enacted the Boland Amendment in December 1982, which forbade the CIA or the Pentagon to provide any funds or training to anyone for the purpose "of overthrowing the government of Nicaragua." Reagan appealed to Congress in 1983 for funds to "hold the line against externally supported aggression" in Central America. Congressional Democrats accused him of exaggerating the Cuban and Soviet threats, of relying too heavily upon military solutions, and of ignoring serious social and economic problems within Central American countries that bred rebellion. Public opinion polls revealed much popular opposition to American military involvement in Central America and fears of being drawn into another Vietnam-like quagmire. After noisy debates, Congress rejected the Reagan administration's request for $80 million, and then rejected another request for $50 million to support CIA covert operations against Nicaragua. After more noisy debates, Congress, in December 1983, reversed itself and approved $24 million for covert operations.

Meanwhile, the CIA continued its war on the Sandinistas. Contra forces, trained by the CIA at bases in neighboring Honduras, began operations inside of Nicaragua. Other CIA-trained elements attacked various port installations at several sites in Nicaragua. In early 1984, helicopters flown by CIA-trained operatives mined three of Nicaragua's major harbors. When an alarmed Congress learned that CIA-trained forces had mined Nicaraguan harbors, causing damage to merchant ships, it cut off all American aid for the Contras. The

World Court later ruled that the United States had violated international law and that Nicaragua could sue America for damages. The Reagan administration ignored the Court's ruling.

With funding of its secret war in Nicaragua cut off by Congress, the Reagan administration looked elsewhere for money to keep the Contras in the field. Administration officials made a deal with the Saudi Arabians, whereby the United States sold the Saudis 400 Stinger aircraft missiles in return for which the Saudis agreed to provide the contras with $10 million. The administration also persuaded Israel to aid the Contras, and wealthy individual Americans also chipped in money. The Iran-Contra scandal originated in these efforts at creative financing to keep the Reagan administration's proxy war in Nicaragua afloat and to circumvent the will of Congress.

In El Salvador, the war between left-wing guerrillas and a right-wing government continued. Carter had cut off U.S. aid to the government following the murder of three American nuns by government forces. The Reagan administration restored and increased U.S. assistance and sent in forty-five American military advisers to help government forces. The United States backed a government headed by a moderate democrat, Jose Napoleon Duarte. Duarte defeated the candidate of the extreme Right, Roberto d'Aubisson, in a 1984 election and began a reform program. He also tried to curb the excesses of right-wing "death squads" that had murdered thousands of civilians since the war began. But Duarte's forces could not defeat the rebels. The civil war went on.

While the Reagan administration pursued its proxy war against the Sandinistas in Nicaragua and backed the Duarte government in El Salvador, it also fought a brief miniwar for control of a small island, Grenada, located in the eastern Caribbean. Early on the morning of October 25, 1983, some 1,900 U.S. Marines and Army paratroopers stormed ashore. U.S. forces invaded Grenada, ostensibly to rescue several hundred U.S. citizens who were studying medicine there. The main purpose of the invasion was to overthrow a Marxist regime headed by General Hudson Austin, who had recently come to power. What most concerned the Reagan administration was the construction of an airport underway at Point Salines, which was capable of accommodating Fidel Castro's air force when completed. The 9,000 foot runway also could serve as a refueling station for Soviet aircraft ferrying weapons to the Sandinistas. Within four days, U.S. forces had overwhelmed the small Grenadian army and 784 Cuban militiamen who had been working on the airport as a construction battalion. U.S. forces deposed the Austin regime and shipped the Cubans home.

Most Grenadans welcomed the American armed forces as liberators who had rescued them from a tyrannical regime that had taken control of their island and turned it into an outpost of Cuban and Soviet power. The United States installed a friendly interim government and granted it $30 million in military and economic assistance. UN spokesmen and some liberal pundits and politicians within the United States condemned the Grenada operation as being unnecessary, pointless, and wrong. They were drowned out by defenders of Washington's decision to invade the island. Public opinion polls in this country showed that Reagan's actions enjoyed broad popular support. Besides, the Grenada operation was not just about Grenada, it was also about Lebanon and the Middle East. By staging a brief, dramatic, and low-casualty rescue operation only two days after 241 U.S. Marines were blown up in their barracks in Beirut, the Grenada miniwar diverted Americans' attention from that horrible tragedy and began to erase bitter memories of previous U.S. foreign policy failures.

REAGAN: THE FIRST TERM

Liberal intellectuals took to the mainstream media to frequently savage Ronald Reagan. They were offended by both the conservative agenda that he so effectively promoted and by his seeming lack of some of the abilities normally associated with occupants of the Oval Office. Historian John Wiltz called him "the least cerebral" of modern presidents. His detractors portrayed him as a kind of ceremonial president: while he looked and acted the part, an inner circle of elite advisers made policy and ran the country. Reagan was poorly read, intellectually incurious, and appeared to lack the ability to think analytically or to make hard judgments among policy options presented by his advisers. He tended to disengage himself from the details of his day-to-day administration. On occasion, he dozed off at Cabinet meetings while his advisers debated policy options. He often could not remember the names of his advisers or visiting dignitaries. He sometimes appeared dependent on his wife Nancy for advice and guidance, and the First Lady was fiercely protective of her husband's presidency and image. President Reagan sometimes confused events that had transpired in the celluloid world of Hollywood films with historical reality. His knowledge of the world appeared impressionistic and anecdotal rather than conceptual and factual. He often was given to misstatements. During his presidency, Reagan's staffers became adept at damage control, at putting the proper "spin" on his more ludicrous remarks, such as his claim that trees cause smog. At times, Reagan appeared to be an old actor playing the role of President rather than functioning as the chief executive of the world's preeminent power.

As his liberal detractors ridiculed his intellectual and administrative shortcomings, they underrated the man's remarkable political talents. Elitist intellectuals might have scoffed at the old actor's simplistic ideas, but Reagan understood that average American citizens could not care less whether the President of the United States possessed a powerful mind or had mastered all of the intricacies of a policy or program. They wanted a leader, not a policy wonk as Chief executive. President Reagan also had a clear vision of the direction in which he wanted to move the government, the country, and its people, and he was determined to succeed. He was determined to reverse the fifty-year trend, whereby the federal government assumed increasing responsibility for underwriting the economic security and general welfare of the population. He wanted to slash taxes and eliminate government regulations, which he believed had shackled the entrepreneurial energies of the American people for a half-century. He was also determined to restore American military primacy in the world and to contain Soviet expansionism as Americans had done in the 1940s and 1950s, before the Vietnam debacle had sapped their will to contain Communism. And if he could, he would win the Cold War and destroy the Soviet Union.

Demonstrating great political skill, Reagan largely succeeded in moving Congress and the American people in accordance with his conservative vision. He retained the trust, admiration, and affection of a majority of his fellow citizens for most of his presidency. He did not destroy the welfare state, if that was his intent, but he trimmed its sails. The social service state was pared down, and the social contract was attenuated. Under his leadership, the economy, after enduring a bitter recession in 1982, rebounded strongly. Inflation was brought under control, and long-term stable growth for the rest of the decade ensured a prosperous economy. Reagan strengthened the armed forces, and Americans were treated with new respect in the world by both friends and foes. Most Americans became more optimistic about both their present conditions and the future of the nation. Reagan's stirring leadership and eloquent speeches helped lift the malaise that had fastened itself on the nation during the era of limits. Ronald Reagan proved to be the most popular, successful president since Dwight David Eisenhower.

But there was a dark underside to the Reagan record. Huge deficits in the federal budget and in international trade roared out of control. While yuppies prospered, the number of Americans living in poverty increased. The number of homeless Americans proliferated. Rich Americans became richer, while poor Americans became poorer. Ronald Reagan presided over a major redistribution of national income away from the poor and toward the rich. The Reagan administration had scant interest in civil rights or ecological concerns. Drugs poured into the country, and crime rates soared. Although popular with a large majority of the population, the Reagan presidency was a controversial one, and it had its legions of critics and detractors.

THE ELECTION OF 1984

Reagan's landslide reelection victory on November 6, 1984, reaffirmed his remarkable personal popularity. His forty-nine-state sweep expressed voter approval of the strong economic recovery and the country's powerful military buildup. The seventy-three-year-old incumbent garnered 525 electoral votes, the largest total in history. Former Vice President Walter Mondale, the Democratic Party candidate, carried only his home state of Minnesota and the District of Columbia. Reagan got 52.7 million votes (59 percent) to Mondale's 36.5 million (41 percent). The Republicans gained thirteen seats in the House and won seventeen of thirty-three Senatorial elections, retaining a 54 to 46 majority. In state and local races, beyond the reach of Reagan's influence, Democratic candidates fared much better.

President Reagan's smashing victory crossed all regional and most demographic lines. The Democrats appeared to have no remaining regional base of support. In the once Solid South, every state went for Reagan by decisive majorities. In the West and Southwest, Reagan won easily. The Northeast, once the stronghold of both moderate Republicans and liberal Democrats, voted for Reagan. He also swept the industrial states of the Great Lakes and the Midwestern farm belt, despite continuing economic problems in both of those regions. All age groups voted for him. He did especially well among young, first-time voters, ages eighteen to twenty-one. Baby boomers, voters in their twenties and thirties, many of whom had voted for neoliberal Gary Hart in the Democratic primaries, voted 2 to 1 for Reagan. Half of all union members voted for the President, even though Mondale's chief backers were the AFL-CIO leadership.

Class and ethnic differences were visible in the voting returns. Middle-class and wealthy voters overwhelmingly supported Reagan. Less affluent voters generally supported

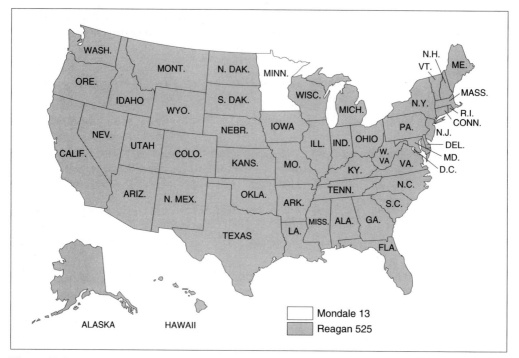

Figure 13.4   The electoral vote, 1984.   *Source:* Moss, *Moving On,* p. 337. Public Domain map.

Mondale. Ninety percent of blacks voted for Mondale as did 60 percent of Hispanics. Election results showed that Hispanics were an emerging political force, comprising large voting blocs in populous states with large chunks of electoral votes, such as in California, Texas, and Florida.

At the outset of the election campaign, Reagan appeared vulnerable to charges that Reaganomics unfairly favored the rich and hurt working-class and poor people. His Middle East policy had failed in Lebanon, and 241 Marines had lost their lives. His Central American policy was controversial, and the Soviets had broken off arms control talks. There had been several scandals involving administration members in conflict-of-interest cases. But the elderly incumbent mounted a buoyant and an energetic campaign. His reelection bid was well financed, and it employed slick television commercials that emphasized the restoration of the national economy and national pride, while avoiding specific issues. His commercials stressed the themes of redemption, family values, and patriotism. His chief speech writer, Peggy Noonan, wrote the best line of his campaign: "America is back; it's morning again." Garry Wills suggested that Reagan's popularity derived from nostalgia, from a popular yearning for a sense of restoration of a lost community.

Reagan also was helped significantly by what Democratic Congresswoman Pat Schroeder had grumpily called the "Teflon presidency": the public and most of the established media did not hold Reagan personally accountable for his policy failures or for wrongdoing by members of his administration. For the duration of the 1984 campaign, it almost appeared as though the American people and the media were determined to enjoy a successful, popular presidency, no matter what, after so many scandals and so many failures. Reagan, especially during his first term, probably enjoyed the most favorable press of any modern president. As journalist Bill Moyers observed, Americans voted for Reagan because they wanted "to feel good."

Mondale tried to focus his campaign on issues, but he never found one that enabled him to cut the president's huge lead. Public opinion polls showed that voters disapproved of many of Reagan's specific policies but that they were voting for him because they liked and trusted him. Given world and national conditions, probably no Democrat could have beaten Reagan in 1984. Mondale also hurt whatever slim chance he might have had to win by announcing bluntly to American voters at the outset of his campaign that he intended to raise taxes if he won. Given the anathema with which American voters viewed taxes, such candor amounted to committing political hari-kari. Polls showed that most Americans believed that they were better of economically in 1984 than they had been in 1980, and that they were pleased to find the nation at peace. Compounding Mondale's problems, he came across poorly on television. His droopy-eyed appearance and the nasal twang in his voice projected negativism and pessimism. In contrast, Reagan, the Great Communicator, exuded energy, goodwill, and unrelentingly cheerful optimism.

In defeat, the Democrats made history twice. First, Jesse Jackson, the first serious African-American candidate for president, conducted a spirited primary campaign, getting 18 percent of the vote and winning 373 delegates to the Democratic Convention. Second,

Figure 13.5   The Democratic Party made history in 1984 when it chose Geraldine Ferraro, a member of Congress, as its first female vice-presidential candidate.
Source: AP/Wide World Photos.

Mondale's running mate, Representative Geraldine Ferraro, the first woman vice-presidential candidate on a major party ticket, conducted a historic campaign. But their candidacies proved to be ideas whose time had not yet come. Ferraro was on the defensive during much of her campaign because of her inexperience, because of her violations of campaign spending laws, and because of her husband's questionable business practices. She neither strengthened a weak Democratic ticket nor enabled Mondale to exploit the "gender gap." Jackson's campaign proved too radical and divisive. His associations with Black Muslims and his anti-Semitic remarks alienated many liberal and Jewish voters. Jackson's promised "rainbow coalition" of all disadvantaged Americans failed to congeal, and his political base never reached much beyond the African-American community.

BIBLIOGRAPHY

A sizable historical and journalistic literature has already accumulated for the 1980s. F. Clifton White, in *Why Reagan Won: A Narrative History of the Conservative Movement, 1964–1981,* tells the story of the conservative movement from the Goldwater debacle to Reagan's successful bid for the presidency in 1980. Haynes Johnson, in *Sleepwalking through History: America in the Reagan Years,* offers a critical account of the Reagan era. The most informed account of the Reagan presidency is Lou Cannon's *President Reagan: The Role of a Lifetime.* President Reagan has written a substantial memoir, *An American Life.* A fine recent study, Stephen Vaughn's *Ronald Reagan in Hollywood: Movies and Politics,* explores the important relationships between Reagan's film and political careers. Two important books that interpret the public career of Ronald Reagan are Garry Wills's *Reagan's America: Innocents at Home* and Michael P. Rogin's *Ronald Reagan: The Movie.* A good account of the early years of the Reagan presidency is Laurence I. Barrett's *Gambling with History: Reagan in the White House.* P. C. Roberts, in *The Supply-Side Revolution,* defends Reaganomics. T. B. Edsall, in *The New Politics of Inequality,* challenges the president's economic policies. Strobe Talbott's *Deadly Gambit* is a lucid, fascinating analysis of the arcane complexities of arms control. Edward N. Luttwack, in *Making the Military Work,* offers a critical study of 1980s' military policies. *Central America: Anatomy of Conflict,* by R. S. Leiken, ed., contains useful studies of that important region. *Visions of America* is a lively account of the 1984 election. Edmund Morris has written a creative biography of Reagan using fictive devices to illuminate the "inner man." It is titled *Dutch: A Memoir of Ronald Reagan.*

14

Thawing the Cold War

Coming off of his landslide victory over the hapless Democratic challenger, Ronald Reagan was at the apogee of his power and popularity as he began his second term. The old actor rode tall in the saddle in January 1985 as his second term got underway. His situation could be compared to the great Franklin Roosevelt's in 1937 and the revered Dwight Eisenhower's in 1957, when they had begun their second terms following landslide victories over opponents who realistically had no chance of defeating such popular incumbents.

Working with the Democratic leadership in Congress, the Reagan administration had significant domestic legislative achievements. The most significant was the enactment of the 1986 Tax Reform Act, the first complete overhaul of the modern income system since its inception during World War II. The immigration system was reformed, easing some of the problems caused by the millions of illegal immigrants who were residing within the United States. The Reagan administration was not very responsive to the AIDS epidemic, and its much publicized war on drugs failed miserably.

The U.S. economy continued its strong performance during Reagan's second term. Inflation remained under control, and oil supplies were plentiful. The economy maintained its strong growth rate, averaging 3 percent to 4 percent per annum and generating millions of new jobs. The Great Bull Market of the 1980s roared on; stocks continued their climb to record levels. Many U.S. corporations enjoyed record sales and profits. Despite its overall strong performance, serious problems continued to plague the economy. Annual federal budget deficits were huge and growing larger. During Reagan's presidency the national debt tripled, from $1 trillion to $3 trillion! Annual trade deficits also rapidly expanded. Most worrisome was the growing inequality of American life. Differentials between upper-income families and lower-income families widened. The rich grew richer, and the poor grew poorer.

During his second term, Reagan had to face many serious international problems. Global financial crises threatened as several Third World nations sank ever deeper into debt. International terrorism was a growing problem. The most important foreign policy achievement of the Reagan presidency was the thawing of the Cold War. The signing of a nuclear arms control treaty and the return of cordial relations with the Soviet Union were the high points of the old Cold Warrior's second term.

THE SECOND TERM

President Reagan began his second term in January 1985, convinced that most Americans endorsed both his domestic and foreign policies. He was determined to provide more of the same. He also reorganized his White House staff with not entirely happy results. His capable Chief of Staff James Baker switched jobs with Secretary of Treasury Donald Regan. Regan never developed the rapport with the president that Baker had enjoyed, nor did he have the ability to compensate for or protect Reagan from his shortcomings as had Baker. Two other personal advisers also departed: Michael Deaver and Edwin Meese who, along with Baker, had formed a "Troika" that was responsible for much of the Reagan presidency's legislative successes during the first term. Deaver went into business for himself. He formed a public relations firm to cash in on his White House connections and promptly ran afoul of laws forbidding influence peddling. Meese became Attorney General of the United States, where he succeeded in establishing the lowest ethical and legal standards for the nation's top law enforcement office since the days of Warren G. Harding. Meese was in continual conflict with Congress because of some of his unsavory associations and because of the slipshod manner in which he handled his personal finances. Both Deaver's and Meese's activities contributed to what became known as the "sleaze factor" in the Reagan presidency, especially during the second term.

President Reagan made tax reform his top legislative priority. The federal tax system had become exceedingly complex over the years as Congress had factored in many exemptions and loopholes favoring corporations and wealthy individual taxpayers. Polls showed strong popular support for revising a tax structure that former President Carter had called a "disgrace to the human race" and Reagan had termed "un-American."

Bipartisan support for tax revision gradually emerged in Congress, led by Democratic Congressman Daniel Rostenkowski, Republican Senator Robert Packwood, and Democratic Senator Bill Bradley. In the summer of 1986, Congress passed the Tax Reform Act that brought with it the first fundamental overhaul of the modern federal income tax system since its inception during World War II. The tax reform law was the most important domestic accomplishment of Reagan's second term. The act simplified the tax code by eliminating many tax shelters and deductions. It reduced multiple tax brackets on individuals to just three, at rates of 15, 28, and 33 percent. It also restored a measure of fairness to a tax system that had long been skewed in favor of the wealthy. It removed 6 million low-income Americans from the federal tax rolls and lowered the tax burden for a majority of taxpayers. The new law shifted some of the tax burden to the business community by closing loopholes and eliminating write-offs and exemptions. Many corporations that had paid little or no federal income tax would pay more under the new law. The Tax Reform Act represented another triumph for supply-side economics. President Reagan predicted that lower taxes would translate into greater consumer spending, expanded productivity, and greater prosperity. Critics predicted that the tax law would hurt business enterprise and slow economic growth.

Reagan shared in another major achievement when his administration supported a landmark immigration bill passed by Congress in October 1986. The bill revamped the 1965 act by offering legal status to millions of aliens living illegally in the United States. It also required employers to ask for identification verifying the citizenship of job applicants, and it levied fines on employers who hired illegal aliens. This legislation appeared to help solve some of the most pressing problems posed by the inability of the nation to police its borders effectively and to control the immigration process.

Despite his continuing popularity and despite some legislative successes during his second term, President Reagan failed to accomplish one of the major goals of the resurgent conservative movement—a realignment of the nation's major political parties. During the midterm elections, held in November 1986, the Democrats regained control of the Senate and increased their already large majority in the House of Representatives. The new Democrat-controlled Congress that convened in January 1987 had the votes to prevent any further cuts in social spending and refused to vote for additional increases in military spending. The new Congress also proved unresponsive to repeated efforts by the Reagan administration to get it to enact his conservative social agenda, particularly constitutional amendments banning abortion and permitting prayer in public schools. In spite of their successes in capturing the White House, Republicans remained the minority party nationally. In 1987, Democrats controlled Congress, two-thirds of state legislatures, and a majority of state governorships, and Democratic mayors and other locally elected officials outnumbered Republican officeholders by a 3 to 1 margin nationally.

An urgent problem that Reagan was slow to respond to was the AIDS epidemic, which swept the country during the mid-1980s. This hideous illness, for which there was no cure nor even an immunizing agent, believed by many experts to be invariably fatal to all who contracted the virus, each year killed thousands of mostly gay males all across the nation. For years the administration refused to even publicly acknowledge the disease, and it was, at least in the eyes of those most concerned about fighting AIDS, painfully slow to support increased research and study of the dread illness. Administration officials mainly called for mandatory testing of categories of people thought to be at risk or who held positions of public responsibility. Meanwhile, the disease continued to wreak devastation and blight the lives of the vulnerable. AIDS threatened to become a worldwide epidemic, and it struck the people of several Central and East African nations with special fury.

A serious health problem that Reagan showed more interest in was the growing epidemic of drug use in America. He came to Washington in 1981 committed to waging a war on drugs and to bringing the international drug trade under control. Drug traffic in marijuana, cocaine, and heroin flourished in the mid-1980s. The United States was the world's major consumer of illicit drugs. The immense costs of America's gargantuan drug habit included thousands of deaths annually, health problems for millions, huge increases in urban crime, corruption in the criminal justice system, and loss of productivity. Efforts to enforce drug laws and American-financed efforts to eradicate drug crops at their source in Asia and Latin America continued to be ineffective. One of the major reasons for the failure of the Reagan administration's war against drugs, popularized by First Lady Nancy Reagan, was its inability to slow the great American appetite for drugs. All efforts to curtail the supply of drugs were doomed to fail until a measure of control could be imposed on the demand.

After years of activity and having spent $3 billion, Reagan announced early in 1988 that the war against drugs had been won. His claim was preposterous; all of the evidence confuted his claim. According to contemporary surveys, 25 million Americans regularly used marijuana, 6 million regularly used cocaine (particularly "crack" cocaine), and another 1 million were heroin addicts. Public opinion polls showed that Americans considered the drug epidemic the nation's number one domestic problem. The federal policy of criminalizing drug use and interdicting the supply either at the source or at the point of entry into this country was failing as the Reagan presidency ended. Some experts suggested that an alternative policy that focused on educating people, especially young people, about the hazards of drug use, one that relied on therapies, counseling, and community support groups to wean people from drug dependencies, promised better results over the long term.

THE "GO-GO" ECONOMY

The U.S. economy continued to perform strongly through the second term of Reagan's presidency. Inflation remained under control and oil supplies were plentiful; indeed, world oil markets were glutted. When inflation and higher taxes were taken into account, motorists were filling their tanks with cheap and plentiful gasoline. Growth rates averaged 3 percent to 4 percent per annum; many corporations enjoyed record sales and profits, and they continually expanded production. Millions of new jobs were created. The stock market continued to push through record highs, as the Great Bull Market of the 1980s roared on. Consumer spending and consumer confidence remained high.

Despite its continuing strong performance, serious problems continued to plague the American economy. Old problems got worse. New problems arose. Sometimes both old and new problems were exacerbated by administration policies and priorities. Individual and corporate indebtedness continued to grow. The corporate takeover mania that gripped Wall Street during the Reagan era also proved worrisome. New tax laws and the Reagan administration's relaxed attitude toward corporate mergers encouraged takeovers. Most of these corporate buyouts were severely "leveraged," that is, they were financed by consortia of bankers and brokerage houses that often sold huge portfolios of "junk bonds" (high-yield, high-risk securities issued by companies with low credit ratings) to raise the vast sums of capital needed to buy out shareholders at above-market prices. Once the corporate raiders acquired operating control of the company, they often had to sell off its profitable assets to raise the sums required to meet the huge interest payments on the indebtedness that they had incurred when they bought out the former stockholders.

These leveraged buyouts (LBOs) did not necessarily make the economy more productive or competitive; indeed, they often left companies weaker and in serious debt with no funds for research and the development of new products. Aggregate net capital investment also was not enhanced by these takeovers and mergers; about the only people who got richer were the lawyers, accountants, and brokers who arranged these multibillion dollar deals. Toward the end of the Reagan era, several investigations exposed some of the financial wizards who had put together corporate takeover deals as criminals who had violated laws against insider trading. The two biggest names were Ivan Boesky and Michael Milken, both of whom served years in jail, paid millions of dollars in fines, and saw their business careers and personal reputations destroyed.

Budget deficits continued to grow, exceeding $200 billion in 1986. During Reagan's presidency, the national debt tripled—from $1 trillion to $3 trillion. By 1989, each American's share of the national debt exceeded $12,000. Paying the interest due annually on the national debt became the third largest item in the federal budget, after Social Security and defense. The massive indebtedness came about as a result of a tacit political arrangement between the Reagan White House and many Democrats in Congress. They had both agreed to support large increases in military spending, modest cuts in social spending, and deep tax cuts.

The national debt became so large during the 1980s that servicing it absorbed a large portion of the net savings accrued by individuals and businesses each year. Pressures on interest rates were somewhat alleviated by the fact that foreign investors, particularly Germans, Japanese, and Saudi Arabians, bought up about 20 percent of the U.S. debt each year. Even so, the U.S. government had to take so much money from the private capital markets to fund the debt each year that funds available for investment in research, product development, new technologies, and increased productive capacity were significantly curtailed. There was a link between the huge federal indebtedness and declining American industrial competitiveness in the world's marketplaces. Both the U.S. government and the private sector had become dependent on large annual infusions of foreign capital.

In December 1985, Congress enacted the Gramm-Rudman Act, a measure that required automatic annual reductions in the budget deficit if the president and Congress failed to agree on cuts. The following year, the Supreme Court nullified the law, and the deficit for 1986 came in at a record $226 billion. Congress then enacted a modified version of Gramm-Rudman, but then the White House and Congressional legislators agreed to accounting procedures that effectively gutted the law. Several large spending programs were declared "off budget" and were not included when figuring the deficit in order to evade Gramm-Rudman limits. The 1987 deficit was somewhat smaller, but it took a record crash of the stock market on October 19, 1987, and fears of impending recession to force Reagan and Congress to try seriously to reduce the budget deficit. They were forced to come up with a combination of proposed spending cuts and tax increases, amounting to $76 billion over two years, a politically painful dose of fiscal medicine for both Republicans and Democrats as the 1988 elections approached.

Trade deficits also had expanded rapidly between 1980 and 1985, as imports increased by 41 percent, while exports decreased slightly. Every week during the Reagan presidency, American consumers spent about $1 billion more buying imported goods than foreigners spent buying American-made products. To offset that imbalance in international trading, huge amounts of American securities, real estate, factories, and other tangible assets were purchased by foreign investors who had to recycle their surplus dollars. By the end of Reagan's presidency, foreign corporations owned American banks, investment houses, fast-food restaurants, motion picture studios, landmark skyscrapers, thousands of acres of farm land, publishing firms, and supermarket chains. U.S. assets in foreign countries totaled less than the U.S. assets owned by foreigners. Until the early 1970s, America had been the world's leading creditor nation. By the end of the Reagan era, America had become one of the world's leading debtors.

Other economic trends alarmed Americans. Increasing numbers of American manufacturing concerns moved their operations overseas to escape from unionized workers and high taxes, and they took thousands of good jobs with them. While some foreigners continued to buy American properties, other foreign competitors steadily increased their share of American domestic markets for autos, electronic products, cameras, textiles, and shoes. Many of these developments reflected a new reality: the economic lives of nations were increasingly intertwined. By the mid-1980s, it was painfully evident that the American economy was intricately plugged in to the world economic system. Henceforth, more and more of the economic and financial activities of Americans would be influenced by decisions made in corporate boardrooms in Tokyo, Riyadh, Hong Kong, and Bonn. But many Americans, who tended to intermingle nationalistic feelings with economic activity, felt threatened by what appeared to them losses of autonomy and signs of relative economic decline.

Another sign of economic and financial trouble in America that surfaced in the late 1980s—disasters in the savings and loan industry—was entirely home grown. To a considerable extent, the savings and loan debacle was an unintended consequence of bipartisan good intentions. Deregulation was a policy idea that was first implemented during the Carter years, in the airline and trucking industries. The Reaganauts embraced and expanded upon deregulation in the name of greater competitiveness and productivity, plus economy in government. Under the influence of supply-side economic theory, federal agencies relaxed or abolished rules and regulations affecting the operations of a wide range of American industries. One of these industries was the savings and loan bank business. Historically, savings and loans (S & Ls) lent money to individuals to buy homes in local areas where the banks were located. Home mortgages tended to be low-risk, low-profit investments. Savings and loans banks were noted for being safe, sound, and a little dull.

At the urging of the Reagan administration, Congress deregulated the savings and loan industry in 1982. Consequently, S & Ls could offer a much wider range of loans; they could invest depositors' funds in commercial real estate, undeveloped land, and just about any kind of high-risk project. They also could lend funds for projects nationally and even internationally. Even if these high-risk operations went bust and the banks collapsed, the existence of the Federal Savings and Loan Insurance Corporation (FSLIC) meant that bankers would not incur personal liabilities and that depositors would get their money back from the government.

In many parts of the nation, especially in the Southwest and West, the new era of deregulation in the S & Ls attracted into the banking industry a generation of incompetent, crooked buccaneers. These morally challenged financiers proceeded to invest billions of dollars of depositors' funds in a bewildering variety of dubious projects, knowing that they might reap huge profits from their high-risk undertakings but that they ran no risk of incurring personal responsibility for any losses because of the existence of the FSLIC. Deregulation of the savings and loan industry eventually reaped a financial holocaust that left the taxpayers of America saddled with a tab that ran into hundreds of billions of dollars.

In California, a real estate speculator, Charles Keating, acquired control of a small savings and loan company headquartered in Orange County called Lincoln Federal Savings and Loan. Keating quickly built Lincoln Savings into a multibillion dollar operation by offering high interest rates to large depositors (the FSLIC insured individual bank accounts up to $100,000) and then investing the money in a series of highly speculative enterprises. He also paid himself lavish salaries and perks; soon Keating was a multimillionaire enjoy-

Figure 14.1   Charles Keating (center) enters federal court for the Lincoln Savings and Loan Association case. Photo by Reuters/Ralph Alswang/Archive Photos.   *Source:* Archive Photos.

ing a princely lifestyle. He also worked various scams on his depositors, including selling them junk bonds that were not covered by the FSLIC, although he wrote misleading letters to them telling them that they were.

Within a few years, Lincoln Savings went bankrupt. Intervention by federal officials might have limited the fallout, but Keating made large contributions to the campaigns of influential senators, including Alan Cranston, California's senior senator and one of the most powerful lawmakers on Capitol Hill. Cranston and other senators persuaded bank examiners to allow Keating to stay in business perhaps a year longer than he might have if the politicians had not interceded on his behalf. Before it shut down, the bankrupt Lincoln Savings accumulated more than $2.7 billion in liabilities. The FSLIC had to pick up the tab for the insured depositors. In two subsequent court trials, Keating was convicted of multiple counts of fraud and conspiracy to commit fraud. He received prison sentences totaling more than twenty years. By the end of the Reagan presidency, over 300 savings and loan banks had failed. The total cost of these bankruptcies to the taxpayers eventually exceeded $200 billion. Taxpayers paid the final installments during the Clinton presidency on one of the worst financial scandals in American history.

Although the economic expansion of the "go-go" years of the 1980s was real and impressive, it also was selective and spotty, excluding large numbers of Americans. The chief regional beneficiaries of the Reagan boom years were the Northeast and California. Both regions were on the cutting edge of the computer revolution, and both had extensive military and aerospace industries. In these areas, good jobs at good salaries abounded; real estate prices for both residential and commercial properties shot upward.

But in the states of the upper Midwest, the site of the traditional smokestack industries, economic conditions deteriorated. Agricultural and energy-producing states also slumped during the 1980s. While the Northeast and West Coast boomed, much of the rest of the country was mired in a decade-long recession. Real wages, adjusted for inflation, continued to stagnate in many parts of the country during the 1980s. In fact, real take-home pay for factory workers declined slightly from 1975 to 1987.

There were other victims of Reaganomics during the 1980s. Revenue sharing with state and local governments, enacted by Richard Nixon in 1972, was cut during the Reagan presidency. Infrastructure repairs to roads and bridges were neglected. Cities, strapped for funds by shrinking tax bases and increasingly needy populations, were especially hard hit by these losses of federal funds. Consequently, essential urban social services deteriorated.

During the 1980s, income differentials between upper-income and lower-income families widened. The number of poor women and children increased. Poverty was increasingly feminized because of a sharp increase in the number of unwed mothers; the rate of children living with a never-married mother increased threefold during the 1980s. By the end of the 1980s, one-fourth of the children born in the United States were born to an unwed mother. The Reagan administration, although not directly responsible for the rapid rise of poor unmarried women with children, made matters worse for them by cutting funds for the Women-Infants-Children program (WIC), which had provided both prenatal and postnatal care to low-income women.

During the 1980s, the poverty rate in America regressed to approximately where it had been in the mid-1960s, about 13 percent. But poverty in America had changed by the mid-1980s. Whereas the elderly had composed a majority of the poor people of America in the mid-1960s, by the mid-1980s, most of the poor consisted of single mothers, children, and young men with meager educational and job skills. A sizable proportion of the 1980s' poor worked full time or part time for minimum wage. Millions of new jobs created during the 1980s were full-time or part-time service-sector jobs that paid only minimum wages.

Homeless people constituted a growing proportion of the 1980s' impoverished population. The homeless, the poorest of the poor, came from many backgrounds: the unemployed, the mentally ill, drug and alcohol abusers, those with serious medical problems (including AIDS), racial minorities, runaways, dysfunctional Vietnam veterans, and women fleeing abusive husbands. Many of the homeless struggled to maintain a precarious existence, living on the streets of large cities and begging for food and money. Sometimes aggressive panhandlers frightened or angered prosperous shoppers as they walked along sidewalks or entered stores. If yuppies represented the glittering successes of the Reagan era, the homeless represented the abject failures. In the new Gilded Age of the late twentieth century, the homeless were the prime victims of recrudescent Social Darwinism. Nobody knew exactly how many homeless there were in America in the 1980s. Estimates ranged from a low of 200,000 to more than 1 million. President Reagan, while expressing his per-

Figure 14.2   Some of the many street people who live on top of the steam vents of the Philadelphia sidewalks, get comfortable for the night. Such street people suffer malnutrition and exposure. The moist air of the vents provides warmth, but also prevents cuts and ulcers from healing, sometimes resulting in gangrene. Photo by Putsy Kennedy. *Source:* AP/Wide World Photos.

sonal sympathy for the plight of the homeless, proposed no new federal programs to alleviate their suffering or to get them off of the streets. What assistance there was for the pathetic armies of the homeless mostly came from local governments, private charities, churches, and compassionate individuals.

THE REAGAN COURT

President Reagan had long opposed most civil rights laws and had supported a constitutional amendment outlawing busing to achieve school integration. The Supreme Court in 1983 blocked attempts by the Justice Department to restore tax benefits to segregated private schools and colleges. When the Voting Rights Act of 1965 came up for renewal, Reagan advised Congress to kill it. Congress renewed it by a large majority.

In the field of civil liberties, Reagan, like most conservatives, believed that the court system had long favored the rights of accused criminals over law-abiding citizens who were often victims of violent crimes. During the 1980s, both Congress and the states, responding to widespread popular concerns, took a stronger law-and-order line. Longer, mandatory sentences were imposed for many crimes. Many states reinstituted the death penalty for heinous crimes. Jail populations rapidly increased, and the construction of new prison facilities lagged behind demand. By the end of the 1980s, over 1 million Americans were incarcerated, the highest rate of incarceration for any country in the Free World.

Over the course of his presidency, Reagan appointed over 400 federal judges; these jurists constituted about 60 percent of all sitting federal judges in 1989. The president also appointed a chief justice and three associate justices to the Supreme Court. The administration searched for strict constructionists whose constitutional views incorporated the right-wing social agenda, including opposition to affirmative action programs, abortion, and pornography. In addition, Reagan wanted jurists who favored harsher penalties for accused criminals. Reaganite judges also were expected to support efforts to restore prayer in the public schools and to favor the death penalty. Most of the 400 Reaganite judges were young or middle-aged white males with conservative judicial philosophies.

The president's appointments to the Supreme Court allowed him to reshape that venerable institution. In 1981, he appointed Sandra Day O'Connor and in 1986 he selected Antonin Scalia as associate justices. Both O'Connor and Scalia were conservatives. Reagan also replaced retiring Chief Justice Warren Burger with Associate Justice William Rehnquist, the most conservative member of the Court. Reagan's efforts to add a third justice to the Supreme Court in July 1987 proved embarrassing to the elderly chief executive. His first nominee, Appellate Judge Robert Bork, was rejected by the Senate because of his extreme views concerning First Amendment rights. Reagan's second choice, Douglas Ginsburg, was forced to withdraw his name from consideration after revealing to the press that he had smoked marijuana while a student and later while teaching at Harvard Law School. Reagan's third choice, Anthony Kennedy, also was a judicial conservative and a popular choice. He was unanimously confirmed by the Senate in February 1988.

Gradually the Reagan appointees on the Supreme Court shifted the tenor of its decisions in a conservative direction. The Reagan Court chipped away at some of the rights of

Figure 14.3   Members of the Supreme Court pose for their portraits Friday, December 3, 1993, in Washington. Standing from left, are: Associate Justices Clarence Thomas, Anthony Kennedy, David Souter, and Ruth Bader Ginsburg. Seated, from left, are: Associate Justices Sandra Day O'Conner, Harry Blackman, Chief Justice William Rehnquist, Associate Justices John Paul Stevens and Antonia Scalia. Photo by Marcy Nighswander.   *Source:* AP/Wide World Photos.

the accused established in previous decisions. For example, the Court now permitted the use of illegally seized evidence in court in some instances. It also undermined affirmative action. In *City of Richmond v. J. A. Croson Company* (1989), the Court nullified a government "set-aside" program that reserved a proportion of government contracts for minority businesses.

FOREIGN POLICY

During his second term, President Reagan had to face many serious international problems. Global financial crises threatened as Third World nations sank ever deeper into debt. The collective debt of Argentina, Brazil, and Mexico approached $250 billion, most of it owed to U.S. and European banks. The possibility of these countries ever repaying their debts in full appeared nil, and default, which could derange international financial transactions and trade, and do serious harm to major U.S. banks, remained a constant danger.

International terrorism was another mounting problem. Between 1981 and 1986, thousands of people were kidnapped, injured, or killed by terrorist attackers. The U.S. State

Department estimated that about 700 major terrorist assaults occurred in the world in 1985. Many terrorists had their roots in the bitter conflicts in Lebanon between Christian and Arab factions and in the continuing battle to the death between Israelis forces and Palestinian fighters. Arab terrorist organizations, dedicated to the destruction of Israel and to attacking its Western supporters, frequently targeted Americans. The slaughter of the U.S. Marines in Beirut in 1983 was the most serious of many Muslim terrorist attacks against Americans. In June 1985, Lebanese Muslim terrorists hijacked an American jetliner and held thirty-nine Americans hostage for seventeen days. In October 1985, four members of the Palestinian Liberation Army seized an Italian cruise ship, the *Achille Lauro,* killing an elderly American in a wheelchair. In April 1986, American military installations in West Germany were bombed by Palestinian terrorists supported by Libya. In retaliation, American bombers attacked targets in and near the Libyan capital of Tripoli. Public opinion within the United States supported the air strike, but most of America's European allies, their citizens often the victims of terrorist assaults and kidnappings, called the bombing counterproductive and likely to provoke further terrorist attacks.

In South Africa, a racist white minority maintained a segregationist rule over black, Asian, and mixed-race people that composed 86 percent of the population. The Reagan administration, following a policy it called "constructive engagement" toward the South African apartheid regime, refrained from public criticism and tried to nudge it toward democracy. The policy produced few positive results, and South Africa was racked by violence in the mid-1980s as government security forces violently repressed black demonstrators. Angry and frustrated blacks retaliated with terrorist attacks of their own.

Critics of "constructive engagement" believed that only economic pressure could force the South African government to dismantle apartheid. Within the United States, fourteen states and forty-one cities passed divestiture laws restricting or prohibiting the investment in South Africa of pension funds and requiring the selling off of current holdings in South African securities. The divestiture issue activated protests on college campuses. Some universities, responding to protests, ordered partial or full divestment. In October 1986, Congress, overriding a presidential veto, imposed strict economic sanctions on South Africa, including a boycott of South African products and a ban on new U.S. loans and investment in that country. A few prominent American corporations voluntarily sold off their South African operations. Within South Africa, acts of civil disobedience and demonstrations, followed by violent reprisals from government security forces, continued during 1987 and 1988.

The Reagan administration also had to confront a crisis in the Philippines, the former Pacific colony and longtime ally of the United States. For several years, a corrupt military dictator, Ferdinand Marcos, whom the United States had supported, had been losing power. Communist rebels were gaining strength in several regions of the country. Pressure from U.S. officials forced Marcos to permit elections that had been suspended since he took office. In February 1986, he was challenged by Corazon Aquino, the widow of an assassinated political opponent of Marcos. Both sides claimed victory in an election marked by violence and fraud. American officials, worried about the declining Philippine economy and the rising Communist insurgency in a strategically important country, pressured Marcos to resign. He fled Manila in March 1986, and Aquino assumed office. She worked to restore political democracy, to revamp the economy, to maintain friendly relations with the United States, and to remove the threat of Communist insurgency. During her first two years of power, Aquino had succeeded in restoring political democracy, and the economy was growing after years of stagnation. But she had to survive two right-wing coup attempts led by army elements wanting to restore Marcos to power. The Communist insurgency was growing, and American military personnel stationed in the Philippines were attacked.

THE IRAQI-IRANIAN WAR

The continuing Iraqi-Iranian War reached menacing proportions in 1987. After six years of fighting that claimed nearly 2 million lives, the stalemated war spilled into the Persian Gulf and threatened vital oil shipments that flowed daily from Gulf oil fields to Europe, Japan, and the United States. Iraq attacked Iran's oil-export terminals and also struck Iranian tankers carrying oil from the Gulf. Iran could not strike Iraqi oil shipments directly, because Iraq's oil traveled through pipelines to terminals on the Mediterranean Sea and Black Sea, but the Iranians undertook reprisals by attacking ships hauling oil from Kuwait, a small, oil-rich Arab emirate that was bankrolling Iraq's war against Iran.

Soviet entry into the Gulf, along with both Iraqi and Iranian threats to the shipment of oil in the Gulf, caused President Reagan to send a large fleet of U.S. Navy vessels to the region and to provide naval escorts for oil convoys. In what amounted to armed intervention into the shipping war, the United States agreed to reflag and escort tankers carrying oil produced by Kuwait. In the summer of 1987, the *Stark,* a U.S. guided missile frigate on station in the Gulf, was attacked, apparently by accident, by an Iraqi plane, with the loss of thirty-eight lives. Then, on July 3, 1988, there occurred an even more ghastly accident when a U.S. cruiser, the *Vincennes,* fired a missile that brought down an Iranian airliner, killing all 290 people aboard. Radar operators aboard the American destroyer misidentified the airliner; they thought that it was an Iranian fighter closing in on their ship for an attack.

The United States feared that a victory by either Saddam Hussein's secular Iraqi regime or Khomeini's Islamic fundamentalist Iranian government would make the winner the dominant power in the Middle East. To prevent either side from winning the war—a victory that could threaten the political stability of Saudi Arabia, Kuwait, and other moderate Arab regimes and disrupt the flow of oil to the United States and its allies—the United States, behind an official facade of neutrality, secretly aided whichever side appeared to be losing. In the early years of the war, Washington helped the Iranians, but after 1986, the United States backed Saddam Hussein. There had been several incidents involving attacks on merchant shipping by Iranian speedboats, and several ships had been damaged by mines lain by Iranians. American ships and helicopter gunships had retaliated for some of the Iranian attacks, sinking speedboats and damaging an Iranian oil platform in the Gulf. In April 1988, there occurred a series of clashes between American and Iranian naval units. As a consequence of American intervention in the Persian Gulf, Iran and the United States were engaged in a small-scale, undeclared naval war.

The Iraqi-Iranian War ended suddenly in August 1988, when Ayatollah Khomeini accepted a UN-proposed cease-fire. At the time, Iraq had gained the upper hand, and Iranian enthusiasm for war had subsided after six years of slaughter. Although he had seized the initiative in the lengthy, brutal struggle, Saddam Hussein, weary of the long war, readily consented to the cease-fire. Mutual exhaustion after years of bloodletting had brought about an end to the war; neither side, however, was prepared to abandon the conflicting territorial claims that had provoked the war. During the war, the Iraqis had used poison gas against the Iranians and were feverishly at work developing nuclear weapons. Despite these ominous indicators, the Reagan administration continued to back Iraq, considering that country a necessary counterforce to the Iranian threat. U.S. support of Hussein in the late 1980s would be one of the background causes of the 1991 Persian Gulf War.

As the war between Iraq and Iran ground to a close, the interminable Arab–Israeli conflict took a violent turn. Palestinians living in the West Bank and in Gaza took to the streets to protest continuing Israeli occupation of the two territories. Roving bands of Palestinian youths, armed with rocks and Molotov cocktails, clashed with Israeli army squads. This Palestinian *intifidah* ("uprising") continued intermittently through 1988 and 1989, resulting in the deaths of hundreds of Palestinians and perhaps a dozen Israeli soldiers. The Israeli government, headed by Prime Minister Yitzhak Shamir, refused to consider any resolution of the conflict that would establish a Palestinian state in the territories. He also refused to meet with Yasir Arafat and the PLO, the only organization that represented a majority of the Palestinians. The Reagan administration backed the Shamir government's refusal to meet with PLO leaders, but it did favor some kind of political arrangement in the occupied territories that would give the Palestinians limited autonomy.

CENTRAL AMERICA

The Reagan administration continued its support of the Contra rebels fighting to overthrow Nicaragua's Sandinista regime. In the summer of 1985, Congress narrowly approved $100 million in support of the Contras. The administration's policy continued to draw criticism from the media and from liberal Democrats in Congress. Public opinion polls showed a majority of Americans opposed to Contra aid and fearful that U.S. troops would be sent to fight the Sandinistas if the Contra rebels failed. Meanwhile, the intermittent, low-intensity civil war continued.

A peaceful alternative to civil war in Nicaragua surfaced late in 1987, when President Oscar Arias Sanchez of Costa Rica, speaking for the leaders of four Central American republics meeting in Guatemala City, proposed a plan calling for an end to U.S. military backing of the Contras, the restoration of democracy in Nicaragua, and negotiations between the Sandinista government and Contra leaders leading to a cease-fire. Arias was awarded the 1987 Nobel Peace Prize for his efforts to end the war. Reagan administration officials expressed a willingness to let Arias try to implement his plan, and Nicaraguan leader Daniel Ortega Saavedra appeared willing to accept some of the proposals. In April 1988, both sides agreed to a temporary cease-fire, and Congress voted for $48 million in humanitarian aid for the Contras. In nearby El Salvador, efforts to begin negotiations between the Duarte government and the Marxist rebels continued to fail, and the civil war in that impoverished, tormented country went on.

THE IRAN-CONTRA SCANDAL

President Reagan's personal popularity remained high throughout the first half of his second term. Public opinion polls showed that most Americans remained optimistic about their own and their nation's prospects and that they strongly endorsed Reagan's style of presidential leadership. But two weeks after the midterm elections in the fall of 1986, the worst political scandal since Watergate erupted in Washington. Americans were shocked to learn that the Reagan administration had entered into secret negotiations with Iranian officials. These negotiations had led to deals that involved selling them arms in exchange for the release of American hostages held captive in Lebanon by pro-Iranian Muslim terrorists. Two weeks after Americans had learned of the arms-for-hostages deals with Iran, Attorney General Edwin Meese told a stunned press conference audience that his investigators had discovered that profits from the Iranian arms sales had been sent to Contra rebels fighting in Nicaragua, even though Congress had enacted legislation forbidding American military aid to the rebel fighters.

At a hastily called press conference, President Reagan gamely denied that U.S. arms had been traded to Iran for hostages. He insisted that a relatively low-level operative with the National Security Council, Marine Lieutenant Colonel Oliver North, was mainly responsible for both the dealings with Iran and the Contra arms sales, and that only North's immediate superior, a national security adviser, Vice Admiral John Poindexter, knew of his activities. Reagan's statements were simply not credible. For the first time in his presidency, his integrity and competence were seriously questioned by the citizenry. His public approval rating dropped precipitously, from 67 percent to 46 percent.

The origins of the Iran-Contra scandals went back to 1981, when President Reagan ordered CIA director William Casey to organize an anti-Sandinista force among Nicaraguan exiles living in Honduras. Over the next several years, these forces, called Contras, waged a guerrilla war against the Sandinista forces. The U.S. Congress, concerned about reports that the Contras had killed many civilians within Nicaragua and had also sown mines in Nicaraguan harbors, damaging merchant ships belonging to other countries, enacted the Boland Amendment. The Boland Amendment limited U.S. aid to the Contras to $24 million and forbade the use of any U.S. funds for the purpose of trying to overthrow the Sandinista government, a government that the United States officially recognized.

Reagan, passionately committed to the goal of overthrowing the Sandinistas and, in his view, eliminating a Communist threat to Central America, and contemptuous of the Democrat-controlled Congress, instructed the CIA, the National Security Council, and the Pentagon to circumvent Congressional restrictions on aiding the Contra forces. In the summer of 1984, Congress, responding to the Reagan administration's efforts to continue its clandestine proxy war in Nicaragua, tightened the Boland Amendment. It forbade the CIA or any other U.S. government agency from aiding the Contras.

The tighter version of the Boland Amendment failed to deter the president and his men. Casey, National Security Adviser Robert McFarlane, and one of McFarlane's aides, Marine Lieutenant Colonel Oliver North, persuaded a handful of American allies to provide funds for the Contras. Nations contributing monetary support for the rebels included Israel, South Africa, Saudi Arabia, South Korea, and Taiwan. At the same time they raised funds from U.S. allies for the Contra cause, Casey, North, and others also solicited additional funds from wealthy American citizens to support the rebels.

While President Reagan and his subordinates were circumventing the will of Congress and violating the Boland Amendment by continuing the war in Nicaragua, which Congress was trying to stop and for which there was little popular support in the United States, the administration also began an involvement with Iran aimed at freeing U.S. hostages being held in Lebanon by pro-Iranian Muslim terrorists. President Reagan was personally concerned with freeing the hostages, and he had been deeply moved when the families of seven American citizens held hostage in Lebanon had pleaded with him to arrange for the release of their loved ones. Reagan also was aware of the major political dividends that would accrue to him and to the Republican Party in the upcoming elections if he could somehow get the hostages home.

In July 1985, Iranian arms dealer Manucher Ghobanifar met with McFarlane. Ghobanifar claimed to represent a moderate faction within the Iranian government that wanted to improve relations with the United States. He proposed to McFarlane that the United States, working through Israeli middlemen, arrange for the delivery to Iran of TOW antitank missiles, which the Iranians desperately needed in their ongoing war with Iraq. In return, the moderates in the Iranian government would work to arrange the release of some of the American hostages. A few months later, President Reagan authorized the sale of 100 TOW missiles to Iran in an effort to obtain the release of some of the hostages. At the time that he authorized the sale of the weapons, Reagan understood that the United States was trading arms for hostages. He also knew that it was against the law and contrary to U.S. policy, which he had publicly affirmed, to sell weapons to Iran because of its support of international terrorism.

But no hostages were freed after this transaction. Ghobanifar told McFarlane that the Iranians wanted an additional 400 missiles in exchange for the release of a single hostage. McFarlane arranged for the missiles to be sent, and on September 15, 1986, one of the American hostages, Benjamin Weir, was set free. In November, Ghobanifar was back with another deal: send Iran 100 HAWK surface-to-air missiles and five American hostages would be freed. In December, President Reagan signed a secret document, called a finding, which approved and justified the proposed sale. The finding described the transaction as an arms-for-hostages deal. At the time the deal was made, Oliver North wrote a memorandum equating the 100 HAWK missiles to the five American hostages that were supposed to be released, but no hostages were released.

Even though the several arms sales to Iran had yielded only one released hostage, Reagan's enthusiasm for the project remained undiminished. Admiral Poindexter, who replaced McFarlane as National Security Adviser in December 1985, working through North, arranged for another shipment of arms to Iran. This time 3,000 TOW missiles and another 100 HAWK missiles would be sent in exchange for the remaining six Americans still held captive by terrorists in Lebanon. Both Secretary of State George Schultz and Secretary of Defense Caspar Weinberger opposed the arms-for-hostages transactions because they were illegal, because they were contrary to stated U.S. foreign policy, and because they did not serve the national interest. Vice President George Bush, although not a major player in the transactions, attended several meetings at which the arms-for-hostages deals were discussed. Bush never gave any indication that he opposed them.

Oliver North came up with the plan to divert the profits from the sale of arms to the Iranians to the Contras. Did President Reagan direct North to send the money to the Contras? Reagan later could not remember if he had approved the funds; Poindexter testified that the president ordered North to use the money to buy arms for the Contras. In February 1986, a sale of 1,000 TOW missiles to the Iranians netted a profit of about $8 million. North gave the money to a retired air force major general, Richard Secord, to buy arms for the Contras. No hostages were released; in fact, two more Americans in Lebanon were taken hostage. After at least four arms shipments to the Iranians, more Americans than ever were held hostage. But Reagan's enthusiasm for the cause remained undiminished. On July 26, Iran arranged for the release of another American hostage, Lawrence Jenco, a Catholic priest. Another shipment of missiles was sent to Iran, but it resulted in no further prisoners being freed. On November 2, just before the midterm elections, a final arms shipment was sent to Iran through Israeli middlemen, which produced the release of another hostage, David Jacobsen. But all of the arms deals with the Iranians did not net the Reagan administration its hoped-for political boost. Instead, the sales generated a serious Election Eve political crisis for the president and his men.

The cover on the bizarre secret schemes was blown in late October and early November. On October 5, 1986, a plane hauling weapons to the Contras was shot down by the Sandinistas, and they captured an aircrewman, American Eugene Hasenfus. Hasenfus confessed to his captors that he was part of a secret American program to aid the Contras. On November 1, the Lebanese magazine *Al Shiraa* ran a story about the U.S. arms-for-hostages deals with Iran. Iranian officials quickly confirmed the story and told the world that the so-called moderates were agents of the Khomeini government. The Iranians bragged that they had tricked the Americans into selling them modern weapons that were urgently needed for their war against the Iraqis. Three weeks later, Edwin Meese made his stunning announcement that money from the sale of arms to Iran had been diverted to the Contra war effort against the Sandinistas.

In some ways, the fallout from the Iran-Contra scandal was worse than Watergate. It severely damaged U.S. foreign policy. The American policy of taking a hard line against terrorism had been exposed as hypocritical. The Saudis and other moderate Arab states felt an acute sense of betrayal over the news that U.S. officials had sold antitank and antiaircraft missiles to Khomeini's government in the hope of securing the release of seven Americans being held hostage in Lebanon by groups of Islamic fundamentalists controlled by Teheran. At home, conducting a clandestine foreign policy in Central America against the express wishes of Congress, a policy contrary to public opinion and in violation of federal law weakened Reagan's ability to govern effectively. The essence of the Iran-Contra scandal involved officials high in the Reagan administration selling weapons to an outlaw regime to raise money used for illegal purposes. Constitutional scholars realized that an important principle was at stake. By circumventing the congressional ban on aid to the Contras, the architects of the Iran-Contra scandal had also circumvented Article I of the U.S. Constitution, which vested all control over appropriating public moneys in Congress. Following the Iran-Contra disclosures, Reagan's chances of getting his legislative program through the Democrat-controlled Congress were sharply reduced. The Iran-Contra scandal badly wounded the Reagan presidency, eroding both its power and popularity.

In the aftermath of the scandalous revelations about trading arms for hostages and aiding the Contras, there were several official investigations of their details. A federal court appointed an Independent Counsel to investigate the scandal. President Reagan appointed a commission headed by former Senator John Tower to investigate the affair. Congress also appointed committees to investigate the scandals. The Tower Commission's report was made public in March 1987. It portrayed Reagan as an out-of-touch president who had surrounded himself with irresponsible advisers pursuing ideologically driven policies that hurt the national interest. It charged Reagan with pursuing policies that ran counter to his promise to be tough on terrorists and with undermining the nation's power and prestige.

Reagan responded on March 4 with a speech to the American people in which he tried to restore his faltering hold on events. He acknowledged responsibility for the Iran-Contra scandal, but he insisted that it was not his intent to trade arms for hostages and that he knew nothing about using some of the money obtained from Iran to buy arms for the Contras. In effect, he denied all responsibility for any wrongdoing by admitting that he did not know what was going on within his own administration. He was forced to plead a fool's defense to avoid being branded a knave. Reagan's speech neither improved his image nor enabled him to regain the political initiative.

Following the Tower Commission's report, the combined Congressional committees began holding televised hearings that ran through the summer of 1987. At times, the hearings evoked memories of the Watergate scandals, as Congressmen tried to follow the money trail, to find out how the profits from arms sales to Iran were channeled to the Contras, and to find out who profited from all of these bizarre transactions.

Two of the witnesses appearing before the committees, retired Air Force Major General Richard Secord, who had been recruited by Colonel North to run the Contra weapons supply system, and former National Security Adviser Robert McFarlane, who had arranged the arms sales to Iran, both implicated the President in their testimony. They insisted that Reagan was repeatedly briefed about the arms sales to Iran and that he approved of the efforts to get the hostages released. They also implicated CIA Director William Casey, who had just died and who may have been the mastermind behind the Iran-Contra operations. Casey may have worked through Colonel North and Vice Admiral Poindexter to avoid Congressional oversight and public disclosure as required by law. The two key witnesses to appear before the Committee, Colonel North and Admiral Poindexter, both insisted that they had kept President Reagan uninformed about the details of the Iranian negotiations and that they never told him about the government's involvement in shipping arms to the Contras. They also admitted that they had deliberately misinformed Congress and the press about their actions—actions that they believed served the national interest and accorded with the President's wishes. The flamboyant, unrepentant North was clearly the star of the televised hearings. He passionately defended his actions as moral and patriotic, even if they did defy Congress and break the law.

The Committee hearings were seriously flawed. They were hastily conducted, and investigators lacked crucial documents that would have enabled them to get to more of the truth about the Iran-Contra scandals. Key witnesses lied or gave evasive answers. The investigating committees clearly did not have the stomach to press their investigations too close to Reagan, nor to consider the possibility of impeaching him, even though there was

Figure 14.4   Lt. Col. Oliver North. Photo by Lana Harris.   *Source:* AP/Wide World Photos.

considerable evidence suggesting that he had knowingly and deliberately broken laws. The Congressmen and Senators knew that most Americans could not care less whether funds from arms sales were diverted to aid the Contras. While resenting the arms sale to Iran, many Americans also could see Reagan's good intentions; he was trying to free the hostages, even if the means chosen were dubious. The lawmakers also feared political reprisals at the hands of the people if they stood guilty once again of regicide. Besides, there was no "smoking gun" in the Iran-Contra scandal that irrefutably implicated the President. Liberals, who were most outraged by the scandal, given their low estimations of Reagan, found his defense plausible. They could believe that he really was an out-of-it, aging former actor who did not know what was going on inside of his own administration.

The committees issued a joint 450-page report on November 18, 1987, that was scathingly critical of the President. It bluntly accused Reagan of not obeying his oath to uphold the Constitution and the laws of the land, and it said that he bore "the ultimate responsibility" for the wrongdoing of his aides. The Congressional report also provided the most accurate accounting to date of how nearly $48 million raised from the arms sales had been distributed. In a sweeping criticism of the officials involved, the report stated that the

Iran-Contra affair was "characterized by pervasive dishonesty and inordinate secrecy." It also voiced the suspicion that the President knew more about the arms sales and Contra funding efforts than he acknowledged. It also challenged the credibility of Colonel North's and Vice Admiral Poindexter's testimony. Without citing specific individual actions or naming specific laws, the report asserted that "laws were broken" in the Iran-Contra affair. The report concluded that the President's protestations of ignorance could not absolve him from responsibility, because the scandal had occurred on his watch.

Coming a year after the original revelations, the report failed to elicit much public interest. White House spokesmen dismissed the report as containing nothing new. But the Iran-Contra revelations had severely damaged Reagan's presidency and his personal reputation. They also seriously crippled his crusade to overthrow the Sandinistas. Public opinion polls revealed that a majority of Americans believed that the president knew about the government's involvement in the Contra arms shipments, and President Reagan's popularity ratings remained far lower than they had been before the news of the scandal had broken.

In March 1988, the independent counsel, Lawrence Walsh, issued grand jury indictments to North, Poindexter, Secord, and several others involved in the Iran-Contra scandals. All were charged with multiple offenses, including conspiracy, fraud, theft, perjury, and covering up illegal operations. At his trial in 1990, Poindexter repudiated his testimony previously given before the combined congressional committees. He stated that President Reagan was in charge of the Iran-Contra operations from the beginning and that he had ordered him, North, and others to break the law.

Former President Reagan was called to testify at Poindexter's trial. In answers to 127 questions addressed to him, Reagan frequently gave confused and vague answers, and often he could not remember the names of subordinates or their activities. He insisted that he was not involved in any wrongdoing and that he did not know what his subordinates were doing when they traded arms for hostages or diverted the profits to the Contras. It was a humiliating performance by Reagan who, some observers believed, exhibited early signs of Alzheimer's disease, which he later contracted. Poindexter was convicted of five felonies, including perjury. Oliver North was convicted of obstructing Congress and of destroying confidential documents. The trials of the Iran-Contra conspirators concluded this shabby episode that marred the reputation and undermined the popularity of Ronald Reagan during his final two years in office.

THE SLEAZE FACTOR

While Iran-Contra investigations raised troubling questions about the integrity and competence of high government figures, other scandals rocked the Reagan administration. In December 1987, former White House adviser Michael Deaver, who operated a political consulting service, was convicted on three counts of perjury for denying that he improperly used his White House connections to help clients. In February 1988, Attorney General Edwin Meese became the latest in a long line of Reagan administration officials to be accused of conflict-of-interest activities and improper conduct. The charges against

Meese stemmed from his alleged financial relations with a small company that had received a defense contract. He came under further attack for his alleged awareness of a proposal to bribe Israeli officials to guarantee that Israeli armed forces would not attack a planned oil pipeline construction project in the Middle East. Further problems for Meese developed at the Justice Department, when several top officials resigned in April 1988 because they feared that Meese's mounting problems prevented him from exerting strong leadership of the department and also hindered several ongoing Justice Department operations. Despite his troubles and declining credibility, Meese continued to enjoy the support of President Reagan, who gave his longtime friend and adviser a strong vote of confidence.

On top of these revelations of wrongdoing and improprieties at high levels in the White House came the incredible disclosure in 1988 through the memoirs of Donald Regan, Reagan's former chief of staff, that the President had permitted his wife Nancy, after she had consulted with an astrologer, to influence his scheduling. Journalists wrote of a "sleaze factor" pervading the administration. By the end of Reagan's presidency, allegations of illegal and unethical activities tarnished the reputations of more than 100 White House officials.

Reagan administration officials were by no means the only politicians plagued by scandal in 1987 and 1988. The leading contender for the Democratic presidential nomination, Gary Hart, had to abandon his campaign for seven months when a newspaper reporter disclosed that Hart had spent an adulterous weekend with a woman, an attractive fashion model. When Hart belatedly reentered the race in 1988, he found that he had lost all of his organization and most of his popular support. He soon gave up his now hopeless candidacy. Another Democratic presidential hopeful, Senator Joseph Biden of Delaware, had to withdraw when reporters learned that he had frequently plagiarized the speeches of other politicians and falsified his academic record.

THAWING THE COLD WAR

During President Reagan's second term, both the United States and the Soviet Union urgently needed to stabilize the nuclear arms race in order to free their people and the planet from the spiraling cost and danger of such a competition. Ronald Reagan, the quintessential Cold Warrior, alarmed and dismayed most of his conservative supporters when he began to soften his hard-line approach to the Soviet Union. He authorized the resumption of arms negotiations with the Soviets, which began again in March 1985. A dramatic moment in world history occurred when Soviet leader Mikhail Gorbachev and President Reagan met in Geneva from November 24 to November 27, 1985, the first summit conference since Carter had journeyed to Moscow in 1979. But their six hours of private talks were inconclusive. They achieved no major agreements on arms control. The major block was Reagan's insistence that America would continue development of the Strategic Defense Initiative (SDI). Gorbachev complained to Reagan that the SDI project violated provisions of SALT I. The Soviet leader also demanded that the United States would have to abandon the SDI before he would agree to any cuts in nuclear weaponry or sign any arms control agreements. At the summit's conclusion, Reagan and Gorbachev produced a four-and-one-half page communiqué pledging to accelerate arms control negotiations.

The summit was an exercise in global public relations by both sides. But it also was a historic event, giving further diplomacy a needed impetus. A budding friendship between the two world leaders was the main outcome of their private meetings. The personal relationship between the two men was secured when Reagan told Gorbachev, a Hollywood movie buff, stories about his days as an actor. Reagan's anecdotes about Jimmy Stewart, John Wayne, Humphrey Bogart, and other movie icons captivated the Soviet leader. President Reagan toned down his anti-Communist rhetoric, saying that Gorbachev was a man with whom he could do business. In the Soviet press, a new image of Reagan as a man who could be reasoned with had replaced a hostile version, in which he had often been compared to Hitler. But the great expectations generated by the Geneva summit failed to materialize.

At a hastily called summit meeting in Reykjavik, Iceland, in October 1986, Gorbachev proposed that both sides cut their stockpiles of strategic missiles by 50 percent in exchange for which the United States would abandon the SDI. Reagan responded by making an even more amazing offer, one that he made on his own initiative and one that astonished and frightened all of his advisers. He offered to eliminate all U.S. missiles but insisted that the Soviets accept American development and deployment of the SDI. Gorbachev could not accept the SDI, so Reagan then abruptly ended the conference, much to the relief of his advisers.

During the next year, Reagan replaced many of his hard-line, anti-Communist advis-

Figure 14.5   On December 8, 1987, President Reagan and Mikhail Gorbachev signed the INF treaty to eliminate an entire class of weapons, intermediate-range missiles.   *Source:* National Archives.

ers with a new breed of more flexible, pragmatic bureaucrats. Frank Carlucci replaced Weinberger in the Defense Department. Army General Colin Powell became the new head of the National Security Council. And Senator Howard Baker replaced Donald Regan as the President's Chief of Staff. These men favored reaching arms control agreements with the Soviets. First Lady Nancy Reagan, concerned over her husband's place in history in the aftermath of the Iran-Contra scandal, urged him to seek a major arms control agreement with Gorbachev. She wanted an accommodation with the Soviet Union to be the chief legacy of the Reagan presidency.

A year after the Reykjavik meeting, joint arms control efforts finally resulted in a major agreement between the two superpowers. Gorbachev journeyed to the United States, and he and Reagan signed a historic treaty in December 1987. The agreement eliminated an entire class of weapons, intermediate-range thermonuclear ballistic missiles, which had been located mostly in Europe. Both sides had, in effect, accepted the "zero option" originally proposed by Reagan in 1983. The agreement, known officially as the Intermediate Nuclear Forces (INF) Treaty, was the first nuclear arms control agreement ever reached that required the destruction of deployed nuclear weapons systems. It also provided for inspectors of both powers to observe the dismantling and destruction of the intermediate-range missiles. The signing of the INF Treaty and the return of cordial relations with the Soviet Union represented President Reagan's most important diplomatic achievements. The old Cold Warrior, after years of racheting up the the Cold War, was now thawing it.

The signing of the INF Treaty and the return of détente with the Soviets also held out the promise of future agreements that would cut strategic weaponry on both sides. Negotiators from both countries continued to work on a Strategic Arms Reduction Treaty (START). The Soviets also announced that they were ending their costly, futile war in Afghanistan. In addition to phasing out the Afghan adventure, Gorbachev undertook a worldwide scaling back of Soviet foreign policies. He indicated that the Soviets might end their economic and military support of the Sandinistas, urged the PLO to recognize Israel's right to exist, pressured Hanoi to pull its troops out of Kampuchea, pulled Soviet forces back from the Sino–Soviet border regions, and urged the Soviet satellites in Eastern Europe to reform their economies and become more involved with the nations of Western Europe.

The sudden and quite remarkable turnabout in U.S.–Soviet relations culminated in Reagan's triumphant visit to the Soviet Union in June 1988. To anyone familiar with Reagan's long record of fervent anti-Communism, his appearance in the heart of "the evil empire" was genuinely astonishing. When asked if he still believed that the Soviet Union was the "focus of evil in the modern world," Reagan responded, "They've changed." He spoke to the Soviet people on television and warmly embraced his friend Mikhail Gorbachev at the site of Lenin's tomb. After such acts of reconciliation, no one appeared to care whether the United States and the Soviet Union still had 30,000 nuclear warheads aimed at each other. Gorbachev made another visit to the United States in December, just before Reagan's presidency ended. Good pals "Ron" and "Gorby" staged a photo opportunity in front of the Statue of Liberty. Even the First Ladies, Nancy Reagan and Raisa Gorbachev, who had taken a chilly dislike to each other since their first meeting, exchanged warm smiles. At the highest official levels, the Cold War had thawed.

Figure 14.6   President Ronald Reagan speaks with Soviet leader Mikhail Gorbachev during arrival ceremonies at the White House in December 1987. (Gorbachev is in gray, and Reagan is in black.)
Source: AP/Wide World Photos.

THE ELECTION OF 1988

As candidates in both parties geared up for the 1988 elections, the race for the presidency appeared wide open. For the Republicans, the major contenders included Vice President George Bush, Senate Republican leader Robert Dole, and former "televangelist" Pat Robertson. For the Democrats, a large field of candidates sought their party's nomination, including Congressman Richard Gephardt of Missouri, Senator Albert Gore of Tennessee, Governor Michael Dukakis of Massachusetts, and charismatic black leader Jesse Jackson.

When the lengthy primary process finally ran its course in June, the survivors were Reagan's sixty-four-year-old Vice President George Bush and Massachusetts Governor Michael Dukakis. Jesse Jackson, who had finished a strong second in the primary balloting to Dukakis, sought the vice presidency. Dukakis chose instead an elderly conservative Senator from Texas, Lloyd Bentsen. George Bush easily survived a mini-controversy over his selection of youthful Senator J. Danforth Quayle of Indiana as his vice-presidential running mate. Quayle was thought to be too young and inexperienced to be a heartbeat away from the presidency.

The Republicans conducted a richly financed and an efficient campaign. The Bush campaign easily won what media analysts have called the "battle of the sound bites," that is, the vivid ten- to twenty-second pronouncements uttered daily by the candidates as they campaigned across the nation that would be picked up on the evening television news programs and beamed into millions of living rooms nightly until Election Day. Bush also found most of the "hot" electoral buttons to push during the contest with Dukakis. He projected a vision of a "kinder, gentler nation," and he encouraged Americans to help one another and shine forth from "a thousand points of light." He pledged "no new taxes," and when questioned about his commitment, he responded a la a popular Clint Eastwood movie character with "read my lips." Bush also waged a long, relentless assault on Dukakis as an exemplar of all that was wrong with contemporary liberalism. He charged that Dukakis was weak on foreign policy and national security matters. The most notorious attack commercial pandered to racist fears by including a mug shot of Willie Horton, a black convicted murderer and rapist who committed another murder while on a weekend furlough from prison. The commercial implied that Dukakis, who was governor when Horton was serving time in a Massachusetts prison, was soft on crime.

Dukakis disdained negative campaigning, and he refused to even respond to the Bush attacks. Dukakis tried to focus his campaign on the issues. His approach failed, and his campaign never caught fire. He never found a telling issue or a rousing theme that resonated

Figure 14.7   The Reverend Jesse Jackson campaigning for the presidency in 1988.   *Source:* St. Louis Mercantile Library. Used with permission.

among the voters. During two televised debates between the candidates, Dukakis failed to cut into Bush's lead or to even slow his momentum.

On Election Day, the Bush–Quayle ticket buried Dukakis and Bentsen, winning 54 percent of the popular vote to 46 percent, 48,000,000 votes for the Republicans to 41,000,000 for the Democrats. Bush carried forty of the fifty states and had a 426 to 112 advantage in the electorate vote. Dukakis's defeat could be attributed in part to the continued flight of white voters, who comprised over 80 percent of the electorate. Since 1948, the only Democratic presidential candidate to receive a majority of the white vote was Lyndon Johnson. Dukakis got about 38 percent of the white vote in 1988. The once solidly Democratic South was now solidly Republican, as was most of the Midwest and the West. Millions of blue-collar workers, once a Democratic mainstay, voted for Bush.

Despite being beaten in the presidential vote, the Democrats retained control of both houses of Congress, two-thirds of state governorships, and thirty-six state legislatures. Although they had lost five of the last six presidential elections, the Democrats in 1988 retained considerable political power at the local, state, and Congressional levels. Voter turnout in 1988 was the lowest since 1924. Of the estimated 183 million Americans eligible to vote, only 91.6 million (50.1 percent) bothered to vote, by far the lowest percentage of any of the world's prosperous democratic nations.

The factor that had ensured Bush's victory was that he was Reagan's heir apparent. True, the old leader had lost some of his luster in the wake of the Iran-Contra scandal and the "sleaze factor." Toward the end of his presidency, Reagan clearly showed the effects of aging, failing health, mental deterioration, and fatigue. Dukakis and other Democratic leaders also called attention to a long list of national problems that eight years of conservative Republicanism had either created or neglected: monstrous federal budget deficits, increased numbers of poor people, indifference to civil rights, environmental degradation, scant interest in consumer protection or safety in the workplaces of America, the decline of unions, the decline of the public schools, and the fact that one-third of American families could not afford adequate health insurance. The Democrats also raised a basic question of fairness. They charged that Reaganomics had favored the rich and affluent classes at the expense of the middle classes, working classes, and poor. Democrats also called attention to a series of Reagan foreign policy failures in Central America and the Middle East.

But the majority of voters in 1988 no longer supported liberal programs, nor did they look to the Democrats for presidential leadership on either domestic or foreign policy. For most Americans, talk of national debts involved incomprehensibly large numbers that did not seem to have any relevance or negative impacts on their daily lives. Most voters in 1988 were not poor or members of a minority, and they did not appear very concerned about the folks who were. Eight years of Reagan's rule had coincided with the longest sustained period of economic growth in U.S. history. During the decade, nearly 20 million new jobs were created.

Even though he had numerous failures and shortcomings, Ronald Reagan remained by far the most popular man in public life. He presided over a peaceful, prosperous America. Relations with the Soviet Union were better than at any time since World War II. The 1988 election amounted to a referendum on Reaganism. A large majority of the electorate concluded that George Bush was more likely than Michael Dukakis to keep the nation at peace and to keep the good times rolling.

BIBLIOGRAPHY

The most thorough account of the Iran-Contra scandal that rocked the Reagan administration in 1986 and 1987 is Theodore Draper's *A Very Thin Line: The Iran-Contra Affairs.* Bob Woodward, in *Veil,* offers a well-done account of the Iran-Contra affair in which Woodward contends that it was masterminded by CIA director William Casey. Seth P. Tillman's *The United States and the Middle East: Interests and Obstacles* is a balanced treatment of American policy in that troubled region. Stansfield Turner, in *Terrorism and Democracy,* provides a thoughtful study of one of the most serious and agonizing problems that U.S. presidents have to deal with. Michael Mandelbaum's *Reagan and Gorbachev* is a good account of their personal diplomacy. Roy Gutman's *Banana Diplomacy* is a critical study of U.S. foreign policy in Nicaragua and El Salvador in the 1980s. Michael Schaller was the first historian to write an account of the Reagan years. His *Reckoning with Reagan: America and Its President in the 1980s* is a balanced study of what happened and why it happened during the Reagan presidency.

15

The American People in the 1990s

The last decade of the twentieth century was both an exciting and a frightening era for most Americans. They had to cope with rapid, fundamental transitions both at home and abroad. With the sudden and unexpected collapse of Communism, the disintegration of the Soviet Union, and the end of the Cold War, Americans found themselves in a novel post–Cold War era without precedent and without guidelines. At the same time Americans groped for new strategic roles in the post–Cold War world, they also had to adapt to the rapidly evolving world economy. Increasing globalization each year integrated more and more elements of the American economy with the rest of the world.

As Americans confronted a transformed global situation abroad, at home they had to deal with changing demographics, a fragmented social order, cultural warfare, and ideologized politics. Many Americans expressed dismay over environmental degradation, decaying inner-city public schools, and rising inequality.

During the early 1990s, Americans suffered a relatively mild economic recession that probably cost George Bush his chance to become a two-term president. The economy recovered by 1993, and a sustained period of growth and rising prosperity began that extended into 2000. The strongest bull market in U.S. financial history carried stocks to record levels and made many people rich. However, a combination of financial crises in many Pacific Rim countries, a near collapse of the Brazilian and Russian economies, and continuing stagnation among many European economies caused a 20 percent drop in stock market equity values during the summer of 1998. But continuing strong consumer demand kept the U.S. economy growing and enabled the market to rebound, and in 2000 it surged on to record levels. Within the United States, unemployment and inflation remained low. The prosperous and growing economy annually generated large numbers of good jobs. Millions of

American families enjoyed unprecedented good times. Young people entering the job markets during the late 1990s experienced their best opportunities in decades. Even so, as the American economy was increasingly integrated into the burgeoning global economy, the terms of competition became fiercer. Competitive pressures kept wages down, and people had to work harder than ever to keep their jobs.

A DEMOGRAPHIC PROFILE FOR THE 1990s

Census takers, combing the country during 1990, discovered that dramatic changes had occurred in the nation's demographic profile during the go-go years of the 1980s. In 1990, the national population totaled 247 million, nearly a 10 percent increase over 1980. By 2000, the population had approached 275 million, and the median age had reached thirty-five, making Americans one of the oldest national populations on the planet. One of the most important findings of the 1990 census was that the advance wave of baby boomers had entered middle age. The fastest growing age groups continued to be older Americans. This "graying of America" raised serious issues. How well would society be able to maintain its oldest citizens, and at what cost? Corporations found their pension costs inflating out of control.

The Social Security system, although fiscally solvent for the foreseeable future, barring catastrophe, was increasingly strained. Young workers had to pay higher Social Security taxes to fund pensions paid to an ever-higher proportion of retirees. Many of the retirees were far more affluent than the workers paying their Social Security pensions. In the early 1990s, many retirees also were drawing generous pensions relative to the amounts that they had contributed to the Social Security system during their working years. Social Security taxes increased by 25 percent during the 1980s. Many young working people in the 1990s remained openly skeptical over whether Social Security benefits would be there for them when they reached retirement age. There also were special problems with Medicare and Medicaid, both funded through the Social Security system. By 1995, it was clear that Medicare costs had to be trimmed sharply, or the system would verge on bankruptcy early in the next century. Despite the fiscal crisis in the Medicare and Medicaid programs, partisan political posturing delayed any serious efforts to resolve it. In the fall of 1998, Republicans insisted that the budget surplus go for tax relief as well as fixing Medicare. President Clinton insisted that the budget surplus be used to repair Social Security first. Partisan politics continued to hamper efforts to fix Social Security in 2000.

The 1990 census confirmed that Americans remained a people on the move. Migration patterns that originated during World War II continued. The Sunbelt states retained their magnetic abilities to attract new residents from the Northeast and Midwest. Population increases in Sunbelt states stretching from South Carolina to Southern California continued to account for most of the nation's population growth in the 1980s. California, fueled by immigration from Mexico and the Asia/Pacific Islands, added 5 million people and accounted for 25 percent of the total population growth during the decade. Continuing population shifts from the Northeast and Midwest to the South and Southwest also meant that the locus of political power continued to shift in the same direction. In the new House of

Representatives, elected in 1992, California gained seven seats, Florida gained three, and Texas gained two. Several of the older states in the Northeast and Midwest lost representation. The 1990 census also revealed that the national population continued to gravitate toward the nation's urban centers. Most of the decade's population growth occurred in cities containing more than 100,000 people.

In addition, the 1990 census reflected the growing variety of household living arrangements in America. The number of traditional families, of married parents with children, continued to decline. Nuclear families made up only about one-fourth of the nation's households in 1990. Almost as many households were made up of a person living alone. The number of single mothers heading a household increased rapidly during the decade, especially among minority populations. In 2000, there were nearly 15 million single-parent families, most of them headed by a woman who had never married. During the 1990s, the number of people choosing not to marry increased rapidly. In 2000, approximately 13 percent of American households were poor, about the same proportion as could be found in this country in 1965. Since the national population had increased by 75 million during that thirty-three-year period, there were about 4 million more poor families living in the United States in 2000 than in 1965.

The large increase in poor, single-parent families during the 1990s had ominous implications for millions of American children. Observers noted that in addition to the usual adolescent disaffection, some of which adults suspected was designed simply to annoy them—peculiar dress, weird hairstyles, tattoos and piercings, and a taste for bad music—many young people exhibited genuine confusion, anguish, and despair. In 2000, the rates for teenage eating disorders, drug use, depression, and suicide were all rising. A new and terrifying dimension of youthful pathology appeared during 1998 and 1999, when several teenage and even younger boys went on shooting rampages at their schools, wounding and killing their fellow students and teachers. Adolescents were one of the highest-risk groups for contracting AIDS. At the same time teenage pathologies were rising at an alarming rate, SAT scores were dropping. Young people also had to deal with a declining public school system and diminishing opportunities for higher education. Economy-minded Congresses reduced the amounts of money available for student grants, loans, and work-study programs. Competition intensified for enrollment in elite universities and for good jobs.

THE DECLINE OF THE MIDDLE CLASSES

Despite generally good times during most of the 1990s, many serious, intertwined economic problems, exacerbated by the recession that struck during the early 1990s, continued to vex the American people. The annual trade deficit exceeded $100 billion in 1999. Annual federal deficits continued to run up huge amounts of red ink. The national debt reached $4 trillion in 1992 and $5 trillion in 1996. That year, annual interest payments on the national debt reached $250 billion and consumed 16 percent of all federal spending. In 1998, for the first time in nearly thirty years, the federal government, after years of fiscal restraint, tax increases, cuts in military spending, cuts in social spending, and steady economic growth, managed to produce a budget surplus of $80 billion. The surpluses grew steadily in 1999 and 2000.

During the recession, unemployment rose; it reached 7.8 percent during the summer of 1992, meaning that about 9 million workers were without jobs. Housing starts, new car sales, and business investment plummeted. Consumer confidence dropped. The Federal Reserve Board slashed interest rates to thirty-year lows, but the economy did not pick up. The first recession to afflict the American people in a decade had two major causes: cuts in military spending in the aftermath of the Cold War and the collapse of commercial real estate markets in the wake of the overexpansion of the 1980s. A further cause derived from the spending binge that Americans had gone on during the go-go decade of the 1980s. Their bills came due in the early 1990s, and the economy contracted.

More important, the long-term structural weaknesses of the U.S. economy that had first appeared during the early 1970s persisted into the 1990s. The employment shift from industrial to service-sector jobs continued, with many of the latter positions low paying and unskilled. Large corporate employers, facing increasingly stiffer worldwide competition, continued to streamline their operations. As they computerized and downsized, they layed off thousands of workers, not only production workers but also managerial personnel, especially middle management types whose work could be done more efficiently by computers.

The most serious long-term structural weakness that had eroded the economic underpinnings of millions of American middle-class families since 1973 was the slow rate of economic growth. From 1890 to 1970, the U.S. economy grew at an annual rate of 3.5 percent, adjusted for inflation. That high rate of economic growth, sustained over much of the twentieth century, more than any other single factor created a large and prosperous middle-class society. Since 1970, including the boom years of the 1980s, the annual rate of growth has averaged 2.2 percent. This sharp decline (37 percent) in long-term annual growth rates has had a devastating impact on many middle-class families. Real income for the middle

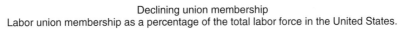

Declining union membership
Labor union membership as a percentage of the total labor force in the United States.

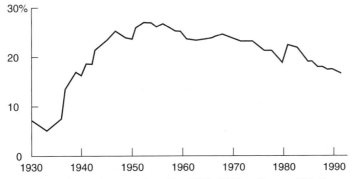

Figure 15.1   Labor union membership, 1930–1990.   *Source:* U.S. Bureau of Labor Statistics, Department of Labor.

classes has been declining since 1973. During those years, the annual share of national income earned by the middle classes also has been declining. Slower rates of growth meant declining economic opportunity and lowered social mobility for all but affluent families.

By the mid-1990s, the U.S. economy had fully recovered from recession and was performing strongly. From 1995 to 2000, the economy grew at an annual rate of 4 percent, its best performance since the period 1983–1984. The U.S. economy remained the largest and strongest national economy in the world. By 1996, American industry once again led the world in productive efficiency. Aided by a weak dollar and quotas imposed on Japanese imports, American automakers improved their domestic market share, which reached 75 percent in 1996, up from 68 percent in the late 1980s. By the mid-1990s, U.S. automakers were turning out fuel-efficient, reliable vehicles that were as good as the foreign competition, and they often cost thousands of dollars less. American automakers dominated the markets for minivans, light trucks, and off-road vehicles. In the late 1990s, large, powerful, and expensive sports utility vehicles were the vehicles of choice for those who could afford them.

In the late 1990s, American high-tech industries flourished. U.S. electronics companies continued to lead the world in diverse fields such as desktop computers, software applications, and telecommunications. Even though overall American companies ran a large annual trade deficit, U.S. high-tech industries enjoyed a growing annual trade surplus that exceeded $60 billion in 1997. High school and college graduates entered one of the strongest job markets for young people in decades. With the strongest economies of Europe stagnating—facing rising indebtedness, inflation, and high employment rates—and with the Japanese economy in a deep, seemingly permanent recession, the continuing strong American economic performance appeared even more impressive.

In the summer of 1997, Thailand, Hong Kong, South Korea, Indonesia, and several other Asian countries experienced turmoil in their financial markets that suddenly reversed years of robust economic growth and rising prosperity. The Asian financial disasters drove down stock values and devalued currencies, bringing many large banks and corporate conglomerates in these nations to the verge of bankruptcy. Several countries received financial assistance from the International Monetary Fund, at a price—they were forced to implement harsh austerity programs to stop the financial hemorrhaging. In Indonesia, mass unrest in the wake of economic decline forced the aging autocrat Suharto to resign. These financial and economic crises deepened the recession that had already engulfed Japan and threatened to slow the Chinese juggernaut. Even the American powerhouse felt the effects of the Asian meltdown. By the summer of 1998, the growth rate of the U.S. economy was slowing, stock values had plunged by nearly 20 percent, and businesses that sold goods and services on Asian markets were hurting. The U.S. farmers who sold grain and beef to Asians were especially hard hit.

A NATION OF IMMIGRANTS

During the decade of the 1980s, 6 million legal immigrants entered the country. No one knows how many illegal immigrants entered during the same period, but conservative estimates put the figure at hundreds of thousands per annum. If the estimated illegal immigrants are added to the legal immigrants, between 9 million and 10 million people emigrated to America during the 1980s, the largest number for any decade in American history. Europeans represented only 12 percent of the 1980s' immigration. Experts estimate that the rate of immigration established during the 1980s continued into the 1990s and may even have increased because of the prosperous and growing U.S. economy. Most of the immigrants emigrated from a Hispanic country within the Western Hemisphere or from a Pacific Island or Asian nation. If it were not for the continuing high rate of immigration to the United States, given the low fertility rates prevailing among American women, its population would be slowly declining.

Most of the arriving immigrants clustered in a few states and cities. According to the 1990 census, California was home to two-thirds of the Asian-American population and over one-third of the Hispanic-American population. In New York, Los Angeles, San Francisco, Chicago, and other great cities, the new Hispanic and Asian populations settled into ethnic neighborhoods. They brought their distinctive manners, cultural mores and styles, and unique languages, cuisine, dress, and music. America's large cities became home to the most culturally diverse populations in world history, and they continued to increasingly take on the qualities of cosmopolitan economic and cultural centers.

While cultural diversity brought energy and vitality and made America's large cities the most vibrant urban centers in the world, it also brought tensions, dislocations, and serious problems and pressures. African Americans were most vulnerable to the economic competition posed by striving newcomers. The huge influx of new people during the 1980s and 1990s triggered an upsurge of nativism. Drives to repeal bilingual education and to make English the official national language reflected this resurgent nativism. In 1994, California voters approved overwhelmingly Proposition 187, a ballot initiative that barred undocumented aliens from access to public schools, health clinics, and all other social services. Federal courts declared most of the initiative's provisions unconstitutional, and it was never enforced. Governor Pete Wilson of California tried unsuccessfully to parlay nativist attacks on immigrants and efforts to repeal affirmative action programs into a drive to win the Republican nomination for president in 1996. He failed to generate much support among the party faithful and quickly pulled out of the contest. In 1998, California voters, by a nearly two-thirds majority, approved an initiative that essentially ended bilingual instruction in the public schools.

BLACK AND WHITE, BUT NOT TOGETHER

Festering ethnic tensions exploded in May 1992, when a California jury acquitted four white police officers who were charged with savagely beating an African American suspect, Rodney King. A bystander had videotaped the incident, and portions of the tape were repeatedly broadcast to the nation. To nearly all who observed the gruesome sequences, the television camera presented compelling images of police brutality. The verdict to acquit the four policemen, rendered by a politically conservative suburban jury containing no African American members, ignited the most violent race riot in the nation's history in south-central Los Angeles. Thousands of businesses were looted and destroyed, many of them burned. Fifty-four people were killed, thousands more were injured, and over 17,000 were arrested. The cost of the riot exceeded $1 billion. The Los Angeles police, poorly led and confused, initially were slow to respond to the riot and allowed events to get out of control. National Guard troops had to be rushed to Los Angeles to quell the rioters. Within a few days, order was restored, but only after enormous property damage and loss of life had occurred.

The riot was reminiscent of the 1965 Watts upheaval when mobs of angry black rioters burned and looted neighboring businesses. But there also were significant differences. The 1965 riot had pitted blacks against whites. The 1992 riot had much more complex ethnic dynamics reflecting the ethno-racial diversity of the nation's second largest city. Blacks attacked other blacks as well as whites. Hispanics attacked whites. Blacks and Hispanics both attacked Asians, mostly Korean store owners. Gangs of African American and Hispanic thugs also engaged in violence and looting. No simple analysis sufficed to account for the ominous upheaval. The King verdict obviously triggered the riot, but the underlying causes appeared to be a potent mix of ethno-racial antagonisms, poverty, and government neglect, all exacerbated by a severe economic recession that hit poor people, working-class people, and small businessmen especially hard.

In 1995, an ironic sequel to the Rodney King case occurred in the tormented city of Los Angeles. From January to October, a former star athlete turned television sportscaster and film actor, O. J. Simpson, stood trial for the murder of his former wife Nicole Brown Simpson and her friend Ronald Goldman. After a lengthy trial, a jury acquitted Simpson of all charges.

Because of the political and cultural contexts in which the trial occurred, it acquired a significance that far transcended the guilt or innocence of one prominent individual. The O. J. Simpson murder trial became the most famous media event in American history. Virtually all of the major media provided constant coverage of the trial for months. Cable TV watchers could catch analyses and perspectives on the trial from ex-judges, ex-prosecutors, and ex-defense lawyers. At times there were so many newly minted pundits commenting on the case that a comedian called the trial "the full employment act for lawyers." Millions of Americans became personally involved in the "trial of the century." Attorneys for both sides and the judge, Lance Ito, often played to the ever-present television cameras. Due process became judicial theater, a media circus, and Hollywood showbiz. A terrible tragedy became a mass spectacle. A brutal double murder became prime-time entertainment, a real-life whodunit. Despite its obvious dangers for Simpson, it was the role of a lifetime for an actor of relatively modest attainments.

In the eyes of a substantial majority of viewers and expert commentators, the state presented a strong case based on physical evidence that implicated Simpson beyond a reasonable doubt in the two murders. Simpson had no alibi, and the defense presented no creditable alternative explanation that challenged the prosecution's claim that Simpson killed both victims. The fact that Simpson, a rich and famous man, whose resources matched those that Los Angeles county could allocate for the trial, hired a battery of high-priced attorneys to mount a successful defense proved to many Americans the dubious proposition that he was immune to the justice system. They believed that he was not held accountable for his murderous actions. Simpson's acquittal also reinforced the widely held cynical notion that in America there was one standard of justice for the rich and another, harsher standard for the poor. The antics of attorneys on both sides, the often erratic behavior of Judge Ito, and most of all, the outcome of the trial suggested to many observers that the American system of criminal justice had been tried and convicted of an infamous miscarriage of justice. The jury system appeared to sacrifice impartial justice to political goals and ethnic agenda. The trial raised an ominous question: Could the traditional jury system work in a racially polarized society?

The trial also raised the specter of domestic violence. The prosecution, although failing to convince the jury that Simpson was a murderer, did show that he had frequently battered and brutalized his wife prior to their divorce. Statistics showed that domestic violence was the leading cause of injury to women each year in this country. During 1994, over 1,400 women died as a result of domestic violence.

Looming over all aspects of the trial was the ugly reality of racism. Because the murder victims, Nicole Brown Simpson and Ronald Goldman, were white and Simpson was a black celebrity, racial attitudes in this country became central to the outcome of the trial and how people viewed that outcome. The jury—consisting of nine African Americans, eight of them women, a Hispanic male, and two white women—reached a verdict of acquittal within four hours. The jurors rushed to judgment without seriously considering the mountain of evidence, much of it quite complex and technical, presented by 133 witnesses who testified during the long trial. Polls showed that 87 percent of black Americans agreed with the jury's verdict, but 65 percent of whites believed Simpson to be guilty as charged.

The black-white racial chasm that existed in this country was highlighted on October 4, 1995, when the clerk of the court read the jury's verdict, witnessed by a huge nationwide television audience. Around the country, wherever crowds of black Americans had gathered to hear the verdict, they broke into cheers and hugged each other at what appeared to them to be a triumphant deliverance. Wherever crowds of whites had gathered to hear the verdict, they stood in stunned silence or stared in disbelief at what appeared to them to be a brutal miscarriage of justice. These differential responses dramatically demonstrated beyond a reasonable doubt that white and black Americans stared uncomprehendingly at each other from across a vast cultural divide.

Seemingly lost in all of the furor over the verdict of acquittal in a criminal trial was the fact that Simpson still faced civil suits brought by the families of the murder victims, accusing him of the "wrongful deaths" of Nicole Brown Simpson and Ronald Goldman. The subsequent civil trials were conducted in a West Los Angeles courtroom before a mostly white middle-class jury that did not include a single African American. A tough old judge excluded the television cameras, kept a rigid order, and did not allow Simpson's attorneys to accuse the Los Angeles police of a racist conspiracy to frame Simpson as Judge Ito had permitted during the criminal trial. Simpson, nearly bankrupt from the costs of the first trial and having lost all opportunities to earn big money, could not afford a high-powered defense for his civil trials. On February 4, 1997, Simpson was convicted of responsibility for the "wrongful deaths" of Nicole Brown Simpson and Ronald Goldman. Their survivors were awarded a total of $33.4 million in compensatory and punitive damages. Simpson's attorneys promptly appealed both of the verdicts and the damage awards. There was far less media coverage and public interest in the civil trial and little noticeable reaction to the verdicts or awards.

Two weeks after the conclusion of the first Simpson trial, another dramatic event accentuated the black-white racial divide rending the American social fabric. The controversial leader of the Nation of Islam, Louis Farrakhan, led a "Million Man March" on Washington. About 500,000 black men gathered on the mall in front of the Washington Monument. For the huge gathering, it was a day of atonement and renewal, an affirmation of their black manhood. For most of the participants, it was a deeply moving experience. Strangers listened to speeches, chatted, sang, cried, and hugged one another. Time will tell whether the event was merely a spectacular public happening, a Woodstock for African Americans, or a profound turning point in black culture, when inspired men returned to their neighborhoods, determined to live righteous lives and to make a positive contribution to society. The march also demonstrated how far America had yet to travel to achieve Martin Luther King's vision of an individualistic, integrated, color-blind society, a society "in which people were judged not by the color of their skin but by the content of their character."

THE ASSAULT ON AFFIRMATIVE ACTION

Affirmative action had been controversial from its origins during the heyday of Lyndon Johnson's Great Society in 1965. From the outset, there were white men who protested that affirmative action was unfair and amounted to reverse discrimination. Some, such as Allen Bakke, had taken their cases to court. Political leaders in the late 1960s, such as Ronald Reagan and George Wallace, lambasted affirmative action. Wallace was especially bitter, ridiculing "pointyhead" white liberal bureaucrats in Washington, D. C., who sent their children to expensive private schools and at the same time promulgated programs that forced desegregation and affirmative action on ordinary white people.

But affirmative action remained official government policy until the mid-1990s, when a complex set of factors, including arguments over women's, immigrants', and other minorities' rights, economic recession, and fierce white male resentment, combined to revive the debate on the issue. By the mid-1990s, its critics had perceived that affirmative action policies had evolved into a kind of zero-sum game in which gains for women, blacks, and Hispanics came at the expense of Asians, other "unprotected" minorities, and non-Hispanic white males. The battle over affirmative action also became politicized and intensely emotional. Liberal admissions officers, passionately embracing an ideology of diversity and group rights, battled their opponents who were equally committed to an ideology based on merit and individual opportunity.

In the mid-1990s, the battle was joined over admissions to elite universities and professional schools. The University of Texas Law School, under court order, abandoned its use of affirmative action criteria for admissions. In 1995, all nine campuses of the University of California scrapped their affirmative action admissions policies that had been in place for over twenty years. The first classes admitted in the fall of 1997 under the new color-blind admissions policies showed a sharp, system-wide reduction in the number of entering African-American and Hispanic students. A sizeable number of African American and Hispanic students who had been admitted under the new system chose to attend other elite universities, fearing that they would not be welcome at the University of California campuses.

A FRAGMENTED SOCIETY

During the 1980s and 1990s there occurred a dramatic transformation in the ethnic and racial composition of the American population, the greatest since immigrants from Southern and Eastern Europe flooded into America during the first fifteen years of the twentieth century. According to the 1990 census, one in four Americans claimed African, Hispanic, Asian, or Native American ancestry. African Americans represented 12 percent of the total; Hispanic Americans represented 9 percent of the total; Asian Americans represented 3 percent of the total; and Native Americans represented 1 percent of the total population of 247 million. By 2000, the nation's population approached 275 million, constituting a mosaic of Native Americans, African Americans, Hispanic Americans, Asian Americans, and European Americans. Each of these large ethno-racial groups, in turn, consisted of an array of subgroups differentiated by region, national origins, religion, education, gender, age, and class. Because of the continuing high rate of immigration, both legal and illegal, to America, the percentage of foreign-born people had exceeded 10 percent by 2000, the highest since the 1920s, up from 5 percent in 1970.

In 2000, more than 2 million people identified themselves as Native Americans, more than twice the 1970 total. This figure reflected not only a rapid natural increase in the Amerindian population but also the growing numbers of people of mixed-race ancestry eager to affirm their ethnic roots. A network of tribal-controlled colleges and universities provided Native Americans with relevant educations and cultural sustenance. Many tribes energetically pursued various business ventures, from growing wild rice to operating profitable gambling casinos. In August 1998, near New London, Connecticut, on Mashantucket Pequot Tribal Nation land, the 550 surviving Pequots, grown rich as Arabian sheiks on profits from their Foxwood Casino complex, proudly unveiled a magnificent museum and research center. The museum, built at a cost of nearly $200 million, celebrated the resurrection of a once-powerful Native American people who had struggled for centuries to survive at the margins of the dominant European society that had conquered and nearly obliterated them during the seventeenth century. The centerpiece of the museum was a recreated Pequot village on a summer day in 1550 on the eve of the European arrival. Fifty-one life-size figures were shown weaving mats, sharpening arrows, and constructing wigwams. It is a work of restoration authentic in every detail, both beautiful and tragic, for it recreates an intact, flourishing society and culture on the eve of its destruction.

Despite much progress during the 1990s, Native Americans remained the nation's poorest, most oppressed major ethnic group. Both on reservations and in urban America, unemployment, alcoholism, accidents, and suicide continued to take their toll on the nation's most vulnerable people.

Fed by continuing high rates of immigration, the Asian American population continued to grow rapidly during the decade of the 1990s. People from Korea, the Philippines, Vietnam, China, India, and other countries continued to come to the United States in large numbers. In 2000, 11 percent of Los Angeles's 3.5 million residents were Asians, more than double the proportion a decade earlier. Strengthened by family cultures and prizing academic success, Asian Americans showed high rates of college attendance and upward mobility. However, Asian American communities experienced generational tensions as young people got caught between the tug of traditional ways and the lure of American popular culture.

In the mid-1990s, African Americans remained divided along class lines. At one end of the social spectrum, a large and growing class of black professionals and businesspeople enjoyed affluent lifestyles. In 1998, 12 percent of college students were black, roughly equal to their ratio of the general population. In 2000, nearly half of African Americans in the workforce held middle-class jobs.

At the other end of the spectrum could be found the impoverished inner-city blacks, representing one-fourth of the African American population of approximately 30 million. The poorest of the poor, representing perhaps 10 percent of the African American population in 2000, comprised the "underclass" trapped within the drab and menacing confines of the inner cities. Although intact families, thriving churches, and other strong institutions could be found in the inner city, this culture of decency often was overwhelmed by a staggering array of social pathologies. As factory jobs that were once open to urban workers disappeared, inner-city unemployment rates soared to 50 percent to 60 percent ranges. Lacking the education and skills for good jobs that were no longer available locally, young people faced life on mean streets or held marginal service-sector jobs in car washes or fast-food restaurants. Inner-city pathologies such as high crime rates, drug abuse, welfare dependency, and teenage pregnancies derived from more fundamental problems—the lack of good educational and job opportunities.

As the twentieth century ended, the nation's 23 million Hispanics, more than double the total in 1975, represented America's fastest growing minority. Hispanic Americans are themselves an extraordinarily diverse group; they include 16 million Mexican Americans concentrated in California and the American Southwest; 1 million Cuban Americans mostly living in South Florida; and between 1 million and 2 million immigrants from the Caribbean region and Central America, living mostly on the East Coast or in California. The Hispanic-American population also includes 2 million Puerto Ricans who are American citizens by birth.

Most Hispanics, regardless of their national origins, emigrated to America in search of a better life for themselves and their families. Millions have found success. Hispanic family, church, and cultural institutions have sustained hardworking people struggling to make it in America. But life remained harsh for millions of Hispanic families. In 2000, 20 percent of Mexican Americans and one-third of Puerto Ricans lived in poverty. Hispanic communities were often devastated by alcohol and drug abuse, soaring crime rates, and high rates of school dropouts and teenage pregnancies.

As American society grew more fragmented in the 1980s and 1990s, the ideal of a common national culture proved ever more elusive. Americans appeared to share only consumerist cultural experiences such as shopping at malls and watching prime-time television programs. To many first- and second-generation immigrant families, becoming an American was defined primarily in residential and economic terms: reside in the country, get a good education, and then obtain a well-paying, high-status job. Make money, buy a home in the suburbs, provide well for your family, and enjoy the good life based on consumerist values. Questions of politics and nationality were ignored or downplayed. Futurists predicted that America would become the world's first post–national political entity, one in which transnational to local cultural identities would gradually replace traditional nationalistic and political identities.

CULTURE WARS

But among others, debates erupted, as groups hitherto marginalized or excluded from the mainstream of American life demanded cultural as well as political equality. The multiculturalism controversy took many forms. High school and college course offerings became contested arenas. Newly empowered advocates for women, African Americans, Hispanic Americans, Asian Americans, Native Americans, gays and lesbians, and fundamentalist religious groups demanded that high schools and colleges revise their curricula. Multiculturalists challenged course reading lists that continued to privilege DWEMs (dead, white, European males). Stanford University revised its undergraduate curriculum to include more studies of non-Western cultures. Professors of literature revised reading lists to include works by women, persons of color, and Third World writers. History professors hastened to rewrite textbooks to give more space to previously neglected or excluded non-elite groups.

Culture wars raged on other fronts as well. Congressional conservatives tried to eliminate federal funding for the arts, humanities, and public television. The National Endowment for the Arts and The National Endowment for the Humanities managed to survive the onslaught, but on drastically reduced budgets. The Corporation for Public Broadcasting survived more or less intact.

The multiculturalist reforms provoked a backlash. Traditionalists insisted that these efforts at more inclusive scholarship eroded any sense of a shared national identity. Critics feared that all of that counting by race, ethnicity, gender, sexual preference, age, and religious affiliation could lead to a Balkanization of American society. They worried lest a heedless rush to multiculturalism would destroy the basic unity of the most successful pluralistic society in world history. Some professors and teachers expressed dismay at working in repressive environments in which newly empowered champions of multiculturalism and "politically correct" speech imposed a new bureaucratic orthodoxy that stifled academic freedom and encouraged an aggressively litigious culture of victimization. In extreme form, "p. c." (politically correct) suggested that it was not possible to say anything without offending someone.

A number of voices resisted all efforts to polarize Americans into warring factions and insisted that multiculturalism's many positive contributions could be retained, while rejecting its extremist claims. In this view, the cultures carried by ethnically and racially defined communities could be appreciated without expecting individuals to define themselves narrowly as members of the descent-based community into which they were born. David Hollinger, one of the nation's most imminent historians, distinguished sharply between biology and culture, complaining that multiculturalists too often assumed that a person's values and tastes flowed from skin color or face shape. In a brilliant and timely little book, *Postethnic America: Beyond Multiculturalism,* Hollinger offered his cosmopolitan and inclusive vision of a dynamic, pluralistic society embracing all people of whatever descent:

> Postethnicity prefers voluntary to prescribed affiliations, appreciates multiple identities, pushes for communities of wide scope, recognizes the constructed character of ethno-racial groups, and accepts the formation of new groups as part of the normal life of a democratic community.[1]

Hollinger's vision offered a cultural space big enough to include all warriors.

WOMEN AND WORK

By the late 1990s, women had smashed through all remaining sexist barriers to higher education and the workplace. In many fields, long virtually closed to women, such as medicine, law, engineering, and business management, many women energetically pursued productive careers. In 2000, one-fourth of all doctors and lawyers were women. There also were huge increases in the number of women holding public office in the 1980s and 1990s. President Reagan had appointed Sandra Day O'Connor to the Supreme Court in 1991. President Clinton added Ruth Bader Ginsburg to the Court in 1993. Clinton also appointed several women to Cabinet rank, including Madeleine Albright, the first woman Secretary of State. In 1996, the number of working mothers with children exceeded the number of mothers with children not working outside of the home. By 2000, women constituted virtually half of the total workforce.

But even as increasing numbers of women moved into formerly male-dominated occupations and professions, disparities continued in the pay that they received for performing comparable work. Women who worked full time in 2000 earned about seventy-five cents for every dollar a man earned. Experts offered several explanations to account for continuing pay inequities for women: women included most of the newer entrants into the job market; they had more interruptions in their work careers; they more likely worked in occupations that were not unionized; they sometimes traded higher pay for more convenient or flexible hours; and, of course, they were victims of continuing discrimination. Many women still confronted a segregated job market in the late 1990s. Sixty percent of working women held "pink-collar" jobs.

Many women who had reached managerial positions in business in the late 1990s felt that they were paying too high a personal price for their professional successes. Others complained that they could not fulfill family obligations at home and perform their jobs at the highest levels. Felice Schwartz, the head of a research institute that studied women in business, suggested that these woman might pursue a slower career track in business to have

---

[1]David A. Hollinger, *Postethnic America: Beyond Multiculturalism* (New York: Basic Books, 1995), p. 116.

more time for family responsibilities. But mainstream feminists denounced Schwartz's so-called "mommy track." They claimed that it perpetuated the very second-class status of women in business that they were trying to surmount.

Long-term structural changes in the economy adversely affected working women. The rise of service industries and the implementation of new technologies created millions of new jobs for women but also created new limits and liabilities. For example, computers degraded the labor and status of many clerical employees. Automated offices became the sweatshops of the 1990s. And many businesses, to cut costs, increasingly hired part-time and temporary clerical workers who typically received less pay and fewer benefits than full timers.

Long-term structural changes in family relations affected working women more adversely than economic changes. In the 1990s, the divorce rate continued to rise, as did the

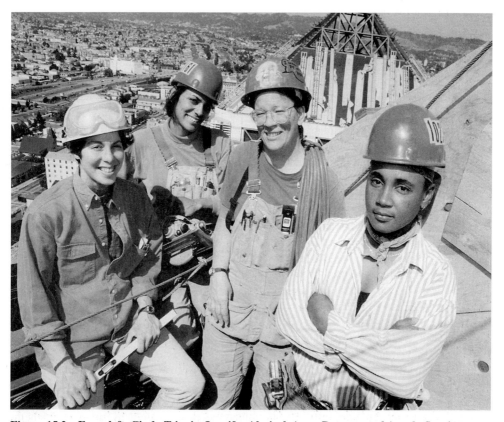

Figure 15.2   From left, Cindy Tsingis, Jennifer Almirol, Anna Detzner, and Angela Saucier stand recently on the rooftop of a construction project overlooking Oakland, California. The women, at work on the city's new federal building, make up only eight percent of the workforce, which is considered well above normal and a symbol of the growing numbers of women building careers in construction. Photo by Olga Shalygin. *Source:* AP/Wide World Photos.

numbers of women living alone and the numbers of single-parent households headed by women. In 2000, about half of women workers had never been married or had been divorced and had not remarried. Much of the increase in the number of poor households within the United States in the 1990s has been attributed to the rapid increase in the number of single-parent households headed by a woman.

Cultural changes also have accompanied the advent of women into the workplaces of America. Most notably, there have been changes in women's consciousness. Most younger women in the late 1990s felt that they were equal to men in the marketplace and had greater ambitions and expectations than previous generations of women. But traditional values and stereotypes also exhibited strong staying powers. Advertisers no longer celebrated domesticity as women's only appropriate realm, but they still insisted that the busy career woman had to keep her weight down and look pretty. Women spent far more of their incomes on clothes, beauty aids, and diet and exercise programs than did men.

THE INFORMATION SUPERHIGHWAY

Electronic technologies continued to develop at an exponential rate during the 1990s. By 1994, 80 percent of American homes contained VCRs. Hollywood, which had feared the loss of box-office receipts, discovered a lucrative new market, not only for new movies but for old ones as well. By the mid-1990s, videos appeared everywhere—in malls, banks, supermarkets, fast-food restaurants, apartments, airplanes, and trauma centers. Even freeway traffic was monitored on the omnipresent tube. The advent of camcorders meant that family photo albums were often replaced by a library of videotapes documenting important moments in the lives of families, in-laws, and friends.

Refinements and innovations in the realm of computer technology had the greatest impact on American life. By the mid-1990s, more than one-third of American households possessed at least one personal computer. Computers revolutionized the way in which Americans worked and played in the 1980s and 1990s. Millions of young people spent more time playing Nintendo games than they spent hours in school. Computers created the modern electronic office. Even small businesses kept records, sent out bills, and did direct-mail advertising on a single desktop computer. The concept of work itself was transformed during the 1990s, as a new class of telecommuters worked at home using computers, electronic mail (e-mail), and fax machines.

The advent of the Internet was the most dramatic development occurring in information technology during the 1990s. In 2000, an estimated 210 million people in 160 countries were wired into the Internet, and the numbers were growing at an exponential rate. A child of the Cold War, the Internet originated within the Pentagon in 1969 as an effort to develop a secure system of communications that could survive a nuclear attack. By the mid-1980s, the military had surrendered control of the Internet, and civilians had launched themselves into cyberspace. At first, Internet users mainly communicated through e-mail. In 1991, the World Wide Web arrived, enhancing the commercial possibilities of the Internet. Soon, thousands of entrepreneurs were peddling their wares in cyberspace, many of them selling pornography and get-rich-quick schemes. SPAM and junk mail quickly became part of the growing cyber lexicon. By 2000, Amazon.com, founded in 1996, claimed to have a customer base of 11,000,000 and its founder, Jeff Bezos, was estimated to be worth $10 billion. People banked, bought new homes and cars, planned vacations, and invested in stock markets, all on-line, by logging on to the proper Websites. Museums, libraries, universities, and many other institutions soon developed elaborate databases. Websites and chat rooms proliferated. Self-appointed seers held forth on every conceivable subject. By the late 1990s, so many high school and college students were writing research papers using "on-line" sources, that professors had to develop special software to detect plagiarism and cheating.

Its champions hailed the advent of the Information Superhighway as a giant leap toward the democratization of knowledge. Vice President Al Gore was an enthusiastic champion of the Information Superhighway. He spoke eloquently of wiring into the Internet all classrooms in the country. Thoughtful educators pointed out that instantaneous access to information was available only to those who could afford computers and the monthly fees to be plugged in. During the 1990s, the gap between the information haves and have-nots widened. Only a small percentage of U.S. households, mostly those in the upper-income brackets, could afford the computers, modems, telephone connections, and gateway software necessary to get on the Information Superhighway. The information gap also was ethno-racial as well as economic: proportionally far fewer African Americans and Hispanic Americans had access to computers at home, school, or work than did whites and Asian Americans. An electronic elite had emerged, and those who, for reasons of class and culture, could not join the club were more disadvantaged than ever.

In September 1998, the developing Internet enjoyed its finest moment. The 445-page Starr Report, complete with fifty-one pages of excruciating details documenting President Clinton's sexual relations with young White House intern Monica Lewinsky, was released on the Internet before it was available to the conventional electronic and print media. Millions of Internet users logged on to read the report before newspapers, news magazines, and television stations could present even edited versions of it. Enterprising Internet operators even set up a website, *Firstpenis.com,* to keep track of the unfolding scandal.

THE GOOD EARTH

American environmentalists had much to celebrate during the mid-1990s. Many of the nation's rivers, lakes, and waterways were cleaner than they had been since the advent of the American Industrial Revolution. Air pollution had been reduced by one-third. The air over Los Angeles, which had been one of the worst smog-choked cities in the country, showed the lowest level of pollutants in nearly fifty years. Lead emissions from gasoline had been practically eliminated. Many bird species that had been on the verge of extinction, including the magnificent bald eagle, the peregrine falcon, and the California condor, made amazing comebacks. Thousands of cities and towns across the land possessed recycling centers; Americans annually recycled billions of dollars worth of metals, glass, wood, and paper products. When Congressional Republicans in 1995 tried to freeze or roll back environmental initiatives, they had to retreat in the face of strong public disapproval of their anti-environmental stance. However, despite much progress on several fronts, environmentalists perceived that much remained to be done. Millions of Americans continued to breath dirty air every day of their lives. Many rivers and lakes remained unsafe for fishing and swimming. Toxic waste dumps abounded, some of them near residential areas and parks where children played.

It also was clear during the 1990s that environmentalists had to take an increasingly international approach to what were now understood as global problems. The first major international action on an environmental issue occurred in 1987, when delegates from thirty-four nations met in Montreal to sign an agreement to phase out ozone-damaging fluorocarbons. Among other consequences, the Montreal protocol amounted to a death sentence for aerosol spray cans. In 1991, the United States signed a treaty banning all development in Antarctica for fifty years. The following year, Americans signed an international agreement on global warming, according to environmental scientists the most pressing of the world's environmental problems. The world's growing concern about global warming was highlighted in 1998 with the advent of the worst El Niño in twenty years. Record rain fall totals, severe flooding, record heat waves, the worst droughts in decades, and destructive storms all served in the minds of concerned environmentalists to foreshadow the greater global disasters that were inevitable unless the trend toward global warming was reversed in the near future.

BIBLIOGRAPHY

The economic, social, and cultural history of the 1990s is covered best in the pages of the *New York Times,* other fine newspapers, weekly newsmagazines such as *Time* and *Newsweek,* and in the *Atlantic Monthly.* Well-informed journalists, whether writing for daily, weekly, or monthly media, provide the first rough draft of what will be refined, deepened, and broadened by scholars in subsequent years. There also are many fine books already in print concerned with important topics of recent history, many of these books done by scholars working in fields other than history. Those concerned about the many troubling world environmental problems of the 1990s will want to read *Crossroads: Environmental Priorities for the Future* by Peter Borelli, ed. Kevin Phillips, a conservative political analyst, has written *The Politics of Rich and Poor,* which is concerned with the social inequities derived from the economic policies of the 1980s and 1990s. For the matter of women's pay issues, see Sarah M. Evans' and Barbara J. Nelson's *Wage Justice: Comparable Worth and the Paradox of Technocratic Reform.* Ellis Close, in *The Rage of a Privileged Class: Why Are Middle Class Blacks So Angry?* offers an important and a disturbing book. See also William Wei's *The Asian American Movement* for a good study of an important group of Americans that lacks an extensive historical literature.

16

The Post–Cold War World

The opening of the Berlin Wall on November 9, 1989, was the first in a series of stunning events that culminated in the collapse of the Soviet Union and the end of the Cold War that had been the focus of American foreign policy for nearly a half-century. As the world's only remaining superpower, the United States suddenly found itself incontestably the most powerful nation on earth. With the demise of the Soviet Union, Americans appeared to inhabit a less dangerous world. While that was true in that the danger of an all-out nuclear war between the superpowers that might have destroyed the planet had vanished, there remained many unstable regions in the world riven with ethnic conflicts, genocidal assaults, and terrorist attacks. As citizens of the only nation with the economic resources, military assets, and political will to intervene in some of these trouble spots, Americans endured periodic involvements in these small but vicious wars that plagued the last decade of the twentieth century. Americans received a horrific reminder that they inhabited a dangerous world on the morning of August 7, 1998, when two powerful car bombs exploded within minutes of each other outside of U.S. embassies in Nairobi, Kenya, and Dar es Salaam, Tanzania, killing more than 200 people and injuring thousands.

At the same time that Americans tried to define new strategic roles in the post–Cold War world, they also had to adapt to the rapidly evolving world economy. Increasing globalization each year integrated more and more elements of the American economy with the rest of the world. Decisions made in the boardrooms of American-based multinational corporations had important international repercussions. Decisions made in Tokyo, Berlin, and Beijing, often affected the kinds of consumer goods that Americans could buy, the interest rates they paid, and whether they kept their jobs.

Within the nation, a searching debate over the role of the state dominated domestic politics during the 1990s. The steady rise of the national state had been one of the major themes of twentieth-century U.S. national history. Ronald Reagan was the first twentieth-century president that endeavored to downsize the national government, although his efforts largely failed. But his cuts in social spending and rhetorical attacks on the welfare state transformed the terms of political debate within this country and prepared the ground for the Republican "earthquake" that followed. With the election of a Republican-controlled Congress in 1994, the conservative assault on the positive state accelerated. Liberal defenders of the welfare state found themselves on the defensive within the most conservative political climate since the 1920s. In his State of the Union Address in January 1997, President Clinton acknowledged the advent of the new domestic order when he noted that, "The era of big government is over."

THE PATRICIAN AS PRESIDENT

George Herbert Walker Bush's presidency was noteworthy, mainly for the absence of many new initiatives emanating from the White House. Bush clearly lacked Reagan's sense of ideological mission, nor did he appear capable of articulating a compelling vision that would inspire his fellow citizens or provide them with a sense of direction. His presidency began with a series of political gestures. He met with the leaders of the Democratic opposition to tell them that he wanted a cooperative relationship with Congress rather than continue the partisan confrontational style of his predecessor. He also met with African-American leaders to assure them of his sympathetic understanding of their problems. By these actions, Bush signaled that his administration would be more moderate and conciliatory than Reagan's had been. The new President and his unpretentious wife Barbara also showed their fellow Americans that life in the Bush White House would be comfortable, low key, and family oriented. Patrician informality and concern for the sensibilities of ordinary Americans would be in; Hollywood-style nouveau riche glitz and glamour was out.

Bush's first budgetary proposals sent to Congress in February 1989 offered a few programs to combat drug abuse and improve the nation's public schools. He also sought additional funding for child care, clean air, AIDS research, and the homeless. In keeping with his campaign promises, he sought no new taxes to pay for these programs; indeed, he proposed a tax cut—he wanted Congress to reduce the capital gains tax by 15 percent. He insisted that, even with his tax cut, his new funding proposals could be paid for, the deficit reduced, and the bankrupt savings and loans banks resuscitated by the increased revenues flowing into the federal treasury from accelerated economic growth. Few economists outside of his administration shared Bush's faith in the miraculous powers of supply-side economics. They feared that the new president might be practicing his own brand of "voodoo economics."

Bush's presidency was dominated by two overriding concerns: the savings and loan crisis and reducing the huge federal deficits. Bush proposed a rescue plan to either close or sell the bankrupt S & Ls and repay depositors. Congress created a new agency, the Resolution Trust Corporation (RTC), to sell off the assets of the failed thrifts to solvent banks,

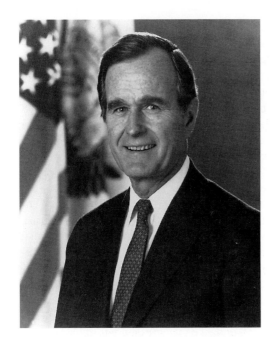

Figure 16.1   George Bush, forty-first president.
Source: The White House Photo Office.

often on very favorable terms. At the same time, the FSLIC was folded into the Federal Deposit Insurance Corporation (FDIC) to provide the billions needed to bail out depositors.

The new president acknowledged that, "Our will is strong, but our wallet is weak," that is, Bush insisted that straitened fiscal circumstances precluded new federal initiatives, however desirable, that cost much money. The Reagan legacy included a prosperous economy, but its prosperity could only be sustained by huge deficit spending—deficit spending by the federal government, by business, and by individual consumers. Reagan's tax cuts had compounded the federal government's enormous debt problems.

In the spring of 1991, Bush, under heavy pressure from Congress to reduce the federal debt, conceded the need to accept some new taxes. His concession promptly outraged his conservative supporters and many citizens who had voted in good faith for Bush and his no-new-taxes promise. This acute sense of betrayal felt by conservatives contributed to Bush's electoral defeat in 1992. In October 1991, the Bush administration and the Democratically controlled Congress finally agreed on a combination of tax hikes and budget cuts that promised modest reductions in the budget deficits over the next four years.

Around the time that the president and Congress worked out their budget deal, the economy slipped into a recession, the first in nearly a decade. Despite complaints emanating from many workers who had lost their jobs, congressional Democrats, and even some Republicans, Bush denied for months that the economy had lapsed into recession, and then he appeared unable to devise a program of economic restoratives. The recession, combined with Bush's denials and inept response, seriously undermined his popularity with American voters.

Bush also inherited a host of serious social problems from his predecessor. The most feared pathology was the ongoing AIDS epidemic. By 1990, the disease had claimed over 110,000 lives, and an estimated 1.5 million people had tested HIV-positive. Most of the AIDS-infected cases involved gay males, but in the early 1990s, the proportion of AIDS cases among African American and Hispanic American intravenous drug users grew rapidly. The number of women infected with the AIDS virus also was increasing. Despite huge sums spent on research, there appeared to be no prospect for an early cure or even the development of an effective vaccine. However, some progress occurred in the development of drugs and therapies that suppressed or delayed the onset of AIDS symptoms.

Bush continued the war on drugs that had begun during Reagan's years without noticeable success. He pushed for more stringent drug testing in the workplaces of America, for better enforcement of existing drug laws, and for additional measures taken to interdict the flood of illicit drugs pouring into the country from Mexico, Peru, and Colombia. Despite stepped-up efforts on all three fronts, drugs, especially "crack" cocaine, remained popular and widely available within the United States. There also was a connection between widespread crack use and the rising level of violence amidst the inner cities of America. Violent turf wars between rival gangs of drug dealers took hundreds of lives annually. Even though the Bush administration spent billions of dollars on its war on drugs, it made no effort to curb the great American appetite for drugs.

THE SUPREME COURT IN THE 1990s

By the late 1980s, the Supreme Court, because of the presence of three Reagan appointees—Sandra Day O'Connor, Antonin Scalia, and Anthony Kennedy—had taken a conservative turn. In *Webster v. Reproductive Health Care Services* (1989), the Court, by a 5 to 4 majority decision, sustained a Missouri statute that restricted abortions. In *Rust v. Sullivan* (1990), the Court upheld a federal law that prohibited personnel at federally funded health clinics from discussing abortion with their clients. In *Planned Parenthood v. Casey* (1992), the Court, by a 5 to 4 decision, upheld a Pennsylvania law requiring a twenty-four-hour waiting period and informed consent before an abortion could be performed. Although the conservative Supreme Court placed restrictions on women's access to abortion, it never challenged *Roe v. Wade,* which established that women have a constitutional right to abortion. In other important constitutional areas, the Court adhered to liberal precedents. In *Texas v. Johnson,* a 5 to 4 majority ruled that burning an American flag as a form of protest was protected free speech under the First Amendment.

With the retirement from the Court in 1990 and 1991 of William Brennan and Thurgood Marshall, two elderly liberal associate justices, President Bush had the opportunity to add additional conservative jurists to the Supreme Court. His first appointment, David Souter, an obscure federal judge from New Hampshire, was quickly confirmed by the Senate with little opposition. Bush's second appointment, Clarence Thomas, a conservative African American jurist, was narrowly confirmed by the Senate in October 1991 by a 52 to 48 vote.

Judge Thomas had to survive challenges from many Senators dissatisfied with his evasive answers to their questions concerning his views on abortion and other issues. In dramatic televised hearings before the Senate Judiciary Committee, Thomas also had to refute charges brought by Oklahoma University law professor Anita Hill, that he had sexually harassed her when she had worked for him at two federal agencies in 1982 and 1983. The nation witnessed three days of often sexually explicit testimony. The close Senate vote to confirm Thomas was not appreciably affected by the hearings; nearly all of the negative votes were cast by Senators who would have voted against Thomas had Hill never made her charges.

The controversy attending Thomas's confirmation hearings brought to the fore the troubling matter of sexual harassment of women in the workforce and political system, both of which remained male dominated at the higher levels. The hearings also heightened public disgust with the performance of Washington politicians and made people more aware of the seriousness of the problems women faced in the workplaces of America.

The insensitive treatment accorded to Hill by some Republican male Senators who were bent on discrediting her testimony revived the moribund feminist political movement. Patricia Ireland, a spokeswoman for NOW, vowed that women would seek to replace male office holders with qualified women. Using as their rallying cry "they still don't get it," mostly liberal Democratic women entered mainstream politics in unprecedented numbers during the 1992 elections.

Figure 16.2   With the addition of George Bush's nominees, David Souter and Clarence Thomas, the Court took on a strong conservative tone. Photo by Joseph H. Bailey.
Source: National Geographic Society. Joseph H. Bailey © National Geographic Society.

THE END OF THE COLD WAR

The advent of the Bush presidency coincided with dramatic developments occurring in the international realm that brought about the most fundamental changes in American foreign policy since World War II. The most important of these changes was the decline of Communism, as evidenced by the disintegration of the Soviet empire in Eastern Europe and then the disintegration of the Soviet Union itself. The Soviet revolution, which had convulsed the world in 1917 and had been one of the most potent shapers of twentieth-century history, disintegrated. The Cold War, which had been the dominant reality of international life for nearly a half-century, suddenly ended. It ended when the Soviet Union had to withdraw from international competition because of severe internal economic weaknesses.

Although conservative spokesmen were quick to say that the rapid U.S. military buildup in the 1980s, the Reagan Doctrine, and Reagan's bold rhetorical attacks on Communism brought about the demise of Communism and the Soviet Union, it appeared more likely that Communism had simply imploded. Communism mainly collapsed from within. Washington's aggressive strategies and the pressures of trying to compete with Americans probably hastened the Soviet collapse. While the Soviet Union clearly was the ultimate loser in a long, historic struggle for world supremacy, the American victory had its costs. The American people endured secret radiation experiments, spying by their own government, anti-Communist witch-hunts, and fear of nuclear annihilation. The U.S. government also spent $4 trillion on nuclear weapons during the life of the Cold War!

The sudden demise of Communism caught official Washington by complete surprise. Neither the CIA, nor any of the other American intelligence agencies, nor any of the myriad of experts inhabiting prestigious U.S. strategic institutes and "think tanks" perceived that the Soviet system was on the verge of collapse until it disintegrated. Communism failed primarily because it did not work. It failed to deliver on its promises of material abundance and social equality. It also failed to transform humanity and reshape society and history. The workers' paradise failed to materialize. The basic failure was economic. Communism's political and ideological failures derived from its economic dysfunctions. Communism never achieved legitimacy among most of the Soviet people, and it finally had to be scrapped, consigned to the dustbin of history.

Ironically, Mikhail Gorbachev inadvertently destroyed the Soviet Union while trying to save it. He understood that the Achilles' heel of the Soviet empire was its stagnating economy and lagging technology, especially in the areas of computer technology and information processing. By the mid-1980s, Gorbachev perceived that the Soviet Union could no longer maintain the arms race with the United States and feed its own people. In a effort to revive a failing system, Gorbachev proclaimed an era of *perestroika* (economic restructuring) and *glasnost* (openness). Economic controls were loosened, and censorship was lifted. A civic awakening occurred. Government was reinvented and revitalized. An elected parliament supplanted party *aparatchiks*.

Although Soviet politics were liberalized, the economy continued to deteriorate. Continuing economic rot forced Gorbachev to pull Soviet troops out of Afghanistan, ending a nine-year war in that country. In July 1989, Gorbachev repudiated the Brezhnev doctrine that had given Soviet troops the right to intervene in Eastern European countries. He cut loose from client governments in Poland, Czechoslovakia, East Germany, Hungary, Bulgaria, and Romania. Once the people of these countries understood that Soviet tanks no longer protected their rulers, they promptly overthrew all of those hated regimes. The Stalinist dominoes toppled in rapid succession.

The most dramatic event heralding the collapse of the Soviet empire in Eastern Europe occurred on November 9, 1989, when the Berlin Wall that had so long served as a hated symbol of the impasse between East and West was breached. Thousands of East and West Germans crossed the former barrier as the long-standing division of their country began to end. With the borders between East and West Germany fully open, the Communist government of East Germany collapsed. A democratic government quickly replaced it, and on October 3, 1990, East Germany peacefully reunited with West Germany. A reunified Germany remained in NATO, and the Warsaw Pact disintegrated. Since disputes between the Soviets and Americans over Germany had been the major causes of the Cold War that began during the mid-1940s, it was historically appropriate that the reunion of Germany signaled the beginning of the end of that long conflict.

The American leaders, Reagan and his successor George Bush, supported the Gorbachev revolution. Many U.S. corporations quickly penetrated the Soviet Union. McDonald's opened a large restaurant just off of Red Square. But it was the Germans who led the

Figure 16.3   As the Soviet Union began to fall apart, Mikhail Gorbachev lost public confidence and was eclipsed by Boris Yeltsin.   *Source:* AP/Wide World Photos.

drive to dominate East European and Soviet markets in the immediate aftermath of the Cold War. Gorbachev and the West Germans cut a deal: the Germans would provide about $30 billion to prop up the ailing Soviet economy, and in return, Gorbachev would accept a speedy German reunion and the end of the Warsaw Pact. Within the declining Soviet Union, Gorbachev's liberal reforms and retreat from the empire alarmed powerful elements. On August 19, 1991, Stalinist reactionaries among the Red Army, the KGB, and the bureaucrats who controlled the Soviet economy attempted a military coup. It failed, because of its own ineptitude and because 40,000 citizens of Moscow defied the putschists and rallied around the courageous populist leadership of Boris Yeltsin.

THE REAPPEARANCE OF RUSSIA

The death of the Soviet Union was officially proclaimed on December 21, 1991, by Boris Yeltsin and several other leaders who announced the formation of a new federation of sovereign states. The former USSR had mutated into an eleven-republic Commonwealth of Independent States, three independent Baltic nations, and an independent Georgia. On December 26, major European powers and the United States officially recognized the Russian republic under Yeltsin's leadership as the de facto successor to the defunct Soviet Union. Presiding over nothing, Gorbachev resigned on December 27.

Since its reappearance as a nation, Russia has remained mired in economic stagnation without the institutional base or competitive strategy required to develop a dynamic capitalistic economy. Exogenous factors such as falling world commodity prices, particularly for oil, and turmoil in Asian financial markets have hurt Russia. Political instability and the fiscal strategies pursued by the Yeltsin government have been more damaging. Since 1992, Yeltsin has pursued an anti-inflationary program that has three key elements—cutting spending, increasing tax collection, and privatizing the economy by selling off state-owned enterprises; keeping a strong ruble by maintaining exchange rates; and promoting trade and foreign investment in Russia.

The results have all been ruinous. Russia's economy has been decimated. The nation has been in a 1930s'-style depression since the early 1990s. Real GDP has fallen 40 percent to 50 percent since 1990; investment has shrunk by 80 percent. Eighty percent of the 150 million Russian people lived in poverty in 2000.

The Russian economy and government are controlled by a capitalist elite, most of them former Communist bureaucrats, that acquired ownership of formerly state-owned enterprises for a fraction of their value. This coterie of billionaires concealed income, evaded taxes, and moved an estimated $200 billion in assets out of the country. The Yeltsin government frequently refused to pay workers or send pensioners their monthly stipends, and the domestic economy has been starved for capital. Science and technology have been gutted. Most foreign investment has been channeled into securities, not direct investment. Russia has dropped into the ranks of a Third World exporter of raw materials. In 1999–2000, its once mighty armed forces have deteriorated to the point where they could not suppress a rebellion of a few thousand Islamic militants raging in Chechnya, a collapsed ministate located in the Caucasus Mountains.

BUSH AND THE POST–COLD WAR WORLD

As the Soviet Union receded from the world stage, Europe, led by a reunified Germany, moved to form a European community free of tariffs, travel restrictions, and monetary impediments. In December, 1991, Europeans approved a foundational treaty, the Treaty of Maastricht, which created the European Union, and established a three-stage process for the creation of a single European currency. During the 1990s, the European Union evolved into the world's largest economic superpower, a gigantic market of over 370 million people in

Figure 16.4   Post-Cold War Europe, 1992.   *Source:* U.S. State Department.

15 countries, with ever more countries clamoring to get in. The "euro" made its debut as a transnational currency January 1, 1999.

Along the Pacific Rim, Japan, although suffering a series of financial and economic setbacks in the 1990s, remained an economic and a financial giant. America's Asian/Pacific trade in 1998, over half of it with the Japanese, was much larger than its trade with Europe. China, its economy freed from Communist shackles, had the world's fastest growing major economy. By the summer of 1998, the Chinese GDP had reach an estimated $1.6 trillion, making it the third largest economy in the world. China, with its rich resources, vast population, and dynamic economy, appeared to have an unbounded future.

U.S. foreign policy in Latin America also benefited from the end of the Cold War. Gorbachev announced that Soviet aid to prop up the Cuban economy, which had been running at $5 billion per annum, would be drastically curtailed. In the post–Cold War era, Castro appeared to be an aging caudillo clinging to power in an impoverished insular backwater country within a hemisphere that had long since abandoned dictatorship of either the Leftist or Rightist variety and had turned instead to U.S.-style liberal democracy.

In Nicaragua, the Sandinistas also felt the impact of the end of the Cold War. The Soviet Union, which had subsidized the Sandinistas to the tune of $500 million a year, was forced to turn off the aid spigot. In early 1990, the Sandinistas permitted free elections under international supervision to take place in Nicaragua. To their dismay, a coalition of anti-Sandinista forces, led by Violetta Chamorro, won. Abandoned by their Soviet patron and repudiated by the people of Nicaragua, the Sandinistas peacefully surrendered their power. Chamorro became Nicaragua's first freely elected president in more than sixty years.

While supporting the spread of democracy in Nicaragua, the United States also settled some scores in Panama. In December 1989, the United States sent military forces into Panama to overthrow dictator Manuel Noriega and to install a pro-American government. Noriega had previously worked with the CIA. He later broke with the Americans, supported the Sandinistas, and got rich as a drug trafficker for the Medellin cartel. Previously, U.S. federal grand juries had indicted Noriega for drug smuggling, gun running, and money laundering. Noriega was captured and brought to the United States for trial. Public opinion polls showed that the Panamanian intervention, which was of dubious legality since Panamanian officials had not requested U.S. assistance, was overwhelmingly popular with Americans. President Bush's popularity soared.

China also felt the impact of rising anti-Communism. In April 1989, thousands of Chinese students and intellectuals gathered in Beijing's Tiananmen Square to demand democracy for China. The pro-democracy movement spread rapidly, and soon demonstrations sprouted in Nanjing, Shanghai, and other Chinese cities. Americans strongly supported the pro-democracy forces. For a time, Chinese authorities appeared uncertain about how to respond to the challenge because of the extensive coverage that the pro-democracy movement received in the world's media. But on the morning of June 4, 1989, Deng ordered the Chinese army to crush the drive for democracy. A brutal massacre ensued, which claimed the lives of at least 1,000 people. Dissident democrats were hunted down and jailed en masse. The nascent pro-democracy movement was violently suppressed. President Bush publicly condemned the Chinese regime's slaughter of its own people, however, he would take no actions that might jeopardize the friendly relations carefully cultivated between the Chinese and American governments since Richard Nixon's historic journey to Beijing in 1972.

While Communist regimes were collapsing in Eastern Europe, Rightist authoritarian regimes also were succumbing to the world democratic revival. In Chile, in 1989, General Pinochet's regime gave way to a democratically elected government. In South Africa, Frederick DeKlerk became prime minister in August 1989. Within a few months, he released African National Conference leader Nelson Mendela from prison, where he had languished for more than twenty-five years. In 1991, as DeKlerk began dismantling apartheid, President Bush lifted American sanctions. In April 1994, there occurred one of the most thrilling moments in modern world history, a kind of political miracle: South Africa held its first elections in which all South Africans could vote. Mendela was elected president, and a multiracial parliament was chosen. Democracy had trumped apartheid. Ballots had bested bullets.

Elsewhere in Africa, famine threatened millions of people, especially in Somalia, where years of civil war had destroyed any semblance of government. In December 1992, when warring Somali factions diverted UN-sanctioned food relief shipments to black markets, Washington sent in 30,000 troops to protect food deliveries. Under President Clinton, the U.S. mission expanded to include restoring order and state building. Eighteen U.S. Marines were killed while fighting the forces of Somali warlord Mohammed Farah Aidid. Yielding to public pressure to bring the troops home, Clinton withdrew all American forces from Somalia in 1994. Somalia quickly resumed its anarchic ways.

WAR IN THE PERSIAN GULF

During January and February 1991, in the first major military action of the new post–Cold War era, America and its allies fought a war in the Persian Gulf against Iraq. The war had a long preparation time, and it derived in part from previous U.S. Middle Eastern diplomatic policies. During the Iraqi-Iranian War, America often aided Iraq to prevent an Iranian victory that Washington feared could threaten the oil-rich Saudis. During the late 1980s, America sent the Iraqis nearly a billion dollars' worth of agricultural, economic, and technical aid. These aid packages included high-tech equipment such as advanced computers and lasers that could be used to produce weapons of mass destruction, including nuclear bombs.

Soon after Iraq's war with Iran ended in a draw under the terms of an agreement brokered by UN representatives, Kuwait, which along with Saudi Arabia had bankrolled Iraq's war with the Iranians, increased its production of oil in violation of OPEC rules. World oil prices dropped, hurting Saddam's government, already deeply in debt and dependent on oil revenues for sustaining the Iraqi economy. Saddam also was angered by the Kuwaitis and Saudis for their refusal to forgive Iraq's huge indebtedness to them. He asserted claims to Kuwaiti territory based on maps predating the 1919 political settlement that had created the modern nation-state of Iraq. Saddam also may have harbored grandiose ambitions of becoming the dominant power in the Gulf area.

Even as Iraq prepared for war, U.S. leaders did not anticipate military action in the region. Washington was preoccupied with the historic events that brought the Cold War to a sudden end. Its policies in the Gulf region still turned on the notion that Iraq was the major counterweight to Iranian revolutionary aggression. On the eve of Iraq's invasion of Kuwait, the American ambassador to Baghdad, April Gillespie, told Saddam that the United States would not become involved in regional disputes, although it would defend its vital interests. Saddam apparently interpreted Gillespie's remark as a green light for aggression.

On August 2, 1990, Iraqi forces suddenly occupied Kuwait and threatened neighboring Saudi Arabia, possessor of more than one-fifth of the world's proven oil reserves. Bush, determined to force Saddam Hussein to withdraw his forces from Kuwait, forged an international coalition under UN auspices to thwart Iraqi aggression. Bush also persuaded Soviet leader Mikhail Gorbachev to abandon his former Iraqi clients and to support the UN initiative.

The United Nations promptly enacted Resolution 661, authorizing a trade embargo against Iraq. The international community clamped a tight economic boycott on Iraq and deployed a military force of some 250,000 troops to defend Saudi Arabia from possible attack. Most of these forces, dubbed Operation Desert Shield, were American troops under the command of U.S. Army General Norman Schwarzkopf. But Schwarzkopf's forces also included a sizable representation from Great Britain, France, and several Arab countries, including Saudi Arabia, Egypt, Syria, and the United Emirates.

Initially, Bush appeared willing to use military force defensively to protect Saudi Arabia and other possible Iraqi targets from attack and to let economic pressures force Saddam out of Kuwait. But almost from the beginning of Gulf military operations, Pentagon planners were preparing for offensive military action. Bush soon became convinced that the boycott would not work, or else it would take too long. During November, 550,000 soldiers representing some twenty countries gathered in and near Saudi Arabia.

Many liberal Democrats opposed military action against Iraq. They believed that the economic boycott should be given a chance to work, and they also did not want America to go to war without congressional approval. The United Nations enacted Resolution 629 on November 29, which set January 15, 1991, as a deadline for Iraqi withdrawal from Kuwait and authorized the use of force to drive the Iraqis from Kuwait if they did not leave by that date. On January 12, both the House and the Senate, after passionate debates and by narrow majorities, enacted resolutions formally approving the use of American military force in the Gulf.

On January 16, 1991, the war in the Persian Gulf, Operation Desert Storm, commenced when President Bush ordered an Allied air assault on Iraqi targets. Deploying an impressive arsenal of high-tech weaponry, America and its allies waged a destructive five-week air war against the Iraqis. Priority targets included Iraqi chemical, biological, and nuclear production, command and control facilities, and airfields.

On February 23, 1991, General Schwarzkopf ordered his forces, now 700,000 strong, to attack Iraqi positions in Kuwait and Southern Iraq. Two hundred thousand American, British, and French armored forces roared across the undefended Iraqi border with Saudi Arabia 200 miles to the west of Kuwait. They smashed into the elite Republican Guard forces and quickly demolished them. Within four days, Allied forces had overwhelmed the Iraqis, whose fighting capabilities had been seriously eroded by the weeks of air attacks that had preceded the invasion. President Bush offered a cease-fire, and the Iraqis quickly accepted it. At war's end, the Allied forces occupied Kuwait and held Southern Iraq.

Only 148 Americans were killed and 467 wounded during the short war, but an estimated 100,000 Iraqi soldiers and civilians died. In addition to light casualties, the dollar costs of the war to Americans also proved light because the $30 billion tab for the war was picked up by wealthy U.S. allies that did not send combat forces.

Americans erupted in frenetic celebration over a victory that had been achieved so quickly and at such a low cost. Parades and celebrations, which had not been seen since 1945, welcomed home the conquering heroes. President Bush's approval ratings soared beyond 90 percent. The Gulf War made a national hero of General Schwarzkopf, the commander who had led Allied forces to a quick victory. The Gulf War was the most popular one since the Spanish-American War. In the first major crisis of the post–Cold War era, America had asserted its leadership, and the Soviets had followed the United States' lead.

The war also received saturation-level media coverage. American home audiences followed the war around the clock on the Cable News Network (CNN). But the U.S. military tightly controlled television reportage, and American TV viewers saw only a censored version of the war. Most TV journalists willingly allowed themselves to be manipulated by the military in exchange for access to war stories. Reporters were allowed in the field only with military escorts who controlled what they saw and who they interviewed. The televised version of the Gulf War that was presented to American audiences was a sanitized affair. Americans saw little of the gory realities of a war that included large numbers of civilian casualties and the slaughter of tens of thousands of Iraqi soldiers.

The immediate U.S. policy goal in the Persian Gulf War was liberating Kuwait. Larger American strategic goals included keeping the vast Middle Eastern oil reserves in friendly hands and destroying Saddam Hussein's capacity to wage offensive war or to achieve paramountcy in the Persian Gulf region. U.S. officials also were determined to terminate Iraq's ability to develop weapons of mass destruction. Concern about Iran also entered into the foreign policy calculus.

Even though the Persian Gulf War was pronounced a great success, critics observed that while the Allied coalition succeeded in driving the Iraqis out of Kuwait, it failed to bring down Saddam Hussein. Bush encouraged ethnic Kurds and Shiite Muslims within Iraq to rebel, but when they did, Washington allowed Saddam to crush them. Bush's reluctance to continue the war derived from Saudi fears that if Saddam were deposed, Iraq would disintegrate. The Saudis preferred a defanged Saddam presiding over a stable Iraq than chaos and civil war on their border. The Saudis also feared Iranian hegemony in the region in the wake of an Iraqi collapse. Years later, both President Bush and his former National Security Adviser Brent Scowcroft acknowledged that at the time they expected that Saddam Hussein would be overthrown in the face of a crippling military defeat.

The short war had a negligible impact on the American economy. Domestic oil prices dropped, but the economy remained mired in recession. President Bush's high approval ratings at the time of the war dissipated during the next six months, as the U.S. economy remained in the doldrums. There was a poignant aftermath to the war. Hundreds of Persian Gulf veterans developed a variety of symptoms, including fatigue, nausea, joint pain, and memory loss after serving in the combat zone. Medical experts believed that many of these

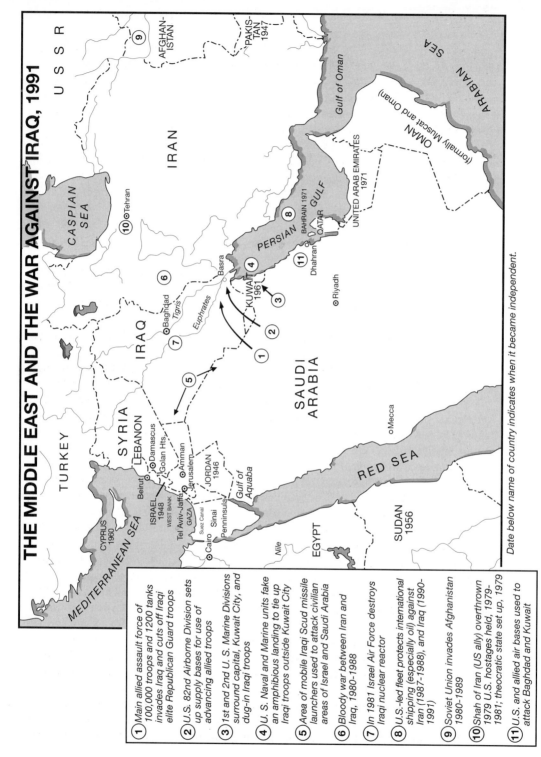

THE MIDDLE EAST AND THE WAR AGAINST IRAQ, 1991

① Main allied assault force of 100,000 troops and 1200 tanks invades Iraq and cuts off Iraqi elite Republican Guard troops

② U.S. 82nd Airborne Division sets up supply bases for use of advancing allied troops

③ 1st and 2nd U. S. Marine Divisions surround capital, Kuwait City, and dug-in Iraqi troops

④ U. S. Naval and Marine units fake an amphibious landing to tie up Iraqi troops outside Kuwait City

⑤ Area of mobile Iraqi Scud missile launchers used to attack civilian areas of Israel and Saudi Arabia

⑥ Bloody war between Iran and Iraq, 1980-1988

⑦ In 1981 Israel Air Force destroys Iraqi nuclear reactor

⑧ U.S.-led fleet protects international shipping (especially oil) against Iran (1987-1988), and Iraq (1990-1991)

⑨ Soviet Union invades Afghanistan 1980-1989

⑩ Shah of Iran (US ally) overthrown 1979 U.S. hostages held, 1979-1981; theocratic state set up, 1979

⑪ U.S. and allied air bases used to attack Baghdad and Kuwait

Date below name of country indicates when it became independent.

Figure 16.5   The Middle East and the war against Iraq, 1991.   *Source:* Public Domain map.

veterans were suffering from the effects of having been exposed to chemical and biological agents released when Allied forces destroyed Iraqi poison gas storage facilities.

Because of the Soviet collapse and the smashing Iraqi defeat, Israel felt more secure than at any other time since the Jewish state was founded. Responding to American pressures, Israeli leaders agreed to participate in an international conference convened in Madrid in December 1991 to try to resolve the Palestinian issue and to achieve a comprehensive Middle East peace treaty. Delegates from several Arab nations and representatives of the Palestinians engaged in dialogues with Israeli envoys. In the spring of 1993, the talks were placed on hold as Israeli security forces fought with Palestinian militants in the occupied territories.

THE ELECTION OF 1992

In the summer of 1990, the economy slid into a recession, the first downturn in eight years, ending the longest period of growth and prosperity in modern American history. Its major causes included a combination of private and public indebtedness, excess productive capacity, and declining consumer confidence. Other causes included low rates of savings and investment, a slump in the world economy that hurt American export sales, and cuts in military and aerospace spending in the post–Cold War era.

Although the recession was not a severe one, the American people reacted very negatively to it. The economic downturn undermined Bush's popularity. The President compounded his political troubles by refusing to acknowledge that the economy had been hit by a recession until six months after its onset. It was the slow recovery from the recession coupled with Bush's political failures that put the long-term Republican hold on the White House in jeopardy. The state of the economy and jobs for the people became the dominant issues in the 1992 elections.

In the fall of 1991, when Democratic leaders declared their candidacies for their party's 1992 presidential nomination, the most prominent names decided not to run because they had concluded that George Bush was unbeatable. Their withdrawals opened the door for a young, energetic governor, William Jefferson "Bill" Clinton, of Arkansas. Clinton, during the 1980s, had been critical of both conservative Republican economic policies and of what he called liberal Democratic "tax and spend" alternatives. He had served as chairman of the Democratic Leadership Council, a group of moderate Democratic leaders intent on winning control of the national party. They were the tribunes of what they called a "third way"; they sought a middle ground between the extremes of statist liberalism on the Left and unrestrained free market capitalism on the Right.

Early in the campaign, during the New Hampshire primary, Clinton was forced to respond to allegations that he had had an affair with a woman who had worked in the governor's office in Little Rock. These allegations nearly destroyed his candidacy before it got going. He also acknowledged smoking marijuana while a college student, but he claimed that he did not inhale and had broken no laws. More seriously, he appeared to have manipulated the selective service system to avoid military service during the Vietnam War era. Another disturbing quality emerged as Clinton campaigned in the early Democratic primaries. His answers and explanations to the myriad of accusations that came his way seemed designed more to evade or appease than to clarify. This political Artful Dodger soon acquired the nickname "Slick Willie."

Nevertheless, Clinton moved ahead quickly in the Democratic primaries. He rather easily defeated two weak rivals, former Massachusetts Senator Paul Tsongas and former California Governor Jerry Brown. Clinton demonstrated resiliency, an ability to hit back at detractors, and, most of all, an impressive grasp of the important issues facing the American people in 1992. At the Democratic Convention in Madison Square Garden in New York City in July, the delegates proceeded to nominate the first baby-boomer ticket in American political history; forty-five-year-old Bill Clinton for president and forty-two-year-old Albert Gore for vice president. In his crisp acceptance speech, Clinton pronounced an end to spendthrift liberalism and special-interest politics. He called for welfare reform, affordable health care for all Americans, a tax cut for the middle class, higher taxes for rich people, tax breaks for small businesses, and sharp reductions in military spending. Polls taken shortly after the Democratic Convention gave Clinton a substantial lead over George Bush.

A strong third-party candidate, maverick Texas billionaire populist H. Ross Perot, entered the 1992 campaign. While Bush and Clinton battled their way through the primaries, Perot's electronic grassroots campaign was fueled by voter outrage at a political system that could not address the real problems facing ordinary Americans, much less solve them. The feisty Texan enlivened the political landscape with his presence during the election of 1992. By May, Perot was outpolling both Clinton and Bush in some national surveys. Suddenly, in mid-July, Perot announced that he was withdrawing from the presidential race, and he threw his support to Bill Clinton, who, Perot claimed, had taken up his issues.

During the fall campaign, Clinton attacked what he called the "trickle-down" economic policies of the Reagan and Bush administrations, while carefully avoiding the label of liberal big spender. He portrayed himself as "an agent of change" to appeal to Perotistas. Clinton called for welfare reform to get the votes of Reagan Democrats. He repeated his proposals made at the Democratic Convention for affordable health care for all Americans, taxing the rich, and tax breaks for the middle class.

Bush made a strenuous bid for reelection. He tried to run on his foreign policy record, but in 1992, in the post–Cold War era, the American people considered foreign policy issues secondary or peripheral. Bush blamed the Democratically controlled Congress for political gridlock, the lingering recession, and the runaway deficits. Mostly he concentrated his fire on Bill Clinton. He charged Clinton with being an old-fashioned tax and spend liberal disguised as a moderate. He questioned Clinton's character and his judgment. He challenged Clinton's patriotism for being a draft avoider and even questioned his loyalty for having visited the Soviet Union. "Who do you trust?" became the focal point of Bush's campaign in its frantic final weeks. However, Bush's shrill attacks on Clinton had little impact on voters' behavior.

In the final month of the campaign, the mercurial Perot leaped back into the fray. Once again, the election became a three-way contest. The election results confirmed the lead that Clinton had long maintained in the polls. He received 43.7 million votes to Bush's 38.1 million and Perot's 19.2 million. He carried thirty-two states and the District of Columbia with a total of 370 electoral votes to 168 for Bush and none for Perot. For the first time since 1977, the Democrats won control of both the White House and Congress.

Clinton's moderate campaign partially restored the old Democratic coalition that had been ripped to shreds by Nixon and Reagan. Clinton retained the African American vote. Hard times and Bush's failed policies brought many Reagan Democrats back to the fold. Clinton got much political mileage out of his oft-repeated slogan, "It's the economy, stupid!" He probably won the election by carrying Ohio, Illinois, Michigan, and Pennsylvania, all of which had gone to Bush in 1988. Clinton also received a majority of the women's and youth vote. Clinton and Gore, both moderate Southerners, also chipped away at the Solid South, which had been solid for Republicans in recent presidential elections. They carried their home states of Arkansas and Tennessee, and they also picked up Louisiana and Georgia. In addition, they carried normally Republican California with its huge bloc of fifty-four electoral votes.

The Democrats picked up one Senate seat, giving them a 58 to 42 edge. The large Democratic majority in the House of Representatives shrank a little, from 266 to 166 to 260 to 174. Although the shift in relative strength of the major parties was slight, the year 1992 represented one of upheaval in Congressional voting. Elections for the House were held for the first time under the reapportionment brought about by the 1990 census. Demographic trends underway since World War II continued to prevail. Sunbelt states such as California, Arizona, Texas, and Florida were the big winners, gaining many additional seats. The Northeastern states and the old industrial states of the Upper Midwest continued to be the big losers, losing the seats that the Southern Rim states gained. Political power in America continued to flow to the South, the Southwest, and the West.

Many voters perceived legislators as being more concerned about office perks than serving the public. More incumbents resigned or were defeated in primary elections than for any election since 1946. Women, African Americans, Asian Americans, and Hispanics were elected to the House of Representatives in record numbers. In the Senate, women scored a major breakthrough: five women, all of them Democrats, won seats. Carol Moseley Braun from Illinois became the first African American woman to serve in the Senate. California sent two women to the Senate, and Colorado sent Native American Ben Nighthorse Campbell.

THE DEMOCRATS RETURN

As in 1960, the 1992 election wrought both a change of party in the White House and a generational shift along the corridors of power. With Clinton and Gore in office and with over 100 new members of Congress in place, the baby boomers assumed national leadership. Clinton made good on his pledge to diversify the upper echelons of the executive branch by selecting many women and minority candidates. Women headed the Environmental Protection Agency and the Council of Economic Advisers. Janet Reno was chosen as the first woman Attorney General. Clinton's determination to select women for important offices also reflected the influence of his wife Hillary Rodham Clinton, who aspired to be the most influential First Lady since Eleanor Roosevelt.

The new president quickly became embroiled in a controversy with the Pentagon over his proposal to allow openly gay and lesbian people to serve in the armed forces. Because of the deeply ingrained hostility within the military services toward openly gay and lesbian people serving on active duty, Clinton was forced to delay the implementation of this reform. In July 1993, Clinton announced a compromise policy that had the support of the Joint Chiefs of Staff: the military would no longer ask prospective recruits questions about their sexual orientation and would no longer employ security forces to hound suspected gays and lesbians out of the armed forces. However, gays and lesbians serving in the military could not engage in overt homosexual behavior on or off military duty stations; in addition, open acknowledgment of gay or lesbian preferences would be grounds for dismissal from military service. This "don't ask, don't tell, don't pursue" compromise failed to satisfy gay and lesbian activists, who vowed to continue their campaign to achieve equality within the armed forces in the courts, and it angered those who opposed any change in the anti-gay and lesbian policies of the military services. Evidence also surfaced in the late 1990s that military security forces continued to harass suspected gay and lesbian personnel despite the new policy.

Clinton also displayed a tendency to abandon or delay many of his campaign commitments, giving rise to the fear that he was less an "agent of change" than a canny politician who exploited popular resentment against the performance of a lackluster incumbent and the economic downturn to get elected. Republicans in the Senate and opposition from his own party leaders in both Houses forced him to abandon his proposal to give tax breaks to small businesses and to reduce the size of his promised stimulus package.

Although the recession was clearly over in the spring of 1993 and the economy was growing again, the high rate of unemployment refused to go down, remaining fixed at 7 percent. Thirty-six million Americans lived in poverty. More Americans than ever before were

Figure 16.6   Baby boomers in the White House. President Bill Clinton and First Lady Hillary Rodham Clinton.   *Source:* The White House Photo Office.

receiving food stamps. In the post–Cold War era, cuts in military and aerospace spending brought massive layoffs at prime defense contractors such as Boeing, McDonnel-Douglas, and Lockeed. American businesses both large and small were forced to become more efficient to meet the rigors of world economic competition in the 1990s. They laid off workers and mid-level managers to become more cost-effective operations. Companies replaced human workers with computers and computer-driven machines.

Millions who continued to work had to worker harder and longer than ever before. Pressures on workers to be more productive were unrelenting and intensifying. Record numbers of workers filed disability claims in the 1990s, their ailments linked to stress or to disabling injuries caused by spending too many hours on computer terminals. Millions of workers and their families in the cutthroat 1990s suffered serious declines in the quality of their lives. They worked harder than their parents, endured more stress, and were less well compensated.

The continued decline of trade unions also contributed to the deteriorating status of working people. In 1998, scarcely 15 percent of American workers belonged to unions, down from a high of 35 percent reached during World War II. Beset by corporate downsizing, the wholesale transfer of jobs overseas, harsh union-busting tactics, and increasingly conservative Congresses that were indifferent or hostile to trade union interests, unions have been powerless to lift the wages of most workers or to even protect their jobs. Adjusted for inflation, wage levels in unionized industries have been stagnant for over twenty years, as productivity and corporate profits have soared.

In August 1993, a Democratic Congress enacted a five-year economic renewal program that incorporated some of Clinton's proposals. It raised the top marginal income tax rates from 31 percent to 36 percent, eased taxes on low-income families, and provided funding for education, retraining, and apprenticeship programs aimed at upgrading workers' skills. The program also brought about modest reductions in the deficits that continued to exceed $200 billion annually in 1994 and 1995.

Clinton also expected the North American Free Trade Agreement (NAFTA) to boost efforts at economic renewal. Negotiated by the Bush administration, NAFTA incorporated Mexico into a free trade zone already created by Canada and the United States during Reagan's presidency. NAFTA aroused both strong support and fierce opposition. Liberal Democrats and trade union leaders led the opposition, insisting that NAFTA would send thousands of U.S. jobs south of the border. NAFTA supporters argued that NAFTA would create jobs by opening up Mexican markets to a greater array of U.S. products. With strong support from Republicans, NAFTA carried Congress, giving Clinton a political victory over the liberal wing of his own party.

Congress also approved a new round of tariff reductions on manufactured goods under the General Agreement on Tariffs and Trade (GATT) that had been in place since the end of World War II. In 1994, Clinton followed these victories by reducing trade barriers with major Pacific Rim nations. In 1995, he became embroiled in a nasty trade dispute with Tokyo over its refusal to allow American companies to sell automotive spare parts to the Japanese. Only after Clinton threatened to impose sanctions that would have severely hurt the sale of Japanese luxury automobiles to the United States did the Japanese make concessions.

Polls taken during the 1992 election showed that public concern about the rising tide of crime, especially violent crime, was second only to economic worries. Congress, in 1993, enacted the Handgun Violence Prevention Act. In 1994, it enacted the most costly, far-reaching crime bill in American history. It provided $30 billion to fund increased law enforcement, crime prevention, and prison construction, extended the death penalty to fifty additional federal crimes, and banned the sale of certain kinds of assault rifles.

In October 1993, following the lead of Hillary Rodham Clinton, the Clinton administration undertook the mammoth task of health-care reform. A task force unveiled a complex plan that had three main goals: to provide coverage for the 45 million Americans who had no health insurance, to hold down costs, and to preserve the high quality of available health care for all Americans. The plan would have drastically restructured the existing health care system. All Americans would be enrolled in large, regional health alliances. Individuals could enroll in either a fee-for-service plan, enabling them to choose their own physicians, or in less expensive health maintenance organizations (HMOs) where they would see doctors on the HMO staff. Employers would pay 80 percent of workers' insurance costs. Self-employed workers would buy their own insurance, and Medicaid would continue to cover the poor. To cover the plan's estimated $100 billion in added costs, Congress would enact large tax increases on tobacco products. The administration's health-care reform proposal instantly attracted legions of critics but relatively little support. After six grueling months of hearings, the administration conceded defeat on health-care reform and settled for some token reforms to contain costs. The big losers were the families who had no health insurance in 1994. These working-class families represented one-fifth of the U.S. population under age sixty-five.

THE REPUBLICAN EARTHQUAKE

The 1994 mid-term elections amounted to a popular referendum on Clinton's performance during his first two years in office. A sizable majority of voters used the occasion to voice their dissatisfaction with the first yuppie president. Clinton brought energy, enthusiasm, and good intentions to his job. He possessed an affable personality and considerable political skills. But he made mistakes, and his image was tarnished by scandals. Most of all, he failed to provide strong leadership or to project a coherent vision for the nation. He failed to get most of his important programs through a Democratic Congress. There appeared to be two President Clintons—the moderate New Democrat and the paleoliberal committed to discredited tax and spend policies. Clinton also was hurt by popular anger at government and politicians generally, fears about rising crime rates, unresolved social issues, cultural conflicts, and continuing economic insecurities and discontents. The elections produced one of the most significant transformations in recent political history. The 1994 midterm elections completed the political transition that had begun with Ronald Reagan's electoral victory in 1980.

The elections brought a Republican Congress to power, the first since 1952. Clinton was the first Democratic president to face a Republican-controlled Congress in a half-century. The shock troops leading this Republican political "earthquake" were a group of seventy-three mostly young conservative reformers, many of whom had strong ties to the

Religious Right. New Speaker of the House of Representatives Newt Gingrich was the leader of the Republican revolt. A controversial politician, Gingrich had for years been the House minority leader. He quickly became the second most powerful politician in Washington.

Gingrich read the election results as a mandate for implementing his "Contract with America," a conservative agenda for the 1990s, with a balanced budget, phasing out welfare, and deep tax cuts as its top priorities. In 1995, the most activist Congress in decades enacted legislation that reformed the way the House worked, curtailed affirmative action programs, cut foreign aid, Medicare, and taxes, and reduced budget deficits. Following Gingrich's lead, the 104th Congress set out to downsize the federal government and to dismantle the welfare state.

Clinton could only watch passively as the Republicans seized the legislative initiative. Clinton was forced to adopt a defensive political strategy—of trying to fend off Republican efforts to cut deeply or destroy liberal programs whenever he sensed that he had

Figure 16.7   President Clinton listens to House Speaker Newt Gingrich of Georgia during a meeting in the White House Cabinet Room on Tuesday, September 12, 1995, with members of the bipartisan Congressional leadership to discuss the federal budget. The President said Tuesday that the White House and Congress won't reach an agreement on the budget before the fiscal year ends. Photo by Wilfredo Lee. *Source:* AP/Wide World Photos.

public opinion on his side, and of trying to position himself to win reelection within an increasingly conservative political environment. Twice in the fall of 1995, Republican enthusiasm for deep tax cuts and achieving a balanced budget by 2002, which Clinton opposed, caused a partial shutdown of the federal government. When Clinton vetoed an appropriations bill, some national parks and museums were forced to shut down, and some recipients reported delays in getting Social Security and Medicare payments. Public anger focused mainly on Republicans, who were seen as ideological zealots and irresponsible politicians whose refusal to compromise caused serious problems for many citizens. Gingrich's and Congress's approval ratings plummeted, and Clinton's soared. Clinton had finessed the Republicans and slowed their efforts to eliminate the welfare state.

In 1996, both President Clinton and the Republican-controlled Congress sought a centrist middle ground that produced several important new programs and policies. The minimum wage was increased. A major telecommunications bill replaced government regulation of the industry, permitting open competition among telephone and cable TV companies. Congress also transformed federal agricultural policy, establishing a program that over seven years gradually removed restrictions on farmers and phased out subsidy payments going back to the New Deal era of the 1930s.

The most important legislation enacted by Congress ended the federal welfare program that dated back to the New Deal. The Welfare Reform Act of 1996 returned the program to the states, along with block grants. According to its provisions, many aid recipients were required to find work and to be off welfare within two years. The act also restricted eligibility for welfare to five years during a person's lifetime. The defederalizing of welfare was the most significant downsizing of the federal government in modern times, and it further attenuated the social contract that was at the heart of what remained of the welfare state. It also signaled that, henceforth, state and local governments would have greater responsibilities and would be required to spend more money for social programs. The federal government would have less responsibility and would spend less.

THE ELECTION OF 1996

Several prominent Republicans sought their party's presidential nomination in 1996. The contenders included Lamar Alexander, a Southern moderate, and publishing magnate Steve Forbes, who used the family fortune to finance his campaign promoting a flat tax and balanced budget. Pat Buchanan was back for another go, pushing his populist attack on NAFTA and on multinational corporations and trying to attract the Religious Right with his condemnation of abortion. But Bob Dole, the Senate majority leader, emerged as the party's nominee by capturing a block of key Southern primaries. He ran on a platform intended to attract all Republican factions: deep tax cuts, deregulation, economic growth, a balanced budget, and continued derogation of social programs to the states. He chose former football star Jack Kemp as his running mate.

President Clinton ran a well-funded, smoothly orchestrated centrist campaign tailored to appeal to middle-class suburban voters. He went after the "soccer mom" vote, suburban women whose political concerns focused on families and children. Clinton also attracted strong support from major segments of the business community, particularly from Silicon Valley, telecommunication, multimedia, and entertainment companies. Clinton and Vice President Gore promoted education, job training, and computer literacy as building bridges to the twenty-first century Information Age.

Dole tried to raise the character issue. He called attention to the Whitewater scandals involving a failed real estate development and a defunct savings and loan bank that occurred in Arkansas when Bill Clinton was governor. Because there was no smoking gun, irrefutable evidence of wrongdoing or lawbreaking by either Bill or Hillary Rodham Clinton, and because it happened long before Clinton became president, Dole got little political mileage out of raising the matter. Another scandal occurred during the final weeks of the campaign that cost Clinton some votes and perhaps prevented the Democrats from regaining control of the House of Representatives. Evidence surfaced that the Clinton campaign had illegally raised campaign funds from foreign sources, including Chinese officials.

Clinton and Gore nevertheless coasted to an easy victory in November. They received 49 percent of the vote to Dole's 41 percent and the maverick Ross Perot's 8 percent. Perot had come back for another run, but this time he provided only a colorful footnote to a lackluster campaign. The Democrats accrued 379 electoral votes to 159 for Dole-Kemp, and they carried seven of the eight most populous states with their huge clusters of electoral votes. Dole and Kemp carried twenty-five states, the same number as Clinton and Gore, but they were mostly Southern, Midwestern, and Mountain states. The Republicans retained control of both branches of the Congress, but by reduced majorities.

In what proved a rather dull campaign in which Dole never had a realistic chance of winning, never found an issue or a language to reach voters where they lived, and never mounted an effective attack on either Clinton's character or his performance in office, economic issues probably were the decisive factors. In 1996, the American economy was prosperous and growing. Unemployment and inflation were both low. Dole's age, disability, and sardonic personality probably worked against him. Clinton's youth, energy, empathy, and relentlessly upbeat rhetoric was too much for Dole, Kemp, and the Republicans to overcome.

The election took place within a generally conservative climate of opinion reminiscent of the 1920s. Apathy and even cynicism about politics and politicians prevailed, especially among younger citizens, who viewed the American democratic political process with a mixture of amused contempt and horror. Despite saturation-level multimedia coverage, there was a low level of citizen interest or involvement in the campaigns. Scarcely half of the folks eligible to vote bothered to do so on Election Day. It was clear that it simply did not matter to almost half of the American citizens eligible to vote whether Bill Clinton was reelected or replaced by Bob Dole.

THE IMPEACHMENT OF PRESIDENT CLINTON

Political gridlock and endless partisan politicking characterized the first two years of Bill Clinton's second term of office. The Republicans in control of Congress, chastened by adverse public reactions to their anti-governmental zeal and outmaneuvered politically by the

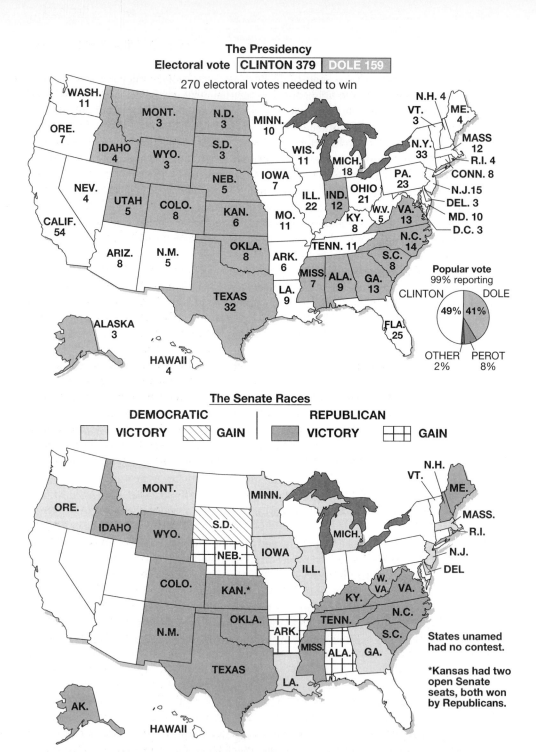

The Presidency

Electoral vote | CLINTON 379 | DOLE 159

270 electoral votes needed to win

WASH. 11
ORE. 7
MONT. 3
IDAHO 4
WYO. 3
N.D. 3
S.D. 3
MINN. 10
WIS. 11
MICH. 18
N.H. 4
VT. 3
ME. 4
N.Y. 33
MASS 12
R.I. 4
CONN. 8
N.J. 15
NEV. 4
UTAH 5
COLO. 8
NEB. 5
IOWA 7
ILL. 22
IND. 12
OHIO 21
PA. 23
DEL. 3
MD. 10
D.C. 3
CALIF. 54
KAN. 6
MO. 11
KY. 8
W.V. 5
VA. 13
ARIZ. 8
N.M. 5
OKLA. 8
ARK. 6
TENN. 11
N.C. 14
S.C. 8
TEXAS 32
LA. 9
MISS. 7
ALA. 9
GA. 13
ALASKA 3
HAWAII 4
FLA. 25

Popular vote
99% reporting
CLINTON — DOLE
49% 41%
OTHER 2%   PEROT 8%

The Senate Races

DEMOCRATIC
VICTORY   GAIN

REPUBLICAN
VICTORY   GAIN

States unamed had no contest.

*Kansas had two open Senate seats, both won by Republicans.

Figure 16.8   The 1996 presidential and senate races—Americans again vote for divided government. *Source:* The New York Times Co., 1996. Reprinted with permission.

President, who co-opted many of their wedge issues, lost momentum. Newt Gingrich was narrowly reelected Speaker of the House of Representatives. He was also reprimanded and fined $300,000 for violating House rules and for "misleading" his colleagues about using tax-exempt donations for political purposes. Clinton was content to propose modest programs to help the middle classes, none of which Congress enacted. Congress also failed to enact a $368 billion settlement against the major tobacco companies to recover the costs of treating smoking-related illnesses, which also included fines for concealing from the public scientific evidence in their possession that proved smoking was hazardous to people's health. The one significant achievement of both Congress and the White House came in May 1997, when they reached a historic agreement on a balanced budget. Because the economy continued to perform strongly, the federal government produced a balanced budget for the fiscal year 1998, the first in nearly thirty years.

Mostly the news out of Washington concerning Clinton's second term focused on a myriad of scandals that plagued the president and at times implicated several Cabinet members and Vice President Al Gore. Many of the scandals stemmed from illegal fund-raising practices during the 1996 presidential campaign. Gore allegedly solicited funds by making illegal phone calls from the White House. The vice president denied that these calls violated the law, because "no controlling legal authority" forbade the practice. There also was evidence that on April 6, 1996, Gore had knowingly attended a fund-raising luncheon held at a Buddhist temple in Hacienda Heights, California. He admitted attending the luncheon, but he denied that he had known in advance that it was a fund-raiser. In July 1997, the Senate convened a special investigating committee, chaired by Republican Senator Fred Thompson of Tennessee, to hold hearings into potentially illegal fund-raising practices relating to both the 1994 and 1996 electoral campaigns. Specifically, the senators wanted to learn if the Chinese government, through illegal campaign contributions, tried to influence the outcome of the 1996 election.

In January 1998, the fund-raising scandals were relegated to the back pages by sensational discoveries that President Clinton had had an eighteen-month-long sexual relationship with Monica Lewinsky, a twenty-one-year-old White House intern from Beverly Hills, which had begun on November 15, 1995. The affair attracted the attention of independent counsel Kenneth Starr, who for three years had been conducting an investigation into possible improper and illegal activity by both Bill and Hillary Rodham Clinton, going back to the days of Whitewater and including several White House scandals. Starr received formal authority on January 16 from a federal court to expand his investigation to determine if Clinton had broken any laws during his efforts to conceal the liaison with Lewinsky. On January 27, Starr formally convened a grand jury inquiry into the affair.

Lewinsky herself was in legal jeopardy, because on January 7, 1998, she had denied under oath that she had had sexual relations with the President in a pretrial deposition that she gave in the Paula Jones case. Jones had first surfaced in February 1994, when she stated that in 1991, while she was a state employee, Governor Bill Clinton of Arkansas had invited her to his hotel room and made a crude demand for oral sex. Jones testified that she had refused Clinton's demand and quickly left the room. At the time Jones came forward with her accusations, President Clinton had denied them all. Jones's lawyers then filed a sexual harassment suit against Clinton. The President had also given a deposition at the

**Figure 16.9   Former White House intern Monica Lewinsky and her attorney William Gins-
burg head to their car from the Wanamaker Building in Philadelphia on Monday, April 6,
1998. Ginsburg was born in the Philadelphia area. Photo by Dan Loh.**   *Source:* AP/Wide
World Photos.

Jones pretrial hearing, in which he denied under oath ever having a sexual relationship with
Lewinsky. On January 26, President Clinton went on television to deny that he had had a
sexual liaison with her. Looking the American people squarely in the eye and wagging his
right index finger, he emphatically stated, "I did not have sexual relations with that woman,
Ms. Lewinsky." Thereafter, he stonewalled the matter, refusing to answer questions or to
discuss the situation further in public. In April 1998, a judge dismissed Jones's suit, observing that even if her account were true, Clinton's behavior, while tacky and coarse, did
not constitute sexual harassment. Months later, on November 13, Clinton agreed to pay
Paula Jones $850,000, and she agreed to drop her efforts to reinstate her case.

    Kenneth Starr, with unlimited resources at his disposal, continued his investigation
of the affair. While Starr's team of experienced prosecutors methodically subpoenaed witnesses and compiled evidence, the President ostentatiously went about conducting the public's business as usual. He and his spokespersons publicly proclaimed that they were coop-

erating with Starr's investigation and that they too wanted the scandal resolved as quickly as possible. Behind the scenes, for seven months, both Clinton's legal advisers and political operatives did everything they could to thwart, discredit, and delay Starr's investigation. Hillary Clinton, on *Good Morning America,* spoke vaguely of a "vast right-wing conspiracy" that had set out to destroy her husband for partisan and ideological reasons. Clinton's lawyers repeatedly tried to find legal grounds to prevent Secret Service agents and senior aides from testifying before the grand jury. The courts kept quashing the legal arguments, and witnesses continued to be compelled to testify. Clinton's power and room for maneuver were both eroded.

As the investigation moved forward, polls periodically showed that Clinton's approval rating remained high. The economy remained strong and prosperous, and the nation was at peace. A majority of those polled viewed Clinton as a capable chief executive. They separated his character flaws and the alleged misdeeds of his private life from his public performance. The same polls also showed that Kenneth Starr remained unpopular with a majority of voters. They did not think that having a sexual relationship with an intern and lying about it, even if proven true, were grounds for impeachment. One series of polls was flatly contradictory: a majority of respondents stated that they believed Clinton had perjured himself, and they also stated that they believed perjury was an impeachable offense. However, that same majority, when asked, did not think Clinton should be impeached for perjury. People also indicated that they were bored, embarrassed, and disgusted by the matter. It had become a distraction; they wanted the politicians to put it behind them and to get on with conducting the nation's business.

On July 17, prosecutors issued a historic subpoena compelling the President's testimony before the grand jury pursuant to a criminal investigation in which he was a suspect. Starr withdrew the subpoena on July 29, when the President agreed to testify from the White House with his lawyers present. On August 6, Lewinsky, granted immunity from prosecution, testified before the grand jury. She told prosecutors that she had had a sexual relationship with the President, contradicting her testimony in the Paula Jones hearing. She also told prosecutors that she and Clinton had discussed how to keep their affair a secret, but that he had never told her to lie nor helped her find a job to keep her quiet.

Clinton testified on August 17. Later that evening, he spoke briefly to the American people. During his four-minute speech, he admitted that he had had "a relationship that was inappropriate" with Lewinsky. He gave no details, nor did he say that it was a sexual relationship. He insisted that he had not committed perjury when he denied under oath at the Paula Jones hearing that he had had sexual relations with Lewinsky, although he acknowledged that his testimony was misleading. But half of his speech was devoted to an angry attack on Kenneth Starr. The speech proved disastrous for the President. It not only failed to end the matter, it ensured its indefinite perpetuation. Most prominent media editorialists and political leaders, including Democratic supporters of the White House, doubted that the president was sincerely repentant, and they criticized his attacks on Starr. In the wake of his speech, mainstream media editorialists and leading Democratic senators condemned the President's behavior and his attempts over the past seven months to deceive both Congress and the American people about it.

On September 9, Starr delivered his report to the House of Representatives, which contained what he considered "substantial and credible information that may constitute grounds for impeachment of the president of the United States." Starr reported that he had gathered evidence showing that Clinton may have committed perjury, tampered with witnesses, obstructed justice, and abused the power of his office. Starr's report set the stage for high political drama reminiscent of the days of Watergate, when a Senate committee discovered that President Nixon had secretly tape-recorded White House conversations. Clinton's stone wall had crumbled.

The most perilous moment of Clinton's presidency and perhaps the defining episode of his public life had arrived. The report landed like a bomb on official Washington, for it posed the threat that President Clinton could be removed from office. On September 10, Congress voted overwhelmingly to make public the Starr Report and most of the supporting evidence that his prosecutors had gathered during their seven-month-long investigation. That evening, the Starr Report went out over the Internet. The next day, both the electronic and print media presented the Starr Report to the public in its entirety or in edited form, with extensive commentary, analysis, and interpretation. On September 21, a videotape of the President's testimony to the grand jury was broadcast to the nation. Clinton's political fate was now in the hands of Congress and public opinion.

After the release of the Starr Report, thousands of pages of supporting testimony, and the videotape; polls showed that two-thirds of Americans still thought that Clinton was doing a good job as president, and they did not want him to be impeached, but his personal ratings had sunk to all-time lows. Clinton the president was praised for a job well done; Clinton the fallible human being was condemned for immorality and for dragging the hallowed office of the presidency into the muck. Many Republicans and a few Democrats called for Clinton's resignation.

To live television coverage by all major networks and CNN, the Republican Party leadership in the House set the impeachment process in motion. The Starr Report was sent to the House Judiciary Committee, which promptly created a special subcommittee to examine the report. On October 5, by a strict 21 to 16 party-line vote, the House Judiciary Committee recommended that the House of Representatives open a formal investigation into grounds for impeaching President Clinton. Three days later, Congress voted 258 to 176 to authorize a formal impeachment inquiry. Thirty-one Democrats joined with the Republican majority in authorizing the impeachment inquiry. In an atmosphere poisoned by intense partisan acrimony, for only the third time in American history the House Judiciary Committee began hearings to determine whether there were grounds for impeaching a president.

On November 3, as the House Judiciary Committee prepared to hold its historic hearings, the 1998 midterm elections were held. Given the timing and the dramatic contexts in which these elections occurred, pundits and politicians gave them extraordinary significance: they would amount to a referendum on the impeachment process. The fate of a presidency hung in the balance. The results surprised the experts and confounded the Republican Right, which was determined to destroy Clinton if it could. After almost a year dominated by scandals that put the White House in jeopardy and put the Democrats on the defensive, the Democrats made unexpected gains on Election Day. They picked up five seats in the House and broke even in the Senate. The Republicans retained control of Congress, but by a smaller majority. In contested House districts, where Republicans made Clinton's alleged immoral and criminal behavior the chief issue, Democratic candidates won more often than they lost. For the first time since 1934, a president's party had gained seats at midterm.

Revealing the disconnection between the American public and the Washington political culture, only 36 percent of those eligible to vote turned out on Election Day. In many states, the turnout was less than 20 percent. The percentage of young people (ages eighteen to twenty-nine) voting also was less than 20 percent. Voter turnout in 1998 was the lowest since 1942, when the nation was at war. Again defying the conventional wisdom, Democrats capitalized on the low voter turnout. They were particularly successful in persuading blacks, union members, and women to vote. Despite the fact that there were six news stories about the scandal for every news story about electoral politics, exit polls revealed that most voters were not interested in the scandal and that it was not a factor in determining how they voted. In all, only about 73 million Americans voted. And the largest number of eligible Americans in history opted not to vote—120 million!

If the election signified anything other than that citizen cynicism and apathy about national politics were worse than ever, it was probably on the whole a victory for incumbents and the status quo. The nation was prosperous, and the economy was strong, having survived the Asian meltdown and the collapse of the Russian and Brazilian currencies. What hurt Republicans most was their capitulation to Clinton on federal spending priorities. Outmaneuvered and fearful of being blamed if another governmental shutdown occurred, the Republican Congress enacted all of Clinton's budget proposals during the Congressional session that ended three weeks before the election. Lacking bold leaders and alternative issues, many Republican voters stayed home on Election Day. In the immediate aftermath of the election, Newt Gingrich, who had rocketed to power and national prominence with the Republican "earthquake" in 1994, was forced to resign the Speakership of the House. The scandal had claimed its most prominent victim. Ironically, the man who had orchestrated the attacks on Clinton was himself consumed by the fires that he had ignited.

Electoral setbacks did not deter the Republican majority on the House Judiciary Committee. Tom DeLay, the Republican House Whip, stepped into the breach left by Gingrich's resignation. The former pest exterminator rallied Republicans to continue the assault on Clinton. On November 18, the House Judiciary Committee, under the leadership of Chairman Henry Hyde, formally convened the impeachment inquiry. Kenneth Starr testified before the Committee the next day. On December 8 to December 10, White House lawyers appeared before the committee to present its defense. On December 11 to December 12, again along strict 21 to 16 party-line votes, the House Judiciary Committee approved four articles of impeachment. The first two articles charged Clinton with perjury, the third article charged him with obstruction of justice, and the fourth article charged him with abuse of power. The committee, also by a straight party-line vote, rejected a censure resolution proposed by the Democratic members.

The drama built as the full House of Representatives opened formal impeachment hearings on December 18. On December 19, William Jefferson Clinton became only the second president in American history to be impeached. (The first was Andrew Johnson in 1868.) The House passed two articles of impeachment: Article 1 charged that Clinton had committed perjury in his grand jury testimony of August 17. It passed by a vote of 228 to 206. Article 2 charged that the President had obstructed justice. It passed by a vote of 221 to 212. Few Democrats voted for either article.

December 19 was one of the weirdest days in the history of the Republic—an enfeebled president took the nation to war on the very day that he was impeached by Congress! He ordered aircraft and missile attacks on Iraq that began four days of intense aerial warfare aimed at degrading Saddam's command and control facilities, his elite Republican Guard forces, and his capacity to build and use weapons of mass destruction, particularly chemical and biological agents. The previous year, Hollywood had produced the wickedly satiric movie *Wag the Dog,* in which a president, to deflect attention from a sex scandal that might cost him his reelection, arranges to have a prominent Hollywood producer create a fake war on television! Although there was no compelling evidence to support the charge, some prominent politicians and pundits suspected that Clinton had timed the attacks on Iraq to rally public support and to deflect attention from the impeachment proceedings.

On January 7, 1999, the Senate impeachment trial of President Clinton opened, presided over by Chief Justice William Rehnquist, with the Senators themselves impaneled as a 100-person jury to hear the case and to render a verdict. Concerned about public opinion, both Senate majority leader Trent Lott and Democratic leader Tom Daschle were determined to conduct a prompt, fair trial and to proceed in a civil, decorous manner in contrast to the impassioned partisan divisions that had characterized the House debates over impeachment. From January 14 to January 16, the thirteen Impeachment Managers from the House, led by Henry Hyde, presented their cases. From January 19 to January 21, a battery of lawyers representing the president, led by Charles Ruff, presented its defenses. The Impeachment Managers argued that Clinton should be convicted on both articles and removed from office. Clinton's defense team presented a dual line of defense: the President was not guilty of either charge, and even if he were, they did not rise to the level of impeachable offenses under the Constitution. The chief issue that caused conflict during the Senate trial and aroused partisan passions was whether to call witnesses, particularly Monica Lewinsky. Lott and Daschle worked out a compromise, whereby the Impeachment Managers got to depose three witnesses—Lewinsky, Vernon Jordan, a powerful friend of the President's, and Sydney Blumenthal, a White House aide. Both sides then used excerpts from those depositions to bolster their closing arguments.

As the Senate trial went forward, there occurred another bizarre bit of political theater. Clinton appeared before a joint session of Congress to present his State of the Union address. It was Clinton at his best; his speech lasted more than an hour. Ignoring the scandals swirling around him and ignoring the ongoing trial that would determine whether he would remain in office to complete his second term, President Clinton offered an extensive array of poll-tested modest programs and initiatives—targeted tax cuts, support for education, and proposals for keeping Social Security and Medicare solvent for the foreseeable future without requiring either tax increases or cuts in benefits. While Democrats cheered, clapped, whistled, and shouted their support, Republicans often sat quietly in their seats, yawned, or twiddled their thumbs. Given the realities of a weakened lame-duck presidency, the poisonous partisan atmosphere prevailing in Washington, and most of all, Republican control of Congress, virtually none of Clinton's lengthy laundry list of proposals stood any chance of becoming public policy.

As the five-week-long trial in the Senate ran its course, polls consistently showed that two-thirds of Americans did not want President Clinton convicted and removed from office. An even larger percentage consistently showed that they approved of the way he performed his job. All of the nation's most influential newspapers, led by the *New York Times, Washington Post,* and *Los Angeles Times,* opposed Clinton's conviction and removal from office. All Democratic Senators and several Moderate Republican Senators indicated that they would vote to acquit Clinton. Since the Constitution required a two-thirds vote to convict, Clinton's acquittal was a foregone conclusion. The vote, when finally taken, was anti-climatic.

On February 12, 1999, the Senate voted to acquit William Jefferson Clinton. The Senate rejected the perjury charge, 55 to 45, and it split 50–50 on the obstruction of justice charge. Many Moderate Republican and Democratic Senators were clearly uncomfortable with their votes for acquittal, because they believed that there was considerable evidence to substantiate the charges of perjury and obstruction of justice against President Clinton brought by the House, and by their votes, they were acquitting him of all charges. However, they had no choice, because they did not want to remove him from the office to which he had been twice elected by the people for criminal behavior that did not threaten the workings of the American government or its Constitutional system. They were voting to save the presidency and the Constitution, not the man whom many distrusted and despised. After the votes were taken, an effort by Senator Dianne Feinstein of California to offer a resolution of censure was quickly defeated.

Shortly after the votes for acquittal, Clinton spoke briefly to the American people. He apologized once more for what he had said and done, for what he had put the American people through, and, for the first time, he acknowledged that his words and deeds had contributed to the sordid sequence of events that had disrupted the normal routines of government. The often surreal story that had dismayed and disgusted most Americans for over a year and had plunged the nation into a prolonged constitutional crisis had finally played itself out.

Following the verdicts for acquittal, the scandal was over in the important sense that the constitutional crisis had passed and Clinton would serve out the remainder of his second term. But there were leftover aspects of the case that cropped up *post hoc* to remind Americans that the President of the United States was a seriously flawed human being. Kenneth Starr and his team of prosecutors continued their investigations. On April 12, Federal Judge Susan Webber Wright, the jurist who had presided over Paula Jones's pretrial hearing, cited Clinton for civil contempt. Judge Wright ruled that Clinton had lied when he denied that he had had sexual relations with Monica Lewinsky. Wright's ruling, which the President's attorneys did not appeal, added juridical credibility to the impeachment proceedings.

The origins of the impeachment controversy lay in the collision of two essentially irrational forces. First was Clinton's pattern of dishonest, ruthless, and occasionally illegal political practices stemming from his Arkansas days, which carried into the White House. These practices were coupled with his history of philandering. Second was his conservative Republican political enemies, who went after him when his affair with Lewinsky became public knowledge. They believed that he was now vulnerable and could be destroyed through the Constitutional process of impeachment and removal from office. As they attempted what amounted to a peaceful assassination, they did not anticipate that a large majority of the American people would rally to Clinton's defense. Had it not been for the strong public support for this beleaguered President, he probably would have been convicted and removed from office.

There were several sources of conservative hostility toward Clinton. One source of conservative animosity was an expression of the ongoing "culture wars." Conservatives were fighting a battle over the 1960s and its legacy. Clinton was the first baby-boomer president, the first acknowledged pot-smoking, draft-dodging, and affair-having leader to make the White House. Conservatives saw him as a sinister threat to the moral order. Another source of conservative fury directed at Clinton was political, a response to his ability to co-opt the best parts of the conservative agenda—issues such as crime, welfare reform, and balancing the budget. He maneuvered the Republicans into contending with Democrats over issues where conservative positions were less popular than his, for example, Social Security and troubling social issues such as abortion and homosexuality. A third and probably the most potent source of conservative hostility toward Clinton was personal. To them, he was a con artist, "Slick Willie," a clever demagogue who faked an empathetic concern for the problems of ordinary Americans. They regarded his "I feel your pain" act as exactly that, a fraud, rather than an expression of natural sympathy. Ironically, conservative hatred of Clinton resembled liberal hostility toward Ronald Reagan. Liberal pundits simply could not accept the notion that Reagan's popular appeal might be genuine and issue based. Generally, liberal intelligentsia chalked up Reagan's broad popular appeal to the mesmeric powers of an old actor tricking the naive and gullible masses (a power they would never grant him as an actor). Some conservative intellectuals such as William Bennett, with no other way of explaining Clinton's popular appeal, denounced the American people for having been taken in by a charlatan and for their loss of a capacity for moral outrage.

Because historians will be explaining and assessing these dramatic events for decades to come, any immediate accounting is risky and must necessarily be tentative and subject to revision. There was a fundamental anomaly—the scandals amounted to a prolonged constitutional crisis that seemed to have no impact outside of the cocooned world of Washington politics. While the President and the Republican majority in Congress were locked in mortal combat, most Americans happily went about their business, and for most Americans, business had never been better. The major electronic and print news media gave the crisis saturation-level coverage from start to finish, yet most Americans could not care less, or so they said, and they denounced the news media for their obsessive devotion to tabloid politics.

One outcome is certain. The first thing all future history texts will say about Bill Clinton is that *he is the only elected president ever to be impeached.* This fact will be the tin can tied to President Clinton's historical reputation that will rattle and bang throughout the ages. This fact will be his chief legacy. It will overpower all other things for which Clinton and his defenders might want to take credit: the most powerful sustained binge of prosperity in American history, spectacular gains in the securities markets, a sharp reduction in violent crime, welfare reform, a balanced budget, crafting a foreign policy that promoted world peace and prosperity, and moving the Democratic Party to the political center where the voters are, thereby displacing the Republicans and marginalizing the liberal troglodytes of his own party.

History also will judge President Clinton to have been irretrievably damaged in the eyes of his family, friends, supporters, and the nation at large. Clinton lost all moral authority to lead, and he survived in office as a severely wounded lame-duck president. Both his power and the power of the presidency were substantially eroded. Given the mutual lack of trust, the poisonous partisanship, and the substantive issue differences between them, it is unrealistic to expect that the Republican-controlled Congress and President Clinton can work cooperatively during the remainder of his presidency to enact legislation dealing effectively with education, drug abuse, crime, tax cuts, Social Security, Medicare, or the myriad of other pressing problems confronting the American people.

If anything positive could be gleaned from the year-long political train wreck, it was the manifest political maturity of the American citizenry, a large majority of whom quickly concluded that a capable President should not be removed from office for matters pertaining to his private life, even if they were sordid and repellent. The fact that the national government survived the year-long crisis strong and intact reaffirmed the good sense of the citizenry, the stability of American political institutions, and the fundamental soundness of the U.S. Constitutional system.

CLINTON AND THE POST–COLD WAR WORLD

Upon taking office in January 1993, Clinton reversed Bush's priorities. For Clinton, an unreconstructed domestic policy wonk, internal affairs took priority over foreign policy issues. In the conduct of foreign affairs, Clinton was handicapped by his lack of experience and his failure to appoint strong leaders to key positions. The Clinton administration also faced the daunting task of developing and implementing effective foreign policies in the post–Cold War era, of redefining America's global role in a new environment without precedents and guidelines to follow.

Because Clinton and his foreign policy advisers lacked clear objectives and did not have a consistent set of criteria to apply, Washington could never decide when or how much U.S. power and prestige to commit to situations that did not involve vital national interests. A pattern of *ad hoc* responses to crises as they arose characterized Clinton's approach to foreign policy. Initially, he tried to downplay international politics and the use of military force. He focused U.S. foreign policy on economic issues, on promoting world recovery from recession and stimulating economic growth. In the area of foreign economic policy, he had major achievements. He supported NAFTA, normalized relations with Vietnam, and negotiated trade agreements with Pacific Rim nations. Ironically, a President who initially tried to avoid the use of military force, ordered more military intervention than any other modern president.

The shortcomings of the Clinton approach to foreign affairs were glaringly evident in Bosnia and Herzegovina, where the largest war in Europe since World War II raged on. Vi-

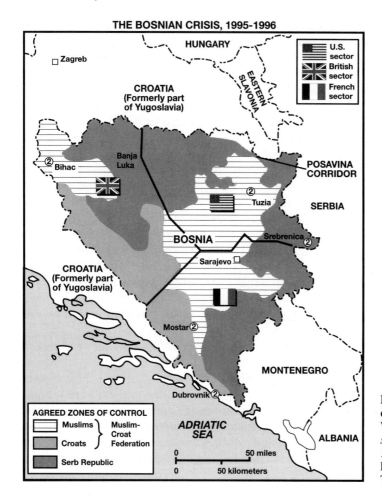

THE BOSNIAN CRISIS, 1995-1996

Figure 16.10   The Bosnian crisis, 1995–1996.   *Source:* Walter LaFeber, *America, Russia, and the Cold War, 1945– 1996,* 8th ed. Copyright © 1997. Reprinted with permission of The McGraw-Hill Companies.

cious ethnic fighting among the Serbs, Bosnian Muslims, and Croats had killed over 100,000 people and generated over 3.5 million refugees. Even though the Bosnian Muslims were clearly the victims of aggression and atrocities and were hindered in their efforts at self-defense by an arms embargo, Washington appeared more concerned with avoiding significant military involvement and confining the conflict to the petty successor states of the now-defunct Yugoslav federation than aiding the Bosnians. Despite feeble UN efforts to broker a cease-fire and negotiate a settlement that would have divided Bosnia and Herzegovina into a patchwork of ethnic regions, the murderous warfare raged on in 1994 and 1995.

In the fall of 1995, Washington, after years of dithering, finally took action. However, the initiative was taken by Assistant Secretary of State Richard Holbrooke, who persuaded Clinton and Secretary of State Warren Christopher to come aboard. Holbrooke understood that the United Nations and the Europeans were incapable of effective action in Bosnia. He brought the leaders of the three warring factions to Dayton, Ohio, in December, brokered a cease-fire, and worked out a complex political settlement to be implemented gradually. The settlement involved sending a NATO force of 60,000 troops, 20,000 of which were U.S. combat soldiers, to police the cease-fire and to allow the political settlement to gradually take hold. A vocal majority in Congress and among the American public opposed sending U.S. forces to Bosnia, because no vital U.S. interest appeared to be at risk and because prospects for achieving a political solution appeared problematic. Military leaders were reluctant to place American forces in a dangerous and violent region where they could incur casualties.

The NATO military intervention succeeded in maintaining a cease-fire, but as the new century began, the confederated Bosnia, in which the three groups—the Croats, Bosnian Muslims, and Serbs—were supposed to live together, had failed completely. Bosnia still had no functioning central government. The country had, in effect, been partitioned. Few refugees had been able to return to their homes. Most prominent war criminals remained ostentatiously at large. The 5,000 U.S. troops that remained in Bosnia had little to do except drink beer, play volleyball, and work out in gyms. Informed observers feared that the uneasy truce would once again explode into ethnic violence if the soldiers were withdrawn.

While Bosnia-Herzegovina endured an uneasy peace, ethnic conflict erupted into war in nearby Kosovo, a Yugoslav province inhabited by 1.8 million ethnic Albanians, who constituted 90 percent of the region's population. The conflict had been building for years. In 1989, the Yugoslav leader, Slobodan Milosevic, revoked the autonomy that the Kosovars had enjoyed since 1974. As the Belgrade regime became more repressive, the Kosovars, following the moderate leadership of Ibrahim Rugova, attempted to create a parallel government that would permit at least a semblance of autonomy within the Yugoslav federation. In 1991, more militant Kosovars founded the Kosovo Liberation Army (KLA); its leaders were committed to achieving independence from Yugoslavia and one day uniting with Albania to create a Greater Albanian nation. KLA terrorists sporadically attacked Serbian soldiers and police stationed in Kosovo. The Serbs retaliated brutally, trying to eliminate the KLA and its supporters. They failed; in the spring of 1998, the KLA began a full-scale rebellion against Serbian authority. Milosevic responded by escalating the violence against the Kosovars. NATO, led by the United States, attempted to impose a settlement of the conflict along the lines of the Dayton Accords of 1995 that had brought a cease fire to Bosnia-Herzegovina.

On March 22, 1999, efforts by Secretary of State Madeleine Albright to broker a settlement between Milosevic and the KLA at Rambouillet, a suburb of Paris, failed. The proposed agreement called for autonomy for the Kosovars to be guaranteed by the insertion of a NATO peacekeeping force that would include 4,000 U.S. soldiers. Albright made it clear to Milosevic that failure to sign the accord would bring NATO aerial assaults on Yugoslavia. The Yugoslav leader showed his contempt for the agreement by not even bothering to show up; his defiance humiliated and infuriated Albright.

On March 24, NATO, commanded by U.S. Army General Wesley K. Clark, began an aerial war, against the Milosevic government to induce him to return to the bargaining table and sign the Rambouillet accords. Albright and Clark clearly underestimated Milosevic.

They assumed that a few days of precision bombing with high-tech cruise missiles and laser-guided "smart bombs" against carefully selected military targets would persuade the Serb leader to return to the bargaining tables prepared to sign. Instead, the canny and ruthless Milosevic escalated his campaign of "ethnic cleansing" against the hapless Kosovars. He knew that most Serbs regarded Kosovo as sacred soil, and they would support his efforts to retain control over it by standing up to NATO aggression. Milosevic also wanted to maintain control of the massive Trepca mining complex located within Kosovo that annually brought in millions of dollars of hard currency.

Within a few weeks NATO confronted a humanitarian catastrophe of biblical proportions. An estimated 800,000 Kosovars were driven from their homes and forced into exile in neighboring Macedonia, Albania, and the Yugoslav province of Montenegro. The presence of these pitiful refugees threatened to destabilize these small, poor multiethnic countries. Another 600,000 Kosovars were driven from their homes and villages, but remained inside the province, hiding in mountain forests and canyons. They had become refugees within their own country. Thousands, mostly young men, had been murdered, another 100,000 Kosovars were missing, and hundreds of villages, towns, and cities had been razed. NATO, the United Nations, and numerous international aid agencies rushed to provide food, clothing, shelter, and medical care to the Kosovars driven out of their own country.

NATO's gradually escalating air war, OPERATION ALLIED FORCE, wrought serious damage to the Serbian infrastructure and industrial capacity. Accidental bombings, including hitting the Chinese embassy and a hospital, claimed hundreds of civilian casualties. But NATO could not stop the horrid process of ethnic cleansing in Kosovo. In fact, the Allied war effort allowed Milosevic to strengthen his hold on power and to escalate his efforts to rid Kosovo of the Kosovars.

For its duration, Operation Allied Force did not want for critics. Senator John McCain, a Vietnam war hero and a candidate for the Republican presidential nomination in 2000, called for sending ground combat forces to Kosovo. He doubted that air power alone could win the war in Kosovo. However, President Clinton, whose nation furnished the pilots and planes that accounted for 90 percent of the sorties flown during NATO's air war, had ruled out sending in ground combat forces, thus foreclosing that option at the outset of the war. Administration spokesmen would not even acknowledge that NATO was at war. They preferred to call OPERATION ALLIED FORCE a form of coercive diplomacy that would bring Milosevic to the bargaining table. Domestic politics appeared to drive U.S. foreign policy in southern Europe and limit NATO's strategic options.

While the war raged in Kosovo, questions about its effectiveness abounded. NATO had started the war with minimal contingency planning. When Milosevic refused to buckle after a few days of bombing and missile attacks, NATO strategists appeared to have no operational plan to put in place. The air war quickly took on an *ad hoc* improvisational quality: as planes became available, fly more sorties and see what happens. It became a pain endurance contest: Which would break first Milosevic or NATO's will?

There was scant legal basis for the military intervention under extant international law. NATO was a defensive military alliance originally created in 1949 to combat the Soviet menace. Serbian forces had committed no acts of aggression against any NATO mem-

Figure 16.11   Ethnic Albanian Kosovar refugees wait to be placed in a tent after crossing into Macedonia at a refugee camp near the village of Blace, 15 miles (25 km) northwest from Skopje, Saturday, April 24, 1999. Hundreds of thousands of ethnic Albanian Kosovars, many with accounts of atrocities committed by Serbian forces, have left their home province through national and regional borders since NATO began airstrikes against Yugoslavia on March 24th. Photo by Boris Grdanoski.   *Source:* AP/Wide World Photos.

ber. The war violated the United Nations charter, which authorized the use of force only in the case of cross-border attacks. However horrific the results of ethnic cleansing might be, Kosovo was an integral part of the sovereign Yugoslav nation. The war also violated the United States Constitution. Congress had not authorized the use of U.S. combat forces in Kosovo. The American people had been given no opportunity to debate the pros and cons of a U.S. war in southern Europe.

President Clinton and Secretary of State Albright maintained that military intervention in Kosovo was justified on humanitarian grounds and that NATO also sought to preserve stability in Europe. But most foreign policy experts could see no vital U.S. economic or geopolitical interests engaged in what was essentially an internal conflict within the remnants of the Yugoslav Federation.

Outside of NATO's orbit, world public opinion condemned the war. To much of the world, NATO appeared to be a bully—the world's most powerful military alliance trying to impose its will and values on a small nation that refused to be intimidated. Russia, traditionally an ally of the Serbia, denounced the bombing and made a public show of solidarity with Milosevic's government. China, outraged at the attack on its embassy, called for a halt to all bombing and threatened to veto any UN resolution authorizing a peacekeeping force in Kosovo.

The American public, horrified by televised images of the hordes of hapless Kosovars streaming into squalid refugee camps in Macedonia and Albania, initially supported the war. But public support was lukewarm from the outset and diminished as the war dragged on. The American people gradually disengaged from the war despite massive and mostly favorable media coverage. On April 30, six weeks into the air war, and with the plight of the Kosovars worse than ever, the Republican-controlled Congress defeated a resolution of support for the air war. Within the nation, there were signs of growing antiwar sentiment such as scattered protest demonstrations and full-page ads in major newspapers.

The War in Kosovo ended after 78 days of bombing. A combination of factors brought Milosevic to sign an agreement that differed little from the Rambouillet formula that he had rejected previously. Patient diplomacy conducted by Assistant Secretary of Defense Strobe Talbot persuaded Russian president Boris Yeltsin to align Russia with NATO despite powerful domestic opposition. President Martti Ahtisaari of Finland and Russian envoy Viktor Chernomyrdin, meeting with Milosevic, brokered the deal. Increasingly effective tactics by NATO pilots, coordinating their attacks with KLA fighters, inflicted major damage on Yugoslav armed forces fighting in Kosovo. Milosevic, isolated diplomatically, his army in Kosovo increasingly battered, calculated that the NATO offer was the best he was likely to get. Besides, he had accomplished his two major goals—consolidating his hold on power in Yugoslavia and at least temporarily ridding Kosovo of much of its indigenous Albanian population.

President Clinton claimed victory for a righteous cause and a stable Europe. NATO's credibility as an aggressive military alliance was maintained. Air power was vindicated. But to many observers, OPERATION ALLIED FORCE appeared to be a military victory that produced mostly political failures. NATO had blundered into a war that lasted far longer and required a commitment of far more military assets than had been planned—against a pipsqueak power led by a tyrant, who first called NATO's bluff and then embarrassed the leaders of the world's mightiest military alliance by absorbing their best shots for nearly three months.

NATO finally obtained UN sanction for its peacekeeping operations, belatedly giving a fig leaf of legitimacy to the enterprise. NATO troops, including 7,000 U.S. soldiers, were deployed in Kosovo as the 40,000 or so Serbian forces exited. As part of the agreement, an undisclosed number of Russian soldiers were also deployed, formally working with the NATO forces, but not under their command. The pro-Serbian Russian troops complicated the staggeringly delicate and difficult problems facing the peace keepers.

NATO's postwar goals were to protect and assist the Kosovars as they returned to their homes. But many of the traumatized Kosovars living in makeshift refugee centers in Macedonia, Montenegro, Albania, and elsewhere did not want to return to Kosovo. After ethnic cleansing—with its mass murders, wholesale destruction of their homes and communities, and massive uprootings of a large part of an entire population, the Kosovars did not feel safe, even with UN peacekeepers on hand. A large number of returning Kosovars found no homes, farms, businesses, or villages to return to. Some returning Kosovars, bitter and seeking reprisal, attacked the small remaining Serbian population, even though most of these Serbs had neither joined nor supported Milosevic's campaign of terror against their Albanian neighbors. Many Kosovars, radicalized by their horrendous experiences, turned to the KLA, having abandoned the moderate strategies of Rugova. These Kosovars will be satisfied only if Kosovo becomes independent. The current agreement does not support independence for the Kosovars, even as a distant goal. NATO leaders have consistently rejected an independent Kosovo because they see it as a prescription for eternal political instability in the Balkans.

As the new century dawned, President Clinton and Secretary of State Albright continued to characterize the military interventions in Bosnia and Kosovo as humanitarian and strategic victories. But the political price was steep—an estimated 300,000 people killed, 3 million more displaced, *de facto* partitions of countries occurred, Western protectorates of indefinite duration involving thousands of U.S. forces created, and $30 billion spent. The NATO goal of peaceful multiethnic democratic nations living in harmony with one another appeared increasingly unattainable and divorced from harsh and enduring Balkan realities.

On another front, the hijackings and other terrorist acts that had tormented the presidencies of Carter and Reagan declined during the early 1990s. Suddenly, in February 1993, terrorism struck the United States when a powerful explosion ripped through the World Trade Center in New York City, killing five people and injuring scores of others. In 1995, following a dramatic trial, a militant sheik and four of his Shiite fundamentalist followers were convicted of the bombing. In April 1995, Americans discovered to their horror that they did not have to import terrorists, when a car bomb of tremendous explosive power utterly demolished a nine-story federal building in Oklahoma City, killing 168 people in all, many of them children who were enrolled in a preschool housed on the second floor. The FBI soon arrested Timothy McVeigh and Terry Nichols, who were charged with the crime. Both men had loose ties with the militia movement, an extreme right-wing fringe group that viewed governmental efforts to impose a measure of gun control as part of a larger conspiracy by the federal government to extinguish freedom in America. Both were convicted of mass murder. McVeigh was sentenced to die for his crimes, and Nichols was given a life sentence without parole. In March 1996, FBI agents, acting on a tip from his brother, arrested fifty-three-year-old Theodore Kacyznski, as the suspected Unabomber, a serial killer who had waged a campaign of terror bombing since 1979 that had killed three people and injured twenty-three others in sixteen separate incidents. In 1998, after a trial in federal court, in Sacramento, California, Kacyznski, who admitted that he was the Unabomber, was sentenced to life imprisonment without parole.

Homegrown terrorist assaults reached new levels of horror in 1998 and 1999, when angry, hateful, and seriously troubled schoolboys gunned down fellow students and teachers in a rash of schoolyard massacres that took place in various cities across the country. The worst slaughter occurred at Columbine High School in Littleton, Colorado, a prosperous, middle-class suburb of Denver where most families were living out their version of the American Dream. On Tuesday morning, April 20, 1999, Eric Harris and Dylan Klebold, both seniors, arrived on campus armed with an arsenal of high-powered weaponry consisting of automatic pistols, automatic rifles, sawed-off 12-gauge shotguns, and dozens of pipe bombs. They proceeded to murder twelve students and a teacher in cold blood and to wound dozens more of their classmates, and then they took their own lives. In the aftermath of the worst school massacre in U.S history, bewildered, frightened, and grieving survivors and their families struggled to cope with the inexplicable tragedy.

While terrorists recruited from various Middle Eastern countries bombed the World Trade Center, Washington's efforts to bring peace to the Middle East progressed. Building on the previous attempts of Presidents Reagan and Bush, Clinton's Secretary of State Warren Christopher urged Israeli and Palestinian leaders to continue the dialogue begun at Madrid following the smashing Allied victory in the Persian Gulf War. In September 1993, following secret talks, there occurred a startling and historic breakthrough. Israel and the Palestine Liberation Organization (PLO) announced an accord granting the Palestinians limited autonomy in the Gaza Strip and in areas of the West Bank. In return, Yassir Arafat, the PLO's leader, renounced terrorism and recognized Israel. On September 13, 1993, in Washington, as a beaming Bill Clinton looked on, Israeli Prime Minister Yitzhak Rabin and Yassir Arafat signed the accord and shook hands. Despite sporadic efforts by Palestinian militants to disrupt the peace process, the Israeli–PLO Accord remained in place, and the PLO steadily increased its capacity to govern in the territories. Progress was stalled in 1996 with the election of conservative Israeli Prime Minister Benjamin Netanyahu and the continuing inability of Arafat's security forces to control Palestinian terrorist activity.

On October 20, 1998, a new agreement was hammered out at the Wye Conference Center in Queenstown, Maryland. Israel agreed to turn over additional West Bank lands to the Palestinians, who agreed to eliminate language from the PLO charter calling for the destruction of Israel. Both President Clinton and especially mortally ill King Hussein of Jordan were instrumental in getting Netanyahu and Arafat to accept the agreement. Militants in both Israel and in lands under the control of the Palestinian authority protested strongly. Sporadic violence continued, and the peace process went forward by fits and starts. Netanyahu's government fell in the wake of the Wye accords. The new Israeli Prime Minister, Ehud Barak, elected in April, 1999, was committed to completing the peace process with the Palestinians and resolving the remaining border dispute with Syria if he could.

While Arabs and Israelis struggled to find a *modus vivendi,* U.S. China policy showed signs of serious strain. Since President Nixon opened the gates to improved relations with China in 1972, all subsequent presidents, whether Republicans or Democrats, have followed similar policies toward the emerging giant. They have all attempted to promote trade and cultural exchanges, have accepted China's human rights violations, and have tried to influence Chinese foreign policy—with very mixed results. President Clinton's China policy of constructive engagement came under heavy fire from the Republican-controlled Congress during his second term. There were allegations of illegal efforts by Chinese officials to influence the outcome of the 1996 presidential election. In the spring of 1999, FBI agents discovered evidence of Chinese nuclear espionage within the United States that evidently had been going on since the 1980s.

The Chinese government continued its efforts to suppress political dissent and religious freedom, to stamp out the vestiges of traditional Tibetan culture, and to intimidate Taiwan. In October, 1999, after lengthy negotiations, Chinese leaders agreed to open certain industries to foreign investment in exchange for U.S. support of China's efforts to join the World Trade Organization (WTO). Washington's China policy was premised on the assumption that political liberalization would follow in the train of economic liberalization.

2000 AND BEYOND

According to historian Eric Foner, the decade of the 1990s was characterized by two central developments. The first was the triumphant growth of U.S.-style corporate capitalism and the simultaneous emergence of the United States as the pre-eminent power in the world. The second was the ongoing battle within the country between the empowered and those who sought empowerment, between the haves and those who wanted to have more. And that second development, the continuing struggle between those who had it made and those who wanted to make it, was essentially a battle to define just what kind of country this rich, hegemonic power was and ought to be.

During the 1990s, American business and political leaders worked cooperatively to promote the growth of a global free market. In 1995, the World Trade Organization (WTO) replaced the General Agreement on Trade and Tariffs (GATT), which had been in place since the end of World War II. Headquartered in Geneva, WTO bureaucrats, meeting behind closed doors, cut deals, usually with corporate lobbyists hovering just outside. WTO officials all embraced the American ideology of the global free market—capital, natural resources, and workers were only factors of production—in their endless quest for trade and profits.

A backlash that had been building for years against the WTO's secretive ways and narrow views exploded in Seattle during the first week of December, 1999. Seattle hosted a World Trade Organization conference where delegates planned to set an agenda for the next round of trade talks. Thousands of protestors representing a broad spectrum of activist groups converged on the normally sedate Northwestern city, including environmentalists, progressive trade unionists, economic nationalists, anarchists, farmers, and college students.

The protestors succeeded in dramatically blowing the cover behind which the WTO had operated since its inception. Televised images of violence in the streets of Seattle dramatically pushed the World Trade Organization into public consciousness for the first time. Never again would it be able to conduct its business beyond the purview of concerned publics. Since the WTO was unable to reach an agreement on an agenda for future talks, the conference was a disaster for the United States as the host nation, and for President Clinton.

Some saw a revival of the 1960s protest spirit among the mostly young activists. That may be the case, but of much greater significance was the fact that the WTO provoked opposition from groups across a broad ideological spectrum that had little in common except their anti-WTO animus. In the streets of Seattle, Rightwing economic nationalists linked arms with Leftwing labor activists and Naderite environmentalists. In the Twenty-First century, the old political paradigms of Left and Right may be replaced by *ad hoc* coalitions of committed activists for whom the old ideological boundaries will either be blurred or ignored.

As troubles in Seattle subsided, the 2000 presidential election began in earnest. In a series of primary battles fought during the spring, Vice President Al Gore secured the Democratic party nomination. He easily fended off a weak challenge by former Senator and star athlete Bill Bradley. Texas governor George W. Bush, the son of former president

George Bush, secured the Republican Party nomination. Governor Bush's main competition came from Arizona Senator John McCain, a certified Vietnam war hero, who seized the mantle of reform by campaigning hard against "politics as usual" and the money-dominated system of campaign financing. McCain surprised both Bush and the pundits by winning the New Hampshire and Michigan primaries. But the feisty governor was able to contain the McCain insurgency by holding on to the core conservative Republican constituencies. With their respective party nominations secured by March, 2000, both Gore and Bush began their campaigns for the White House. Their contest promised to be long, costly, and close.

Experts concerned about the future of the small planet we inhabit fear that rapid world population increases and severe environmental problems pose far more serious long-term threats to our living standards and general sense of well-being than do political and economic problems. On January 1, 1999, the world's estimated population reached 6 billion people. Demographers predict that by the year 2020 the world's population will reach 8 billion. The consequences of such population growth will all be dire. Mass immiseration, especially in Third World countries, will breed extremist political and religious movements that ensure a turbulent future. Surging populations will also use up huge quantities of the earth's finite resources, wipe out millions of acres of rain forests necessary to cool and purify the planet, and extinguish thousands of species of plants and animals, thereby reducing earth's biodiversity. The world's supply of arable farm land and fresh water will continue to diminish. Global warming looms as a serious danger.

As Americans enter the new millennium, they face many challenges at home and abroad. To survive and possibly flourish, they must remain committed to finding new ways of coping with the daunting future now exploding among them.

BIBLIOGRAPHY

As previously mentioned in the introduction to the bibliographic essay in Chapter 15, recent history is best covered in the many fine daily, weekly, and monthly print news media. You might want to reference that introduction for the specific publications listed. Additionally, *The National Review* covers recent history from a conservative perspective, and the *New Republic* covers the same events from a moderate liberal perspective. There is an extensive literature on the AIDS epidemic. One of the best books about AIDS is Randy Shilts's *And the Band Played On.* On contemporary drug problems plaguing Americans see Erich Goode's *Drugs in American Society.* There is a growing literature on all of the historic changes occurring in Eastern Europe and the Soviet Union. See Robert O. Crummey, ed., *Reform in Russia and the USSR* and William E. Griffith, ed., *Central and Eastern Europe: The Opening Curtain.* Two American Sovietologists, Robert Jervis and Seweryn Bailer, eds., present diverse looks at the post–Cold War world in *Soviet-American Relations after the Cold War.* For American–Japanese relations, see Akira Iriye's and Warren I. Cohen's, eds., *The United States and Japan in the Postwar World.* For recent developments in Central America, consult John A. Booth's and Thomas W. Walker's *Understanding Central America.* Judith Miller and Laurie Mylorie, in *Saddam Hussein,* offer an informative study that sheds light on the motivations of the Iraqi leader and the genesis of the Persian Gulf crisis. Recently, President Bush and his former National Security Adviser Brent Scowcroft published a joint memoir, *A World Transformed.* It is the most important book yet written about the end of the Cold War. A recent study that looks to the future of international relations is Paul Kennedy's *Preparing for the Twenty-First Century.*

Appendices

APPENDIX A

The Declaration of Independence

When in the Course of human events, it becomes necessary for one people to dissolve the political bands which have connected them with another, and to assume among the Powers of the earth, the separate and equal station to which the Laws of Nature and of Nature's God entitle them, a decent respect to the opinions of mankind requires that they should declare the causes which impel them to the separation.

We hold these truths to be self-evident, that all men are created equal, that they are endowed by their Creator with certain unalienable Rights, that among these are Life, Liberty and the pursuit of Happiness. That to secure these rights, Governments are instituted among Men, deriving their just powers from the consent of the governed, That whenever any Form of Government becomes destructive of these ends, it is the Right of the people to alter or to abolish it, and to institute new Government, laying its foundation on such principles and organizing its powers in such form, as to them shall seem most likely to effect their Safety and Happiness. Prudence, indeed, will dictate that Governments long established should not be changed for light and transient causes; and accordingly all experience hath shown, that mankind are more disposed to suffer, while evils are sufferable, than to right themselves by abolishing the forms to which they are accustomed. But when a long train of abuses and usurpations, pursuing invariably the same Object evinces a design to reduce them under absolute Despotism, it is their right, it is their duty, to throw off such Government, and to provide new Guards for their future security.—Such has been the patient sufferance of these Colonies; and such is now the necessity which constrains them to alter their former Systems of Government. The history of the present King of Great Britain is a history of repeated injuries and usurpations, all having in direct object the establishment of an absolute Tyranny over these States. To prove this, let Facts be submitted to a candid world.

He refused his Assent to Laws, the most wholesome and necessary for the public good.

He has forbidden his Governors to pass Laws of immediate and pressing importance, unless suspended in their operation till his Assent should be obtained; and when so suspended, he has utterly neglected to attend to them.

He has refused to pass other Laws for the accommodation of large districts of people, unless those people would relinquish the right of Representation in the Legislature, a right inestimable to them and formidable to tyrants only.

He has called together legislative bodies at places unusual, uncomfortable, and distant from the depository of their public Records, for the sole purpose of fatiguing them into compliance with his measures.

He has dissolved Representative Houses repeatedly, for opposing with manly firmness his invasions on the rights of the people.

He has refused for a long time, after such dissolutions, to cause others to be elected; whereby the Legislative Powers, incapable of Annihilation, have returned to the People at large for their exercise; the State remaining in the mean time exposed to all the dangers of invasion from without, and convulsions within.

He has endeavoured to prevent the population of these States; for that purpose obstructing the Laws of Naturalization of Foreigners; refusing to pass others to encourage their migration hither, and raising the conditions of new Appropriations of Lands.

He has obstructed the Administration of Justice, by refusing his Assent to Laws for establishing Judiciary powers.

He has made Judges dependent on his Will alone, for the tenure of their offices, and the amount and payment of their salaries.

He has erected a multitude of New Offices, and sent hither swarms of Officers to harass our People, and eat out their substance.

He has kept among us in time of peace, Standing Armies without the Consent of our legislature.

He has affected to render the Military independent of and superior to the Civil power.

He has combined with others to subject us to a jurisdiction foreign to our constitution, and unacknowledged by our laws; giving his Assent to their acts of pretended Legislation:

For quartering large bodies of armed troops among us:

For protecting them, by a mock Trial, from punishment for any Murders which they should commit on the Inhabitants of these States:

For cutting off our Trade with all parts of the world:

For imposing taxes on us without our Consent:

For depriving us in many cases, of the benefits of Trial by Jury:

For transporting us beyond Seas to be tried for pretended offences:

For abolishing the free System of English Laws in a neighbouring Province, establishing therein an Arbitrary government, and enlarging its Boundaries so as to render it at once an example and fit instrument for introducing the same absolute rule into these Colonies:

For taking away our Charters, abolishing our most valuable Laws, and altering fundamentally the Forms of our Governments:

For suspending our own Legislature, and declaring themselves invested with Power to legislate for us in all cases whatsoever.

He has abdicated Government here, by declaring us out of his Protection and waging War against us.

He has plundered our seas, ravaged our Coasts, burnt our towns, and destroyed the lives of our people.

He is at this time transporting large Armies of foreign Mercenaries to complete the works of death, desolation and tyranny, already begun with circumstances of Cruelty & perfidy scarcely paralleled in the most barbarous ages, and totally unworthy of the Head of a civilized nation.

He has constrained our fellow Citizens taken Captive on the high Seas to bear Arms against their Country, to become the executioners of their friends and Brethren, or to fall themselves by their Hands.

He has excited domestic insurrections amongst us, and has endeavoured to bring on the inhabitants of our frontiers, the merciless Indian Savages, whose known rule of warfare, is an undistinguished destruction of all ages, sexes and conditions.

In every stage of these Oppressions We have Petitioned for Redress in the most humble terms: Our repeated Petitions have been answered only by repeated injury. A Prince, whose character is thus marked by every act which may define a Tyrant, is unfit to be the ruler of a free people.

Nor have We been wanting in attention to our British brethren. We have warned them from time to time of attempts by their legislature to extend an unwarrantable jurisdiction over us. We have reminded them of the circumstances of our emigration and settlement here. We have appealed to their native justice and magnanimity, and we have conjured them by the ties of our common kindred to disavow these usurpations, which, would inevitably interrupt our connections and correspondence. They too have been deaf to the voice of justice and of consanguinity. We must, therefore, acquiesce in the necessity, which denounces our Separation, and hold them, as we hold the rest of mankind, Enemies in War, in Peace Friends.

We, therefore, the Representatives of the United States of America, in General Congress, Assembled, appealing to the Supreme Judge of the world for the rectitude of our intentions, do, in the Name, and by Authority of the good People of these Colonies, solemnly publish and declare, That these United Colonies are, and of Right ought to be Free and Independent States; that they are Absolved from all Allegiance to the British Crown, and that all political connection between them and the State of Great Britain, is and ought to be totally dissolved; and that as Free and Independent States, they have full Power to levy War, conclude Peace, contract Alliances, establish Commerce, and to do all other Acts and Things which Independent States may of right do. And for the support of this Declaration, with a firm reliance on the protection of divine Providence, we mutually pledge to each other our Lives, our Fortunes and our sacred Honor.

APPENDIX B

Amendments to the United States Constitution Since 1945

The Twenty-Second Amendment

The Twenty-Second Amendment, a belated slap at Roosevelt by a Republican-dominated Congress, limits the president to two terms in office. Ironically, the two presidents to which it has applied were Republicans, Dwight D. Eisenhower and Ronald Reagan.

Amendment XXII [1951]

No person shall be elected to the office of the President more than twice, and no person who has held the office of President, or acted as President, for more than two years of a term to which some other person was elected President shall be elected to the office of the President more than once.

But this Article shall not apply to any person holding the office of President when this Article was proposed by the Congress, and shall not prevent any person who may be holding the office of President, or acting as President, during the term within which this Article becomes operative from holding the office of President or acting as President during the remainder of such term.

The Twenty-Third Amendment

The Twenty-Third Amendment allows residents of the District of Columbia to vote in presidential elections.

Amendment XXIII [1961]

Section 1. The District constituting the seat of Government of the United States shall appoint in such manner as the Congress may direct:

A number of electors of President and Vice President equal to the whole number of Senators and Representatives in Congress to which the District would be entitled if it were a State, but in no event more than the least populous State; they shall be in addition to those appointed by the States, but they shall be considered, for the purposes of the election of President and Vice President, to be electors appointed by a State; and they shall meet in the District and perform such duties as provided by the twelfth article of amendment.

Section 2. The Congress shall have the power to enforce this article by appropriate legislation.

The Twenty-Fourth Amendment

The Twenty-Fourth Amendment prevents the states from making payment of a poll tax a condition for voting. Common at the time among Southern states, the poll tax was a capitation (poll, or head) tax on individuals. A poll tax receipt was often required in order to vote. It was designed to prevent uneducated people, especially blacks, who were unaccustomed to saving receipts, from voting.

Amendment XXIV [1964]

Section 1. The right of citizens of the United States to vote in any primary or other election for President or Vice President, for electors for President or Vice President, or for Senator or Representative in Congress, shall not be denied or abridged by the United States or any State by reason of failure to pay any poll tax or other tax.

Section 2. The Congress shall have the power to enforce this article by appropriate legislation.

The Twenty-Fifth Amendment

The Twenty-Fifth Amendment, inspired by President Eisenhower's heart attack and President Johnson's abdominal surgery, provides for the temporary replacement of a president who is unable to discharge the duties of the office.

Amendment XXV [1967]

Section 1. In case of the removal of the President from office or his death or resignation, the Vice President shall become President.

Section 2. Whenever there is a vacancy in the office of the Vice President, the President shall nominate a Vice President who shall take the office upon confirmation by a majority vote of both houses of Congress.

Section 3. Whenever the President transmits to the President pro tempore of the Senate and the Speaker of the House of Representatives his written declaration that he is unable to discharge the powers and duties of his office, and until he transmits to them a written declaration to the contrary, such powers and duties shall be discharged by the Vice President as Acting President.

Section 4. Whenever the Vice President and a majority of either the principal officers of the executive departments, or of such other body as Congress may by law provide, transmit to the President pro tempore of the Senate and the Speaker of the House of Representatives their written declaration that the President is unable to discharge the powers and duties of his office, the Vice President shall immediately assume the powers and duties of the office of Acting President.

Thereafter, when the President transmits to the President pro tempore of the Senate and the Speaker of the House of Representatives his written declaration that no inability exists, he shall resume the powers and duties of his office unless the Vice President and a majority of either the principal officers of the executive departments, or of such other body as Congress may by law provide, transmit within four days to the President pro tempore of the Senate and the speaker of the House of Representatives

their written declaration that the President is unable to discharge the powers and duties of his office. Thereupon Congress shall decide the issue, assembling within 48 hours for that purpose if not in session. If the Congress, within 21 days after receipt of the latter written declaration, or, if Congress is not in session, within 21 days after Congress is required to assemble, determines by two-thirds vote of both houses that the President is unable to discharge the powers and duties of his office, the Vice President shall continue to discharge the same as Acting President; otherwise, the President shall resume the powers and duties of his office.

The Twenty-Sixth Amendment

The Twenty-Sixth Amendment corrected a historic injustice: young men could be drafted and sent to war at age eighteen but were not allowed to participate in the nation's democratic processes until they were twenty-one. It extended the vote to eighteen year olds.

Amendment XXVI [1971]

Section 1. The rights of citizens of the United States, who are 18 years of age or older, to vote shall not be denied or abridged by the United States or any state on account of age.

Section 2. The Congress shall have the power to enforce this article by appropriate legislation.

The Twenty-Seventh Amendment

The Twenty-Seventh Amendment has a curious history. It was originally proposed as part of the Bill of Rights to allay citizen fears that politicians would vote themselves fat pay raises while in office. It lay quiet for two centuries until congressional scandals forced Congress in 1992 to quickly resuscitate it. It was speedily ratified and became law on May 7, 1992.

Amendment XXVII [1992]

No law, varying the compensation for the services of the Senators and Representatives, shall take effect, until an election of Representatives shall have intervened.

APPENDIX C

Presidential Elections Since 1944

YEAR	CANDIDATES RECEIVING MORE THAN ONE PERCENT OF THE VOTE (PARTIES)	POPULAR VOTE	ELECTORAL VOTE
1944	FRANKLIN D. ROOSEVELT (Democratic)	25,606,585	432
	Thomas E. Dewey (Republican)	22,014,745	99
1948	HARRY S. TRUMAN (Democratic)	24,179,345	303
	Thomas E. Dewey (Republican)	21,991,291	189
	J. Strom Thurmond (States' Rights)	1,176,125	39
	Henry Wallace (Progressive)	1,157,326	0
1952	DWIGHT D. EISENHOWER (Republican)	33,936,234	442
	Adlai E. Stevenson (Democratic)	27,314,992	89
1956	DWIGHT D. EISENHOWER (Republican)	35,590,472	457
	Adlai E. Stevenson (Democratic)	26,022,752	73
1960	JOHN F. KENNEDY (Democratic)	34,226,731	303
	Richard M. Nixon (Republican)	34,108,157	219
1964	LYNDON B. JOHNSON (Democratic)	43,129,566	486
	Barry M. Goldwater (Republican)	27,178,188	52
1968	RICHARD M. NIXON (Republican)	31,785,480	301
	Hubert H. Humphrey (Democratic)	31,275,166	191
	George C. Wallace (American Independent)	9,906,473	46
1972	RICHARD M. NIXON (Republican)	45,631,189	521
	George S. McGovern (Democratic)	28,422,015	17
	John Schmitz (American Independent)	1,080,670	0
1976	JAMES E. CARTER, JR. (Democratic)	40,274,975	297
	Gerald R. Ford (Republican)	38,530,614	241
1980	RONALD W. REAGAN (Republican)	42,968,326	489
	James E. Carter, JR. (Democratic)	34,731,139	49
	John B. Anderson (Independent)	5,552,349	0
1984	RONALD W. REAGAN (Republican)	53,428,357	525
	Walter F. Mondale (Democratic)	36,930,923	13
1988	GEORGE H. W. BUSH (Republican)	47,917,341	426
	Michael Dukakis (Democratic)	41,013,030	112
1992	WILLIAM JEFFERSON CLINTON (Democratic)	43,682,624	370
	George H. W. Bush (Republican)	38,117,331	168
	H. Ross Perot (Independent)	19,217,213	0
1996	WILLIAM JEFFERSON CLINTON (Democratic)	47,401,185	379
	Bob Dole (Republican)	39,397,469	159
	H. Ross Perot (Independent)	8,845,294	0

APPENDIX D

Population of the United States Since 1940

1940	132,000,000
1950	151,000,000
1960	179,000,000
1970	205,000,000
1980	227,000,000
1990	247,000,000
2000 (est.)	275,000,000

APPENDIX E

Presidents, Vice Presidents, and Cabinet Officers Since 1945

PRESIDENT AND VICE PRESIDENT	SECRETARY OF STATE	SECRETARY OF TREASURY	SECRETARY OF WAR	POSTMASTER GENERAL	ATTORNEY GENERAL	SECRETARY OF INTERIOR
33. Harry S. Truman (1945) Alben W. Barkley (1949)	James F. Byrnes (1945) George C. Marshall (1947) Dean G. Acheson (1949)	Fred M. Vinson (1945) John W. Snyder (1946)	Robert P. Patterson (1945) Kenneth C. Royall (1947) **Secretary of Navy** James V. Forrestal (1945) **Secretary of Defense** James V. Forrestal (1947) Louis A. Johnson (1949) George C. Marshall (1950) Robert A. Lovett (1951)	R. E. Hannegan (1945) Jesse M. Donaldson (1947)	Tom C. Clark (1945) J. H. McGrath (1949) James P. McGranery (1952)	Harold L. Ickes (1945) Julius A. Krug (1946) Oscar L. Chapman (1949)
34. Dwight D. Eisenhower (1953) Richard M. Nixon (1953)	John Foster Dulles (1953) Christian A. Herter (1959)	George M. Humphrey (1953) Robert B. Anderson (1957)	Charles E. Wilson (1953) Neil H. McElroy (1957) Thomas S. Gates (1959)	A. E. Summerfield (1953)	H. Brownell, Jr. (1953) William P. Rogers (1957)	Douglas McKay (1953) Fred Seaton (1956)
35. John F. Kennedy (1961) Lyndon B. Johnson (1961)	Dean Rusk (1961)	C. Douglas Dillon (1961)	Robert S. McNamara (1961)	J. Edward Day (1961) John A. Gronouski (1963)	Robert F. Kennedy (1961)	Stewart L. Udall (1961)
36. Lyndon B. Johnson (1963) Hubert H. Humphrey (1965)	Dean Rusk (1963)	C. Douglas Dillon (1963) Henry H. Fowler (1965) Joseph W. Barr (1968)	Robert S. McNamara (1963) Clark M. Clifford (1968)	Lawrence F. O'Brien (1965) W. Marvin Watson (1968)	Robert F. Kennedy (1963) N. deB. Katzenbach (1965) Ramsey Clark (1967)	Stewart L. Udall (1963)
37. Richard M. Nixon (1969) Spiro T. Agnew (1969) Gerald R. Ford (1973)	William P. Rogers (1969) Henry A. Kissinger (1973)	David M. Kennedy (1969) John B. Connally (1970) George O. Shultz (1972) William E. Simon (1974)	Melvin R. Laird (1969) Elliot L. Richardson (1973) James R. Schlesinger (1973)	Winton M. Blount (1969)	John M. Mitchell (1969) Richard G. Kleindienst (1972) Elliot L. Richardson (1973) William B. Saxbe (1974)	Walter J. Hickel (1969) Rogers C. B. Morton (1971)

38. Gerald R. Ford (1974) Nelson A. Rockefeller (1974)	Henry A. Kissinger (1974)	William E. Simon (1974)	James R. Schlesinger (1974) Donald H. Rumsfeld (1975)	William B. Saxbe (1974) Edward H. Levi (1975)	Rogers C. B. Morton (1974) Stanley K. Hathaway (1975) Thomas D. Klepper (1975)
39. James E. Carter Jr. (1977) Walter F. Mondale (1977)	Cyrus R. Vance (1977) Edmund S. Muskie (1980)	W. Michael Blumenthal (1977) G. William Miller (1979)	Harold Brown (1977)	Griffin B. Bell (1977) Benjamin R. Civiletti (1979)	Cecil D. Andrus (1977)
40. Ronald W. Reagan (1981) George H. W. Bush (1981)	Alexander M. Haig, Jr. (1981) George P. Shultz (1982)	Donald R. Regan (1981)	Caspar W. Weinberger (1981)	William French Smith (1981)	James G. Watt (1981) William Clark (1983) Donald P. Hodel (1985)
41. Ronald W. Reagan (1985) George H. W. Bush (1985)	George P. Shultz (1985)	James B. Baker III (1985)	Caspar W. Weinberger (1985)	Edwin Meese III (1985)	Donald P. Hodel (1985)
42. George H. W. Bush (1989) J. Danforth Quayle (1989)	James B. Baker III (1989)	Nicolas Brady (1989)	Richard Cheney (1989)	Richard Thornburgh (1989)	Manuel Lujan (1989)
43. William Jefferson Clinton (1993) Albert Gore (1993)	Warren Christopher (1993) Madeleine K. Albright (1996)	Lloyd Bentsen (1993) Robert E. Rubin (1995)	Les Aspin (1993) William J. Perry (1994) William S. Cohen (1997)	Janet Reno (1993)	Bruse Babbitt (1993)

Secretary of Energy	Secretary of Agriculture	Secretary of Veteran Affairs	Secretary of Commerce	Secretary of Labor	Secretary of Health and Human Services	Secretary of HUD	Secretary of Education	Secretary of Transportation
James Walters (1989) Hazel O'Leary (1993) Federico Peña (1997) Bill Richardson (1998)	Clayton Yeutter (1989) Mike Espey (1993) Dan Glickman (1995)	Edwin Derwinski (1989) Jesse Brown (1993) Togo West, Jr. (1998)	Robert Mosbacher (1989) Ron Brown (1993) Mickey Kantor (1996) William Daley (1997)	Elizabeth Dole (1989) Robert Reich (1993) Alexis Herman (1997)	Louis W. Sullivan (1989) Donna Shalala (1993)	Jack Kemp (1989) Henry Cisneros (1993) Andrew Cuomo (1997)	Richard Riley (1993)	Samuel K. Skinner (1989) Federico Peña (1993) Rodney Slater (1997)

Source: From Unger, pp. 826–828. Reprinted with permission of Prentice Hall.

APPENDIX F

Immigration to the United States by Region and Selected Countries of Last Residence Since 1941

REGION AND COUNTRY OF LAST RESIDENCE	1941–50	1951–60	1961–70	1971–80	1981–89	1984	1985	1986	1987	1988	1989
All countries	1,035,039	2,515,479	3,321,677	4,493,314	5,801,579	543,903	570,009	601,708	1,601,516	643,025	1,090,924
Europe	621,147	1,325,727	1,123,492	800,368	637,524	69,879	69,526	69,224	67,967	71,854	94,338
Austria-Hungary	28,329	103,473	26,022	16,028	20,152	2,846	2,521	2,604	2,401	3,200	3,586
Austria	24,860	67,106	20,621	9,478	14,566	2,351	1,930	2,039	1,769	2,493	2,845
Hungary	3,469	36,637	5,401	6,550	5,586	495	591	565	632	707	741
Belgium	12,189	18,575	9,192	15,329	6,239	787	775	843	859	706	705
Czechoslovakia	8,347	918	3,273	6,023	6,649	693	684	588	715	744	526
Denmark	5,393	10,984	9,201	4,439	4,696	512	465	544	515	561	617
France	38,809	51,121	45,237	25,069	28,088	3,335	3,530	3,876	3,809	3,637	4,101
Germany	226,578	477,765	190,796	74,414	79,809	9,375	10,028	9,853	9,923	9,748	10,419
Greece	8,973	47,608	85,969	92,369	34,490	3,311	3,487	3,497	4,087	4,690	4,588
Ireland	19,789	48,362	32,966	11,490	22,229	1,096	1,288	1,757	3,032	5,121	6,983
Italy	57,661	185,491	214,111	129,368	51,008	6,328	6,351	5,711	4,666	5,332	11,089
Netherlands	14,860	52,277	30,606	10,492	10,723	1,313	1,235	1,263	1,303	1,152	1,253
Norway-Sweden	20,765	44,632	32,600	10,472	13,252	1,455	1,557	1,564	1,540	1,669	1,809
Norway	10,100	22,935	15,484	3,941	3,612	403	388	367	372	446	556
Sweden	10,665	21,697	17,116	6,531	9,640	1,052	1,171	1,197	1,168	1,223	1,253
Poland	7,571	9,985	53,539	37,234	64,888	7,229	7,409	6,540	5,818	7,298	13,279
Portugal	7,423	19,588	76,065	101,710	36,365	3,800	3,811	3,804	4,009	3,290	3,861
Romania	1,076	1,039	2,531	12,393	27,361	2,956	3,764	3,809	2,741	2,915	3,535
Soviet Union	571	671	2,465	38,961	42,898	3,349	1,532	1,001	1,139	1,408	4,570
Spain	2,898	7,894	44,659	39,141	17,689	2,168	2,278	2,232	2,056	1,972	2,179
Switzerland	10,547	17,675	18,453	8,235	7,561	795	980	923	964	920	1,072
United Kingdom	139,306	202,824	213,822	137,374	140,119	16,516	15,591	16,129	15,889	14,667	16,961
Yugoslavia	1,576	8,225	20,381	30,540	15,984	1,404	1,521	1,915	1,793	2,039	2,464
Other Europe	8,486	16,350	11,604	9,287	7,324	611	719	771	708	785	741
Asia	37,028	153,249	427,642	1,588,178	2,416,278	247,775	255,164	258,546	248,293	254,745	296,420
China	16,709	9,657	34,764	124,326	306,108	29,109	33,095	32,689	32,669	34,300	39,284
Hong Kong	—	15,541	75,007	113,467	83,848	12,290	10,795	9,930	8,785	11,817	15,257

India	1,761	1,973	27,189	164,134	221,977	23,617	24,536	24,808	26,394	25,312	28,599
Iran	1,380	3,388	10,339	45,136	101,267	11,131	12,327	12,031	10,323	9,846	13,027
Israel	476	25,476	29,602	37,713	38,367	4,136	4,279	5,124	4,753	4,444	3,494
Japan	1,555	46,250	39,988	49,775	40,654	4,517	4,552	4,444	4,711	5,085	5,454
Korea	107	6,231	34,526	267,638	302,782	32,537	34,791	35,164	35,397	34,151	33,016
Philippines	4,691	19,307	98,376	354,987	477,485	46,985	53,137	61,492	58,315	61,017	66,119
Turkey	798	3,519	10,142	313,399	20,028	1,652	1,690	1,975	2,080	2,200	2,538
Vietnam	—	335[1]	4,340	178,820	266,027	25,803	20,367	15,010	13,073	12,856	13,174
Other Asia	9,551	21,572	63,369	244,783	557,735	55,998	55,595	56,179	51,793	53,717	74,458
America	354,804	996,944	1,716,374	1,982,735	2,564,698	208,111	225,519	254,078	265,026	294,906	672,639
Canada & Newfoundland	171,718	377,952	413,310	169,939	132,296	15,659	16,354	16,060	16,741	15,821	18,294
Mexico	60,589	299,811	453,937	640,294	975,657	57,820	61,290	66,753	72,511	95,170	405,660
Caribbean	49,725	123,091	470,213	741,126	759,416	68,368	79,374	98,527	100,615	110,949	87,597
Cuba	26,313	78,948	208,536	264,863	135,142	5,699	17,115	30,787	27,363	16,610	9,523
Dominican Republic	5,627	9,897	93,292	148,135	209,899	23,207	23,861	26,216	24,947	27,195	26,744
Haiti	911	4,442	34,499	56,335	118,510	9,554	9,872	12,356	14,643	34,858	13,341
Jamaica	—	8,869	74,906	137,577	184,481	18,997	18,277	18,916	22,430	20,474	23,572
Other Caribbean	16,874	20,935	58,980	134,216	111,384	10,911	10,249	10,252	11,232	11,812	14,417
Central America	21,665	44,751	101,330	134,640	321,845	27,626	28,477	30,086	30,366	31,311	101,273
El Salvador	5,132	5,895	14,992	34,436	133,938	8,753	10,093	10,881	10,627	12,043	57,628
Other Central America	16,533	38,856	86,338	100,204	187,907	18,873	18,354	19,205	19,739	19,268	43,645
South America	21,831	91,628	257,954	295,741	375,026	38,636	40,052	42,650	44,782	41,646	39,812
Argentina	3,338	19,486	49,721	29,897	21,374	2,287	1,925	2,318	2,192	2,556	3,766
Colombia	3,858	18,048	72,028	77,347	99,066	10,897	11,802	11,213	11,482	10,153	14,918
Ecuador	2,417	9,841	36,780	50,077	43,841	4,244	4,601	4,518	4,656	4,736	7,587
Other South America	12,218	44,253	99,425	138,420	210,745	21,208	21,724	24,601	26,452	24,201	33,541
Other America	29,276	59,711	19,630	995	458	2	2	2	11	9	3
Africa	7,367	14,092	28,954	80,779	144,096	13,594	15,236	15,500	15,730	17,124	22,485
Oceania	14,551	12,976	25,122	41,242	38,401	4,249	4,552	4,352	4,437	4,324	4,956
Not specified	142	12,491	93	112	582	295	12	8	63	72	86

APPENDIX G

Chronology of Significant Events Since 1945

1945	The Big Three meet at Yalta
	Battle of Iwo Jima takes place
	Roosevelt dies; Truman becomes president
	Germany surrenders
	Battle of Okinawa takes place
	Potsdam conference is held
	Japanese cities are bombed with atomic weapons
	Japan surrenders; World War II ends
	United Nations is founded in San Francisco
1946	Nuremburg war crimes trials are held
	Atomic Energy Commission is created
1947	Truman Doctrine is announced
	Major league baseball is desegregated
	HUAC investigates Hollywood
	Marshall Plan for European recovery is inaugurated
	National Security Act is enacted
	Taft-Hartley Act is enacted
1948	Berlin blockade occurs
	Truman orders the armed services desegregated
	Truman is elected president
1949	NATO is created
	Soviets explode an atomic device
	Chinese revolution succeeds
	Alger Hiss is convicted of perjury
1950	Truman orders work to begin on the hydrogen bomb
	Senator Joseph McCarthy launches his anti-Communist campaign
	Korean War begins
	NSC-68 is implemented
	David Riesman's and others' *The Lonely Crowd* is published
	J. D. Salinger's *Catcher in the Rye* is published
1952	Dwight D. Eisenhower is elected president
1953	Eisenhower appoints Earl Warren as Chief Justice of the Supreme Court
1954	Supreme Court rules on *Brown v. Board of Education of Topeka,* Kansas
	Geneva conference partitions Vietnam at the seventeenth parallel
	Army–McCarthy hearings take place
1955	Montgomery bus boycott ignites the modern civil rights movement
	AFL and CIO merge
	"Summit" conference is held at Geneva
1956	Elvis Presley's first superhit, "Heartbreak Hotel," is recorded
	Federal Highway Act is passed
	The Suez crisis occurs
	Soviet tanks crush the Hungarian revolution
1957	School desegregation crisis occurs in Little Rock
	First modern Civil Rights Act is enacted
	Jack Kerouac's *On the Road* is published
	Soviets launch *Sputnik*
1958	NASA is established
	U. S. Marines hit the beaches in Lebanon
1959	Castro comes to power in Cuba
	Nikita Khrushchev visits the United States
1960	U-2 incident causes impending summit meeting to be canceled
	Kennedy–Nixon debates are televised
	John F. Kennedy is elected president
1961	Bay of Pigs fiasco takes place
	CORE organizes freedom rides to the South

(continued)

	Berlin Wall is built
	Peace Corps is created
	Alliance for Progress is implemented
1962	James Meredith desegregates the University of Mississippi
	Cuban missile crisis takes place
1963	Martin Luther King Jr. leads demonstrations in Birmingham
	Nuclear Test Ban Treaty is signed
	March on Washington to support civil rights bill takes place
	Ngo Dinh Diem is assassinated in Saigon
	John F. Kennedy is assassinated in Dallas
	Lyndon Johnson accedes to the presidency
1964	Civil Rights Act is enacted
	Beatles hold first American concert
	Johnson announces the beginning of a War on Poverty
	Gulf of Tonkin incidents occur
	Johnson is elected president
	Free Speech Movement at Berkeley campus of the University of California inaugurates era of student protest
1965	Malcolm X is assassinated
	Voting Rights Act is enacted
	United States intervenes in the Dominican Republic
	Race riots in Watts occurs
	The United States goes to war in Vietnam
	Federal aid to public education is enacted
	Medicare and Medicaid are enacted
	Immigration Act is enacted
1967	Major race riots occur in Newark and Detroit
1968	Communists launch the Tet Offensive
	Johnson announces that he will not seek reelection
	Martin Luther King Jr. is assassinated
	Robert Kennedy is assassinated
	Nixon is elected president
1969	Secret bombing of Cambodia begins
	Warren Burger is appointed Chief Justice of the Supreme Court
	Vietnamization is announced
	Woodstock festival is held
1970	Cambodia is invaded
1971	Lieutenant William Calley is convicted of war crimes
	Pentagon Papers are published
1972	Nixon visits China
	Nixon visits the Soviet Union and signs SALT I
	Watergate break-in takes place
	Nixon is reelected in a landslide victory
1973	American involvement in the Indochina War ends
	Nixon's secret White House taping system is discovered
	Supreme Court decides *Roe v. Wade*
	Yom Kippur War takes place
	First energy crisis occurs
	Agnew resigns from the vice presidency
1974	Nixon resigns from the presidency
	Gerald Ford assumes the presidency
	President Ford pardons Nixon
1975	Saigon falls to the Communists
1976	Jimmy Carter is elected president
1977	Panama Canal treaties are finalized
1978	Supreme Court delivers *Bakke* decision
	Revolution in Iran takes place

(continued)

Chronology of Significant Events Since 1945 (continued)

1979	Camp David Accords are reached
	U. S. hostages are taken in Teheran
	United States and China resume normal diplomatic relations
	USSR invades Afghanistan
	Carter Doctrine is announced
	Sandinistas triumph in Nicaragua
1980	Ronald Reagan is elected president
1981	Ronald Reagan is inaugurated as the fortieth president of the United States
	Reaganomics is implemented
	U. S. military buildup begins
1982	Covert aid to contras in Nicaragua begins
	Congress enacts Boland Amendment
1983	U. S. deploys intermediate-range Pershing missiles in Western Europe
	Reagan proposes SDI (Star Wars)
	Muslim terrorist kills 241 U. S. Marines in Beirut
	The United States invades Grenada
1984	Reagan is reelected by a landslide margin
1985	Geneva summit takes place
	Gramm-Rudman Act is enacted
	The United States becomes a debtor nation for the first time since 1915
1986	Tax Reform Act is passed
	The United States adopts economic sanctions against South Africa
	Reykjavik summit takes place
	Immigration Reform Act is passed
	Democrats regain control of the Senate
1987	The United States intervenes in the Persian Gulf shipping war
	Iran-Contra scandal is revealed
	Stock market crashes
	The United States and the Soviet Union sign the INF treaty
	The Soviet Union begins scaling back its international commitments
1988	George H. W. Bush is elected president
1989	Tiananmen Square massacre takes place
	The Cold War ends
	United States invades Panama to overthrow and capture Manuel Noriega
1990	Violetta Chamorro is elected president of Nicaragua
	Germany is reunited
	Iraq invades Kuwait
1991	Persian Gulf War occurs, and Kuwait is liberated
	Clarence Thomas becomes an associate justice of the Supreme Court
	Middle East peace conference occurs
	The Soviet Union disintegrates
1992	South Africa votes to end apartheid
	Bill Clinton is elected president
1993	Ruth Bader Ginsburg is appointed to the Supreme Court
	Israeli–PLO agreement
1994	Republicans win control of Congress
1995	The O. J. Simpson murder trial becomes the "trial of the century"
	Terrorists bomb the federal building in Oklahoma City
1996	U. S. troops are sent to Bosnia-Herzegovina
	Bill Clinton is reelected president of the United States
1997	The federal budget is balanced for the first time in nearly thirty years
1998	President Clinton is impeached by the House of Representatives
1999	President Clinton is acquitted of all impeachment charges by the Senate
	NATO attacks the Yugoslav Federation
2000	Americans and much of the world welcome the Third Millenium

Index